Fifth Edition

Clinical Mental Health Counseling in Community and Agency Settings

Samuel T. Gladding
Wake Forest University

Deborah W. Newsome
Wake Forest University

Pearson

330 Hudson Street, NY, NY 10013

Director, Teacher Education & the Helping Professions: Kevin M. Davis
Portfolio Manager: Rebecca Fox-Gieg
Content Producer: Janelle Rogers
Content Project Manager: Pamela D. Bennett
Media Project Manager: Lauren Carlson
Portfolio Management Assistant: Anne McAlpine
Executive Field Marketing Manager: Krista Clark
Executive Product Marketing Manager: Christopher Barry
Procurement Specialist: Deidra Smith
Cover Designer: Melissa Welch
Cover Photo: Johnér/Shutterstock Offset.com
Full-Service Project Management: Sadika Rehman, iEnergizer/Aptara®, Ltd.
Composition: iEnergizer/Aptara®, Ltd.
Printer/Binder: LSC Communications
Cover Printer: LCS Communications
Text Font: 10/12 ITC Garamond Std.

Library of Congress Cataloging-in-Publication Data available upon request.

ISBN 13: 978-0-13-438555-6
ISBN 10:   0-13-438555-1

*In memory of Shirley Ratliff, a clinical mental health counselor
and an inspirational professional who touched my heart deeply
and gave me many new insights.*

—Samuel T. Gladding

*In memory of Dr. Thomas M. Elmore (December 28, 1926–October 29, 2012),
my mentor, teacher, colleague, and friend. Dr. Elmore exemplified what it
means to be a counselor, in every sense of the word.*

*I also dedicate this book to our students—past, present, and future—who
make it a privilege and an honor to serve as a counselor educator.*

—Deborah W. Newsome

PREFACE

Clinical mental health counseling is an exciting, evolving, and challenging profession. If you are just now embarking on the journey of becoming a professional clinical mental health counselor (CMHC), you are in for an exciting ride! We hope that this text, which addresses many of the 2016 standards of the Council for Accreditation of Counseling and Related Educational Programs (CACREP), will provide you with a strong foundation on which to develop skills and knowledge in the field.

When we wrote the fourth edition of *Clinical Mental Health Counseling in Community and Agency Settings* (2014), the 2009 CACREP standards had just been adopted. The standards no longer recognized community counseling and mental health counseling as separate specialization areas. Instead, the specializations were merged into one: clinical mental health counseling (CMHC). Counselor education programs that had separate community counseling and mental health counseling tracks were given time to transition into the new single CMHC track. As of July 1, 2013, CACREP recognizes only CMHC programs that have met the accreditation standards. To that end, we have focused exclusively on clinical mental health counseling in this fifth edition to provide you with a strong base in this specialty area.

Societal changes, changes in the global economy, high rates of unemployment and underemployment, rapid advances in technology, increased incidences of cyberbullying, issues confronting veterans, and an increased emphasis on treating clients from a holistic perspective (which is not always an easy task when clinicians are working in managed care environments) represent just a few of the ways changes in our world compel changes in the way we practice as clinical mental health counselors. We recognize that the CMHC profession will continue to evolve and that by the time you read this text, even more changes will have taken place. The *Diagnostic and Statistical Manual-5 (DSM-5)* was published in May 2013. The American Counseling Association (ACA) revised its code of ethics in 2014. Unanticipated changes to the world of clinical mental health counseling are inevitable. However, in the midst of change, clinical mental health counselors will continue to perform a broad range of therapeutic services among diverse client populations in a variety of settings. Clinical mental health counselors will use evidence-based approaches that promote prevention, early intervention, wellness, and advocacy, taking into account the client, the environment, and the interaction between the two. Clinical mental health counselors will continue to develop skills in working with crisis and trauma. Furthermore, they will continue to work with teams of other mental health and medical professionals to provide the best possible care for their clients.

In the fifth edition of this text, we address these and other topics. We examine the history and professional foundations of counseling, legal and ethical issues, counseling with diverse populations, multiple roles and functions of clinical mental health counselors, and the many settings in which clinical mental health counselors practice.

NEW TO THIS EDITION

The fifth edition features new content, which reflects some of the ongoing developments in the clinical mental health counseling field, including the following:

- Over 200 references have been added or updated, bringing this edition of the book current with the research in the field of mental health counseling.

- References to the *DSM-TR-IV* have been replaced by references to the *DSM-5*, making the diagnosis of clients current with the latest standards in the field.
- References to the American Counseling Association (ACA) 2005 *Code of Ethics* have been replaced with a focus on the 2014 *ACA Code of Ethics*.
- References to the 2009 CACREP Standards have been replaced with references to the 2016 CACREP Standards.
- The book has been streamlined from 16 to 15 chapters to make it more in line with semesters, which are usually 15 weeks long. (In making this change, the separate chapters on the history of counseling and identity as a mental health counselor were combined.)
- More than two dozen tables, figures, and boxes have been added to summarize important material in the book.
- Key words and concepts in each chapter have been boldfaced to help students recognize them.
- Parts of previous chapters have been moved around and expanded upon to make them more congruent in the chapters in which they have been placed. For instance, "coaching" has been moved from Chapter 13 on college and career counseling and placed in Chapter 15 next to private practice, which is more likely to be a setting that employs this clinical mental health specialty. Likewise, in Chapter 8, the last half of the chapter, dealing with crises and disasters, has been moved to the front of the chapter since counselors are more likely to be involved in these activities than matters pertaining to suicide.
- Chapter lengths have been evened out, providing a more uniform flow to the text.
- An epilogue has been added to contrast where the field of counseling and mental health counseling was when it was first formulated in the late 1970s with where it is today.

ORGANIZATION OF THE TEXT

The content is designed to address pertinent topics in clinical mental health counseling. Contents are organized in four parts:

- **Part 1: Historical and Professional Foundations of Clinical Mental Health Counseling.** In Part 1 of the text, we focus on the historical foundations of counseling, beginning with a recounting of the historical roots of the profession and an exploration of the concept of professional identity, particularly the specialty area of clinical mental health counseling. We describe credentialing and licensure policies associated with the profession (Chapter 1). In Chapter 2, ethical and legal issues, with a focus on those that pertain to clinical mental health counseling, are examined. In Chapter 3, we address counseling issues related to diversity. It is crucial for counselors to develop skills in working with people of different ethnic and racial backgrounds, sexual orientations, levels of ability, and social class. Other areas of diversity, including gender and adulthood, are discussed elsewhere in the text.
- **Part 2: Roles and Functions of Clinical Mental Health Counselors.** Clinical mental health counselors are responsible for developing the knowledge and skills needed to conduct a broad array of counseling services. Part 2 opens with a general description of the counseling process and specific descriptions of activities that occur

during the initial, working, and closing stages of counseling. In Chapter 5, we give specific attention to two general functions that counselors need to conduct skillfully: assessment and diagnosis. This chapter is followed with a description of holistic approaches to counseling, which are becoming more prevalent in many clinical settings. In Chapter 7, we focus on four important services clinical mental health counselors provide: consultation, advocacy, client outcome evaluation, and program evaluation. Part 2 concludes by addressing the significant topics of crisis and disaster response, suicide assessment and intervention, and the need to maintain counselor effectiveness, manage stress, and avoid burnout.

- **Part 3: Working with Specific Populations.** Clinical mental health counselors work with groups, couples, families, and individuals of varying ages. In Chapter 9, ways to work with groups are discussed, and in Chapter 10, ways of working with couples and families are covered. In Chapter 11, we focus on counseling children and adolescents, giving attention to developmental issues, counseling techniques, and specific counseling concerns that face this age group. In Chapter 12, issues related to counseling adults at different developmental levels are discussed. In addition to focusing on counseling throughout the adult life span, special attention is given to working with older adults, especially concerns related to the discriminatory practice of ageism and to the specific counseling needs of women and men.

- **Part 4: Clinical Mental Health Counseling: Settings and Services.** Clinical mental health counselors are employed in many different for-profit and nonprofit settings that operate in both public and private sectors. Chapter 13 explores the ways clinical mental health counselors work in college settings and the services they offer in career counseling, regardless of settings. In Chapter 14, we describe several settings in which clinical mental health counselors might be employed, including community agencies, healthcare facilities, child and family agencies, and other specialized clinical settings. Finally, Chapter 15 discusses the work counselors engage in when they are in employee assistance settings, private practice, and managed care environments. The practice of coaching is also included in this chapter since some private practitioners engage in this activity.

The content of the fifth edition is based on current research and practices germane to clinical mental health counseling. Information presented in the chapters is supplemented with narratives supplied by mental health professionals employed across counseling settings, who share their views of the rewards and challenges associated with the services they provide. In addition, case studies in each chapter, many of which were written by graduate students practicing in the field, provide opportunities for students to grapple with challenging issues faced by clinical mental health counselors. Finally, boxes, figures, and tables summarizing or clarifying information are included in individual chapters.

ALSO AVAILABLE WITH MYCOUNSELINGLAB®

This title is also available with MyCounselingLab, an online homework, tutorial, and assessment program designed to work with the text to engage students and improve results. Within its structured environment, students see key concepts demonstrated through video clips, practice what they learn, test their understanding, and receive feedback to guide their learning and ensure they master key learning outcomes.

- **Learning Outcomes and Standards measure student results.** MyCounselingLab organizes all assignments around essential learning outcomes and national standards for counselors.
- **Video- and Case-Based Assignments develop decision-making skills.** Students watch videos of actual client-therapist sessions or high-quality role-play scenarios featuring expert counselors. They are then guided in their analysis of the videos through a series of short-answer questions. These exercises help students develop the techniques and decision-making skills they need to be effective counselors before they are in a critical situation with a real client.
- **Licensure Quizzes help students prepare for certification.** Automatically graded, multiple-choice Licensure Quizzes help students prepare for their certification examinations, master foundational course content, and improve their performance in the course.
- **Video Library offers a wealth of observation opportunities.** The Video Library provides more than 400 video clips of actual client-therapist sessions and high quality role-plays in a database organized by topic and searchable by keyword.
- **Comprehensive online course content.** Filled with a wealth of content that is tightly integrated with your textbook, MyLab lets you easily add, remove, or modify existing instructional material. You can also add your own course materials to suit the needs of your students or department. In short, MyLab lets you teach exactly as you'd like.
- **Robust gradebook tracking.** The online gradebook automatically tracks your students' results on tests, homework, and practice exercises and gives you control over managing results and calculating grades. The gradebook provides a number of flexible grading options, including exporting grades to a spreadsheet program such as Microsoft Excel. And, it lets you measure and document your students' learning outcomes and performance by standard.

ACKNOWLEDGMENTS

It takes the efforts of a community to rewrite a textbook. We want to thank our professional colleagues in the various communities in which we have worked—academic communities, clinical communities, and professional communities, including the American Counseling Association and its divisions. We also acknowledge the dedicated mental health professionals who supplied narratives or personal interviews for the text, including Kristina M. Acosta, John Anderson, Tom Buffkin, Kelli Coker, Robin Daniel, Pat DeChatelet, Ann Dixon Coppage, Paige Greason, Jay Hale, Donna Hampton, Peggy Haymes, Tania Castillero Hoeller, Pamela Karr, Anya Lainas, Nick Mazza, Peg McEwen, Ellen Nicola, Mary Claire O'Brien, Peg Olson, Patti Patridge, Edward Shaw, Elizabeth Vaughan, and Laura Veach.

Several of our current and former graduate students contributed case studies for various chapters, including Kavitha Dharmalingam, Elisabeth Harper, Corrine Harris, Lolly Hemphill, Katie Lee Hutson, Karen Kegel, Shahnaz Khawaja, Beth Montplaisir, Amanda Rich Morgan, Kevin Varner, and Brittany Wyche. Throughout the course of the text revision, Wake Forest research and teaching assistants Kavitha Dharmalingam, Teresa Prevatte, and Brittany Wyche provided invaluable assistance. Also we wish to thank James Raper and Kavitha Dharmalingam, who combined with Dr. Newsome to write Chapters 9 and 15 respectively in the fourth edition of this text. Their research, writing, and expertise on these matters contributed greatly to the comprehensiveness and readability of the book then and we have built on their work since.

We would also like to thank the reviewers who provided helpful comments and suggestions for strengthening the text. They are Joyce A. DeVoss, Northern Arizona University; Amy L. Reynolds, University at Buffalo; David A. Scott, Clemson University; Oscar Flores Sida, University of Nevada Las Vegas; and Carlos Zalaquett, Ph.D., LMHC, Lic., University of South Florida and The Pennsylvania State University. In addition, we recognize and are grateful for the contributions of the staff at Pearson, especially Kevin Davis. Thank you as well to our project manager at Aptara, Sadika Rehman. The patience and flexibility of these individuals made the project manageable.

We are especially thankful for the contributions of our spouses (Claire Gladding and David Newsome) for their patience and encouragement during the text revision. We appreciate our children, our families, and our friends for the humor, love, support, and sensitivity they provide on an ongoing basis. Finally, we are fortunate to work with several very special colleagues and students, who listen, challenge, and inspire. Thank you to the faculty, staff, and counseling students at Wake Forest University for their ongoing support.

ABOUT THE AUTHORS

Samuel T. Gladding is a professor in the Department of Counseling at Wake Forest University in Winston-Salem, North Carolina. He is a fellow in the American Counseling Association and its former president (2004–2005). He has also served as president of the Association for Counselor Education and Supervision (ACES), the Association for Specialists in Group Work (ASGW), the American Association of State Counseling Boards, and Chi Sigma Iota. He is the former editor of the *Journal for Specialists in Group Work*, a past member of the American Counseling Association Foundation, and a past member of the North Carolina Board of Licensed Professional Counselors.

Dr. Gladding has authored numerous professional publications, including 45 books. In 1999, he was cited as being in the top 1% of contributors to the flagship periodical of the American Counseling Association: the *Journal of Counseling and Development*. A National Certified Counselor (NCC), a Certified Clinical Mental Health Counselor (CCMHC), and a Licensed Professional Counselor (North Carolina), Dr. Gladding's specialty in counseling is creativity. He is married to Claire Tillson Gladding and is the father of three adult sons. In his spare time, he enjoys swimming, writing poetry, listening to music, and reading humor and history.

Deborah W. Newsome is an associate professor in the Department of Counseling at Wake Forest University in Winston-Salem, North Carolina, where she serves as the clinical mental health program director. She served on the Executive Board of the Association for Assessment in Counseling and Education (AACE) for six years and is a member of several divisions of the American Counseling Association (ACA). She is a National Certified Counselor (NCC), a Licensed Professional Counselor (LPC), and a Licensed North Carolina School Counselor. She teaches courses in clinical mental health counseling, counseling skill development, assessment, and career development and counseling. She also supervises graduate students' clinical experiences and volunteers at a local nonprofit counseling center.

Dr. Newsome has coauthored three books and over 25 book chapters and journal articles. She received Wake Forest University's Graduate Student Association Faculty Excellence Award twice. She and her husband, David Newsome, are the parents of two young adults—David, Jr., and Jennifer. Debbie is an avid runner and swimmer and enjoys playing the flute for various community organizations.

BRIEF CONTENTS

CONTENTS

Historical and Professional Foundations of Clinical Mental Health Counseling

CHAPTER 1

History of and Professional Identity in Clinical Mental Health Counseling

LiliGraphie/Shutterstock

CHAPTER OVERVIEW

From reading this chapter, you will learn about

- A chronological overview of the history of professional counseling
- Counseling in the 21st century
- Projected trends in clinical mental health counseling
- What it means to be a professional counselor and, more specifically, a clinical mental health counselor
- Other therapeutic professionals with whom clinical mental health counselors work and levels of helping

As you read, consider

- What it means to be a clinical mental health counselor
- How world events, governments, and personalities have shaped the counseling profession
- What projections for the future of clinical mental health counseling you consider most pressing and why

There is a quietness that comes
*   in the awareness of presenting names*
*   and recalling places*
*   in the history of persons*
*   who come seeking help.*
Confusion and direction are a part of the process
*   where in trying to sort out tracks*
*   that parallel into life*
*   a person's past is traveled.*
Counseling is a complex riddle
*   where the mind's lines are joined*
*   with scrambling and precision*
*   to make sense out of nonsense,*
*   a tedious process*
*   like piecing fragments of a puzzle together*
*   until a picture is formed.*

Reprinted from "In the Midst of the Puzzles and Counseling Journey," by S. T. Gladding, 1978, *Personnel and Guidance Journal, 57,* p. 148. Copyright © S. T. Gladding.

- Reasons why the specialties of community counseling and mental health counseling merged in 2009 into a single specialty area—clinical mental health counseling
- The professional organizations with which you may want to affiliate

The following story was popular when I (Gladding) first entered the counseling profession: A young man took a stroll by a river. As he was walking, he noticed an old woman flailing her arms in the midst of the river and yelling for assistance. Without hesitation, he jumped into the water, swam out, grabbed her, and pulled her to safety. Just as she was recovering, a boy floated past in dire straits. Again, the young man dove into the water and rescued the boy in the same brave way he had rescued the older woman. To the young man's chagrin and to the amazement of a small crowd that was gathering on the banks of the stream, a third person, a middle-aged executive, came floating by yelling for help. The young man was a hero once more with his rescue of the businessman.

Exhausted, the young man then started walking upstream. As he did, a bystander asked him, "Aren't you going to stay to rescue others who may fall in the river and need you?"

The young man replied, "No. I'm going farther up the river to find out why these people are falling in."

The story illustrates a key component of counseling in general and clinical mental health counseling in particular. Counseling focuses on prevention whenever possible, on altering people's environments to make them hospitable as opposed to hostile, and on providing direct services when needed.

HISTORICAL ROOTS OF CLINICAL MENTAL HEALTH COUNSELING

Clinical mental health counseling evolved over time from the discipline of counseling. Prior to 2009, clinical mental health counseling was not recognized as a distinct specialty area in the counseling field. Instead, accreditation standards recognized two specialties: community counseling (a minimum of 48-semester-hour degree) and mental health counseling (a minimum of 60-semester-hour degree).

Community counseling and its accompanying degree came first, at least conceptually. The term was initially coined by Amos and Williams (1972) and later by Lewis and Lewis (1977) to identify counseling activities that took place outside other established domains, such as educational settings. In 1984, the Association for Counselor Education and Supervision (ACES) Committee on Community Counseling described community counseling as a process and orientation that favored using a multifaceted approach that was developmental and educative, that emphasized prevention, that took into account the effects of the community on the client, and that sought to empower clients through advocacy (Hayes, 1984). In 1975, there was a push to establish a division for counselors who worked in community and agency settings. However, a specific division for community counseling was not established.

While this activity was occurring, in June 1978, the American Mental Health Counselors Association (AMHCA), which had been founded in 1977, was accepted as a division of the American Personnel and Guidance Association (APGA, now the American Counseling Association [ACA]; Weikel, 1996). The new division had 12,000 members by the early 1980s and published a journal, *The Journal of Mental Health Counseling* (originally known as the *AMHCA Journal*). The first training standards for mental health counselors were prepared by Seiler, Brooks, and Beck (1987), and the 1988 Council for Accreditation of Counseling and Related Educational Programs (CACREP) standards recognized mental health counseling as a specialty area. By 1994, CACREP had accredited four mental health counseling programs and 77 community counseling programs (Sweeney, 1995). Through the 1990s, the number of mental health specialty programs grew, as did the number of accredited community counseling programs. Yet mental health counseling had an ACA division, AMHCA, and CACREP standards, while community counseling had neither.

In 2009 CACREP discontinued accrediting community counseling as a program since it had no standards, lacked a division, and conceptually in many ways seemed to overlap with mental health counseling. In place of these two specialties one emerged: clinical mental health counseling. To help counselor education programs that had community counseling programs, a period of transition was built into the 2009 standards so institutions of higher education with community counseling programs could make a transition to become clinical mental health programs or finish graduating those in their programs and discontinue.

Today, clinical mental health counselors still provide services to a wide spectrum of people in a variety of settings. Across settings, professional clinical mental health counselors emphasize wellness, prevention, personal growth, psychoeducation, treatment, and empowerment. Graduate education and clinical training prepare clinical mental health counselors to provide a full range of services for individuals, couples, families, adolescents, and children. The core areas of mental health education programs approved by CACREP include the following:

- Diagnosis and psychopathology
- Psychotherapy
- Psychological testing and assessment
- Professional orientation
- Research and program evaluation
- Group counseling
- Human growth and development
- Counseling theory
- Social and cultural foundations
- Lifestyle and career development
- Supervised practicum and internship

BOX 1-1

Practicing counselors are concerned about pathology, but not from a myopic perspective. People develop difficulties (and in many cases pathology) at various times during their developmental life span. Effectively dealing with pathology does not preclude using a developmental framework. Furthermore, an understanding of the developmental course of numerous disorders is an important aspect of prevention, accurate diagnosis, and treatment.

(Hinkle, 1999, p. 469)

A CHRONOLOGICAL OVERVIEW OF PROFESSIONAL COUNSELING

The counseling profession and its specialty areas have evolved over the years. Thus, in understanding clinical mental health counseling, it is important to look at it in the context of the development of counseling. Therefore, it is vital to examine the history of counseling in the broadest context possible. Historical events and circumstances that have shaped the counseling profession and consequently the specialty area of clinical mental health counseling are presented here. Understanding the past can lead to a better appreciation of the present and future trends of the profession.

One way to chart the evolution of counseling is to trace important events and influences through the decades of the 20th century and into the 21st century. Keep in mind that the development of professional counseling, as well as clinical mental health counseling, was and continues to be a process. Therefore, some names and events will not fit neatly into a rigid chronology. Even so, this overview will provide you with a strong understanding of the historical foundations of professional counseling and which of those directly influenced the foundations of clinical mental health counseling.

The Case of Noah

Noah has always enjoyed reading about the lives of famous people. He finds it interesting and insightful. Now he has been asked to read about the history of counseling. He wonders if it is worth his time—after all, it is not as if counselors are famous people.

Noah has a point. Very few people who have entered the counseling profession are well known. Why then read about how counseling developed? Learning that history will not be as exciting as reading about Abraham Lincoln or Eleanor Roosevelt.

Before 1900

Counseling is a relatively new profession (Aubrey, 1977, 1982). It developed in the late 1890s and early 1900s and was interdisciplinary from its inception. Some of the roles carried out by counselors were and are shared by individuals in other helping professions (Herr & Fabian, 1993).

Before the 1900s, most counseling was informal, characterized by sharing advice or information. In the United States, counseling developed from a humanitarian concern to improve people's lives in communities adversely affected by the Industrial Revolution of the mid- to late 1800s (Aubrey, 1983). The social welfare reform movement (now known as social justice), the spread of public education, and various changes in population makeup of the time (e.g., the influx of a large number of immigrants) also influenced the growth of the new profession (Aubrey, 1977; Goodyear, 1984).

Most of the pioneers in counseling identified themselves as social reformers and educators. They focused on teaching children and young adults about themselves, others, and the world of work. Initially, these helpers were involved primarily in child/adult welfare, educational/vocational guidance, and legal reform. Their work was built on specific information and lessons, such as moral instruction on being good and doing right and developing interpersonal skills (Nugent & Jones, 2009). They saw needs in American society and took steps to fulfill them. These individuals were not called counselors; in fact, "no mention of counseling was made in the professional literature until 1931" (Aubrey, 1983, p. 78). Classroom teachers and agency administrators were the main practitioners.

Major Events Prior to 1900

- Counseling informal and characterized by sharing of advice and information
- Developed out of the social welfare reform movement
- Most early pioneers in counseling were social reformers and educators

1900–1909

Counseling began as an infant profession in the early 1900s, when the helping process was largely dominated by Freud's psychoanalytic theory and behaviorism. During this decade, three persons emerged as leaders in counseling's development: Frank Parsons, Jesse B. Davis, and Clifford Beers.

Frank Parsons is called the "founder of guidance." He focused his counseling work on prevention and growth. Parsons has been characterized as a disciplined scholar, a persuasive writer, a tireless activist, and a great intellect (Davis, 1988; Zytowski, 1985). Parsons was a true "Renaissance man" with a colorful life career in multiple disciplines, including that of lawyer, engineer, college professor, social worker, and social activist (Hartung & Blustein, 2002; Pope & Sweinsdottir, 2005). However, he is best known for founding **Boston's Vocational Bureau** in 1908, which represented a major step in the development of vocational guidance.

At the bureau, Parsons worked with young people who were in the process of making career decisions. He theorized that **choosing a vocation** was a matter of relating three factors: a knowledge of the world of work, a knowledge of self, and the use of true reasoning to match the two. To facilitate this process, Parsons devised a number of procedures to help his clients learn more about themselves and the world of work. His efforts provided the foundation on which modern career counseling is based (Kiselica & Robinson, 2001).

For Frank Parsons, choosing a vocation was a matter of relating three facts:

- A knowledge of the world of work
- A knowledge of self
- True reasoning to match the two

Parsons's book *Choosing a Vocation* (1909), published a year after his death, was quite influential, especially in Boston. For example, Boston school superintendent Stratton Brooks designated 117 elementary and secondary teachers as vocational counselors (Nugent &

Jones, 2009). The "Boston example" soon spread to other major cities as school personnel recognized the need for vocational planning. By 1910, 35 cities had emulated Boston's example (Lee, 1966). Parsons's contributions as a scholar and as an activist had a profound influence on the emerging counseling profession.

Jesse B. Davis was the first person to set up a systematized guidance program in the public schools (Aubrey, 1977). As superintendent of the Grand Rapids, Michigan, school system, he suggested that classroom teachers of English composition include lessons in guidance once a week to help prevent problems and build character. Influenced by progressive American educators such as Horace Mann and John Dewey, Davis believed that proper guidance would help cure the ills of American society. What he and other progressive educators advocated was not counseling in the modern sense but a forerunner of counseling: **school guidance** (a preventive educational means of teaching students how to deal effectively with life events). Davis's focus on prevention continues to be a key component of counseling in the 21st century.

A third figure who significantly affected the emerging counseling profession was **Clifford Beers**. Beers, a former Yale student, was hospitalized for mental illness several times during his lifetime. He found conditions in mental institutions deplorable and exposed them in his book, *A Mind That Found Itself* (1908), which became a bestseller. Beers used his book to advocate for better mental health facilities and reform in the treatment of mentally ill individuals. His work had an especially powerful influence on the fields of psychiatry and clinical psychology, where many of the practitioners referred to their activities as "counseling" (Hansen, Rossberg, & Cramer, 1994). Beers's work was the impetus for the mental health movement in the United States and for advocacy groups that exist today, including the National Mental Health Association and the National Alliance for the Mentally Ill.

Major Events 1900–1909

- Frank Parsons developed a theory of career decision making
- Jesse B. Davis set up a systemized guidance program in the public schools
- Clifford Beers started the mental health movement in the United States

1910s

The contributions of Parsons, Davis, and Beers during the initial decade of the century led to the emergence of several "firsts" during the next decade. The first university-level course in vocational guidance was offered at Harvard University in 1911. The first citywide school guidance program was established in Grand Rapids, Michigan, in 1912, and in 1913, the **National Vocational Guidance Association (NVGA)**, the first national professional organization in the counseling field, was founded (Hershenson, Power, & Waldo, 1996). The NVGA was the forerunner of the American Counseling Association (ACA). The NVGA initiated the publication of counseling-related bulletins, magazines, and journals. Its publications evolved over the years, focusing initially on vocational guidance and culminating in the current ACA flagship journal, the *Journal of Counseling and Development*. NVGA was important because it established an association offering guidance literature and provided an organization for people interested in vocational counseling. Complementing the founding of NVGA was congressional passage of the **Smith-Hughes Act of 1917**. This legislation provided funding for public schools to support vocational education.

An interest in testing, especially group testing, emerged during this decade as a result of World War I. To screen its personnel, the U.S. Army commissioned the development of numerous psychological instruments, among them the **Army Alpha and Army Beta intelligence tests**. Several of the army's screening devices were used in civilian populations after the war, and **psychometrics** (psychological testing) became a popular movement and an early foundation upon which counseling was based.

Aubrey (1977) observes that because the vocational guidance movement developed without an explicit philosophy, it quickly embraced psychometrics to gain a legitimate foothold in psychology. Reliance on psychometrics had both positive and negative effects. On the positive side, it gave vocational guidance specialists a stronger and more "scientific" identity. On the negative side, it distracted many specialists from examining developments in other behavioral sciences, such as sociology, biology, and anthropology.

Major Events of the 1910s

- Founding of the National Vocational Guidance Association, the first national professional organization in the counseling field
- Establishment of the first university course on guidance at Harvard
- Development of the Army Alpha and Army Beta intelligence tests
- Increased use of psychometrics in vocational guidance

1920s

The 1920s were relatively quiet for the developing counseling profession. This was a period of consolidation. Education courses for counselors almost exclusively emphasized vocational guidance during the 1920s. The dominant influences on the emerging profession were the progressive theories of education and the federal government's use of guidance services with war veterans.

A notable event was the certification of counselors in Boston and New York in the mid-1920s. Another turning point was the development of the first standards for the preparation and evaluation of occupational materials (Lee, 1966). Along with these standards came the publication of new psychological instruments, including Edward Strong's **Strong Vocational Interest Inventory (SVII)** in 1927. The publication of this instrument set the stage for future directions for assessment in counseling (Strong, 1943).

A final noteworthy event of the decade was Abraham and Hannah Stone's 1929 establishment of the first marriage and family counseling center in New York City. Other centers developed throughout the nation, marking the onset of marriage and family counseling.

Major Events of the 1920s

- Influence of progressive theories of education on counseling
- Use by the federal government of guidance services with war veterans
- Publication of the Strong Vocational Interest Inventory
- Beginning of the specialty of marriage and family counseling

1930s

The 1930s were not as quiet as the 1920s, in part because the Great Depression influenced researchers and practitioners to emphasize helping strategies and counseling methods that related to employment. A highlight of the decade was the development of the first theory of counseling, which was formulated by **E. G. Williamson** and his colleagues (including John Darley and Donald Paterson) at the University of Minnesota. Williamson modified Parsons's theory and used it to work with students and the unemployed. His emphasis on a directive, counselor-centered counseling approach came to be known by several names, including the **Minnesota Point of View** and **trait-factor counseling**. Williamson's (1939) pragmatic approach emphasized the counselor's teaching, mentoring, and influencing skills.

One premise of Williamson's theory was that persons had **traits** (e.g., aptitudes, interests, personalities, achievements) that could be integrated in a variety of ways to form **factors** (i.e., constellations of individual characteristics). Counseling was based on a scientific, problem-solving, empirical method that was individually tailored to each client to help him or her stop nonproductive thinking and become an effective decision maker (Lynch & Maki, 1981). Williamson's influence dominated counseling for the next two decades, and he continued to write about the theory into the 1970s (Williamson & Biggs, 1979).

Another major occurrence was the broadening of counseling beyond occupational concerns. The seeds of this development were sown in the 1920s, when Edward Thorndike and other psychologists began to challenge the vocational orientation of the guidance movement (Lee, 1966). The work of John Brewer built upon this change in emphasis. His 1932 book, *Education as Guidance*, proposed that every teacher be a counselor and that guidance be incorporated into the school curriculum. Brewer believed that all education should focus on preparing students to live outside the school environment. His emphasis helped counselors see vocational decisions as just one part of their responsibilities. Although Brewer's work initially had the most relevance for counselors who worked in schools, it later affected counselors working in communities.

During the 1930s, the U.S. government became more involved in counseling. For example, in 1938 Congress passed the **George-Dean Act**, which created the Vocational Education Division of the U.S. Office of Education and an Occupational Information and Guidance Service (Sweeney, 2001). Furthermore, the government established the U.S. Employment Service, which published the first edition of the ***Dictionary of Occupational Titles* (DOT)** in 1939. The *DOT*, which became a major source of career information for vocational counselors, described known occupations in the United States and coded them according to job titles.

Major Events of the 1930s

- Dominance of E. G. Williamson's counselor-directed theory of counseling in working with the unemployed and college students
- Broadening of counseling beyond career choices—e.g., more incorporation of guidance in schools
- More involvement of the U.S. government in vocational education—e.g., establishment of the U.S. Employment Service and publication of the *Dictionary of Occupational Titles*

1940s

Three major influences in the 1940s radically shaped the practice of counseling: the theory of Carl Rogers, World War II, and the government's involvement in counseling after the war. **Carl Rogers** rose to prominence in 1942 with the publication of *Counseling and Psychotherapy*, which challenged the directive, counselor-centered approach of Williamson as well as major tenets of Freudian psychoanalysis. Rogers espoused a **nondirective counseling approach** that focused on the client. His ideas were widely accepted by some but harshly criticized by others. Rogers advocated giving clients the responsibility for their own growth. He thought that if clients had an opportunity to be accepted and heard, they would begin to know themselves better and become more congruent (i.e., genuine). He described the role of the counselor as being nonjudgmental and accepting. In this role, the counselor served as a mirror, reflecting the verbal and emotional manifestations of the client.

Aubrey (1977) notes that before Rogers, the literature in counseling was very practical, dealing with topics such as testing, cumulative records, orientation procedures, vocational issues, and the goals and purposes of guidance. With Rogers, there was a new emphasis on the importance of the counseling relationship, skills, and goals. Guidance, for all intents and purposes, suddenly disappeared as a major consideration in the bulk of the literature and was replaced by a concentration on counseling. The Rogers revolution had a major impact on both counseling and psychology. In addition to Rogers's nondirective, person-centered theory, a considerable number of alternative systems of psychotherapy emerged during this decade (Corsini, 2008).

With the advent of World War II, the U.S. government needed counselors and psychologists to help select and train specialists for the military and for industry. The war also influenced the way vocations were looked at for men and women. During the war, many women worked outside the home. Women's contributions to work and to the well-being of the United States during the crisis of war made a lasting impact. Traditional occupational sex roles began to be questioned, and greater emphasis was placed on personal freedom and vocational choice.

Also during the war, mental health professionals worked successfully with a large number of military personnel who suffered emotional breakdowns. The **National Institute of Mental Health** was established, and in 1946 the **National Mental Health Act** was passed, which authorized funds for research and training to prevent and treat mental health disorders (Hershenson et al., 1996).

After the war, the U.S. Veterans Administration (VA) funded the training of counselors and psychologists by granting stipends and paid internships to students engaged in graduate study. Monies made available through the VA and the GI Bill (benefits for veterans) influenced teaching professionals in graduate education to define their curriculum offerings more precisely. Counseling, as a profession, began to move further away from its historical alliance with vocational development.

Major Events of the 1940s

- Creation and prominence of Carl Rogers's theory
- Trend to look at the work of men and women differently, with more women in the workforce
- Establishment of the National Institute of Mental Health
- Passage of the National Mental Health Act
- Veterans Administration funding for the education of counselors and psychologists

1950s

"If one decade in history had to be singled out for the most profound impact on counselors, it would be the 1950s" (Aubrey, 1977, p. 292). Indeed, the 1950s produced at least four major events that dramatically affected the history of professional counseling:

- The establishment of the American Personnel and Guidance Association (APGA)
- The establishment of Division 17 (Society of Counseling Psychology) within the American Psychological Association (APA)
- The passage of the National Defense Education Act (NDEA)
- The introduction of new guidance and counseling theories

AMERICAN PERSONNEL AND GUIDANCE ASSOCIATION.   APGA grew out of the **Council of Guidance and Personnel Association (CGPA)**, a loose confederation of organizations "concerned with educational and vocational guidance and other personnel activities" (Harold, 1985, p. 4). CGPA operated from 1935 to 1951, but its efforts did not lead its members to any specific course of action. APGA was formed in 1952 with the purpose of formally organizing groups interested in guidance, counseling, and personnel matters. Its original four divisions were the American College Personnel Association (Division 1), the National Association of Guidance Supervisors and Counselor Trainers (Division 2), the NVGA (Division 3), and the Student Personnel Association for Teacher Education (Division 4). During its early history, APGA was more of an interest group than a professional organization because it did not originate or enforce standards for membership (Super, 1955).

DIVISION 17.   In 1952, the **Society of Counseling Psychology (Division 17)** of APA was formally established. It was initially known as the Division of Counseling Psychology. Its formation required dropping the term *guidance* from what had formerly been the association's Counseling and Guidance Division. Part of the impetus for the division's creation came from the VA, but the main impetus came from APA members interested in working with a more "normal" population than the one seen by clinical psychologists (Whitely, 1984).

Once created, Division 17 became more fully defined. Super (1955), for instance, distinguished between counseling psychology and clinical psychology, holding that

counseling psychology was more concerned with normal human growth and development and was influenced by both vocational counseling and humanistic psychotherapy. Despite Super's work, counseling psychology had a difficult time establishing a clear identity within APA (Whitely, 1984). Yet the division's existence had a major impact on the growth and development of counseling as a profession. In fact, luminaries in the counseling profession such as Gilbert Wrenn and Donald Super held offices in both Division 17 and in APGA divisions for years and published in the periodicals of both.

NATIONAL DEFENSE EDUCATION ACT.   A third major event was the passage in 1958 of the **National Defense Education Act (NDEA)**, which was enacted following the Soviet Union's launching of its first space satellite, *Sputnik I*. The act's primary purpose was to identify scientifically and academically talented students and promote their development. NDEA provided funds for upgrading school counseling programs, establishing counseling institutes, and training school counselors through Title V-A and Title V-B. By 1958, the number of school counselors had grown to 12,000. The boom in numbers of school counselors continued into the next decade. During this same time period, counselor educators considered offering programs in clinical settings as well as school settings.

NEW THEORIES.   Several new counseling theories emerged during the 1950s. Prior to that time, four main theories had influenced the work of counselors: (a) psychoanalysis and insight theories (e.g., Sigmund Freud); (b) trait-factor or directive theories (e.g., E. G. Williamson); (c) humanistic and client-centered theories (e.g., Carl Rogers); and, to a lesser extent, (d) behavioral theories (e.g., B. F. Skinner). Debates among counselors usually centered on whether directive or nondirective counseling was more effective, and almost all counselors assumed that certain tenets of psychoanalysis (e.g., defense mechanisms) were true.

During the 1950s, debate gradually shifted away from this focus as new theories of helping began to emerge. Applied behavioral and cognitive–behavioral theories, such as Joseph Wolpe's systematic desensitization and Albert Ellis's rational emotive therapy, began to gain influence. In addition, Eric Berne began to develop his theory of transactional analysis. Donald Super's work in career development and advances in developmental psychology made an impact as well (Aubrey, 1977). By the end of the decade, the number and complexity of theories associated with counseling had grown considerably. Counselors implemented these theories in settings outside the educational environment.

Major Events of the 1950s

- Establishment of the American Personnel and Guidance Association
- Creation of the Division of Counseling Psychology within the American Psychological Association
- Passage of the National Defense Education Act and creation of more counseling positions in schools
- Generation of a number of new counseling theories:
  - Behavioral and cognitive–behavioral theories; systematic densensitization, e.g., Joseph Wolpe; and rational emotive therapy, e.g., Albert Ellis
  - Transactional analysis, e.g., Eric Berne
  - Career counseling, e.g., Donald Super

1960s

The initial focus of the 1960s was on counseling as a developmental profession. **Gilbert Wrenn** set the tone for the decade in his widely influential book, *The Counselor in a Changing World* (1962a). His emphasis, reinforced by other prominent professionals such as Leona Tyler and Donald Blocher, was on working with others to resolve developmental needs. Wrenn's book influenced counselors throughout the 1960s in regard to the **influence of culture on counseling**, and he, along with Tyler, became one of the strongest counseling advocates in the United States.

The impact of the developmental model in counseling lessened, however, as the decade continued, primarily because of three events: the Vietnam War, the civil rights movement, and the women's movement. Each event stirred up passions and pointed out particular needs within our society. Many counselors directed their attention to social issues related to these events.

Other powerful influences that emerged during the decade were the **humanistic counseling theories** of Dugald Arbuckle, Abraham Maslow, and Sidney Jourard. Also important was the phenomenal growth of the **group counseling** movement (Gladding, 2016b). The emphasis of counseling shifted from a one-on-one encounter to small-group interaction. **Behavioral counseling** grew in prominence with the appearance of **John Krumboltz**'s *Revolution in Counseling* (1966), which promoted learning as the root of change. Aaron Beck, a psychiatrist trained in psychoanalysis, developed **cognitive therapy**, which focused on helping people confront negative automatic thoughts and core beliefs. Thus, the decade's initial focus on development shifted somewhat with the expansion of a "cornucopia of competing counseling methodologies" (Aubrey, 1977, p. 293).

Professionalism within APGA increased during the 1960s. In 1961, APGA published a code of ethics for counselors (Nugent, 1981). In 1969, Division 17 of APA, which had further clarified the definition of a counseling psychologist at the 1964 Greyston Conference, began publishing a professional journal, *The Counseling Psychologist*, with Gilbert Wrenn as its first editor. This journal, along with the *Personnel and Guidance Journal* (now the *Journal of Counseling and Development*), accepted articles representing a wide range of counseling interests.

Particularly important to the evolution of community and agency counseling was the passage of the 1963 **Community Mental Health Centers Act**. This landmark act authorized the establishment of a nationwide system of community mental health centers (CMHCs) that would serve the needs of America's newly deinstitutionalized mentally ill population by focusing on outpatient, community-based services (Winegar, 1993). These centers opened up new counseling employment opportunities outside educational settings. For instance, **substance abuse and addiction counseling** (initially called drug abuse counseling) began in the 1960s, and services were offered in community mental health centers. Marriage and family counseling became more prominent because of the increase in America's divorce rate (Hollis, 2000). Many counselor education programs changed their focus from preparing counselors for work in schools to preparing counselors for work in community agencies (Hershenson et al., 1996).

A final noteworthy milestone was the establishment of the **ERIC Clearinghouse on Counseling and Personnel Services (ERIC/CAPS)** at the University of Michigan. Founded in 1966 by Garry Walz and funded by the Office of Educational Research and Improvement at the U.S. Department of Education, ERIC/CAPS provided multiple sources of information about counseling activities and trends in the United States and throughout the world. It sponsored conferences on leading topics in counseling that brought national professional counseling leaders together.

Major Events of the 1960s

- Strong advocates for counseling such as Gilbert Wrenn and Leona Tyler
- Increased sensitivity to the role of culture in counseling brought about by the Vietnam War, the civil rights movement, and the women's movement
- APGA's first code of ethics and more precise defining of counseling along with new publications *The Counseling Psychologist* and *Personnel and Guidance Journal*
- Passage of the Community Mental Health Centers Act
- Establishment of the ERIC Clearinghouse on Counseling and Personnel Services (ERIC/CAPS) at the University of Michigan

1970s

The 1970s saw the emergence of several trends that affected the development of clinical mental health counseling. Among the most important were the rapid growth of counseling outside educational settings, the formation of helping skills programs, the beginning of licensure for counselors, and the further development of APGA as a professional organization for counselors.

DIVERSIFICATION IN COUNSELING SETTINGS. The rapid growth of counseling outside educational institutions started in the 1970s, when mental health centers and community agencies began to employ significant numbers of counselors. Before this time, the majority of counselors had been employed in educational settings, usually public schools. But the demand for school counselors decreased as the economy underwent several recessions and the number of school-age children began to decline. In addition, the number of counselor education programs increased from 327 in 1964 to about 475 by 1980 (Hollis & Wantz, 1980). This dramatic rise in the number of counselor education programs meant that more counselors were competing for available jobs.

The diversification of counseling resulted in specialized training in counselor education programs and in the development of new concepts of counseling. For example, Lewis and Lewis (1977) used the term **community counselor** to describe a professional counselor who could function in multidimensional roles regardless of employment setting. Many community counseling programs were established, and counselors became more common in such agencies as mental health clinics, hospices, employee assistance programs, psychiatric hospitals, rehabilitation centers, and substance abuse centers. The **American Mental Health Counselor Association (AMHCA)** was founded in 1976. AMHCA quickly became one of the largest divisions within APGA and united mental health counselors into a professional organization in which they defined their roles and goals.

HELPING SKILLS PROGRAMS. The 1970s saw the development of **helping skills programs** that concentrated on relationship and communication skills. Initiated by Truax and Carkhuff (1967) and Ivey (1971), these programs taught basic counseling skills to professionals and nonprofessionals alike. The emphasis was humanistic and eclectic. It was assumed that certain fundamental skills should be mastered to establish satisfactory personal interaction. A bonus for counselors who received this type of training was that they could teach the skills to others rather easily. Counselors could now consult by teaching some of their skills to those with whom they worked, including teachers and paraprofessionals.

STATE LICENSURE. By the mid-1970s, state boards of examiners for psychologists had become more restrictive. Some of their restrictions, such as barring graduates of education department counseling programs from taking the psychology licensure exam, caused considerable tension, not only between APA and APGA but also within the APA membership. The result was APGA's move toward state and national licensure for counselors. In 1976, Virginia became the first state to adopt a professional counselor licensure law. It was followed quickly by Arkansas and Alabama before the decade ended. It should be noted that California passed a marriage, family, and child counselor law in 1962. However, the California law defined the term *counselor* broadly and later replaced the term with the word *therapist*, which was strictly defined and which ultimately disenfranchised counselors. It was not until 2010 that California passed a professional counselor licensure law.

A STRONG APGA. During the 1970s, APGA emerged as an even stronger professional organization. Several changes altered its image and function, one of which was the building of its own headquarters in Alexandria, Virginia. APGA also began to question its professional identification because personnel and guidance seemed to be outmoded ways of defining the organization's emphases.

In 1973, the **Association for Counselor Education and Supervision (ACES)**, a division of APGA, outlined the standards for a master's degree in counseling. In 1977, ACES approved guidelines for doctoral preparation in counseling (Stripling, 1978). During the decade, the membership of the organization increased to almost 40,000, and five new divisions were chartered: AMHCA, the Association for Specialists in Group Work, the Association for Religious and Value Issues in Counseling, the Association for Non-White Concerns in Personnel and Guidance, and the Public Offender Counseling Association.

Major Events of the 1970s

- Growth in the number of counselor education programs
- Development of helping skills programs
- Beginning of state licensure for counselors
- The creation of new divisions within APGA (now ACA)

1980s

The 1980s saw the continued growth of counseling as a profession, exemplified by proactive initiatives from counselors associated with APGA and Division 17. Among the most noteworthy events of the decade were those that standardized the training and certification of counselors, recognized counseling as a distinct profession, increased the diversification of counselor specialties, and emphasized human growth and development.

STANDARDIZATION OF TRAINING AND CERTIFICATION. The move toward standardized training and certification of counselors began early in the decade and grew stronger yearly. In 1981, the **Council for Accreditation of Counseling and Related Educational Programs (CACREP)** was formed as an affiliate organization of APGA. It refined the standards first proposed by ACES in the late 1970s and initially accredited four programs and recognized others that had been accredited by the California State Counselor Association and ACES (Steinhauser & Bradley, 1983). In 1987, CACREP achieved membership in the Council on Postsecondary Accreditation (COPA), thereby putting it on a par with such accreditation bodies as APA (Herr, 1985). CACREP standardized counselor education programs for master's and doctoral programs in the areas of school, community, mental health, marriage and family counseling/therapy, and personnel services for college students. The inclusion of community counseling in CACREP accreditation further strengthened this specialty within the profession.

Complementing the work of CACREP, the **National Board for Certified Counselors (NBCC)**, which was formed in 1982, began to certify counselors on a national level. The NBCC developed a standardized test and defined eight major subject areas in which counselors should be knowledgeable: (a) human growth and development, (b) social and cultural foundations, (c) helping relationships, (d) groups, (e) lifestyle and career development, (f) appraisal, (g) research and evaluation, and (h) professional orientation. To become a **national certified counselor (NCC)**, examinees were required to pass a standardized test and meet experiential and character reference qualifications. In 1984, NBCC set up standards for certifying career counselors, and as a result, many individuals became national certified career counselors (NCCCs). By the end of the decade, there were approximately 17,000 NCC professionals.

Finally, in collaboration with CACREP, the **National Academy of Certified Clinical Mental Health Counselors (NACCMHC)**, an affiliate of AMHCA, continued to define training standards and certify counselors in mental health counseling, a process it had begun in the late 1970s (Seiler et al., 1987; Wilmarth, 1985). It also began training supervisors of mental health counselors in 1988. Both programs attracted thousands of new professionals into counseling and upgraded the credentials of those already in the field.

COUNSELING AS A DISTINCT PROFESSION. The evolution of counseling in the 1980s as a distinct helping profession came as a result of issues, events, and forces both inside and outside APGA (Heppner, 1990). Inside APGA, there was a growing awareness among its leaders that the words *personnel* and *guidance* no longer described the work of its members. In 1983, after considerable debate, APGA changed its name to the **American Association for Counseling and Development (AACD)** to "reflect the changing demographics of its membership and the settings in which they worked" (Herr, 1985, p. 395). The name change symbolized the rapid transformation in identity that APGA members had experienced through the implementation of policies regarding training, certification, and standards. External events that influenced APGA to change its name and ultimately its focus included legislation, especially on the federal level, that recognized mental health providers and actions by other mental health services associations.

Moreover, professional commitment among members of AACD increased. **Chi Sigma Iota**, an international academic and professional honor society, was formed in 1985 by Tom Sweeney to promote excellence in the profession. It grew to more than 100 chapters and 5,000 members by the end of the decade (Sweeney, 1989). Furthermore, liability insurance policies, new counseling specialty publications, legal defense funds, legislative initiatives, and a variety of other membership services were made available to AACD members (J. Myers, personal communication, 1990). By 1989, over 58,000 individuals had become members of AACD, an increase of more than 18,000 members in 10 years.

CONTINUED DIVERSIFICATION OF COUNSELING. During the 1980s, counselors became even more diversified. Large numbers of counselors continued to be employed in primary and secondary schools and in higher education in a variety of student personnel services. Mental health and community counselors were the two largest blocks of professionals outside formal educational environments. In addition, the number of counselors swelled in mental health settings for business employees, older adults, and married persons and families. Symbolic of that growth, the Association for Adult Development and Aging (AADA) and the International Association for Marriage and Family Counselors (IAMFC) were organized and chartered as divisions of AACD in 1987 and 1990, respectively.

Strong membership in AACD divisions dedicated to group work, counselor education, humanistic education, measurement and development, religious and value issues, employment and career development, rehabilitation, multicultural concerns, offender work, and military personnel further exemplified the diversity of counseling during the 1980s. Special issues of AACD journals focused on such topics as violence, the gifted and talented, creative arts, and prevention, as well as other timely topics. These publications helped broaden the scope of counseling services and counselor awareness.

INCREASED EMPHASIS ON HUMAN GROWTH AND DEVELOPMENT. Counseling's emphasis during the 1980s on human growth and development took several forms. For example, new emphasis was placed on **developmental counseling** across the life span (Gladstein & Apfel, 1987). New behavioral expressions associated with Erik Erikson's first five stages of life development were formulated (Hamachek, 1988). An increased emphasis on the development of adults of all ages was most clearly represented by the formation of AADA and by the development of curriculum guides that infused gerontological counseling into counselor preparation programs.

A second way that human growth and development was stressed was through increased attention to gender issues and sexual orientation (see, for example, O'Neil & Carroll, 1988; Pearson, 1988; Weinrach, 1987). **Carol Gilligan**'s (1982) landmark study on the development of moral values in females, which helped introduce **feminist theory** into the counseling arena, forced human growth specialists to examine the differences between genders more thoroughly. There was greater emphasis on moral development as research in the area increased (Colangelo, 1985; Lapsley & Quintana, 1985).

Finally, the challenges of working with different ethnic and cultural groups were discussed intensely (Ponterotto & Casas, 1987). The Association for Multicultural Counseling and Development (AMCD) assumed a leadership role in these discussions, but multicultural themes, such as the importance of diversity, became a central issue among all groups, especially in light of the renewed racism that developed in the 1980s (Carter, 1990).

Overall, the increased emphasis on human growth and development highlighted the need for counseling in a variety of settings. The innovations of the 1980s enhanced the professional status of community counselors in a number of areas, and the actual number of community counselors graduating from counselor education programs began to exceed the number of school counselors for the first time in history.

Major Events of the 1980s

- Emergence of counseling as a unique profession
- Standardization of counselor education curricula through CACREP
- Certification of counselors nationally through NBCC
- More emphasis on human growth and development
- Increased attention to gender and multicultural issues

1990s

Changes in the evolution of the counseling profession continued into the 1990s. One change that was significant was the 1992 decision by the American Association for Counseling and Development (AACD) to modify its name and become the **American Counseling Association (ACA)**. The new name better reflected the membership and mission of the organization. Three new divisions within ACA were founded: the American College Counseling Association in 1991; the Association for Gay, Lesbian, and Bisexual Issues in Counseling in 1996; and Counselors for Social Justice in 1999. By the end of the decade, ACA had 18 different divisions.

Issues related to multiculturalism and diversity continued to be emphasized in the 1990s. In 1992, Sue, Arredondo, and McDavis published a set of **multicultural competencies and standards** to guide professionals who were working with people of different ethnicities. This important publication set the stage for a larger debate about the nature of multiculturalism. Some leaders in the field adopted a more inclusive definition of multicultural counseling, taking into account differences in language, socioeconomic status, gender, sexual orientation, physical abilities, race, culture, and ethnicity. Much discussion occurred, and continues to occur, about what diversity and counseling entail within a pluralistic society (Weinrach & Thomas, 1998).

Another noteworthy factor that had particular significance for community and mental health counselors also occurred in 1992. For the first time, counseling was included as a primary mental health profession in the healthcare human resource statistics compiled by the Center for Mental Health Services and by the National Institute of Mental Health (Manderscheid & Sonnenschein, 1992). This recognition put counseling on a par with other mental health specialties such as psychology, social work, and psychiatry. By the beginning of the 21st century, there were approximately 100,000 certified or licensed counselors in the United States (Pope & Wedding, 2008).

The provision of health care in general, including mental health care, significantly affected the counseling profession during the 1990s. The explosive growth of **managed care** organizations during the decade has been described as a revolution in the private mental health care delivery system (Winegar, 1993). Conglomerates emerged, and many counselors became providers for **health maintenance organizations (HMOs)**. Consequently, the number of independent counselors decreased, as did the number of sessions a counselor could offer under managed healthcare plans.

In addition, there was a renewed focus within the decade on counseling issues related to the whole person. Counselors became more attuned to social and environmental factors that affect mental health and well-being and recognized the importance of **contextualism**, or organism–context interaction (Thomas, 1996). These factors include spirituality, family environment, social environment, and global conditions, among others.

Other developments within the decade included the following:

- The merger of NACCMHC with NBCC to credential counselors
- The growth of CACREP- and APA-accredited programs in counselor education and counseling psychology, on both the master's and the doctoral levels
- An increase in the number of counseling-related publications by ACA, APA, commercial publishers, and the ERIC Clearinghouse on Counseling and Student Services (ERIC/CASS)
- The growth of Chi Sigma Iota to over 200 chapters and 20,000 members
- The growth of state counselor licensure laws

Major Events of the 1990s

- Explosive growth in managed health care
- Change of names and an increase in divisions within the American Association for Counseling, which became the American Counseling Association
- Increased emphasis on diversity, contextual, and cultural factors in counseling
- Growth in counseling-related associations such as Chi Sigma Iota, counseling publications, and number of states with counseling licensure laws

2000–2009

In 2002, the counseling profession formally celebrated its 50th anniversary as a profession under the umbrella of the American Counseling Association. However, within the celebration was a realization that the profession is ever changing and that professional emphases during the 21st century would change with the evolving needs of clients and society. The changing roles of men and women, innovations in media and technology, trauma and crises, and issues of aging, poverty, and social justice, among other topics, captured the profession's attention as the new century began (Lee & Walz, 1998; Webber & Mascari, 2016). For clinical mental health counselors, the manner in which mental health care was provided and funded, particularly as it related to managed care organizations, continued to be a prominent area of concern. Other important topics affecting counseling included trauma and violence, and the influence of technology. Particularly distinctive in the decade was an emphasis on evidence-based counseling; dealing with conflict, trauma, and crises; professional identity as a counselor; and working with special populations.

EVIDENCE-BASED COUNSELING.   The need to select counseling interventions based on outcome research became even more prominent during the first decade of the 21st century. Counselors were (and are) expected to select **evidence-based interventions** that answer Gordon Paul's well-known question, "What works best with this particular client, with this particular problem, with this particular counselor, in this particular setting?" Counselors are constantly challenged to refine, implement, and evaluate interventions that are empirically based.

Counselors at the beginning of the century started using more types of therapies— some traditional, some alternative, and some that had been developed earlier for use in other disciplines but only recently had become part of the counseling world. Examples of such therapies included eye movement desensitization and reprocessing (EMDR; especially useful for trauma victims and clients with posttraumatic stress disorder, or PTSD), hypnosis, neurofeedback (a form of brainwave feedback), and postmodern therapies such as narrative approaches. As the worlds of science, psychology, and mental health and well-being converged, counselors received training in effective biological, psychological, and ecological approaches.

DEALING WITH CONFLICT, TRAUMA, AND CRISES.   Perhaps one of the most pressing concerns of the 21st century has been finding ways to deal with conflict, violence, and trauma (Goodman, 2015). In the 1990s, heightened concern about conflict and safety emerged during a rash of school shootings and the Oklahoma City bombing, which resulted in the deaths of many innocent people (Daniels, 2002). A defining moment in conflict and violence then occurred on September 11, 2001, when terrorists crashed commercial airliners into the World Trade Center towers in New York City and into the Pentagon in Washington, DC. These acts signaled the beginning of an active, new emphasis in counseling on preparing and responding to trauma and tragedies such as those associated with Hurricane Katrina; the Iraq and Afghanistan Wars; the Virginia Tech shootings; the December 26, 2004, tsunami in Southeast Asia; and random acts of violence across the United States (Webber & Mascari, 2016). Counselors became increasingly aware of the need to develop crisis plans and strategies for working with different populations affected by violence and tragedy. ACA created a Crisis Response Planning Task Force to prepare counselors to implement disaster mental health services on a large scale (Kaplan, 2002). Many clinical mental health counselors participated in disaster relief training coordinated by the American Red Cross. Perhaps more than ever before, counselors recognized the need to develop skills in helping clients cope with violence, trauma, tragedy, and other, less visible, signs of trauma.

The wars in Iraq and Afghanistan created an increased need for counseling professionals to develop skills to work effectively with military families and veterans. A military-funded study of the mental health of troops deployed in Iraq indicated that soldiers returning from deployment, particularly those who were deployed more than once, often exhibit a range of mental health symptoms, ranging from anxiety and sleeplessness to severe depression and PTSD (Shanker, 2008). Federal legislation paved the way for more counselors to work with veterans, and counselors began making strides in being recognized as health providers by the U.S. Department of Veteran Affairs and the Department of Defense.

PROFESSIONAL IDENTITY.   Although the counseling profession is over 100 years old, "counseling as a profession is just coming into its own in terms of parity and respect among peer professions, legislators, and the public" (Erford, cited in Shallcross, 2012c). A key issue addressed at the turn of the century was the need for counselors to develop an even stronger professional identity in order to gain recognition and respect among the general public and other helping professions (Reiner, Dobmeier, & Hernández, 2013). Unfortunately, what professional counselors do is still misunderstood by many, and increasing the recognition of what counselors do is a must if society is to benefit. Developing a unified profession in which professionals were identified as counselors first and as specialists second was crucial. In 2005, ACA and 29 major counseling organizations formed the task force **20/20: A Vision for the Future of Counseling** to address the issue of professional identity (Kaplan & Gladding, 2011). The group also developed a set of "consensus issues" for advancing the future of counseling.

SPECIAL POPULATIONS. Finding effective ways to work with older adult clients, people with addictions, refugees and immigrants, and the millennial generation represented just a few of the populations mental health counselors began to address at the beginning of the 21st century (Rollins, 2008). Innovative ways of engaging members of these groups and others were created and expanded upon. Certainly, the burgeoning force of technology and the continued impact of managed care organizations are ongoing issues in the field of clinical mental health counseling.

Major Events of the 2000s

- Movement to select counseling interventions based on outcome research
- Emphasis on finding ways to deal with conflict, violence, and trauma
- Formation of 20/20: A Vision for the Future of Counseling to address the issue of professional identity
- Increase in working with special populations such as older adults, people with addictions, refugees and immigrants, and millennials

2010 to Present

So how do we build on the past, focus on the present, and look toward the future to consider what lies ahead for the counseling profession? A few years before this text was written, Lynne Shallcross (2012c) interviewed several leaders in the counseling field to get their views about what might take place in the next decade. The article coincided with the celebration of ACA's 60th anniversary as a professional organization. Although no one claims to have a crystal ball, counseling leaders interviewed by Shallcross listed several projections for the counseling profession during this decade and the years ahead that are still relevant. Among them and others are the following:

- Continued unification and solidification of the counseling profession
- Progression toward licensure portability
- Greater emphasis on the globalization of counseling, which includes recognizing global changes (e.g., financial instability, climate changes, population aging, advances in technology)
- A focus on systemic theories, including relational-cultural theory, feminist approaches, and postmodern-constructivist paradigms
- Emphasis on understanding and responding ethically to rapidly evolving technology, including social media, cyberbullying, online counseling, online counseling programs, and distance certified counselors

- A focus on understanding the complex connections between mental health and neuro-biology, neuroplasticity, spirituality, and environmental-cultural factors
- A need to respond to increased demands for evidenced-based accountability
- Continued emphasis on holistic, wellness-based counseling
- Continued emphasis on trauma-based interventions
- A focus on finding ways to effectively counsel the rapidly growing aging population
- Promotion of social justice by confronting social inequities and oppressive systems of power
- Emphasis on working effectively with veterans and military families
- Emphasis on counseling within the context of a financially unstable era; in particular, career counseling that focuses on working with people who are unemployed and underemployed

Topics covered here include a focus on uniformity of counselor education standards; license portability; the internationalization of counseling; the promotion of social justice; biopsycho-social aspects of life; health care; immigration and oppressed populations; and TRICARE, military veterans, and the VA.

UNIFORMITY OF COUNSELOR EDUCATION STANDARDS. Because counseling started off as a confederation, there were many competing entities that vied to set its standards. As mentioned earlier, ACES initially took the lead in drawing up standards but relinquished the duty to CACREP once it was formed. CACREP, in turn, has been vigilant over the years in not only setting standards but also revising them to keep them culturally relevant. For a while, CACREP and the Council on Rehabilitation Counseling (CORE) competed in drawing up standards, but now the two organizations are united. Adding to the prestige of counseling and its unity, the NBCC announced in 2015 that it would no longer certify counselors who were not graduates of CACREP programs after the year 2022.

LICENSE PORTABILITY. License portability is an increasingly discussed topic among counselors and one that different professional counseling groups and a number of states are addressing. As a result of the process by which licensure was gained from 1977 to 2010, state licensing boards have a patchwork of statutes and rules that often preclude the possibility of licensed counselors in one state having the ability to transfer their license to another state. **Portability** involves being able to be licensed in a different state from the one in which a professional originally received a license without having to complete an application process from scratch. Basically, it is the recognition that the license a professional received in one state is acceptable and valid for practice in another state. The American Association of State Counseling Boards (AASCB), which is composed of all states that license counselors, ACES, ACA, AMHCA, and NBCC have all made proposals for facilitating the process and continue to work together and with states to make it easier to transport a professional counselor's license across state lines.

INTERNATIONALIZATION OF COUNSELING. The American Counseling Association and counselors in general have begun to recognize that counseling is not just an American phenomenon but rather is international in scope (and often spelled "counselling"). Evidence of this growing awareness can be seen in a number of actions. First, ACA is publishing books on counseling from a global perspective, the latest being *Counseling Around the World* (Hohenshil, Amundson, & Niles, 2013). Second, ACA is partnering with other international counseling associations to hold professional development and educational conferences. Three recent examples are the ACA–Asian Pacific Counseling Conference in Singapore in 2015 and 2016, the combined ACA–Canadian Counselling and Psychotherapy Association Conference in Montreal in 2006 and 2016, and the ACA–Irish Counseling and Psychotherapy Conference in Dublin in 2016.

PROMOTION OF SOCIAL JUSTICE AND MULTICULTURAL COUNSELING.   Social justice (the fair and just relation between individuals and society) has become a major concern of the counseling profession and is on the forefront of counselor and counseling association initiatives. In the mid-teen years of the 21st century, the AMCD drew up *Multicultural and Social Justice Counseling Competences* (MSJCC) (Ratts et al., 2015). This document revised the *Multicultural Counseling Competencies* (MCC) developed by Sue et al. (1992) and offers counselors a framework to implement multicultural and social justice competencies into counseling theories, practices, and research. Developmental domains within this text reflect the different layers that lead to multicultural and social justice competence: (a) counselor self-awareness, (b) client worldview, (c) counseling relationship, and (d) counseling and advocacy interventions. A visual as well as conceptual emphasis is placed on privileged and marginalized clients and counselors in regard to actions, skills, knowledge, and beliefs and guides professionals in implementing programs and actions related to social justice and multiculturalism on multiple levels.

BIOPSYCHOSOCIAL ASPECTS OF LIFE.   There is a recognition of the increasing intersection between physical, mental, and environmental dimensions of health and the need for more formal training in biopsychosocial aspects of life as well as psychopharmacology. The connections between biological, psychological, and social dimensions of health and their intersection with environmental factors is becoming increasingly important in working with clients who are living with primary depression, bipolar disorders, and substance abuse disorders.

HEALTH CARE.   A focus in counseling is on health insurance and government services for the uninsured. Counselors are faced with situations where there are needs but little or no care is available. Thus they must advocate with insurance and government agencies for client access to services, reimbursement, and improvements to public health. Mental health and substance use disorder services will be among multiple mental health care categories that need increased attention from counselors and greater coverage in society.

WORKING WITH IMMIGRANTS AND OTHER OPPRESSED POPULATIONS.   There are over 38 million immigrants, both legal and illegal, living in the United States, and the number is growing. Many of them are stressed because of their status. At least 11 million are undocumented. In addition, a number are oppressed as a result of the prejudice that exists in the wider society and owing to their lack of skills, limited knowledge of the country, fear of institutions such as the police, and inability to access health care services and other basic needs. Counselors will need to help this population in the upcoming years for the sake of the individuals' mental health and the well-being of society (Hanna & Cardona, 2013).

OFFERING MORE SERVICES TO VETERANS AND BECOMING MORE INTEGRATED AS A PART OF TRICARE.   The Department of Veterans Affairs' new **Choice Program** allows veterans to obtain a wide range of health care—including mental health—from non-VA providers. On

December 10, 2016, Congress passed H.R. 6416, a package of veterans' health and education benefits, which included language authorizing the Department of Veterans Affairs to hire counselors with a CACREP doctoral degree. In addition, the 2015 **National Defense Authorization Act (NDAA)** made modifications to the TRICARE program. Under the new law, TRICARE independent practitioner status is extended to a broader group of state-licensed counselors. Any applicant graduating from a CACREP or regionally accredited institution will qualify until January 2021, after which time only CACREP-accredited institutions will qualify. As of January 1, 2017, all applicants must have passed the National Clinical Mental Health Counseling Examination (NCMHCE).

Major Events of the 2010s

- Continued unification and solidification of the counseling profession
- Progress toward licensure portability
- Greater emphasis on the globalization and internationalization of counseling
- Greater awareness of the relationship between physical, mental, and environmental health, i.e., the biopsychosocial aspects of life as well as psychopharmacology
- More work with immigrants and oppressed populations
- Increased awareness and participation in health insurance
- More services to veterans and more involvement with TRICARE and the VA's Choice Program

Without question, there are many topics besides the ones listed here and many unknown challenges that clinical mental health counselors will face. The future, in some ways, appears daunting. In other ways, it is exciting and replete with opportunities.

To ensure that clinical mental health counselors have the support needed to counsel effectively while advocating for the profession and for clients, it is important for all counselors to become affiliated with professional organizations, including ACA and its divisions. Currently, the ACA has 20 **specialty divisions**, which provide clinical mental health counselors with opportunities to develop skills in areas of interest:

1. National Career Development Association—founded in 1913, formerly the National Vocational Guidance Association
2. Association for Humanistic Counseling—founded in 1931, formerly the Student Personnel Association for Teacher Education, Association for Humanistic Education and Development, and Counseling Association for Humanistic Education and Development
3. Association for Counselor Education and Supervision—founded in 1938, formerly the National Association of Guidance Supervisors and Counselor Trainers
4. American School Counselor Association—founded in 1953
5. American Rehabilitation Counseling Association—founded in 1958, formerly the Division of Rehabilitation Counseling
6. Association for Assessment and Research in Counseling—founded in 1965, formerly the Association for Measurement and Evaluation in Guidance

7. National Employment Counselors Association—founded in 1966
8. Association for Multicultural Counseling and Development—founded in 1972, formerly the Association for Non-White Concerns in Personnel and Guidance
9. International Association of Addictions and Offender Counselors—founded in 1972, formerly the Public Offender Counselor Association
10. Association for Specialists in Group Work—founded in 1973
11. Association for Spiritual, Ethical, and Religious Values in Counseling—founded in 1974, formerly the National Catholic Guidance Conference
12. American Mental Health Counselors Association—founded in 1976
13. Military and Government Counseling Association—founded in 1984
14. Association for Adult Development and Aging—founded in 1986
15. International Association of Marriage and Family Counselors—founded in 1989
16. American College Counseling Association—founded in 1991
17. Association for Lesbian, Gay, Bisexual, and Transgender Issues in Counseling—founded in 1996
18. Counselors for Social Justice—founded in 1999
19. Association for Creativity in Counseling—founded in 2004
20. Association for Child and Adolescent Counseling—founded in 2013

In addition to these divisions within ACA, clinical mental health counselors should also consider joining Chi Sigma Iota (international counseling honor society) and some national mental health associations as well as state licensure groups. They are discussed next.

CHI SIGMA IOTA.   Chi Sigma Iota (CSI) is the international honor society for professional counselors, counselor educators, and students in counselor education programs. CSI was founded in 1985 by Dr. Tom Sweeney. Its mission is to promote scholarship, research, professionalism, leadership, and excellence in counseling, and to recognize high attainment in the pursuit of academic and clinical excellence in the profession of counseling (CSI, 2016). CSI is one of the largest associations of professional counselors in the world. Over 110,000 members have been initiated since its inception. In 2016, CSI had 387 campus-based chapters and was initiating over 6,000 new members each year. Campus-based chapters sponsor many activities and projects designed to promote the counseling profession. CSI is committed to promoting leadership in the profession, too, and publishes the *Journal of Counselor Leadership and Advocacy.*

CSI membership requirements are listed on their website (www.csi-net.org). Membership is open to students and graduates of counselor education programs. To become a member, individuals must have completed at least one semester of full-time graduate course work, have earned a grade point average of 3.5 or higher, and be recommended for membership by their chapter.

OTHER PROFESSIONAL AND MENTAL HEALTH ORGANIZATIONS.   Clinical mental health counselors may choose to affiliate with a number of other professional organizations, besides ACA, committed to promoting mental health and wellness. Examples include the National Alliance on Mental Illness (NAMI), Mental Health America (MHA), and state-based associations for licensed professional counselors (e.g., the Licensed Professional Counselors Association of Georgia, the Licensed Professional Counselors Association of North Carolina). Licensed professional counselors associations exist in many states.

PROFESSIONAL IDENTITY

Just as everyone has a history, everyone has a specific identity. There is a uniqueness in an identity, such as a surname or social security number, and often people have multiple more-informal identities, such as being a son, a sister, a spouse, and a parent. These identities help others recognize and even classify people in everyday life or in business transactions. **Professional identity** refers to the philosophy, training model, and scope of practice that characterize a particular profession. A critical task for all counselors, including clinical mental health counselors, is to assume a professional identity and be able to explain that identity to others (Remley & Herlihy, 2016).

It is important to understand something of the uniqueness of clinical mental health if an individual is going to become a clinical mental health counselor. It is crucial, as well, to know about the other therapeutic professionals with whom clinical mental health counselors work. Professional credentialing is also important, for it further defines the roles and functions of clinical mental health counselors in particular. Professional affiliation is vital, too. Affiliations affect participation in professional organizations. They help clinical mental health counselors acquire new colleagues, cutting-edge therapy information, and continuing education. It is through becoming involved with other professionals that clinical mental health counselors become more knowledgeable and learn of opportunities for growth.

Defining Professional Helping

There are a number of ways of helping. In the mental health field three levels of helping relationships stand out: nonprofessional, paraprofessional, and professional. To practice at a certain level requires that helpers acquire the skills necessary for the task.

The first level of helping involves **nonprofessional helpers**. Helpers at this level are usually untrained and good-hearted volunteers who try to assist those in need in whatever ways they can. Nonprofessional helpers possess varying backgrounds as well as diverse degrees of wisdom and skill. No specific educational requirements are involved, and the level of helping differs greatly among people in this group.

A second and higher level of helping encompasses **generalist human services workers**. These individuals are usually human services personnel who have received some formal training in human relations skills but work as part of a team rather than as individuals. People on this level often work as mental health technicians, probation personnel, and youth counselors. When properly trained and supervised, generalist human services workers can have a major impact on facilitating positive relationships that promote mental health throughout a social environment.

Finally, there are **professional helpers**, also called **therapeutic professionals**. These persons are educated to provide assistance on a preventive, developmental, and remedial level. They hold advanced degrees in one of the main helping professions. People in this group include social workers, psychologists, psychiatrists, psychiatric nurses, and clinical mental health counselors, among others. Individuals on this level have specialized training in honing their clinical skills and have had supervised internships to help them prepare to deal with a plethora of situations. (See Table 1–1.)

Defining Professional Counseling

Although the term *counseling* is used often in society, it is important to define what the term means, especially when focusing on clinical mental health counseling. The term was loosely

TABLE 1–1   Three Levels of Helping

Category	Individuals Involved	Helping Skills
Nonprofessional helpers	Friends, untrained volunteers	Vary greatly; no formal training in helping skills
Generalist human services workers	Probation personnel, mental health technicians, youth counselors	Have basic helping skills; often work as part of a team
Professional helpers, or "therapeutic professionals"	Psychiatrists, social workers, psychologists, clinical mental health counselors	Advanced skilled training; assist at preventive, developmental, and remedial levels

defined for a long time but was professionally defined in the early part of the 21st century. In 2010, delegates of the task group 20/20: A Vision for the Future of Counseling reached a milestone by arriving at a consensus definition. Twenty-nine of the 31 representative organizations—including ACA and all but 2 of its 20 divisions, along with the American Association of State Counseling Boards, the Council for the Accreditation of Counseling and Related Educational Programs, the National Board for Certified Counselors, the Council of Rehabilitation Education, the Commission of Rehabilitation Counselor Certification, and the Chi Sigma Iota International Honor Society—endorsed a formal definition of counseling (Kaplan, Tarvydas, & Gladding, 2014). The definition is only 22 words long but it is comprehensive. Specifically, **professional counseling** is defined as "a professional relationship that empowers diverse individuals, families, and groups to accomplish mental health, wellness, education, and career goals" (ACA, 2016). This definition contains a number of key points for clinical mental health counselors and consumers to consider that have been more implied than stated overtly before:

- Counseling deals with wellness, personal growth, career, education, and empowerment concerns. To that end, counseling services may focus on adjustment, existential issues, psychological health and well-being, and achieving goals in settings such as home, work, and school. Counselors are concerned with social justice and, as a part of that process, advocate for those who are oppressed and powerless.
- Counseling is conducted with persons individually, in groups, and in families. Clients seen by counselors live and work in a wide variety of settings. Their problems may require short-term or long-term interventions that focus on just one person or are conducted with multiple individuals who may or may not be related to each other.
- Counseling is diverse and multicultural. Counselors work with clients from varied cultural and socioeconomic backgrounds. People from minority and majority cultures are helped in a variety of ways depending on their needs, which may include addressing larger societal issues, such as discrimination, prejudice, and power imbalances.

Implied in the definition and understood on some level prior to the adoption of it is that counseling is a dynamic process. Counselors not only focus on their clients' goals, but also help clients accomplish them. This dynamic process uses a variety of theories and methods that are tailored to meet the needs of clients, which makes counseling lively and engaging: a rehearsal for action.

In addition to defining counseling in general, ACA has **counseling specialties**. Counseling specialties are areas within counseling that focus on particular populations, settings, or issues and require advanced knowledge and skills. Among the specialties within counseling are those dealing with educational settings such as schools or colleges and those pertaining to situations in life such as marriage, mental health, rehabilitation, aging, assessment, addiction, and careers. Becoming a specialist is founded on the premise that professional counselors must first meet the requirements for the general practice of professional counseling. Clinical mental health counseling is one example of a specialty area.

Legal Recognition of Counseling as a Profession

Now that we have clarified professional helping and the definition of counseling, we will turn our attention to how counseling and counselors became recognized. Professional identity and professional credentialing depend on **legal recognition**. As recently as 1960, counseling and counselors did not have a strong enough identity as a profession to be recognized legally. In that year, a judge ruled in the case of *Bogust v. Iverson* that a counselor with a doctoral degree could not be held liable for the suicide of one of his clients because counselors were "mere teachers" who received training in a department of education.

It was not until 1971, in an *Iowa Law Review* note, that counselors were legally recognized as professionals who provided personal as well as vocational and educational counseling. The profession was even more clearly defined in 1974 in *Weldon v. Virginia State Board of Psychologists Examiners*. The judgment rendered stated that counseling was a profession distinct from psychology. As stated earlier, the initial state law that regulated counseling was passed in Virginia in 1976. It classified counseling as a generic profession with specialties, such as community or school counseling (Swanson, 1983). In the same year, the U.S. House of Representatives further refined the definition of counseling and recognized the profession in H. R. 3270 (94th Congress, 1976) by stating that counseling is "the process through which a trained counselor assists an individual or group to make satisfactory and responsible decisions concerning personal, educational and career development."

PROFESSIONAL IDENTIFICATION THROUGH CREDENTIALING

With the recognition of counseling as a separate professional entity, there was a need for regulation through **credentialing** procedures. Some credentials are more valued than others. While a number of credentials are conferred by the counseling profession, and others are provided by states to regulate who can legally practice in that state, both types of credentialing are needed to be recognized and respected. Four types of professional credentialing exist: inspection, registration, certification, and licensure.

Inspection

In the **inspection** process "a state agency periodically examines the activities of a profession's practitioners to ascertain whether they are practicing the profession in a fashion consistent with the public safety, health, and welfare" (Swanson, 1983, p. 28). Many state agencies that employ counselors, such as mental health centers, are subject to having their personnel and programs regularly inspected. Such an inspection may include a review of case notes on treatment during a specific period, a review of agency procedures, and personal interviews.

Registration

Registration requires practitioners to submit information to the state concerning the nature of their practice. Usually a professional organization, such as a state division of ACA, assumes the responsibility for setting standards necessary to qualify as a registrant and maintains a list of names of those who voluntarily meet those standards. This method is employed as a way to gain legal recognition for counselors who use the title "registered professional counselor."

Certification

Certification is a professional, statutory, or nonstatutory process "by which an agency or association grants recognition to an individual for having met certain predetermined professional qualifications. Stated succinctly, certification . . . is a 'limited license,' that is, the protection of title only" (Fretz & Mills, 1980, p. 7). In this case, a state or national board or department issues a certificate to an individual in a specialty. Certification basically implies that the person meets the minimum skills necessary to engage in that profession and has no known character defects that would interfere with such a practice. Often states require candidates for certification to pass a competency test and submit letters of reference before a certificate is issued. School counselors were among the first counselors to be certified.

Licensure

Licensure is "the statutory process by which an agency of government, usually a state, grants permission to a person meeting predetermined qualifications to engage in a given occupation and/or use a particular title and to perform specified functions" (Fretz & Mills, 1980, p. 7). Licensure differs in purpose from certification but requires similar procedures in terms of education and testing for competence. Once licensure requirements are established, individuals cannot practice a profession legally without obtaining a license (Wheeler & Bertram, 2015). Licensure is almost exclusively a state-governed process, and those states that have licensure have established boards to oversee the issuing of licenses. A licensee is designed to protect the public and the profession. A licensee who commits an offense that violates the legal or ethical codes adopted by the board to regulate practice is subject to the board's disciplinary authority which may include revocation or suspension of a license. In general, the licensing of professional helpers is always under scrutiny from the public, other professions, and state legislatures. (See Table 1–2.)

IDENTIFYING AND DEFINING THERAPEUTIC PROFESSIONALS

To facilitate collaboration among professional helpers, often called *therapeutic professionals*, it is important to have an understanding of their backgrounds and training, as well as why they have the titles they do and what services they offer. Therapeutic professionals can be defined as "mental health professionals trained to help people with problems that manifest behaviorally or psychologically and that may have roots in physical, psychological, or spiritual dimensions" (MacCluskie & Ingersoll, 2001, p. 3). The problems people experience may range from situational or developmental concerns to more severe psychological disorders. Attempts in the past have been made to define specific mental health professions based on the severity of client problems. However, professional definitions based strictly on client diagnosis can be misleading. Although the counseling profession focuses on providing

TABLE 1–2 Four Types of Professional Mental Health Credentials

Type	Activity Involved	Reason
Inspection	Process whereby a state agency periodically examines the activities of a profession's practitioners	Ascertains whether professionals are practicing the profession in a fashion consistent with public safety, health, and welfare
Registration	Process whereby practitioners voluntarily submit information to the state concerning the nature of their practice	Provides a way to gain legal recognition for a profession from a state
Certification	Process by which an agency or association grants recognition to an individual for having met certain predetermined professional qualifications	Is broader than a state license and not subject to state politics; provides referrals; recognizes counseling specialties
Licensure	Statutory process by which an agency of government, usually a state, grants permission to a person meeting predetermined qualifications to engage in a given occupation and/or use a particular title, and to perform specified functions	Protects the public from nonqualified mental health practitioners; recognizes a profession and its practices

services that are developmental and preventive in nature, clinical mental health counselors also are trained to work with clients experiencing a wide range of concerns, including problems described in the *Diagnostic and Statistical Manual of Mental Disorders* (*DSM-5*; American Psychiatric Association, 2013). Thus, it is more helpful to categorize different therapeutic professions by their training emphases and requirements, recognizing that similarities as well as differences exist among the various professions.

In this section, a brief overview of the therapeutic professions of social work, psychiatry, psychiatric mental health nursing, psychology, and clinical mental health counseling is provided.

Social Work

Social workers usually earn a master's of social work degree (MSW), although some universities award a bachelor's degree in social work. Some social workers elect to pursue additional training at the doctoral level. The National Association of Social Workers (NASW) offers credentials for members who demonstrate advanced clinical and educational competencies. The practice of clinical social work is regulated by licensure laws in all 50 states.

Regardless of their educational background, social workers on all levels have completed internships in social agency settings. Social workers participate in a variety of activities, too, including helping individuals, groups, and communities enhance social functioning. Important goals include negotiating social systems and advocating for change. Some social workers administer government programs for those who are underprivileged and disenfranchised. Others engage in individual, group, and family counseling, emphasizing a systems and contextual approach, rather than following a medical model. Social workers are employed in a variety of settings, including schools, medical and public health environments, and mental health and substance abuse settings.

Psychiatry

Psychiatry represents a specialty area within the school of medicine. **Psychiatrists** typically earn a medical degree (MD) and then complete a four-year residency in psychiatry. To earn the license to practice, they must pass both a national and a state examination. Psychiatrists may specialize in areas such as child or geriatric psychiatry, psychopharmacology, or a particular mode of therapy (Gerig, 2014). Psychiatrists are represented by the American Psychiatric Association.

There is some dispute within the field of psychiatry related to preferred models of training. Some psychiatrists primarily follow a strict **biomedical model** and spend most of their time with clients prescribing medications and evaluating their effects. Other psychiatrists adhere to a **biopsychosocial model**, which acknowledges the interaction of behavioral, psychological, and social factors in development and mental health. Until recently, psychiatrists were the only therapeutic professionals who had the authority to prescribe medication. However, psychiatric mental health nurses are now able to prescribe medication, and in a few states, such as New Mexico, Illinois, and Louisiana, some psychologists now have legal rights to prescribe psychopharmacological medications. Psychologists who have the authority to prescribe medications are trained as medical psychologists and hold a postdoctoral master's degree or equivalent in clinical psychopharmacology (Cherry, 2016).

Psychiatric Mental Health Nursing

Psychiatric mental health nurses (PMHNs) are accredited by the American Nurses Credentialing Center. Advanced practice registered nurses (APRNs) earn master's or doctoral degrees in psychiatric mental health nursing. They assess, diagnose, and treat individuals or families with psychiatric disorders; contribute to policy development; practice evaluation; and participate in healthcare reform (American Psychiatric Nurses Association, 2016). Advanced psychiatric nurses hold a master's degree or higher in psychiatric mental health nursing and are able to assess patients, diagnose disorders, provide psychotherapy, and prescribe medications. They may choose to specialize in child and adolescent mental health nursing, gerontological psychiatric nursing, forensics, or substance abuse disorders. Advanced PMHNs sometimes choose to work as consultants, work collaboratively with primary care providers, or work in an academic setting. Psychiatric mental health nurses with master's degrees also have rights to prescribe psychotropic medication (Cherry, 2016).

Psychology

Psychology programs are accredited by the American Psychological Association (APA). Most **psychologists** earn a PhD (doctor of philosophy) or PsyD (doctor of psychology). Areas of specialization within the field include clinical, social, cognitive, developmental, counseling, and school psychology. All states license psychologists, although requirements for licensure differ from state to state.

Since the 1940s, psychologists have been viewed as experts in psychological assessment—a view that has led to disagreement among therapeutic professionals about who should have access to various assessment instruments. In February 1996, responding to attempts by state psychology licensure boards to restrict assessment practices of other trained professionals, the **National Fair Access Coalition on Testing (FACT)** was formed. FACT is a nonprofit organization that advocates for equitable access to testing services for all appropriately trained professionals who have demonstrated competence in administering and interpreting assessment instruments (FACT, 2015). Throughout the years, FACT has helped ensure that counselors' rights to administer and interpret tests have been protected.

Counseling psychology is a specialization area that is represented by Division 17 of APA. Division 17 was founded in 1946 to facilitate personal, vocational, educational, and interpersonal adjustment (Society of Counseling Psychology, 2007). Counseling psychologists have doctoral degrees and are employed in universities as well as a range of human service settings. There are 68 accredited counseling psychology programs in the United States. Counseling psychology shares common roots and emphases with the field of professional counseling.

Clinical Mental Health Counseling

A **clinical mental health counselor** is a therapeutic professional who has earned a 60-semester-hour degree in clinical mental health counseling; has become a national certified counselor (NCC), and with time may become a certified clinical mental health counselor (CCMHC); and has obtained a license to practice counseling in the state where he or she resides. Clinical mental health counselors usually affiliate with AMHCA and ACA.

Some of the specific topics clinical mental health counselors are trained to help with include career and lifestyle issues, marriage and family concerns, addictions, stress management, crisis intervention, disaster relief, mental health disorders, developmental concerns, and grief and loss. Clinical mental health counselors help people develop psychologically, socially, spiritually, and educationally. They recognize the importance of biological, cultural, social, emotional, and psychological interactions. Whereas other helping professions may include counseling as a **secondary service** (peripheral or less important service), the **primary service** (i.e., main service) counselors provide is counseling with individuals, groups, couples, and families (Remley & Herlihy, 2016). Counselors also provide professional services that include assessment, diagnosis, referral, education, consultation, and advocacy. (See Table 1–3.)

TABLE 1–3 Five Related Helping Professions

Profession	Degree	Emphases
Social worker	BA, MSW, DSW	Negotiates social systems and advocates for change; provides social services; may do counseling
Psychiatrist	MD	Diagnoses psychological disorders in patients; may have a biopsychosocial focus; prescribes medications; may do counseling
Psychiatric mental health nurse	MS, PhD	Assesses patients; diagnoses disorders; provides psychotherapy; prescribes medications; may do counseling
Psychologist	PhD, PsyD	May specialize in clinical, counseling, social, developmental, cognitive, and school psychology; provides diagnosis, psychometrics, research, and counseling; psychology shares a long history with counselor education but is distinct
Clinical mental health counselor	MA	Provides primary service counseling with individuals, groups, couples, and families in such areas as career and lifestyle issues, marriage and family concerns, addictions, stress management, crisis intervention, disaster relief, mental health disorders, developmental concerns, and grief and loss

The Case of Tameka

Tameka recently graduated from a state university with an undergraduate degree in psychology. After working as a mental health technician in a local mental health agency for two years, Tameka has decided to apply to graduate school. She is unsure whether to apply to a program that prepares students to become clinical social workers, clinical mental health counselors, or counseling psychologists. Although she has researched several programs online, she is uncertain of the advantages and disadvantages associated with each profession. Furthermore, she is confused by what appears to be a strong overlap among the professions. How would you help her make an informed decision?

CLINICAL MENTAL HEALTH PRACTICE SETTINGS AND SERVICES

Clinical mental health practice settings include mental health centers, work sites, hospital environments, substance abuse programs, employee assistance programs, universities, and individual practices. Other settings that employ clinical mental health counselors include geriatric centers, government programs including Veterans Affairs centers, businesses and industries, religious institutions, health maintenance organizations, shelters for domestic violence victims, hospice programs, and programs for people living with HIV/AIDS.

Clinical mental health counselors do not work with clients in isolation. They recognize the importance of **client–environment interaction**. This approach to counseling, which is strengths-based and empowering, addresses the idea that a comprehensive approach including clients' environments is more effective than a single-service approach. Thus clinical mental health counselors provide services in four areas:

- Direct client services
- Indirect client services
- Direct community services
- Indirect community services

Examples of each service component are illustrated in Figure 1–1. Clinical mental health counselors recognize that clients' psychological health is affected by the immediate ecological systems in which they live, including family, educational, and work environments. Psychological well-being also is affected by broader sociocultural forces, including the political environment, cultural background, and global influences. Consequently, all systems and their interactions need to be considered when clinical mental health counselors work with clients.

	Client Services	Systems Services
Direct	• Individual counseling • Crisis intervention • Substance abuse counseling • Family counseling	• Parent education programs • Stress management workshops • Conflict mediation workshops • Lobbying for social change
Indirect	• Advocating for clients • Referring clients to appropriate human service agencies	• Influencing public policy • Influencing systems that affect clients (e.g., educational systems, mental health systems)

FIGURE 1–1 Direct and Indirect Services Provided by Clinical Mental Health Counselors
Source: Adapted from Lewis, Lewis, Daniels, and D'Andrea, 2003.

Summary and Conclusion

This chapter began with the story of a hero who went from being a rescuer to becoming a deliverer of preventive services. The story illustrates the assumptions of those who work as clinical mental health counselors: that it is important to focus on people's environments as well as their symptoms, that a multifaceted approach to treatment is better than one that is based on a single-service plan, and that prevention is more efficient than remediation. The chapter then briefly reviewed other premises of the counseling profession and traced its evolution into the 21st century with topics and issues that are now of utmost importance.

Clinical mental health counseling is concerned with wellness, development, and situational difficulties, as well as with helping people who have more serious mental health issues. The history of counseling shows that the profession has an interdisciplinary base. It began with the almost simultaneous actions of Frank Parsons, Jesse B. Davis, and Clifford Beers to provide, reform, and improve services in vocational guidance, mental health treatment, and character development of children. Counseling is interlinked with but distinct from psychometrics, psychology, and sociology. Noteworthy events in the history of counseling include the involvement of the government in counseling during and after World War I, the Great Depression, World War II, and the launching of *Sputnik*. Ideas from innovators such as John Brewer, E. G. Williamson, Carl Rogers, Gilbert Wrenn, Leona Tyler, Thomas Sweeney, and others have shaped the development of the profession and broadened its horizon. The emergence and growth of the American Counseling Association (rooted in the establishment of the National Vocational Guidance Association in 1913) has been a major factor in the growth of the profession, especially since the 1950s.

Community counseling programs emerged in universities in the 1970s. Community counseling was officially recognized as a specialty area in 1981, with the establishment of CACREP. Mental health counseling programs were recognized by CACREP in the early 1990s. With the adoption of the 2009 CACREP standards, the two specialty areas ceased and programs with community counseling were given an opportunity to become clinical mental health counseling programs. The reasons: clinical mental health counseling had standards and an association (AMHCA) while community counseling had neither. In the 21st century, clinical mental health counselors can be found working with many different populations in a wide range of settings, including mental health centers, medical settings, Veterans Affairs centers, correctional institutions, businesses, and private practice.

The importance of developing a professional identity as a clinical mental health counselor who practices in community and agency settings concluded the chapter. Levels of helping were described. The definition of counseling, legal recognition of it, and types of credentialing of counselors and other therapeutic professionals were presented. Four categories of professional helpers—psychiatrists, social workers, psychiatric nurses, and psychologists—were defined, and the ways they are similar to and different from clinical mental health counselors were highlighted. The emphasis of each of these groups of professionals was laid out along with their educational requirements. The chapter ended with a discussion of direct and indirect services clinical mental health counselors provide in the client environments in which they practice.

MyCounselingLab

Start with the Topic 10 Assignments: *History of Counseling* and then the Topic 11 Assignments: *Licensure and Credentialing* and the Topic 6 Assignments: *Current Trends in Counseling*.

CHAPTER 2

Ethical and Legal Aspects of Counseling

Kaspars Grinvalds/Shutterstock

CHAPTER OVERVIEW

From reading this chapter, you will learn about

- How ethics, morality, and the law are defined
- The purpose of ethical codes and their limitations
- Ways to make ethical decisions, particularly when there is an ethical dilemma
- The relationship between the law and counseling
- Ethical and legal concerns that clinical mental health counselors may confront

As you read, consider

- Your personal values and how they may affect the way you work with clients
- How you will go about making ethical decisions
- How you will act when ethical codes and the law are in conflict
- How you will handle ethical and legal concerns when they arise

In the cool grey dawn of early September,
I place the final suitcase into my Mustang
And silently say "good-bye"
  to the quiet beauty of North Carolina.
Hesitantly, I head for the blue ocean-lined coast
  of Connecticut.
Bound for a new position and the unknown.
Traveling with me are a sheltie named "Eli"
  and the still fresh memories of our last counseling session.
You, who wrestled so long with fears
  that I kiddingly started calling you "Jacob,"
  are as much a part of me as my luggage.
Moving in life is bittersweet—
like giving up friends and fears.
The taste is like smooth, orange, fall persimmons,
  deceptively delicious but tart.

Reprinted from "Bittersweet," by S. T. Gladding, 1984, *Counseling and Values, 28*, p. 146. Copyright © S. T. Gladding. Reprinted with permission.

Clinical mental health counseling is a profession that is guided by ethical and legal codes. These codes are based on values, which are at the core of counseling relationships. All goals in counseling, whether for lifestyle modification or symptom relief, are undergirded by values systems. Values held by the counselor and by the client affect many aspects of the counseling process. Clinical mental health counselors need to be aware of their personal and professional values and beliefs if they are to act responsibly, ethically, and legally (Ametrano, 2014).

Counselors who are unclear about their personal values, ethics, and legal responsibilities, as well as those of their clients, can cause harm despite their best intentions (Remley & Herlihy, 2016). Therefore, it is vital for counselors to be aware of their own values and understand professional counseling guidelines before they attempt to work with clients. Ethical counselors demonstrate professional knowledge, concern, and good judgment in their work with clients. They are cautiously prudent in what they suggest and proactive in seeking consultation from other professionals when questionable circumstances arise. In this chapter, ethical standards are covered as well as legal constraints and mandates that guide the counseling process.

DEFINITIONS: ETHICS, MORALITY, AND LAW

The terms *ethics* and *morality* are often used synonymously, and in some ways their meanings are similar. Both deal with "what is good and bad or the study of human conduct and values" (Van Hoose & Kottler, 1985, p. 2). However, each term has a distinct meaning.

Ethics can be defined as "a philosophical discipline that is concerned with human conduct and moral decision making" (Van Hoose & Kottler, 1985, p. 3). Ethics are normative in nature and focus on principles and standards that govern relationships between individuals, such as relationships between counselors and clients. **Morality**, on the other hand, involves judgment or evaluation of actions. It is associated with words such as *good, bad, right, wrong, ought,* and *should* (Brandt, 1959; Grant, 1992). Even though some moral principles tend to be universally shared, moral conduct is defined within the context of a culture or society (Remley & Herlihy, 2016).

Kitchener (1984) describes **five moral principles** that form the foundation for ethical guidelines and provide clarification for ethical decision making. These principles are as follows:

- **Autonomy**, which allows an individual the freedom of choice and action. Counselors are responsible for helping clients make their own decisions and act on their own values. Counselors also are responsible for helping clients consider the ramifications of their decisions and for protecting them from actions that may lead to harm of self or others.
- **Nonmaleficence**, which refers to not harming other people. Nonmaleficence, which is one of the oldest moral principles in the profession, is defined by the dictate followed by ancient Greek physicians to "above all, do no harm." Counselors are to refrain from actions that may intentionally or unintentionally harm others.
- **Beneficence**, which is a proactive concept that implies doing things that contribute to the welfare of the client. When practicing beneficence, it is important for counselors to avoid taking a paternalistic approach toward clients that undermines their autonomy (Cottone & Tarvydas, 2016).
- **Justice**, which refers to treating all people fairly. The concept of justice implies that counselors should not discriminate on the basis of race, socioeconomic status, gender, sexual orientation, or any other variable. Counselors need to examine the degree to

which justice is carried out through the policies of agencies, institutions, and laws that affect mental health practices (Cottone & Tarvydas, 2016).

- **Fidelity**, which means that counselors are loyal to their clients, honor their commitments, and fulfill their obligations.

A sixth principle, **veracity**, is also considered key to ethical practice (Barnett & Johnson, 2015; Remley & Herlihy, 2016). Veracity refers to truthfulness and integrity. It forms the foundation of a trusting relationship. Together, these six principles provide a fundamental framework for guiding clinical mental health counselors in making judgments about what actions they should take to promote their clients' welfare.

The concept of professional ethics can be further clarified by differentiating between mandatory ethics and aspirational ethics (Corey, Corey, Corey, & Callanan, 2015). **Mandatory ethics** are followed when clinical mental health counselors comply with the required minimal standards of the profession. **Aspirational ethics**, in contrast, are followed when counselors make decisions based on internalized principles and ideals of the profession, not just external considerations. Clinical mental health counselors are guided by aspirational ethics when they make choices in accordance with the higher principles behind the literal meaning of ethical codes. Counselors guided by aspirational ethics are extremely self-aware and continually engage in self-monitoring (Granello & Young, 2012).

Law, which differs from ethics and morality, is a set of rules that govern particular activities in society (Wheeler & Bertram, 2015). Law is created by legislation, court decision, and tradition, as in English common law. Laws codify the minimum standards of behavior that society will tolerate, whereas ethics represent ideal standards (Remley & Herlihy, 2016). The practice of clinical mental health counselors is guided by ethical and legal standards, and counselors need to be well informed about both.

The law does not dictate what is ethical in a given situation; rather, it dictates what is legal. Sometimes what is legal at a given point in history is considered unethical or immoral by significant segments of society. A classic example of such a discrepancy is found in the segregation patterns that people of color endured in the United States between the end of the Civil War and the 1950s. These practices were legal; however, they were without ethical or moral rationale.

Ethical codes are not intended to supersede the law; instead, they typically clarify existing law and policy (Cottone & Tarvydas, 2016). At times, however, conflicts between the legal system and ethical codes of conduct occur (see Figure 2–1). Although laws tend to be more objective and specific than ethical or moral codes, interpretations of laws change over time and are often situationally dependent. For example, the law mandating a counselor's duty to warn a third party of potential imminent danger (e.g., the Tarasoff case in California) was not upheld by the Texas Supreme Court, which ruled that mental health professionals have no common law duty to warn identifiable third parties of a client's threats against them (Wheeler & Bertram, 2015).

Clinical mental health counselors need to be aware of legal issues that are applicable to their counseling situations and to the states in which they practice. They also need to work to reconcile differences in legislative and ethical standards. Furthermore, when counselors act as consultants or advocates for clients, the counselors should be aware of the potential for legal change and have sound principles on which to advocate for modification of existing systems.

Remley and Herlihy (2016) provide a model for professional practice that integrates moral and ethical principles, ethical and legal codes, and outside sources of help. The model, depicted in Figure 2–2, illustrates the balance between the internal beliefs and values

		Example
1. Ethical & legal	Following a just law	Keeping a client's confidences that are also protected by law from disclosure
2. Ethical & illegal	Disobeying an unjust law	Refusing to share client records that may damage the client but are subpoenaed by a judge
3. Ethical & alegal	Doing good where no law applies	Offering free service to clients who cannot afford to pay
4. Unethical & legal	Following an unjust law	Following the Federal Trade Commission's edict that ethical codes cannot prohibit the use of testimonials in ads for counseling services
5. Unethical & illegal	Breaking a just law	Disclosing confidential information protected by law from disclosure
6. Unethical & alegal	Doing harm that no law prohibits	Promoting client dependency to enhance one's own feeling of power or security

FIGURE 2–1   Interactions between Ethics and the Law
Sources: Cottone & Tarvydas, 2016; Thompson, 1990; Welfel, 2016.

that drive the counselor and the external forces that guide and support counseling practice. Clinical mental health counselors are committed to developing a deep awareness of personal values and professional moral and ethical principles, a thorough understanding of ethical and legal codes, and a willingness to participate in consultation, supervision, and continuing education opportunities.

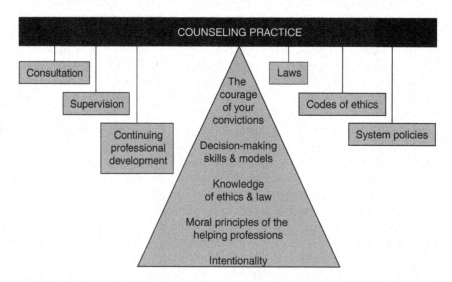

FIGURE 2–2   Professional Practice—Built from Within and Balanced from Outside the Self
Source: From *Ethical, Legal, and Professional Issues in Counseling* (3rd ed.), by T. P. Remley, Jr., and B. Herlihy, 2010, Upper Saddle River, NJ: Merrill/Prentice Hall. Copyright © 2010 by Prentice Hall. Reprinted and electronically reproduced by permission of Pearson Education, Inc.

ETHICS AND COUNSELING

Purpose of Ethical Codes

The key reason for having a code of ethics is to establish norms and expectations for practitioners, thereby minimizing the risk of harm to others (Welfel, 2016). Many mental health professions have established codes of ethics that provide guidelines for practitioners, including the American Counseling Association (ACA, 2014), the National Board for Certified Counselors (NBCC, 2012), the American Mental Health Counselors Association (AMHCA, 2015), the National Association of Social Workers (NASW, 2008), and the American Psychological Association (APA, 2010). Typically, ethical codes consist of general statements that stipulate counseling duties to enhance client welfare. Codes of ethics serve several purposes. Ethical codes educate practitioners about sound ethical conduct, provide a mechanism for accountability, and serve as catalysts for improving practice (Herlihy & Corey, 2015). They help clarify professionals' responsibilities to clients and society and protect clients and members of the profession from unethical or incompetent practice. Also, the establishment of codes and standards helps protect a profession from outside regulation by providing a method for self-regulation.

The *ACA Code of Ethics* (2014) represents the seventh version of the counseling profession's ethical code. The original version was initiated by Donald Super and was adopted by the American Personnel and Guidance Association (APGA) in 1961. It has been revised periodically since then. In addition to the *Code of Ethics*, ACA produces the *Ethics Desk Reference for Counselors* (Barnett & Johnson, 2015) and an *Ethical Standards Casebook* (Herlihy & Corey, 2015). Clinical mental health counselors are encouraged to examine journal articles, books, and podcasts devoted to the topic of ethics in counseling.

Within ACA, several divisions have developed separate codes of ethics, a practice that potentially can create confusion among practitioners (Remley & Herlihy, 2016). Many clinical mental health counselors are members of AMHCA or other ACA divisions that have their own ethical codes. Professional counselors who belong to multiple associations, hold national certifications, and are members of various divisions within ACA are expected to comply with several different codes, which can be problematic and unwieldy. Remley and Herlihy (2016), as well as other counseling professionals, have recommended that a single, universally accepted code of ethics be established for the counseling profession. However, until this occurs, clinical mental health counselors are responsible for understanding and adhering to the different ethical codes that govern the organizations to which they belong. In particular, counselors will want to be familiar with the ethical codes established by ACA (2014), AMHCA (2015), and NBCC (2012), as well as with any ethical standards created by the states in which they practice.

The *ACA Code of Ethics*

The 2014 *ACA Code of Ethics* is a comprehensive document that illustrates the point that counseling has developed into a mature professional discipline. The current ethical code delineates five core professional values: (a) enhancing human development throughout the life span; (b) honoring diversity and embracing a multicultural approach in support of the worth, dignity, potential and uniqueness of people within their social and cultural contexts; (c) promoting social justice; (d) safeguarding the integrity of the counselor–client relationship; and (e) practicing in a competent and ethical manner (ACA, 2014). These core **professional values** align with the aforementioned ethical principles that guide ethical behavior and decision making: **autonomy**, **nonmaleficence**, **beneficence**, **justice**, **fidelity**, and **veracity**.

The 2014 *ACA Code of Ethics* is available online at www.counseling.org/Resources/aca-code-of-ethics.pdf. The code consists of nine sections that address specific counseling issues.

- *Section A: The Counseling Relationship* focuses on the nature of the relationship between counselors and clients. Trust is at the heart of the counseling relationship, and counselors are responsible for safeguarding their clients' rights to privacy and confidentiality (Barnett & Johnson, 2015). This section emphasizes client welfare as the counselor's primary responsibility, and counselors are expected to act in the best interest of their clients. The twelve topics that address the counseling relationship include:

  - Client Welfare (Standard A.1)
  - Informed Consent (Standard A.2)
  - Clients Served by Others (Standard A.3)
  - Avoiding Harm and Imposing Values (Standard A.4)
  - Prohibited Noncounseling Roles and Relationships (Standard A.5)
  - Managing and Maintaining Boundaries and Professional Relationships (Standard A.6)
  - Roles and Relationships at Individual, Group, Institutional, and Societal Levels (Standard A.7)
  - Multiple Clients (Standard A.8)
  - Group Work (Standard A.9)
  - Fees and Business Practices (Standard A.10)

- Termination and Referral (Standard A.11)
- Abandonment and Client Neglect (Standard A.12)

  Throughout Section A, counselors are reminded to consider the role of culture and other diversity issues as they work with clients. To work effectively with diverse populations, counselors need to be aware of their personal values and beliefs to ensure that they do not inadvertently impose those values and beliefs on their clients. Counselors are responsible for safeguarding client welfare from the beginning of the counseling relationship through the termination of the relationship (Remley & Herlihy, 2016).

- *Section B: Confidentiality and Privacy* outlines the client's right to privacy in a counselor–client relationship. Limitations to confidentiality are addressed, as are considerations in working with groups, families, children, and clients lacking the capacity to give informed consent. Requirements regarding client records are described, and guidelines are prescribed to protect client confidentiality when counselors are conducting research, training, or consultation.

- *Section C: Professional Responsibility* provides guidelines related to professional knowledge and competence, advertising and solicitation, presentation of credentials, public responsibility, and respect for others who work in the mental health field. Counselors are expected to facilitate access to counseling services and to practice in a nondiscriminatory manner. They are encouraged to provide some portion of service for which there is little or no financial gain. Also, counselors have a responsibility to engage in self-care activities to ensure that they are able to meet their professional responsibilities (Barnett & Johnson, 2015).

- *Section D: Relationships with Other Professionals* focuses on counselors' interactions with other mental health workers. Counselors often cooperate with a wide range of professionals in order to provide their clients with the best possible care. This section focuses on relationships with colleagues, employers, and employees. It also describes ethical considerations related to consultation.
- *Section E: Evaluation, Assessment, and Interpretation* presents guidelines on selecting, using, scoring, and interpreting assessment instruments. The section also addresses expectations related to informed consent, disclosure of assessment results, and diagnosing (or refraining from diagnosing) mental health disorders. The section discusses conditions of assessment administration, diversity issues in assessment, assessment security, and forensic evaluation. The use of obsolete assessment and outdated results is prohibited.
- *Section F: Supervision, Training, and Teaching* provides guidelines for counselor educators and trainers, counselor education programs, and students and supervisees. It addresses expectations and responsibilities of supervisors, counselor educators, students, and counselor education programs. Faculty diversity, student diversity, and multicultural competence are also addressed in this section.
- *Section G: Research and Publication* describes the responsibilities of researchers. Included among those responsibilities are providing informed consent and protecting the rights of research participants. Section G also deals with plagiarism, the reporting of research results, authorship credit, and guidelines for publication.
- *Section H: Distance Counseling, Technology, and Social Media* represents a new section in the 2014 *Code of Ethics*. It focuses on the ethical use of technology and social media with clients. The section addresses knowledge and legal considerations related to the use of technology in counseling, informed consent and security, client verification, the distance counseling relationship, and electronic records and web maintenance. The section also includes guidelines for the use of social media and emphasizes the need to clearly distinguish between personal and professional virtual presence (Barnett & Johnson, 2015).
- *Section I: Resolving Ethical Issues* addresses ways to resolve ethical issues, including how to handle conflicts between ethics and the law, suspected violations, and cooperation with ethics committees.

OVERVIEW OF CHANGES MADE IN THE 2014 *ACA CODE OF ETHICS*. The 2014 *Code of Ethics* addresses many complex issues that represent the changes in society that have occurred since the 2005 *Code of Ethics* was adopted. In particular, the 2014 *Code of Ethics* makes it clear that professional values supersede counselors' personal values. These professional values are outlined in the revised code's preamble and are expected to guide counselors' practice, teaching, supervision, and research (Meyers, 2014). All changes made to the *ACA Code of Ethics* were designed to protect the public and reflect emerging issues. The following points represent changes incorporated in the 2014 *Code of Ethics*:

- Professional values are clarified and highlighted. Counselors may not refuse to see clients based on their own personal values.
- A major emphasis is placed on the use of technology in the counseling profession. Not only was a new section to the code added, but guidelines about the use of technology are also infused throughout the 2014 code.

- The code provides guidelines for the use of social media. Counselors are expected to distinguish between their personal online presence and their professional one (Meyers, 2014).
- The definition of "relationship" has been expanded to prohibit counselors from having personal virtual relationships with clients.
- The 2014 code has eliminated the end-of-life exception to the referral rule. Counselors may no longer refuse to counsel clients who are terminally ill and are considering physician-assisted or self-inflicted death. Counselors will need to consult with attorneys in states where physician-assisted dying is illegal (Meyers, 2014).
- Counselors' *duty to inform* is clarified, particularly with respect to a client who has a life-threatening disease that may put a third party at risk.
- The 2014 code expands the concept of *pro bono* services.
- The 2014 code clarifies counselors' responsibilities with mandated clients.
- The role of confidentiality is expanded. The responsibility to protect confidentiality begins before a counselor starts working with a client and continues after a client's death.
- The 2014 code describes updated requirements for counselor educators and researchers.

In general, the 2014 *Code of Ethics* needs to be looked at in its entirety (Meyers, 2014), with the goal being for counselors to act thoughtfully, mindfully, and ethically.

NBCC Code of Ethics

Many clinical mental health counselors choose to become nationally certified. A prerequisite for becoming a nationally certified counselor (NCC) is formally agreeing to abide by the *NBCC Code of Ethics*. The *NBCC Code of Ethics* was developed in 1982 and revised in 1987, 1989, 1997, 2005, and 2012. It can be accessed through the NBCC website (www.nbcc.org). The NBCC ethical code consists of seven sections, many of which parallel the standards found in the 2014 ACA code. The seven sections include a total of 95 directives.

In 1997, the NBCC was the first counseling organization to adopt standards for ethical practice of Internet counseling. The standards were updated frequently owing to the evolving world of technology. In accordance with the evolution of technology in counseling, the NBCC adopted the *Policy Regarding the Provision of Distance Professional Services* (2016b), which replaces all previous editions. This document can be accessed through the NBCC website.

Many ethical considerations related to the use of technology in counseling have evolved in recent years, and technological advances occur faster than changes in codes of ethics (Wheeler & Bertram, 2015). Therefore, clinical mental health counselors need to seek information about technological changes and carefully consider ethical and legal situations that may affect their counseling practice.

Limitations of Ethical Codes

Ethical codes are necessary but not sufficient for promoting ethical behavior. Ethical standards are general and idealistic in nature, seldom answering specific questions (Remley & Herlihy, 2016). No ethical code can address every situation or potential dilemma. Consequently, clinical mental health counselors are responsible for exercising sound judgment and decision-making skills in their work with clients. Counselors are guided by ethical guidelines but cannot rely on them exclusively.

Several limitations exist in any ethical code. The following are among those most frequently listed (e.g., Corey et al., 2015):

- Some issues cannot be resolved by a code of ethics.
- Some codes are ambiguous, making them open to interpretation.
- Enforcing ethical codes is difficult.
- There may be conflicts within the ethical codes as well as among different organizations' codes.
- Some legal and ethical issues are not covered in codes.
- Sometimes conflicts arise between ethical and legal codes.
- Ethical codes need to be examined from a cultural perspective, recognizing that some may be adapted to specific cultures.
- Ethical codes do not address every possible situation, nor do they provide solutions for all situations.
- Ethical codes are historical documents. Thus, what may be acceptable practice at one point in time may later be considered unethical.
- Knowledge of ethical codes does not necessarily equate with ethical practice.

Ethical codes are useful in many ways, but they have their limitations. Counselors need to be aware that they will not always find all the guidance they want when consulting these documents. Nevertheless, whenever an ethical issue arises in counseling, the counselor should first consult ethical codes to see whether the situation is addressed.

Making Ethical Decisions

It is not unusual for counselors to experience situations in which ethical guidelines are unclear, yet an ethical decision must be made. Making sound ethical decisions is challenging for even the most seasoned counselors (Barnett & Johnson, 2015). Most counselors go through a set of four strategies before arriving at a way to separate their personal values from their professional values. The four steps in the process are marginalization, separation, assimilation, and integration (Ametrano, 2014). In **marginalization**, counselors, especially those just learning about professional ethics, are basically unaware of their personal, let alone professional, values. Thus, they are somewhat clueless about what should be done in a matter such as suicide. In **separation**, counselors have well-developed personal morals and values but they are not aware of professional ethics. Thus in a matter such as suicide they would make a decision on whether they believe suicide is right or wrong. In **assimilation**, counselors adopt new professional ethics and abandon former cultural values. Again, using suicide as an ethical dilemma, counselors in the assimilation stage would follow a code of ethics to the letter, forgetting previously held values. Finally, in **integration**, counselors adopt the new profession's values while retaining important aspects of their own personal values. Thus they would consider the specifics of what is involved in the matter of suicide along with the profession's values to protect the client and involve family when appropriate.

As indicated, in the absence of clear ethical guidelines, relying strictly on personal value judgments or doing what "seems right" is not adequate because not all value judgments are equally valid (Kitchener, 1984). The 2014 *ACA Code of Ethics* states that when counselors are faced with an ethical dilemma, they should use and document an ethical decision-making model that takes into account relevant ethical standards and laws, deliberates potential risks and benefits of following a particular course of action, and selects a decision based on the welfare of all involved (Barnett & Johnson, 2015).

As stated earlier, Kitchener's (1984) seminal work on ethical decision making emphasizes the need for counseling professionals to develop a deeper understanding of the foundations of ethical decision making. The moral/ethical principles of autonomy, nonmaleficence, beneficence, justice, fidelity, and veracity are fundamental to the decision-making process. All these principles involve intentional decision making by counselors throughout the counseling process. Of these principles, some experts identify nonmaleficence as primary. It involves removing present harm as well as preventing future harm. It is the basis on which counselors respond to clients who may endanger themselves or others. It also underlies the mandate to respond to colleagues' unethical behavior.

Among the many existing decision-making models, some are theoretically or philosophically based, others are practice based, and some draw from both theory and practice. Decision-making models bring order and clarity to the reasoning process, thereby helping counselors resolve ethical dilemmas more effectively. It is important to examine models outlined by Corey et al. (2015); Forester-Miller and Davis (1996); Remley and Herlihy (2016); Welfel (2016); and Wheeler and Bertram (2015), to name just a few. The 2014 *ACA Code of Ethics* does not endorse a particular decision-making model but specifies that counselors need to be knowledgeable about an ethical decision-making model and be able to implement it when encountering ethical dilemmas (ACA, 2014, Standard I.1.b).

An example of a legal and ethical decision-making model was created by Wheeler and Bertram (2015). It includes dimensions that are critical for making legal and ethical decisions and is presented in Figure 2–3.

Other Guidelines for Acting Ethically

Several guidelines for acting in ethically responsible ways, initially outlined by C. D. Swanson (1983), can be used to help counselors assess their thoughts and actions. The first is *personal and professional honesty*. Counselors need to be open with themselves and with their clients. Hidden agendas and unacknowledged feelings hinder relationships and place counselors on shaky ethical ground. One way to overcome personal or professional honesty problems that may hinder acting ethically is to receive supervision.

A second guideline is *acting in the best interest of clients*. This ideal is easier to discuss than to achieve. At times, a counselor may impose personal values on clients and ignore what the client really wants. At other times, a counselor may fail to recognize an emergency and too readily accept the idea that the best interest of the client is served by doing nothing. For example, a counselor who wonders whether a client is in danger of self-harm or suicide might determine that the danger is minimal and thus would not seek consultation or take additional steps to ensure that the client is safe.

A third guideline is *acting without malice or personal gain*. It may be challenging to empathize or build rapport with certain clients. For example, it may be difficult for a counselor to overcome personal biases in working with mandated sex offenders. On the flip side, counselors must also be careful to remain professional and maintain boundaries with clients who are especially likable and personable. Errors in judgment may occur when boundaries are blurred or crossed (Wheeler & Bertram, 2015).

A final guideline is *justifying an action*, which refers to making a judgment of what should be done based on all pertinent information. To make such a decision, counselors

1. **Define the problem, dilemma, and subissues.**
   What are the core concerns (legal, ethical, clinical, or a combination)?

2. **Identify the relevant variables.**
   Who are the people, and how might they influence the outcome of the particular dilemma at issue?
   What are the issues, dynamics, and multicultural considerations?

3. **Review/consult the law, ethics codes, and institutional policy.**
   What federal and state laws, ethics codes (especially the *ACA Code of Ethics*), and applicable institutional policy apply to the facts?

4. **Be alert to personal influences.**
   What personal values, bias/prejudice, or countertransference may be affecting perception?

5. **Obtain outside perspective.**
   Whenever possible, engage in colleague consultation and/or supervision and/or obtain legal advice.

6. **Enumerate options and consequences.**
   What are the possible courses of action and intended consequences?
   Also consider the unintended consequences. Remember to involve the client in the decision making, unless clinically inappropriate (e.g., where client involvement would likely trigger violence against a third party).

7. **Decide and take action.**
   Implement the decision and be prepared to reconsider options.

8. **Document decision making and follow-up actions.**
   Provide written evidence of clinical and ethical decision making and results of implementation.

FIGURE 2–3 Legal and Ethical Decision-Making Model
Source: Reprinted with permission from *The Counselor and the Law: A Guide to Legal and Ethical Practice* (7th ed.), by A. M. Wheeler and B. Bertram, 2015, Alexandria, VA: American Counseling Association. Copyright © 2015 by the American Counseling Association. No further reproduction authorized without written permission from the American Counseling Association.

need to understand current practices and standards of care. There are several ways clinical mental health counselors can do this, including reading the professional literature, attending seminars and conferences, and becoming actively involved in local, state, and national counseling organizations.

The ACA *Ethical Standards Casebook* (Herlihy & Corey, 2015) can be especially helpful in many counseling situations. It presents case studies describing questionable ethical situations and provides guidelines and reflection questions to assist counselors in making ethical responses. The text examines a wide range of ethical issues, including client rights and informed consent, multicultural counseling concerns, confidentiality, competence, working with multiple clients, counseling minor clients, working with clients who may harm themselves, counselor education and supervision, and the relationship between law and ethics.

Another helpful resource for clinical mental health counselors is the *Ethics Desk Reference for Counselors* (Barnett & Johnson, 2015), which is divided into two parts. In the first part, the authors focus on each section of the 2014 *Code of Ethics*. They describe the intent (i.e., essential elements) of specific ethical standards, outline common dilemmas and conflicts associated with each standard, and provide a checklist to help counselors be ethically proactive. In the second part of the book, the authors highlight ways to make sound ethical decisions associated with such areas as culture and diversity, confidentiality, boundaries and multiple relationships, the use of technology, competence, suicidal clients, supervision, termination, and abandonment.

Clinical mental health counselors have many resources to access when confronted with ethical questions or dilemmas. When in doubt about what to do in a given situation, it helps to consult with colleagues, seek supervision, and refer to principles, guidelines, casebooks, and professional codes of ethics. The ACA professional affairs staff may be contacted also when ethical concerns arise. The staff can be emailed directly at ethics@ counseling.org.

Unethical Behavior

Although most counselors strive to adhere to ethical standards, situations occasionally arise when such is not the case. When clinical mental health counselors are aware that unethical behavior is being practiced by another counselor, action needs to be taken. Failure to act condones the unethical behavior and can be detrimental to both the clients and the profession. Even though the primary purpose of the *ACA Code of Ethics* is to guide our own behavior, not to judge the behavior of others, we are mandated as professionals to address unethical behavior appropriately (Remley & Herlihy, 2016). The caution against judging too quickly must be balanced against the obligation to address practices of peers that are viewed as unethical.

The *ACA Code of Ethics* (2014) states, "When counselors have reason to believe that another counselor is violating or has violated an ethical standard and substantial harm has not occurred, they attempt to first resolve the issue informally with the other counselor, provided such action does not violate confidentiality rights that may be involved" (Standard I.2.a). The phrases "have reason to believe" and "resolve the issue" deserve careful attention. First, it is important to avoid making decisions based on secondhand information or rumors. Only direct knowledge of unethical behavior obligates a counselor to take action. Second, counselors are expected to consult with the colleague who is suspected of violating an ethical standard to resolve the issue.

According to the ACA guidelines, a counselor should initially attempt to address issues of misconduct informally with the counselor whose behavior is in question. In many cases, especially if the privacy of an involved party is at risk, it is best to consult with a trusted professional before taking this step (Remley & Herlihy, 2016). Addressing the issue informally involves confrontation in a caring context, which ideally will lead the counselor in question to seek help. If an informal approach is unsuccessful or unfeasible, it may be necessary to report the offense. According to the 2014 code, "If an apparent violation has substantially harmed or is likely to substantially harm a person or organization and is not appropriate for informal resolution or is not resolved properly, counselors take further action depending on the situation" (Standard I.2.b). Examples of appropriate action include reporting the perceived violation to state or national ethics committees, voluntary national certification bodies, state licensure boards, or the appropriate institutional authorities.

Prior to making a decision to report a suspected ethical violation, clinical mental health counselors are advised to consult with other professionals. Remley and Herlihy (2016, p. 210) recommend that the following conditions have been met before making a report:

- The issue cannot be resolved directly with the counselor because of the circumstances or because attempts at resolution have been unsuccessful.
- You have direct knowledge that a serious ethics violation has occurred that is causing or has caused substantial harm.
- You have consulted with colleagues who agree that a report must be made.
- You are willing to participate in a hearing and to testify if a hearing is conducted.
- You are prepared to defend yourself if a counterclaim is filed against you.

The ACA Ethics Committee is responsible for managing formal reports of unethical practice on the part of ACA members. Responsibilities of the Ethics Committee include educating members about the *ACA Code of Ethics*, periodically reviewing and recommending revisions to the code, receiving and processing complaints of reported ethical violations of ACA members, providing interpretations of the ACA ethical guidelines, and recommending appropriate disciplinary actions when ethical violations are substantiated (ACA, 2014).

BOX 2–1   Unprofessional, Unethical, or Illegal Professional Behavior

No one knows how often counselors actually engage in unprofessional, unethical, or illegal practice-related behaviors. . . . Data compiled by the American Counseling Association [ACA, 2014] indicate that there are 140,000 licensed professional counselors. The relative infrequency of licensing board discipline, lawsuits, criminal arrest, or censure by ethics committees compared with the number of counselors suggests that formal accusations of questionable behavior are rare. In our experience, even when there is an accusation against a mental health professional, the resolution often favors the professional. We would be remiss, however, in not stating the obvious: Counselors and other mental health professionals sometimes do engage in behaviors that result in harm to the very people we are in practice to serve: our clients.

(Wheeler & Bertram, 2015, pp. 1–2)

Counselors are responsible not only for acting in ways that are personally and professionally ethical but also for engaging in behavior that is lawful. At times, ethical and legal standards are in conflict. In the next section, we explore legal issues that affect the mental health profession, followed by descriptions of some of the more common ethical and/or legal issues that clinical mental health counselors encounter.

THE LAW AND COUNSELING

The profession of counseling is governed by legal standards as well as by ethical ones. The word *law* can be defined as a set of rules enacted by a legislative body. Laws, often called **statutes**, govern most activities in society (Wheeler & Bertram, 2015). The law plays a pervasive role in the personal and professional lives of counselors and affects almost all areas of counselor practice. Wheeler and Bertram (2015) remind us that counselors need to understand the basic concepts of the legal system, the general body of law affecting professional practice, and the impact of professional conduct and ethical guidelines.

The legal system of the United States is not static. Interpretations of law evolve over time and frequently are situationally contingent. Although no general, comprehensive body of law regulates mental health professions, a number of court decisions and statutes have direct bearing on the counseling profession. Court decisions based on rulings that interpret a law according to a specific case establish what is known as **case law** (Cottone & Tarvydas, 2016). For example, the 1993 Napa County, California, case involving Gary Ramona illustrates a legal decision of this nature. In a widely publicized trial, Ramona sued his daughter's therapists, "charging that by implanting false memories of sexual abuse in her mind they had destroyed his life" (Butler, 1994, p. 10). Ramona was awarded $475,000 after the jury "found the therapists had negligently reinforced false memories" (Butler, 1994, p. 11). The legal concept on which the case was decided was **duty to care**—a legal obligation of health providers to not act negligently.

Another important legal case that affected the counseling profession was the 1996 U.S. Supreme Court decision in *Jaffee v. Redmond* (1996), which maintained that communications between licensed psychotherapists and their patients are **privileged** and do not have to be disclosed in cases held in federal court (Remley, Herlihy, & Herlihy, 1997). The importance of the case for counseling is that a legal precedent was set regarding privileged communication between a master's-level clinician (in this case, a social worker) and the client. The court decision affirmed the importance of protecting confidential communications between "psychotherapists" (the term used in this particular ruling) and their clients, thereby establishing a precedent that makes it more likely for judges to extend privilege in cases involving licensed counselors and clients (Glosoff, Herlihy, & Spence, 2000).

The law supports licensure or certification of counselors as a means of ensuring that those who enter the profession attain at least minimal standards. As the licensing of professional counselors has expanded to all states, the importance of defining the practice of counseling has become even more important. State legislatures have endorsed **practice act** counseling statutes that delineate, from a legal perspective, what professional counselors can and cannot do (Wheeler & Bertram, 2015). Practice acts differ from state to state, making it necessary for clinical mental health counselors to be cognizant of the legal regulations that govern their practice within their particular state. These differences can be confusing to counselors and to the clients they serve. National licensing standards and licensure portability would clarify licensed counselors' scope of practice across states, and there is considerable activity on a number of fronts to enact portability.

Criminal, Civil, and Administrative Law

Clinical mental health counselors are affected by the legal system through criminal, civil, and administrative law, in addition to case law. **Criminal law** applies to acts that are considered crimes against society and are prosecuted by the government, not by individuals (Wheeler & Bertram, 2015). Such acts are punishable by fines, imprisonment, or, in extreme cases, the death penalty. Fraud, civil disobedience, being an accessory to a crime, and contributing to the delinquency of a minor are examples of criminal offenses for which some mental health professionals have been found liable.

Civil law applies to acts committed that affect the civil rights of individuals or other bodies (Wheeler & Bertram, 2015). Civil matters are settled in court when one individual brings suit against another, with sanctions applied to compensate the wronged individual. Civil liability is based on the concept of **tort**—a term that refers to a wrong that legal action is designed to set right. Intentional torts include such things as battery, defamation of character, and invasion of privacy. Unintentional torts often involve negligence, which refers to situations in which the mental health professional does not carry out his or her responsibilities in accordance with the standards of care outlined by the profession. The most common cause of legal liability for mental health professionals is **malpractice**, which means that a counselor has been negligent in carrying out professional responsibilities or duties (Cottone & Tarvydas, 2016).

Administrative law is created by government administrative agencies that develop regulations to help define the laws, or statutes, that are passed by a legislative body (Wheeler & Bertram, 2015). A federal regulation that has many implications for mental health professionals is the Health Insurance Portability and Accountability Act (HIPAA, 1996). HIPAA includes many standards and rules that address client and patient privacy and security. The HIPAA Privacy Rule was enacted on the federal level to address concerns related to the transmission of healthcare information, either electronically or on paper. The HIPAA Security Rule "dovetails with the HIPAA Privacy Rule and requires technical, administrative, and physical safeguards to protect the security of protected health information in electronic form" (Wheeler & Bertram, 2015, p. 108). HIPAA rules apply to all *covered entities*. To determine whether they are considered covered entities under HIPAA, clinical mental health counselors can visit the website for the Centers for Medicare and Medicaid Services at www. cms.gov/Regulations-and-Guidance/HIPAA-Administrative-Simplification/HIPAAGenInfo/ AreYouaCoveredEntity.html.

In 2009, an additional regulatory act was passed, called **HITECH** (Health Information Technology for Economic and Clinical Health). This act established new privacy and security compliance requirements, incentives for adopting electronic health records, and steeper penalties for violating the regulations (Wheeler & Bertram, 2015). Counselors and other mental health professionals must encrypt their laptops and other electronic devices to ensure that clients' confidentiality is not breached. HITECH violations are reported to the U.S. Department of Health and Human Services and are posted on the department's website. Examples of violations include having an unencrypted laptop stolen from a covered entity's office, having thumb drives or other mobile electronic devices that are unencrypted stolen, and sending an email to multiple patients or clients without concealing the patients' identities (Wheeler & Bertram, 2015). In a world where theft and hacking occur frequently, clinical mental health counselors need to take every precaution to ensure that their clients' confidential records cannot be retrieved from other parties.

Malpractice

Professional malpractice is regulated by state law and therefore usually applies only when a person is credentialed according to state statute. However, counselors can still be held legally negligible or guilty of intentional infliction of distress, even in cases when the term *malpractice* does not technically apply (Wheeler & Bertram, 2015). Clinical mental health counselors are expected to exercise due care or face potential liability for failing to perform their professional duties.

BOX 2–2   What Is Meant by Due Care?

===

Due care refers to the concept of duty. It means that the counselor has a legal obligation to act in the best interest of the client. Clients trust their counselors to act in the clients' best interest, thereby establishing a *fiduciary relationship* between the two parties.

Areas of potential malpractice for counselors include, but are not limited to, the following (Vacc & Loesch, 2000; Wheeler & Bertram, 2015):

- Making a faulty diagnosis (e.g., attributing a physically based problem to a psychological condition)
- Failing to take adequate precautions for a suicidal client
- Failing to take action when someone other than the client is in danger
- Improperly certifying a client in a commitment hearing
- Engaging in behavior inappropriate to the accepted standards of the profession
- Providing services for which competence has not been established
- Breaching confidentiality
- Promising a "cure"
- Taking advantage of the counseling relationship for personal gain, monetary or otherwise
- Failing to use a technique that would have been more helpful
- Failing to receive informed consent
- Failing to explain the possible consequences of counseling interventions

There are several proactive ways to avoid malpractice and to protect oneself from liability. To avoid malpractice, clinical mental health counselors need to adhere to professional codes of ethics and provide counseling services viewed as acceptable by the profession. Regardless of how careful counselors are, however, malpractice lawsuits can still occur. Therefore, carrying professional liability insurance is essential. Reading journal articles and texts that address legal issues in counseling, such as *The Counselor and the Law: A Guide to Legal and Ethical Practice* (Wheeler & Bertram, 2015), is another way clinical mental health counselors can be proactive. Being aware of legal issues and obtaining legal advice when questions arise are essential ways counselors can protect themselves should their actions be challenged (Remley & Herlihy, 2016).

Other Reasons for Court Appearances

A relatively small number of counselors have to appear in court to face liability charges. More frequently, counselors find themselves in court for other reasons. For example, a counselor may be asked to serve as an **expert witness**, "an objective and unbiased person with specialized knowledge, skills, or information, who can assist a judge or jury in reaching an appropriate legal decision" (Remley, 1992, p. 33). Expert witnesses serve voluntarily and are compensated financially for their services. Counselors who intend to serve as expert witnesses are advised to take courses, observe other experts in court, and read pertinent written materials to be prepared to serve in that capacity (Remley & Herlihy, 2016).

A counselor may also be summoned to appear in court through a **court order** (e.g., a subpoena to appear in court at a certain time in regard to a specific case). Subpoenas are issued with the intent of having the counselor testify on behalf of or against a present or former client. Because the legal system is adversarial, counselors are wise to seek the advice of attorneys before responding to court orders. In so doing, counselors may come to understand the law, court proceedings, and options they have in response to legal requests. Counselors who have been subpoenaed are advised to work with their attorneys to determine the minimum level of response that is required (Barnett & Johnson, 2015). Also, counselors are wise to consult with other counselors before appearing in court. Participating in webinars and listening to podcasts that focus on legal issues in counseling can help clinical mental health counselors be prepared to face court appearances.

The Case of Luke

Luke is a six-year-old boy whose parents separated 11 months ago. He has been seeing you for counseling at a mental health agency for 6 months. Luke is living with his mother, who brought him to counseling after he began wetting the bed and withdrawing from friends and other activities. You have met with Luke for eight sessions, using nondirective play therapy as a primary intervention tool. During the course of therapy, Luke reveals that when his father was home, he was much happier. He draws a picture of his mother looking angry, and then he draws a large black X over her face. He says that he is mad at his mother and wants to live with his father.

You have kept careful records of each session, following HIPAA guidelines and the guidelines of your agency. Last week, you received a subpoena to appear in court next month, when the divorce will be finalized and custody decisions will be made. What concerns do you have? Will you reveal all your written documents? What responsibilities do you have to Luke, his mother, his father, and the legal system?

COMMON ETHICAL AND LEGAL CONCERNS

Counselors in all settings deal with many issues that have ethical and legal ramifications. A number of authors (e.g., Corey et al., 2015; Cottone & Tarvydas, 2016; Remley & Herlihy, 2016; Welfel, 2016; Wheeler & Bertram, 2015) have written texts that describe ethical and legal concerns that affect mental health practitioners. These topics are frequently addressed in professional development and continuing education activities. The purpose of this section is not to provide a comprehensive overview of all the ethical and legal issues clinical mental health counselors may encounter; instead, it is to provide information about some of the more common concerns that affect the practice of clinical mental health counseling—shared communication, informed consent, roles and relationships with clients, professional competence, and technology. Other issues—including record keeping, mandated counseling, payment issues, professional responsibilities, counseling minors, and managed care—are addressed in other chapters.

Privacy, Confidentiality, and Privileged Communication

The relationship between counselors and clients is based on trust, which is a cornerstone of the counseling relationship (ACA, 2014). For communication to occur freely, clients must have both their privacy and the information shared in sessions protected. Ethical and legal issues related to trustworthy communication include privacy, confidentiality, and privileged communication.

Privacy is the client's right to determine what information about him- or herself will be shared with others (Remley & Herlihy, 2016; Wheeler & Bertram, 2015). It is a broad term that includes not only the confidences shared during counseling sessions but also the fact that the client is participating in counseling. Several factors can jeopardize a client's privacy right, including the need to wait in a general reception area, use of credit cards for bill payment, disposal of records, taping of sessions, and other documentary or business activities associated with the counseling setting (Cottone & Tarvydas, 2016). Professional mental health counselors must use foresight and take the necessary steps to protect the dignity and privacy of their clients.

Confidentiality is a professional's promise not to disclose information revealed within the counselor–client relationship, except under specific, mutually understood conditions (Barnett & Johnson, 2015). The assurance of confidentiality is considered one of the most fundamental obligations of counselors. Counselors should discuss confidentiality and its limits with clients before counseling begins. Except in certain situations, counselors may share confidential information only with the direct written consent of clients or their legal guardians. It is the counselor's responsibility to clarify for clients those circumstances in which breaching confidentiality is either permissible or required (see Standard B.2, 2014 ACA Code of Ethics). Such times occur when obligations to other individuals and society override the ethical responsibility of confidentiality.

A landmark court case that reflects the importance of limiting confidentiality is *Tarasoff v. Board of Regents of the University of California* (1976). In this case, a graduate student, Prosenjit Poddar, who was a voluntary outpatient at the student health services on the Berkeley campus of the University of California, informed the psychologist who was counseling him that he intended to kill his former girlfriend, Tatiana Tarasoff, when she arrived back on campus. The psychologist notified the campus police, who detained and questioned the student about his proposed activities. The student denied any intention of killing Tarasoff, acted rationally, and was released. Poddar refused further treatment by the psychologist, and no additional steps were taken to deter him from his intended action. Two months later, he killed Tarasoff. Her parents sued the psychologist, the psychiatrist, the outpatient treatment center affiliated with the university, the campus police, and the University Board of Regents for failing to notify the intended victim of a threat against her. The California Supreme Court ruled in their favor, indicating that a therapist has a duty to protect the public that overrides any obligation to maintain client confidentiality.

Thus, there is a limit to how much confidentiality a counselor can or should maintain. The ruling in the *Tarasoff* case, sometimes called **duty to warn**, implies that counselors need to take reasonable action to help protect potential victims from serious and foreseeable harm. Subsequent court decisions expanded on the *Tarasoff* doctrine of duty to warn, by extending the duty to warn to others who might be injured by a negligent act and individuals whose property has been threatened (Remley & Herlihy, 2016). There are limitations to the duty, however. For example, several courts have "declined to impose liability in the absence of a readily identifiable victim" (Wheeler & Bertram, 2015, p. 136). Also, mandatory duty does not exist in all states (e.g., Florida, Texas). Again, clinical mental health counselors need to be aware of the state laws that govern their practice and recognize that case law regarding the duty to warn/protect is subject to change. If confidence is breached, either intentionally or unintentionally, the concern potentially becomes a legal as well as an ethical issue for counselors.

When counselors are faced with the duty to warn, they should consult with colleagues and supervisors to determine a course of action that is ethically and legally sound. The counselor may be obligated to breach confidentiality by contacting authorities or government agencies (Barnett & Johnson, 2015). A number of additional limitations to confidentiality and privileged communication have been cited in the literature. A summary of the more common exceptions is presented in Figure 2–4. Because of the

Potential Exceptions to Confidentiality and Privileged Communication	
To protect others from harm	• When there is suspected abuse or neglect of a child, an elderly person, a resident of an institution, or another vulnerable individual • When the client poses a clear and imminent danger to self or others • When the client has a fatal, communicable disease and the client's behavior is putting others at risk of contracting the disease *Note:* Standard B.2.c. states that counselors *may* disclose information to third parties who are potentially at risk. The decision to disclose depends on state laws, the counselor's ability to confirm the presence of a life-threatening disease, the client's willingness to voluntarily disclose, and whether the person(s) at risk are identifiable.
To help improve client services	• When working under supervision (the client should know that the counselor is being supervised) • When consulting with colleagues or peers (e.g., treatment teams) • When clerical assistants handle confidential information (e.g., managed care) • When other mental health professionals request information and the client has provided written consent to share
Other possible exceptions	• When clients raise the issue of their mental health in legal proceedings • When counselors need to defend themselves against a complaint made to a licensure or certifying board or in a court of law • When the client is involved in civil commitment proceedings • When ordered by a court (the counselor should request privilege on behalf of the client, although the right to privilege may be legally overridden, depending on the circumstances)

FIGURE 2–4   Potential Exceptions to Confidentiality and Privileged Communication
Sources: Barnett & Johnson, 2015; Corey et al., 2015; Glosoff, 2001; Welfel, 2016.

differences in state statutes and individual circumstances, clinical mental health counselors will want to verify the limitations that are applicable to their counseling practice. If confidentiality must be broken, it is good practice to talk with the client about the need to share information and to invite the client to participate in the process when feasible (Remley & Herlihy, 2016).

Privileged communication "is a legal term that refers to the protection of confidentiality between two parties" (Wheeler & Bertram, 2015, p. 104). The right of privilege belongs to the client, not the counselor. For privilege to be recognized, the communication must have been made in confidence with intent that the information remain confidential. If a third party is involved, the information generally, but not always, is not privileged. Typically, state law governs whether privilege exists in a counselor–client relationship (Hermann, 2011). On the federal level, the U.S. Supreme Court set a precedent for protecting confidential communications by ruling, as was mentioned earlier, that the confidences shared between a social worker and her client were privileged and not subject to disclosure (*Jaffee v. Redmond*, 1996).

Although the concept of privilege appears to be relatively straightforward, in reality it is complex and somewhat confusing. One major reason for the confusion is that laws regulating privilege and its exceptions vary from state to state. Furthermore, new laws are enacted, and existing statutes are modified on a regular basis. Consequently, counselors must be familiar with statutes and case law and must participate in continuing education events to stay abreast of new developments. Counselors need to be aware of situations in which privilege is waived. Examples include when a client initiates a malpractice suit or licensure board procedure against a counselor or when a defendant claims insanity as a defense in a criminal case (Wheeler & Bertram, 2015).

Issues of privacy, confidentiality, and privilege are among the ethical and legal queries most often received by the ACA Ethics Committee. To illustrate, in 2010 and 2011, ACA's Risk Management Helpline received 205 inquiries about these issues, representing 31% of the total number of ethical inquiries (Wheeler & Bertram, 2015). Specific areas of inquiry include subpoenas; counseling minors; couple, family, and group counseling; custody issues; substance abuse records; counseling of public offenders; confidentiality after a client's death; and issues related to technology.

Elaine's Ethical Dilemma

Elaine is a full-time counselor working in a clinical mental health agency that serves children and adults. She has a 17-year-old female client who has recently ended a physically abusive relationship with her boyfriend. The client's ex-boyfriend is an 18-year-old male, and they dated for two years before breaking up six months ago.

Elaine's client has told Elaine that if she sees her ex-boyfriend, she will kill him and would view her own actions as self-defense. The state in which Elaine practices does not have a duty-to-warn law, but it does have laws regarding client confidentiality. What is her legal obligation to her client, the ex-boyfriend, and herself as a counselor? What is her ethical obligation to her client, the ex-boyfriend, and herself as a counselor? What factors might be important for her to consider? What ethical concerns will she need to consider? Use an ethical decision-making model to help answer these questions.

Informed Consent

Clients have a number of legal as well as ethical rights in counseling, but they frequently do not know about them. One of the counselor's first tasks is to learn what rights clients have and to inform the clients of those rights. The process of **informed consent** refers to clients' right to know what they are getting into when they engage in counseling. It allows them to make informed decisions about their treatment and the release of confidential information. Informed consent provides clients with information about how the counseling process works and makes them active partners in the counseling relationship (Remley & Herlihy, 2016).

In most cases, informed consent is both verbal and written. The *ACA Code of Ethics* specifies the nature of informed consent as follows:

> *A.2.a. Informed Consent.* Clients have the freedom to choose whether to enter into or remain in a counseling relationship and need adequate information about the counseling process and the counselor. Counselors have an obligation to review in writing and verbally with clients the rights and responsibilities of both counselors and clients. Informed consent is an ongoing part of the counseling process, and counselors appropriately document discussions of informed consent throughout the counseling relationship. (ACA, 2014)

Two criteria are central to the concept of informed consent: disclosure and free consent (Glosoff, 2001). **Disclosure** refers to providing clients with the information they need to make informed decisions about entering into counseling, remaining in counseling, and sharing personal information. **Free consent** means that clients choose to engage in an activity without undue pressure or coercion. For informed consent to be legally recognized, clients must demonstrate **capacity** (i.e., the ability to make rational decisions) and know that they are free to withdraw consent at any time, except in court-ordered situations. When working with minors and others unable to legally provide informed consent, special considerations are necessary.

Professional disclosure statements prepared by counselors are contracts that formalize the informed consent process. The *ACA Code of Ethics* (2014) specifies the elements that ethically are part of informed consent procedures and therefore need to be included in disclosure statements:

- The purposes, goals, techniques, procedures, limitations, and potential risks and benefits of the proposed services
- The counselor's qualifications, including credentials, relevant experience, and approach to counseling
- Arrangements for continuation of services if the counselor dies or becomes incapacitated
- The implications of diagnosis and the intended use of tests and reports
- Information about fees and billing
- Confidentiality and its limits
- Clients' rights to obtain information about their records and to participate in ongoing counseling plans
- Clients' rights to refuse any recommended services and be advised of the consequences of refusal

In addition to preparing a comprehensive, understandable professional disclosure statement for clients to sign, counselors need to talk with clients face-to-face to clarify any information that may be confusing. Ongoing discussion throughout the counseling process helps ensure that client and counselor are working together effectively. Informed consent begins when counseling is initiated, but the process should continue throughout the time the client is in counseling (Barnett & Johnson, 2015; Remley & Herlihy, 2016).

Because of the requirements of HIPAA, informed consent represents a legal as well as an ethical concern. Therefore, mental health professionals need to be familiar with HIPAA requirements for informed consent disclosure statements and ensure that their procedures are in compliance with the law.

Professional Boundaries and Roles with Clients

A key aspect of acting ethically and legally as a counselor includes defining, maintaining, and respecting professional boundaries. As Wheeler and Bertram (2015) point out, counselors have a "unique responsibility, defined both ethically and legally, to manage the boundary between professional counselor and client, including any other co-occurring roles that connect the counselor to the client" (p. 183). Although the most obvious boundary violation occurs when a counselor engages in a sexual relationship with a client, a wide range of boundary issues exist. Mental health professionals need to exercise caution to ensure that professional boundaries are maintained and not blurred or crossed. Boundaries help provide structure to the professional relationship and protect the welfare and vulnerability of clients (Remley & Herlihy, 2016).

Often, boundary issues can be viewed in the context of dual or multiple relationships. The 2014 *ACA Code of Ethics* delineates a number of prohibited counselor–client interactions. Specifically, Standard A.5 prohibits counselors from having sexual and/or romantic relationships with current clients, their romantic partners, or their family members. This prohibition applies to in-person as well as virtual interactions or relationships. Even after the counseling relationship has ended, counselors should not engage in romantic or sexual relationships for at least five years since the last professional contact. Even then, the counselor needs to consider carefully the impact a relationship might have on the former client. The reverse is also true: Counselors should not counsel people with whom they have had a prior romantic relationship. In general, clinical mental health counselors should refrain from entering into counseling relationships with friends, family members, students, fellow workers, and others with whom they have a preexisting relationship. To maintain healthy boundaries in existing counseling relationships, mental health professionals are advised to avoid socializing or conducting business with clients.

BOX 2–3   Receiving Gifts from Clients

Standard A.10.f provides the following guidelines about receiving gifts from clients: Counselors understand the challenges of accepting gifts from clients and recognize that in some cultures, small gifts are a token of respect and showing gratitude. When determining whether or not to accept a gift from clients, counselors take into account the therapeutic relationship, the monetary value of the gift, a client's motivation for giving the gift, and the counselor's motivation for wanting or declining the gift.

(ACA, 2014)

Although the principles underlying the ethics of counselor–client relationships seem clear, implementing them is sometimes difficult. Indeed, it may be impossible to avoid all forms of multiple relationships, particularly in small, isolated communities. Remley and

Herlihy (2016) note that many intersecting worlds exist, even in urban environments, and that people's political affiliation, ethnic identity, religious affiliation, sexual orientation, and substance-dependence recovery status all can potentially lead to relationship or boundary concerns. To avoid exploitation or other difficulties that may result from unavoidable multiple relationships, counselors need to recognize the complexity of therapeutic relationships, exercise sound clinical judgment, attend to self-care, and engage in ongoing self-evaluation and peer consultation. When the counseling relationship extends beyond conventional guidelines (e.g., attending a client's ceremony, purchasing a product or service provided by the client, visiting a client's ill family member in the hospital), counselors need to exercise professional precaution and provide documentation of the boundary extension (ACA, 2014, Standard A.6.b. and Standard A.6.c.).

Professional Competence

Another area that has particular legal and ethical significance for clinical mental health counselors is that of **professional competence**. Section C.2.a of the *ACA Code of Ethics* (2014) addresses professional competence in this manner:

> Counselors practice only within the boundaries of their competence, based on their education, training, supervised experience, state and national professional credentials, and appropriate professional experience. Whereas multicultural counseling competency is required across all counseling specialties, counselors gain knowledge, personal awareness, sensitivity, and skills pertinent to being a culturally competent counselor in working with a diverse client population.

The concept of counselor competence is multidimensional. On one hand, it can be defined according to minimum requirements and minimum performance levels required by outside sources (e.g., licensure boards or graduate counseling programs). It also can be viewed as an ideal state of maximum knowledge and skills toward which counselors strive. Remley and Herlihy (2016) remind us that competence is not an either/or concept; rather, it is multileveled and spans a continuum. Competence means having sufficient knowledge, skill, and experience to counsel an individual effectively (Barnett & Johnson, 2015).

Counselors are required to practice within their boundaries of competence; however, those boundaries are not always easy to delineate. Boundaries of competence involve the levels of training, experience, and credentialing required to perform certain procedures or interventions (Cottone & Tarvydas, 2016). From a legal standpoint, competence refers to the capability of providing the accepted standard of care required for working in a particular situation. **Standard of care** can be defined as "a level of care that is consistent with the degree of learning, skill, and ethics ordinarily possessed and expected by reputable counselors under similar circumstances" (Wheeler & Bertram, 2015, p. 26). For example, standard-of-care procedures are demonstrated when a clinical mental health counselor with trained, supervised experience in cognitive–behavioral therapy and anxiety disorders selects a cognitive–behavioral intervention to use with a client dealing with panic disorder.

Professional competence can be developed and maintained through education, formal training, and supervised practice in particular areas. It is important to recognize the impossibility of universal competence: No single professional counselor will be competent in all areas. When counselors attempt to expand their competencies, whether in a new practice area or with a new population of individuals, they need to evaluate the time, training, and supervision that will be required to develop the skills needed to work effectively with their clients.

Competent practice also involves an ability to work with diverse populations. Both the ACA and the NBCC codes of ethics state that counselors have the responsibility to respect the diversity of their clients and act in ways that are nondiscriminatory. A counselor who does not have the training and supervised practice needed for working with culturally diverse clients may be practicing unethically by providing services to them (Remley & Herlihy, 2016). Clinical mental health counselors have an ethical obligation to develop the knowledge and skills needed to work in a culturally diverse society. The *Multicultural Competencies and Standards* (Sue, Arredondo, & McDavis, 1992) initially provided guidelines for practicing culturally sensitive counseling with diverse populations. In 2015, the *Multicultural and Social Justice Counseling Competencies* were developed and revised the *Multicultural Competencies and Standards* (Ratts, Singh, Nassar-McMillan, Butler, & McCullough, 2015). These standards are now the norm for practicing culturally sensitive counseling. Mental health professionals need to be aware of their own cultural values, prejudices, and biases and be intentional about learning ways to work effectively with clients from different cultural backgrounds.

The professional value of honoring diversity is one that in the past has caused some confusion among counselors and counselors-in-training. Counselors are to "refrain from referring prospective and current clients based solely on the counselor's personally held values, attitudes, beliefs, and behaviors" (ACA, 2014, Code A.11.b.) In other words, if a counselor holds a belief that same-sex partnerships are not acceptable, that counselor does not have the option of refusing to counsel a person with a sexual orientation that differs from his or her own orientation. Several recent court cases centered on counselors or counselors-in-training who declined to counsel lesbian, gay, bisexual, and transgender (LGBT) clients. Examples include *Ward v. Wilbanks* (a.k.a. Ward v. Polite, 2012), *Keeton v. Anderson-Wiley* (2011), and *Bruff v. North Mississippi Health Services* (2001). In the first two cases, two counseling students were dismissed from their programs because they refused to counsel LGBT clients. In both of these cases, faculty offered the choice of completing remediation plans, but the students declined. The students brought suit against their universities, but the courts upheld the decisions of dismissal (Remley & Herlihy, 2016). In the case of *Bruff v. North Mississippi Health Services*, a counselor referred a client who wanted help with her same-sex marriage. The counselor's religious beliefs were the basis for referral. The client filed a complaint, and the counselor lost her job.

These examples beg the question: How do I work effectively with clients whose values and beliefs differ from my personal values and beliefs? According to Standard A.11.b., counselors need to "seek training in areas in which they are at risk of imposing their values onto clients, especially when the counselor's values are inconsistent with the client's goals or are discriminatory in nature" (ACA, 2014). In addition to seeking training, counselors are encouraged to **bracket**, which is the intentional separation of "a counselor's personal values from his or her professional values . . . in order to provide ethical and appropriate counseling to all clients" (Kocet & Herlihy, 2014, p. 182).

Often, counselors will find themselves in situations in which the needs of a particular client are greater than their professional competence. When this occurs, the best course of action is to refer that client to someone with the necessary training. For example, if a client with an eating disorder comes to you for counseling, and you do not have the specialized training to work with this client, it would be in the client's best interest for the counselor to refer the client to counselors who specialize in that area. At other times, counselors may need to refer clients on the basis of personal factors affecting their competence, such as stress, illness, or some form of impairment (Remley & Herlihy, 2016). The key to practicing responsibly is being aware of one's capabilities and level of functioning and making sound judgments based on that awareness. Standard C.2.e states that counselors should "take reasonable steps to consult with other counselors, the ACA Ethics and Professional Standards Department, or related professionals when they have questions regarding their ethical obligations or professional practice" (ACA, 2014).

End-of-Life Decisions

Issues related to end-of-life decisions, particularly as they apply to physician-assisted suicide when individuals request a hastened death, raise both legal and ethical concerns. As stated earlier, even though the *ACA Code of Ethics* (2014) provides support for a client's right to choose options to end suffering caused by terminal illness, as well as support for counselor involvement in working with these clients, end-of-life issues present a plethora of moral, ethical, and legal questions (Wheeler & Bertram, 2015). The *ACA Code of Ethics* purpose statement notes that "reasonable differences of opinion can and do exist among counselors with respect to the ways in which values, ethical principles, and ethical standards would be applied when they conflict." Even when a counselor is fully aware of his or her own perspective, the issue may be clouded by a number of factors, including (a) who the client is (i.e., the patient or a family member), (b) who has legal competence to determine what course of action is in the best interest of the patient/client, (c) state laws, (d) the values of the client and other caretakers, and (e) the values of the counselor who is providing services (Wheeler & Bertram, 2015). Standard B.2.b states that counselors have the option of breaking or not breaking confidentiality. Before taking any course of action, clinical mental health counselors who work with clients making end-of-life decisions need to engage in consultation and/or supervision throughout the decision-making process.

The Case of Daniel

Your client is an 18-year-old Japanese American male named Daniel Hayashi, who was referred to you by his high school counselor. Daniel has been diagnosed with an incurable form of cancer. Though his cancer can be treated with chemotherapy and radiation to extend his life for an indefinite amount of time, Daniel feels hopeless about his future. He has stopped doing schoolwork and no longer looks forward to attending college. He told his school counselor of his plans to take his life, which in his culture is not forbidden and has historically been seen as an honorable decision. Daniel has not told his parents of his plan. Daniel's cultural background makes him somewhat skeptical of counseling. He is satisfied with his choice to take his life and is seeing you reluctantly.

Your own Judeo-Christian background leads you to view suicide as morally unacceptable. Your personal beliefs are that life should be protected at all costs. How can you honor Daniel's cultural beliefs while maintaining your own sense of morality? Where is the line between morals and ethics? Does this situation present an ethical dilemma? If so, what ethical principles are at odds? How does the ACA Code of Ethics *address this situation? How would you proceed ethically?*

THE USE OF TECHNOLOGY

Of the many developments that have profoundly influenced the mental health profession, those related to technology have been especially salient. The widespread availability of computer networking and the Internet in the 1990s dramatically increased the use of technology in counseling (Oravec, 2000). As noted by Walz (2000), "All counselors must come to grips with this exponentially expanding medium and decide for themselves what to do and what not to do" (p. xii). That statement, issued almost two decades ago, has even greater implications now. Email, text messaging, social media, cell phones, instant messaging, and tweeting are just a few of the many forms of technological communication that affect the practice of counseling. There are many potential ethical and legal considerations that clinical mental health counselors need to consider when using technology in their practice.

Online counseling, Internet therapy, cybercounseling, and technology-assisted distance counseling are commonly used terms to describe the process of counseling with individuals, families, or groups using the Internet (Haley & Vasquez, 2009). Online counseling can occur through email interaction, chat room counseling, instant messaging, and FaceTime. Voice over IP (VoIP) programs such as Skype, which allows real-time speaking over the Internet using a microphone and webcam, are also forms of cybercounseling (Haley & Vasquez, 2009). When the counseling occurs during the moment of connection, it is called **synchronous counseling**. When there is a time lapse between client–counselor communications, the counseling is **asynchronous**. Skyping and instant messaging are examples of synchronous counseling, whereas email counseling and text messaging are examples of asynchronous counseling.

Several professional organizations have addressed ethical and legal concerns associated with technology-assisted counseling, as well as other technological concerns associated with the client–counselor relationship, in their ethical codes. Among the associations issuing guidelines have been the ACA (2014) *Code of Ethics*, the AMHCA (2015) *Code of Ethics*, and NBCC's (2016b) *Standards for Distance Professional Services*. In addition, legal statutes as well as regulations prescribed by state licensure boards govern technology-assisted counseling.

Rather than discuss the array of ethical and legal issues that are inherent in technology-assisted counseling, we pose a list, which certainly is not all inclusive, of steps clinical mental health counselors can take to protect their clients from harm and to protect themselves from acting unethically or illegally. The list is compiled from recommendations offered by ACA (2014); AMHCA (2015); Barros-Bailey and Saunders (2010); Bradley, Hendricks, Lock, Whiting, and Parr (2011); Kaplan et al. (2009); and Wheeler and Bertram (2015).

Using Technology-Assisted Counseling Responsibly

- Establish methods to ascertain a client's identity. This recommendation is easier said than done, especially if no webcam is involved. Creating and exchanging a confidential password or other means of security offers some protection, but counselors still cannot be certain with whom they are communicating (and vice versa).
- Transfer client information electronically to authorized third-party recipients only when both the counselor and the authorized recipient have secure transfer and acceptance capabilities.
- Make sure that clients provide informed consent before engaging in any form of technology-assisted counseling. Informed consent considerations should include a description of the risk and benefits associated with technology-assisted counseling. In particular, concerns related to privacy, expectations of response time, emergency plans, and security configurations need to be addressed. Many counselors

meet face-to-face with clients and also provide access to their professional email or cell phone information. In such cases, counselors need to let clients know that email, cell phone calls, and texts should be used only for setting and/or canceling appointments.

- Make sure that adequate security configuration is available. Many counseling practices use encryption to protect client confidentiality. If you do not know how to use encryption, technology experts and websites can be helpful (e.g., see "How Encryption Works" at www.howstuffworks.com/encryption.htm).
- Provide technology-assisted counseling only in practice areas that are within your expertise.
- Do not provide technology-assisted counseling to clients in states where doing so would violate local licensure laws.
- Have a plan should emergency situations arise. For example, let the client know whom to contact in case of emergency (e.g., calling 911 or contacting the person on call if you are working in an agency).
- Consult with others who are more experienced in using technology-assisted counseling. Employee assistance programs can be good resources, as they are quickly becoming experts in Internet counseling.
- Refer to written resources, such as the *Ethical Standards Casebook* (Herlihy & Corey, 2015) and other publications, to become well versed in technology-assisted counseling.
- If you choose to become a distance credentialed counselor, a credential offered by NBCC, participate in their training program.

Social media networking presents an entire set of new potential ethical concerns to the clinical mental health counseling profession. For example, at the beginning of 2016, Facebook had 1.65 billion monthly active users per month and was the most popular social network worldwide (Statista, 2016). Wheeler and Bertram (2015) state, "Engaging in social media between counselor and client without advance thinking and use of sound informed consent may cause harm to both client and counselor" (pp. 114–115). Two of many concerns associated with social media and counseling are the following:

- *Breach of confidentiality or invasion of privacy:* Counselors who interact with clients on social networking sites such as Facebook or MySpace run the risk of breaching confidentiality. Such breaches pose ethical and possibly legal problems. For example, disclosing confidential information on a public network violates federal laws, specifically, the HIPAA Privacy Rule and a significant post-HIPAA regulation from the Health Information Technology for Economic and Clinical Health Act (HITECH, 2009; Wheeler & Bertram, 2015). HITECH was enacted to establish additional privacy and security requirements regarding electronic health records.
- *Boundary violations:* Social media interactions may inadvertently create boundary issues. If a counselor uses Facebook for nonprofessional reasons, privacy settings are essential, and even then profile information may become public by default (Schaffer, 2010). Wheeler and Bertram (2015) advise against "friending," "liking," or "poking" on Facebook, which are inappropriate in counseling relationships. Clinical mental health counselors need to inform clients that it is their policy to refrain from friending clients on Facebook in order to protect the counseling relationship and preserve confidentiality (i.e., to protect the client's welfare).

Keeping up with advances in technology and remaining proactive in deciding how to use technology is a major task and responsibility of clinical mental health counselors.

The Case of Selena

Selena worked with a 20-year-old client for six months on issues related to anxiety and depression. The client made excellent progress and terminated counseling appropriately, letting Selena know that she would contact her if she needed additional help. One year later, the client contacted Selena's Facebook page and requested to add her as a friend. How should Selena respond? What reasons might the former client have for contacting Selena? What are your thoughts about counselors maintaining online social media pages?

Summary and Conclusion

The mental health profession is influenced by ethical and legal constructs that affect the counselor–client relationship and the practice of counseling. Counselors, like other mental health professionals, have established codes of ethics to guide them in the practice of helping others. The *ACA Code of Ethics* and the *NBCC Code of Ethics* are two primary documents that professional counselors should consult when they face ethical dilemmas. Clinical mental health counselors should also consult the AMHCA *Code of Ethics* and the codes associated with other organizations to which they belong. Acting ethically is not always easy, comfortable, or clear, but it is a crucial part of maintaining professional integrity and of protecting the rights and welfare of clients.

In making ethical decisions, counselors rely on personal values as well as on ethical standards and legal precedents. Following a decision-making model and documenting reasons for selecting certain actions promotes ethical practice. To help with ethical dilemmas, clinical mental health counselors should consult with professional colleagues, seek supervision, and refer to casebooks and other professional literature.

In addition, clinical mental health counselors should be well informed about state and national legislation and legal decisions that affect the counseling profession. Counselors are liable for civil and criminal malpractice suits if they violate client rights or societal rules. One way to protect themselves legally is for counselors to review and follow the ethical standards of the professional organizations with which they are affiliated and to operate according to recognized standard practices. Clinical mental health counselors also need to have professional liability insurance in the event that their practices are questioned.

Ethical standards and legal codes reflect current conditions and are ever-evolving documents. They do not cover all situations, but they do provide important guidelines for practice. Clinical mental health counselors will want to be especially aware of ethical and legal obligations that relate to confidentiality, informed consent, professional boundaries and multiple relationships, professional competence, end-of-life issues, and technology. Because codes and legal statutes are not static, clinical mental health counselors need to be cognizant of changes to ethical and legal guidelines.

MyCounselingLab

Try the Topic 7 Assignments: *Ethical and Legal Considerations.*

CHAPTER 3

Clinical Mental Health Counseling in a Diverse Society

Rawpixel.com/Shutterstock

CHAPTER OVERVIEW

From reading this chapter, you will learn about

- Terminology associated with multicultural counseling and diversity and factors that influence the practice of multicultural counseling
- Implications related to counseling distinct populations in a culturally diverse world
- Issues related to sexual orientation and gender identity
- Issues faced by people with disabilities
- Issues related to socioeconomic status and social class

As you read, consider

- What personal beliefs, values, and attitudes you have that might inhibit your ability to work effectively with diverse populations
- In what ways you can develop the awareness, knowledge, and skills necessary to counsel diverse clients
- What cultural immersion experiences you can participate in to enhance your ability to understand people who differ from you
- What ethical concerns might arise for clinical mental health counselors working with specific populations

I walk among groups of uniformed people
in a bustling, well-planned, unfamiliar land
*   that looks in many ways like my own.*
As I hear the sound of language
*   alien to my ear*
*   I futilely search for meaningful words*
*   but end up with disappointments.*
I am a foreigner
*   different from the rest*
*   in looks, in style, and in expectations,*
I stand out as a visitor in Osaka
*   who still veers right instead of left*
*   to avoid the crowds in subways.*
Amidst it all, I am filled with new awareness
*   as I step from cultural shelters*
*   into a driving rain*
*   to become drenched in falling water*
*   and flooded with a rush of feelings.*
The challenge of understanding
*   both myself and others*
*   comes with each encounter.*

Reprinted from "Visitor in Osaka," by S. T. Gladding. Copyright 2002 by S. T. Gladding. Reprinted by permission.

The effectiveness of counseling depends on many factors, but among the most important is the ability of the counselor and client to understand and relate to each other. Effective clinical mental health counselors acknowledge differences among people and seek to improve their competence in counseling diverse populations (Robinson-Wood, 2017). Ethnicity, race, gender, religion, sexual orientation, age, ability levels, and socioeconomic background represent only some of the factors in which people differ. Being able to address the needs of the growing number of clients from diverse backgrounds may be one of the most challenging tasks clinical mental health counselors face (Lee & Park, 2013).

In this chapter, some of the many issues related to counseling distinct populations in a culturally diverse world are addressed. As the U.S. population becomes increasingly more diverse, it is imperative for clinicians to develop the awareness, knowledge, and skills needed to interact successfully with people from different backgrounds. Methods that work well with one client may be irrelevant or even inappropriate for other clients. Indeed, what may be valued and viewed as a strength in certain cultures may be devalued and viewed as a weakness in others (Harris, Thoresen, & Lopez, 2007). Therefore, counselors must be lifelong learners and implementers of new and effective methods of working with a wide range of clients. Topics covered in this chapter include working with culturally and ethnically distinct clients, sexual minority clients, clients with differing abilities, and clients who are economically disadvantaged.

CULTURE AND ETHNICITY

Many distinct racial and ethnic groups live in the United States. According to the Census Bureau, European Americans make up the largest group (approximately 62%), with four other distinct groups—African Americans, Native Americans, Asian Americans, and Hispanic or Latinos/-as—composing the majority of the rest of the population (approximately 38%). Of this last group, people of Hispanic or Latino origin (which technically refers to ethnicity rather than race) make up 17% of the U.S. population, with African Americans composing 13%, Asian Americans more than 5%, and Native Americans around 1%. More than 7.5 million individuals (over 2% of those reporting) now identify with more than one racial/ethnic background, and the multiple heritage population growth is more than four times that of any other group (Henriksen & Maxwell, 2016). Clearly, the United States is a nation of multiple ethnic and racial groups!

Several factors influence the practice of multicultural counseling, including understanding a client's identity, education, age, religion, socioeconomic status, and experiences with racism. A guide that can help counselors systematically consider various cultural influences is the ADDRESSING model (Hays, 2016). Letters of the model stand for the following factors:

- **A**ge and generational influences
- **D**evelopmental disabilities
- **D**isabilities acquired later in life
- **R**eligion (and/or spirituality)
- **E**thnicity (may include race)
- **S**ocial status (or social class)
- **S**exual orientation
- **I**ndigenous heritage
- **N**ational origin
- **G**ender (and gender socialization)

Cross-cultural encounters in counseling are enhanced when clinical mental health counselors respect their clients and take these factors into account.

About a quarter of those who initially present for counseling at mental health facilities are from minority cultural and ethnic groups (Cheung, 1991). Yet researchers have consistently found that clients from minority groups who enter counseling tend to be less satisfied with the services they receive than are clients from majority groups. Some 50% of minority-culture group members who begin counseling terminate after one session, as compared with about 30% of majority-culture clients (Sue & Sue, 2016). Several hypotheses have been proposed to explain why minority-culture clients underutilize counseling services. One explanation is that minority clients do not find traditional settings or psychotherapy helpful. They may distrust the counseling process, considering it intrusive, dehumanizing, or stigmatizing (Buser, 2009; West-Olatunji, 2001). To meet the needs of racial and ethnic minority populations more effectively, clinical mental health counselors need to develop cultural competencies characterized by a respectful understanding of different ethnic and racial groups, including their histories, traditions, beliefs, and value systems (see Box 3–1).

BOX 3–1   Six Foundational Concepts of Multicultural Counseling

Courtland Lee (2013, pp. 5–6) outlines six basic concepts of multicultural counseling. These concepts can guide your work as you meet the challenges of cross-cultural encounters.

- **Culture** refers to any group of people who identify with one another on the basis of a common purpose, need, or similarity of background.
- Cultural differences influence all human interactions.
- All counseling can be considered cross-cultural.
- Multicultural counseling emphasizes all forms of human diversity.
- Culturally competent counselors develop the awareness, knowledge, and skills to work effectively with people from culturally diverse backgrounds.
- Culturally competent counselors are globally literate.

Defining Culture and Multicultural Counseling

Culture can be defined in several ways. The term can be conceptualized as a combination of "**ethnographic variables** such as ethnicity, nationality, religion, and language, as well as **demographic variables** of age, gender, place of residence, etc., **status variables** such as social, economic, and educational background and a wide range of formal or informal memberships and affiliations" (emphasis added; Pedersen, 1990, p. 550). Personal cultural backgrounds, which include each of these variables, structure our behaviors, thoughts, perceptions, values, and goals. Cultural elements help create the lenses through which people view and experience the world.

An individual's cultural identity is often complex and not readily apparent. People's identities are embedded in multiple levels of experiences and contexts (Robinson-Wood, 2017; Sue, Ivey, & Pedersen, 1996). The salience of various cultural elements differs from person to person. For example, one person may base his or her cultural identity on shared physical characteristics, whereas another person may identify more with shared history and beliefs. Furthermore, many people have multiple group-referenced identities, such as being an aging lesbian African American female. To facilitate empathic understanding, clinical mental health counselors can intentionally help clients articulate their cultural identities and the associated values and beliefs they consider important.

Just as the word *culture* is multifaceted, the terms *multicultural* and *multicultural counseling* have been conceptualized in numerous ways. There is no universal definition of **multicultural**, although accrediting groups such as the Council for Accreditation of Counseling and Related Educational Programs (CACREP) have chosen to define the term broadly. Defined broadly, multiculturalism takes into account differences in areas such as language, social class, race, ethnicity, gender, sexual orientation, religion, and level of ability (Lee, 2013). Multiculturalism recognizes the unique qualities of various groups as well as individual differences within groups. West-Olatunji (2001) emphasizes that **multicultural counseling** refers to "multiple perspectives or multiple cultural viewpoints within the counseling relationship in which none are dominant or considered more 'normal' than others" (p. 418).

Recognizing that all people are unique cultural beings and that no two people experience culture in exactly the same way, how, then, do counselors approach multicultural counseling? Historically, counselors have taken either an etic or an emic approach to the issue. The **etic** perspective emphasizes the universal qualities of counseling that are culturally generalizable. In contrast, the **emic** perspective focuses on the indigenous characteristics of each cultural group that influence the counseling process, emphasizing counseling approaches that are culturally specific. Neither approach is singularly sufficient. The etic approach has been criticized for emphasizing universality to the extent of ignoring important cultural differences. The emic approach has been criticized for overemphasizing specific, culturally appropriate techniques to facilitate client change. Conceivably, the most constructive approach to multicultural counseling is one that merges etic and emic perspectives by focusing on both universal themes and specific cultural considerations.

As counseling professionals and researchers continue to build on the foundation of multicultural knowledge, one point remains clear: Clinical mental health counselors need to develop cultural sensitivity and competency to work effectively with clients who differ from them. Counselors who disregard cultural differences and operate under the assumption that all counseling theories and techniques are equally applicable to all clients are, according to Wrenn (1962b), **culturally encapsulated**. Insensitivity to the actual experiences of clients from different cultural backgrounds can lead to discrimination as well as to ethical misconduct.

Five themes have emerged from multicultural counseling publications during the past two decades, according to D'Andrea and Heckman (2008):

1. Sensitivity to the significant ways that cultural factors affect human development
2. Awareness of the competencies practitioners need to acquire to promote the healthy development of clients from diverse populations
3. Consideration given to the professional training strategies that help foster the development of cultural competence among professionals
4. A broad knowledge of the research findings related to multicultural issues
5. An understanding of the present and future challenges for counselors in a society that continues to be in a state of rapid flux in its racial/cultural demography (p. 259)

Challenges and Issues in Multicultural Counseling

Becoming a competent multicultural counselor can present both challenges and opportunities for a practitioner. Skillful multicultural counseling involves being sensitive and flexible, tolerating ambiguity, and understanding and accepting different worldviews (Locke, 2001). **Worldview** refers to the way people perceive their relationship to the world, including nature, other people, objects, and religious experiences. Worldviews influence people's thoughts, feelings, behaviors, and perceptions (Hays & Erford, 2014; Sue, 1981).

One challenge related to multicultural counseling is the ability to recognize difficulties that arise from living in poverty and with discrimination. Poverty is a variable that intersects with aspects of cultural identity, including race, sexuality, gender, and ethnicity (Robinson-Wood, 2017). Historically, members of ethnic minority groups in the United States have an average income that is lower than the average income of majority-group members. A disproportionate number of minority-group families have limited financial resources. When people live in an environment characterized by poverty and powerlessness, they may exhibit behaviors and attitudes that appear dysfunctional but are, in fact, healthy coping mechanisms for living in that environment (West-Olatunji, 2001). Clinical mental health counselors need to be aware of the multiple environmental and societal factors that affect their clients, some of which are culturally based and others that are not (see Box 3–2).

BOX 3–2 A Call to the Profession

We cannot assume that racism will disappear just by our being good people, or by leaving people of color to deal with it. We cannot assume that sexism will disappear just by our being good people, or by leaving women to deal with it. We cannot assume that homophobia will disappear just by our being good people, or by leaving lesbian women and gay men to deal with it. We cannot assume that discrimination against the "differently-abled" will disappear just by our being good people, or by leaving people who are differently-abled to deal with it. We can no longer tolerate the barriers that have kept us separate for so long. To take pleasure and strength in the particular heritage to which we were born is fine; to buttress our own identities by humiliating or demonizing or rendering invisible those of other heritages is a sure recipe for our own disaster. Alone, we will be mystified, silenced, invalidated; we will burn out in the struggle. But together, we can help each other pull down the walls that separate us and demolish the invisible barriers that keep us from the connection that is our human birthright.

(Locke, 2001, pp. 245–246)

Two pressing issues that affect counseling in a diverse society are prejudice and racism. They are closely related but have been defined differently. **Prejudice**, according to Allport's (1954) classic definition, is a negative bias toward a particular group of people. **Racism** is based on prejudicial beliefs, which maintain that racial groups other than one's own are inferior (Casas, 2005). Prejudice is mainly attitudinal in nature, whereas "racism extends the negative attitude into behavior that discriminates against a particular group" (Utsey, Ponterotto, & Porter, 2008, p. 339). Racism demeans all who participate in it and is a form of projection usually displayed out of fear or ignorance. **Cultural racism** occurs when one cultural group considers another group inferior, and the first group has the power to impose its standards on the other group. **Institutionalized racism** refers to the established use of policies, laws, customs, and norms to perpetuate discrimination and prejudice. It may be difficult for those who are part of a majority group to recognize their own racism, although doing so is vital to the development of cultural self-awareness (Orozco, Lee, Blando, & Shooshani, 2014).

Another challenge in multicultural counseling is the dominance of theoretical approaches based on Western philosophical assumptions and cultural values (Sue & Sue, 2016). Some dominant **Western values** include individualism, autonomy, action-oriented approaches to problem solving, strong work ethics, and an emphasis on rigid time schedules (Axelson, 1999; Sue & Sue, 2016). A liability of these values in counseling is that theories built around them may not always be applicable to clients from other cultural traditions. Indeed, such culture-bound values may contradict the value systems of other cultural groups, and imposing them on racial/ethnic minorities may be detrimental. Clinical mental health counselors are challenged to move beyond Eurocentric biases that characterize traditional counseling theories and develop new conceptual frameworks that are more appropriate and culturally relevant for all clients.

A fourth factor that is particularly relevant to counseling ethnic minorities and immigrants is the client's level of acculturation/enculturation (Yoon, Langrehr, & Ong, 2011). **Acculturation** can be defined as "cultural adaptation that occurs as a result of contact between multiple cultures" (Miller, 2007, p. 118). It can be conceptualized as cultural socialization to the majority culture. In contrast, **enculturation** involves the retention of one's culture of identity. For example, immigrants from Vietnam may intentionally retain their cultural values, customs, and worldviews and take steps to socialize their children and grandchildren accordingly (Yoon et al., 2011). Acculturation and enculturation are not mutually exclusive. Individuals can develop cultural orientations to both the majority culture and their culture of origin.

Cultural pluralism is the term used to describe minority groups that participate fully in the dominant society yet maintain their distinct cultural differences (Hays & Erford, 2014). On a societal level, people benefit from cultural pluralism. Culturally sensitive counselors are aware of the different ways in which ethnic minorities and immigrants, as well as other minority groups, navigate the processes of acculturation, enculturation, and cultural pluralism. Economic disadvantages, racism, value differences, and levels of cultural identity all can potentially influence the client–counselor relationship and the effectiveness of counseling.

Developing Multicultural Counseling Competencies

In 1996, the Association for Multicultural Counseling and Development (AMCD) published a document, *Operationalization of the Multicultural Counseling Competencies* (Arredondo et al., 1996), which was designed to help counselors work effectively in an ethnically diverse society. These competencies were originally posited by Sue, Arredondo, and McDavis in their seminal article, "Multicultural Counseling Competencies and Standards: A Call to the Profession" (1992). The multicultural counseling competencies (MCCs) were endorsed by many professional counseling associations. In 2015 the *Multicultural and Social Justice Counseling Competencies* (MSJCC), which revised the competencies developed by Sue et al. (1992), offered counselors a framework to implement multicultural and social justice competencies into counseling theories, practices, and research (Ratts et al., 2015). All of these documents contributed to changes in ACA's *Code of Ethics* (2014) and counseling accreditation standards (CACREP, 2016).

Overall, multicultural competencies are organized into four categories: (a) counselor self-awareness, (b) knowledge of clients and their worldviews, (c) counseling relationship, and (d) counseling and advocacy interventions. Ethnically responsive counselors are professionals who have intentionally found ways to grow and develop in each of these categories.

The counselor self-awareness category includes counselors being aware of their own beliefs, attitudes, and feelings associated with cultural differences—for example, racism, sexism, heterosexism, and other areas of difference (Sue & Sue, 2016)—as well as being cognizant of their own cultural values and biases. The process of self-awareness is facilitated when counselors ask themselves questions such as, "How do I see myself as a member of my cultural group?" "How do I see other people in my cultural group?" and "How do I perceive people who differ from me in regard to race, ethnicity, sexuality, and other areas?"

In addition to developing self-awareness, counselors need to acquire a knowledge base of clients and their worldviews. This information guides their work in a diverse society. To that end, C. C. Lee (2001) offers the following suggestions:

- Acquire an understanding of how economic, social, and political systems affect the psychosocial development of ethnic and other minority groups.
- Acquire general knowledge about the histories, experiences, customs, and values of people from diverse groups. Understand how these contexts influence personal and social development.
- Read the literature and use the media to learn about the lifestyles, customs, values, and traditions of different ethnic groups. For example, view diversity-focused films about specific cultures to understand and experience these cultures vicariously. Literature can provide tremendous insight into a wide range of cultural experiences.
- Experience ethnic diversity firsthand by interacting with people in their cultural environments. For example, you can attend festivals, ceremonies, and places of worship that represent different cultural environments. Counselor educators can invite people from other cultures to speak about their experiences, either individually or as part of a panel.

Although it is unrealistic to expect counselors to be knowledgeable about all cultures, they can intentionally learn about different ethnic groups, particularly those that they are most likely to encounter in counseling.

Counselors must also acquire relationship skills to help people resolve problems or make decisions in ways that are consistent with the realities of their clients' cultural experiences. C. C. Lee (2001) suggests that relationship skills should be grounded in three premises:

1. Ethnic diversity is real and should not be ignored.
2. Ethnic differences are not deficiencies. Counselors need to meet clients where they are, recognizing differences and responding accordingly.
3. Counselors need to avoid stereotypes and consider the multiple contexts that affect client development.

With these premises in mind, clinical mental health counselors are advised to take several factors into account when counseling people from diverse ethnic groups, including kinship influences, language preference, gender-role socialization, religious/spiritual, cultural privilege, and help-seeking attitudes and behaviors (Lee, 2001, 2013).

When possible, counselors should communicate with clients in their preferred language. When this is not feasible, a referral to a bilingual counselor may be appropriate (see Box 3–3).

BOX 3–3   A Voice from the Field: Counseling and Advocating for Latino/-a Clients

As a new bilingual practitioner working with Latino/-a clients and their families, I learned that I was expected not only to be a counselor but also to serve as an advocate for clients who were not able at times to speak for themselves; that is, to speak English. I was faced with the dual challenges of establishing myself as a beginning counselor and creating a safe environment for my clients. Being a bilingual counselor allows me the opportunity to use my language skills to counsel Spanish-speaking clients in a more direct and empathic way than would occur through using a translator. A blessing indeed, but it also has proved to be a bit of a struggle getting my peers to view me as a trained therapist. They initially viewed me as a *translator*, asking, "What are they [the family members] saying?" rather than as a *counselor*, asking, "What do you think is going on with this family?"

As an advocate for my clients, I often must help them understand that my role is to help them with mental health issues, not to pass judgment regarding their immigration status in the United States. Through my continued work with Latino/-a clients, I have experienced the joy of facilitating the removal of cultural and emotional *paredes* (walls) within individuals and families.

Tania Castillero Hoeller, MA Ed, LPC, NCC,
Casa Guadalupe, Catholic Social Services

Finally, there are counseling and advocacy interventions. In this fourth category, counselors

- Employ empowerment theories
- Help clients develop a critical consciousness by understanding situations in society
- Assist clients with developing self-advocacy skills that promote multiculturalism and social justice
- Use advocacy techniques to address the historical events and persons that shape and influence society
- Promote support for clients through relationships and collaboration

Becoming Ethnically Responsive Counselors: Integrating Awareness, Knowledge, Skills, and Advocacy

Developing multicultural counseling competencies is a complex process that integrates personal growth with learning and skill development (Orozco et al., 2014). One training technique that helps counselors improve their multicultural counseling skills while increasing sensitivity and understanding is Pedersen's (2002) **triad role-play model**. In the role play, participants take the roles of counselor, client, and problem. They simulate a counseling session in which they strive to

- Articulate the problem from the client's cultural perspective
- Anticipate resistance from a culturally diverse client
- Diminish defensiveness by studying the counselor's personal defensive responses
- Learn and practice recovery skills when culturally related problems occur

Pedersen recommends that counselors-in-training film their role plays to facilitate greater learning. By discussing the videotaped role plays, students can enhance their understanding of how cultural differences can affect the counseling process.

USE OF THEORIES.   Another way counselors can develop skills in working with people from different cultures is by intentionally examining and implementing existing theories that have cross-cultural applications. For example, existential counseling is a holistic approach that has applications across cultures and socioeconomic groups (Epp, 1998). Existential theory deals with the meaning of life, freedom, human relationships, and the ultimate realities of life and death. These basic human conditions transcend culture and, for many clients, are primary counseling concerns.

An exciting development in multicultural counseling is the renewed emphasis on theories specifically designed for different cultures. For example, traditional Asian psychotherapies (e.g., yoga, meditation), which have existed for more than 3,000 years, have become more popular in the West (Walsh, 2000). Many of these Eastern traditions stress existential and transpersonal health and development, rather than pathology, using such techniques as mindfulness, meditation, and yoga. These practices can have beneficial effects on wellness and psychological growth, whether used alone or in concert with other approaches.

Culturally sensitive counselors are able to evaluate the relevance of their theoretical orientations, recognizing that approaches that are helpful for some clients may be ineffective for other clients (Lee, 2013). Moreover, although a plethora of literature addresses helpful ways to counsel specific cultural groups, counselors need to remember that there are more within-group differences than between-group differences. In other words, not all people from a cultural group share the same reality; thus, using "cookbook" approaches to working with diverse clientele is ill-advised.

CONVEYING CULTURAL EMPATHY.   An essential component of working effectively with culturally diverse clients is the counselor's ability to communicate cultural empathy (Chung & Bemak, 2002). For cultural empathy to be conveyed, Chung and Bemak (2002) make the following recommendations:

- Demonstrate a genuine interest in learning more about the client's culture. Become knowledgeable about the historical and sociopolitical background of clients, and demonstrate sensitivity about specific cultural issues.
- Convey genuine appreciation for cultural differences between the client and the counselor.
- Recognize the cultural meaning clients attach to phenomena, and use that understanding to facilitate client empowerment, strengthen the therapeutic alliance, and enhance counseling outcomes, a practice known as **broaching** (Day-Vines et al., 2007).
- Incorporate culturally appropriate interventions and outcome expectations into the counseling process. Implement indigenous healing practices from the client's culture if possible.
- Understand and accept the context of family and community for clients of different backgrounds.
- Recognize the psychosocial adjustment that must be made by clients who have moved from one environment to another.

- Be sensitive to oppression, discrimination, racism, and microaggressions that are encountered by many people, often on a regular basis.
- Be prepared to advocate for and empower clients who feel underprivileged and devalued. (pp. 156–157)

Counselors who are able to convey cultural empathy are more likely to develop therapeutic relationships with clients from different cultural backgrounds, thus increasing the likelihood of positive counseling outcomes.

The Case of Khadijah

Khadijah is a 30-year-old Muslim woman who is a recent refugee from Afghanistan, where her father and two brothers were killed by the Taliban. She has been in the United States for two months. She is frequently harassed because of her head covering and long dress (traditional Muslim attire in Afghanistan). She has been taunted and accused of being a terrorist. Last week, she was told by someone in her neighborhood that she should "go back to her jihadist despotic relatives." This occurred in the presence of her 13-year-old daughter, who was dressed in similar traditional clothing. Since that incident, her daughter has refused to dress in an appropriate Islamic manner and has started challenging her parents when they insist that she do so. Khadijah has sought counseling to help her deal with the family conflict, the anger she feels about the taunts and accusations, the trauma of losing her father and brothers in Afghanistan, the culture shock of being in America, and general feelings of helplessness and depression.

What are your initial impressions about Khadijah? What aspects of her story have you come in contact with before? What, if anything, makes you feel uncomfortable or nervous? If you were Khadijah's counselor, what are some things you might do at the outset?

SEXUAL ORIENTATION AND GENDER IDENTITY

In addition to focusing on ways to become an ethnically responsive counselor, it is important to consider other issues related to counseling in a diverse society. People frequently have multiple identities, some of which are more visible than others. In this section, counseling issues related to sexual orientation and gender identity are covered.

Sexual orientation represents just one of many dimensions that make up an individual's identity. Unlike ethnicity, however, sexual orientation is, in many ways, an "invisible identity" (Bringaze & White, 2001). Consequently, counselors may not be aware of a client's sexual orientation unless the client chooses to reveal it. Sexual minority percentages, which are difficult to determine precisely, range from 5% to 15% of the population (Miller & House, 2005; Moursund & Kenny, 2002). One of the reasons it is difficult to obtain accurate statistics on the prevalence of sexual minorities is that "many surveys rely on self-report data and some people may not feel safe disclosing their sexual orientation and/or gender identification" (Singh & Chun, 2013, p. 195). Because of the stigmatization that continues to be associated with sexual minority identity in our society, many lesbian, gay, bisexual, and transgender individuals experience discrimination and lack of acceptance. Even though non-heterosexual individuals are more likely to seek counseling than their heterosexual counterparts, they report being less satisfied with their counseling experiences and are more likely to terminate early (Miller & House, 2005).

Professional mental health organizations forbid discrimination based on sexual orientation. For example, the *ACA Code of Ethics* (2014) mandates that professional counselors do not condone or engage in discrimination against clients based on their "age, culture, disability, ethnicity, race, religion/spirituality, gender, gender identity, sexual orientation, marital status/partnership, language preference, socioeconomic status, or any basis proscribed by law" (Standard C.5). To work effectively with lesbian, gay, and bisexual clients (hereafter referred to as LGB), practitioners need to develop a clear understanding of their own sexual identity, knowledge about issues related to LGB identity development and lifestyles, and skills for working competently with this population. In this section, information is presented about sexual orientation and sexual identity, special concerns related to working with LGB clients, and implications for counseling. Later in the section, counseling issues related to working with transgender individuals are discussed. Transgender individuals are those whose gender identity differs from their biological sex. Although transgender persons may have experiences similar to those of LGB populations, they also have "social and psychological dimensions unique to their identity" (Palma & Stanley, 2002, p. 74).

Definitions and Terminology

Although research strongly indicates that sexual orientation is biological in origin, some people continue to refer to sexual orientation as **sexual preference**, a term that implies choice and needs to be avoided. The suggested terminology is **sexual orientation** (also called **affectional orientation**), which refers to past, present, and ideal feelings about who is attractive and desirable in sexual and/or romantic ways. Sexual orientation—which can be heterosexual, homosexual, bisexual, or questioning—is a multidimensional construct that many researchers believe exists on a continuum ranging from exclusively homosexual to exclusively heterosexual. The classic Kinsey studies (Kinsey, Pomeroy, & Martin, 1948) were among the first studies to suggest that people endorse sexual orientation along a continuum rather than "strictly in a bipolar fashion" (Savage, Harley, & Nowak, 2005).

It is important to avoid making generalizations about sexual orientation because generalities may not necessarily represent the experience of a specific client (Orozco et al., 2014). For the sake of clarity, in this chapter the term **gay** refers to men who are sexually oriented to other men, **lesbian** refers to women who are sexually oriented to other women, and **bisexual** refers to individuals who are sexually oriented to both men and women. **Queer** is a term that in years past was considered derogatory and pejorative. In recent years, however, the term has been reclaimed by many youth and individuals who identify outside the heteronormative or gender binary community (Singh & Chun, 2013). **Questioning** individuals are those who are beginning to explore their sexual understanding and orientation (Falkner & Starkey, 2009). These terms represent just a few of the many terms that are part of the language of sexual minority communities. More complete definition of terms can be accessed on the website for ACA's Association for Lesbian, Gay, Bisexual, and Transgender Issues in Counseling (ALGBTIC), where you can download the *ALGBTIC Competencies for Counseling LGBQQIA Individuals* (www.algbtic.org/).

Counselors need to select terminology prudently in their work with all clients, including sexual and gender minority clients. In particular, referring to someone as **homosexual** is discouraged because of the psychopathological connotations ascribed to that term in early editions of the *Diagnostic and Statistical Manual of Mental Disorders* (American Psychiatric Association, 1968), in which homosexuality was classified as a mental illness. Because the use of language can be either affirming or offensive, counselors need to be cognizant of their use of language. The best way to determine how clients self-identify is simply to ask.

Researchers distinguish among the terms **sexual attraction**, **sexual behavior**, and **sexual identity**. A person may be erotically attracted to someone of the same sex but engage exclusively in heterosexual behavior. Sexual identity, on the other hand, includes both the affectional and sexual dimensions of self that are evidenced by thoughts, feelings, and behaviors (Palma & Stanley, 2002). It is based on attraction, interests, and self-identification and can be viewed across a life span of development rather than as a constant in a person's life (Falkner & Starkey, 2009). The development of sexual identity is a dynamic process that is influenced by personal, contextual, and cultural experiences. Issues related to sexual identity development are often of specific concern to LGB clients, particularly when they have experienced prejudice, oppression, discrimination, and/or rejection.

Homophobia and Heterosexism

Prejudicial beliefs and attitudes, principally homophobia and heterosexism, have pervasive adverse effects on sexual minority clients, as well as on society as a whole. **Homophobia** refers to an antigay bias, or a fear of individuals who are perceived as lesbian, gay, or bisexual. Homophobic attitudes are evidenced by the stereotyping and denigrating of LGB individuals. In extreme cases, these negative, derogatory responses become violent, resulting in harassment and hate crimes. As many as 92% of gay men and lesbian women have experienced antigay verbal abuse, and some 24% report being victims of physical violence (Orozco et al., 2014). The fatal beating of Matthew Sheppard, a Wyoming college student, is a tragic but well-known example of a hate crime perpetrated against someone because he was gay. Cyberbullying can also lead to tragic outcomes. For example, in September 2010, two Rutgers freshmen secretly hid a camera in the room of Tyler Clemente, another Rutgers freshman. These two students filmed Clemente engaging in a sexual act with another man. They then posted the images on the web. Soon after the incident was broadcast on the Internet, Clemente committed suicide by jumping off the George Washington Bridge. Clinical mental health counselors are responsible for combating homophobia (also called **homoprejudice**) when it is evidenced in any form.

Perhaps a more insidious form of discrimination and prejudice is **heterosexism**, which refers to the viewpoint that heterosexuality is the only acceptable sexual orientation. Heterosexism has been further defined as a pervasively oppressive institutional preference for heterosexuality (Ritter & Terndrup, 2002). The heterosexist stance continues to be the societal norm in the United States, as evidenced by prevailing attitudes that reinforce heterosexual privilege. Heterosexism is evidenced when, for example, workplaces do not provide healthcare or bereavement benefits for same-sex partners or institutions fail to recognize same-sex life commitments as legal. Even more subtle forms of heterosexism may be evidenced in counseling agencies, when intake forms include blanks for *spouse*, or when counselors assume that their clients are heterosexual. Some researchers use the term **homonegativity** to encompass the concepts of both homophobia and heterosexism. More succinctly, homonegativity can be defined as negative thoughts and feelings about sexual minorities (Worthington, Dillon, & Becker-Schutte, 2005).

Although general trends indicate that people are more accepting of minority sexual identities than they have been in past years, many LGB individuals continue to encounter homonegativity on a regular basis (see Box 3–4). Counselors need to be aware of their own beliefs and responses, oppose discrimination, demonstrate affirmation, and acquire the knowledge and skills for counseling effectively with LGB clients. Indeed, legal and ethical issues abound when a counselor refuses to counsel sexual minority clients, which constitutes a violation of the standard of care in the counseling community. For example, in *Bruff v. North Mississippi Health Services, Inc.* (2001), a federal appeals court upheld the job termination of a counselor who asked to be excused from counseling a lesbian client on relationship issues because the client's sexual orientation conflicted with the counselor's religious beliefs (Hermann & Herlihy, 2006).

BOX 3–4   Negative Consequences of Stereotyping and Labeling

When society categorizes an individual using only one dimension of humanness, a significant part of that person is omitted. This omission leads to stereotyping and labeling, which have a significant and detrimental impact on the individual. Examples of such stereotyping and labeling include, "He is a dumb jock; what is he doing with a philosophy major?" "She's a woman; she shouldn't do that kind of work." "He's gay; he should not be working with children." "She is married; she couldn't possibly be bisexual." All of these statements focus on only one aspect of the individual. By focusing on an isolated aspect, the person in each of these examples is minimized and reduced to that one aspect—an unfair and inaccurate characterization of the whole person. The more holistic approach to human behavior focuses on the integration of all aspects of the individual, including the emotional, social, intellectual, spiritual, and physical dimensions of each person.

(Miller & House, 2005, pp. 435–436)

Sexual Identity Development and Coming Out

MODELS OF IDENTITY DEVELOPMENT.   Several theoretical explanations of minority sexual identity development have been proposed, each with unique counseling implications. Identity models help explain the cognitive, emotional, and behavioral changes that occur as an individual moves toward identifying him- or herself as gay, lesbian, or bisexual. One of the first models, developed by Cass (1979, 1984), proposed a six-stage model that provides a framework for understanding sexual minority identity development. Cass's six phases are identity confusion, identity comparison, identity tolerance, identity acceptance, identity pride, and identity synthesis.

Whereas Cass's model was based on a study of gay men, other models have been developed that point out different developmental paths experienced by women. In particular, lesbian women often experience feelings of connectedness and attraction to women before associating those feelings with a specific sexual orientation (Bringaze & White, 2001). McCarn and Fassinger (1996) developed a model of lesbian identity development, which occurs over four phases: awareness, exploration, deepening commitment, and internalization/synthesis. Bisexual identity development, which has not been researched as extensively as gay or lesbian identity development, involves dimensions that are unique to the bisexual experience and need to be taken into consideration during counseling (Horowitz & Newcomb, 1999). Bisexuality does not imply promiscuity—a misconception held by some individuals. Instead, someone who is bisexual is attracted to more than one gender (The Bisexual Index, 2016). Clinical mental health counselors benefit their clients and themselves when they are sensitive to issues that affect sexual minority identity development, as well as to issues that affect identity development overall.

It is helpful to view sexual identity development as a process that is unique for each individual and is influenced by multiple personal and contextual factors (Palma & Stanley, 2002). Movement from one stage of development to another may be fluid and nonlinear, with no one formula or path that is "best." Bringaze and White (2001) emphasize that the process of achieving a positive lesbian, gay, or bisexual identity can take many years, with some people getting stuck during the process and never developing a positive, integrated identity. Counselors need to take into account each client's unique sociocultural background, experiences, and perspectives and meet that client where he or she is in regard to sexual identity formation.

SEXUAL AND ETHNIC MINORITY IDENTITY.   Lesbian, gay, and bisexual individuals from ethnic minority groups may face a unique set of issues that differ from those faced by other LGB clients. In some ways, LGB people of color face particular struggles when they attempt to function in several communities simultaneously (Orozco et al., 2014). They may be more likely to face social discrimination on many levels, which can lead to psychological distress. For example, Latino communities largely reject sexual minority identities (Sager, 2001). In Latino communities, **familism**, or the primary importance of family, is often valued above individual needs. Coming out in a Latino family may accentuate feelings of guilt and alienate clients from their families, churches, and communities. Consequently, LGB Latino/-a clients may "face the difficult choice of remaining closeted in the heterosexist Latin American community or dealing with racism in the LGB and European American communities" (Sager, 2001, p. 25). The fear of rejection, cultural disinheritance, and loss of ties to one's ethnic community can make it especially difficult for clients from Latino and other ethnic groups to develop healthy, integrated sexual identities.

The Case of Manuel

Manuel, an 18-year-old Latino, is your client at a university counseling center. During the third session, he tells you that he has struggled with issues related to his sexual orientation for several years. You are the first person he has shared this with, and he approaches the topic with great anxiety. He says that in his culture, gay and lesbian individuals are ostracized and that his father would disown him if he knew that his son was gay.

In small groups, discuss ways you would respond to Manuel. What are the key issues in this case? What more information do you need? How can you work with Manuel on issues related to sexual orientation and other issues of diversity? Remember, you are the first person he has talked with about his struggles. How can you affirm Manuel as he works through issues related to sexuality? As you read the next section, consider concerns Manuel might face if he decides to come out.

COMING OUT.   A key component of minority sexual identity development is the coming-out process. **Coming out**, or letting other people know that one is lesbian, gay, or bisexual, is not a one-time event, but instead is an ongoing process, affected largely by an individual's life circumstances. The process may begin at any age and can be especially difficult for adolescents, who may be more vulnerable and subject to ridicule. At any age, making the decision to reveal one's sexual orientation to others can have serious consequences, both positive and negative (Winter, 2002). Clinical mental health counselors can help clients sort through the various issues associated with that decision and examine the risks and benefits associated with coming out.

It is generally accepted that coming out is positively associated with mental health and relationship satisfaction (Orozco et al., 2014). Coming out contributes to identity acceptance, integration, and authenticity. However, coming out also carries with it the risk of abandonment, ridicule, and disapproval. Practitioners have an obligation to assist clients in carefully assessing potential risks as they consider the option of disclosure to others in their lives (Lemoire & Chen, 2005). The process may be psychologically painful, as the old sense of self is grieved before the new sense of self emerges. Practitioners can help clients cope with coming-out issues by providing emotional support; a safe space; and a genuine, nonjudgmental attitude. Counselors can take concrete steps to help clients with the coming-out process through the use of role play, cognitive rehearsal, and bibliotherapy. Providing information about support groups, hotlines, churches that are gay-affirming (i.e., fully accepting), and other community resources can benefit LBG clients grappling with coming-out issues.

Other Counseling Issues and Implications

Because of the pervasiveness of homonegativity in our society, LGB clients often enter counseling to help them come to terms with their orientation. However, the issues clients bring to counseling may or may not be related to sexual identity, and counselors need to avoid making premature assumptions about presenting concerns. With this caution in mind, some specific issues are unique to sexual minority clients. Often, LGB clients struggle to understand themselves and their relationships within a predominantly heterosexual society. Internalized homophobia and negative self-image, interpersonal relationships, career-related concerns, and conflicted religious values are just a few of the issues that LGB clients may choose to work on in counseling.

INTERNALIZED HOMOPHOBIA AND NEGATIVE SELF-IMAGE. Internalized homophobia occurs when a lesbian, gay, or bisexual individual internalizes negative societal attitudes about sexual minorities (Robinson-Wood, 2017). Such internalization can result in cognitive dissonance, low self-esteem, depression, and other forms of psychological distress. Typically, a person's internalized messages are tied to childhood experiences, family roles, religious beliefs, and societal expectations. LGB individuals often receive negative messages from many sources, including friends, family members, churches, and schools. Counselors can help clients explore and articulate the internalized messages they have received about being gay, lesbian, or bisexual. By encouraging the exploration of thoughts and feelings, counselors can then help clients challenge inaccuracies and reconstruct meanings about sexuality that are more positive and acceptable (Bringaze & White, 2001).

For clients to explore thoughts and feelings about their sexual orientation, they need to sense unconditional positive regard on the part of the counselor. They may test the counselor to determine his or her stance toward sexual minorities. Clinical mental health counselors can be proactive by establishing an environment in which clients feel safe exploring issues related to sexual identity. To that end, several researchers (e.g., Black & Underwood, 1998; Miller & House, 2005; Palma & Stanley, 2002; Robinson-Wood, 2017; Winter, 2002) provide the following suggestions:

- Demonstrate respect for the client's current experiences and presenting issues. These issues may or may not be related to sexual orientation.

- Be sincere, open, genuine, and ethical, respecting confidentiality and honoring differences.
- Explore personal issues related to sexuality and heterosexism. Covert, unexplored issues or attitudes are likely to affect the counseling experience negatively.
- Be aware of societal prejudices and oppression, and advocate for an LGB-affirmative environment. Offices with books, brochures, and symbols that are relevant to LGB individuals suggest that the counselor is affirming and nonjudgmental.
- Be sensitive to nonverbal or covert client messages that may signal permission for the counselor to address issues related to sexual identity.
- Be knowledgeable about sexual identity development issues. Provide support, normalize feelings, and validate confusion and ambiguity.
- Help clients explore feelings. Many LGB clients, especially adolescents, feel isolated, guilty, afraid, ashamed, and angry. Listen empathically, providing a safe space in which feelings can be validated.
- Be aware of the potential for depression and self-esteem issues.
- Provide accurate information about sexually transmitted diseases, such as HIV and AIDS.
- Be informed about community resources and support groups, and share that information with LGB clients.
- Attend seminars and workshops on counseling sexual minorities.

FAMILY RELATIONSHIPS.   Relationships with family members, particularly in regard to disclosure, can present unique sources of concern for LGB clients. When family members are supportive and accepting of sexual minority clients, relationships are enhanced, and clients report a higher degree of life satisfaction and adjustment (Bringaze & White, 2001). Unfortunately, however, many families do not support nonheterosexual orientations, and counselors need to help clients evaluate the pros and cons of disclosure. Disadvantages associated with not coming out to family members include having to monitor and censor one's interactions, as well as guilt associated with being unauthentic. On the other hand, when family values and cultural messages are such that an "out" sexual minority client will be alienated from his or her family, it may be in the client's best interest to avoid disclosure.

Clinical mental health counselors can help clients explore the realistic consequences of coming out to family, and if the client decides to disclose, the counselor can facilitate the process through rehearsal, empty-chair activities, and/or letter writing (Bringaze & White, 2001). Counselors also may be in a position to help families work through questions and confusion that arise in relation to their family member's sexual orientation.

OTHER RELATIONSHIPS.   Relationships with heterosexual friends and colleagues also may be sources of concern for LGB clients. Palma and Stanley (2002) point out that there often is a time lag between disclosure of one's sexual identity and the acceptance and/or affirmation that friends and colleagues are capable of providing. Counselors can help clients develop appropriate expectations of others by reminding them of the time it took for the clients to acknowledge their own sexual identity.

Associating with other people who are lesbian, gay, or bisexual can be especially helpful for LGB clients. Social and professional groups that provide support have been established in most urban areas and can serve as powerful resources for LGB clients. Groups exist that address multiple issues, including heterosexism, legal concerns, aging, health, and religion. Counselors in rural communities may have fewer local resources and thus need to be aware of resources available nationally, in nearby cities, and online.

LGB couples may seek counseling to work through relationship issues. Although some issues are common to same-sex and heterosexual couples (e.g., finances, communication problems) and are responsive to traditional therapeutic interventions, others are unique to gay and lesbian couples. Unfortunately, same-sex couples have fewer visible role models and may experience unique difficulties in regard to roles and relationships definition. Attempting to define roles in the same ways they are defined in heterosexual relationships can be counterproductive or detrimental.

RELIGIOUS CONCERNS. Many religious communities—particularly some conservative Christian denominations, Mormons, and Muslims—view homosexuality as sinful, and it may be difficult for LGB clients to find a place of worship where they are accepted and affirmed. It may be especially difficult for LGB clients to reconcile their sexual orientation with the beliefs of their faith. Accordingly, LGB clients may perceive it impossible to be a sexual minority and also religious, leading to an identity struggle referred to as **cognitive dissonance** (Mahaffy, 1996). When places of worship exhibit homonegativity, either actively or passively, LGB clients are likely to experience religious rejection, which may result in high levels of psychological distress (Berecz & Helm, 1998; Ritter & Terndrup, 2002). Feelings of shame, guilt, unworthiness, isolation, and loss, and feeling cut off from one's religious community, can be devastating and demoralizing.

There are several ways in which LGB individuals cope with religious rejection. They may choose to leave their church or other place of worship, deny or compartmentalize their sexual identity, change their sexual identity, or integrate their faith with their sexuality (Lease, Horne, & Noffsinger-Frazier, 2005; Mahaffy, 1996). Ideally, LGB persons are able to achieve identity integration so that they can embrace their sexual orientation in an affirming faith-based community. Counselors can help LGB clients discuss their religious beliefs and religious concerns and share resources with them about religious communities that affirm sexual minorities.

BOX 3–5   Reparative or Conversion Therapy

Reparative therapy, also called *conversion therapy* or *reorientation*, is the practice of attempting to change a client's sexual orientation from lesbian, gay, bisexual, queer, or questioning to that of heterosexual (ALGBTIC, 2012). The ACA—as well as organizations such as the American Psychological Association, the American Psychiatric Organization, and the National Association of Social Workers—opposes the promotion of reparative therapy. Studies have shown that efforts to change an individual's sexual orientation do not work and can cause significant psychological harm. Dr. Robert Spitzer, a well-known psychiatrist who published a study that supported the use of reparative therapy, recently recanted his claims in an open apology letter in which he stated, "I believe I owe the gay community an apology for making unproven claims of the efficacy of reparative therapy. I also apologize to any gay person who wasted time and energy undergoing some form of reparative therapy because I believed that I had proven that reparative therapy works with some 'highly motivated' individuals" (see Rudow, 2012).

CAREER CONCERNS.   Career choice, workplace benefits and stresses, and career advancement may present unique challenges to LGB clients (Orozco et al., 2014). Sexual minority clients may not be able to integrate their personal lives into the workplace as easily as their heterosexual counterparts can. They are more likely to face **work discrimination**, which refers to unfair and negative treatment based on personal attributes that are unrelated to job performance (Chung & Bemak, 2002). Although many companies have adopted corporate nondiscrimination policies, discrimination in the workplace is still a reality. Counselors can help LGB clients examine their perceptions of discrimination and evaluate potential coping strategies, which may include open confrontation or changing jobs. In other situations, clients may decide not to come out in the workplace, in which case counselors can help the clients cope with the additional stress that accompanies nondisclosure (Orozco et al., 2014). Counselors are encouraged to engage in social advocacy for LGB clients, including lobbying for the inclusion of sexual orientation in companies' nondiscrimination policies (Pope et al., 2004).

Working with Transgender Clients

The term **transgender**, sometimes called **transgendered** or **trans**, was coined in the late 1980s by gay men as a way to describe their desire to live as women (Prosser, 1997). The definition of *transgender* has evolved since then. Transgender individuals are people whose gender identity and expression conflict with their biological manifestation of sex. Male-to-female (MTF) transgender persons are born with male genitalia but experience their lives "gendered primarily as females" (Mostade, 2009, p. 308). For female-to-male (FTM) transgender individuals, the reverse is true. **Genderqueer** individuals do not identify with the traditional labels of male or female (Singh, Hays, & Watson, 2011). **Transsexual** individuals pursue hormonal treatment and/or sex reassignment surgery so that their externalized gender identification will match their internal gender identification. The *DSM-5* uses the term **gender dysphoria** to describe individuals who experience incongruence between their expressed/experienced gender and their assigned gender. The word *disorder*, which implies a mental health condition and was used in the previous edition of the *DSM*, has been eliminated. A lack of knowledge, understanding, and acceptance of transgender people often results in **transphobia** and **transprejudice**, manifested by societal stigma, marginalization, and discrimination (Singh, Boyd, & Whitman, 2010).

Media attention has provided visibility for transgender persons. Movies such as *Midnight in the Garden of Good and Evil*, *Boys Don't Cry*, *Normal*, and *Transamerica* have enabled activists to challenge public intolerance and prejudice (Carroll, Gilroy, & Ryan, 2002). Watching movies like these can build empathy for and understanding of the issues faced by transgender persons.

For counselors to work effectively with transgender clients, they need to build a knowledge base that will help them understand transgender issues. In addition, counselors need to examine their own values, beliefs, and biases. Working with transgender individuals where they are, recognizing that their main issue may not involve their gender identification, is crucial. When a client is considering hormonal and surgical intervention, trained mental health professionals can help the client explore options. Helping clients who are struggling with this decision can be especially challenging (Mostade, 2009).

Clinical mental health counselors are in a position to serve as advocates for LGBT clients. Joining ALGBTIC, a division of ACA, is one way counselors can advocate for sexual minority clients. Counselors also can take proactive steps to counteract bias on all fronts, whether it exists in relation to a person's sexual orientation, gender, ethnicity, or any other characteristic subject to discrimination.

DIFFERING ABILITIES

Nearly 58 million Americans reported a disability in 2010 (U.S. Census Bureau, 2012). That translates to 19% of the population, or nearly one of every five people. Disabilities differ in level of severity and are manifested in a variety of ways. They may be physical, emotional, cognitive, and/or behavioral in nature. Three broad categories of disabilities include physical, cognitive, and psychiatric. Examples of **physical disabilities** include sensory loss (e.g., blindness, deafness); orthopedic impairments, amputations, and congenital disabilities (e.g., spinal bifida); and chronic illness (e.g., multiple sclerosis, diabetes, chronic heart disease). Examples of **cognitive disabilities** include developmental disabilities, Alzheimer's disease, learning disabilities, and other cognitive impairments. **Psychiatric disabilities** include a range of mental disorders, including mood disorders, psychoses, and substance abuse or dependence. Because of the increasing number of people with disabilities, clinical mental health counselors are likely to provide services to clients with one or more disabilities (Smart, 2013).

In addition to variation in types of disabilities, there is much divergence in regard to age of onset, cause, severity, and manifestation of the disability. Consequently, the population of individuals with disabilities constitutes an extremely diverse group. Furthermore, people with disabilities represent the only minority group of which a person may unexpectedly become a member at any time (Foster, 1996). Often, people without disabilities are unaware of the marginalization and segregation experienced by individuals with disabilities (Emam, 2016). Discrimination against anyone disabled is referred to as **ableism**.

BOX 3–6 Respecting People Who Are Differently Abled

People with disabilities, like all people, want to participate fully in the society in which they live. The desire to achieve and to be successful is not diminished by a disability; indeed, the opportunity to work and contribute to the support of self and family is considered a basic right in a free, democratic society, and as American citizens, people with disabilities have a right to equality of opportunity of education, employment, transportation, housing, health care, and leisure. A person's disability should not interfere with full participation in any of these activities.

(Martin, 1999, p. 25)

Definitions and Terminology

The Americans with Disabilities Act of 1990 (ADA) defines **disability** as a physical or mental impairment that substantially limits a major life activity. The Supreme Court narrowed the ADA definition of disability by ruling that for a person to be considered substantially limited, the impairment must prevent or severely restrict the individual from doing activities that are of central importance to most people's daily lives, and that the impairment must be permanent or long term (Thomas, 2002). Disability status is dynamic, because of the transitory nature of health and the connection between a person's level of functioning and the barriers in his or her environment (Fujiura, 2001). Furthermore, disability is a "common and natural fact of life" and should be considered within the context of the multiple identities and roles that constitute an individual's life span (Smart & Smart, 2006, p. 29).

When working with people who are disabled, counselors must put the client first, not the disability. One way to accomplish this is by avoiding labels and stereotyping. Related to this concept is the need to choose language respectfully, making sure that terms are not pejorative or dehumanizing. For example, it is better to refer to someone who is differently abled as a "person with a disability" rather than as a "disabled person" (Martin, 1999). Similarly, terms like "physically or mentally challenged" should be avoided. Because there are literally hundreds of physical and mental conditions that qualify as disabilities, no single source of information on terminology provides suggestions that are appropriate for all people. Therefore, counselors will want to check with clients to determine their preferences regarding terminology and language use.

The degree to which a disability impedes an individual's functioning is situational. The presence of a disability and its subsequent effects vary, depending on the individual and the circumstances. For example, two people may have the same type of spinal cord injury but react and adapt to the injury differently. Likewise, someone may have epilepsy that is well controlled by medication, so that the disease does not pose a major impediment to the activities of daily living. Counselors can determine the degree to which a disability poses a barrier by carefully assessing and evaluating clients and the environments in which they live and work. Through careful assessment, stereotyping and overgeneralization can be avoided. Indeed, many individuals view their disability as a valued part of their identity and would not choose to eliminate the disability if such an option were viable (Smart & Smart, 2006).

Factors Associated with Increased Rates of Disability

A number of demographic, socioeconomic, and medical trends have been linked with rising rates of disabilities. These factors—which include aging, poverty, medical advances, and emerging medical conditions—are summarized in Figure 3–1. To meet the minimum standards of practice, clinical mental health counselors, in addition to rehabilitation counselors, need to become proficient in working with clients with disabilities (Smart, 2013).

Attitudes and Myths about Disabilities

Misconceptions about and biases toward individuals with disabilities often reflect lack of knowledge and negative stereotyping. Such societal attitudes are often subtle and may include reactions of sympathy, pity, or discomfort expressed verbally or nonverbally. Some of the negative attitudes and myths that may be held by members of society who are not currently disabled include the following (Martin, 1999; National Victim Assistance Academy [NVAA], 2002; Orozco et al., 2014; Tyiska, 1998):

- *The charity or helplessness myth:* People with disabilities are suffering and should be extended charity instead of rights and responsibilities. This attitude implies people with disabilities are not capable of making decisions for themselves and need others to manage their lives.
- *The spread phenomenon myth:* If one disability is present, there must be other disabilities as well.

> - **Aging.** Approximately three of every four Americans over the age of 80 have a disability of some type, and over half of this age group have a disability classified as severe. With longevity continuing to increase, there also comes an increase in disabilities associated with the aging process.
> - **Poverty.** Poverty has been linked to disability as both a consequence and a cause. People with disabilities are much more likely to be living in poverty than the general population is. They often are at a substantial disadvantage in regard to employment, access to private health insurance, and levels of educational achievement.
> - **Medical advances.** Due to medical advances, survival rates for spinal cord and severe brain injury, as well as other medical conditions, have improved dramatically. Also, survival rates for low-birth-weight infants have increased 70-fold during the past 25 years, affecting the prevalence of developmental disabilities.
> - **Emerging conditions.** Over the past years, certain medical conditions have either emerged as new syndromes (e.g., chronic fatigue syndrome) or increased in incidence (e.g., asthma, autism, attention-deficit/hyperactivity disorder, bipolar disorder). It is unclear whether the higher numbers represent an increase in prevalence or an increase in the recognition and reporting of such conditions.

FIGURE 3–1   Factors Associated with Increased Disability

- *The dehumanization or damaged merchandise myth:* A person with a disability is less than a full member of society or is inferior in some way.
- *The feeling no pain myth:* People with disabilities are immune from pain and suffering or have no feelings.
- *The disabled menace myth:* Because they are perceived as "different," people with certain disabilities are considered unpredictable and dangerous (e.g., group homes for adults with mental retardation are feared in some neighborhoods).

Negative attitudes and perceptions tend to undermine self-advocacy efforts and increase the vulnerability of people with disabilities. To counteract this effect, counselors who work with people with disabilities need to take lead roles in helping change negative societal attitudes, beginning with an examination of any personal attitudes that might interfere with effective interactions and interventions (see Figure 3–2).

Federal Regulation Related to Disability

Through the years, federal legislation has taken a key role in protecting the civil rights of people with disabilities. For over two decades, several federal initiatives have been enacted as laws designed to provide education and related services to individuals with disabilities. The Americans with Disabilities Act of 1990 (ADA) and its subsequent amendments provide a clear, comprehensive mandate for the elimination of discrimination against individuals with disabilities. Specifically, the ADA was enacted to protect people with disabilities from discrimination in employment, public accommodations, transportation, and telecommunication. Other examples of proactive legislation include the Individuals with Disabilities in Education Act, the Rehabilitation Act (including Section 504), and the Fair Housing Act. Additional information about the rights of people with disabilities can be obtained from the U.S. Department of Justice (*A Guide to Disability Rights Laws*; www.ada.gov/cguide.htm; cf. Smart, 2013). To provide effective preventive and remedial services, counselors must actively seek to understand the laws, regulations, and programs that affect people with disabilities.

- Treat the person with dignity and respect.
- Ask the person how to communicate most effectively with him or her.
- Address and speak directly to the person, even if he or she is accompanied by a third party.
- When introduced to a person with a disability, you may shake hands. People with limited hand use or who wear an artificial limb can usually shake hands.
- If you offer assistance, wait until the offer is accepted, and then listen to or ask for instructions.
- With regard to most accommodations, take your cue from the individual.
- Do not tell the person that you admire his or her courage or determination for living with the disability.
- When speaking to a person who uses a wheelchair or crutches, place yourself at eye level whenever possible to facilitate the conversation.
- When communicating with a person who is hard of hearing and who prefers to lip-read, face the person. Make sure you have the person's attention before you begin speaking. Speak slowly and distinctly, in a normal tone of voice without shouting.
- When using a sign language interpreter, have him or her sit next to you so that the person who is hearing impaired can easily shift his or her gaze back and forth.
- When meeting with someone who is visually impaired, indicate your presence verbally, identify yourself by name, and speak in a normal tone of voice. If other people are present, ask them to identify themselves.
- If someone has a developmental disability, give that person time to respond. Talk slowly and calmly, using easy-to-understand language.
- Obtain expert consultation on how to communicate effectively with individual victims with developmental disabilities and people with serious mental illness.

FIGURE 3–2   Suggestions for Interacting with People Who Have Disabilities
Sources: National Victim Assistance Academy, 2002; Tyiska, 1998.

Counseling Goals and Interventions

One way to conceptualize counseling people with disabilities is by considering three categories: prevention or primary intervention, intervention, and postvention or rehabilitation (Livneh & Wosley-George, 2001). In **prevention**, the emphasis is on preventing disease or disability before it occurs. Programmatic efforts are levied at increasing public awareness of specific activities or situations that are likely to lead to physical and/or emotional problems (e.g., stress, unhealthy behaviors). **Intervention** refers to direct, time-limited strategies that often are implemented in crisislike situations, such as with spinal cord injury, myocardial infarction, or severe psychological distress. **Postvention**, also called **rehabilitation counseling**, focuses on helping people with permanent or chronic physical, cognitive, and psychiatric disabilities cope successfully and adjust to life with those disabilities. Clinical mental health counselors may be involved in each of these three phases of service.

The major goal of rehabilitation counseling is to help individuals with disabilities maximize their potential in terms of acceptance, independence, productivity, and inclusion (Martin, 1999). Interventions can be targeted toward the individual client or toward the environment in which the client lives and works. **Client-aimed interventions** include personal adjustment counseling, vocational counseling, behavioral modification, and skill development in performance of the activities of daily living (ADLs). In contrast, **environment-aimed interventions** are targeted toward barriers in the external environment that may need modification to meet the client's goals. Examples include helping the client find ways to use assistive aids (e.g., hearing aids, prostheses, and wheelchairs), facilitating the removal of architectural barriers, and helping a client find a group home (Livneh & Wosley-George, 2001). Both types of interventions often are carried out by counselors involved in rehabilitation work.

Training, Roles, and Functions of Rehabilitation Counselors

Many rehabilitation counselors belong to the American Rehabilitation Counseling Association (ARCA), a division of ACA, whose mission is to enhance the development of people with disabilities and promote excellence in the rehabilitation counseling profession. Other professional organizations for counselors who specialize in working with clients with disabilities include the National Rehabilitation Counseling Association (NRCA) and the National Association of Rehabilitation Professionals in the Private Sector (NARPPS).

Rehabilitation counselors carry out several roles and functions in serving clients with disabilities. Initially, the role of the counselor is to assess the client's current level of functioning and the surrounding environmental influences that either hinder or assist functionality. Based on the results of that assessment, counselors help clients formulate goals. Depending on the nature of the goals, counselors may need to carry out several different roles. Versatility is important, as the counselor will not only provide services directly but also coordinate services with other professionals and monitor clients' progress in gaining independence and self-control.

Hershenson (1998) describes five different functions of rehabilitation counselors: counseling, consulting, coordinating services, case management, and critiquing effectiveness. In making decisions about what services to provide, Hershenson suggests that counselors take into account the client's personality (e.g., motivation, outlook on life, and reaction to the disability), interpersonal skills and socialized behavior, learning capacities, and personal and work goals, as well as the extent of available supports and barriers. To achieve desired goals, the rehabilitation counselor may need to counsel with the client about specific coping issues, consult with the client's family and employer about expectations, coordinate a skills training program, engage in case management to monitor the delivery of services, and conduct an ongoing critique (evaluation) of the effectiveness of the interventions. Throughout the process, the counselor needs to be aware of the various systems and subsystems that influence the client's well-being. How do those systems and subsystems promote or impede rehabilitation? What physical and attitudinal resources or barriers do they present? It may be necessary to work with the client's friends, family, and employers to redesign the environment to maximize access and opportunities (Wright & Martin, 1999).

Counseling Issues and Implications

Although it would be inappropriate and inaccurate to make any all-encompassing statements regarding counseling people with disabilities, the nature of the issues presented may differ from those presented in other counseling situations. Livneh and Wosley-George (2001) note the prevalence of specific themes that may emerge during the process, such as independence versus dependence, personal loss, coping with crises, and maintaining employment. Some of the common problems that arise in the personal and interpersonal domains are illustrated in Figure 3–3. Other counseling issues that may confront people

Personal Domain	Interpersonal Domain
• Lack of motivation	• Increased dependence (financial, medical, psychosocial, other)
• Reluctance to participate in rehabilitation tasks	
• Increased depression and/or anxiety	• Impaired social and/or vocational roles
• Damaged body image	• Changing family dynamics and relationships
• Insult to self-concept	• Disruption of social life
• Loss of sense of control	• Negative attitudes toward disability
• Loss of reward and pleasure sources	• Societal rejection and/or social isolation
• Loss of physical and economic independence	• Disuse or lack of appropriate social skills
• Difficulty accepting and adjusting to the disability	• Decreased sexual activity
• Inability to access the environment	

FIGURE 3–3   Common Issues in the Personal and Interpersonal Domains
Source: Based on information in Livneh and Wosley-George, 2001.

with disabilities include coping with and adjusting to an acquired disability, family concerns, career-related concerns, and abuse.

COPING WITH AN ACQUIRED DISABILITY.   When someone sustains an unexpected disability, whether through bodily injury or the onset of a disease, that individual is suddenly faced with an array of physical and emotional challenges. Individuals who become disabled may feel lost, terrified, and confused about what the future holds. In such cases, a primary counseling goal is to help the client make order out of chaos, recognizing that acceptance and adjustment take time. Frequently, the client is faced with grief and loss issues, much like those experienced after a death. Livneh and Evans (1984) outline 12 phases of adjustment associated with an acquired disability: shock, anxiety, bargaining, denial, mourning, depression, withdrawal, internalized anger, externalized aggression, acknowledgment, acceptance, and adjustment/ adaptation. Different interventions are appropriate for different phases. It is important for counselors to be aware of the adjustment process and work *with* it rather than against it. At times, client behaviors may seem bizarre or confusing, but that may be necessary for progress.

During the initial stages after a disability is sustained, crisis intervention and supportive counseling are often called for. Offering support and reassurance, listening and attending, and allowing the client to ventilate feelings can be especially helpful. Also, it is important to recognize that the client may be using defense mechanisms and that those mechanisms serve a purpose. Without them, "reality could overwhelm the individual, and the situation could be perceived as being impossible to address" (Rothrock, 1999, p. 210). In time, the client can deal more effectively with the reality of the disability.

As counseling progresses, the counselor needs to help the client develop resources for accepting, coping, and adjusting to life with a disability. One way to encourage clients to utilize their own coping abilities is to find out what helped them cope with difficult events in the past. Modifications of previously successful coping behaviors can facilitate adjustment to the new lifestyle. For example, if a client has a supportive family, inviting the family to participate in counseling sessions can help with decision making and make life more manageable.

Cognitive therapy may help a client with a disability reinterpret life experiences in a manner that enhances resilience and a sense of coherence (Lustig, Rosenthal, Strauser, & Haynes, 2000). A strong sense of coherence increases the chances that a person will mobilize available resources and seek new resources when handling stressful situations. A client's sense of coherence is determined by his or her perceptions of (a) comprehensibility (the degree to which the world is perceived as predictable, ordered, and explicable); (b) manageability (the degree to which a person believes that he or she has the resources needed to handle a demand); and (c) meaningfulness (the belief that demands are worthy of investment and commitment). People with a strong sense of coherence are able to cope more effectively with stressors and thereby are more likely to adjust better to life with a disability (Lustig et al., 2000). Perceptions associated with a sense of coherence may be either adaptive or dysfunctional. The goal of cognitive therapy is to help clients modify assumptions and perceptions that are maladaptive so that adjustment and quality of life are enhanced.

Adjusting to an acquired disability takes time and perseverance. Counselors can facilitate the process by fostering independence rather than dependence, finding ways to turn failures into learning experiences, respecting their clients as fellow human beings, and helping them take ownership of their rehabilitation.

FAMILY ISSUES. Disabilities in family members can affect family functioning in numerous ways. Family responses to disability vary, depending in part on which phase of adaptation the family is in. Three common phases include the crisis phase, the chronic phase, and the terminal phase (Orozco et al., 2014; Roland, 1994). Families in the **crisis phase** are either waiting for a diagnosis or have just received information about a family member's disability. Family members often deal with feelings of shock, denial, anger, and depression. During this phase, counselors can provide the family with supportive counseling characterized by empathic listening and attending. A primary goal during the crisis phase is to help the family consider what will remain the same and what will need to change as a consequence of the disability and then determine how to manage that change as it occurs.

Families in the **chronic phase** are coping with the day-to-day issues related to the disability (Roland, 1994). The degree to which adjustment and coping are needed is affected by numerous factors, including the nature and severity of the disability and the temperament and stamina of family members. Useful counseling interventions during this phase include helping family members find ways to manage stress, building on client strengths, developing realistic expectations, and anticipating problems before they arise so that they can be managed more effectively.

Certain disabilities, such as some types of aggressive cancer and amyotrophic lateral sclerosis (ALS), have a prognosis different from that of other disabilities, and in most cases, the condition is terminal. Family members typically need support as they deal with the many different emotions associated with anticipated loss. Counselors can help families prepare for their loved one's death by making connections with hospice and other community resources. During the **terminal phase**, the primary caretakers frequently are under a tremendous amount of stress, and family interactions may be strained. Counselors can help to normalize the tension and encourage family members to find ways to take care of themselves as well as their loved one during this difficult time.

CAREER AND ECONOMIC ISSUES. Although legislation to empower people with disabilities has made important strides to equalize rights and opportunities for people with disabilities, statistics show that there still are significant lifestyle and economic gaps between people with disabilities and those without disabilities. Consider the following 2010 National Organization on Disability findings:

- Only 21% of working-age people with disabilities report being employed, compared to 59% of those who do not have disabilities.
- People with disabilities are much more likely to be living in poverty.
- People with disabilities are less likely to access health care.
- People with disabilities are less likely than those without disabilities to socialize with friends, neighbors, and relatives.
- Only 54% of adults with disabilities access the Internet, whereas 85% of adults without disabilities access the Internet.

These findings represent more than numbers. Although many people with disabilities are unable to work for medical reasons, other individuals are able to pursue meaningful work if necessary accommodations and incentives are provided. Professional counselors who counsel clients with disabilities need to be skilled in career counseling, cognizant of the types of skills that can be acquired through rehabilitation training, and open to reconstructing traditional definitions of work in relation to meaningfulness and purpose.

The specific nature of a client's disability affects the type of career counseling that needs to take place. For example, a person with emotional or communicative disabilities may not interview well. In such cases, nontraditional job-seeking strategies, such as networking, may be helpful. Skills training and practice may help the client become more adept at interpersonal interactions. In other situations, a disability might not keep a client from performing a particular job if adaptations are provided. Then the counselor's role may include increasing client awareness of vocational options, particularly as they relate to the ADA.

Rehabilitation counselors and clinical mental health counselors work with an increasing number of people with severe psychiatric disabilities, which can include schizophrenia, chronic recurrent affective disorders, and severe personality disorders. These individuals may experience deficits in social skills, personal management, symptom and medication management, cognition, and coping with stress. Many of them have been unsuccessful in seeking employment; in fact, people with serious mental illnesses have the highest unemployment rate of any group with disabilities (Bazelon Center for Mental Health Law, 2009). The demands of working with this population are complex and can present a strong challenge to mental health workers. To help people with severe mental disorders become and remain contributing members of society, rehabilitation, vocational training, and assistance in work settings are essential. Counselors who work in settings for psychiatric rehabilitation need additional training to meet the myriad needs of people with severe psychiatric disabilities.

ABUSE.   Unfortunately, individuals with disabilities are victimized at a higher rate than that of the general population. Women with disabilities—regardless of age, race, or class—are assaulted, raped, and abused at a rate two times greater than that of women without a disability, and the risk of being physically or sexually assaulted for adults with developmental disabilities is four to ten times higher than it is for other adults (NVAA, 2002). Also, children with disabilities are more likely to be maltreated than children without disabilities (Child Welfare Information Gateway, 2012). Counselors working with people with disabilities need to be alert to any signs indicating abuse and advocate for the rights of their clients.

OTHER ISSUES. Cultural values and expectations influence beliefs about disabilities. In some cultures, mistaken beliefs about causal factors can lead to greater stigmatization of people with disabilities. For example, some Latino families have a fatalistic view about their lives, which may make rehabilitation more difficult. In a similar vein, some Asian cultures attribute disability to the behavior of one's ancestors, making the disability a source of shame. Within certain Native American tribes (e.g., the Dine'h), attributional beliefs may be attached to specific disabilities, such as the belief that seizures are caused by incest between siblings (Orozco et al., 2014). Culturally based beliefs and attitudes like these can complicate the counseling process and need to be addressed sensitively.

SOCIOECONOMIC STATUS AND SOCIAL CLASS

Economic disparities are increasingly prevalent within the United States as well as globally. Social class affects people from all backgrounds, including racial, ethnic, gender, and other areas of diversity. As such, social class can be considered a specific cultural identity (Thompson, Cole, & Nitzarim, 2012). Many clients are unemployed, underemployed, and/or dependent on the government for financial support. In the United States there is a wide gap between the superwealthy (i.e., the top 1–10%) and the rest of America (Liu & Watt, 2013). The concept of social class, poverty, classism, and economic disadvantage is not new, but until recently social class has been "relatively ignored within psychotherapy research" (Thompson et al., 2012, p. 208).

BOX 3–7 The Working Poor

The man who washes cars does not own one. The clerk who files cancelled checks at the bank has $2.02 in her own account. The woman who copyedits medical textbooks has not been to a dentist in a decade. This is the forgotten America. . . . Whether you're rich, poor, or middle class, you encounter them every day. They serve you Big Macs and help you find merchandise at Wal-Mart. They harvest your food, clean your offices, and sew your clothes.

David Shipler, *The Working Poor: Invisible in America,* 2004

Definitions and Terminology

To help clarify counseling considerations related to social class and socioeconomic status, we have compiled a list of terms commonly associated with these cultural variables.

- **Socioeconomic status (SES)** classifies people according to social and economic dimensions. Indicators of SES include income, occupation, education level, use of public assistance, and access to health care.
- **Social class** is typically based on components of SES and is hierarchical in nature. Phrases such as *low SES, economically disadvantaged, middle class, upper class,* and *superwealthy* are often used to describe social class. Social class may be fluid; thus, it is necessary to consider the life span of an individual to determine ways social class has influenced a person's worldview. Social class is directly related to classism (Liu & Watt, 2013).
- **Classism** refers to oppression, discrimination, or marginalization experienced by people who are negatively affected by socioeconomic disparity (Pope & Arthur, 2009).

- **Privilege** is a term that has ramifications when considering all types of diversity. **Social class privilege** is a benefit or advantage given to a person by reason of social position (Liu, Pickett, & Ivey, 2007). It is an attitudinal variable that is often unrecognized by the people who have it.
- **Poverty threshold** is the amount of cash income minimally required to support families of various sizes. Poverty rates are highest for families headed by single women, particularly if they are Black or Hispanic.

SES as a Risk Factor

Lower SES is associated with a wide range of physical and mental health problems (Pope & Arthur, 2009). The association can be explained in part by an interconnection of factors that affect physical and psychological well-being. For example, people who live in lower-income or impoverished neighborhoods face environmental challenges that contribute to an increase in physical and mental health problems. Impoverished communities often have few supermarkets, an abundance of liquor and tobacco stores, dilapidated housing, transportation problems, and limited access to health care. High crime rates, violence, and chaos also characterize environmentally disadvantaged communities. Lower-income neighborhoods tend to have fewer recreation areas, such as parks, pools, and organized sports programs, too (Liu & Watt, 2013). It is easy to see how these factors can have deleterious effects on both physical and mental health.

In his book *Social Perspective: The Missing Element in Mental Health Practice* (2012), U'Ren points out that the least affluent members of society have the poorest mental health. Many mental health conditions—including anxiety, depression, and substance abuse—are connected to difficult life circumstances. Examples of difficult life circumstances include family fragmentation, workforce discrimination, a lack of social cohesion, and poor public health policies (Pope & Arthur, 2009). Clinical mental health counselors need to recognize the many environmental factors that influence mental health and incorporate a systemic perspective into their work with economically disadvantaged clients.

Poverty and Social Class Fluidity

Poverty can become a vicious cycle for many clients. Unemployment, underemployment, economic depression, educational barriers, and other factors can be self-perpetuating. Clinical mental health counselors can advocate for economically disadvantaged groups and social justice in multiple ways. The following actions can be helpful.

- Provide psychoeducation about mental health issues to people in impoverished neighborhoods and describe ways that counseling can address these concerns.
- Provide information about accessible resources that can be used by people with limited financial resources (e.g., transportation, food, housing, healthcare options).
- Consider the possibility of out-of-the-office counseling with clients who have limited access to counseling services. It is helpful to collaborate with churches and other community organizations to make counseling services available to vulnerable populations.
- Educate school personnel, government leaders, healthcare providers, and mental health providers about the ways SES and social class affect people's mental and physical health.

A repressed economy, unemployment, overextended mortgages, and exploitative financial institutions can negatively affect people who were considered middle class into a situation where they are economically strapped and may have to foreclose on their homes. The stories of these individuals represent the fluidity of social class. Consider the case of Robert and Tameka Blanton.

The Case of Robert and Tameka Blanton

Robert and Tameka were living the American dream. They and their two children lived in a suburban neighborhood in a large, two-story house. Robert worked as a building contractor and made a good income. Tameka, who had earned a BA in psychology, chose to stay at home with their two children. When the Blantons bought their home, their down payment was minimal and their mortgage high, but with the building business booming, they were certain that finances would not be a problem.

Then an economic recession hit. There were more houses on the market than buyers, and bids for construction plummeted. Within a short period of time, the Blantons were living off their savings. A little while later, they lost their home to foreclosure and moved in with Tameka's parents. Robert took whatever construction jobs he could find, and Tameka tried to find work, but she had been out of the workforce for 10 years, and no one was hiring. Eventually, the Blantons were able to rent a small apartment in an urban neighborhood but still were barely making ends meet. The couple fought frequently over finances, and the children could not understand why they had to change schools. Robert exhibited signs of depression, and Tameka began having panic attacks. Many of the people with whom they had previously socialized distanced themselves from the couple. Stressed and distressed, Robert and Tameka talked about seeking counseling, but they did not think that they could afford to do so.

In what ways are the variables of social class, SES, and their current economy affecting Robert and Tameka's mental health? If they were able to go to counseling, what particular issues should be considered? If you were the counselor, how would you proceed?

Counseling Implications

As in all cases of cross-cultural counseling, clinical mental health counselors need to be sensitive to the culture of social class and the negative effects of classism as they work with clients. Liu and Watt (2013) suggest that counseling competency develops from (a) knowing the social class and classism concerns relevant to the communities and populations likely to be served; (b) exploring and understanding how values, beliefs, and cultural norms are affected by social class; and (c) recognizing and celebrating the ways in which economically disadvantaged individuals have survived and sometimes flourished (p. 260). Counselors can advocate for their clients, empower them, and teach them self-agency skills. Lui and Watt (2013) describe interventions based on Liu's (2011) social class worldview model. Intervention steps include these:

- Step 1: Help clients identify and understand their economic culture.
- Step 2: Help clients identify the social class messages they have received.
  - Identify social class behaviors, lifestyles, and material possessions that are pertinent to the current situation.

- Step 3: Identify clients' experiences with classism, and help them move toward an adaptive, realistic, and healthy expectation about themselves.
- Step 4: Help clients integrate their experiences of classism.
  - Help clients take action and make changes. (pp. 273–274)

Social class is a cultural identity that traverses gender, sexual orientation, race, ethnicity, and many other constructs associated with diversity. Classism and social biases can have negative effects on the clients with whom you work.

Summary and Conclusion

In this chapter, counseling issues related to four areas of diversity have been examined: culture and ethnicity, sexual orientation, disability, and social class and socioeconomic status. A wealth of material in the professional literature portrays the general concerns of each group and describes the counseling theories and techniques most appropriate for cross-cultural counseling.

Although information about a particular population may appear unrelated to other populations, it is not. A common theme is that counselors who work with a variety of clients must be knowledgeable about them collectively and individually to deal effectively with their common and unique concerns. All too often, stereotypes and prescribed roles are assigned to members of distinct ethnic and racial groups, sexual minorities, people with disabilities, and people who are economically disadvantaged. To be culturally responsive, it is important for counselors to develop multicultural competencies in four primary areas: awareness, knowledge, skills, and advocacy. Overcoming prejudices, fears, and anxieties and learning new skills based on accurate information and sensitivity are major challenges of counseling in a multicultural and pluralistic society.

When working with diverse populations, counselors need to be sensitive to the range of concerns that affect their clients. Counselors must also realize the limitations and appropriateness of the counseling interventions they employ. Effective counselors concentrate on increasing their sensitivity to global issues as well as to individual concerns. By intentionally being culturally responsive, clinical mental health counselors have a unique opportunity to serve as advocates for their clients by denouncing all forms of stigmatization, marginalization, and oppression, while finding ways to facilitate individual and collective empowerment.

MyCounselingLab

Try the Topic 12 Assignments: *Multicultural Considerations*.

PART **2**

Roles and Functions of Clinical Mental Health Counselors

CHAPTER 4

The Counseling Process

SpeedKingz/Shutterstock

Your words splash heavily upon my mind
  like early cold October rain
    falling on my roof at dusk.
The patterns change like an Autumn storm
  from violent, rumbling, crashing sounds
    to clear, steady streams of expression.
Through it all I look at you
  soaked in past fears and turmoil;
Then patiently I watch with you in the darkness
  for the breaking of black clouds
    that linger in your turbulent mind
And the dawning of your smile
  that comes in the light of new beginnings.

Reprinted from "Autumn Storm," by S. T. Gladding, 1975,
Personnel and Guidance Journal, 54, p. 149. Copyright
© Samuel T. Gladding.

CHAPTER OVERVIEW

**From reading this chapter, you will
learn about**

- Factors that influence the counseling
  process
- Three stages of counseling: the initial
  phase, the working phase, and the
  closing phase
- The importance of structure and
  initiative in counseling
- Working with reluctant, resistant, or
  ambivalent clients
- Case conceptualization, documentation,
  treatment plans, and client records
- Counseling interventions, skills, and
  techniques
- Risk management

As you read, consider

- What information needs to be gathered
  during initial sessions
- How you would work with a resistant
  or reluctant client
- What is meant by *case conceptualization*
- How you write a treatment plan
- What interventions you have used with
  clients and what skills you would like
  to hone
- How you end a counseling relationship
  and what methods of follow-up seem to
  be most effective

C linical mental health counselors promote client well-being on multiple levels by providing prevention services and treatment for a wide range of clients in diverse settings. Counselors are trained to assess and diagnose, provide crisis intervention, and work with individuals, groups, couples, and families.

In this chapter, a general description of the counseling process is given. We begin with a brief description of physical factors that affect the counseling environment and thus the counseling process. Next, attention turns to the initial, working, and closing stages of counseling. Counselor and client behaviors associated with each stage are highlighted, including establishing rapport, conceptualizing cases, developing treatment plans, and ending the counseling relationship.

A key component of working effectively with clients is maintaining careful records of counseling activities. Throughout the chapter, specific documentation procedures associated with the different stages of counseling are addressed, including professional disclosure statements, intake interviews, treatment plans, and case notes. Keep in mind that assessment and diagnosis, two primary skills used by clinical mental health counselors, often begin at the onset of the counseling process.

BOX 4–1   What Do You Think?

Some people are attuned to their physical surroundings and are affected by the environments in which they are living or working. Other people are relatively oblivious to physical surroundings. Even though the degree of sensitivity people have toward their surroundings is neither a positive nor a negative trait—it is just a predisposition—it behooves counselors to be aware that some of their clients will be affected by the physical setting in which counseling occurs. Which type of person are you? Are you affected by the sights, smells, and sounds that surround you, or do you tend to be less aware of your immediate physical environment? As a clinical mental health counselor, what factors related to the physical setting in which you practice are within your control?

THE PHYSICAL SETTING OF COUNSELING

The physical settings in which clinical mental health counselors work vary in size, comfort, and appearance. How much control counselors have over their working environments varies as well, depending on the agency or organization. Counseling can occur almost anywhere, but some physical settings help promote the process better than others. Environmental factors can influence individuals physically, psychologically, and emotionally. Thus, it is important to consider physical elements that enhance or detract from the counseling process.

Pressly and Heesacker (2001) reviewed counseling-relevant literature on various physical conditions that affect counseling, including accessories, color, room design, and other factors. Although there are no universal qualities that compose the "ideal" counseling setting, certain features appear to be more conducive to the counseling process than others.

Aesthetic Qualities and Room Design

People are influenced by room appearance in different ways. Both counselors and clients are usually affected by room décor at some level. According to some researchers (e.g., Frank & Frank, 2004; Nasar & Devlin, 2011), a healing setting plays a role in the therapeutic process. Three variables that can create a **healing environment** include **safety**, **personalization**, and

softness. A soundproof room that elicits feelings of comfort can help a client feel safe. Personalization refers to an office that includes mementos, personal items such as photographs, and diplomas or certificates (Nasar & Devlin, 2011). Softness refers to soft surfaces and textures, including such things as sofas, comfortable chairs, movable furniture, and lamps.

Pressly and Heesacker (2001) discuss personalizing an office by displaying artwork, photographs, and objects that counselors consider meaningful or attractive. Research has shown that people prefer texturally complex images of natural settings to posters of people, urban life, or abstract works. Plants, which represent growth, can enhance the office's appeal. Preference for office colors varies, depending on the age and sex of clients. Children and young adults tend to associate light colors with positive emotions and dark colors with negative emotions. Neutral colors are soothing and practical and may be preferred when space is shared with other counselors.

Lighting research indicates that although brightly lit rooms may enhance general conversation, softer light is more conducive to intimate conversation. Lighting that highlights furniture, artwork, and plants can be especially effective and give the office a "softer" appearance. In addition to lighting, room temperature influences the mental concentration of counselors and clients. In places where clinical mental health counselors can control the thermostat, keeping the temperature within a comfortable range, while being sensitive to client differences, is preferable (Pressly & Heesacker, 2001).

The room design itself also affects the counseling process. Whenever possible, the counseling room should be private and free from distracting sounds or smells. Research on furniture placement indicates that most clients prefer an intermediate distance between themselves and the counselor. What is considered optimal, however, is influenced by a number of factors, including cultural background, gender, and the nature of the relationship. Clients may feel a greater degree of autonomy and comfort in offices where they have some control over the furniture arrangement. For example, couches and movable chairs allow clients to place themselves in positions that are comfortable. Also, it is important for counseling offices to be physically accessible to individuals with disabilities.

The arrangement of the furniture depends on what the counselor is trying to accomplish. A desk can be a physical and symbolic barrier to the development of a therapeutic relationship. Comfortable chairs, couches, a small table, and lamps are often found in counseling offices. The table can be used for many purposes, such as making a box of tissues available to clients.

Regardless of the arrangement within the room, counselors should not be interrupted during counseling sessions. Phone calls should be held, cell phones should be turned off, and in some cases, a "Do Not Disturb" sign should be hung on the door. Auditory and visual privacy are mandated by professional codes of ethics and facilitate maximum self-disclosure. A white noise machine outside the doors may help block sounds coming from inside the counseling office.

INITIAL SESSIONS: BUILDING A COUNSELING RELATIONSHIP

Counseling is a process that occurs over time. Although counseling is not linear, it can be conceptually helpful to divide the process into three stages: initial, working, and closing. Various tasks and responsibilities are associated with each stage, including securing informed consent, conducting intake interviews, and record keeping. Throughout the counseling process, practitioners aspire to establish and maintain a positive counseling alliance with their clients.

During the first few sessions of the counseling process, counselors focus on building a therapeutic relationship and helping clients explore issues that directly affect them. In initial sessions, counselors assess the seriousness of the concern presented, provide structure to the counseling process, help clients take initiative in the change process, develop initial case conceptualizations, and create treatment plans.

The Case of Anne

Anne, a 35-year-old accountant, has recently been feeling unfulfilled at work and in her marriage of 10 years. The activities she used to enjoy, such as listening to music and going on walks, are no longer appealing to her. She finds herself withdrawing from social interactions, experiencing sleeping difficulties, and feeling constantly agitated during the day. One of her friends has recommended that she seek counseling. Anne is skeptical but is willing to do what it takes to start feeling like herself again. She has never been to counseling before and is a little nervous about the first appointment. She does not know what to expect from the process and is concerned that the counselor will think she is unstable.

If you were Anne's counselor, what are some things you would take into consideration during the initial counseling sessions? What steps might you take to help alleviate her anxiety about the counseling process? What will you need to do to help Anne understand the counseling process and feel safe?

Seriousness of the Presenting Problem

The counseling process and the direction it takes are influenced by the seriousness of the client's presenting problem. In particular, the intake interview can help counselors determine the nature, severity, and duration of the presenting issue. There is a relationship between initial levels of self-reported disturbance and the course of treatment (Leibert, 2006). Clients with more severe issues are likely to need more sessions to make effective life changes. In some cases, clients with certain disorders (e.g., schizophrenia, borderline personality disorder, antisocial personality disorder) may not respond well to traditional talk therapies or individual counseling, although group counseling or other modes of therapy may be helpful. Additional factors that affect ways counselors select appropriate treatment modalities include the client's level of functioning, psychosocial stressors, and cultural background.

Structure

Clients and counselors sometimes have different perceptions about the purpose and nature of counseling. Clients often do not know what to expect from the process or what is expected of them. By providing structure to the process, counselors can help clarify expectations and prevent misunderstandings. Structure in counseling, which also is called **role induction**, refers to counselor–client understanding about the conditions, procedures, and nature of counseling. It helps protect rights, define roles, provide direction, and verify obligations of both parties.

Structure is especially important at the beginning of counseling. Clients often seek counseling when they are in a state of crisis or flux, which can leave them feeling out of control. To help clients regain stability and find new directions in their lives, counselors provide constructive guidelines. Counselors' decisions about how to establish structure are based on their theoretical orientation to counseling, their areas of expertise, and the personalities and cultural backgrounds of their clients. It helps for counselors to be flexible and to negotiate the nature of the structure with their clients on an ongoing basis.

Establishing practical guidelines is essential to the structure-building process. **Guidelines** include time limits (such as a 50-minute session), action limits (for the prevention of destructive behavior), role limits (what will be expected of each participant), and procedural limits (the client's responsibility to work on specific goals or needs). Guidelines also provide information on fee schedules, billing, and other related concerns. In general, structure promotes counseling development by providing a framework in which the process can take place.

At the outset, counselors must provide clients with an opportunity to give informed consent to participate in counseling. Informed consent has ethical and legal implications. Glosoff (2001), citing several sources, suggests using an informed **consent content checklist** to guide the counseling process, which includes the following topics:

- *Counselor's background and professional affiliations.*   Include education, areas of specialization, licensure and certification, professional affiliations, and contact information for appropriate regulatory or certification boards and professional organizations.
- *Therapeutic process issues.*   Describe the nature of the counseling process and counseling relationships, boundaries of the professional relationship, your theoretical orientation and how that affects the counseling process, and clients' right to participate in ongoing counseling plans.
- *Risks, benefits, and alternatives.*   Make sure clients understand that therapeutic results cannot be guaranteed. Discuss the limitations, potential risks, and benefits of counseling. Explain the client's right to refuse recommended services and to be advised of potential consequences of that refusal.
- *Fees.*   Describe fees associated with services, cancellation and no-show policies, arrangements with any managed care organizations, and issues related to insurance reimbursement.
- *Confidentiality and privileged communication.*   Describe confidentiality and its limits, information that may need to be shared with insurance companies, plans for dealing with any exceptions to confidentiality that may arise, and clients' right to obtain information about their records. Include information about any supervisory or peer consultation arrangements, too.
- *Structure of the counseling relationship.*   Describe the frequency and length of sessions, approximate duration of counseling, any known limitations to the length of treatment, and procedures for termination.
- *Diagnostic labels.*   How will diagnostic labels be used? How do insurance companies use diagnostic labels to determine reimbursement? What are the potential ramifications of diagnostic labels (e.g., preexisting conditions)? What are your limitations to control what insurance companies do with the information you provide them?
- *Emergency situations and interruptions in counseling.*   What are the normal hours of operation? What constitutes an emergency, and what should clients do if you cannot be reached? Explain what happens when you are on vacation and discuss ways to handle unexpected interruptions in counseling services.
- *Involuntary clients.*   What information will be shared, with whom, and for what purposes? How will participation in counseling affect legal issues (e.g., parole)? Involuntary clients have the right to refuse treatment but need to be informed of the legal consequences of making that choice.

To help ensure the provision of informed consent, clinical mental health counselors need to prepare a **professional disclosure statement**, which provides information to clients about the counselor and about the counseling process. Such statements, like the one in Figure 4–1, typically define a counselor's qualifications and theoretical orientation as well as

---

LPC Professional Disclosure Statement

Deborah W. Newsome, PhD, LPC, NCC
Office: xxx-xxx-xxxx

I am pleased that you have chosen me as your counselor. The purpose of this document is to provide you with information about my background, our professional relationship, and the counseling process.

Qualifications

I hold a PhD in Counseling and Counselor Education, which I received in December 1999 from the University of North Carolina at Greensboro. I have been a licensed professional counselor (LPC) in North Carolina since October 2001 (License # 3900) and a licensed North Carolina School Counselor since December 1999. I also am a National Certified Counselor (Certificate #48370). I have worked as a professional counselor and a counselor educator for seventeen years.

Counseling Background

I have worked as a counselor, supervisor, and educator in a variety of settings, including public schools, universities, and clinical mental health centers. My educational background, which includes an emphasis on human development and family studies, prepared me to conduct family, individual, and group counseling with children, adolescents, and adults. As a counselor educator at Wake Forest University, I teach courses in counseling skills, career development and counseling, and clinical mental health counseling and supervise graduate students' clinical experiences.

I view counseling as a process in which I help clients focus on strengths to help them initiate and maintain change in their lives. Issues often addressed in counseling include, but are not limited to:

• Family changes
• Child behavior and school problems
• Stress management
• Grief and loss
• Communication problems
• Career development
• Depression
• Anxiety
• Child and adolescent developmental issues

To help clients resolve issues, I draw from several theoretical bases, including existential, humanistic, and cognitive–behavioral approaches. I use techniques and counseling procedures from these and other theoretical orientations to meet the specific needs of my clients. When I work with families, I follow a systemic approach, helping family members examine rules, roles, and boundaries that are a part of their particular family system. When counseling children and adolescents, I use cognitive–behavioral approaches, expressive arts, and bibliotherapy to facilitate the exploration of thoughts, feelings, and behaviors. In working with adults, I typically use humanistic, existential, psychodynamic, and cognitive approaches to help clients gain new perspectives and deal more effectively with life issues.

If we enter into a professional counseling relationship, we will work together to identify counseling goals. We will reexamine and evaluate those goals periodically. When necessary, we will adjust counseling goals to ensure that you are getting the most out of the counseling sessions.

FIGURE 4–1 Sample Professional Disclosure Statement

(Continued)

Session Fees and Length of Service

I will render services in a professional manner consistent with the accepted clinical standards of care. Sessions will last 50 minutes. My fee is $100 per session, payable by check or cash at the end of each session. If you have insurance coverage, you are responsible for submitting the request for reimbursement to your insurance company. In cases of special need, I will work with you to develop a payment plan, which may include a sliding scale fee. The determination to use a sliding scale will be considered on a case-by-case basis.

Use of Diagnosis

Some health insurance companies will reimburse clients for counseling services and some will not. In addition, most require a diagnosis of a mental health condition and indicate that you must have an "illness" before they will agree to reimburse you. Some conditions for which people seek counseling do not qualify for reimbursement. If a qualifying diagnosis is appropriate in your case, I will inform you of the diagnosis before we submit the diagnosis to the health insurance company. Any diagnosis made will become part of your permanent insurance records.

Confidentiality

All of our communication becomes part of the clinical record, which is accessible to you upon request. I will keep confidential anything you say as part of our counseling relationship, with the following exceptions: (a) you direct me in writing to disclose information to someone else, (b) it is determined you are a danger to yourself or others (including child or elder abuse), or (c) I am ordered by a court to disclose information, in which case I will work with you, your attorney, and/or the magistrate to reach an agreement about what must be disclosed. Other than these circumstances, our relationship and the information you share will not be disclosed without your full knowledge and written consent.

Complaints

Although clients are encouraged to discuss any concerns with me, you may file a complaint against me with the organization below should you feel I am in violation of any of these codes of ethics. I abide by the *ACA Code of Ethics* (www.counseling.org/Resources/aca-code-of-ethics.pdf).

North Carolina Board of Licensed Professional Counselors
P.O. Box 77819
Greensboro, NC 27417
Phone: 884-622-3572 or 336-217-6007
Fax: 336-217-9450
E-mail: Complaints@ncblpc.org

Acceptance of Terms

We agree to these terms and will abide by these guidelines.
Client: _____ Date: _____

Counselor: _____ Date: _____

FIGURE 4-1 (*continued*)

the purposes, expectations, responsibilities, methods, and ethics of counseling. Professional disclosure statements differ, depending on the state licensure requirements, counseling settings, and populations served (e.g., agencies or private practices, adults or children, involuntary or voluntary clients). As counselors develop new competencies, they modify their disclosure statements to reflect their new areas of expertise.

Initiative

Initiative can be conceptualized as the motivation to change. Many clients come to counseling on a voluntary or self-referred basis. They experience tension and concern about themselves or others, and they are willing to work hard in counseling sessions. Other clients, however, are more reserved about participating in counseling. Change is hard, and people typically do not like to be vulnerable. It takes time to develop trust in the counselor and in the counseling process. Thus, these clients may appear reluctant or resistant to change. Counselors need to be sensitive to the various reasons clients come to counseling (e.g., court-referred, referred by others, or complying with a partner's wishes). Counselors can empathize by saying something like, "If I were forced to participate in counseling, I wouldn't be very happy about it. I don't like people telling me what to do. I'm wondering what you are feeling right now" (Harris, 2013).

The Case of Luke

Luke, who is 57 years old, has been feeling irritable and tired for about six weeks. His wife, Carmen, suggested that he go see a counselor. Luke is skeptical about counseling and blames his irritability on his job. However, he is willing to go to counseling to appease Carmen, who continues to suggest that he get help.

During the first two counseling sessions, Luke spends most of the time talking about his frustration with his job. He also says that he is annoyed by the way his wife "nags me to get professional help." He does not see any reason to try to examine his personal issues. He says that if he can just hold on to the job for a few more years, he will be able to retire, and then everything will be fine. He does not want to talk about his feelings or about options for change.

As Luke's counselor, what could you do to help with the counseling process? Read the next section about reluctant and resistant clients, and see if you have any additional ideas about how to proceed.

RELUCTANT AND RESISTANT CLIENTS. In many cases, **reluctant clients** are people who really do not want to be there. They may fear the unfamiliar, be apprehensive about the process, or be mandated to attend. Often, children, adolescents, and court-referred clients present as reluctant clients. They do not wish to be in counseling, let alone talk about themselves. Many non-mandated (and sometimes mandated) reluctant clients terminate counseling prematurely and report dissatisfaction with the process (Gladding, 2018).

The concept of resistance and **resistant clients** has changed over time (Hagedorn, 2011). A client may appear resistant because change in general is difficult. A client may also appear resistant because of a perceived disconnect with the counselor. Resistance can be displayed in many ways, including the following:

- *Noncompliance* (e.g., not following through with homework assignments, showing up late for appointments, or missing them altogether)
- *Avoidance* (e.g., displaying in-session extremes expressed as outbursts against the counselor, debating, attempting to derail or detour conversation with such terms as "I don't know" or by changing the subject, manipulating the session by waiting until the end of the session to bring up important information)

**Example: Procrastinating on Major Projects of
a College Student**

Benefits of Behavior	Disadvantages of Behavior
• Gives me more time to do the things I want to do. • I work best under pressure. • I like staying up all night to finish a project.	• I feel anxious until the project is finished. • I feel guilty when I know I should be working on something. • My life seems disorganized. • My grades are sometimes lower because of carelessness that comes from rushing.
Benefits of Changing Behavior	Disadvantages of Changing Behavior
• Life will feel more structured. • I will be able to manage my time better. • I will get more sleep, and feel more rested. • I will be able to do the things I want to do without feeling guilty. • I will have time to go back over what I've done before it is due and make corrections.	• I will have to make a schedule for myself. • I will have to say no to some of the things my friends want to do. • I am afraid that I won't work well unless I am under pressure.

FIGURE 4–2   Motivational Interviewing Behavior Matrix

- *Ambivalence*   (e.g., having mixed feelings about the proposed change, such as smoking cessation)

Various theoretical frameworks approach resistance in different ways. One way to help resistant or ambivalent clients is **motivational interviewing**, which encourages counselors to roll with client resistance rather than confront it (Miller & Rollnick, 2013). Although motivational interviewing initially was developed for use in addiction counseling, it can be applied to many change-related issues, such as losing weight, managing procrastination, and changing negative habits. Figure 4–2 depicts an intervention that clinical mental health counselors can use with clients who appear resistant to or ambivalent about change.

Directly related to motivational interviewing is the **transtheoretical model of change**, developed by Prochaska and associates (e.g., Prochaska, DiClemente, & Norcross, 1992; Prochaska & Norcross, 2014). This model describes five different levels of readiness for change: precontemplation, contemplation, preparation, action, and maintenance. A description of each level is provided in Figure 4–3. Assessing a client's readiness for change according to these levels informs decisions regarding treatment and interventions.

Whereas some clients enter counseling already in the preparation stage, others may still be in the precontemplation or contemplation stage, denying either the existence or the seriousness of a problem. Reluctant clients typically are in one of these last two stages of readiness. For such clients, processes that increase emotional arousal and provide support are more likely to be effective than are approaches that focus on tasks or behavioral schedules (Petrocelli, 2002). To be effective, clinical mental health counselors need to be aware of a client's level of readiness and motivation and be knowledgeable about specific tasks and interventions suitable for that level.

Stage of Change	Characteristics	Possible Interventions
Precontemplation	Client is unaware that a problem exists.	Awareness exercises Support Motivational interviewing Feedback Education
Contemplation	Client is aware that a problem exists but denies that the problem is serious or requires treatment.	Exploration of values, personal goals, and desired changes Motivational interviewing Exploration of strategies for making changes Promoting ownership and responsibility
Preparation	Client has taken small steps toward change, indicating potential commitment.	Exploration of reasons for and against changing Strengths and weaknesses inventory Gestalt techniques
Action	Client has demonstrated commitment to change through overt behaviors.	Behavioral strategies (e.g., rehearsal, reinforcement, tasks, ordeals, and homework)
Maintenance	Client has made positive changes in the desired area and is attempting to change his or her lifestyle and to maintain those changes.	Continuing support Reinforcement management Follow-up contracts Support groups Relapse prevention

FIGURE 4–3   The Stages of Change
Sources: Adapted from Petrocelli, 2002; Prochaska et al., 1992; Young, 2013.

The Case of Robin

A 30-year-old client, Robin, comes to your office for counseling. She quit work seven years ago to stay home with her two children. Her partner, Leah, works as a financial investor. Robin smokes marijuana two or three times a day (self-report) but "never in front of the children." She has been smoking marijuana for 14 years on a daily basis. Leah is concerned about the effect Robin's habit is having on their children. She persuaded Robin to get help.

Robin admits to smoking marijuana regularly, but she says that it does not affect her ability to be a good mother. She adamantly states that she can quit any time she wants to but claims that pot smoking helps her relax and be a more patient parent. She says that the only reason she is here today is to appease Leah.

What level of change is Robin in? Would you be able to serve her effectively? If so, what would you do as her counselor? What steps might you take to increase her motivation to change?

HELPING CLIENTS INITIATE CHANGE.   There are several ways counselors can help clients initiate change. One way is to anticipate the anger, frustration, defensiveness, or ambivalence that some clients display. Indeed, such responses are to be expected with involuntary clients, as well as with other clients who are fearful of the helping process. Counselors who anticipate client resistance are better prepared to deal effectively with it when it is encountered (Young, 2013).

A second way to promote client initiative is to show acceptance, empathy, and unconditional positive regard, thereby strengthening the therapeutic relationship, which is probably the most powerful predictor of successful client outcome (Seligman & Reichenberg, 2014). An empathic, nonjudgmental approach helps promote trust and open communication. When open communication exists, clients are more likely to be honest with themselves, and the counselor and client are better able to recognize and express reasons for what manifests as resistance or noncompliance.

A third way counselors can help clients gain initiative is by using therapeutic confrontation, which involves pointing out discrepancies in clients' beliefs, actions, words, or nonverbal behaviors (Young, 2013). Clients are responsible for responding to the confrontation. There are three primary ways of responding: denying the confrontation, accepting some aspect of the confrontation as true, and fully accepting the confrontation and agreeing to try to resolve the inconsistency. Doing something differently or gaining a new perspective on a problem is a beneficial result of confrontation, especially when things the client has tried in the past have not worked. Counselors need to use confrontation gently and therapeutically, not as a way to beat clients over the head or to express their own frustration. A counselor might use phrases such as, "I wonder if there could be something else going on here," or "I hear you say that you love your partner, but your facial expression is showing a lot of anger. Help me understand what you are experiencing."

Counselors can also use language, especially metaphors, to break through resistance or reluctance. Metaphors can help reduce threat levels by providing images, offering fresh insights, challenging rigidity, and overcoming tension (James & Hazler, 1998). For example, a counselor might say, "Carrying that heavy bag of guilt must really be taking its toll on you. I wonder what it would be like to put it down?"

Although helping clients take the initiative for their personal growth and change ideally occurs during initial sessions (or even the initial session), client resistance can be evidenced at any point during the counseling process. Clinical mental health counselors can help clients move forward by recognizing resistance when it is demonstrated and helping clients assume ownership for the change process. On the flip side, counselors also need to look in the mirror and ask, "Is there something I am doing that is hurting the therapeutic relationship? Am I looking at the world from my client's perspective? Am I being culturally sensitive?" Although resistance can manifest itself in multiple ways and at unexpected times, the *source* of resistance may derive from either the client or the counselor.

Initial Counseling Interviews

The counseling process begins with the initial session, which serves as the foundation for subsequent interventions. Initial sessions set the tone for the counseling process and strongly influence the likelihood of future sessions.

In the first session, both counselors and clients work to determine whether it is reasonable to develop a counseling relationship. By being honest, open, and self-aware, counselors should quickly assess whether they are capable of working with the clients' issues. Also, clients must ask themselves if they feel comfortable with and trust the counselor before they can enter into the relationship wholeheartedly. Although the client–counselor relationship evolves over time, clients are likely to form perceptions about the quality of the relationship early, and those perceptions tend to remain stable (Seligman & Reichenberg, 2014).

Frequently in clinical settings, the initial session is used primarily to gather information about the client for the purpose of assessment and diagnosis. Counselors who are employed by medical, mental health, correctional, rehabilitation, and social agencies are likely to conduct formal intake interviews to gather information and form diagnostic impressions. Usually, these agencies have intake questionnaires designated for initial session use (see Figure 4–4). Examples of topics addressed during intake interviews include the following:

- *Identifying information about the client* (e.g., age, race, birth date, marital status, occupation, contact information)
- *The presenting concern(s) and level of client distress* (i.e., intensity or severity of concern)
- *History of the presenting concern* (i.e., onset of concern, duration and frequency, surrounding events)
- *Family background* (e.g., marital status, number of children, other relatives in the home, influences of family on presenting concern)
- *Personal history* (i.e., educational, medical, vocational, other)
- *Previous counseling experiences* (i.e., duration, outcome, what was helpful or not)
- *Risk assessment* (e.g., suicidal or homicidal ideation)
- *Clinical impression and/or diagnosis* (i.e., case conceptualization, current level of functioning)
- *Client's goals for counseling* (i.e., what the client wants to happen in counseling, to what degree the client believes the problem is changeable)

Although intake interviews tend to be structured and focused, counselors must be attentive to relationship-building skills throughout the session. In some settings, the intake forms are lengthy and prohibit building rapport unless the counselor takes definite steps to counteract that possibility. For example, the counselor may begin the interview by stating something like this:

> During the first session, it is important for me to ask several questions to get a clearer picture of what brings you here and to be able to make decisions about what might be most helpful for you. Please bear with me through the process, even though it may seem rather formal and structured. At times, I will ask you to explain things in more detail. If there are questions you would rather not answer, please let me know, and we'll move on to another question.

Another way to deal with lengthy intake forms is to ask clients to complete the forms before coming to the first session. In such cases, the forms can be mailed directly to the clients (with their permission), or they can go to the counseling site prior to the appointment date. If counselors ask clients to complete intake forms in advance, the counselor can encourage the client to elaborate on the information provided in the first session, thus facilitating case conceptualization.

I.   **Identifying data**
   A. Client's name, address, and telephone number through which the client can be reached—This information is important in the event the counselor needs to contact the client between sessions. The client's address also gives some hint about the conditions under which the client lives (e.g., large apartment complex, student dormitory, private home).
   B. Age, sex, marital status, occupation (or school class and year)—Again, this is information that can be important. It lets you know when the client is still legally a minor and provides a basis for understanding information that will come out in later sessions.

II. **Presenting problem(s), both primary and secondary**
   It is best when the presenting problem(s) are presented in exactly the way the client reported them. If a problem has behavioral components, these should be recorded as well. Questions that help reveal this type of information include these:
   A. How much does the problem interfere with the client's everyday functioning?
   B. How does the problem manifest itself? What are the thoughts, feelings, and behaviors that are associated with the problem?
   C. How often does the problem arise? How long has the problem existed?
   D. Can the client identify a pattern of events that surround the problem? When does it occur? With whom? What happens before and after its occurrence?
   E. What caused the client to decide to enter counseling at this time?

III. **Client's current life setting**
   A. How does the client spend a typical day or week?
   B. What social, recreational, and religious activities does the client engage in?
   C. What is the nature of the client's vocational and/or educational situation?

IV. **Family history**
   A. Father's and mother's ages, occupations, personality descriptions, relationships of each to the other and each to the client and other siblings
   B. Names, ages, and birth order of brothers and sisters; relationships between client and siblings
   C. Any history of mental disturbance in the family
   D. Descriptions of family stability, including number of jobs held, number of family moves, etc. (to provide insights in later sessions when issues related to client stability and/or relationships emerge)

V.   **Personal history**
   A. Medical history—any unusual or relevant illness or injury from prenatal period to present
   B. Educational history—academic progress through grade school, high school, and post–high school; includes extracurricular interests and relationships with peers
   C. Military service record
   D. Vocational history—where the client has worked, at what types of jobs, for what duration, and with what relationships with fellow workers
   E. Sexual and marital history—description of any current relationship with spouse or partner; identification of any children

FIGURE 4–4   Sample Intake Interview
Source: Adapted from *Counseling Strategies and Interventions* (8th ed.), by L. S. Cormier and H. Hackney, 2012, Upper Saddle River, NJ: Pearson. Copyright 2012 by Pearson Education. Reprinted and electronically reproduced by permission.

F. Any past experiences with and reactions to counseling
G. Personal goals in life

VI. Description of the client during the interview
   A. What was the client's physical appearance, including dress, posture, gestures, facial expressions, voice quality, and general presentation?
   B. How did the client relate to you in the session—i.e., readiness of response, motivation, warmth, distance, passivity, etc.?
   C. Were there any perceptual or sensory functions that intruded upon the interaction? (Document your observations.)
   D. What was the general level of information, vocabulary, judgment, and abstraction abilities displayed by the client?
   E. What were the streams of thought and the regularity and rate of talking? Were the client's remarks logical and connected?

VII. Summary and recommendations
   You will want to acknowledge any connections that appear to exist between the client's statement of a problem and other information collected in this session.
   A. What type of counselor do you think would best fit this client?
   B. If you are to be this client's counselor, which of your characteristics might be particularly helpful? particularly unhelpful?
   C. How realistic are the client's goals for counseling?
   D. How long do you think counseling might continue?

FIGURE 4–4 *(continued)*

In other clinical mental health settings, the intake interview is less structured. In an unstructured interview, the counselor has a general concept of topics to cover, but the questions are geared toward the individual needs of the client. With less formal initial interviews, it often is not necessary to follow a particular sequence in gathering the needed information; instead, the counselor follows the client's lead. An advantage to a less structured interview is that it can be intentionally adapted to meet the client's unique needs. However, unstructured interviews have more room for error and may result in spending too much time on relatively minor issues (Whiston, 2017). To help counteract this problem, counselors can prepare an informal form with major headings, such as *Identifying Information, Presenting Concern, History of the Concern*, and other topics that are typically covered during an initial interview. Having something tangible to refer to helps ensure that no major topics are inadvertently omitted.

Regardless of the type of intake interview conducted, counselors will use a combination of closed and open questions to gather information about the client. **Closed questions** can be effective in eliciting a large amount of information in a short time, but they do not encourage elaboration, which might be needed. An example of a closed question is, "How long have you been separated from your husband?" In contrast, an **open question** typically begins with words such as *what, how,* or *could* and allows the client more latitude to respond. "I wonder how you feel about that?" and "Could you tell me more?" are examples of open questions. Both types of questions can be used effectively by counselors during intake interviews to gain information and engage the client's participation (Young, 2013).

Another form of communication used by counselors during initial sessions is a request for clarification, which helps ensure that the counselor understands what the client is saying. These requests require the client to repeat or elaborate on material just covered. For example, a counselor might say, "Please help me understand what you mean when you say that you feel jittery," or "You say that you feel out of control all of the time. Can you tell me more about that?"

When counselors are working with clients who differ from them in areas of diversity, it is especially important to ensure that the counselor understands what the client means.

Relationship Building during Initial Sessions

During the initial interview, it is important to make clients feel comfortable, respected, supported, and heard. For this to occur, counselors need to set aside their own agendas and focus exclusively on the clients by actively listening to, showing genuine interest in, and accepting their stories and presenting concerns. This type of behavior helps establish rapport.

The counselor can go even further in building rapport by intentionally using specific helping skills, such as reflecting feelings, summarizing, clarifying, and encouraging. It is critical for counselors to develop a repertoire of helping skills and an ability to use them appropriately throughout the counseling process. Ivey and Ivey (2007) state that the two most important skills for rapport building are basic **attending behavior** and **client-observation skills**. A counselor needs to focus on what the client is thinking and feeling and how the client is behaving. Establishing and maintaining rapport is vital for the disclosure of information, the initiation of change, and the ultimate success of counseling.

Inviting clients to talk about their reasons for seeking help is one way to initiate rapport. These noncoercive invitations to talk are called **door openers**, which contrast with judgmental or evaluative responses known as **door closers**. Appropriate door openers include inquiries and observations such as "What brings you to see me?" and "What would you like to talk about?" These unstructured, open-ended invitations allow clients to take the initiative in the session (Cormier, 2016). In such situations, clients are more likely to talk about priority topics. In contrast, a door closer blocks therapeutic dialogue—for example, "You really feel like you want to focus on your difficulty with time management *again*? We've already discussed that topic a lot. What if we move on to something different?"

The amount of talking that clients engage in and the insight and benefits derived from the initial interview are enhanced when the counselor appropriately conveys empathy, encouragement, support, caring, attentiveness, acceptance, and genuineness. Of all these qualities, empathy is the most important.

EMPATHY. Empathic counselors are able to share clients' experiences through deep and subjective understanding. Of particular importance is being able to perceive the cultural frame of reference from which the client operates and which guides the client's perceptions. This type of empathy, called **culturally sensitive empathy**, helps bridge the cultural gap between the counselor and the client (Chung & Bemak, 2002).

Carl Rogers (1987) describes two factors that make empathy possible: (a) realizing that "an infinite number of feelings" do not exist and (b) having a personal security from which "you can let yourself go into the world of this other person and still know that you can return to your own world. Everything you are feeling is 'as if" (pp. 45–46). Being able to empathize with clients at this level involves a combination of innate skill, intentionality, and learned skills.

Empathy is expressed through active listening, which is the intentional use of attending skills that enable the counselor to respond to the client's verbal and nonverbal messages and emotional experiences. Counselors can make responses at several levels that reflect different degrees of empathy. A scale formulated by Carkhuff (1969), *Empathic Understanding in Interpersonal Process*, provides a classic measure of these levels. Each of the five levels either adds to or subtracts from the feeling and meaning inherent in a client's statement:

1. The verbal and behavioral expressions of the counselor either do not attend to or detract significantly from the verbal and behavioral expressions of the client.
2. Although the counselor responds to the expressed feelings of the client, the counselor does so in a way that does not capture the depth of those feelings.
3. The expressions of the counselor in response to the expressions of the client are essentially interchangeable.
4. The responses of the counselor add noticeably to the expressions of the client in a way that lets the client feel heard and understood at a deeper level.
5. The counselor's responses add significantly to the feeling and meaning of the client's expressions in ways that go beyond what the client was able to verbalize.

Responses at the first two levels are not considered empathic; in fact, they inhibit the creation of an empathic environment. For example, if a client expresses distress over the loss of a job, a counselor operating on either of the first two levels might reply, "Well, you might be better off in a different line of work." Such a response misses the pain that the client is feeling.

At Level 3, a counselor's response is rated as "interchangeable" with that of the client. For example, the client might say, "It's been five years since Jim died, and I still find myself crying when I think about him," and the counselor responds, "You still get sad when you think about Jim."

At Levels 4 and 5, a counselor adds either "noticeably" or "significantly" to what the client says. It is this ability to *go beyond* what clients say that distinguishes counseling from conversation or other less therapeutic forms of behavior (Carkhuff, 1972). For example, in response to the client who describes crying about Jim, a Level 4 response might be, "You cared deeply about Jim. It sounds as though you miss him a lot." Level 5 responses typically are made during long-term therapeutic relationships (Neukrug, 2016). They express to the client a deep understanding of the feelings—or the feelings behind the feelings—that are contributing to the client's current situation. The client's reaction determines whether or not a counselor's response accurately reflects the client's implicit message.

During the initial phase of counseling, counselors are involved in developing a therapeutic relationship and assessing the clients' problems and the possible causes of those problems. During the initial sessions, counselors work with clients to determine what will help them heal, change, and cope more effectively with life. The work carried out during the initial sessions leads to the collaborative establishment of therapeutic goals, which are recorded in the form of a treatment plan. To facilitate the development of a treatment plan, counselors use the data gathered during initial sessions to develop a case conceptualization.

Case Conceptualization

Case conceptualization, also known as **case formulation**, provides a way for a counselor to link the client's presenting problems to a treatment plan. It also serves as a way to tailor interventions to specific client needs (Sperry, 2005a). Definitions of case conceptualization include these:

- Making sense out of complex clinical data by analyzing case information, formulating hypotheses, and making treatment decisions (Falvey, 2001)
- A method of summarizing diverse case information in a coherent "map" that sheds light on the client's basic pattern of behavior (Sperry, 2005b)
- Developing core clinical hypotheses to understand client issues—hypotheses that are consistent with the data gathered during initial sessions but are subject to change, based on new information (Ingram, 2012)

Developing clinical hypotheses "is the heart of case formulation" (Ingram, 2012, p. 11). A counselor's theoretical orientation will influence the hypotheses formed, case conceptualizations, and treatment planning. Theoretical orientation is important. However, Ingram recommends taking an integrative approach to hypothesizing that is not wedded to a particular theory. She goes on to state that it is important to test out hypotheses and remain open to the possibility that a hypothesis may be incorrect. In other words, "Flirt with your hypotheses; don't marry them" (Ingram, 2012, p. 12). Case conceptualization needs to be culturally competent, dynamic, and used to create treatment plans that follow logically from hypotheses. Sperry (2005b) recommends that case conceptualization be client-focused rather than theory-focused so as to maximize the match between a client's issues and the treatment interventions provided.

Developing the complex cognitive skills needed to conceptualize client cases effectively needs to be done intentionally. Often, beginning counselors have a vague idea of what case conceptualization entails, but the concept is abstract and difficult to articulate. When counselors-in-training present cases to their practicum or internship groups, the client information they share with the group, their clinical decision-making process, and the feedback they receive from group members regarding what might be going on with a particular client all contribute to the development of case conceptualization skills. Clinical mental health counselors need to hone their conceptualization skills by consulting with colleagues, receiving supervision, and reading publications that focus on the topic. Being able to conceptualize cases, being open to new client information, and using those skills to formulate treatment plans are essential for practicing effectively in managed care environments (Sperry, 2005b).

Client Records

Throughout all phases of the counseling process, accurate and timely documentation is an essential part of a clinical mental health counselor's work. There are a number of helpful sources that clinicians can refer to for assistance in record keeping and documentation. Also, most agencies have guidelines for maintaining client records, and counselors need to familiarize themselves with those guidelines.

WHAT ARE CLIENT RECORDS?   The term **client records** refers to all client information that is needed for effective service delivery (Barnett & Johnson, 2015). Although most client records are in printed or electronic form, client records also include any video- or audio-tapes of client–counselor interactions. The number and types of forms vary depending on the needs of the client, agency, and practitioner. Piazza and Baruth (1990) note that most client records fall within one of the following six categories: (a) identifying or intake information, (b) assessment and diagnostic information, (c) the treatment plan, (d) case notes (also called **staff notes**), (e) the termination (closure) summary, and (f) other data (e.g., signed consent for treatment, copies of correspondence, consent for release of information forms). Identifying information, assessment information, and treatment plans are usually documented during initial counseling sessions; case notes provide a written record of treatment and intervention; and termination documentation is compiled at the end of the counseling process. Client records provide documentation of what transpires between a counselor and a client. They protect the interests of both parties and promote continuity of care.

REASONS FOR CAREFUL RECORD KEEPING.   For many counselors, completing paperwork can be tedious and less fulfilling than actually working with clients. However, well-organized and accurate records "are the most effective tool counselors have for establishing client treatment plans, ensuring continuity of care in the event of absence, and proving that quality care was provided" (Wheeler & Bertram, 2015, p. 203).

Whereas many years ago, it was not uncommon for mental health professionals to refrain from keeping client records, accurate and complete records are now considered the professional standard of care. The *ACA Code of Ethics* (2014) outlines requirements for record keeping and documentation in Section B.6. There are several reasons counselors need to create a record of all counseling services. Some of those reasons include the following:

- The *ACA Code of Ethics* (2014) requires counselors to "create and maintain records of documentation necessary for rendering professional services" (Section B.6.a).
- Careful documentation helps protect counselors if malpractice allegations are made.
- Inadequate or incomplete documentation may be harmful to the client as well as to the counselor.
- In the event that the primary counselor is unable to provide services, client records can ensure appropriate continuity of care.
- Funding sources require documentation that verifies the need for services as well as the nature of the services rendered.
- Utilization review, peer review, and quality assurance review, which often are based on client records, are essential to the work that occurs in many clinical settings. (Barnett & Johnson, 2015, Mitchell, 2007)

CONFIDENTIALITY AND ACCESS TO CLIENT RECORDS.   Counselors are responsible for ensuring the safety and confidentiality of any client records they create, maintain, or destroy. This means that counselors make sure client documents are secured in locked files or saved in protected computer programs. Counselors also need to review state laws regarding record maintenance and storage of client records (Barnett & Johnson, 2015). All client charts and other client information need to remain in the agency or office, not be taken home. Also, when client records are disposed of because they are outdated or invalid, they should be shredded before being thrown away or recycled (Welfel, 2016). Furthermore, counselors need to take necessary precautions when eliminating records that have been stored electronically.

The 2014 *ACA Code of Ethics* stipulates that "counselors ensure that records and documentation kept in any medium are secure and that only authorized persons have access to them" (Standard B.6.b). When case notes and other client records are created and/or stored on a computer, there needs to be a security component that ensures the protection of information. In addition to basic concerns related to electronic storage and transmittal of data, counselors need to be aware of regulations related to HIPAA. Although not every counseling setting is a HIPAA-covered entity, it is likely that HIPAA requirements will continue to influence the maintenance, storage, and transmission of client records (Wheeler & Bertram, 2015). All records, including electronic, paper, and oral, are covered by the HIPAA privacy rule (Remley & Herlihy, 2016).

Whereas the content of client records technically belongs to the mental health professionals, clients have the right to access copies of their records and control their dissemination (Welfel, 2016). Therefore, counselors have an ethical and a legal obligation to provide competent clients access to their records if requested, unless the content would be detrimental to client welfare. Also, clients have the right to demand that copies of clinical records be transferred to other professionals. It is important for clinicians to keep clients' access rights in mind as client records are created.

If counselors need to transfer or disclose client records to legitimate third parties, written consent should be obtained from the clients. Standard B.3.e. of the 2014 ACA Code of Ethics stipulates that counselors are to take precautions to protect the confidentiality of all information transmitted through the use of any medium. When counselors receive client permission to submit documentation of services rendered, it is best to disclose only the information considered necessary for processing reimbursement and in a manner that meets federal and state laws. Moreover, when documentation is transmitted electronically, the electronic media needs to be secure, off limits to unauthorized persons, and HIPAA-compliant (Barnett & Johnson, 2015).

Client records can be subpoenaed in litigation situations, sometimes despite client objection and/or claims of privilege. **Subpoenas** are court orders that cannot be ignored. When subpoenas are issued, counselors should consult with their employment supervisors, a lawyer, and their liability insurance agency (e.g., Healthcare Providers Service Organization, or HPSO) before turning over records or appearing in court (Remley & Herlihy, 2016). If records must be turned over, copies of the originals should be sent and should not include documentation from other professionals. In some cases, the attorneys who issued the subpoenas will allow counselors to write and submit treatment summaries rather than copies of the actual case notes themselves.

SUGGESTIONS FOR RECORD KEEPING.   R. M. Mitchell (2007) provides numerous recommendations for documenting intake sessions, treatment plans, and case notes:

- Make notes grammatically clear and correct.
- Use precise language, avoiding jargon, clichés, and qualifiers.
- Enter only the information that is pertinent to the client's situation. The record should be logical, beginning with assessment and moving to a plan, case notes, case reviews, and termination.
- Write legibly and in an organized manner.
- Eliminate unfounded opinions or assumptions.
- Logically relate the recorded intervention to the treatment plan.

- Avoid including personal feelings in client records.
- Describe the client's behavior, or quote what was said during the session.
- Do not use correction fluid or tape. If you need to alter a document, use a pen to draw a single line through the entry. Above the line, write *error* and *corrected entry*; then add the correct information.
- Write notes within 24 to 48 hours of the session.
- Document outcomes of sessions.
- Sign each record, including your full name and credentials. In some cases, it is necessary to obtain a cosignature (e.g., that of a supervisor or medical director).

In addition to these suggestions, Remley and Herlihy (2016) suggest writing notes with the assumption that they will become public information at some later date. However, the counselor should not be so cautious that insufficient information is recorded.

Careful record-keeping procedures will serve counselors well in any of the clinical settings in which they work. Although the process is somewhat time-consuming, it benefits counselors and clients. In particular, keeping accurate professional records facilitates the provision of quality services to clients and provides self-protection for counselors (Remley & Herlihy, 2016).

THE WORKING PHASE OF COUNSELING

In the initial phase of counseling, counselors concentrate on gathering information and getting their clients involved in the helping process. The initial sessions of counseling conclude with a treatment plan that serves as the basis for the next phase of counseling—the action, or working, phase. During this phase, specific objectives are defined, and interventions for achieving those objectives are implemented. It is important to remember that the division between the initial phase and the working phase is arbitrary. For example, assessment, although associated with the initial phase of counseling, continues through all phases of counseling. Treatment plans, which usually come at the conclusion of the initial phase of counseling, also signify the beginning of the working phase of counseling.

Treatment Plans

Treatment plans help set the course for further counseling interventions. They are required by managed care organizations and many insurance companies for service approval and reimbursement. A **treatment plan** explains why the client is receiving services and what is going to take place in counseling. It lists measurable and desired outcomes of treatment and is sometimes called a **plan of care**, **service plan**, **habitation plan**, **residential plan**, or **case management plan**, depending on the type of services provided and the agency providing those services.

Treatment planning is a complex process that outlines a relationship among problem definition, treatment goals, theory, and research (Parsons, 2009). A well-written treatment plan often includes the following (Mitchell, 2007):

- *Problem statement.* The presenting problem or concern is clearly described. *Example:* Depression due to marital difficulties.
- *Goal statement and expected date of achievement.* List specific, measurable goals that relate to the presenting problem(s). Include expected dates that goals will be

accomplished. *Example:* Keep a journal describing thoughts, feelings, and behaviors for the next two weeks. Address partner with "I messages" when disputes occur rather than walking away.

- *Treatment modality.*   Describe the interventions that will be used to help meet the stated goals. The best interventions are evidence based. To be a billable service, the intervention must be provided by a professional who is considered qualified by the funding source. *Example:* Meet weekly with a group of women experiencing relationship-related depression. The group will be facilitated by a licensed professional counselor.
- *Clinical impression or diagnosis.*   Clinical impressions need to accurately reflect the client's mental health as described in the assessment. Diagnostic terms, when used, should be listed according to *DSM* or *International Classification of Diseases* codes. A client's condition must not be overstated or understated. *Example:* 300.02 Generalized Anxiety Disorder.
- *Names and credentials.*   List the names and credentials of people who participated in the development of the treatment plan. Also list the name of the assigned clinician. The person who writes the plan needs to sign and date it.

Treatment plans should represent a collaborative, ongoing effort between client and counselor.

Interventions, Skills, and Techniques

Counseling interventions are outlined in the treatment plan and are determined by several factors, including the nature of the presenting problem, client characteristics (e.g., cultural background, age, gender, personality), counselor characteristics, theoretical orientation, training, and the organization in which the counselor works. For example, a counselor with a strong psychodynamic orientation is likely to interact and intervene differently with clients than a counselor with a cognitive–behavioral orientation.

Within the mental health profession, evidence-based research is conducted to determine what interventions tend to yield the best outcomes for specific conditions. There is a demand from consumers and professionals to provide empirical evidence of the efficacy of counseling. Pressure from managed care companies also has prompted a focus on evaluating treatment outcomes (Hill & Beamish, 2007).

Outcome research indicates that, in general, counseling is effective across settings and theoretical orientations. What, then, leads to successful outcomes? A summary of counseling research reveals that client outcome is determined by client variables, a set of common curative factors, and specific interventions applied to particular problems (Granello & Witmer, 2013). It is important for counselors to provide the most effective treatments possible by selecting interventions and techniques that have been demonstrated as effective.

Following in the tradition of the medical profession, which adopts procedures or protocols based on research for treatment of specific problems, the American Psychiatric Association, the American Psychological Association, the psychiatric nursing profession, and the ACA have independently made strong efforts to summarize outcome research to guide mental health practices. One responsibility of clinical mental health counselors is to find ways to integrate research and practice so that the interventions they select coincide with professional standards of care. When interventions are informed by research, successful outcomes during the working phase of counseling are more likely. For example, Hill and Beamish (2007) summarize outcome research reviewing treatment outcomes for obsessive–compulsive disorder. Delineating standards of care, based on outcome research, enhances the professional credibility of clinical mental health counselors. At the same time, however, it is important to remember that not all clients experience the same problem in the same way, and focusing too much on immediate problem resolution rather than taking a more broad-based approach to healthy emotional functioning may be counterindicated (Vacc & Loesch, 2000).

Lambert and Bergin (1994) suggest that the common curative factors of effective counseling can be organized into three categories (see Figure 4–5): (a) **support factors** (e.g., the therapeutic alliance, trust, empathy, catharsis), (b) **learning factors** (e.g., cognitive learning, affective experiencing, feedback), and (c) **action factors** (e.g., reality testing, rehearsal, mastery efforts). During the working phase, counselors may find it beneficial to use various combinations of these factors to help clients make positive changes. Earlier in the chapter, support factors that facilitate the development of a therapeutic client–counselor relationship were examined. In this section, particular attention will be given to three of the learning and action factors: **cognitive learning** (ways of thinking), **affective experiencing** (ways of feeling), and **rehearsal** (ways of behaving).

COGNITIVE LEARNING.   Often, clients come to counseling with distorted or dysfunctional cognitions, making them more susceptible to problems in relationships and life events. Cognitive distortions affect the way people think, feel, and act on multiple levels. Clinical mental health counselors can help clients change distorted or unrealistic cognitions by offering

Support Factors	Learning Factors	Action Factors
Catharsis	Advice	Behavioral regulation
Identification with therapist	Affective experiencing	Cognitive mastery
Mitigation of isolation	Assimilation of problematic experiences	Encouragement of facing fears
Positive relationship	Changing expectations for personal effectiveness	Taking risks
Reassurance	Cognitive learning	Mastery efforts:
Release of tension	Corrective emotional experience	• Modeling
Structure	Exploration of internal frame of reference	• Practice
Therapeutic alliance	Feedback	• Reality testing
Therapist/client active participation	Insight	Success experience Working through
Therapist expertness	Rationale	
Therapist warmth, respect, empathy, acceptance, genuineness		
Trust		

FIGURE 4–5   Common Factors across Therapies Associated with Positive Outcomes
Source: From "The Effectiveness of Psychotherapy," by M. J. Lambert and A. E. Bergin, in A. E. Bergin and S. L. Garfield (Eds.), *Handbook of Psychotherapy and Behavior Change* (4th ed., pp. 143–189), 1994, New York: Wiley. Copyright © 1994 by John Wiley & Sons. Reprinted with permission.

them the opportunity to explore thoughts and beliefs within a safe, accepting, and nonjudgmental environment.

Cognitive distortions are negative, inaccurate biases that can result in unhealthy misperceptions of events. For example, a worker may assume that her boss considers her less capable than others, when in reality, the boss is pleased with the worker's performance. Cognitive theorists have identified several types of distortions, including exaggerating the negative, minimizing the positive, overgeneralizing, catastrophizing, and personalizing. Cognitive distortions also are evidenced when people engage in all-or-nothing thinking or **selective abstraction** (i.e., taking a detail out of context and using it to negate an entire experience). Such perceptions can result in negative automatic thoughts, which then negatively affect emotions and mood states. Counselors can teach clients to evaluate and challenge the validity of their cognitions (Beamish, Granello, & Belcastro, 2002). Teaching clients ways to correct faulty information processing can help them view situations more realistically. Viewing situations more realistically can have a positive impact on clients' affective and behavioral responses.

The Case of Simon

Simon met with his boss to discuss his end-of-the-year evaluation. Simon's boss pointed out many of Simon's strengths, including his strong organizational skills, his dependability, his willingness to help the company achieve its goals, and his overall work ethic. The boss suggested that some coworkers did not consider Simon a team player—through the years he has demonstrated a desire to work independently whenever possible. (Simon states that he can get more work accomplished that way.) The boss went on to suggest that Simon engage in teamwork when opportunities presented themselves. He said that he considered the need to interact more with colleagues an "area of growth" for Simon.

Simon told you, his counselor, that he received a "terrible evaluation" and that his skills and efforts at work were not appreciated by anyone. He asked you if he should begin looking for other work. Does Simon appear to have any cognitive distortions, and if so, what are they? How would you help Simon think about his evaluation more realistically?

The goal of cognitive learning and restructuring is to help clients formulate new cognitions that are more realistic and adaptive (Beck, 1995). One way counselors can help clients modify cognitions is through the process of **reframing**, which offers another probable and positive viewpoint of what a situation is or why an event might have happened. Such a changed point of view provides the client with an opportunity to respond differently to the situation. For example, if an adolescent client insists that his mother is always worrying and nagging him, the counselor might be able to help the client reframe the situation by suggesting that it sounds like his mother is concerned about his well-being and appears to care about him very much.

AFFECTIVE EXPERIENCING. Just as it is important to help clients examine their cognitions, or to think about their thinking patterns, it also is important to help clients recognize and explore the emotions they experience. Although numerous emotions are common to the human experience, people experience emotions uniquely. Seligman and Reichenberg (2014, pp. 141–143) describe eight dimensions that characterize emotions:

- *Primarily emotional, physical, or a combination.*   Emotions are physically embedded. For example, worry (an emotion) can lead to nausea and/or headaches (physical symptoms).
- *Overt, covert, or a combination of both.*   Overt feelings are evident to other people, whereas covert feelings are kept inside and are not revealed.
- *Positive, negative, or neutral.*   Joy, happiness, and amusement are positive emotions. Shame, worry, and guilt are negative emotions. Curiosity is an example of a neutral emotion. However, emotions that typically fall into one category may be experienced differently by certain people. For instance, John's expression of anger may result behaviorally in intimidation, which gives him a feeling of power and control. In contrast, Courtney may turn her anger inward, believing that outward expressions of anger are not acceptable.
- *Level of intensity.*   The intensity with which emotions are felt varies, depending on the person and the circumstances. Intense expression of negative emotions can lead to misunderstandings and relationship difficulties.
- *In or out of awareness.*   Some people are more aware of their emotional states than are others. People who are unaware of their emotions often experience problems in relationships. Feelings that are considered "unacceptable" (e.g., envy, shame, rage) may be particularly challenging for clients.
- *Appropriateness for context and stimulus.*   Emotional expression that may be appropriate in one context may not be appropriate in another. For example, expressing anger when an infant is crying in a restaurant may be inappropriate, whereas expressing anger toward someone who has put you down may be both healthy and appropriate.
- *Congruence.*   When emotions are expressed congruently, verbal and nonverbal behaviors match. People can unknowingly sabotage their communication efforts when emotions and behaviors are incongruent. For example, if someone tells his partner he is sorry, but his facial expression and tone do not match the words, the apology will not be well received.
- *Helpful or harmful.*   Depending on the way and the context in which they are expressed, emotions may enhance lives and relationships or contribute to struggles intra- and interpersonally.

Counselors can use a number of skills and techniques to increase clients' emotional awareness. The skill of accurately reflecting feelings is used by many counselors to help clients focus on emotions they may be avoiding (Young, 2013). Helping clients identify the feeling associated with a particular incident, reflecting the feeling back to them, and then encouraging them to determine where in their body that feeling is experienced can help clients develop emotional awareness. By asking them to think of a time in their lives when they had the same bodily sensations and emotional feelings they just experienced, counselors can assist clients in exploring patterns of emotional responses. Also, many Gestalt techniques, when used properly, provide powerful ways for clients to connect with their emotions. However, in some cases, interventions that focus on emotions are not recommended, particularly when clients are in high levels of distress or are psychotic.

Simply releasing emotions (**catharsis**) can have some value in counseling, but catharsis should not be the final goal. When clients experience emotional release in counseling, counselors will want to work through underlying beliefs, thoughts, and patterns of behavior (Corey, 2013). The goal of increasing affective experiencing, then, is to help clients connect their emotions with cognitions and behaviors in a way that leads to new insights and changed behavior.

REHEARSAL. Whereas cognitive learning focuses on thoughts and affective experiencing focuses on emotions, rehearsal focuses on client behavior. Counselors can help clients maximize the possibility of accomplishing their goals by giving them opportunities to rehearse or practice new behaviors. Just as practicing benefits athletes and performance artists, so can it benefit clients dealing with particular issues, such as assertiveness and social skill deficits. Clients can rehearse in two ways: overtly and covertly (Cormier, Nurius, & Osborn, 2017). **Overt rehearsal** requires clients to verbalize or act out what they are going to do. For example, if an adult daughter is working on becoming more assertive with her overbearing parent, she can rehearse what she is going to say and how she is going to act before she actually encounters the parent. **Covert rehearsal** involves imagining and reflecting on the desired course of action. For example, individuals who have to give a speech can first imagine the conditions under which they will perform and then reflect on how to organize the subject matter for presentation. Imagining the situation beforehand can alleviate unnecessary anxiety and help improve performance.

Another way to help clients practice and generalize the skills learned in counseling sessions is by assigning homework. Homework provides clients with opportunities to work on particular skills outside the counseling session and has numerous advantages (Hay & Kinnier, 1998; Hutchins & Vaught, 1997), such as the following:

- Keeping clients focused on relevant behavior between sessions
- Helping them see clearly what kind of progress they are making
- Motivating clients to change behaviors
- Helping them evaluate and modify their activities
- Helping clients assume more responsibility for their own behaviors
- Celebrating a breakthrough achieved in counseling

Many counselors use homework to get clients to help themselves. For homework to be most effective, it needs to be relevant to the situation and specifically tied to some measurable behavior change (Okun & Kantrowitz, 2015; Young, 2013). Counselors need to follow up with clients to ensure homework assignments are completed, determine their level of effectiveness, and modify assignments as needed.

Cognitive learning, affective experiencing, and rehearsal are just a few of the many interventions counselors use during the working phase of counseling. Throughout the process, effective counselors will continue to employ basic helping skills (e.g., active listening, reflecting, clarifying, summarizing, probing, being immediate, and confronting) and specific theory-grounded techniques (e.g., the empty-chair technique) to help clients make progress toward their goals. As counseling progresses, it is important to work with clients to reevaluate goals and progress, making changes when necessary.

After each counseling session, counselors need to write case notes to record what occurred.

Case Notes

Each time a counselor meets with a client, the counselor is responsible for documenting the activity. This documentation is sometimes referred to as a **case note**, **clinical entry**, **process note**, **progress note**, **group note**, or **service log**. Prior to the advent of managed care services, the primary purpose of case notes was to enable counselors to record information about the content of the counseling session and to guide professional practice. This purpose still is paramount. However, 21st-century clinical mental health counselors must write case notes with the understanding that the content may be used to determine reimbursement for services. Furthermore, case notes are required by the *ACA Code of Ethics* (2014). They protect counselors from litigation issues. Also, they are in keeping with professional expectations. Some of the general information included in most case notes includes the following:

- *Confirmation of a service.*   What did the counselor do during the session? What did the client do? Use verbs to describe the services rendered (e.g., *focused, identified, discussed, recommended*).
- *Verification of the information implied within the billing code.*   The content of the case note should confirm the date of service, length of session, and type of service provided.
- *An original, legible signature.*   Some notes need cosignatures. To determine whether a cosignature is necessary, counselors need to read and comply with the state licensure and funding source regulations.

Many acceptable formats can be followed when writing case notes. Examples of three useful formats are presented in Figure 4–6. In many instances, the agency for which a counselor works will have a predetermined outline that is to be followed when writing case notes, and it is incumbent on the counselor to adhere to that format. Remley and Herlihy (2016) remind us that the primary purposes of case notes are to provide quality services to clients and to document decisions made and actions taken by counselors.

Documenting Work with High-Risk Clients

Special considerations need to be taken when clinical mental health counselors work with clients classified as high risk. Examples of **high-risk cases** include clients who are potentially violent, suicidal, homicidal, or engaged in criminal behavior. Clients who have experienced or committed abuse also are considered high risk.

If a counselor determines that a client is potentially dangerous, three things must be done: (a) explain how the conclusion was reached, (b) take action, and (c) document the action (Mitchell, 2007). There are a number of actions a counselor might take, depending on the situation. In some cases, it is necessary to notify the potential target and/or appropriate law enforcement agencies. Other action options include consulting with a psychiatrist and taking steps toward an involuntary hospitalization. Before taking action, it is prudent to consult with coworkers, a supervisor, and a lawyer and then to document those consultations. Take any threat of suicide or homicide seriously, and write down the client's exact words (as closely as possible) when documenting the threats. In some cases, suicidal and homicidal safety plans can be clinically useful; however, in litigation, a contract does not always protect the clinician (Mitchell, 2007). If a client threatens to kill or harm someone, the counselor has a **duty to warn**. If confidentiality is broken for this reason, counselors need to document the decision and justify it. Practitioners should involve clients in the documentation process when feasible because it can "enhance the service relationship [and] promote empowerment" (Mitchell, 2007, p. 68).

STIPS Format (from Prieto & Scheel, 2002)	
Signs and symptoms	Record the client's current level of functioning and clinical signs and symptoms, especially as they relate to the presenting issues. Record any changes from previous level of functioning. Note observable client behaviors (e.g., appearance, affect, speech).
Topics of discussion	Describe the major issues discussed in the session. Include any developments that have occurred since the previous session.
Interventions	Record specific interventions used during the session. Interventions should relate to the identified problem and treatment goals. Track client's completion of homework assignments, and record any new assignments. Summarize progress clients have made toward established goals.
Progress and plans	Record plans for the next session, including specific topics of discussion, planned interventions, and anticipated outcomes. Note any changes to the overall treatment plan.
Special issues	Record any newly developed or ongoing critical issues that need to be tracked (e.g., suicidal ideation, homicidal threats, concerns about referrals, suspected abuse). Document ways these issues are being handled (e.g., consultation, supervision, reporting to outside agencies).
Goals and Action Plan Format (from Piazza & Baruth, 1990)	
Goals for the session	State goals for the session that relate to the client's treatment plan and are connected to previous sessions. Goals should be flexible to accommodate more pressing concerns when necessary.
Goal attainment	Describe the techniques and interventions used in the session, and evaluate their effectiveness. If the interventions were ineffective, what could have been done differently?
Clinical impressions	Record clinical impressions based on client behavior and statements. Avoid recording subjective impressions that are not supported by data.
Action plan	State plans for the next session. These plans will be used to provide the goal statement for that session.
SOAP Format (from Cameron & Turtle-Song, 2002)	
Subjective	Record information about the problem from the client's perspective (and from that of significant others). Include the client's feelings, thoughts, and goals. Describe the intensity of the problem and its effect on relationships.
Objective	Record factual observations made by the counselor. Observations include any physical, interpersonal, or psychological findings noted by the counselor (e.g., appearance, affect, client strengths, mental status, responses to the counseling process).
Assessment	Summarize clinical thinking about the client's issues. This section synthesizes and analyzes data from the subjective and objective observations. When appropriate, include the *DSM* diagnosis. (Section may also include clinical impressions used to make a diagnosis.)
Plan	Record plans for future interventions and a prognosis. Include the date of the next session, proposed interventions, and anticipated gains from treatment.

FIGURE 4–6   Three Sample Formats for Case Notes

If a counselor suspects abuse, neglect, or current criminal behavior, it is advisable to discuss the case with a lawyer and contact the proper authority if a report is required. When documenting any concerns about abuse, be sure to record the client's words and behaviors rather than express unsubstantiated opinions. By sticking to the facts and avoiding impressionistic or defamatory statements, objectivity is maintained and counselors are in a better position to carry out next steps. A general rule of thumb is to be precise and specific in all documentation. When an abused child is in therapy, Mitchell (2007) recommends that clinicians work with the child's attorney and make attempts to have records sealed or reviewed only by the judge involved in the case.

BOX 4–2   Recommendations for Risk Management Documentation

- Document what the client said or did that suggested that he or she was engaging in, or considering engaging in, a high-risk activity.
- Document the severity of any threat of high-risk behavior, based on your clinical expertise.
- Record options you considered taking, based on your assessment.
- Explain what options you ruled out and why, thereby explaining your clinical rationale.
- Consult with colleagues, supervisors, and/or attorneys whenever possible, and document that consultation.
- Document the option you chose, including specific actions you took to implement that option.
- Document what occurred after that action was taken.

Source: Adapted from Wheeler and Bertram, 2015, p. 1.

CLOSING COUNSELING RELATIONSHIPS

Why Closing Is Important

Closing the counseling relationship, sometimes called **termination**, is the last phase of counseling and refers to the decision made by the client, counselor, or both parties to stop counseling. It is probably the least researched and most neglected phase of counseling. Many counselors assume that closing a relationship with a client will occur naturally, with satisfying outcomes for both parties. Goodyear (1981) states that "it is almost as though we operate from a myth that termination is a process from which the counselor remains aloof and to which the client alone is responsive" (p. 347).

But the closing of a counseling relationship has an impact on all involved. Closing often produces mixed feelings for both the counselor and the client. Unless it is handled properly, closing has the power to harm as well as heal.

Historically, addressing the process of closing the counseling relationship has been avoided for several reasons. Ward (1984) suggests two of the more prominent reasons. First, closing is associated with loss, which on the surface may seem contradictive to counseling's emphasis on growth and development. Second, closing is not directly related to the microskills that facilitate counseling relationships. Therefore, some counselors may not be prepared to attend fully to the ending of a counseling relationship.

However, ending the counseling relationship serves several important functions. First, ending the counseling experience signals that something important has been completed.

Throughout life, individuals enter into and leave a succession of experiences, including jobs, relationships, and life stages. Growth and adjustment depend on the ability to make the most of these experiences and learn from them. For someone to begin something new, a former experience must be completed and resolved (Perls, 1969). Counselors who manage the closing process appropriately can help clients learn healthy ways to end relationships for the purpose of moving on to the next stage of life.

Second, closing gives clients the opportunity to maintain changes already achieved and generalize problem-solving skills to new areas. Successful counseling results in significant changes in the ways clients think, feel, or act. These changes are rehearsed in counseling, but they must be practiced in the real world. When the counseling experience ends, the client has the opportunity to do just that. The client can always go back to the counselor for any needed follow-up, but closing is the natural point for the practice of independence to begin. It is a potentially empowering experience for clients that enables them to address the present in an entirely new or modified way. When the counseling relationship ends, the client is given the opportunity to put "insights into actions" (Gladding, 1990, p. 130). In other words, what seems like an exit becomes an entrance.

Finally, closing serves as a reminder that the client has matured (Vickio, 1990). Besides offering clients new skills and/or new ways of thinking, an effective closing marks a time in clients' lives when they are less absorbed by and preoccupied with personal problems and better able to deal with outside people and events. This ability to handle difficult situations may result in healthier relationships and lives that are more balanced and satisfying. Having achieved a successful resolution to a problem, a client now has new insights and abilities that are stored in memory and may be recalled and used in the future.

Timing of Closing

Knowing how and when to terminate a counseling relationship is important. If the relationship is ended too soon, clients may lose the ground they gained in counseling and regress to earlier behaviors. If closing is never addressed, clients can become dependent on the counselor and fail to resolve difficulties and to grow as persons. There are, however, several pragmatic considerations related to the timing of closing a counseling experience (Cormier, 2016; Young, 2013):

• *Have clients achieved behavioral, cognitive, or affective goals?*   When clients and counselors have a reason to believe that particular goals have been reached, the timing of closing is easier to determine. Setting up contracts, treatment plans, goals, and objectives during the initial counseling sessions is key to determining whether goals are met.

• *Has the client developed better coping skills?*   Related to this question is the level of the client's initial distress. Has it been reduced? In what ways can that be observed?

• *Is the counseling relationship no longer helpful?*   If either client or counselor senses that what is occurring in counseling sessions is no longer helpful, ending the counseling relationship is appropriate. The counselor can talk to the client about referral possibilities if the reason for lack of progress is due to a counselor–client mismatch.

• *Has the context of the initial counseling arrangement changed?*   In cases where there is, for example, a move or a prolonged illness, closing (as well as a referral) should be considered.

Overall, there is no one right time to close a counseling relationship. The "when" of termination must be determined in accordance with the uniqueness of the situation and with overall ethical and professional guidelines.

PREMATURE CLOSING. In many cases, clinical mental health counselors may be expected to provide time-limited services to clients. In these situations, counselors need to explain the time limits at the outset of counseling. If the client reaches the end of an HMO-imposed time limit before being ready to end the relationship, the counselor can negotiate with the service provider for additional sessions, refer the client to alternative sources for help, ask the client to pay out-of-pocket, or provide pro bono services. The *ACA Code of Ethics* (2014) makes it clear that counselors cannot abandon their clients (Section A.12). However, the *Code of Ethics* also stipulates that it is permissible for counselors to discontinue services in the following circumstances:

- It is clear that the client is no longer benefiting from counseling.
- The client does not pay the designated fees.
- The counselor is in jeopardy of harm by the client or another person with whom the client has a relationship.
- Agency limits do not allow services to continue.
- An appropriate referral is made, but the client declines the referral.

Standard A.11.d states, "When counselors transfer or refer clients to other practitioners, they ensure that appropriate clinical and administrative processes are completed and open communication is maintained with both clients and practitioners" (ACA, 2014). Although counselors cannot insist that a client accept a transfer or referral for services, they can talk with the client about options, demonstrate respect for the client's opinions, and honor the client's decision in a professional manner.

Facilitating Closing

Counseling relationships vary in length and purpose. It is vital to the health and well-being of the client to review the counseling process and client progress on a regular basis (Young, 2013). Individuals need time to prepare for the end of meaningful relationships. There may be some sadness even if the relationship ends in a positive way. Ending the therapeutic relationship should not necessarily be presented as the zenith of the counseling experience. Clinical mental health counselors can help normalize the closing process by acknowledging it as both an ending and a beginning.

Ideally, counselor and client should agree on when it is time to end the counseling relationship (Young, 2013). Often, verbal messages may indicate a readiness to terminate. For example, a client may say, "I really think I've made a lot of progress over the past few months," or a counselor may state, "You appear to be well on your way to no longer needing my services." Statements of this nature suggest recognition of growth or resolution. At other times, client behaviors signal that it is time to end the counseling relationship. Examples include a decrease in the intensity of work; more humor; consistent reports of improved coping skills; verbal commitments to the future; and less denial, withdrawal, anger, mourning, or dependence (Shulman, 2016; Welfel & Patterson, 2005).

How much time should counselors and clients devote to the closing process? Cormier (2016) believes that when a relationship has lasted more than three months, the final three to four weeks should be spent discussing the impact of termination. During this time, counselors can help clients review their accomplishments and give them credit for the gains they have made. Shulman (2016) suggests that in general, one-sixth of the time spent in a counseling relationship should focus on the upcoming termination. Although the exact amount of time spent in closing is a matter of judgment, there needs to be a time of preparation. Ideally, when the counseling relationship ends, clients will feel confident about living effectively without the support of the therapeutic relationship (Young, 2013).

To help with the closing process, counselors can use a procedure called **fading**, in which counseling appointments are spaced over increasing lengths of time. Counselors can also help with closing by encouraging clients to articulate ways they will utilize their newly developed coping skills in upcoming life experiences.

The Case of Heather

Heather, a 17-year-old adolescent, has been in counseling with you for 12 sessions. Her counseling goals included managing test-taking anxiety and overcoming her fear of public speaking. You and Heather have used several strategies to help her accomplish her goals, including deep-breathing exercises, cognitive and behavioral rehearsal, and thought-stopping techniques. Heather has made a lot of progress during the 12 sessions, and your last 2 sessions have seemed to be more conversation-oriented than therapy-oriented. You believe that it is time to move toward termination. What issues will you want to consider? How will you approach these issues with Heather? Will the fact that Heather is a minor affect the way you enter into the closing process? How do you think Heather will react to ending the counseling relationship? In what ways might you follow up with her after the closing process is complete?

Documenting Closing

When the counseling process is over, a closing statement, or closing summary, needs to be written and added to the client's record. Mitchell (2007) lists two reasons for carefully documenting termination: (a) the client may return for additional services, and (b) a client or the legal representative may initiate a malpractice suit. Well-written termination summaries, particularly in cases of premature closing, can protect counselors against the accusation of abandonment.

Documentation provides a clinical summary of the course of treatment and its outcomes. Piazza and Baruth (1990) and Mitchell (2007) recommend including the following information in the closing summary:

- A synopsis of the initial assessment, treatment plan, interventions, and outcomes
- An evaluation of the client's current level of functioning
- Reasons for closing
- Summary of progress toward goals, including final diagnostic impressions
- Follow-up plan—When clients are moving from inpatient to outpatient care, an after-care plan is needed that states identifying information about the new counselor and a plan for services.
- Other pertinent information—Whether or not additional information is documented is determined on a client-by-client basis.

As with case notes, the format of the termination summary may be determined by the organization in which a counselor practices. Clinical mental health counselors should be familiar with all record-keeping procedures associated with their work sites.

Following Up

Following up entails checking to see how the client is doing, with respect to the presenting issue, sometime after counseling has ended (Okun & Kantrowitz, 2015). In essence, it is a type of positive monitoring process that encourages client growth (Egan, 2014). The process is important because it reinforces the gains clients have made in counseling and helps both the counselor and the client reevaluate the counseling experience. Follow-up emphasizes the genuine care and concern counselors have for their clients. Short-term follow-up is usually conducted three to six months after a counseling relationship ends. Long-term follow-up is conducted at least six months after termination.

Follow-up may take many forms, but there are four main ways in which it is usually conducted (Cormier et al., 2017). The first is to invite the client in for a session to discuss any progress the client has continued to make in achieving desired goals. A second way is through a telephone call to the client. A call allows the client to report directly to the counselor, although only verbal interaction is possible. A third way is for the counselor to send the client a letter asking about the client's current status. A fourth and more impersonal way is for the counselor to mail or email the client a questionnaire dealing with current levels of functioning. Many public agencies use this type of follow-up as a way of demonstrating accountability. The last two procedures do not preclude the use of more personal follow-up procedures by individual counselors. Although time-consuming, a personal follow-up is probably the most effective way of evaluating past counseling experiences.

Referring and Recycling

Counselors are not able to help everyone who seeks assistance. When counselors realize that situations are unproductive, it is important for them to either terminate the relationship or make a referral. A **referral** involves arranging other assistance for clients when the initial arrangements are not likely to be helpful (Okun & Kantrowitz, 2015). Some of the more common reasons for making a referral include lack of competence on the part of the counselor (as long as the referral is not based on the counselor's personal values), lack of benefit to clients from services, or the possibility that continuing the counseling relationship will result in client harm (Barnett & Johnson, 2015).

Referrals involve a *how*, a *when*, and a *who*. The *how* concerns knowing how to make a referral in a manner that maximizes the possibility that clients will follow through with the referral process. Clients may resist a referral if they feel rejected by the counselor. When counselors refer clients, it is important to follow appropriate clinical and administrative procedures. It also is important to maintain open communication with clients and practitioners (Barnett & Johnson, 2015). When a counselor reaches an impasse with a certain client, the counselor should refer that client sooner rather than later. On the other hand, if the counselor has worked with a client for a while, the counselor should demonstrate sensitivity in discussing the possibility of referral.

The *who* of making a referral involves the person you are recommending to a client. The interpersonal ability of that professional may be as important initially as his or her skills if the referral is going to be successful. A helpful question to ask is whether the new counselor is someone you would feel comfortable sending a family member to see (MacCluskie & Ingersoll, 2001). Another consideration involves insurance panels. When appropriate, counselors can check to ensure that the new counselor will be covered under the client's insurance policy.

Recycling is an alternative when the counselor thinks the counseling process has not yet worked but has the potential to do so. Recycling involves the reexamination of all phases of the therapeutic process. Perhaps the goals were not properly defined, or unhelpful interventions were implemented. Regardless, when the counselor and client reexamine what has occurred in counseling, they can decide how or whether to revise and reinvest in the counseling process. Counseling, like other experiences, is not always successful on the first attempt. Recycling gives both counselor and client a second chance to achieve what each wants: positive change.

Summary and Conclusion

This chapter covered a wealth of material, ranging from the physical settings in which counselors work to specific activities that occur during the actual counseling process. Clinical mental health counselors know how to work with clients throughout the counseling process, including the initial phase, the working phase, and the closing phase.

In the initial counseling sessions, counselors work to establish rapport and set up a structure for success. During this stage, issues related to informed consent are addressed, including the nature of counseling, the counselor's background, fees, and expectations. Counselors also make efforts to get clients to take the initiative in the change process. Clients enter counseling for different reasons, and many clients are reluctant, resistant, or ambivalent. Counselors accept clients where they are, establish rapport, and help provide motivation. During the initial sessions, counselors gather information about clients either formally (e.g., in structured intake interviews) or less formally for the purpose of assessment. At the end of the initial phase, the counselor and client work collaboratively to set goals and design a treatment plan for change. The counselor uses the information acquired during the initial session and subsequent sessions to develop a case conceptualization, which facilitates treatment planning. Case conceptualization needs to be tentative and open to change.

During the working phase of counseling, clients move toward achieving therapeutic goals. The emphasis therefore shifts from understanding to activity. In selecting interventions, effective counselors integrate research with practice. They implement counseling procedures that are most likely to produce positive outcomes. Various common curative factors have been linked with effective counseling, including cognitive learning, affective experiencing, and rehearsal.

In the closing phase, counselors and clients gradually end the therapeutic relationship. An important part of termination is follow-up. In follow-up, client progress is monitored through phone calls, personal interviews, or another format agreed upon by the client and counselor.

Throughout the counseling process, practitioners need to document their interactions with clients. Careful record keeping includes writing treatment plans, case notes, and termination summaries. As clinical mental health counselors provide quality services to their clients, they simultaneously manage the necessary documentation with a high degree of professionalism.

MyCounselingLab

Try the Topic 3 Assignments: *Characteristics of the Effective Counselor.*

CHAPTER 5

Client Assessment and Diagnosis

ESB Professional/Shutterstock

CHAPTER OVERVIEW

From reading this chapter, you will learn about

- Ways clinical mental health counselors use assessment in counseling
- Methods and purposes of assessment
- Guidelines for using assessment
- Clinical diagnosis and commonly used diagnostic systems, including the *DSM-5*
- Biopsychosocial assessment and diagnosis

As you read, consider

- The multiple roles assessment plays in clinical mental health counseling
- What some of the key cultural concerns are that need to be considered when assessing clients
- The purpose of diagnosis
- The benefits and risks associated with diagnosis
- How clinical mental health counselors conduct a biopsychosocial assessment

She works in a world I have never known
*   full of rainbow pills and lilac candles*
*   woven together with simple time-stitches*
A pattern of color in a gray fabric factory
*   where she spends her days*
*   spinning threads*
*   that go to Chicago by night.*
Once with a little girl smile and a giggle
*   she flew to Atlanta in her mind,*
Opening the door to instant adventures
*   far from her present fatigue,*
That was a journal we shared
*   arranging her thoughts in a patchwork pattern*
*   until the designs and desires came together.*

Reprinted from *Patchwork*, by S. T. Gladding, 1974a, *Personnel and Guidance Journal, 53*, p. 39. Copyright © by Samuel T. Gladding.

Clinical mental health counselors are responsible for carrying out many different functions, some of which may depend on the settings in which the counselors work. Two general functions that clinical mental health counselors need to conduct skillfully are assessment and diagnosis. Assessment is an ongoing process in which counselors gather information about clients from several different sources and use that information to make decisions about treatment planning. Diagnosis is closely related to assessment, and is used in many private and public settings to describe clients' conditions, guide treatment planning, and apply for third-party reimbursement. This chapter provides information about assessment and diagnosis and examines issues related to the two processes.

The Case of Michelle

Michelle is a 24-year-old medical student. Recently she was driving home from a spring break vacation with her two best friends when she fell asleep at the wheel. Unable to regain control of the car, she swerved into another lane, colliding head-on with an oncoming car and leaving her friends in serious condition. Michelle survived with minimal injuries, but her two friends have been in the hospital for four weeks. Unable to overcome the guilt of her role in the accident, Michelle has withdrawn from her social network. She is having trouble sleeping at night and often experiences flashbacks during the day. She has lost much of her appetite and states that she does not remember anything from the accident. Her medical doctors believe she may have amnesia from the accident, but people close to her believe she is avoiding any discussion of the accident because of the guilt she feels. She refuses to visit her friends in the hospital because she believes she will be plagued by great anxiety and flashbacks. Since the accident, she has had a sudden and seemingly intractable change in personality, often wishing to spend time alone in her room. Her family worries she may be experiencing posttraumatic stress symptoms following the accident but are unable to get her to open up about her feelings.

If Michelle agreed to go to you for counseling, how would you begin to assess her situation? What hypotheses would you make about her behavior? What else might be going on? What diagnosis or diagnoses might apply? Think about these and other questions as you read this chapter on assessment and diagnosis.

ASSESSMENT IN COUNSELING

Assessment is a multifaceted activity that is integral to the counseling process. Although some people associate assessment with the early stages of counseling, it actually is an ongoing activity that takes place throughout the counseling process, from referral to follow-up (Drummond, Sheperis, & Jones, 2016; Hohenshil, 1996). Formal and informal methods of assessment help counselors gather information to determine the nature of clients' issues, the prevalence of their problems, the clients' strengths and skills, and the likelihood of counseling being beneficial. Systematic assessment helps counselors and clients develop an understanding of the presenting problems and issues, conceptualize the issue(s), select and implement effective interventions, and evaluate progress made in counseling (Whiston, 2017).

Assessment begins with the first counselor–client contact, as the counselor listens to the client's story and observes behaviors. During this initial stage, important data about the client are collected, counselors begin to hypothesize about the nature of the client's concerns, and decisions are made about whether counseling will be beneficial. To gather information about clients, clinical mental health counselors typically conduct intake interviews. In this section, additional information is provided about assessment in counseling, including methods and purposes of assessment, principles of sound assessment, diagnosis, and specific issues related to assessment and diagnosis.

Assessment Defined

The term **assessment** has been defined in numerous ways. Psychological assessment includes a combination of evaluative methods used to gather information about clients. Frequently, the terms **appraisal** and *assessment* are used interchangeably because both processes utilize formal and informal techniques, not just standardized tests (Whiston, 2017). **Psychological testing**, a term often associated with assessment, is just one of several methods counselors use to collect client information. A **psychological test** is defined by Anatasi and Urbina (1997) as an objective, standardized measure of behavior and is usually used for evaluation. Other methods of assessment include interviews, checklists, rating scales, and qualitative or experiential approaches. Counselors integrate and interpret the results of these evaluation methods to increase their understanding of clients and their situations.

As part of their training, clinical mental health counselors take at least one course in appraisal procedures, in which they learn methods and principles of assessment. It would be beyond the scope and purpose of this chapter to describe those methods and principles in depth. However, we do present a brief overview of the topic to highlight important factors related to assessment in counseling.

Methods of Assessment

Assessment procedures may be formal or informal, standardized or nonstandardized, and objective or subjective. Assessment can be used to measure attributes and behaviors in many domains, including personality, cognition, affect, ability, interests, values, and relationships. Clinical mental health counselors can choose from a wide spectrum of methods for assessing clients, including the following:

• *Standardized tests.* Psychological tests that are standardized must meet certain requirements for test construction, administration, and interpretation. Such tests use representative norm groups for scoring and interpretation and typically have been evaluated for reliability and validity. These tests also include uniform standards for administration. Examples of areas measured by standardized tests include aptitude, achievement, personality, interests, values, and skills.

• *Checklists and rating scales.* Checklists and rating scales provide subjective estimates of behaviors or attitudes based on observations made by the client or other observers. With checklists, clients or observers simply mark words or phrases that apply to the clients or their situations. Such tools can provide valuable information to counselors in a relatively brief time. Some checklists are standardized, such as the Symptom

Checklist-90–Revised (SCL-90–R; Derogatis, 1994) and the shorter version of the instrument, the Brief Symptom Inventory (BSI; Derogatis, 1993). These checklists, as well as
less formal checklists, are often used during intake sessions in mental health settings
(Whiston, 2017).

With rating scales, the rater indicates the degree or severity of the characteristic
being measured. For example, clients may be asked to rate their energy level on a graded
scale, from lethargic (1) to energetic (5). Informal rating scales may be used to determine
how clients perceive the intensity of the presenting problem. Standardized rating scales
that are completed by the clients and significant others can be especially helpful for
measuring a wide spectrum of behaviors. For example, the Conners–3 (Conners, 2008)
provides rating scales that are completed by parents and teachers (and by the adolescent,
in the case of older children) and are used to help assess attention-deficit/hyperactivity
disorder (ADHD), aggression, executive functions, and problems such as anxiety and
oppositional behavior.

• *Other inventories.*   Clinical mental health counselors may use a number of other
inventories besides rating scales and checklists to assess client concerns. For example, the
Minnesota Multiphasic Personality Inventory–2 (MMPI–2; Butcher, Dahlstrom, Graham,
Tellegen, & Kaemmer, 1989) is widely used by counselors in mental health settings
(Bubenzer, Zimpfer, & Mahrle, 1990). The MMPI–2 consists of 567 affirmative statements,
to which clients respond in one of three ways: *true, false,* or *cannot say.* In addition to
identifying individuals who may be experiencing psychiatric problems, the MMPI–2 is able
to discern important characteristics such as anger, alienation, depression, and social insecurity. Counselors need extensive training and experience to use the instrument accurately
and appropriately.

Another standardized instrument used by clinical mental health counselors is the NEO
Personality Inventory-3 (NEO-PI-3; McCrae & Costa, 2010). The NEO-PI-3 assesses the Big
Five personality factors: extroversion, agreeableness, conscientiousness, emotional stability
(neuroticism), and openness. Six subfactors, or **facets**, are associated with each primary factor. Clinical mental health counselors can use the NEO-PI-3 to help understand clients, build
empathy and rapport, provide feedback regarding personality traits, and guide treatment
planning (McCrae & Costa, 2010).

The Myers-Briggs Type Indicator (MBTI; Myers, McCaulley, Quenk, & Hammer,
1998) is frequently used in clinical mental health counseling. The MBTI, which is based
on the work of Carl Jung and Jungian theory, is the most widely used personality inventory for normal functioning (Quenk, 2000). The MBTI was initially developed by Kathar-
ine Briggs and her daughter, Isabel Briggs Myers. It is published by Consulting
Psychologists Press and frequently is taken on the computer, yielding a computer-gener-
ated report that is interpreted to clients by counselors. The assessment helps clients
examine differences and similarities of personality types based on four dimensions, which
are depicted in Figure 5–1.

• *Clinical interviews.*   Interviews are commonly conducted by counselors to assess
clients. Interviews can vary in format, ranging from relatively open and unstructured to
highly structured. During the past several years, many structured clinical interviews have
been published for research and practice purposes. Structured clinical interviews can be
especially useful in the current era of managed care, which stresses precision, time-limited
counseling, and demonstrated effectiveness.

EXTRAVERSION (E)	INTROVERSION (I)
• Draws energy from the outer world of people and things.	• Draws energy from the inner world of ideas and impressions.
SENSING (S)	**INTUITION (N)**
• Focuses on the present, on concrete information, and prefers to examine things using the five senses.	• Focuses on the future, with an emphasis on patterns and possibilities.
THINKING (T)	**FEELING (F)**
• Decisions are based primarily on logic and objective analysis.	• Decisions are based primarily on values and subjective evaluation of person-centered concerns.
JUDGING (J)	**PERCEIVING (P)**
• Prefers a planned, organized approach to life, where things are structured and settled.	• Prefers a flexible, spontaneous approach to life, where options are kept open.

FIGURE 5–1   The Four Myers-Briggs Type Indicator Dichotomies

A **structured clinical interview** consists of a list of behaviors, symptoms, and events to be addressed during an interview, guidelines for conducting the interview, and procedures for recording and analyzing information (Vacc & Juhnke, 1997). The questions are usually asked in an ordered sequence and typically are either diagnostic (specifically related to the *DSM*) or descriptive (providing data on emotional, behavioral, and social issues, but not for the purpose of diagnosis). Structured clinical interviews can be helpful in that they use preestablished questions to assess a wide range of behaviors in a consistent manner (Neukrug & Fawcett, 2015). However, the very structure of the interview may limit rapport building and may prevent the client from going into depth about important issues.

Whereas structured clinical interviews specify the order and wording of questions, semistructured interviews are less restrictive. **Semistructured interviews** address the same issues as structured interviews do, but they provide more flexibility in sequence, wording, and interpretation. These interviews use prescribed items, allowing the counselor to obtain necessary information in a timely manner, but also give the counselor leeway if a specific issue needs to be addressed.

Unstructured interviews provide even more flexibility and can be helpful in building rapport. However, they do not allow for the breadth of coverage provided by structured and semistructured interviews. Unstructured interviews also make it more likely that a clinician will spend excessive time focusing on certain items, thereby neglecting other items (Neukrug & Fawcett, 2015).

• *Mental status examination.*   The mental status examination (MSE) has been used by mental health professionals for over 80 years. A skillfully administered MSE provides information about a client's level of functioning and self-presentation. It may be conducted formally or informally during the initial interview and provides a format for organizing objective and subjective data gathered during the interview. Data gathered during the MSE may be used for initial diagnostic impressions.

The MSE assesses behaviors and attitudes that can be organized under the following six categories: (a) appearance, attitude, and activity; (b) mood and affect; (c) speech and language; (d) thought process, thought content, and perception; (e) cognition; and (f) insight and judgment. A brief description of each category is presented in Figure 5–2. When conducted proficiently, the MSE provides biological, social, and psychological information about the client that facilitates diagnosis and treatment planning.

THE MENTAL STATUS EXAMINATION

- **Appearance:** *Appearance* refers to the client's physical presentation, dress, grooming, cleanliness, and presence or absence of any disabilities. It can also include body position, posture, and use of eye contact.
- **Attitude:** *Attitude* refers to the client's approach to the interview and interactions with the counselor. Observations about attitude include tone of voice, facial expressions, attentiveness, and degree of evasiveness in responses. Attitude may change during the course of the interview. Examples of terms used to describe attitude include *cooperative, uncooperative, suspicious, hostile,* and *open.*
- **Activity:** This category refers to the client's level and quality of motor activity. Any observation of tics, tremors, mannerisms, compulsions, and perseveration is documented. Physical manifestations of emotions (e.g., laughing, crying, fist clenching, and grunting) are documented, as well.
- **Mood and affect:** *Mood* refers to the client's predominant internal feeling state, as reported by the client. *Affect* refers to the client's outward expression of an emotional state, as observed by the counselor, and varies in range and intensity.
- **Speech and language:** *Language* refers to the client's ability to comprehend word meanings and express them through writing and speaking. Speech and language defects include *defects of association* (i.e., the way words are grouped to make phrases) and *defects of rate and rhythm of speech* (e.g., pressured or delayed speech patterns).
- **Thought process, thought content, and perception:** During the MSE, thought content and process are inferred from what the client says and what the counselor observes. Disturbances of thought process, content, and perception can include delusions and hallucinations. Appraising a client's thoughts of violence to self or others is a crucial part of thought content assessment.
- **Cognition:** *Cognition* refers to the client's ability to use logic, intellect, reasoning, memory, and other higher-order cognitive functioning. During the MSE, cognition is assessed in a structured manner. Areas to be evaluated include attention, concentration, orientation, memory, and abstract thinking. Counselors can assess attention and concentration by asking clients to count backward by 7s or 3s from 100. Assessment of long- and short-term memory and orientation to person, place, time, and circumstance also helps evaluate cognitive functioning.
- **Insight and judgment:** These are the most advanced areas of mental functioning. **Insight** refers to the degree to which clients are aware of how personal traits and behaviors contribute to their current situations. **Judgment** refers to the ability to make decisions about an appropriate course of action.

FIGURE 5–2 The Mental Status Examination
Sources: Information from Polanski and Hinkle, 2000; Trzepacz and Baker, 1993.

• *Qualitative methods.* Qualitative assessment procedures include card sorts (see Box 5–1), structured exercises, creative activities, genograms, timelines, and other open-ended approaches. These methods are usually less formal than quantitative techniques, allowing for greater counselor and client flexibility and adaptability, which may make them especially suitable for a diverse clientele (Goldman, 1990). Qualitative methods elicit active client participation and provide ways for the counselor to understand the client's current problems within the context of the client's unique developmental history.

BOX 5–1   What Is a Card Sort?

A card sort is a qualitative method of assessment, which also serves as an intervention. It is an activity in which the client sorts cards that contain words describing various possibilities (e.g., vocational options, college choices, other life choices). Clients are asked to separate the cards into categories, such as *yes, no,* or *maybe*. In this way clients are able to organize their ideas and explain their decision-making processes. Through this process, counselors can help clients explore thoughts and feelings about the topics written on the cards.

The active nature of qualitative assessment promotes counselor–client interaction and client self-awareness while revealing information about the client that might otherwise remain unknown. Qualitative assessment activities can serve as interventions as well as tools for gathering data. Participation in such activities can help clients understand relationship patterns (e.g., creating and discussing a genogram), reexamine premature decisions (e.g., card sorts for career guidance), and become more aware of personal challenges and strengths (e.g., timelines, ecomaps).

Purposes of Assessment

The primary goal of assessment is to collect data about clients' behaviors, characteristics, and contexts that will then facilitate clinical decision making and evaluation. With this general purpose in mind, it is helpful to look at some of the specific ways that assessment facilitates counseling throughout the different stages of the process: in early stages for treatment planning, during the treatment phase as an actual intervention, and throughout the process and after termination for evaluation.

ASSESSMENT TO INFORM THE CLINICIAN AND GUIDE TREATMENT PLANNING. At the outset of counseling, clients may talk about a wide spectrum of concerns. One of the goals of assessment during this early stage of counseling is to work with clients to clarify and prioritize the issues. A systematic assessment helps ensure that counselors are helping clients with the most important issues. In addition to helping clients prioritize their concerns, M. E. Young (2013) suggests nine other reasons counselors need to spend sufficient time assessing clients during initial sessions:

• Assessment helps counselors know if they can provide the help the clients need.
• Assessment helps clients set useful goals.
• Assessment helps counselors understand the events related to the problems.

- Assessment provides information about environmental contexts that may be contributing to the problems.
- Assessment helps counselors recognize the uniqueness of individuals. To this end, counselors need to recognize that there is a tendency to view clients and their issues through one's own cultural lenses. Therefore there is a need to take precautions so as to assess clients objectively, respecting differences in cultural backgrounds and values.
- Assessment uncovers the potential for self-harm or violence (e.g., suicidal or homicidal ideation).
- Assessment reveals important historical data. For example, timelines can help counselors understand significant life events portrayed in sequential order.
- Assessment highlights strengths as well as concerns. Often, assessment is thought of as a tool that helps mental health professionals diagnose pathology. However, assessing clients' strengths, resources, and abilities enables counselors to select interventions that capitalize on clients' skills and support systems.
- Assessment helps clients become more aware of the severity of a problem (e.g., substance abuse). Frequently, clients are either unaware or in denial about a particular issue. Assessment is one way to help clients break through denial and begin to recognize the severity of a problem.

In summary, a thorough assessment helps the counselor gain a more complete understanding of the client. Information provided through assessment helps the counselor make sound decisions about treatment goals and intervention strategies. In some settings, such as in managed care environments, early assessment is often used to render a formal diagnosis.

ASSESSMENT AS AN INTERVENTION.   Beyond providing the counselor with information for diagnosis and treatment, assessment methods have the potential to serve directly as interventions. Formal and informal appraisal procedures can encourage client self-exploration and catalyze decision making. For example, discussing the results of a career interest inventory can help clients crystallize their understanding of personal interests, particularly as those interests relate to the world of work. Completing checklists of personal qualities can promote recognition and appreciation of strengths. Instruments like the Five Factor Wellness Inventory (5F-WEL; Myers & Sweeney, 2005b), which is designed to assist individuals in making healthier lifestyle choices, can help clients examine areas of their lives that may be out of balance. Qualitative methods such as card sorts or timelines encourage clients to engage in self-reflection, which can then facilitate movement in new directions. It is the interactive dialogue between counselor and client, either during an activity like a card sort or during the interpretation of the results of a psychological instrument, that transforms the assessment process from an information-gathering activity to a therapeutic intervention.

ASSESSMENT FOR EVALUATION AND ACCOUNTABILITY.   The need to evaluate the effectiveness of counseling has become increasingly important as managed care organizations and other agencies demand accountability. For evaluation to occur, goals and objectives need to be specified clearly during the early stages of counseling. Follow-up assessment can take several forms, including goal attainment scaling, self-monitoring techniques, posttests, client satisfaction surveys, and outcome questionnaires.

Using assessment for evaluation is not a straightforward activity. Counseling is a complex process, and its effectiveness depends on many variables. Also, demonstrating the effectiveness of counseling varies, depending on who completes the outcome measure (e.g., the client, the counselor, or an outside observer). For evaluation to be meaningful, counselors will want to consider measuring change from multiple perspectives, using several different methods.

In addition to outcome evaluation at the conclusion of counseling, assessment can be conducted at various points throughout the process to determine what has been helpful and what needs to be changed. By obtaining objective and subjective feedback from clients, counselors can modify interventions so that clients are more likely to meet their goals.

Principles of Sound Assessment

The process of psychological assessment is both a science and an art. Counselors need to have comprehensive knowledge about psychological assessment instruments and their psychometric properties (e.g., reliability, validity, norming procedures; Drummond et al., 2016). They also need to integrate that knowledge with strong communication and counseling skills as they select, administer, and interpret assessment instruments. To help counselors conduct assessment skillfully, several basic principles need to be considered (Hays, 2013; Hood & Johnson, 2007):

- Determine the purpose of assessment. Focusing on that purpose will help counselors identify which assessment procedures to conduct.
- Involve the client in selecting areas to be assessed and in the interpretation of assessment results.
- When using formal assessment instruments (e.g., standardized tests), make sure that the instruments demonstrate test trustworthiness, which includes validity, reliability, cross-cultural fairness, and practicality (Neukrug & Fawcett, 2015).
- Never rely on a single assessment tool; instead, use multiple methods of assessment. For example, a counselor may use information gained from an intake interview, the Beck Depression Inventory–II, an informal checklist, and outside observers to form an impression about whether a client is depressed.
- Consider the possibility of multiple issues, many of which may be interconnected (e.g., substance abuse, depression, and physical problems).
- Assess the client's environment. Problems occur in a social context and are rarely related to just one factor.
- Evaluate client strengths, as well as areas of concern. Identifying strengths and resources can help shift the focus from the problem to potential solutions.
- Consider alternative hypotheses, rather than simply looking for evidence to support a favorite hypothesis. What else might be going on with the client?
- Treat assessment results as tentative. As more information becomes available, initial assumptions may change.
- Be aware of cultural and personal biases that may influence decisions. Incorporate cultural data, such as measures of acculturation levels, into the assessment process.
- Consider the influence of individual factors—including age, gender, and educational level—on assessment results. In some cases (e.g., career interest inventories), gender-based norms should be used to interpret results.
- Consult with other professionals on a regular basis.
- Provide feedback about assessment results to clients. The feedback process can improve self-understanding and promote change.

Issues Related to Assessment

Counselors are responsible for conducting ethically sound assessment procedures. Several documents have been developed to help guide professionals who use assessment instruments with the public. The *Standards for Educational and Psychological Testing* (AERA, APA, & NCME, 2014) was developed by experts in several fields, including research, measurement, psychology, and counseling. This important document was originally developed in 1999 and was revised in 2014. It addresses a wide range of issues related to assessment practices, including test-user competencies, testing applications, and diversity considerations. Several additional sources are available on the Association for Assessment and Research in Counseling (AARC) website (http://aarc-counseling.org/resources), which can help clinical mental health counselors use assessment instruments responsibly and ethically.

COUNSELOR COMPETENCE.   Before using psychological assessment instruments, counselors need to consider their levels of training and experience. Competent assessment use is stressed in professional codes of ethics and has legal ramifications. Different instruments require different degrees of competence, and counselors need to be able to demonstrate skill in using a particular instrument before administering it. To monitor competence, many test publishers require professionals to provide a record of their educational background before allowing them to purchase assessment instruments. Although there are some exceptions, tests traditionally are categorized by levels (i.e., Levels A, B, and C) and are sold only to those professionals who meet the requirements for a particular level (Neukrug & Fawcett, 2015). Ultimately, the responsibility to select and administer an assessment instrument correctly lies with the individual counselor.

DIVERSITY CONSIDERATIONS.   A number of concerns have been raised about the misuse of assessment instruments with ethnic and racial minorities, people with disabilities, women, people from impoverished backgrounds, and other populations. Indeed, one of the most controversial issues in assessment relates to whether appraisal instruments are fair to people from different racial or ethnic groups (Drummond et al., 2016; Suzuki & Kugler, 2001). When selecting instruments, counselors need to consider a client's cultural background, gender, language, developmental level, and level of physical ability. Clinical mental health counselors will work with diverse populations and need to be skilled in cross-cultural assessment. Specific considerations related to assessing diverse clientele include the following:

- Select instruments that are appropriate for the population being tested; examine the purpose of the test, norming groups, and sensitivity of content. Be aware of cultural limitations of certain appraisal instruments.
- Determine the client's language proficiency, and when possible, use tests that are written in that language.
- When administering tests to individuals with disabilities, do everything possible to ensure that the instrument accurately measures the skills or aptitudes it is designed to measure, rather than any characteristics associated with the disability. Be aware of options available for clients with disabilities who require testing accommodations.
- Consider the potential effects of counselor–client cultural differences on the test-taking process and its results. Be culturally sensitive in establishing rapport, conducting the assessment, and interpreting the results.

Clinical mental health counselors can refer to a number of resources to help them become more effective in cross-cultural assessment. One resource that is of particular importance to counselors is the fourth revision of *Standards for Multicultural Assessment* (Association for Assessment in Counseling and Education, 2012). The document was produced by members of the AACE (now called AARC) and compiles standards associated with multicultural assessment from several documents. It also includes a section on advocacy as it relates to multicultural assessment.

Another helpful resource for developing competence in cross-cultural assessment is *The Handbook of Multicultural Assessment* (Suzuki, Ponterotto, & Meller, 2008). This handbook, which is in its third edition, provides information about general issues related to multicultural assessment as well as specific information related to ethical guidelines and clinical issues.

USE OF RESULTS.   In all situations, client welfare is the counselor's primary consideration. In assessment, issues related to privacy, confidentiality, and communication of results are especially pertinent. Many of the documents listed in this chapter (e.g., the *ACA Code of Ethics* and *Standards for Educational and Psychological Testing*) provide helpful guidelines for using assessment results. ACA's *Code of Ethics* (2014) addresses the use of assessment results in Section E: Evaluation, Assessment, and Interpretation. Section E provides standards in 13 areas of assessment:

- E.1. General (purpose of assessment, client welfare)
- E.2. Competence to Use and Interpret Assessment Instruments
- E.3. Informed Consent in Assessment
- E.4. Release of Data to Qualified Professionals
- E.5. Diagnosis of Mental Disorders
- E.6. Instrument Selection
- E.7. Conditions of Assessment Administration
- E.8. Multicultural Issues/Diversity in Assessment
- E.9. Scoring and Interpretation of Assessments
- E.10. Assessment Security
- E.11. Obsolete Assessments and Outdated Results
- E.12. Assessment Construction
- E.13. Forensic Evaluation: Evaluation for Legal Proceedings

The Case of Farah

Farah is a licensed professional counselor who has worked in a nonprofit agency for four years. She is working with a client, Paul, who wants to know more about his personality. He asks Farah to administer a personality assessment to him. Farah knows that the agency has two computerized personality instruments on its computer for use with clients: the MMPI–2, which she knows she is not qualified to administer, and the NEO-PI-3. Farah learned about the NEO-PI-R during her 2005 master's level appraisals course. She did not take the instrument herself, nor has she ever administered it. She has never seen the NEO-PI-3, which was published in 2010. However, it is a B-level instrument, and Farah thinks that she is qualified to administer B-level instruments. Is Farah qualified to administer the NEO-PI-3 to Paul? What ethical issues relate to this decision? If Farah were your employee, what would you suggest? What do you think Farah should tell Paul?

An issue related to the use of assessment results that directly affects clinical mental health counselors on a regular basis is that of diagnosis. Counselors routinely diagnose and treat clients with problems ranging from developmental concerns to more serious mental health conditions. Almost all settings in which clinical mental health counselors work require a diagnosis for reimbursement of services. A *DSM-5* (American Psychiatric Association [APA], 2013) assessment and diagnosis provides essential information that helps counselors and clients with goal setting and treatment planning. However, diagnostic procedures have the potential for abuse, in that "an inappropriate label could follow a person throughout life, affecting family, social, educational, and occupational status" (Hohenshil, 1996, p. 65). In diagnosis, it is crucial to use person-first language as a mechanism to separate the identity of an individual from any clinical diagnosis, disability, or chronic condition (Granello & Gibbs, 2016). For example, conveying that an individual is a "person who has a disability" is quite different from saying an individual is a "disabled person."

In addition to language, it is important to remember that diagnosis is an ongoing process. Its essential purpose is to aid in treatment planning and intervention, not to label clients.

DIAGNOSIS

Approximately 18% (or 43.6 million) American adults aged 18 and older are affected by mental health disorders in a given year (National Institute of Mental Health, 2014). To treat clients effectively, clinical mental health counselors need to be skilled at assessing and diagnosing clients. Indeed, CACREP (2016) standards require that accredited clinical mental health counseling programs provide evidence that students understand the diagnostic process and can use the principles and practices of diagnosis. Although some professionals believe that diagnosis contradicts a developmental approach to counseling, others maintain that an accurate diagnosis helps counselors determine the proper treatment for a disorder (Seligman, 2009). Many employers, licensing agencies, and insurance companies expect counselors to know how to formally diagnose mental disorders.

Diagnosis, either formal or informal, has always been a part of counseling (Hohenshil, 1996). For example, making a decision about whether a client's problem is a developmental issue or a form of pathology is, in fact, a form of diagnosis. In addition to making informal diagnoses, in recent years clinical mental health counselors have been expected to accrue skills in diagnosing using a formal diagnostic system, such as the *Diagnostic and Statistical Manual of Mental Health Disorders*. Currently, mental health practitioners use the *DSM-5* (APA, 2013), which is the most recent edition of the *DSM*. Clinicians also are expected to know how to use to use diagnostic codes from the *International Classification of Diseases* (*ICD-10*), which coordinate with *DSM-5* diagnoses.

Diagnosis is "the process of comparing the symptoms exhibited by the client with the diagnostic criteria of some type of classification system" (Hohenshil, 1996, p. 66). A diagnosis is not a judgmental label; rather, it is used to describe a client's systems in a way that can be understood by other professionals (Whiston, 2017). The purposes of diagnosis are to provide a common ground for understanding what a diagnostic category means and to help counselors determine efficacious treatment. Seligman (2009, pp. 374–375) outlines several reasons for becoming skilled in diagnosis:

- A diagnostic system provides a consistent framework and set of criteria for naming and describing mental disorders.

- Accurate diagnosis enables counselors to understand client symptoms and anticipate the typical course of a disorder.
- Diagnosis enables counselors to make use of the growing body of research on treatment effectiveness (e.g., what types of interventions are most likely to ameliorate a specific disorder) and develop a treatment plan that is likely to be efficacious.
- Diagnosis provides a common language for mental health professionals, which facilitates parity, credibility, communication, and collaboration.
- Many diagnoses are linked to standardized assessment inventories, such as the MMPI–2 and the Millon Clinical Multiaxial Inventory III, thus providing a direct link between assessment and diagnosis.
- When counselors make diagnoses and treatment plans according to an accepted system, they can more easily demonstrate accountability and are less vulnerable to malpractice suits.
- Using a standardized, accepted system of diagnosis helps counselors obtain third-party reimbursement for services, thereby making counseling more affordable to those who might otherwise not be able to pay.
- Sharing diagnoses with clients, when appropriate, can help them understand their symptoms. Knowing that other people deal with the same symptoms and that information and treatment are available can be reassuring.
- Diagnosis can help counselors determine whether they have the skills and training needed to help a particular client or whether it would be better to refer that client to another mental health professional.

Although it is important for mental health counselors to develop strong diagnostic skills, there also are risks and concerns associated with the diagnostic process. Some of those risks include the following (e.g., see Granello & Young, 2012; Seligman, 2009):

- Diagnostic labels can be stigmatizing if misused and may lead to misperceptions of the person if the diagnosis becomes known.
- Diagnosis is part of the medical illness–cure tradition and is not consistent with a holistic, developmental approach to counseling that emphasizes wellness, multicultural concerns, contextual influences, and strength-based approaches.
- Diagnosis is historically contingent and socially constructed, not absolute reality.
- Diagnosis can lead to pathologizing clients so that they are viewed *as* the disorder (e.g., schizophrenics, borderlines), rather than as persons with particular concerns and symptoms.
- Diagnosis may have a negative impact on people's ability to obtain insurance and, in some situations, affect their employment opportunities.
- The most common diagnostic systems (e.g., the *DSM-5* and the *ICD-10*) are steeped in the Western concept of mental illness and may not be relevant for people from other cultures, although strides have been made to make the *DSM-5* more culturally relevant.
- Attaching a diagnostic label to a client puts the focus of treatment on the individual rather than on the family or the social system. In some cases, this can cause the family to pathologize the individual rather than work collectively on relationships and shared issues (Gladding, 2015).

Although there are risks associated with the process of diagnosis, many of those risks can be avoided by conducting skillful and comprehensive assessments, presenting diagnostic information in such a way that it is understood by clients and families, and honoring client confidentiality. To make proper diagnoses, counselors must receive extensive training and supervision. They should know diagnostic classifications, which are described in the *DSM-5* (APA, 2013).

Using the *DSM-5* in Mental Health Counseling

In the United States, the most widely used system for psychiatric diagnosis is the *Diagnostic and Statistical Manual of Mental Disorders* (*DSM*). Currently in its fifth edition, the *DSM-5* (APA, 2013) includes over 200 diagnoses that are divided into 20 classifications.

WHAT IS A MENTAL DISORDER?   The *DSM-5* (APA, 2013) states that a **mental disorder** is

> a syndrome characterized by clinically significant disturbance in an individual's cognition, emotion regulation, or behavior that reflects a dysfunction in the psychological, biological, or developmental processes underlying mental functioning. (p. 22)

For a syndrome to be considered a mental disorder, two requirements must be met. There must be sufficient evidence that the symptoms represent a dysfunction in the processes underlying mental functioning. Also, the dysfunction must cause harm to the person in regard to psychological functioning that is clinically significant (APA, 2013; First & Wakefield, 2013).

It is important to note that behaviors that are culturally sanctioned are not considered mental disorders. Cultural and religious beliefs must be taken into account when making decisions about whether certain beliefs are delusions. For example, hearing voices may be part of a culturally sanctioned religious experience (Reichenberg & Seligman, 2016). Furthermore, professionals in the counseling field know that many people who seek counseling do not have mental disorders. For example, if Heather is experiencing relationship problems with her partner of five years and is trying to make a decision about whether to stay in the relationship or leave, she does not have a mental disorder unless she exhibits distress, impairment, or significant risk to herself or others.

DSM diagnoses are made based on the clinician's evaluation of certain criteria. Counselors are not trained to work with all the disorders represented in the *DSM*; however, they are expected to be knowledgeable about the disorders and aware of their own areas of competence. For instance, if a client presents with a major neurocognitive disorder, which is characterized by multiple cognitive impairments, the counselor may be part of a treatment team, but the primary treatment will usually come from a physician.

Overview of Mental Disorders and Conditions

In this section, the 20 categories of mental disorders that are described in depth in the *DSM-5* are briefly reviewed (APA, 2013). Two categories that are not considered mental disorders but are listed in Section 2 of the *DSM-5* are also described. People entering the field of clinical mental health counseling need to master *DSM* terminology and differential diagnosis (i.e., distinguishing between similar disorders by comparing their signs and symptoms).

- **Neurodevelopmental Disorders.** Neurodevelopmental disorders first appear in early childhood, often before a child starts school. Disorders manifest in difficulties in personal, social, and academic functioning. Examples include intellectual disabilities, communication disorders, autism spectrum disorders, attention-deficit/

hyperactivity disorder, specific learning disorders, motor disorders, tic disorders, and other neurodevelopmental disorders. One of the more controversial changes made in the *DSM-5* was the combining of Asperger's disorder, childhood disintegrative disorder, and pervasive developmental disorder not otherwise specified under one umbrella. Because autism spectrum disorder occurs on a spectrum, three levels based on the degree of severity and the level of needed support are included in the diagnosis.

- **Schizophrenia Spectrum and Other Psychotic Disorders.** Schizophrenia spectrum and other psychotic disorders all have one common trait: psychotic symptoms, which include delusions, hallucinations, and thought disorders (Reichenberg & Seligman, 2016). The disorders, which range in severity, include schizotypal personality disorder (which is also listed in the category of personality disorders), delusional disorder, brief psychotic disorder, schizophreniform disorder, schizophrenia, schizoaffective disorder, substance/medication-induced psychotic disorder, psychotic disorder due to another medical condition, catatonic disorders, and other specified and unspecified schizophrenia disorders.
- **Bipolar and Related Disorders.** These mood disorders have been separated intentionally from the category depressive disorders due to their differences. Clients with bipolar and related disorders cycle between bouts of mania or hypomania and depression, which at times can be debilitating. Disorders in this category include bipolar I, bipolar II, cyclothymic disorder, substance/medication-induced bipolar or related disorder, bipolar or related disorder associated with another medical condition, and other specified and unspecified bipolar or related disorders.
- **Depressive Disorders.** Clients with depressive disorders experience depressed mood as the primary concern. Examples of depressive disorders include disruptive mood dysregulation disorder (the onset is typically before age six), major depressive disorder, persistent depressive disorder (previously known as dysthymia), premenstrual dysphoric disorder, substance/medication-induced depressive disorder, depressive disorder due to another medical condition, and other specified and unspecified depressive disorders.
- **Anxiety Disorders.** Anxiety disorders are characterized by the shared features of excessive fears and anxiety, combined with behavioral disturbances. Eleven disorders are included in this category: separation anxiety disorder (which typically occurs in childhood), selective mutism (which also typically occurs in childhood), specific phobia, social anxiety disorder, panic disorder, panic attack specifier, agoraphobia, generalized anxiety disorder, substance/medication-induced anxiety disorder, anxiety disorder due to another medical condition, and other specified and unspecified anxiety disorders. The various disorders differ from one another in regard to the fears, anxieties, and avoidant behaviors.
- **Obsessive–Compulsive and Related Disorders.** Disorders in this category can be debilitating and prevent people from participating fully in their lives (Reichenberg & Seligman, 2016). Disorders in this category include obsessive–compulsive disorder, body dysmorphic disorder, hoarding disorder, trichotillomania (hair pulling), excoriation (skin picking), substance/medication-induced obsessive–compulsive and related disorders, obsessive–compulsive and related disorders due to another medical condition, other specified and unspecified obsessive–compulsive and related disorders, and unspecified obsessive–compulsive disorders.

- **Trauma- and Stressor-Related Disorders.** Traumatic life events can have pervasive detrimental effects on people's psychological and physical well-being. Disorders in this category include reactive attachment disorder (which begins in childhood), disinhibited social engagement disorder (which also begins in childhood), posttraumatic stress disorder, acute stress disorder, adjustment disorders, other specified trauma- and stressor-related disorders, and unspecified trauma- and stressor-related disorders.

- **Dissociative Disorders.** Dissociative disorders are characterized by a loss in continuity of experience that can cause individuals to misinterpret identity, surroundings, and memory (Neukrug & Fawcett, 2015). Diagnoses include dissociative identity disorder, dissociative amnesia, depersonalization/derealization disorder, and other specified and unspecified dissociative disorders.

- **Somatic Symptom and Related Disorders.** Previously referred to as somatoform disorders, the disorders in this category are characterized by thoughts, feelings, and behaviors related to somatic (physical) symptoms. Disorders in this category include somatic symptom disorder, illness anxiety disorder, conversion disorder, psychological factors affecting other medical conditions, factitious disorder, other specified somatic symptom and related disorders, and unspecified somatic symptom and related disorders.

- **Feeding and Eating Disorders.** These disorders are characterized by a persistent disturbance of the amount or kind of food individuals ingest. Results can significantly impair physical health or psychosocial functions (APA, 2013). Examples of feeding and eating disorders include pica (eating one or more nonfood substances, such as soil, paper, soap, and chalk, on a persistent basis), avoidant/restrictive food intake disorder, anorexia nervosa, bulimia nervosa, binge-eating disorder, other specified feeding or eating disorders, and unspecified feeding or eating disorders.

- **Elimination Disorders.** These disorders typically occur during childhood, but can manifest at any point in a person's life. The disorders include enuresis (inappropriate elimination of urine) and encopresis (inappropriate elimination of feces). Both disorders may be voluntary or involuntary. Other specified and unspecified elimination disorders are also included in this category. The diagnosis of enuresis or encopresis is not made if the client has neurogenic bladder, spina bifida, or other medical conditions that cause inappropriate voiding or fecal elimination.

- **Sleep-Wake Disorders.** The *DSM-5* classification of these disorders "is intended for mental health and medical clinicians" (those caring for adult, geriatric, and pediatric patients). Ten disorders are included in the category, including insomnia disorder, hypersomnolence disorder, narcolepsy, breathing-related sleep disorders, circadian rhythm sleep-wake disorders, non–rapid eye movement (NREM) sleep arousal disorders, nightmare disorder, rapid eye movement (REM) sleep behavior disorder, restless legs syndrome, and substance/medication-induced disorders. Individuals with sleep-wake disorders experience dissatisfaction with their quality of sleep, which results in daytime distress and impairment. It is often necessary to refer people with sleep-wake disorders to a sleep specialist.

- **Sexual Dysfunctions.** Many factors correlate with sexual dysfunctions, including medical conditions, relationship issues, aging, and cultural or religious factors (APA, 2013). Therefore, it is important for clinicians to take these factors into account before rendering a diagnosis of a particular sexual dysfunction. The diagnoses included in this category include delayed ejaculation, erectile disorder, female orgasmic disorder, female sexual interest/arousal disorder, genito-pelvic pain/penetration disorder, male hypoactive sexual desire disorder, premature ejaculation, substance/medication-induced sexual dysfunction, other specified sexual dysfunctions, and unspecified sexual dysfunctions.

- **Gender Dysphoria.** This disorder was described as gender identity disorder in earlier versions of the *DSM*, but the term was considered pejorative. Individuals with gender dysphoria experience a marked incongruence between their expressed gender and the gender others assign to them. The disorders in this category include gender dysphoria in children, gender dysphoria in adolescents and adults, other specified gender dysphoria, and unspecified gender dysphoria.

- **Disruptive, Impulse-Control, and Conduct Disorders.** People diagnosed with disorders in this category demonstrate a lack of emotional and behavioral self-control. Disorders include oppositional defiant disorder (which typically is exhibited in childhood); conduct disorder; intermittent explosive disorder; pyromania; kleptomania; and other specified disruptive, impulse-control, and conduct disorders.

- **Substance-Related and Addictive Disorders.** In previous editions of the *DSM*, a distinction was made between substance abuse and substance dependence. Now those two categories are merged into one category: **substance use disorder**. The primary reason for merging the two disorders is that substance abuse disorder exists on a continuum (Reichenberg, 2014). Many diagnoses are included in this category, including alcohol-related use disorder; caffeine-related disorders; cannabis-related disorders; hallucinogen-related disorders; phencyclidine use disorder; other hallucinogen use disorders; hallucinogen persisting perception disorder; inhalant-related disorders; opioid-related disorders; sedative, hypnotic, and anxiolytic-related disorders; stimulant-related disorders; tobacco-related disorders; other (or unknown) substance-related disorders; non-substance-related disorders; and gambling disorder. Gambling disorders are considered **behavioral disorders**. It is expected that future editions of the *DSM* will include other behavioral disorders with addictive potential, including Internet gaming, shopping, and pornography.

- **Neurocognitive Disorders.** Neurocognitive disorders are diagnosed when a client exhibits a significant decline in cognitive functioning. The decline is acquired rather than developmental (Reichenberg, 2014). Neurocognitive disorders include delirium and major or mild neurocognitive disorders. Several specifiers are used to help clinicians differentiate among the neurocognitive disorders, most of which are due to medical conditions.

- **Personality Disorders.** Clients with personality disorders demonstrate enduring patterns of functioning that are maladaptive, are inflexible, and significantly impair social and occupational functioning or cause subjective distress (Maxmen & Ward, 1995). The maladaptive behavior is manifested in at least two of the following areas: cognition, interpersonal functioning, affectivity, and impulse control.

Personality disorders can be difficult to diagnose and treat. Because clients' perceptions of their personality disorders typically are **egosyntonic** (i.e., the disorder is an integral part of the self), clients may be less likely to believe that their problems are changeable

(Whiston, 2017). Ten personality disorders are described in the *DSM-5* and are grouped into three clusters: Cluster A (paranoid, schizoid, and schizotypal personality disorders), Cluster B (antisocial, borderline, histrionic, and narcissistic personality disorders), and Cluster C (avoidant, dependent, and obsessive–compulsive personality disorders). People with Cluster A personality disorders often appear odd or eccentric. Clients with Cluster B disorders tend to appear dramatic, emotional, or erratic. In contrast, individuals diagnosed with Cluster C disorders appear anxious or fearful. In addition to the three clusters, a client can be diagnosed with an unspecified personality disorder as well as a personality change due to another medical condition (Neukrug & Fawcett, 2015).

Diagnosis of a personality disorder involves evaluating the client's long-term patterns of functioning, with the particular characteristics of the disorder being evidenced by early adulthood. It is important to take into account the client's ethnic, cultural, and social background to avoid misdiagnosis.

- **Paraphilic Disorders.** Paraphilic disorders refer to an abnormal or unnatural attraction, such as pedophilia (adults attracted to sexual activity with children). To be classified as a disorder, the paraphilia must currently cause distress or impairment to the individual or cause harm or risk of harm to others. Paraphilic disorders include voyeuristic disorder, exhibitionistic disorder, frotteuristic disorder, sexual masochism disorder, sexual sadism disorder, pedophilic disorder, fetishistic disorder, transvestic disorder and other specified and unspecified paraphilic disorders.
- **Other Mental Disorders.** Four disorders are included in this category. They cause symptoms characteristic of mental disorders and cause clients significant distress but do not meet the full criteria for any other mental disorder (Reichenberg, 2014). The four disorders are listed as other specified mental disorder due to another medical condition, unspecified mental disorders due to another medical condition, other specified mental disorders, and unspecified mental disorders.

The following two categories are included in the *DSM-5* as disorders, but they are not mental health disorders. They are included in the *DSM-5* because medication is used in the treatment of mental disorders and other conditions (Reichenberg, 2014).

- **Medication-Induced Mental Disorders and Other Adverse Effects of Medication.** Some medications prescribed for the treatment of mental disorders have the undesired effect of causing movement disorders, such as tremors or muscular rigidity. Other medications can cause symptoms when they are discontinued. Some of the examples of disorders in this category include neuroleptic-induced parkinsonism, medication-induced acute dystonia, tardive dyskinesia, medication-induced postural tremor, and antidepressant discontinuation syndrome. Several other disorders are included in this category, as well. Clinicians need to be aware of the medications their clients are taking so that they can diagnose appropriately.
- **Other Conditions That May Be a Focus of Clinical Assessment.** Oftentimes, clients are in environments that may contribute to their seeking help. In the *DSM-TR-IV* (APA, 2000), these conditions were referred to as V-Codes. Examples include relational problems, psychological or sexual abuse, violence, economic problems, and occupational problems. Clinicians record these problems as *ICD-10* Z Codes, which can be found online at www.icd10data.com/ICD10CM/Codes/Z00-Z99. They are also listed in the *DSM-5*, beginning on page 715.

Diagnosing Using the *DSM-5*

The *DSM-5* includes several changes from the *DSM-TR-IV*, not only in regard to the categories of disorders but also in regard to how to diagnose. The most significant changes include the elimination of the multiaxial system of diagnosis, the alignment of diagnostic codes with *ICD-10* codes, the use of a dimensional approach to diagnosing, a greater emphasis on developmental and lifestyle considerations, and an expansion of gender-related and cultural considerations (Reichenberg, 2014). Rather than go into detail about each of the changes, we provide an overview of ways those changes affect the diagnostic process for clinical mental health counselors.

NONAXIAL SYSTEM OF DIAGNOSIS. Earlier versions of the *DSM* used a multiaxial system of diagnosis. Such a system allowed counselors to organize information based on clients' symptoms, their physical conditions, their levels of coping, current stressors, and a global assessment of functioning. The nonaxial system in the *DSM-5* uses a single diagnostic recording system. Mental health disorders, medical conditions, and psychosocial or environmental issues are listed on one axis. The principal diagnosis, along with the matching *ICD-10* code, is listed first, followed by other mental health disorders that may not be of primary concern. Medical conditions, along with *ICD-10* codes are listed next, followed by other conditions that may be a focus in counseling. These conditions are listed as Z codes in the *ICD-10*. Previously, they were listed as V codes. The global assessment of functioning (GAF) score that used to be listed on Axis V is no longer used. However, an assessment instrument that is being researched, the World Health Organization Disability Assessment Schedule 2.0 (WHODAS 2.0), assesses functioning in six domains and is described in depth in Section 3 of the *DSM-5*. The WHODAS 2.0 provides a way for clinicians to access overall client functioning (Reichenberg, 2014).

DIMENSIONAL APPROACH TO DIAGNOSIS. The *DSM-5* uses a dimensional approach to diagnosis. Mental disorders vary in severity and represent a continuum of behavior. Thus, diagnosis is done using a spectrum approach. For example, a client may meet the criteria for generalized anxiety disorder, but the disorder is considered mild, instead of moderate or severe.

To help with diagnosis, the *DSM-5* has added many specifiers to several disorders to enhance the utility of the diagnosis. Example of those specifiers include the following (Reichenberg, 2014):

- Course (e.g., in partial remission)
- Severity (e.g., mild, moderate, severe)
- Frequency (e.g., daily)
- Duration (e.g., minimum of one year)
- Descriptive features (with minimal insight)

ALIGNMENT WITH *ICD-10* AND FUTURE *ICD* CODES. One of the primary goals of the *DSM-5* was to harmonize mental diagnoses with *ICD* codes, thereby increasing a common language between the World Health Organization (WHO) and the American Psychiatric Association (APA, 2013). The *ICD* codes are used to clarify the diagnosis. For example, consider a client presenting with major depressive disorder. He has suicidal thoughts and has made a previous attempt at suicide. He reports that he has experienced major depression three times within the past year. He meets all the criteria for major depressive disorder. He states that he uses alcohol to self-medicate. He has been divorced from his wife for five years. The recording of his disorder would be as follows:

F33.2 major depressive disorder, recurrent episode, severe (principal diagnosis)

F10.10 alcohol use disorder, mild

Z63.5 disruption of family by separation or divorce

Diagnosis and Treatment

Diagnosis is just one part of a comprehensive assessment that leads to treatment planning. It is a crucial part, however, in that it affects the delivery of counseling services, third-party reimbursement, and professional credibility.

Seligman (2009) developed a model to help counselors integrate assessment, diagnosis, and treatment planning based on the *DSM-IV-TR* diagnostic system. The title of the model is a mnemonic device called DO A CLIENT MAP. The DO A CLIENT MAP is still relevant. Each letter of the mnemonic addresses one of the areas to be considered during diagnosis and treatment planning, thus providing a comprehensive organized guide for working with a client.

1. **D**iagnosis according to the *DSM-5*.
2. **O**bjectives of treatment (written as treatment goals)
3. **A**ssessment procedures (formal and informal procedures)
4. **C**linician characteristics (considerations related to clinical background, gender, ethnicity, and other issues)
5. **L**ocation of treatment (inpatient or outpatient, site)
6. **I**nterventions (theoretical approach and specific interventions)
7. **E**mphasis of treatment (level of support needed; level of directiveness by the counselor; focus on cognitive, behavioral, or emotional areas, or a combination of the three)
8. **N**umbers (individual, group, or family counseling)
9. **T**iming (frequency, pace, and duration of treatment)
10. **M**edication (determine whether a referral for medication is needed)
11. **A**djunct services (additional activities to supplement the counseling process, such as tutoring)
12. **P**rognosis (based on the diagnosis, the severity of the disorder, and the client's levels of support)

Clinical mental health counselors will want to use the *DSM-5* responsibly, recognizing the importance of cultural influences and social context on client behaviors (Whiston, 2017). Counselors will need to examine assessment information and diagnostic criteria critically, so that the diagnostic process is used for its intended purpose: to inform and guide treatment.

Using what you have learned in this chapter, hypothesize what might be going on with Javed. Follow Reichenberg and Seligman's (2016) DO A CLIENT MAP model, and determine how you would address each of the 12 areas. What cultural issues need to be considered? What other issues need to be considered?

The Case of Javed

Javed is a 20-year-old, first-generation American of Pakistani parents. He is a sophomore at a large university. He is nearing the end of his sophomore year and has been a successful student until this past semester.

Javed's roommate, who is his older brother, Majid, has noticed that Javed has been spending more and more time by himself, avoiding contact with social groups. He attends class sporadically and states that he is tired all the time. Javed used to accompany his older brother home every weekend to visit their large extended family, but lately Javed has been making excuses to stay on campus and play the online game World of Warcraft, often until the early hours of the morning. In general, Javed seems irritable and depressed, spending more time alone and doing just enough to get by in his classes.

Javed's mother is also concerned about his behavior. His conversations with her on the phone—formerly a weekly event—have become infrequent, and he seems preoccupied when he talks with her. His mother says she is disappointed and feels slighted. According to her, he avoids her questions about school and about his future plans. He has begun responding in English, refusing to speak in Urdu.

At the end of this semester, Javed will be expected to formally declare a major, and his parents are expecting him to pursue an undergraduate track that will lead him to medical school. Javed is a talented visual artist and spends time drawing elaborate pictures of characters and scenes from World of Warcraft and other online games. His older brother has stated that his artwork is "fantastic and full of imagination" and that he talks about his online life and his love of comic book art more than he talks about his biology classes. Javed has expressed an interest in attending an art class but has found that it conflicts with his hectic schedule as a biology major.

BIOPSYCHOSOCIAL ASSESSMENT AND DIAGNOSIS

The **biopsychosocial (BPS) model** is an approach to medicine and mental health that recognizes the interrelated, integrated roles played by biology, psychology, and social/cultural factors in the maintenance of wellness and the understanding of illness. One of the 2016 CACREP Standards for Clinical Mental Health Counseling (Foundations 5.C.1.c.) states that clinical mental health counselors need to know "the principles, models and documentation formats of biopsychosocial case conceptualization and treatment planning" (CACREP, 2016, p. 24). Moreover, many agencies expect clinicians to be skilled at gathering biopsychosocial information about their clients. Therefore, in this section we outline a formal, generic method of BPS assessment.

BPS assessment, as the name indicates, includes biological, psychological, and social factors that may be contributing to a client's level of well-being. To get an accurate picture of what is going on with clients, clinical mental health counselors need to gather information about each of these areas. Often, information is gathered during intake interviews. However, assessment is a fluid process, and clinical mental health counselors will want to continue monitoring what is going on with clients in these three areas throughout the course of treatment. The outline presented next describes a series of questions and guidelines that can help a counselor conduct a thorough BPS assessment (Gallagher, 2011).

Biopsychosocial Assessment and Reporting

BIOLOGY (BIO)

- What medical conditions does the client have? Examples are numerous, and the client may or may not be getting treatment for medical conditions. Some examples of chronic medical conditions include fibromyalgia, chronic pain, arthritis, Crohn's disease, irritable bowel syndrome, polycystic ovarian syndrome, cancer, and diabetes.
- Has the client had a physical within the past year?
- What genetic factors may be influencing the client's well-being?
- Have the client's thyroid hormone levels been checked? Hyperthyroidism (when the thyroid hormone level is too high) can lead to nervousness, insomnia, palpitations, breathlessness, fatigue, weight loss, and tremors. Hypothyroidism (when hormone levels are too low) can result in hypersomnia, fatigue, loss of interest, concentration difficulties, feelings of hopelessness or helplessness, a preoccupation with death, and weight gain.
- Has the client ever experienced a traumatic brain injury (TBI)? TBI can result in personality changes, speech impediments, cognitive impairments, depression, anxiety, anger, and seizures.
- Is the client on birth control medication? Birth control pills sometimes cause clients to feel depressed, anxious, or out of control.
- Does the client have allergies? Allergies can cause memory impairment, concentration difficulties, depression, and other medical concerns.
- What medications is the client taking, including over-the-counter medications?

PSYCHOLOGICAL (PSYCHO)

- What brings the client to counseling at this time? What is the presenting problem?
- What is the history of the presenting concern? When did it begin, what stressors may be contributing to the problem, and how frequently does the client experience the problem?
- Is the client experiencing a developmental, psychological, or psychopathological concern?
- Does the client have a history of addiction or dependency?
- Is there a family history of addiction or psychiatric disorders?
- What is the client's mental status? The counselor may choose to use the mental status examination to determine the answer to this question.
- Is the client experiencing suicidal or homicidal ideation?

SOCIAL

- What is the client's personal history? (Topics to ask about include parents, siblings, birth order, and the client's relationships. The counselor will also want to find out if the client has experienced trauma or abuse.)
- Who is in the client's support system?
- Does the client have a spouse or partner? What is that relationship like? Who else provides support for the client? Does the client have children? If so, what are those relationships like? What is the client's living situation?
- What cultural factors are relevant to the client's presenting problem?

- What is the client's level of education?
- What is the client's work history?
- Has the client experienced any legal difficulties?
- What is the client's current financial situation?

SUMMARY AND INTERPRETATION OF INFORMATION GATHERED

- Incorporate significant information from each section to inform a diagnosis, if a diagnosis is warranted. Include the symptoms that apply to the diagnosis. Describe related events, history, and perceptions that may inform the diagnosis.

SHORT-TERM GOALS

- What does the client want to happen in counseling? Recognize that these goals may change over time.

DIAGNOSTIC IMPRESSION

- What are your diagnostic impressions based on the BPS assessment? Rendering a diagnosis may not be possible if you are still gathering information, in which case you may want to either defer diagnosis or classify the diagnosis as provisional.
- It may be that no diagnosis is appropriate.
- Write "per history" if the client reports prior diagnoses that are not indicated in his or her current presentation.
- If you are recording a Diagnostic Impression section for your agency, be sure to include information about diagnoses, medical conditions, and other areas of concern. Also recognize that in some cases, the best option is to write, "No diagnosis."

Examples of written BPS assessments can be found online. Reading them will help you gain a better understanding of how all the pieces of the BPS model fit together to inform treatment planning.

Summary and Conclusion

In this chapter, assessment and diagnosis—two essential elements of counseling in most clinical mental health settings—were described. Assessment is a process that occurs throughout counseling and serves several purposes. It helps counselors and clients conceptualize presenting problems, serves to guide treatment planning, acts as an intervention, and helps counselors evaluate treatment progress and outcomes. Counselors can choose from a variety of assessment tools, including standardized tests, rating scales, interviews, the mental status examination, and qualitative approaches. There are a number of sound appraisal principles that counselors will want to follow, including the use of multiple methods to assess clients. Some of the issues that affect the assessment process include counselor competence, assessment of diverse populations, and use of assessment results.

Closely related to the process of assessment is diagnosis. Diagnosis has become increasingly important for clinical mental health counselors over the course of the past few decades. Consequently, clinical mental health counselors need to be familiar with the most commonly used system of diagnosing mental and emotional conditions: the *Diagnostic and Statistical Manual of Mental Disorders* (APA, 2013). The *DSM-5* provides a way for clinicians to assess clients more accurately. Although clinical mental health counselors do not treat all types of diagnoses, they must be familiar with signs and symptoms associated with each so that they can either plan appropriate interventions or make appropriate referrals.

Clinical mental health counselors need to know how to assess clients from a biopsychosocial (BPS) perspective. The components of a BPS assessment and sample questions that can help clinical mental health counselors conduct such an assessment have been provided in the last part of this chapter.

MyCounselingLab

Try the Topic 1 Assignments: *Assessment and Diagnosis*.

CHAPTER 6

Holistic Approaches to Clinical Mental Health Counseling

Samuel Borges Photography/Shutterstock

CHAPTER OVERVIEW

From reading this chapter, you will learn about

- What it means to approach counseling holistically
- The biopsychosocial model, its components, and ways it can be used in counseling
- Ways spirituality can be infused into the counseling process and benefits of mindfulness
- Wellness-based counseling and wellness models used in counseling
- The importance of prevention and ways to design a stress management program

As you read, consider

- In what ways holistic approaches are consistent with the definition of counseling
- What the differences are between spirituality and religiosity
- How mindfulness can be used formally and informally by clients and counselors
- What components of wellness you consider most important and what a personal wellness plan would look like
- Why prevention is considered to be at the core of the counseling profession and what factors hinder the promotion of prevention efforts

Rainbow

With age she has learned
*   to forgive the groups*
*   that mistreated her*
*   because of her color.*
Each Saturday she now bakes bread
*   and takes it to the local mission*
*   where she stays to cut and serve it*
*   with love and a main dish.*
Her grace has overcome years of hatred
*   angry words and hours of sadness*
*   her brightness exudes a subtle warmth*
*   everyone calls her "Rainbow."*

Reprinted from "Rainbow," by S. T. Gladding, 1997. Copyright © by S. T. Gladding.

Approaching counseling from a holistic perspective means that the counselor considers the whole person, including mental, physical, emotional, spiritual, and environmental factors. Clinical mental health counselors address these factors to enhance client wellness, personal growth, and development. They have skills in assessing multiple dimensions of client development and in designing treatment plans to address client needs and, in some cases, pathology. Providing services from a holistic approach complements the philosophical foundations of the counseling profession (Myers & Sweeney, 2008). In this chapter a description is given of the biopsychosocial model. Related topics are then addressed, including spirituality, mindfulness, wellness, and prevention.

THE BIOPSYCHOSOCIAL MODEL

The counseling profession finally has a model sophisticated enough to use across all specialties, modalities, and presenting problems.

(Kaplan & Coogan, 2005, p. 23)

The **biopsychosocial (BPS) model** is an approach to medicine and mental health that focuses on the multiple, interrelated ways biology, psychology, and social/cultural factors are conducive or detrimental to health and well-being. Although the concept does not appear novel, the BPS model has only recently begun to appear in counseling literature. The model was proposed by George Engel (1977), a cardiologist, who viewed the prevailing biomedical model as narrow, reductionist, and linear. He proposed the BPS model as a holistic alternative (Borrell-Carrió, Suchman, & Epstein, 2004). Engel (1977) believed that to adequately respond to people's distress and suffering and to help them feel understood, clinicians need to attend to the biological, psychological, and social dimensions that affect overall health. The model proposed by Engel represents a worldview that includes patients' and clients' subjective experiences as well as biomedical data.

So how does the work of a cardiologist that began almost four decades ago affect the clinical work conducted by mental health practitioners in contemporary society? Kaplan and Coogan (2005) state that counseling needs a comprehensive paradigm that allows assessment and intervention across a range of modalities and specialties. The BPS model represents such a paradigm. It provides a framework for understanding three essential, integrated components that affect the general health and mental health of clients.

The CACREP standards (2016) emphasize the importance of the BPS model to the work of clinical mental health counselors. Section 5.C.1.c of the Clinical Mental Health Counseling Standards—Foundations—states that clinical mental health counselors are expected to know the principles, models, and documentation formats of biopsychosocial case conceptualization and treatment planning. To that end, a brief overview of the three major components of the model is provided here, along with suggestions for assessment and treatment, and a case study that challenges the reader to utilize the BPS model in practice.

Biological Components

Biological components of the BPS model include physical, biochemical, and genetic factors that influence mental health (Kaplan & Coogan, 2005). Because of scientific advances, counselors today have a sound understanding of biogenetics, mind–body interconnections, neurochemicals, and neurodevelopment. Although counselors are not expected to be neuroscientists, they do need a fundamental knowledge of neurological and physiological factors that affect human behavior. In fact, the CACREP 2016 standards include knowledge of neurological factors and foundations in standards specific to human development, clinical mental health counseling, and addiction counseling (Miller & Barrio Minton, 2016). An understanding of the functions of the brain, its development, the role of neurotransmitters, and the effects of psychotropic medications (which affect the mind, emotions, and/or behavior) is imperative. Recent publications, including the *Journal of Mental Health Counseling*, have featured articles on the integration of neurocounseling into the counseling profession (Russell-Chapin, 2016). Counselors can gain more knowledge in this field, which continues to develop at a rapid pace, through continuing education and training. A few of the more pertinent biological factors that affect mental health are explained here, specifically neurotransmitters, the limbic system, and biogenetics.

Neurotransmitters are the chemicals in the brain that account for the transmission of signals from one neuron to the next across synapses. They are produced by glands, such as the pituitary gland and the adrenal glands (Boeree, 2003). Neurotransmitters, which are **messenger molecules**, are released from one neuron to another neuron. They either excite or inhibit the message being sent by the brain across the neurons. In other words, communication between brain cells requires the action of neurotransmitter molecules (Preston, O'Neal, & Talaga, 2010).

Several neurotransmitters have been identified and are known to affect mental health, including regulation, inhibition, and stability. Examples include acetylcholine, serotonin, dopamine, norepinephrine, epinephrine, and gamma-amino butyric acid. Although interactions among the billions of neurons that compose the human brain make it difficult to determine exactly what affects what, certain things about some neurotransmitters are known. For example, a decrease in dopamine is linked to an increase in hyperactivity and irritability (Matthews, 2001). Norepinephrine modulates other transmitters and shares some similarities with dopamine. Serotonin is an inhibitory neurotransmitter that is closely associated with emotion and mood. Too little serotonin can lead to depression, problems with anger control, obsessive–compulsive disorder, other emotional disorders, and suicide. Too little serotonin can have other deleterious effects, including an increased appetite for carbohydrates and sleeping difficulties. A lack of sufficient serotonin has also been associated with migraines, irritable bowel syndrome, and fibromyalgia (Boeree, 2003).

Counselors who have a basic understanding of brain chemistry are in a better position to understand how psychotropic medications work. They can then confer intelligently with psychiatrists and other physicians who work with their clients and who have prescription privileges. Therefore, counselors need to be informed about clients' medication practices and be well versed in the connections between pharmacology and mental health (Barden, Conley, & Young, 2015; Oestmann, 2007).

The **limbic system**, also located in the brain, plays a key role in the way clients feel and express emotions such as rage, fear, aggression, and sexuality (Field, Beeson, & Jones, 2015; Matthews, 2001). It affects memory, the way a person responds to threats, emotional expression, physical health, and well-being. Boeree (2002) describes this **emotional nervous system** in the following way:

> The limbic system is a complex set of structures that lies on both sides and underneath the thalamus, just under the cerebrum. It includes the hypothalamus, the hippocampus, the amygdala, and several other nearby areas. It appears to be primarily responsible for our emotional life, and has a lot to do with the formation of memories. In this drawing, you

are looking at the brain cut in half, but with the brain stem intact. The part of the limbic system shown is that which is along the left side of the thalamus (hippocampus and amygdala) and just under the front of the thalamus (hypothalamus). ("The Limbic System," para. 1)

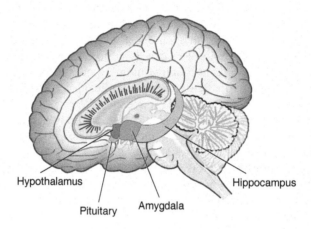

Clients dealing with chronic pain or stress or struggling with cognitive functioning may be especially affected by limbic system responses (Oestmann, 2007). Because clinicians are likely to work with clients experiencing these and other conditions, understanding the relationship between stress and the limbic system is especially pertinent.

Stress results in emotional reactions that may include intense anxiety, an inability to concentrate, irritability, and a range of physical symptoms. Responses to stressors can "jolt the body out of homeostasis" (Oestmann, 2007, p. 131). Two hormones secreted by the adrenal glands are epinephrine (adrenalin) and glucocorticoids (cortisol or hydrocortisone). The decline in an individual's immune system after facing chronic stress is due to the stress hormone cortisol (Nauert, 2008). Buffers such as physical exercise, creative outlets for frustration, a sense of control over events or sources of stress, social support, and a belief that things will improve can help clients cope with stress more effectively.

Genetics plays another key role in the biological component of the BPS model. Many psychiatric conditions have a genetic component that puts individuals at a higher risk for developing certain disorders—for example, autism, anxiety disorders, bipolar disorder, Parkinson's disease, schizophrenia, ADHD, Tourette's syndrome, and alcoholism (Oestmann, 2007). In many cases the specific genes related to the disorders are not yet known, and environmental factors are believed to "activate" the genes in some conditions. Study of genetics and the human genome continues to be an important part of scientific research, and counselors need to stay abreast of the newest developments in the field as well as the psychological components of BPS model.

Psychological Components

Psychological components of the BPS model include patterns of thinking, coping skills, judgment, perceptions, and **emotional intelligence** (i.e., the ability to perceive, understand, and express emotions). Additional psychological factors include general temperament and personality characteristics. Many of the factors included under the psychological umbrella represent areas of specialized knowledge for mental health professionals. For example, several components addressed during a mental status examination are categorized as psychological components.

The BPS model proposes that psychological components can influence biological components and vice versa. For example, a client who is experiencing depression may demonstrate all-or-nothing thinking, concentration difficulties, and a sense of helplessness. Symptoms of the depression may be evidenced physiologically in, for example, sleeplessness, appetite disturbance, and a decreased energy level. Both the psychological and the physical manifestations of the depression may be connected to neurotransmitter imbalances, such as decreased levels of dopamine and serotonin. A thorough assessment of the client's circumstances may indicate a recent marital separation, the death of a parent from cancer within the past year, and the pending outsourcing of the client's job—examples of social factors. The combination of biological, psychological, and social factors in this case coalesced in a way that threatened the client's mental well-being.

Social Components

Social components, which also may be conceptualized as sociocultural components, include family relationships, support systems, work relationships, and the broader cultural environment as it intersects with one's personal cultural identity. Several other social factors include values and beliefs, environmental conditions, lifestyle factors, sociopolitical conditions, and reproductive challenges (Oestmann, 2007). Although some mental health professionals might argue that some of these elements are not really social factors (e.g., reproductive challenges can also be classified as biological or physiological factors), it still is important to consider them when conducting a thorough BPS assessment.

Assessment and Treatment Planning

The purpose of the BPS model is to provide health professionals a way to assess elements of human behavior within a comprehensive whole (Kaplan & Coogan, 2005). The components of the model, as well as factors within those components, interrelate and interact. Clinical mental health counselors can enhance their work with clients by taking each of the three primary components into account when conducting an assessment, conceptualizing a case, and designing a treatment plan. An approach to BPS assessment that enables the clinician to access the major domains of the BPS model is the **BATHE technique**. BATHE is an acronym representing five specific areas of assessment: **B**ackground, **A**ffect, **T**rouble, **H**andling, and **E**mpathy (Lieberman & Stuart, 1999; McCulloch, Ramesar, & Peterson, 1998; Rodriguez, 2004).

The BATHE technique focuses on five specific areas that lay the groundwork for working collaboratively with a client to examine the biological, psychological, and social systems that influence the client's well-being. Each area is briefly described here, and examples of questions that a clinician might ask during the assessment interview are provided. The areas addressed in the interview do not need to be addressed linearly, and clinicians can encourage clients to elaborate on points of particular significance.

- **Background**—The counselor begins to build rapport and establish a collaborative relationship. The general questions suggested here can lead to further examination of biological, psychological, and social factors affecting the client's condition.
  ○ What are your current circumstances?
  ○ What is the reason for your visit today?

○ What do you feel comfortable sharing with me today?

○ What can you tell me that would help me understand your circumstances?

- **Affect**—The counselor attempts to understand the client's current emotional state.
  ○ What are some of the feelings you have right now?
  ○ What feelings have you experienced during the past week?
  ○ On a scale of 1–10, how intense are those feelings? (Ask about each specific feeling.)
- **Trouble**—The counselor explores the client's presenting problem and additional factors that might underlie the problem.
  ○ What troubles you most today?
  ○ What disturbs you most about your current circumstances?
  ○ What is contributing to those circumstances?
  ○ What physical symptoms are you having?
- **Handling**—The counselor assesses the client's coping style and support systems.
  ○ How are you handling this situation?
  ○ How have you handled similar situations in the past?
  ○ Who do you turn to for support?
  ○ How do you find relief?
- **Empathy**—Empathy is conveyed by the counselor to the client in a manner that is perceived by the client. The counselor seeks to convey the message that under the circumstances, the client's response is understandable.
  ○ This situation must be quite difficult for you.
  ○ You are dealing with some really challenging circumstances.

When counseling professionals work in collaboration with a health team, efforts are made to coordinate care. Through this process, the counselor's perceptions and treatment are integrated into a holistic approach to care. Treatment planning within the BPS framework varies according to the presenting concerns, taking into account mind, body, and social environments that affect the client. For example, consider the case of Khun Prasong.

The Case of Khun Prasong (Praz)

Khun Prasong is a 30-year-old second-generation Thai American. His parents immigrated to the United States 40 years ago. Khun Prasong goes by the name Praz, although his parents still call him by his given name. Praz is a civil engineer who often feels anxious about his job performance and about social interactions. His English is excellent; however, he does not have many close friends. He has never married and does not belong to any recreational clubs. Nor has he had a physical checkup in the past 10 years.

Praz reports that he feels sad most of the time. During the past three months, he has lost his appetite, and the activities he used to enjoy are no longer pleasurable to him. He is getting about four hours of sleep a night and says that he feels chronically tired. Praz's parents and only sibling live in Texas, which is 600 miles away.

Using the BPS model as a framework, how would you conceptualize Praz's case? Which issues are most pressing? How would you consider addressing them? What other information would you like to have? What other health professionals would you collaborate with? How would you use the BATHE model to assess Praz?

Clinicians who are guided by a BPS framework recognize that mental health is a dynamic construct. It is not feasible to treat one component of the model without taking into account the other components. In the case of Khun Prasong, it will probably be important to encourage him to get a physical checkup to rule out specific physiological issues. It will also be important to find out more about his social support system and his relationship with his family. What is his connection with the Thai culture? Another important issue is his work: Does he find his job as a civil engineer rewarding? What led him to that field? Are there people in his company with whom he feels comfortable socializing? Certainly, it will be important to evaluate his level of depression, including suicidal ideation. Because of the presenting symptoms associated with depression and anxiety, referring Praz to a reputable psychiatrist is advised. Throughout the counseling process, you will want to continue to assess the biological, psychological, and social factors—positive and negative—that are affecting Khun Prasong's mental health. You will want to work collaboratively with him to determine which areas of concern to address first.

SPIRITUALITY

The biopsychosocial model described in the previous section did not focus on the spiritual component of mental health counseling. However, for hundreds of years, theologians, philosophers, physicians, and, more recently, mental health professionals have recognized the interrelationship of the mind, body, and spirit (Meyers, 2007). It can be argued that a truly holistic approach to counseling follows a biopsychosocial-spiritual model.

Research suggests that the majority of Americans value spirituality and religion (e.g., Cashwell & Young, 2011; Gold, 2010). In recent years "a burgeoning literature has emerged concerning religion and psychotherapy" (Ottens & Klein, 2005, p. 32). Religious and/or spiritual connections can serve as sources of wisdom, community, strength, and health (Harris, Thoresen, & Lopez, 2007). Many mental health professionals recognize spirituality as a cultural and coping factor that has the potential to affect counseling relationships, processes, and outcomes. These professionals also recognize the need to train clinicians to address religious and spiritual issues in counseling (Burke, Chauvin, & Miranti, 2005).

Within the counseling field, there is a long tradition of including spirituality as an important dimension of human life. For example, such luminaries as Victor Frankl, Abraham Maslow, Alfred Adler, and Rollo May emphasized the importance of spirituality in living. Carl Jung recognized spirituality as a vital part of life. He believed that people over the age of 40 were uniquely qualified to explore its many dimensions. Jung recognized the developmental process of spiritual growth over time. In more recent years, Fowler (1981) has described ways faith develops over the life span, beginning in childhood and maturing as one ages.

Although some theorists integrate spirituality and counseling, others have argued to keep the topics separate. Historically, the topics of spirituality and religion were not embraced by the fields of counseling and psychology (Gold, 2010; Myers & Williard, 2003). Several reasons help explain the division between spirituality and counseling. For example, mental health professionals have been "taught to adopt a stance of neutrality and remain objective and unbiased" (Burke et al., 2005). Some professionals have expressed concern that counselors who incorporate spirituality into their clinical work may violate ethical guidelines by imposing their values on clients. Consequently, it may be difficult for clients to bring their spiritual concerns to counseling and difficult for counselors to ask clients about their beliefs. However, being open with clients about spirituality gives them the opportunity to bring spiritual issues into counseling sessions if they choose to do so. Indeed, the shift from viewing spirituality as a topic to be avoided in counseling to now viewing it as an integral part of holistic counseling has been a 180-degree change.

During the past two decades, mental health counseling has given increased attention to spirituality (Cashwell, Bentley, & Yarborough, 2007). Gold (2010) points to three reasons for this increased attention: (a) a more positive professional receptivity to spirituality, (b) a growing acknowledgment of spirituality and religion as multicultural variables, and (c) a greater client demand for clinicians to address issues of spirituality and religion during counseling sessions. He cites Hoogestraat and Trammel (2003), who maintain the following:

- All humans are spiritual beings;
- Spirituality [affects] mental, physical, and emotional health; and,
- It is essential to address spiritual and religious issues in therapy to maintain ethical care. (p. 414)

Terminology

Although multiple definitions of spirituality and religion have been proposed, any definition must be accompanied by qualifications. The Association for Spiritual, Ethical, and Religious Values in Counseling (ASERVIC) conducted a Summit on Spirituality in 1995. During the summit, a description of spirituality was generated, and a list of competencies for integrating spirituality into counseling was devised (Young, Wiggins-Frame, & Cashwell, 2007). The following description of **spirituality** was constructed during the summit:

> [Spirituality is a] capacity and tendency that is innate and unique to all persons. The spiritual tendency moves the individual toward knowledge, love, meaning, peace, hope, transcendence, connectedness, compassion, wellness, and wholeness. Spirituality includes one's capacity for creativity, growth, and the development of a value system. ("Summit Results," 1995, p. 30)

Religion has been defined in multiple ways but is often referred to as the social or organized means by which a person expresses spirituality (Burke et al., 2005; Young et al., 2007). Religiosity often is conceptualized as having more organizational and behavioral components, whereas spirituality is considered to be oriented toward personal experiences that may be transcendent in nature (Jackson & Bergeman, 2011). For many people, both older and younger, religious organizations, rituals, and collective worship provide a means through which spirituality can be outwardly expressed.

Benefits Associated with Spirituality

"A growing body of research has established a relationship between diverse spiritual principles and multiple aspects of health" (Simpson, 2009, p. 299). Studies have demonstrated links between spirituality and physical health, including the ability to cope with illness, facilitation of recovery, and cognitive functioning (Koenig, George, & Titus, 2004; Matthews et al., 1998; Meisenhelder & Chandler, 2002; Woods, Antoni, Ironson, & Kling, 1999). Research also supports links between spirituality and mental well-being. Examples include higher self-esteem, decreased alcohol and drug use, and less depression (Giordano et al., 2015; Sperry, 2012). Many wellness models include spiritual wellness as an important component, with some models conceptualizing spirituality as the core characteristic of a healthy person.

Although positive links between spirituality and well-being have been documented, there are concerns associated with certain religious beliefs. Cadwallader (1991) describes religion as existing on a continuum between life-affirming and life-constricting. In her view, religion can either benefit or damage mental health, depending on the way it functions in a person's life. "Counselors will want to be especially attuned to spiritual coping styles that involve a client feeling punished" (Buser, 2013, p. 167). For example, a client who approaches stress from this perspective may have heightened bulimic behaviors. On the other hand, a healthy sense of religion can lead to self-actualization and positive self-esteem. Because religion can have either positive or negative effects on mental health, depending on the context, it is a counselor's obligation to be willing to discuss the topic and provide support for clients whose religion has negatively affected their psychological well-being (Cashwell, Bentley, & Yarborough, 2007; Yakushko, 2005).

Spirituality and the Counseling Process

During the 1995 Summit on Spirituality and throughout subsequent discussions with counselors, counselor educators, and supervisors, ASERVIC generated a list of nine competencies for integrating spirituality into counseling (Young et al., 2007). Since the 1995 summit, additional competencies have been added, grouped according to categories, and endorsed by ACA. These competencies can be accessed through the ASERVIC website at www.aservic.org/resources/spiritual-competencies/. The current fourteen competencies are categorized under these six domains:

- Culture and worldview
- Counselor self-awareness
- Human and spiritual development
- Communication
- Assessment
- Diagnosis and treatment (ASERVIC, 2009)

To what degree do counselors endorse the competencies for integrating spirituality into counseling? In a random-sample survey that included the original nine spiritual competencies, 505 ACA members, responding to a questionnaire, rated the importance of those competencies. Results indicated that ACA members strongly supported the importance of the competencies for effective counseling practice, with an overall mean rating of 4.2 on a 5-point Likert scale. Sixty-eight percent of the participants strongly agreed that formal training in the area of spirituality was important. On another note, however, 43.5% either strongly disagreed, disagreed, or were neutral in regard to their current ability to integrate those competencies into their practice (Young et al., 2007). The researchers recommend extending counselor training competencies beyond self-awareness, thereby providing counselors-in-training with more direction about how to address spiritual issues within the counseling relationship.

Generally speaking, it is best to encourage clients to take the lead in addressing spiritual issues. Some general assessment questions that can open the door to discussing spiritual issues, if clients choose to go in that direction, include the following:

- Do you have any spiritual or religious beliefs? Help me understand them.
- How do these beliefs affect your relationships?
- Are there religious practices that you follow? What do you like about them, and how are they helpful?

- When you think about your reason for seeking counseling, what personal values or spiritual convictions seem to apply?
- Considering the issue you are facing, what do you imagine (Buddha, Jesus, Muhammad, Moses, Lao Tzu, etc.) might have said about it?
- Are you aware of any ways in which your beliefs may be contributing to the problem? (Cashwell & Young, 2011; Nations, 2006; Warden & Nations, 2016)

Ingersoll (1994) states that counselors interested in working effectively with clients committed to a particular spiritual view can best do so by affirming the importance of spirituality in the client's life, using language and imagery in problem solving and treatment that is congruent with the client's worldview, and consulting with other "healers," such as ministers and other spiritual leaders. This process calls for cultural sensitivity as well as for ethical practices of the highest standards. When spirituality is evidenced in the form of particular religious beliefs—such as Buddhism, Confucianism, Islam, or Christianity—counselors need to be respectful and work with clients to maximize the positive nature of their beliefs and values in connection with the difficulties they are experiencing.

For clinical mental health professionals to work effectively with clients, counselors need to be aware of their own spiritual beliefs. In a nationally representative sample of ACA-affiliated counselors, the majority of respondents valued spirituality in their lives (Kelly, 1995). However, not all counselors consider spirituality a priority. Therefore, counselors should first assess their own spiritual beliefs before assessing the beliefs of their clients. Then the counselors' job is to assist clients in dealing with psychosocial tasks, such as maintaining a meaningful quality of life, coping with loss of function, and confronting existential or spiritual issues as they arise.

The Case of Mike

Mike was a born-again Christian who held strong religious beliefs. He entered a counseling program so he could graduate and help people live their lives in an ethical and spiritual way. His grades were stellar and his classmates thought highly of him. In the middle of his internship, though, he was asked to counsel with a woman who was lesbian and who wanted to have better relationships with her partner and 6-year-old daughter. Mike told his supervisor he simply could not work with this new client and wanted to refer her to a more secular counselor. His supervisor told Mike that simply referring her, especially after he had had a session with her, would not be appropriate. Mike protested and stated his religious faith would not let him counsel with such a person.

If you were the supervisor, what would you do? If you were Mike, what would you do if your supervisor insisted you work with this client? How do you think dilemmas like this one are best resolved?

MINDFULNESS

Mindfulness is a unique approach to mental health that has rapidly attracted attention among many healthcare professionals (Rajeski, 2008). The practice of mindfulness to enhance well-being has been part of the Buddhist tradition for over 2,500 years (Wallace & Shapiro, 2006) and can be considered within the context of spirituality. Although its roots are in Buddhism, the practice of mindfulness has been taught as a secular discipline for over

30 years (Boyce, 2011). A simplified definition of mindfulness is paying attention to the here and now, in a nonjudgmental manner (Kabat-Zinn, 2005). Research studies indicate that mindfulness can reduce stress, treat depression, control chronic pain, treat substance abuse, and help with a myriad of other disorders, including ADHD (Kabat-Zinn, 1990; Schure, Christopher, & Christopher, 2008; Zylowska, 2012). A person can practice mindfulness informally or formally, although many individuals find the formal practice of meditation helpful.

Mindfulness means fully attending in an unbiased, curious manner to what one is experiencing. Three core building blocks of mindfulness include **intention** (practicing mindfulness purposefully), **attention** (paying attention to what is going on at the moment, focusing), and **attitude** (observing what is going on in a nonjudgmental manner; Shapiro, Carlson, Astin, & Freedman, 2006). Mindfulness involves being aware of experiences without filters or distortions, thereby allowing people to avoid being critical of themselves or others.

Being intentionally mindful is the opposite of living life on autopilot. When people are on autopilot, they are not in control of their attention. They act out of impulse or habit, which can lead to difficulties with self-regulation and limit their ability to reach their full potential. Practitioners describe mindfulness as a way to "train the puppy mind"—a mind that tends to be in constant motion and often wanders from one focus to another (Greason, Newsome, Henderson, McCarthy, & Wyche, 2012). Formal and informal practices of mindfulness provide ways to monitor the puppy mind. An oversimplified way of describing mindfulness training includes these steps:

- Intentionally finding an anchor. Often, this anchor is the breath. Mindful breathing means inhaling and exhaling fully. Often, breathing is accompanied by internal counting or by repeating a mantra, such as "relax," "it's okay," or a phrase that is particularly meaningful. Other anchors include specific sounds or body sensations (Zylowska, 2012).
- Observing the present-moment experience with full acceptance
- When focus strays, noticing what has just happened and gently returning attention to the anchor

According to Kabat-Zinn (2005, 2012), mindfulness is a simple but powerful practice that has multiple benefits. From a clinical perspective, mindfulness benefits mental health counselors by enabling them to develop insight and compassion for clients. It is correlated with multicultural awareness and multicultural knowledge as well (Ivers, Johnson, Clarke, Newsome, & Berry, 2016).

Mindful clinicians are able to use "the self" more fully in clinical practice. They are better able to monitor themselves, thus "ensuring the sanctity and effectiveness of the counselor–client relationship" (Cashwell, Bentley, & Bigbee, 2007, p. 74). Mindfulness also benefits clients. Teaching mindfulness to clients enables them to deal more effectively with the pain that often accompanies difficult emotions. Empirical research demonstrates the powerful effects mindfulness can have on people physically and emotionally.

BOX 6–1   The Power of Mindfulness

I first was exposed to the power of mindfulness in my own life. As a yoga practitioner and instructor, I saw how being present for the moment and allowing that moment to be exactly as it was could transform an ugly, dark place into something that could just be a curious "happening" in the moment.

(continued)

When I was in graduate school, I would use my mindfulness skills to notice my tendency to not only ruminate about my dissertation or perseverate over sticky conversations but also to engage in a judgmental "meta-conversation" about my ruminating or perseverating. I would catch myself thinking things along the lines of, "Why are you getting so worked up about this?" or "He probably thinks I'm crazy." Noticing this inner dialogue helped me disengage from believing that the thoughts were true and be more intentional about the actions I needed to take to reach my goals. Rather than feeling bad about myself and eating a bunch of ice cream (my automatic-pilot, self-soothing strategy), with mindfulness I was able to notice that I was having these thoughts and then consciously choose my next step. I might shift my attention to something in the present such as the feeling of my feet on the ground or the sensation of breath in my belly. As I mindfully disengaged, the thoughts, the fears, and the worries would lose their power as I responded to them consciously rather than reacting automatically. They were still there—just with less of a grip on my mind.

As a counselor, I use mindfulness techniques with my clients both informally and formally. Informally, I work to infuse all my sessions with mindful awareness. My practice is to notice both my client's present-moment experience and my own, with full acceptance of what is there. I am always surprised by how much more intuitive and empathic I feel when I am intentionally present in a mindful way.

Formally, I have found that clients respond quite favorably to being taught mindfulness tools, whether through specific programs such as dialectical behavior therapy or mindfulness-based cognitive therapy or simply as an in-session psychoeducational moment. One client experience will always stand out for me—Sarah. When I first met Sarah, she was classically depressed. She hung her head, didn't make eye contact, and saw the world through very dark lenses. During an early session, we discussed the possibility of just observing the feelings of sadness as they arose in her body instead of getting in a battle with the feelings. We practiced this together in my office. We explored what sadness felt like in her body and what thoughts, images, or sensations were associated with the feeling. I also taught her how to shift her attention to an external focus when things were feeling too intense internally. Initially, she didn't understand how "sitting with" her sad feelings could help her feel better, but she was desperate for relief, so she was willing to try. I was incredibly surprised when she returned the next week to report that after a fight with her partner, when she was feeling completely overwhelmed and afraid, she took the moment to practice mindfulness. She sat on the picnic table outside her kitchen and paid attention to the feelings of sadness and anger that arose in her. She also shifted her attention to notice the sensation of the sun on her face. She shared a huge revelation with me—the feelings of anger and sadness changed. They weren't permanent! Not only that, she actually had a moment of feeling joy as the sun warmed her skin. As she described the moment to me, she made eye contact and, for the first time in our relationship, smiled.

Paige B. Greason, PhD, LPCS, Counselor and Counselor Educator

WELLNESS

Within the mental health field, the emphasis on promoting wellness has become increasingly more prominent. ACA emphasizes the promotion of wellness as the foundation of the counseling profession (Tanigoshi, Kontos, & Remley, 2008). Researchers have found that specific practices, such as meditation, promote wellness and cultivate positive emotions while increasing empathy, which is critical for developing a therapeutic alliance as well as associated with positive client outcomes (Leppma & Young, 2016). Wellness involves many aspects of life, including the physical, intellectual, social, psychological, emotional, spiritual, and environmental. Myers, Sweeney, and Witmer (2000) define **wellness** as a way of life oriented toward optimal health and well-being in which body, mind, and spirit are integrated by the individual to live life more fully within the human and natural community. Ideally, it is the optimum state of health and well-being that each individual is capable of achieving. (p. 252)

In an interview published in *Counseling Today* (Rollins, 2008), Thomas Sweeney elaborates on the significance of a wellness approach to counseling. He states, "We need to look at how to enrich instead of fixing that which is broken. Being healthy is to be normal, but being *well* is to optimize that" (p. 33). In other words, the emphasis in counseling is not just on wellness but on *positive wellness*.

A holistic approach to counseling—which addresses the biological, psychological, social, and spiritual components described earlier—focuses on wellness. Wellness-based counseling has been described as **salutogenic** (i.e., health enhancing). A wellness perspective involves assessing all dimensions that affect health and well-being and recognizing the balance of those dimensions. Perhaps in response to the interest in wellness expressed by the general public, an increasing number of mental health practitioners and physicians are adopting holistic, wellness-based practices in their work with clients and patients (Granello, 2013).

Models of counseling-based wellness have evolved from theoretical models to empirically based models that provide an evidence base for practice (Granello & Witmer, 2013; Myers & Sweeney, 2008; Witmer, 2013). Three pioneers in the development of wellness models and inventories for measuring wellness are J. Melvin Witmer, Thomas J. Sweeney, and Jane E. Meyers.

Wellness Models: The Wheel of Wellness and the Indivisible Self

The **Wheel of Wellness** (Myers et al., 2000; Sweeney & Witmer, 1991; Witmer & Sweeney, 1992) is a holistic theoretical model of wellness that was designed to illustrate characteristics associated with healthy people. The Wheel of Wellness is rooted in individual psychology and has its roots in the Adlerian approach to understanding individuals from a holistic perspective (Wolf, Thompson, & Smith-Adcock, 2012). As can be seen in Figure 6–1, the wellness wheel consists of five major life tasks: **spirituality**, **self-direction**, **work and leisure**, **friendship**, and **love**. Spirituality is at the center of the wheel and is considered the most important component of well-being. Twelve subtasks associated with the five major tasks are listed in the spokes of the wheel: sense of worth, sense of control, realistic beliefs, emotional awareness and coping, problem solving and creativity, sense of humor, nutrition, exercise, self-care, stress management, gender identity, and cultural identity. Life tasks are influenced by life forces, including family, community, education, religion, and government. Life forces and life tasks are influenced by external global factors, both natural (e.g., catastrophic events) and human (e.g., war; Myers et al., 2000).

The Wheel of Wellness model is theoretical in nature, but statistical analyses did not support its structure. Consequently, Hattie, Myers, and Sweeney (2004) used findings from those analyses to devise an empirically supported model of wellness: **the Indivisible Self (IS-WEL)**. This model also is grounded in Adlerian concepts, particularly the concept of holism (Myers & Sweeney, 2005a). Counselors can use the model to help clients assess personal wellness and evaluate choices they can make to enhance wellness. For example, counseling utilizing the IS-WEL model offers a structure for providing counseling services that support caregivers of persons with dementia by mobilizing their strengths, improving their coping, and enhancing their overall well-being (Clarke, Adams, Wilkerson, & Shaw, 2016).

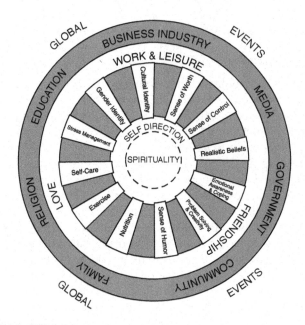

FIGURE 6–1   The Wheel of Wellness
Source: The Wheel of Wellness (p. 10), by J. M. Witmer, T. J. Sweeney, and J. E. Myers, 1998, Greensboro, NC: Authors. Copyright 1998 by Witmer et al. Reprinted with permission.

The IS-Wel model consists of a primary factor of global wellness, five secondary-order factors, seventeen third-order factors, and four contextual scores. The secondary-order factors that compose IS-Wel are (a) the creative self, (b) the coping self, (c) the social self, (d) the essential self, and (e) the physical self. Contextual factors include local context (family, neighborhood, and community), institutional context (policies and laws), global context (world events), and chronometrical context (life span over time).

Ways to Use the Indivisible Self Model in Counseling

1. *Introduction of the wellness model.*   First, clinicians introduce the concept of wellness and what it means. Next, they describe the model itself, often using graphic representations. Finally, the connection between healthy living and overall well-being is discussed.

2. *Assessment of the wellness components.*   Clinicians administer the Five-Factor Wellness Inventory (5F-Wel; Myers & Sweeney, 2005b) to clients. Results are shared and used to provide information about levels of functioning in specific areas of wellness. Clinicians encourage clients to examine their scores, evaluate how those scores match their personal perceptions, and make decisions about what areas could be strengthened.

3. *Development of a personal wellness plan.*   This step can be conducted individually when a clinician is designing counseling interventions with a particular client. When clinicians conduct larger prevention programs for multiple clients, they can use the information gained from the initial assessment to determine which areas of focus might benefit the most people and then design programs accordingly. In either case, the wellness plan

should include specific objectives for change, methods for accomplishing change, and resources for facilitating the process (Myers & Sweeney, 2005a).

4. *Evaluation and follow-up.* Plans for evaluation and follow-up need to accompany whatever prevention (or intervention) strategy is implemented. Counselors can help participants identify markers of change to indicate short- and long-term goal accomplishment and to evaluate the overall success of the program.

Although the counseling literature focuses primarily on the wellness models just described, there are other wellness models that mental health counselors may use with clients. One example is Bill Hettler's (1984) six-dimensional hexagon, which includes spiritual, emotional/social, physical, occupation/leisure, environmental, and intellectual components. Hettler's model emphasizes the importance of striving for a high level of wellness among each of the six dimensions, as well as balancing them effectively to optimize wellness (National Wellness Institute, n.d.).

BOX 6–2 Using Wellness in Counselor Education Programs

A range of literature addresses the importance of integrating wellness in counselor preparation (see Wolf et al., 2012). I teach wellness in most of my courses. As part of the introductory clinical mental health counseling course, I use an activity adapted from D. H. Granello and Young (2012). I ask students to draw a grid that includes four columns: Dimensions of Wellness, Ways That I Regularly Strengthen This Dimension, One Goal I Have for Improving This Dimension, and Obstacles to Reaching My Goal. I then ask the students to include the following rows in their grid: Physical, Emotional, Spiritual, Intellectual, Social, and Other. At the bottom of the grid, students write The Degree to Which I Think I Can Accomplish Each Goal. I ask them to complete the grid, using scaling (1–10) to respond to the last question. At the end of the course, I ask students to respond again to the scaling question, indicating the degree to which each goal was accomplished. I ask students to write themselves letters that describe their personal worth and value. I collect the letters and their wellness plans without reading them and put them in self-addressed envelopes, which are mailed to the students three months later. That gives them an opportunity to examine their wellness goals while at the same time affirming their worthiness as individuals.

Debbie Newsome, PhD, LPC, NCC

PREVENTION

Overall, a cornerstone of the wellness approach and the related holistic approaches described thus far is an emphasis on the prevention of mental health issues. Indeed, one of the defining characteristics of the counseling profession is its emphasis on preventing mental health problems by building on strengths and developing resources that facilitate healthy development. Primary prevention strategies provide the most efficient way to promote mental health among large numbers of people. Consequently, clinicians need to be skilled at designing and implementing prevention programs.

Definition of Prevention

The term **prevention** is used frequently in the medical field but is somewhat more ambiguous to define when it comes to mental health. Indeed, professionals in mental health fields have struggled with its definition (Romano & Hage, 2000). The literal definition of prevention is to

---

Primary prevention—preventive efforts that attempt to reduce the number of new occurrences of a disorder. For example, teaching lessons on ways of appropriately expressing their feelings may prevent people from bottling up all their emotions and taking them out on others in an angry and aggressive way.

Secondary prevention—preventive efforts aimed at people who are at risk of developing a mental health problem or who are exhibiting early symptoms of a disorder. For example, teaching people who are prone to get angry quickly how to quickly and quietly calm themselves before they become out of control may result in their becoming less irate and more in charge of their lives.

Tertiary prevention—preventive efforts (i.e., treatment) directed at reducing the debilitating effects of an existing disorder. For example, helping people who are constantly angry learn the ABCs of rational emotive behavior therapy (REBT) may stop them from doing an emotional bypass and assuming that events cause feelings instead of feelings being connected to thoughts.

FIGURE 6–2 Prevention in Mental Health

stop something from happening (e.g., cancer, depression, or suicide). Gerald Caplan added to this definition as early as 1964 by differentiating among three types of prevention: primary, secondary, and tertiary. **Primary prevention** occurs "before the fact" and refers to prevention efforts that attempt to reduce the number of new occurrences of a disorder. The goal of primary prevention is to keep healthy people healthy by increasing environmental resources or bolstering personal competencies (Scileppi, Teed, & Torres, 2000). **Secondary prevention** is targeted toward people who are at risk of developing a mental health problem or who are exhibiting early symptoms of a disorder. The goal is to work with these individuals to forestall or alleviate problems before they become more severe. **Tertiary prevention** refers to efforts aimed at reducing the debilitating effects of an existing disorder. Tertiary prevention can also be conceptualized as treatment, remediation, or reactive intervention. (See Figure 6–2.)

Although the lines differentiating the three types of prevention are not always distinct, primary prevention and its implementation are focused on here. Primary prevention can include doing something in the present to prevent something undesirable from happening in the future, or doing something in the present that will permit or increase desirable outcomes in the future (Albee & Ryan-Finn, 1993). The following statements provide clarification about the nature of primary prevention (Conyne, 2000, p. 840):

- Primary prevention is intended to decrease the incidences of new cases of any designated disorder.
- Primary prevention occurs through intentionally and collaboratively planned programs that are comprehensive, multilevel, multimethod, and interdisciplinary.
- Primary prevention programs are designed and implemented from a contextual, ecological perspective, taking into account multicultural and societal variables.
- Primary prevention is conducted to reduce risk factors (e.g., stressors, exploitation) while building protective factors (e.g., self-esteem, career aspirations).
- Primary prevention results in an empowered concordance between people and systems. Efforts are made to help make the person–environment fit more satisfying, effective, and productive.

Primary prevention promotes healthy lifestyles by introducing preventive maneuvers that reduce the chances that a health problem will occur (Kaplan, 2000). It involves reducing negative influences, such as toxic lifestyles and environments, and strengthening resistance to stress through the development of coping skills, interpersonal skills, intrapersonal strengths, and support systems. Prevention may involve direct services, aimed at helping people build competencies, and indirect services, targeted toward changing specific environmental factors. Furthermore, prevention efforts can be population based, group based, or individually based.

Rationale for Prevention

Prevention provides the most efficient way of helping promote mental health among the largest number of people. Even though unquestionably there will continue to be a need for reactive interventions—that is, individuals will continue to experience emotional distress, and direct counseling will be needed to help alleviate that distress—greater emphasis on proactive, primary prevention provides opportunities to reach more people before distress is experienced. Albee (2000) argues for increased attention to major preventive efforts for these reasons:

> The data are clear: At least a third of the population of the United States suffers debilitating emotional distress, yet the overwhelming majority of publications, public information, volunteer citizens' groups, news releases, presidential commissions, White House conferences, and so forth focus on individual treatment. To me, this whole situation is a flagrant example of denial. We have pitifully few resources with which to offer one-to-one treatment, yet we deny the importance of primary prevention. And too often when we discuss prevention, it is in terms of small-scale educational or inspirational programs, not major efforts. (p. 846)

Primary prevention is time efficient and cost efficient. Moreover, it takes into account the importance of ecological systems—family, community, institutional, and global. When primary prevention efforts are targeted toward the proximal and distal environments in which people live and work, the likelihood of promoting mental health among individuals, communities, and the society at large is enhanced.

Although the need for prevention theoretically is at the core of professional counseling, there has been a general resistance to implementing large-scale prevention efforts. To illustrate, surveys of mental health journals (e.g., the *Journal of Mental Health Counseling*) reveal that considerably more attention is devoted to treatment of conditions than to preventive counseling (Britzman & Nagelhout, 2011; Kiselica & Look, 1993; Kleist, 1999). Several factors contribute to this resistance. First, only small portions of budgets for mental health services are allocated for large-scale prevention programs (Scileppi et al., 2000). Monetary resources are limited, and from a political perspective, it is difficult to divert scarce resources from people who are already suffering from mental disorders. Similarly, most third-party reimbursement is based on a medical diagnosis and typically does not cover preventive interventions. Also, many training programs for counselors and other mental health workers do not offer specific courses on preventive interventions (Conyne, Newmeyer, Kenny, Romano, & Matthews, 2008). Consequently, even though strong arguments have been made for primary prevention, agencies may lack the funds and mental health workers may lack the knowledge and skills needed to implement comprehensive preventive programs (Romano & Hage, 2000).

Many scholars and practitioners have called for a renewed emphasis on prevention among counseling professionals (e.g., Albee, 2000; Conyne et al., 2008; Kleist, 1999; Romano & Hage, 2000). Prevention outcome research provides strong evidence that prevention is "a highly effective strategy for enhancing the quality of mental health in the community" (Scileppi et al., 2000, p. 80). Prevention efforts targeted toward wellness, health promotion, and resiliency can help people circumvent avoidable problems of living and navigate the unavoidable problems more effectively. For prevention programs to be successful, however, they need to be well designed, skillfully implemented, targeted toward a specific population and/or setting, and culturally sensitive. It also is important, after implementation, to evaluate their effectiveness (Conyne, 1991; Palmo, 2006).

Prevention Models

Various models of effective primary prevention have been described in prevention literature. One such model is Bloom's (1996) configural equation of prevention, which focuses on three broad dimensions:

1. Increasing individual strengths and decreasing individual limitations (e.g., enhancing self-efficacy or teaching stress-reduction techniques)
2. Increasing social supports and decreasing social stresses (e.g., promoting self-help groups or drug information hotlines)
3. Enhancing environmental resources (e.g., community programs) and minimizing environmental pressures (e.g., targeting poverty, providing services following natural disasters)

Albee's incidence formula (Albee & Gullotta, 1997) provides another way to conceptualize the prevention of psychological difficulties. The incidence formula model emphasizes the need to bolster people's coping skills, self-esteem, and support systems. Prevention strategies also can be directed at reducing the negative effects of certain biological conditions (e.g., predispositions to physical and mental conditions) and environmental stressors. Lewis et al. (2003) have adapted Albee's original formula, adding the variables of personal power and powerlessness. An adapted formula is depicted in Figure 6–3.

Preventive programs designed to increase personal attributes and skills and to support and decrease external and internal stressors may be directed toward individuals and/ or the environments in which they live and work. Strategies to increase personal power and decrease powerlessness often involve systemic interventions directed at unjust social conditions.

Examples of exemplary prevention programs are numerous. Efficacious prevention programs have been implemented with preschoolers, older children, adolescents, and adults. Many of the programs directed toward children and youth focus on life skills, such as interpersonal communication, problem solving and decision making, physical fitness and health maintenance, and identity development (e.g., Darden, Gazda, & Ginter, 1996; Ginter, 1999; Palmo, 2006). Prevention programs for adults also address life skills, with some programs geared toward specific concerns, such as eating disorders, violence, parenting, and stress management. Because everyone suffers from physical and emotional stress of some nature, stress management is an especially important area to consider when designing prevention

$$\text{Psychological health} = \frac{\text{Coping skills} + \text{Self-esteem} + \text{Social support} + \text{Personal power}}{\text{Organic factors} + \text{Stress} + \text{Powerlessness}}$$

FIGURE 6–3 An Equation for Psychological Health

programs. Stress management programs can be adapted for all ages and provide a variety of physical and mental health benefits.

STRESS MANAGEMENT

The relationship among stress, coping, and well-being is well documented (e.g., Preston, O'Neal, & Talaga, 2010; Romano, 2001; Shallcross, 2011). **Stress** is a construct that has been defined in multiple ways. It can be viewed as a relationship between the events that happen to us and our physical, cognitive, emotional, and behavioral responses to them (McNamara, 2000). Stress can refer to an internal state, an external event, or the interaction between a person and the environment. A more formal definition, offered by Lazarus and Folkman (1984), describes stress as "a particular relationship between the person and the environment that is appraised by the person as taxing or exceeding his or her resources and endangering his or her well-being" (p. 19). Perceptions of what is stressful vary widely among individuals, with some people viewing certain events as quite stressful and others being nonplussed by them.

Anything perceived as a source of threat, harm, loss, or challenge has the potential to be stressful. Stressors may be chronic (e.g., living in poverty), acute (e.g., death of a spouse), or ongoing daily aggravations (e.g., arguing with siblings). Exposure to stress triggers several physical, emotional, and cognitive changes. Immediate, short-term reactions to stress can potentially motivate people toward action; however, long-term exposure can lead to physical and psychosocial difficulties (Gibson & Myers, 2006; Sharrer & Ryan-Wenger, 2002). Coping with stress is the process by which a person handles stressful situations and the thoughts and emotions they generate.

Prevention programs to help people manage stress effectively typically focus on (a) identifying sources of stress, (b) recognizing the physical and emotional consequences of stress, and (c) learning and implementing adaptive coping responses. McNamara (2000) suggests that counselors include the following eight components in stress management programs:

1. *Education about the causes and consequences of stress.* Education includes helping people recognize sources of stress in their own lives and their cognitive, physical, and emotional responses to stress.
2. *Training in methods to reduce psychological and physical arousal.* Counselors can use deep breathing and relaxation exercises to help people reduce their reactions to stress.
3. *General problem-solving and decision-making skills.* Helping people construct a model for problem solving and decision making can help establish a healthy sense of control.
4. *General cognitive skills.* Cognitive restructuring, including reducing negative or catastrophic thinking, can also provide a sense of control that helps reduce stress.
5. *Physical ways of coping with stress.* Nutrition, physical activity, and sleep quality all affect people's psychological well-being. Developing and practicing good habits in each of these areas can help reduce stress.
6. *Time management.* Time management tools are essential for handling stress effectively. Setting achievable goals, balancing work and leisure, and organizing tasks are examples of time management tools. Additional examples are listed in Figure 6–4.

• Clarify your goals.	What is the most important and why?
• Avoid procrastination.	Establish a routine, and reward yourself for completing tasks.
• Keep a calendar or day timer.	Write down meetings, scheduled events, assignments, etc.
• Break down large tasks into manageable units.	Make plans for completing each unit.
• Keep a daily and weekly "to-do" list.	Prioritize activities and tasks, and check them off when they are completed.
• Recognize the need for balance and flexibility.	Include breaks and recreational times that coincide with your body clock.
• Keep things in perspective.	Worry saps time and energy and is nonproductive. If you find yourself getting anxious, take time to relax and practice deep breathing.

FIGURE 6–4   Time Management Tools

7. *Skills for increasing self-control and self-esteem.*   Anger management skills can be taught to facilitate self-control. Counselors also can help people identify and develop personal strengths, thus building resilience.
8. *Social skills.*   Social skills training includes effective communication, conflict resolution, and assertiveness training.

Stress management programs are often implemented in schools, work settings, universities, and community agencies. Examples of successful programs are numerous. One such example, designed by Ballesteros and Whitlock (2012), outlines a program for helping adolescents and young adults who engage in self-injurious behavior cope more effectively with stress. Clinical mental health counselors need to be able to plan, implement, and evaluate stress management programs for the populations with which they work.

Many chronic stressors—including poverty, discrimination, and prejudice—are systemic in nature and need to be addressed accordingly. Albee (2000) states, "The longer I work in the field of prevention, the more convinced I become that economic, social-class variables are most important in perpetuating stress, social injustice, and exploitation" (p. 850). Lewis et al. (2003) collectively refer to individuals who experience a similar kind of stress for an extended time as **vulnerable populations**. Examples of vulnerable populations include people who are poor, homeless, and unemployed (or underemployed); families undergoing divorce; pregnant teenagers; people with chronic diseases such as fibromyalgia and AIDS; some elderly populations; and other people marginalized by society because of discrimination. To address the needs of vulnerable populations, counselors are urged to engage in advocacy, outreach, and social action.

Summary and Conclusion

In this chapter, an overview of holistic approaches to clinical mental health counseling has been described. Clearly, many of the approaches share commonalities because they all emphasize the importance of the whole person rather than disparate parts.

The biopsychosocial model of counseling has been defined in some depth. The integral role spirituality plays in many of our clients' lives was also discussed, including the ways spirituality can be infused into counseling sessions. Related to spirituality is mindfulness, a practice that can be used by clients and counselors informally and formally. Mindfulness is one way to enrich life experiences and cope with problems in living.

The concepts of wellness and prevention were then dealt with. Wellness-based counseling is designed to improve mental and physical health, taking into account all dimensions that affect health and well-being and recognizing the need to balance those dimensions. Two models of wellness—the theoretically based Wheel of Wellness and the empirically based Indivisible Self model—were presented.

Preventing psychological distress by helping people develop resources and strengths while reducing negative influences is a fundamental value of the counseling profession. Primary prevention programs, which take into account individual and environmental influences, provide the most efficient way of promoting mental health among the largest number of people. The prevention models described in the chapter emphasize the importance of enhancing individual strengths and environmental resources and decreasing individual limitations and social stressors.

Holistic approaches to clinical mental health counseling are strengths-based and help build self-efficacy and resilience. They should be utilized whenever possible.

Dragon Images/Shutterstock

CHAPTER 7

Consultation, Advocacy, and Evaluation

CHAPTER OVERVIEW

From reading this chapter, you will learn about

- Characteristics of effective mental health consultation and the different roles consultants play

- The importance of advocacy on multiple levels

- The need for client outcome evaluation and ways to evaluate client outcomes

- The need for systematic program evaluation and the importance of process evaluation and program outcome evaluation

As you read, consider

- How important consultation is to counseling; the different types of consultation, based on Caplan's model; and your comfort with each

- Why advocacy is important and the types of advocacy you envision yourself being a part of

- Ways you would evaluate client outcomes and reasons you might feel uncomfortable evaluating client outcomes

- Your role in helping with program evaluation and the differences between process evaluation and program outcome evaluation

I read the test data like a ticker tape
  from the New York Stock Exchange.
Your "neurotic" scales are slightly up
  with a large discrepancy in your Wechsler scores.
Myers-Briggs extroversion is in the moderate range
  with an artistic interest expressed in your Strong profile.
At first, like a Wall Street wizard,
  I try to assess and predict your future,
    but in talking about expected yields
      I find the unexpected. . . .
Alone, you long for the warmth of relationships
  as well as for the factual information at hand.
In the process of discussion,
  a fellow human being emerges.
Behind what has been revealed on paper
  is the uniqueness of a person.

Reprinted from "Thoughts of a Wall Street Counselor," by S. T. Gladding, 1986/1995, *Journal of Humanistic Education and Development, 24,* p. 176. Copyright © Samuel T. Gladding.

Clinical mental health counselors carry out many different roles. Even though the amount of time spent in various roles will differ, depending on the counselor and the setting, the roles described in this chapter are all considered important to the work mental health professionals do. Although the topics presented in this chapter may initially appear unrelated—consultation, advocacy, and evaluation—they have a common theme: Each plays a vital part in the well-being of clients and the greater community.

The chapter begins with an overview of consultation. The role of being a consultant is not well conceptualized by many counselors who do not understand its exact nature. Brown (1983) relates the story of a person whose image of a consultant was of "someone who blows in, blows off and blows out" (p. 124). Realistically, consultants are experts in particular areas, such as mental health counseling, who offer indirect and usually atheoretical services to clients, communities, and organizations experiencing problems. Consulting is the term for this service, and it is both similar to and different from counseling.

The second service covered in this chapter is advocacy. It is a process that steps outside the traditional role of counseling by focusing on injustices and environmental conditions that need to change for a client's or a community's welfare to be maximized (Kiselica & Robinson, 2001). ACA adopted a set of advocacy competencies for counselors in 2003. Advocates can engage in a spectrum of activities to address systemic needs, ranging from empowering clients to actively lobbying for social justice. Advocacy for clients and for the profession of counseling has been identified as a professional imperative (Myers, Sweeney, & White, 2002).

In the final two sections of the chapter, evaluation is covered—specifically, the evaluation of client treatment outcomes and the evaluation of programs that are offered in particular settings. Evaluation is an ongoing process that is integral to all aspects of counseling. Continuing, systematic, well-planned evaluation is a vital component of effective mental health service delivery. Evaluation enables counselors to make informed decisions about treatment options and services offered to clients. It provides ways to ensure that services are being implemented as planned and that specific goals and outcomes are being met. Moreover, evaluation makes it possible to demonstrate accountability to clients, other professionals, accrediting agencies, and the community at large.

MENTAL HEALTH CONSULTATION

One key service provided by clinical mental health counselors is consultation. Consultation is a broad area that is used in many fields, including education, psychology, medicine, and business (Brown, Pryzwansky, & Schulte, 2011). According to the 2016 CACREP standards, counselors are expected to have a knowledge of "theories, models, and strategies for understanding and practicing consultation" (Section 2, 5.c). Mental health consultation draws heavily from the work of Gerald Caplan (1917–2008), who is known as the father of the modern practice of mental health consultation (Erchul, 2009). Caplan was a child and community psychiatrist who developed and refined many conceptual models and methods for practicing consultation.

Clinical mental health counselors are called upon to consult with other professionals and organizations. Indeed, consultation is a "cornerstone activity" for almost all helping professions (Carney & Jefferson, 2014; Dougherty, 2014). The skills needed to provide effective consultation are "built on a professional's solid foundation of clinical knowledge and expertise" (Sears, Rudisill, & Mason-Sears, 2006, p. 388). Although some mental health professionals choose to become full-time consultants, most clinical mental health counselors do not. Instead they engage in consultation as a part-time service. Depending on the services rendered, clinical mental health counselors may or may not be directly reimbursed. Most insurance and managed care organizations do not pay for consultation (Sears et al., 2006). That is one reason why clinical mental health counselors in private practice are not as involved in consultation as others in different settings.

What Is Mental Health Consultation?

Put succinctly, **consultation** is "a problem-solving, interpersonal relationship that develops through periodic face-to-face contacts between consultant and consultee" (Erchul, 2003, p. 105). For clarification, the consultant is the professional helper providing consultation. The consultee is the professional working directly with the client who requests help from the consultant. The third party is the client or client system served directly by the consultee.

Some underlying premises of mental health consultation are listed in Box 7–1.

BOX 7–1 Underlying Premises of Mental Health Consultation

- Consultation involves sharing information and ideas, coordinating and comparing observations, and developing tentative hypotheses for action.
- Consultation is based on the recognition that a single form of expertise is not always sufficient to meet a client's needs.
- A lack of objectivity on the part of the consultee can lead to the need for consultation.
- Consultation represents a triadic relationship between the consultant, the consultee(s), and the client or client system.
- Consultation is an indirect relationship in which the consultant works with the consultee, who works with the client or client system.
- The consultative relationship is designed to be nonhierarchical, collegial, and nonauthoritative.
- The consultant and consultee are viewed as experts in their own areas.
- The client's well-being and progress are the responsibility of the consultee.
- The consultee can choose to accept, modify, or reject consultant recommendations.
- The consultative relationship is voluntary, work-related, and systems-oriented.
- The consultative relationship is confidential.
- The purpose of consultation is to help the consultee with the challenges presented by the consultee's client and to increase the consultee's skills for working independently with similar problems in the future.
- Consultation is distinct from therapy.
- It is crucial that consultants maintain clear role boundaries.

Source: Adapted from Sears et al., 2006, p. 402.

In short, common aspects of the consultation process are (a) it is problem-solving focused, (b) it is tripartite in nature, and (c) it emphasizes improvement (Dougherty, 2014; see Figure 7–1).

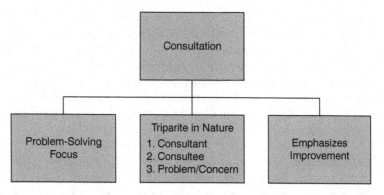

FIGURE 7–1   The Anatomy of Consultation

Caplan's Four Types of Mental Health Consultation

A comprehensive study of consultation indicates that there are many models and styles of consultation, and that the nature of consultation depends on its purpose. Caplan's four types of mental health consultation is an exemplary and comprehensive model of consultation. Although each type of mental health consultation is described separately, counselors may need to be flexible in shifting from one type to another (Sears et al., 2006). Throughout the process, consultants continually assess, conceptualize, and evaluate what is working and what needs to be changed.

CLIENT-CENTERED CASE CONSULTATION.   This approach is the most commonly used form of mental health consultation. The consultee presents a case about a particular client who is experiencing a problem for which the consultee needs treatment recommendations. The primary goal of this form of consultation is to develop a plan to help a specific client. A secondary goal is to provide the consultee with tools to handle similar cases in the future. In many cases, the consultant evaluates the client directly to develop recommendations for the consultee (Sears et al., 2006).

    Case Example: A school counselor (the consultee) is working with a fifth grade student, Megan, who has missed several days of school recently. When the school counselor, Mr. Rolf, talked with Megan, she explained that many derogatory things about her had been posted on a popular social network. Megan reluctantly shared some of the messages and pictures that had been displayed. Mr. Rolf realized that Megan was being cyberbullied, an issue that he has dealt with infrequently. Because he wants to consult with someone who has expertise on the issue, he contacts your agency and asks to consult with you about Megan and the issue of cyberbullying, an area in which you have a great deal of expertise. You meet with Megan to find out more about the situation and then meet with Mr. Rolf to develop recommendations for working with Megan.

CONSULTEE-CENTERED CASE CONSULTATION.   The goal of consultee-centered case consultation is to improve the consultee's ability to work effectively with a particular case as well as with similar cases. Although there are similarities between this type of consultation and client-centered consultation, the primary difference is that the assessment focuses on possible shortcomings in the consultee or in the support systems of his or her organization (Erchul, 2003). A consultant in consultee-centered case consultation typically does not assess the client directly; instead, the consultant builds a relationship with the consultee, assesses the consultee's problem(s) with the case, and intervenes to help alleviate the problem(s). As the consultee talks about the case, the consultant tentatively categorizes the problem(s) as a lack of knowledge, lack of skill, lack of confidence, or lack of professional objectivity. The focus is on improving the consultee's professional functioning in relation to specific cases (Dougherty, 2014).

Case Example: Sabrina, a licensed professional counselor in your agency, is working with an adolescent, Nathan, whose father recently died in a fire. The counselor does not have much direct experience in trauma work and lacks confidence in her skills, even though she has participated in several trauma workshops. Sabrina is unsure about how to work effectively with Nathan. In addition to her lack of confidence, she is concerned about her professional objectivity; her father died suddenly three months ago. Sabrina asks you to consult with her about how to proceed.

PROGRAM-CENTERED ADMINISTRATIVE CONSULTATION.   The goal of program-centered administrative consultation is to help an individual or a group of consultees develop a new program or improve an existing one. The role of the consultant is to work with consultees to assess the existing situation, determine needs, and then develop recommendations for change (Sears et al., 2006). In a formal program-centered administrative consultation, the consultant writes a report that presents findings and specific recommendations.

Case Example: A community mental health agency is concerned that it is not serving certain populations in the community. The agency's director may decide to contact a consultant to determine ways to address the concern. Is the problem related to cost of services, transportation issues, the times services are offered, the professionals offering services, or an unidentified factor or combination of factors? The consultant meets with groups and individuals in the agency to assess the problem and develop a plan(s) to help the agency find ways to provide services more effectively to underrepresented populations.

CONSULTEE-CENTERED ADMINISTRATIVE CONSULTATION.   Consultee-centered administrative consultation differs from program-centered administrative consultation in several ways. The goal of consultee-centered administrative consultation is not to help an organization develop or improve programs. Instead, the consultant's goal is "to assess the consultee and administrative staff to develop more effective professional functioning of an individual, group, or entire organization" (Sears et al., 2006, p. 405). Put another way, the goals of consultee-centered administrative consultation are to help solve problems in organizational policy, enhance the professional competency of staff, and increase the overall level of consultees' professional functioning (Dougherty, 2014). These consultants need to have a sound knowledge of social systems, administrative services, and organizational theory. They also need to be skilled in group work and group processing. Some of these consultants are internal consultants, and others are external (outside) consultants. (See Box 7–2.)

Case Example: A police chief is aware of racial tension among the police officers in his department. Police officers choose to segregate themselves during break times. Moreover, at least two officers have asked to be reassigned to new partners "with whom they have more in common." Racial slurs are not uncommon, and efforts at team building have been unsuccessful. The police chief realizes that the problem needs to be addressed as soon as possible. He calls you to see if you would be willing to serve as an outside consultant, that is, someone who is not already employed by the organization. Your job is to meet with groups and individuals to help them develop diversity skills.

BOX 7–2 Internal and External Consultants

An internal consultant is an employee of the organization or agency. Internal consultants may be employed, for example, as licensed professional counselors who have their own caseloads. Consultation occurs when someone else in the organization—either another mental health professional or someone at the administrative level—asks for help in providing indirect services to a client(s) or client system. In contrast, an external consultant is not a regular employee of the organization or agency. External consultants are often brought into an organization for a specific purpose because of their "presumed objectivity and special expertise" (Sears et al., 2006, p. 18).

Key Characteristics of Successful Consultants

Although some mental health professionals choose to become professional consultants, more frequently consultation is a skill that clinical mental health counselors use within the broader context of the counseling arena (Carney & Jefferson, 2014). Many of the qualities that characterize effective mental health professionals in general also characterize effective consultants. Some of those attributes, described by Sears et al. (2006), include the following:

- *A positive, caring approach.*   Effective consultants are nonjudgmental and sensitive, and they demonstrate genuine concern for all parties involved.
- *Strong communication skills.*   Effective consultants listen carefully to what consultees are saying and validate that communication. The consultants are able to engage with consultees, avoid offering immediate solutions, and work collaboratively rather than offer prescriptive advice.
- *A responsible work ethic.*   In many formal consultative situations, particularly when serving externally, it is important to represent the external organizations responsibly. The way consultants present themselves, interact with others, and follow through with commitments all need to be given careful consideration. Other work factors that demonstrate reliability include flexibility, time efficiency, and a nonauthoritarian attitude.
- *Thorough diagnostic skills.*   Consultation typically involves problem solving. To solve problems, consultants need to be objective, carefully assess relevant variables, and conduct well-planned evaluations.
- *A wealth of content knowledge.*   Effective consultants have a strong understanding of human development theory, specialized knowledge about particular topics, and training in consultative methods. Just as the *ACA Code of Ethics* (2014) mandates counselors practice only within the boundaries of their competence, consultants need to be selective about accepting referrals, accepting only those that are within their areas of expertise.
- *System smarts.*   Consultants need to understand the nature of the systems in which they work. For example, if the recommendations made by the consultant involve

considerable financial expense that cannot be covered by the organization's budget, those recommendations, no matter how appropriate, do not meet the system's feasibility criterion.

Developing a personal consultation style is a lifelong process based on your professional and personal experiences. Developing a consultation style involves examining your personal values and beliefs, becoming aware of your personal and professional limitations, seeking out additional training in consultation, and continually assessing the needs of the organizations and people with whom you are working. Being intentional about developing successful consultation skills can increase your overall effectiveness and influence as a clinical mental health counselor (Dougherty, 2014).

This section ends with a tongue-in-cheek set of recommendations for how to *fail* as a mental health consultant (what you should not do!). These recommendations (see Box 7–3) are adapted from a list of steps taken from Q. Rae-Grant's "The Art of Being a Failure as a Consultant" (cited in Sears et al., 2006, p. 400).

BOX 7–3   How to Fail as a Mental Health Consultant

1. Be a know-it-all.
2. Don't learn anything about the consultee.
3. Be dogmatic and inflexible.
4. Do not accept feedback.
5. Insist on implementing unwanted or unsanctioned change.
6. Conduct therapy with your consultee.
7. Create alliances with various subgroups.
8. Do not follow through with your commitments.
9. Act as a supervisor rather than as a consultant.
10. Act as a therapist rather than as a consultant.
11. Sulk when your recommendations are not taken.

ADVOCACY

In addition to consultation, clinical mental health counselors serve as advocates for their clients and for the profession of counseling. Many of the clients served by clinical mental health counselors are members of vulnerable populations—for example, people who are poor, homeless, and unemployed; families undergoing divorce; pregnant teenagers; people with chronic diseases; and people who have experienced discrimination. To address the needs of vulnerable populations, mental health professionals must engage in advocacy, outreach, and social action.

The 1999 presidential theme for the American Counseling Association was "Advocacy: A Voice for Our Clients and Communities" (see Box 7–4). Since then, the counseling profession has made significant progress in emphasizing ways counselors can advocate for their clients and the systems within which those clients live (Ratts, Toporek, & Lewis, 2010). Advocacy counseling expands the traditional role of individual counseling, which focuses on intrapersonal concerns, to a broader focus that addresses injustice, oppression, and environmental conditions that need to improve for the benefit of an individual or group

(Kiselica & Robinson, 2001; Ratts et al., 2010). In this section, advocacy is defined as it relates to clinical mental health counseling.

BOX 7–4   Advocacy

Advocacy is an important aspect of every counselor's role. Regardless of the particular settings in which counselors work, each of them is confronted again and again with issues that cannot be resolved simply through change within the individual client. All too often, negative aspects of the environment impinge on a client's well-being, intensifying personal problems or creating obstacles to growth. When such situations arise, effective counselors speak up!

(Lewis & Bradley, 2000, p. 3)

What Is Advocacy?

Several definitions of advocacy have been proposed. For example, Toporek (2000) defines **advocacy** as actions taken by counseling professionals to help remove environmental barriers that hamper clients' well-being. Lewis et al. (2003) note that advocacy serves two purposes: (a) to increase clients' sense of personal power, and (b) to foster environmental changes that reflect greater responsiveness to clients' personal needs. C. C. Lee (2007) emphasizes the need for counselors to make advocacy a priority that focuses on addressing systems of oppression that negatively affect clients.

Outreach, empowerment, social justice, and social action are all terms associated with advocacy. **Outreach** refers to initiating behaviors toward people in need for the purpose of making a helpful difference. It involves reaching out to vulnerable populations in their communities and helping them find new ways to cope with stressors. **Empowerment** is a process through which clients gain the resources and skills needed to have more control over their environments and their lives (McWhirter, 1997). **Social justice** "involves promoting access and equity to ensure full participation in the life of a society," particularly for those members who have been marginalized (Lee, 2013, p. 16). **Social action** refers to behaviors designed to promote social justice. Social action can occur on behalf of a client or on behalf of the larger society. It is designed to eradicate social inequities, which may limit or obstruct vulnerable groups' access to basic societal rights. Although the terms social justice and social action are similar, social justice is a belief system that values fair and equal treatment for all members of society. Social action derives from that belief system, resulting in actions taken to promote equal rights for all people. Advocacy counseling can include outreach, empowerment, and social action, which is rooted in the concept of social justice. Advocacy serves to enhance a client's sense of personal power and/or foster change in the broader sociopolitical environment.

Empowering individuals and diminishing societal forces that cause powerlessness among certain groups are ways to promote psychological health. Advocacy counseling can be conceptualized on a continuum, with empowerment of the individual client on one end of the continuum and social action to reduce oppression, discrimination, and other forms of injustice on the other end (Toporek, 2000; see Figure 7–2). Accordingly, the counselor's role as an advocate can range from designing interventions that empower individual clients to taking actions that influence public policy and systemic change.

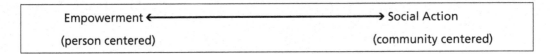

FIGURE 7–2   The Continuum of Advocacy

Empowerment

Facilitating empowerment through counseling is a way to focus on individual clients within the context of their sociopolitical environments. Empowerment refers to efforts of the counselor and the client to identify barriers while simultaneously developing client self-advocacy skills and resources to help overcome those barriers (Toporek, Lewis, & Crethar, 2009). This effort may involve helping a woman who is being abused become aware of the inappropriate use of power and privilege that her partner is claiming. Similarly, it may involve helping a client recognize an environmental barrier (e.g., discrimination in the workplace) and then make a plan to overcome it (Toporek, 2000). Empowerment is a lifelong process that involves critical self-reflection and action, an awareness of the power dynamics in the environment that affect diverse populations, and the development of skills to gain personal power and empower others.

To help counselors understand the concept of empowerment, McWhirter (1994, 1997) designed a 5 Cs model of empowerment for counseling, which includes the following components:

- **Collaboration**, which involves working collaboratively with clients to define the problem and then plan for change. Collaboration also includes taking steps to decrease the inherent power differential between counselor and client.
- **Context**, which refers to acknowledging the role of factors such as poverty, racism, sexism, classism, and other barriers that maintain or exacerbate clients' problems.
- **Critical consciousness**, which is fostered by critical self-reflection and power analysis. The goal is to raise clients' awareness of the social, economic, and other power dynamics that affect their well-being.
- **Competence**, which focuses on clients' strengths, resources, and skills that can be used to help them take action toward problem resolution.
- **Community**, which may be defined broadly to include family, friends, ethnic affiliations, faith connections, organizational affiliations, or other significant bonds. Connection with the community is essential to the empowerment process because it provides resources and support as well as opportunities for the client to "give back" by empowering others.

Key outcomes of empowerment are a client's enhanced sense of personal control and the ability to advocate for oneself. To facilitate self-advocacy in clients, counselors first need to be aware that counseling has the potential to encourage dependence in that it presupposes neediness (McWhirter, 1997). Rather than act as rescuers, effective advocates help clients develop and utilize strengths and resources, both personally and in their communities. In Box 7–5, a clinical mental health counselor describes his role as an advocate when he worked as a mental health practitioner.

BOX 7–5   My First Professional Role in a Clinical Mental Health Setting: Counselor, Advocate, and Team Member

My initial position as a credentialed counselor was that of a mental health practitioner. I worked in a county agency, serving clients with severe and persistent mental illness (SPMI). My position included being part of a team modeled after the Program for Assertive Community Treatment (PACT), a nationally known model developed by Deborah J. Allness, MSSW, MD, and William H. Knoedler, MD. The program is designed specifically for mental health professionals serving the SPMI population within the communities in which they live. Our treatment team was multidisciplinary and met daily to plan and coordinate client care before going out into the community.

I realized that I could apply the principles, theories, and skills learned during my educational training as I worked with clients. However, one of my primary challenges was *patience*, not as much with clients, but rather with systems—the systems and agencies that must be choreographed and coerced in order to provide services. Building rapport and relationships among colleagues and others in the larger support system was (and is) especially important. My role as a clinical mental health counselor was intertwined with the role of being an advocate. I have also learned to advocate for myself as a professional counselor within the context of a dynamic mental health team.

Advocating for clients requires addressing stigmas every day, personal as well as those associated with the health, welfare, and social services systems, and with correctional facilities. In challenging environments, it is paramount to remember that ALL clients have rights, privileges, and expectations. Respecting differences and using power judiciously often meant adjusting MY counseling expectations to a new reality. Working with the SPMI population taught me an important lesson: Maintaining psychiatric stability is often an outcome to be celebrated.

Additional considerations that accompanied the formidable tasks of effective assessment, diagnosing, and treatment planning were client issues of substance abuse, physical illness, intellectual functioning deficits, criminal history, and poor family support. We adopted a team approach that incorporated biopsychosocial assessment, case conceptualization, and realistic treatment plans. The services we provided were designed to increase self-sufficiency rather than build dependence. Although my position as mental health practitioner had its share of struggles, the triumphs I shared each day with clients and team members helped me grow as a person, an advocate, and a counseling professional.

Tom Buffkin, MA Ed, LPC, NCC

Social Action

Counselors committed to social action advocate for change in the context of the larger sociopolitical arena (Toporek et al., 2009). Social action may be directed toward agencies, communities, the legal system, and legislation. Social action can address immediate environmental concerns (e.g., making a specific facility more accessible to people with disabilities) or more global concerns (e.g., legislative or policy issues that adversely affect groups of people). Advocating for mental health parity to ensure that mental healthcare benefits are covered in the same way as other healthcare benefits is one instance of social action. Other examples include advocating for public policy changes on behalf of the homeless and making community presentations to advocate for fair and respectful treatment of lesbian, gay, bisexual, and transgender individuals.

Counselors for Social Justice (CSJ), a division of ACA, provides an organized forum through which counselors can advocate for oppressed populations. CSJ was established in 1999 as an organizational affiliate and officially became an ACA division in September 2002. The mission of CSJ is "to work to promote social justice in our society through confronting oppressive systems of power and privilege that affect professional counselors and our clients and to assist in the positive change in our society through the professional development of counselors" (CSJ, 2011). CSJ promotes individual and collective social responsibility, provides a support network for counselors engaged in social justice activities, and collaborates with other organizations in ACA and the larger community to implement social action strategies.

ACA Advocacy Competencies

As noted earlier, in 2003 ACA adopted a set of advocacy competencies that can be used by practitioners, counselor educators, and counseling students (Goodman, 2009). The competencies were developed by a task force appointed by the 2001 ACA president, Jane Goodman. A three-dimensional competency model can be accessed on the ACA website (www.counseling.org/resources/competencies/advocacy_competencies.pdf).

The competency domains are defined by the extent of client involvement and the level of intervention. The extent of client involvement falls on a continuum, ranging from "acting on behalf of the client" to "acting with the client." Level of intervention also falls on a continuum, which includes the microlevel (client-focused), the mesolevel (community- and systems-focused), and the macrolevel (focused on systemic change in the public arena). Examples of ways counselors might serve as advocates across domains include the following:

- *Client empowerment:*   The counselor helps the client identify strengths and resources and helps the client develop self-advocacy skills.
- *Client advocacy:*   The counselor helps a client gain access to needed services, such as health care or disability assistance.
- *Community collaboration:*   Counselors work with community organizations to bring about change that fosters clients' healthy development.
- *Systems advocacy:*   Counselors intervene at the systemic level to help bring about change. For example, a counselor might be aware of discrimination against the LGBT population at a particular university and works with the university administrators to develop a center designed to educate the campus community around issues of sexual orientation and/or gender identity.
- *Public information:*   Counselors disseminate information to inform the public about "issues of disempowerment or disenfranchisement and create a sense of urgency for change" (Lee & Rodgers, 2009, p. 285). Interventions designed to increase public awareness utilize a variety of media outlets.
- *Social/political advocacy:*   Counselors take actions on behalf of the populations they serve. When counselors are aware of broad issues that are hindering vulnerable populations, they act on the macrolevel by working toward change in public policy (Toporek et al., 2009).

Advocacy Skills and Attributes

A number of skills and attributes are needed to engage in advocacy successfully. At the core of successful advocating is a compassionate spirit that is sensitive to human suffering and committed to helping alleviate that suffering (Kiselica & Robinson, 2001). Compassion and commitment provide the necessary motivation to take action related to an identified need (Myers et al., 2002). Once a need is identified, counselors need skills to identify specific areas to target, keeping the bigger picture in mind. Social change usually does not occur quickly, and when changes are made, it takes time to implement and evaluate those changes. To that end, advocates demonstrate planfulness, persistence, and patience.

To advocate successfully, counselors use many of the same verbal and nonverbal communication skills that are essential to effective counseling. Advocates need to be able to listen and respond empathically to vulnerable clients so that those clients feel understood and heard. Beyond that, counselors need to develop strong skills in persuasion, conflict resolution, compromise, and negotiation (Ezell, 2001). To advocate successfully, counselors must develop skills in communicating effectively with the power sources from which change will originate. For example, when communicating with legislators, it is important to be organized, concise, and concrete. The use of jargon, exaggeration, or rambling hurts a counselor's presentation.

Social justice advocacy begins with self-awareness and a commitment to eradicating social injustices (Lee & Rodgers, 2009). Strong leadership skills, a strategic vision that can be clearly articulated, an ability to collect and utilize data that illustrate the need for social change, and the courage to back up one's convictions are all important characteristics of counselors who advocate in the public arena.

In summarizing skills and practices related to advocacy, Ezell (2001) states that effective advocates do the following:

- Provide vigorous representation for their clients
- Use multiple methods to understand their clients' needs, issues, and problems
- Target specific policies or practices for change
- Map the decision systems responsible for targeted policies and practices
- Recast larger problems into solvable pieces
- Propose concrete solutions to problems
- Utilize several strategies and skills simultaneously and sequentially
- Actively counter negative stereotypes and misbeliefs
- Use the least confrontational tactics necessary to accomplish their objectives
- Exhibit cultural awareness and respect as they relate to colleagues, clients, and decision makers
- Place a high priority on influencing budgets
- Closely monitor the implementation of changed policies and practices (p. 193)

Challenges of Advocacy

Advocacy can be challenging work, particularly if efforts are not made to avoid certain pitfalls. Because of the personal investment involved, advocacy can be emotionally draining and can lead to burnout if professionals do not set limits and boundaries (Ezell, 2001). Accordingly, advocates need to evaluate themselves and their motives, being careful to avoid overzealousness and blind idealism (Kiselica & Robinson, 2001). Out of the desire to help vulnerable populations, it is possible to move ahead too quickly, not respecting existing barriers and perhaps even creating additional ones. Similarly, in attempting to right a wrong, advocates may tend to exaggerate claims about specific problems, an action that is unethical.

In addition to moving too quickly, it also is possible to assume responsibility for too much. McWhirter (1997) notes that "the number of issues that lend themselves to social activism is virtually endless" (p. 10). Focusing on specific issues—such as violence against women, affordable housing, or community assistance for seniors—enables counselors to channel their energies more effectively than attempting to address an assortment of societal ills. Not everyone needs to become a revolutionary; there is room in the field for all levels of intervention (Albee, 2000).

Advocacy for the Profession

Although advocating for client well-being and for social justice is crucial, a related form of advocacy is advocating for the counseling profession itself. This form of advocacy, according to Myers et al. (2002), is a professional imperative. Professional advocacy includes contributing to the development of a strong professional identity, lobbying for professional recognition, and demonstrating professional pride and accountability. It may include working through the political process to influence legislation that affects the profession of counseling, such as obtaining government-funded reimbursement for licensed professional counselors and lobbying for mental health parity. Engaging in professional advocacy helps ensure that counselors are recognized as competent and credible mental health service providers.

To successfully advocate for the counseling profession, clinical mental health counselors need to stay abreast of public policy and take steps to influence the passage of laws when existing conditions adversely affect either their clients or the counseling profession. The ACA Office of Public Policy and Information is an excellent resource for federal legislative initiatives and can be accessed through the ACA website at www.counseling.org/PublicPolicy/.

CLIENT OUTCOME EVALUATION

> *However beautiful the strategy, you should occasionally look at the results.*
> —Winston Churchill

Clinical mental health counseling is a complex process, and to be effective mental health counselors need skills in evaluating the effectiveness of the interventions used with clients. One of the most challenging tasks clinical mental health counselors face is determining "what treatment, by whom, is the most effective for this individual with that specific problem or set of problems, and under which set of circumstances" (Paul, 1967, p. 111). Client outcome research is designed to evaluate the effectiveness of specific interventions. A well-developed research base, combined with clinical judgment, facilitates practitioners in making decisions about how to work best with clients (Sheperis, Young, & Daniels, 2017). Definitions and examples of evidenced-based treatment, evidence-based practice, and other terms associated with outcome research are presented in Box 7–6.

BOX 7–6   Outcome Research Terminology

EVIDENCE-BASED TREATMENT (EBT):   EBTs are identified based on the outcomes of randomized, controlled trials. The research trials are conducted to determine whether the interventions outperform control or alternative interventions. Treatment outcomes are measured in a number of ways and often yield inconsistent results (De Los Reyes & Kazdin, 2008). *Example:* Studying an adolescent treatment program using cognitive behavior therapy (CBT), measuring treatment effectiveness for anger management, and comparing the research results to a nontreatment group.

EVIDENCE-BASED PRACTICE (EBP):   EBP is "a broader term and refers to clinical practice that is informed by evidence about interventions, clinical expertise, and [client] needs, values, and preferences and their integration in decision making about individual care" (Kazdin, 2008, p. 147). *Example:* After considering what the evidence says about using CBT as an intervention for adolescent anger management, the counselor uses clinical expertise and knowledge about the particular group members to adapt the intervention to meet the needs of the group. Clinical judgment plays a key role in decision making regarding interventions.

MODERATORS: Moderators are characteristics that influence the intervention outcome (Kazdin, 2008). They include characteristics of the client, the clinician, and contextual factors. *Examples:* Socioeconomic status, ethnicity, gender, comorbidity, age.

TREATMENT INTEGRITY: The extent to which interventions are delivered in a comprehensive manner by a trained interventionist (Hagermoser, Sanetti, & Kratochwill, 2009). *Example:* A clinician who has been trained in PTSD follows protocol when working with a client diagnosed with PTSD, taking into account clinical adjustment and moderating factors that have been shown to affect treatment effectiveness in different populations.

Definition and Purpose of Client Outcome Evaluation

Client outcome evaluation is a way to evaluate treatment outcomes with specific clients. It is one way clinicians can monitor client progress and make adjustments as needed (Young, 2013). Systematic evaluation of client progress enables counselors to reflect carefully on their counseling methods, assess client change, modify interventions as needed, and inform future decision making. Evaluating with clients the effectiveness of the counseling process during sessions and after the sessions end can benefit clients and counselors alike.

Counselors who fail to employ evaluation procedures place themselves and the counseling profession in jeopardy with the general public, third-party payers, and specific clients who rightfully demand accountability. A failure to evaluate counseling methods and related outcomes also puts counselors in danger of being unethical because they cannot demonstrate that the counseling services implemented have a reasonable promise of success, as the ethical codes of professional counseling associations require (Sexton & Whiston, 1996).

Multifaceted Approaches to Client Outcome Evaluation

How do clinicians measure client outcomes? Measures exist on a spectrum ranging from general to specific but generally address the following interrelated areas (Dharmalingam, Berg, & Hall, 2012):

- *Symptoms:*   Client symptoms are the manifestations of the client's concerns. Examples include depression, anxiety, substance abuse, mania, and violent behavior.
- *Well-being:*   Well-being refers to emotional stability, motivation, energy levels, and general life satisfaction.

TABLE 7–1 Measuring Outcomes: Examples of Evaluation Methods

Measurement	Purpose	Examples
Client satisfaction survey	To evaluate the degree to which clients feel they have received services that are useful	Client Satisfaction Questionnaire-8 (CSQ-8; Attkisson & Greenfield, 1994)
		Service Satisfaction Scale-30 (SSS-30; Attkisson & Greenfield, 1994)
Goal attainment scaling	To help determine the efficacy of services according to preestablished criteria	5-point Likert scale, used to evaluate client progress toward achieving specific goals
Assessment of client functioning	To measure functional status along general or specific dimensions	Global Assessment of Functioning (GAF), using guidelines from the *DSM*
		Life Functioning Scales (Howard, Orlinsky, & Bankoff, 1994)
Assessment of client symptomatology	To rate the frequency or intensity of presenting complaints	Brief Symptom Inventory (Derogatis & Lazarus, 1994)
		Brief Psychiatric Rating Scale (Faustman, 1994)
Alternative assessment approaches	To gather information about clients, using methods other than traditional paper-and-pencil approaches	Performance assessment (i.e., evaluating how a person acts or behaves in given situations)

Sources: Loesch, 2001; Steenbarger and Smith, 1996.

- *Functioning:* How is the client functioning in his or her environment? Functioning can involve interpersonal relationships, work or school behaviors, and goal-oriented behavior.

Using multiple methods to measure client outcomes is preferable to using a single method. For example, clinicians may choose to use measures of client satisfaction, qualitative measures of functioning and/or goal attainment, progress notes, and specific instruments designed to measure change (Young, 2013). Table 7–1 contains some of the methods of measurement, both formal and informal, that are used to evaluate client outcomes.

Additional formal measures used by clinicians to evaluate client outcomes include the following:

- *Client Evaluation of Counseling Inventory (CEC):* Used to measure subjective well-being, presenting symptoms, overall life functioning, quality of life, and the therapeutic alliance (Frey, Beesley, & Liang, 2009).

- *Outcome Questionnaire-45.2 (OQ-45.2):*   Used to measure symptom distress, interpersonal relationships, social roles, and risk assessment (Lambert et al., 1996).
- *Clinical Outcomes in Routine Evaluation (CORE-OM):*   A computerized system designed to measure clients' subjective well-being, problems and symptoms, life functioning, and risk/harm. The system is designed to be used before, during, and at the conclusion of therapy (Barkham et al., 2010).
- *Beck Depression Inventory II (BDI-II):*   Used to monitor client depression (Beck, Steer, & Brown, 1996).

These instruments represent just a sampling of the plethora of instruments that can be used to measure client outcomes. Most can be accessed by clients online and can be completed at regular intervals during the counseling process or at the end of the counseling experience.

Challenges and Benefits of Client Outcome Evaluation

Time (or a lack of it) is one common reason evaluating client outcomes is often overlooked. Counselors are busy people! Many have large client loads, and if the setting in which the counselor works does not require outcome evaluation, it simply may not occur. Also, if clinicians do not value outcome measures, these tasks may be ignored or viewed as additional administrative chores. Streatfield (2012) suggests several reasons clinicians may be resistant to the routine collection of client outcome measures:

- Outcome measures are not therapeutic to the counseling process and may hinder progress.
- There is not enough time to complete the measures.
- The client may not like completing evaluations.
- The outcome data may be misused by supervisors and may negatively affect the counselors' performance evaluation.

However, collecting outcome data before, during, and at the completion of counseling can benefit both the counselor and the client (Streatfield, 2012). When outcome measures are used collaboratively to improve the counseling experience and monitor progress, counselors gain a better understanding of what is working and what could be improved. The use of outcome measures helps clients see the value of their counseling experiences and enhances their investment in the process.

PROGRAM EVALUATION

Program evaluation is related to client outcome evaluation but is broader in its scope and purpose. **Program evaluation** is a systematic collection of information about the activities, qualities, and results of clinical mental health counseling programs so that judgments can be made about overall program effectiveness (Patton, 2008). Program evaluation enables counselors and administrators to know whether the planned services were delivered as expected and whether specific goals and outcomes were achieved (Lewis, Lewis, Packard, & Soufleé, 2001). Evaluation results are then used to make decisions about current and future services, including prevention programs; individual, group, and family counseling services; crisis programs; and outreach efforts.

The Case of Jenny

Jenny is the director of a counseling agency that works primarily with clients who have depression and anxiety. Currently, she has 11 mental health professionals on staff, and several of them have been with the agency for over 10 years. Lately, the client load at the agency has started to decrease. Most of the clinicians are seeing only a couple of clients per day, and group attendance has dropped considerably, to the point that several groups have had to be canceled. Jenny has been unsure about keeping all 11 professionals on staff because financial gains have not been as high as in past years. She has also started to contemplate the performance of the counselors and the effectiveness of their programs. It has been several years since any type of program evaluation has been conducted at the agency. In addition, the accrediting board of the agency has been in contact with Jenny about quality assurance.

What steps should Jenny take to complete a thorough program evaluation? What are some examples of methods that Jenny can utilize to complete a program evaluation? How should Jenny approach discussing program evaluation with her staff? What are some repercussions that may occur if Jenny does not follow through with the program evaluation? Think about these questions as you read about program evaluation, taking into account what you've already read about client outcome evaluation.

Purposes of Program Evaluation

Evaluation typically involves gathering meaningful information on various aspects of a counseling program and using those data to inform program planning and service delivery (Lewis et al., 2003 Loesch, 2001). Evaluation has a quality of immediate utility. In clinical settings, it gives counselors direct feedback on the services they are providing and insight into what new services they need to offer. It also enables clients to have systematic, positive input into a counseling program. In describing counseling program evaluation (CPE), Loesch (2001) clarifies:

> The purpose of CPE is to maximize the efficiency and effectiveness of service delivery through careful and systematic examination of program components, methodologies, and outcomes. It is not the purpose of CPE simply to provide a rationale for what currently exists or is being done. Rather, CPE is used primarily to change counseling service delivery for the better. (p. 513)

Specifically, program evaluation serves the following purposes. First, it aids in administrative decision making. Information gathered about service outcomes helps administrators make informed decisions about which programs to continue to develop and which programs to eliminate or reduce. Second, evaluation can help service providers make improvements in current programs by comparing them with what was originally planned. Third, evaluation provides a way to demonstrate accountability to funding and accrediting agencies, clients, and other stakeholders. Demonstrating such accountability by disseminating evaluation results to policy makers, consumers, and service providers can help agencies gain increased support from the larger community, which is a professional necessity (Lewis et al., 2001).

Steps in Evaluation

For program evaluation to be effective, it needs to be comprehensive and systematic. Consequently, plans for evaluation need to be made at the front end of program design, not afterward. To plan and implement an effective evaluation program, it is helpful to follow a sequential process, such as the following five-step procedure outlined by Burck and Peterson (1975).

According to Burck and Peterson, the first step in formulating an evaluation program involves conducting a needs assessment. A **needs assessment** refers to a set of methods or approaches used to determine if there is a need for a certain program or intervention (Sleezer, Russ-Eft, & Gupta, 2014). Assessments can be conducted through surveys, interviews, focus groups, and other observational or descriptive methods.

Information gathered through the needs assessment is used to identify program goals and performance objectives. Formulating goals and objectives represents the second step in program evaluation. Here, both terminal program outcomes (those that are most immediately recognizable) and ultimate program outcomes (those that are most enduring) are described in terms of measurable performance objectives. In formulating goals and objectives, it is important to identify current program strengths, limitations, and resources, and to then prioritize goals and objectives within that framework.

The third step in evaluation is designing and implementing a program. Program activities are selected to address the specific goals and objectives that have been delineated. To be successful, a program needs "a well-developed plan that integrates content, methods, resources, services, marketing, and evaluation" (Lusky & Hayes, 2001, p. 32).

Program design and implementation lead to the fourth step, which is revising and improving the program. No matter how well a program is planned, responses and outcomes are not always predictable. Consequently, ongoing evaluation of the process is required, accompanied by program revisions when necessary.

The fifth and final step of overall program evaluation is assessing the program's effectiveness in relation to the stated goals and objectives. Inherent in this step is the need to disseminate the findings of the program evaluation to the general public. Such consumer information is vital for potential clients if they are to make informed decisions, and counselors within a clinical program need this kind of feedback to improve their skills and services.

Comprehensive evaluation involves many people, including service providers, administrators, clients, and often the larger community. Each of these stakeholders plays a part in determining how the evaluation is conducted. Their degree of involvement in the process varies, depending on their interests and needs, but "all help determine the nature of effective evaluation practices" (Loesch, 2001, p. 515).

Process and Program Outcome Evaluation

Several different models of evaluation have been described in counseling literature. Most comprehensive models provide ways to evaluate processes and outcomes. In process evaluation, the focus is on the manner in which services are being delivered. The program is evaluated as it is occurring (Hadley & Mitchell, 1995). In outcome evaluation, which occurs after program delivery, the focus is on whether the program produced the desired results. Both are essential components of comprehensive program evaluation.

Process evaluation, also called **formative evaluation**, provides information about how well a program is being implemented (Daniels, Thompson, & Wolf, 2017). During process evaluation, evaluators determine whether the programs are operating in accordance with stated plans, objectives, and expectations. Process evaluation involves ongoing monitoring of what services are being provided, by whom, for whom, to how many, when, and at what cost (Lewis et al., 2001). Examples of questions that might be asked during process evaluation include these:

- What are the goals and objectives of the program?
- What steps have been accomplished for the identified objectives?
- What resources were (are) needed for each step?
- Do the characteristics of the clients being served match those of the target population?
- What target groups are underrepresented? Why?
- Does the number of clients being served match the projected goal? If not, why not?
- How satisfied are the clients with the program offered?
- How satisfied is the staff?
- Are there aspects of the program that need to be altered? If so, how can that be done? (Granello & Young, 2012, p. 237)

Results obtained through process evaluation inform service providers about potential changes that need to be made to enhance program delivery. For example, if a support group for battered women is not being well attended, perhaps the group is meeting at an inopportune time, or perhaps the content used during group meetings is not addressing the most pertinent needs of the participants. By conducting process evaluation, counselors can determine what is or is not working and adapt accordingly.

In contrast, program outcome evaluation provides information about whether, and to what degree, the goals and objectives of the program have been achieved (Daniels et al., 2017). Also called **summative evaluation** or **product evaluation**, this type of evaluation provides one way for counselors and agencies to demonstrate accountability for their services. The focus of program outcome evaluation is on the components of the program being evaluated, not on the clients. Although both process and program evaluation rely on clearly specified objectives, process evaluation objectives usually relate to projected activities, whereas program outcome evaluation objectives are stated in terms of expected results.

Program outcomes can be measured in various ways. Just as multifaceted approaches are suggested for client outcome and process evaluation, so is a multifaceted approach suggested for program outcome evaluation. Some of the questions that need to be considered include these (Daniels, Mines, & Gressard, 1981; Lewis et al., 2001):

- What questions does the evaluation intend to answer?
- For whom is the evaluation intended?
- What are the best available methods for obtaining answers to the questions asked?
- Do the evaluators have the knowledge and expertise needed to complete the evaluations?
- Is the evaluation part of a well-designed research plan?

In some agencies, data gathered through process and program outcome evaluations are used to conduct an efficiency evaluation, which connects the costs of implementing a particular program with the benefits achieved by the participants. In analyzing costs, resources required for program implementation are assessed, including time, effort, and financial expenditures. A key goal of an efficiency evaluation is to determine whether the same results can be achieved with reduced time, effort, or financial cost (Lewis et al., 2001).

Quality Assurance

In many settings, quality assurance (QA) is an ongoing process by which the agency and outside groups monitor the quality of services offered. Because of the demands of accrediting organizations such as the Joint Committee of Accreditation of Healthcare Organizations (JCAHO) and the National Committee for Quality Assurance (NCQA), documented evidence of the quality of care is crucial. **Quality of care** is a multidimensional construct that encompasses access and availability of care, client satisfaction with services, and adherence to recognized standards of care and service delivery (Steenbarger & Smith, 1996). It is in the best interest of clinical mental health agencies and other service providers to document evidence that quality services are being delivered and to seek external accreditation. External accreditation lets the public know that agencies have met certain minimum criteria for service delivery, thereby placing those agencies in a better position to negotiate contracts with third-party providers (MacCluskie & Ingersoll, 2001).

Issues and Challenges of Program Evaluation

In principle, the concept of program evaluation is relatively straightforward. In reality, however, evaluation is a complex process that can pose several challenges. One of the greatest challenges involves the logistics of data collection. Administration and scoring of assessment measures can be tedious and time-consuming, possibly leading to delays in calculating and disseminating results. Another challenge relates to the gathering and interpretation of evaluation data. Finding valid and reliable methods of measuring program effectiveness is a difficult task and varies from setting to setting. Consequently, what one agency considers "effective service" may or may not be truly effective. In addition to methodological concerns, professionals may resist evaluation because of concerns about how the results are going to be used. People do not like to be judged, especially if the results of the evaluation may be used against them. When evaluators take steps to use evaluations constructively rather than punitively and clarify the intended purposes of the evaluation from the outset, those being evaluated are more likely to respond favorably.

Although these challenges can create barriers to program evaluation, they can be overcome if handled sensitively. When evaluation is viewed as an integral component of service delivery that benefits both staff and clients, resistance to the process is minimized, and opportunities for growth and improvement are enhanced.

Summary and Conclusion

Clinical mental health counselors participate in many different roles to meet the needs of their clients and the greater community. In this chapter, an overview of mental health consultation, advocacy, client outcome evaluation, and program evaluation has been provided. Clinical mental health counselors have opportunities to engage in consultation on multiple levels, such as by using Caplan's model, which includes four types of consultation. Characteristics of effective consultants are as crucial as types of consultation and were covered in this chapter.

Another key service provided by clinical mental health counselors is advocacy. Advocacy services go beyond the traditional role of individual counseling by focusing on ways to address social injustices and environmental conditions that impinge on the well-being of individuals and groups. There are many ways counselors can serve as advocates for their clients, ranging from facilitating personal empowerment to becoming involved politically to improving societal conditions. Another dimension of advocacy is advocating for the counseling profession. Professional advocacy benefits clients by ensuring that the counseling profession is recognized as a viable, credible provider of mental health services.

Clinical mental health counselors also play a role in evaluating treatment outcomes for their clients. There are multiple ways to evaluate client outcomes. As a clinical mental health counselor, you must know what is working best for whom and under what conditions.

Finally, the chapter discussed program evaluation. Systematic program evaluation, which occurs throughout the course of service delivery, provides ways to demonstrate accountability and maximize the quality of services provided. Two common types of this form of evaluation are process evaluation, which supplies information about how well a program is being implemented, and program outcome evaluation, which indicates the degree to which service goals and objectives are met.

MyCounselingLab

Try the Topic 14 Assignments: *Research and Evaluation*.

CHAPTER 8

Dealing with Crises, Disasters, and Suicide, while Managing Stress and Avoiding Burnout

Minerva Studio/Shutterstock

CHAPTER OVERVIEW

From reading this chapter, you will learn about

- Different types of crises and ways to provide crisis assessment and intervention, as well as training models for disaster intervention

- Ways to assess suicide risk, risk factors and warning signs associated with suicide, and interventions with clients who may be suicidal, including how to talk with them

- Definitions of compassion fatigue, secondary traumatic stress, and vicarious traumatization

- Ways to manage stress and avoid burnout

As you read, consider

- How you will respond to crisis situations

- What types of training you might participate in to respond to disasters

- The steps needed to conduct a thorough suicide assessment and how you might intervene if you consider a client at extreme or high risk for suicide

- Specific methods you will use to manage stress and avoid burnout

She stands
    leaning on his outstretched arm
        sobbing awkwardly
Almost suspended between
    the air and his shoulder
        like a leaf being blown
            in the wind from a branch of a tree
                at the end of summer.
He tries to give her comfort
    offering soft words
        and patting her head.
"It's okay," he whispers
    realizing that as the words leave his mouth
        he is lying
And that their life together has collapsed
    like the South Tower of the World Trade Center
        that killed their only son.

Reprinted from "September 27th," by S. T. Gladding, 2002. Used with permission.

Although the nature and intensity of problems faced by individuals vary, most people experience a crisis of some type during the course of their life. Working effectively with clients facing crisis situations or with clients considering suicide requires specialized knowledge and skill. These topics, as well as how counselors can practice self-care and avoid burnout, are covered in this chapter.

CRISIS AND DISASTER RESPONSE

Definition of Crisis

Before discussing crisis intervention services, it is important to clarify what is meant by the term *crisis*. Many definitions have been proposed, three of which are given here.

- *Crisis* is a perception or experiencing of an event or situation as an intolerable difficulty that exceeds the person's current resources and coping mechanisms. Unless the person obtains relief, the crisis has the potential to cause severe affective, behavioral, and cognitive malfunctioning. (James, 2008, p. 3)
- *Crisis* is a state of disorganization in which people face frustration of important life goals or profound disruption of their life cycles and methods of coping with stressors. The term *crisis* usually refers to a person's feelings of fear, shock, and distress *about* the disruption, not to the disruption itself. (Brammer, 1985, p. 94)
- A *crisis* is a critical phase in a person's life when his or her normal ways of dealing with the world are suddenly interrupted. (Lewis et al., 2003, p. 117)

The concept of crisis is not simple or straightforward. A **crisis** contains three essential elements: "(1) a precipitating event, (2) a perception of the event that leads to subjective distress, and (3) diminished functioning when the distress is not alleviated by customary coping resources" (Pueleo & McGlothlin, 2014, p. 1). Although a single event may precipitate a crisis, that is, act as the "trigger" for a crisis occurring, a combination of personal traits, environmental factors, and interpersonal support systems are all involved.

One way to determine whether an event will be a crisis or not is through using the **ABCX** and **Double ABCX models of a crisis** (Hill, 1949; McCubbin & Patterson, 1982). In the ABCX model, an event or situation (A) becomes a crisis depending on the resources (B) and perception (C) of an individual or family and the degree of stress (X) from low to high generated by the event or situation. An event that is perceived as relatively minor by one individual, such as an independently wealthy person losing his or her job, may be perceived as a crisis by someone else without many skills or financial resources. The dynamics of such a situation may be seen simply in Figure 8–1, where each element in the diagram affects the others.

As Hill (1949) initially conceptualized the process of a simple crisis, all the factors influence one another. Usually, though, there are multiple factors, hence the refinement of the theory of what creates a crisis to the Double ABCX model. In this model there are double A, double B, and double C factors that represent accumulated or multiple aspects of the elements that go into making a situation a crisis, such as stressors, resources, and coping strategies. People and families build up adaptations to outside influences over time. The timing, intensity, and number of other stressors the person is experiencing can, and usually do, affect the complexity of a potential crisis situation.

Clinical mental health counselors need to be prepared to work with clients and populations who have experienced a crisis (Jackson-Cherry & Erford, 2014). Unfortunately, the

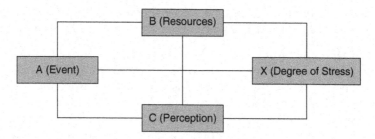

FIGURE 8–1 Hill's ABCX Theory of Elements in a Crisis

need for crisis intervention services continues to increase. One reason more services are needed is the upsurge of large-scale violent acts occurring in the United States, such as the terrorist attacks on New York City and Washington, DC, in 2001; the 2012 shooting at Sandy Hook Elementary School in Newtown, Connecticut; and the 2016 Orlando nightclub blood-bath. Sadly, violent acts occur "with such frequency and indiscriminateness that no one can consider him- or herself safe" (Myer, 2001, p. 3).

Other disasters—including earthquakes, floods, fires, hurricanes, and tornadoes—result in tragic loss of lives and homes. Examples are numerous, such as Hurricane Katrina striking New Orleans in August 2005, Superstorm Sandy wreaking havoc in New Jersey in October 2012, and massive floods in West Virginia and gigantic wild fires in California occurring in June 2016. On an international level, tsunamis, earthquakes, and cyclones have had catastrophic effects on people in many other countries. Automobile and plane accidents, injury, illness, and disease are other examples of traumatic situations that can have devastating effects on victims and their families. It is now recognized "that trauma exposure is relatively common, with about two-thirds of people experiencing a traumatic event during their lifetime" (Goodman, 2015, p. 283).

Experiencing violence, disaster, or any other form of trauma can leave people without sufficient resources for coping. In such cases, crisis intervention services are needed. Crises can affect a large group of people, such as the events just described, but they also can be more individualized, as evidenced when someone is killed in a car crash, is diagnosed with an incurable illness, or commits suicide. When people experience an event or situation as a crisis, either within their communities or intrapersonally, finding ways to resolve the crisis effectively is essential to mental health and well-being.

BOX 8–1

When written in Chinese, the word *crisis* is composed of two characters. One represents danger, and the other represents opportunity.

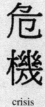

危
機

crisis

James (2008) emphasizes the importance of distinguishing among different types of events or situations that may lead to crises. He classifies crises into four categories.

1. *Developmental crises.*   Developmental crises occur during the normal flow of human growth and maturation. As people move through different developmental stages in their lives, they may experience crisis during certain changes or shifts. For example, a developmental crisis may occur when the last child leaves home, when a person retires, or when an individual reaches birthdays that end in a zero. When the event corresponds to culturally accepted patterns and timetables (e.g., launching children in their early 20s or deciding to retire at 65), it is less likely to be experienced as a crisis than when this does not occur (e.g., teenage pregnancy, delayed puberty, or forced early retirement).

2. *Situational crises.*   A situational crisis occurs when an unexpected, extraordinary event takes place that the person had no way of anticipating or controlling. Examples include automobile accidents, rape, job loss, sudden illness, and death of a loved one. A situational crisis is "random, sudden, shocking, intense, and often catastrophic" (p. 13).

3. *Existential crises.*   An existential crisis is equated with intense, pervasive inner conflict and anxiety associated with the issues of purpose, meaning, responsibility, freedom, and commitment. At times, existential crises are precipitated by **nonevents**, that is, events that do not happen such as realizing that one is never going to have children or make a significant difference in a particular field of work. However, an existential crisis also may occur when a spouse or partner questions the value of the relationship and seriously considers moving in a different direction.

4. *Ecosystemic crises.*   Ecosystemic crises refer to natural or human-caused disasters that overtake a person or group of people who "find themselves, through no fault or action of their own, inundated in the aftermath of an event that may adversely affect virtually every member of the environment in which they live" (p. 14). In many ways, ecosystemic crises are situational crises that have widespread ramifications. Terrorist attacks, the devastation of war, or school violence exemplify human-caused ecosystemic crises with wide-reaching effects. Ecosystemic crises caused by natural phenomena include hurricanes, tornadoes, wildfires, and earthquakes.

Although crises represent highly stressful and disruptive situations, they do not typically lead to mental disorders. Many, but not all, crises are time limited, usually lasting between six and eight weeks, after which the major symptoms of distress diminish. However, crises can have long-term physical and psychological outcomes, depending on how they are resolved. Therefore, timely crisis intervention services are needed to help people resolve crises in ways that will prevent negative outcomes in the future (Cooper, 2014).

Unresolved trauma can, in some instances, lead to the development of **posttraumatic stress disorder (PTSD)**. With PTSD, the trauma lasts in an individual's mind long after the event itself has passed. People with PTSD may exhibit a number of symptoms, including reexperiencing the trauma through flashbacks, avoidance of trauma-related activities, intense fear or helplessness, emotional numbing, and a range of coexisting disorders such as substance abuse, obsessive–compulsive disorder, and panic disorder (APA, 2013). Counselors who work with PTSD clients need specialized training in empirically validated treatments to help reduce the impact of the trauma and improve functioning. In particular, clinicians who work with veterans of foreign wars (such as Vietnam, the Gulf War, Afghanistan, or Iraq) or with people involved in natural or manmade disasters or violence need to be familiar with the signs and symptoms of PTSD and be trained to work effectively with these individuals.

In contrast, when people experiencing crisis or trauma manage to resolve their cognitive, affective, and behavioral reactions effectively, they can change and grow in a positive manner (James, 2008). This phenomenon is referred to as **posttraumatic growth** (Calhoun & Tedeschi, 2013).

Definition of Crisis Intervention

Crisis intervention differs from traditional counseling in that it is a "time-limited treatment directed at reactions to a specific event in order to help the client return to a precrisis level of functioning" (Myer, 2001, p. 5). It is an action-oriented approach used to help clients cope with a particular life situation that has thrown them off course. According to the National Organization for Victim Assistance (NOVA), **goals of crisis intervention** include helping the client defuse emotions, rearrange cognitive processes, organize and interpret what has happened, integrate the traumatic event into his or her life story, and interpret the traumatic event in a way that is meaningful (Bauer, 2001; NOVA, 2016).

Crisis intervention, also called **crisis management**, typically does not last longer than six weeks and may be much briefer. It is not to be confused with more long-term postcrisis counseling, which can include the treatment of PTSD. Long-term trauma counseling, which may be necessary depending on the nature of the crisis and the client's psychological well-being, is another important mental health service, but it is not the focus of this section. Clinicians who engage in long-term trauma work have been clinically prepared to conduct long-term trauma counseling (Levers, 2012).

With that in mind, all clinical mental health counselors need to be prepared to intervene effectively in crisis situations. To that end, the six-step model of crisis intervention presented by James and Gilliland (2017) is presented in Figure 8–2. The model has been used successfully by professionals and trained lay workers to help people cope with many different types of crises.

As can be seen in Figure 8–2, three primary counselor functions are carried out at various stages of crisis intervention: (a) **assessment**, which occurs throughout crisis intervention; (b) **listening**, which is especially important during Steps 1, 2, and 3; and (c) **acting**, which varies in degrees of directiveness and occurs primarily during Steps 4, 5, and 6. Because assessment occurs throughout the intervention process and is the key to effective intervention, it is addressed first.

Crisis Assessment

The first step in crisis intervention is to assess the nature of the crisis. The purpose of crisis assessment is to provide information about (a) the severity of the crisis; (b) the client's current emotional, behavioral, and cognitive status; (c) the coping mechanisms, support systems, and additional resources available to the client; and (d) whether the client is of danger to self and others (James, 2008).

ASSESSING:

Overarching, continuous, and dynamically ongoing throughout the crisis; evaluating the client's present and past situational crises in terms of the client's ability to cope, personal threat, mobility or immobility, and making a judgment regarding type of action needed by the crisis worker. (See crisis worker's action continuum, below.)

Listening →

Acting →

LISTENING: Attending, observing, understanding, and responding with empathy, genuineness, respect, acceptance, nonjudgment, and caring.

1. *Define the problem.* Explore and define the problem from the client's point of view. Use active listening, including open-ended questions. Attend to both verbal and nonverbal messages of the client.

2. *Ensure client safety.* Assess lethality, criticality, immobility, or seriousness of threat to the client's physical and psychological safety. Assess both the client's internal events and the situation surrounding the client, and, if necessary, ensure that the client is made aware of alternatives to impulsive, self-destructive actions.

3. *Provide support.* Communicate to the client that the crisis worker is a valid support person. Demonstrate (by words, voice, and body language) a caring, positive, nonpossessive, nonjudgmental, acceptant, personal involvement with the client.

ACTING: Becoming involved in the intervention at a nondirective, collaborative, or directive level, according to the assessed needs of the client and the availability of environmental supports.

4. *Examine alternatives.* Assist client in exploring the choices he or she has available to him or her now. Facilitate a search for immediate situational supports, coping mechanisms, and positive thinking.

5. *Make plans.* Assist client in developing a realistic short-term plan that identifies additional resources and provides coping mechanisms —definite action steps that the client can own and comprehend.

6. *Obtain commitment.* Help client commit himself or herself to definite, positive action steps that the client can own and realistically accomplish or accept.

Crisis Worker's Action Continuum

| Crisis worker is nondirective | Crisis worker is collaborative | Crisis worker is directive |

(Threshold varies from client to client) (Threshold varies from client to client)

Client is mobile   Client is partially mobile   Client is immobile

The crisis worker's level of action/involvement may be anywhere on the continuum according to a valid and realistic assessment of the client's level of mobility/immobility.

FIGURE 8–2 The Six-Step Model of Crisis Intervention

Source: Crisis Intervention Strategies (5th ed.), by R. K. James and B. E. Gilliland, 2005, Pacific Grove, CA: Brooks/Cole. Copyright © 2005 Wadsworth, a part of Cengage Learning, Inc. Reproduced by permission.

BOX 8–2   Crisis Intervention Terminology Associated with Assessment

EQUILIBRIUM: A state of emotional or mental stability and balance

DISEQUILIBRIUM: A lack of emotional stability or balance

MOBILITY: A state of being able to autonomously change or cope in response to different moods, feelings, emotions, needs, and influences; being flexible or adaptable to the surrounding environment

IMMOBILITY: A state of being incapable of changing or coping in response to different moods, feelings, emotions, needs, and influences; being unable to adapt to the immediate physical and social world

(James, 2008, p. 41)

One method of crisis assessment that provides an efficient model for obtaining information about the severity of the crisis and the client's range of responses is the **triage assessment model** (Myer, Williams, Ottens, & Schmidt, 1992). The model provides a framework for assessing a client's reactions in three domains: affective, behavioral, and cognitive (ABC). Each domain is composed of three categories of reactions that represent the range of responses clients typically experience in crisis situations. To use the model effectively with diverse populations, counselors need to be sensitive to cultural differences, recognizing that reactions may have different meanings in various cultures.

- Responses in the affective domain include anger/hostility, anxiety/fear, and sadness/melancholy. Clients are assessed to determine which of these emotions is being experienced by the client and which appears to be dominant. People in crisis may be experiencing intense emotions and may scream or sob uncontrollably. At the other extreme, clients may appear emotionally numb, withdrawn, or shut down. Impaired emotional expression is an indication of the disequilibrium that usually accompanies crisis experiences. Counselors can help reestablish equilibrium by demonstrating empathy and using reflective listening skills to validate feelings (Cooper, 2014).
- Responses in the cognitive domain include client perceptions of transgression (i.e., violation), threat, and loss. According to Myer (2001), perception of transgression is focused on the present (i.e., what is happening now, during the crisis). Perception of threat is future oriented, and perceptions of loss are focused on the past (i.e., recognizing that something is irrevocably gone). Perceptions may occur in any of several life dimensions: physical, psychological, social, and moral/spiritual.
- Reactions in the behavioral domain are approach, avoidance, and immobility. Clients usually adopt one of these three behaviors in reacting to the crisis. When clients try to implement strategies to address the crisis event, they are using approach behaviors. **Avoidance behaviors** are those by which the client tries to ignore, deny, or escape the crisis event. **Immobility** refers to a set of behaviors characterized by nonproductive, disorganized, or self-defeating attempts to cope with the crisis. Behavioral reactions may be constructive or maladaptive. To determine the helpfulness or harmfulness of the response, counselors can evaluate the potential outcome of the reaction by asking themselves, "Will the behavior aid or hinder the resolution of the crisis?"

During the assessment process, counselors need to be alert to any possibility of suicidal or homicidal ideation. Usually, the potential for violent reactions increases when the client's responses are intense or extreme. If a counselor has reason to believe that a client is a danger to self or others, the counselor needs to assess the situation to determine intent (whether immediate or future), availability of means, lethality of means, and existence of a definite plan.

When assessing each of the three domains, the counselor must determine not only the client's predominant response in each category but also the severity of the reactions on each scale. Myer (2001) suggests that crisis intervention should focus initially on the client's most severe reaction, realizing that the intensity of responses varies throughout the crisis experience and that continued assessment, flexibility, and adaptation are needed.

As stated earlier, assessment takes place throughout the crisis intervention process. Two other counselor functions that occur during crisis intervention are listening and acting. To explain how these functions are enacted, James and Gilliland's (2017) six-step model of crisis intervention is described.

Six-Step Model of Crisis Intervention

Step 1   Defining the Problem.   The first step in the model is to "define and understand the problem from the client's point of view" (James, 2008, p. 39). Core counseling skills—which include empathy, genuineness, and unconditional positive regard—are essential to this step of intervention. Giving clients a chance to tell their stories not only helps with assessment but also helps clients "turn down the volume" of powerful feelings and reengage cognitive processes. An important purpose of crisis intervention is to help clients take steps toward stabilizing emotionally and reengaging cognitively, as described in Box 8–3.

BOX 8–3

Human beings are not wired to think after a crisis; we are wired to act and react. Unfortunately, many important decisions must be made and problems solved in post-crisis moments. Poor choices can complicate and increase the painful impact of surviving a tragedy. The sooner survivors have access to relatively clear thinking, the sooner they can begin making thoughtful decisions. Crisis responders facilitate this reconnection to thinking by helping survivors turn their experience from jumbled fragments into a coherent story.

(Bauer, 2001, p. 242)

Step 2   Ensuring Client Safety.   Ensuring client safety means "minimizing the physical and psychological danger to self and others" (James, 2008, p. 39). Throughout crisis intervention, keeping clients safe must be of primary concern. When people experience traumatic events, their sense of the world as a safe, predictable place is destroyed (Webber & Mascari, 2016). Helping people feel safe is a key factor of crisis intervention. Crisis counselors need to help individuals reestablish, as much as possible, a sense of safety, normalcy, and predictability.

Step 3   Providing Support.   Through words, actions, and body language, the counselor needs to convey to the client genuine caring and support. It is not sufficient for counselors to simply think they are being supportive. Rather, a key goal is to find ways to ensure that the client perceives the counselor as supportive, nonjudgmental, and involved.

Step 4 Examining Alternatives.   The next three steps of crisis intervention involve the use of strategies to help clients make appropriate choices and restore equilibrium. In Step 4 of the model, the counselor helps the client explore a range of options and alternatives. Part of the exploration includes encouraging the client to identify available support sources and coping mechanisms. Identifying resources and coping mechanisms and exercising constructive thinking patterns can help lessen the client's stress and anxiety.

Step 5 Making Plans.   Step 5 logically follows Step 4. Clients are encouraged to select from the different alternatives that were explored and then make specific plans for implementing the selected option. In this step, it is important for counselors to work collaboratively with clients, thereby supporting client independence, power, and self-respect. Clients need an opportunity to restore their personal sense of control, which often is severely shaken in crisis situations.

Step 6 Obtaining Commitment.   In this step, the counselor encourages commitment to definite positive action steps that will help the client move toward pre-crisis equilibrium. Action steps need to be uncomplicated and clearly articulated, thereby increasing the probability of the steps being enacted. It also is essential to make plans for follow-up with the client. Depending on the situation, follow-up may include ongoing counseling or a referral to an appropriate source for continued assistance. Figure 8–3 summarizes the six-step model of crisis intervention.

The six-step model of crisis intervention presents an organized framework to guide counselors as they work with clients who have experienced crisis or trauma. It provides a way to help clients manage the emerging feelings, concerns, and situations that they may experience. Throughout the crisis intervention process, counselors assess the person and the situation to ensure that the client is safe, evaluate resources, and make decisions about how to intervene most effectively. Counselors use effective listening, communication, and problem-solving skills to help clients in crisis regain equilibrium, make sense of their situation, and resolve the crisis in a healthy manner.

Crisis intervention is demanding, intensive work that requires specific skills, attributes, and attitudes on the part of the counselor. Gladding describes a personal experience with intense crisis work in Box 8–4. Prolonged exposure to clients who have experienced tragedy or trauma can lead to compassion fatigue or secondary traumatization (consisting of flashbacks, nightmares, and intrusive thoughts) (Figley, 1995; James, 2008). Finding ways to prevent compassion fatigue or burnout is critical if counselors are going to provide crisis services effectively. Merriman (2015) has found that one way to combat compassion fatigue

Step 1 Defining the Problem	Understand problem from client's perspective
Step 2 Ensuring Client Safety	Minimize danger to self and others
Step 3 Providing Support	Convey genuine warmth and caring
Step 4 Examining Alternatives	Explore a range of options; identify resources
Step 5 Making Plans	Make specific plans for implementing selected option(s)
Step 6 Obtaining Commitment	Commit to definite positive action(s), follow-up

FIGURE 8–3   Six Step Model of Crisis Intervention

is to provide education on it and ways to promote protective factors against it, such as self-care to interns entering the profession. Interestingly, Thompson, Amatea, and Thompson (2014) have found a difference in the factors that contribute to compassion fatigue and burnout. Their research has uncovered the fact that four conditions—perceived working conditions, mindfulness, use of coping strategy, and compassion satisfaction—account for only 31.1% of the variance in compassion fatigue, while these same dynamics explain 66.9% of the variance in burnout. Counselors who report "less maladaptive coping, higher mindfulness attitudes and compassion satisfaction, and more positive perceptions of their work environment" report less burnout (p. 58).

BOX 8–4 Reflections on Counseling After a Crisis

After the September 11 terrorist attacks, I was asked to go to New York City to work as a mental health technician for the American Red Cross. For a week, I worked at the Family Assistance Center on Pier 94. There I saw survivors of the tragedy and worked with them to help process the wide range of feelings—from denial to grief—that they felt. My job was to assist individuals in making applications for death certificates of their loved ones. I was an escort who walked with families from the front of the building to the back and talked with them about what they were feeling, what they had felt, or what they were doing in regard to the emotions that would be coming. I also accompanied families to Ground Zero so they could see for themselves the horror and finality of the event. The view of the site helped many individuals begin the process of grieving in depth as they realized in a stark and striking way that those they had loved and cherished were indeed dead and would not be coming back to them.

From these experiences and other related incidents, I learned a great deal more than I ever anticipated about the nature of counseling, clients, and myself. The lessons I learned have some universal application for persons who enter almost any crisis situation. They are especially applicable to crises that may seem overwhelming initially. In the midst of working with people who are in a crisis, counselors need to make sure they do the following:

- Are mentally healthy to begin with
- Interact in positive and professional ways with colleagues
- Stay flexible and prepare for the unexpected
- Find out about referral resources and support personnel in the community
- Realize the power of small acts of kindness, such as sympathetic words or actions
- Are mindful of the influence of nonverbal actions that lend support to those in need, from giving them tissues to offering them symbols of comfort
- Take care of themselves through physical exercise, journaling, taking in needed nourishment, and debriefing regularly

Counseling after a crisis is a time filled with heavy emotion. It is a time of opportunity as well as one of turmoil. It demands much of counselors. Knowing what to expect can make the experience both positive and productive. The lessons I took away from my experiences in New York City can be applied to many types of crisis situations—both large-scale community trauma and individualized, personal crisis events.

Samuel Gladding, PhD, LPC, NCC, CCMHC

Disaster Mental Health Training

In recent years, increasing attention has been given to disaster mental health (DMH) and to DMH interventions. **Disaster mental health counseling** can be conceptualized as the field application of crisis intervention. Workers in DMH are often called on to help with national and international disaster relief. The ACA, the American Red Cross, the International Critical Incident Stress Foundation (ICISF), NOVA, the Salvation Army, and other organizations assist in training thousands of people annually in crisis intervention services as applied to large-scale disasters.

The types of training for emergency response vary from organization to organization. **Crisis incident stress management (CISM)** is one example of a disaster mental health training model. The CISM model, also known as the Mitchell model, is a comprehensive, integrated, systematic, and multicomponent crisis intervention program (Mitchell, 2012). It is based on crisis intervention, group psychotherapy, community psychology, and peer support. Information about the CISM model can be accessed at CISM International at www.criticalincidentstress.com/. Concepts of the model have been used by emergency personnel since 1974; however, relatively few CISM studies have been conducted.

The American Red Cross trains DMH workers across the continuum of disaster preparedness, response, and recovery. Clinicians interested in participating in this training should contact their local Red Cross division. The ACA is a Red Cross partner and provides training for Red Cross disaster health volunteers at annual ACA conferences. To participate in the training, clinical mental health counselors need to be licensed for independent practice by a state licensure board.

The Salvation Army trains crisis responders to provide emotional and spiritual care to meet the needs of both disaster responders and disaster-affected families and individuals. Their training courses are rated according to difficulty, ranging from basic to advanced.

Yet another form of disaster response, which is supported by mental health experts as the "acute intervention of choice," is **psychological first aid** (PFA; National Child Traumatic Stress Network & National Center for PTSD, 2006). A field operations manual describing PFA can be retrieved through the Veterans Administration website at http://www.ptsd.va.gov/professional/materials/manuals/psych-first-aid.asp. Online training is available for PFA, and information about that training can be accessed at www.nctsn.org/content/psychological-first-aid. The goals of PFA include the following:

- *Protect:* Preserve survivors' and responders' safety, health, and self-esteem.
- *Direct:* Help direct people to appropriate safe places. Help them to prioritize, organize, and plan.
- *Connect:* Facilitate supportive communication with family, community, and service providers.
- *Detect:* Assess, triage, and provide crisis support for people who appear to be at risk for more severe symptoms.
- *Select:* Refer people as needed to mental health, social, spiritual, health, and financial services.
- *Validate:* Inform and normalize the emotional and psychological responses people are experiencing. Validate their concerns, reactions, and ways of coping. (Levers & Buck, 2012, pp. 328–329)

The list of training models described is by no means exhaustive, but it provides a starting point for clinical mental health counselors to learn more about disaster response. Disaster and crisis response are key areas of knowledge and skill for clinical mental health counselors in the 21st century (Webber & Mascari, 2016).

Compassion Fatigue, Secondary Traumatic Stress, and Vicarious Traumatization

Counselors who engage in crisis intervention, disaster response, and trauma work cannot afford to neglect their own well-being, even while they are in the midst of helping others (Shallcross, 2012b; Webber & Mascari, 2016). Much has been written about the effects of crisis and disaster work on helpers. Three terms—*compassion fatigue, secondary traumatic stress,* and *vicarious traumatization*—are all associated with the reactions mental health professionals may experience when they work with clients or communities that have experienced crisis or disaster.

Compassion fatigue is a term coined by traumatologist Charles Figley (1995). He describes compassion fatigue (CF) as a response to helping or being involved with people who experience trauma or extreme predicaments (cited in Tarvydas & Ng, 2012). Figley uses the term interchangeably with **secondary traumatic stress** (STS; Baird & Kracen, 2006). Counselors experiencing CF or STS may exhibit symptoms that resemble PTSD: exhaustion, hypervigilance, avoidance, and numbing (Shannonhouse, Barden, Jones, Gonzalez, & Murphy, 2016). Working long hours in disaster environments can result in fatigue, hunger, and sleeplessness, making counselors more vulnerable to STS.

Vicarious traumatization (VT) is a related condition that also is associated with trauma work. Pearlman and MacIan (1995) define VT as changes that alter mental health professionals' views of themselves, others, and the world. VT is associated with disruptions in helpers' views of safety, trust, esteem, intimacy, and control (Baird & Kracen, 2006).

Mental health professionals need to be aware of the deleterious effects of CF, STS, and VT. In particular, caregivers who have personally experienced trauma are likely to be more vulnerable to these effects. More attention and research needs to be given to all aspects of crisis and disaster mental health response, including ways to support the helpers. Recommended activities that help with self-care and mitigate the negative impact crisis and disaster work can have on counselors include the following:

- Identifying and relying on your support group
- Carrying an index card listing ways you can reduce your own stress before you become overwhelmed
- Listing the triggers that affect you so that you can plan ahead to reduce their impact
- Committing to regular physical exercise, even when working in disaster environments
- Being aware of somatic stressors
- Practicing relaxation exercises, such as diaphragmatic breathing
- Journaling

As a mental health professional, it is important to be aware of the toll all forms of counseling can take on the counselor, as it can lead to burnout if not recognized and managed.

The Case of Terry

Terry has been a counselor for three years. He was initially enthusiastic about coming to work at the mental health center each day. He worked in a large city and thought of his job as like being a physician in an emergency room. There were always crises and he was very good at handling them. He often worked overtime. A few months ago he married Patricia. He loves her and she has asked him to spend more time with her and less time at his job. Her point is that there will always be crises and professional helpers will always be there to assist those in such situations.

Terry is unsure if he should cut back his hours. On the other hand, he wants his marriage to go well. What would you advise he do? Why?

SUICIDE ASSESSMENT AND INTERVENTION

Suicide is a self-inflicted death with evidence (either explicit or implicit) of intent to die. The most recent available statistics show that 41,149 people in the United States complete suicide annually (Drapeau & McIntosh, 2015), and it is estimated that 25 times that many— or approximately 1,000,000 persons—attempt suicide in any given year (Heron, 2016; Quinnett, 2012). And although it is unknown how many people have suicidal thoughts, suicide ideation increases in frequency and severity when a person is experiencing a crisis (Chamberlain, Goldney, Delfabbro, Gill, & Dal Grande, 2009).

In the United States, suicide is the third highest cause of death for people between the ages of 15 and 24, with 10 persons out of 100,000 completing suicide (Drapeau & McIntosh, 2015). It is the second highest cause of death for college students and for people between the ages of 25 and 34 (Centers for Disease Control and Prevention, 2015). Additionally, in 2013 the rate of suicide for adults 65 years of age and older was approximately 16 per 100,000. Men are three and a half times more likely to die by suicide than women, although more women than men attempt suicide (Drapeau & McIntosh, 2015). Additionally, having a mental illness increases one's risk for suicide, with approximately 90% of those who complete suicide having had a diagnosable mental illness and/or substance use disorder (Brent, Baugher, Bridge, Chen, & Chiappetta, 1999; Harris & Barraclough, 1997; Hemingway, 2015). In sum, suicide ideation, attempts, and completion transcend age, ethnicity, sex, and socioeconomic status.

Talking with Clients about Suicide

Professional counselors can expect to counsel at least one client who is contemplating or actively planning suicide (Barnett & Johnson, 2015). Each culture has its taboos, and in the United States (as in much of the Western world) openly talking about topics like money, sex, religion, politics, and suicide can be difficult. Partly because of this taboo, many counselors may be hesitant to talk with clients about suicidal thoughts or prior suicide attempts (Pope, Sonne, & Greene, 2006). Experts in the fields of suicide prevention, assessment, and intervention have long agreed that asking clients about their thoughts of suicide does not increase their risk for suicide. Furthermore, research has found that asking about thoughts of suicide can actually decrease the overall stress and severity of suicidal thinking (Gould et al., 2005).

Counselors need to be aware of their own personal and cultural beliefs about suicide (e.g., suicide is a sin; it demonstrates weakness and/or selfishness; or conversely, it is an attractive option in certain circumstances). These and other beliefs may interfere with a counselor's responsibility to promote client welfare, and counselors need to explore their own beliefs and "check them at the door" when entering their clinical settings (Sommers-Flanagan & Sommers-Flanagan, 1995). They then are in a better position to create a safe environment, free from judgment and criticism, for their clients and increase the chances that clients will feel comfortable enough to disclose information about suicide when asked.

When talking with clients about suicide, counselors do best when using words that are kind and empathic, recognizing that talking about suicide is difficult and frightening for clients. It is also helpful to be direct by naming suicide when needed (e.g., "It's not uncommon for someone feeling down and under a lot of stress to think about suicide, so I'm wondering when was the last time you thought about suicide?"). Even though it can be difficult to talk openly about suicide, counselors must take steps to protect clients from foreseeable harm and to do so in a way that is accepting and affirming.

CLINICAL INTERVIEWING: ASSESSING IDEATION AND PLANS. The presence of thoughts about suicide and more specific plans about completing suicide are understandably two of the most important warning signs for a counselor to assess early in the interview (see Figure 8–4 for a brief list of risk factors and warning signs). It is recommended that counselors question their clients using the nonjudgmental assumption that suicide ideation might have been present at some point by asking, "When was the last time you thought about killing yourself?" or "When was the last time you thought about suicide?" Counselors are cautioned against using euphemisms or code language for suicide (e.g., "hurting yourself"), which can decrease the overall validity of the assessment. For example, a client may not consider suicide to be something that will hurt, but instead as something that will bring joy and relief. When assessing for suicide ideation, Sommers-Flanagan and Sommers-Flanagan (1995) recommend listening for and asking about (a) frequency of thoughts, (b) duration of thoughts, and (c) intensity of thoughts.

When assessing for the presence of a suicide plan, counselors are encouraged to be calm but direct. For example, the counselor can ask, "When you have thought about suicide, what kinds of things have you thought about?" Using a similarly gentle approach, counselors can ask open-ended questions to invite discussion and gain information to help with risk

---

Some Risk Factors for Suicide

- Sex (males more likely)
- Age (elderly and late adolescence)
- Marital status (divorced or widowed)
- Diagnosis (presence of psychiatric or medical illness)
- Prior suicide attempt (the best predictor of a future suicide)
- Family history
- Unemployment
- Access to firearms

Some Warning Signs for Suicide

- Substance abuse
- Significant anxiety and/or agitation
- Social withdrawal
- Active psychosis
- Plans and preparations
- Insomnia
- Immediate "flight into health" (i.e., everything becomes better)
- Talking about death or dying
- Hopelessness

FIGURE 8–4 Risk Factors and Warning Signs for Suicide

assessment. Asking for as much detail as possible about a client's plans will aid in the assessment. Clients may describe plans that are very specific (e.g., "shooting myself on the anniversary of my wedding with my grandfather's revolver") or somewhat vague (e.g., "maybe I'll just take a bunch of pills").

The acronym **SLAP** (Sommers-Flanagan & Sommers-Flannagan, 1995) can assist a counselor in assessing for suicide plans:

- *Specificity:* How detailed and specific are the plans for suicide?
- *Lethality:* How deadly are the means that the client plans to use?
- *Access to means:* How available are the means for suicide?
- *Proximity of social support:* How close by are safe people who can provide support and/or assistance?

It is worth noting that a plan with low lethality does not necessarily indicate that the client has a low risk of suicide or that the counselor should not be concerned. However, a plan that has greater specificity, lethality, and access to means greatly increases the client's risk for completing suicide.

Unfortunately, predicting suicide ideation, attempt, and completion is not an exact science. Fundamentally, there is still much that is not known about why one person will decide to end his or her life when another very similar person, who has experienced similar life events (and even has the same genetic makeup), does not. However, there are ways clinical mental health counselors can responsibly conduct suicide assessments. Suicide assessment can include a clinical interview as well as the administration of objective measures. In the **clinical interview**, a counselor's job is to evaluate known risk factors and warning signs, understand each client's unique situation, and subsequently develop appropriate and responsive interventions to reduce a client's overall risk for suicide. Much of this information is the client's to reveal. In addition to talking with clients about what they might do, counselors can use standardized tests.

Some assessment instruments relevant to suicide include the Beck Depression Inventory–II (Beck, Steer, & Brown, 1996), the Beck Scale for Suicide Ideation (Beck & Steer, 1991), the Brief Reasons for Living Inventory (Ivanoff, Jang, Smyth, & Linehan, 1994), the Hamilton Depression Rating Scale (Hamilton, 1960), the Millon Clinical Multiaxial Inventory–III (Millon, Davis, & Millon, 1997), the Minnesota Multiphasic Personality Inventory–2 (Butcher et al., 1989), the Suicidal Ideation Scale (Rudd, 1989), the Suicide Behaviors Questionnaire (Cole, 1988), and the Suicide Status Form (Jobes, Jacoby, Cimbolic, & Huestad, 1997).

Identifying Risk and Protective Factors

PRIMARY RISK FACTORS. The presence of a prior suicide attempt in a client's history is the best single predictor of a future suicide and thus warrants a counselor's particular attention. Asking about the details of the attempt (e.g., when, where, how; what kept you from completing the act), as well as the surrounding events (e.g., life stressors, family dynamics, mood or illness at the time, substance abuse), is crucial in assessing the client's current risk level. Such a conversation can also provide a counselor with information about the client's current perspective, insight, and use of healthy coping mechanisms to manage internal and external stressors.

As noted in Figure 8–4, there are additional important risk factors for completed suicide, and counselors are encouraged to become sensitized to these risks as well as to remember that having many or all of the risk factors does not mean that a person will attempt or complete suicide in the future. In addition, there are risk factors that may be unique to a specific client population (e.g., children, Hispanics, seniors).

OTHER RISK FACTORS. Two risk factors for suicide that have gained recent attention both in the media and in empirical literature are military veteran status and posttraumatic stress disorder (PTSD). Males who were veterans of the U.S. armed forces were at twice the risk of dying by suicide as a nonveteran comparison group (Kaplan, Huguet, McFarland, & Newsom 2007). These veterans posed a 58% greater risk of dying by using firearms. Another factor, PTSD, has been found to be quite prevalent in veterans of combat. Nye and Bell (2007) reported that one of the elements of PTSD diagnosis—reexperiencing the trauma—was the highest relative predictor of suicide ideation when compared with the remaining criteria for diagnosis.

PROTECTIVE FACTORS. A valid assessment of risk for suicide should also include an understanding of **protective factors**, or the presence of factors that reduce the likelihood of suicide. Protective factors include interpersonal support (e.g., family, friends, care providers, faith-based groups), restricted access to highly lethal means of suicide, investment in effective clinical care, cultural/religious beliefs that encourage self-preservation, and healthy problem-solving and coping skills. The identification and reinforcement of existing protective factors—along with the development of new ones—is important when working with a client who has suicide ideation.

Immediate Interventions

The interaction between counselor and client during the interview can aid in a thorough and valid assessment. In fact, many of the assessment areas just described, when approached by the counselor with unconditional acceptance, are also excellent interventions that can help reduce suicide risk. Imagine a client who has never given voice to thoughts of suicide because of fears of judgment, but who finds a safe place in your office to openly discuss them. A counselor asking, "What has stopped you so far from attempting to end your life?" can help a client remember what has been worth living for and can generate hope.

The use of no-suicide contracts has been replaced with a much more effective and ethical intervention called a **safety plan**. Creating a safety plan involves collaborating with the client to develop a written list of healthy coping responses for the client to engage in when noticing the early signs of suicide ideation. With this list of healthy behaviors, a client can learn to respond to stressors in new ways that will reduce the risk of suicide—for example, calling friends, listening to music, exercising, or calling a crisis support line. The last line of the safety plan should always include calling local law enforcement, a mobile crisis number, or you (depending on your policy about after-hours contact) to help keep the client safe.

Ed Shneidman (1996), a psychiatrist who has often been referred to as the father of suicidology, developed the Ten Commonalities of Suicide (see Figure 8–5). When thinking about interventions, it is useful to consider these common ways in which intense suicide ideation can affect a person. For example, if it is determined that a client is **cognitively constricted** (i.e., has a severely reduced ability to develop options for managing stressors), intervention can be to help the client consider new or renewed ways to manage emotional

1. The common stimulus is unendurable psychological pain (psychache).
2. The common stressor in suicide is frustrated psychological needs.
3. The common purpose of suicide is to seek a solution.
4. The common goal of suicide is cessation of consciousness.
5. The common emotion in suicide is hopelessness–helplessness.
6. The common internal attitude toward suicide is ambivalence.
7. The common cognitive state in suicide is constriction.
8. The common interpersonal act in suicide is communication of intention.
9. The common action in suicide is egression (escape).
10. The common consistency in suicide is with lifelong coping patterns.

FIGURE 8–5 Shneidman's Ten Commonalities of Suicide

pain. Because such pain (a.k.a. "**psychache**") can make it difficult for a client to hear or retain a lot of new information, writing down these new options is often helpful. Similarly, if the client views suicide as a means of escape, a useful intervention is to explore what the client wants to escape from and then consider the ramifications of that escape. In so doing, the client and counselor can collaboratively develop healthier ways of coping.

The Case of Sally

Sally considers herself a competent clinical mental health counselor. She handles herself well in most situations. However, she is quite nervous and unsure of herself when a client threatens suicide. That has only happened to her twice and she was able to work with the clients to find them immediate help. Now she is working with Marsha, who is a cutter and keeps talking about ending her life. Sally has tried to talk rationally with Marsha and convince her that suicide is not a good idea. Marsha has agreed, but in today's session Marsha showed Sally a new and deep cut on her wrist. She also told Sally she had nothing to live for since she is not married and does not have a family. Sally has come to you for a consultation on what to do next. What ideas do you have?

Responding to Risk Assessment

All of these considerations should assist the counselor in developing a balanced and circumspect evaluation of suicide risk. Such an assessment can range from **extreme risk** (i.e., client is unable to agree to a safety plan, has a specific and lethal plan for suicide) or **high risk** (i.e., client has a suicide plan but easily engages in safety planning), to **moderate risk** (i.e., client has thoughts of suicide without a clear plan) and **low risk** (i.e., client has no thoughts of suicide but some risk factors). Each level of assessed risk comes with its own appropriate level of care, including voluntary or involuntary hospitalization (for extreme risk), increased frequency of contact with client and outpatient medical evaluation (for high risk), or greater focus on and management of triggers for thoughts of suicide (for moderate risk). Even with low risk clients, it is useful for the counselor to continue to listen for changes in mood and healthy functioning and to reassess for thoughts and plans for suicide as needed.

INPATIENT TREATMENT. If it is determined that the client is of imminent danger to self (extreme risk), the prospect of voluntary hospitalization should be discussed. Counselors are encouraged to be open and direct with their clients about their rationale for seriously exploring this option. It is not uncommon for counselors to be uncomfortable with presenting the possibility of voluntary commitment to their clients. Counselors often experience anxiety that clients will be angry or resistant, and they well may be. However, once the clinical interview leads the counselor to the conclusion that a client may be in imminent danger, the counselor is responsible for helping that client stay safe. Ideally, the client then is taken to the hospital and is admitted. In such a case, the client should be accompanied by a family member, a trusted friend, or the clinician to ensure safety and appropriate communication of relevant clinical information to hospital professionals. Under no circumstances should the suicidal client be left alone, even briefly.

If the counselor has determined that the client is of immediate danger to self but the client will not agree to voluntary hospitalization, involuntary hospitalization may be necessary. Family members, friends, and, when needed, law enforcement can facilitate this process. At times it is necessary for the counselor to commit the client, even though taking such a step can be detrimental to the counseling relationship. Ultimately, the client's immediate safety needs to be a counselor's primary concern.

OUTPATIENT TREATMENT.   When the danger to self is not assessed to be imminent, outpatient treatment may be the best option. In this situation, "the goal is to obtain follow-up counseling soon—preferably in the next 48 hours, to provide support and re-assess the client" (MacCluskie & Ingersoll, 2001, p. 174). If the counselor's agency cannot provide continued, ongoing services, the counselor is responsible for scheduling the client with another professional at another agency, and follow-up should occur within the next few days. A safety plan should be developed with the client that includes emergency contact information. In many cases, family members need to be consulted, preferably with the client's permission. In cases of inpatient or outpatient treatment, the counselor should consult with other professionals and document all interventions, assessments and rationales, and consultations.

MAINTAINING EFFECTIVENESS AS A COUNSELOR: MANAGING STRESS AND AVOIDING BURNOUT

Clinical mental health counseling provides challenges and opportunities that can be rewarding and life enhancing. However, working therapeutically with clients day after day can also be emotionally draining and stressful. Counselors can successfully manage stress, avoid burnout, and maximize life satisfaction both personally and professionally, but it takes work.

Stress and Burnout in Counseling

BOX 8–5   What Is Counselor Burnout?

Extensive research has led to *burnout* being defined as "a psychological syndrome that develops in response to chronic emotional and interpersonal stress and is characterized by three features: emotional exhaustion; depersonalization (a defense mechanism for caregivers and service providers to gain emotional distance from clients); and feelings of ineffectiveness or lack of personal accomplishment" (Thompson, Amatea, & Thompson, 2014, p. 58). Some signs of burnout include reduced energy levels, feelings of helplessness or hopelessness, cynicism, and resentfulness. Counselors experiencing burnout often feel that they have nothing left to give.

A growing body of evidence suggests that human services workers, including counselors, experience high levels of stress in the workplace (e.g., Edwards, Burnard, Coyle, Fothergill, & Hannigan, 2000; James, 2008; Lee, Cho, Kissinger, & Ogle, 2010; Patrick, 2007). In addition to the typical stressors associated with everyday living, clinicians encounter challenges unique to mental health professionals. A full day of counseling clients can stretch one's emotional and mental resources, particularly when clients are dealing with traumatic problems such as assault, disease, and abuse (MacCluskie & Ingersoll, 2001). Other stressors that often are present in clinical mental health environments include long work hours, work overload, lack of control, low pay, organizational demands, paperwork deadlines, value conflict, hassles related to insurance reimbursement, and job–person incongruity (Maslach, 2003; Skovholt & Trotter-Mathison, 2016). When professional demands are coupled with personal pressures, finding ways to cope effectively can be challenging.

Stress is experienced when a substantial imbalance exists between real or perceived environmental demands and an individual's response capabilities (Baird, 2014; Lazarus & Folkman, 1984). When stress is not dealt with effectively and the imbalance is not corrected, counselors may experience burnout. It is the single most common personal consequence of working as a counselor (Kottler, 1993). People experiencing burnout are emotionally or physically drained to the point that they cannot perform functions meaningfully. Symptoms of excessive stress and burnout can be manifested in several areas, including the following (James, 2008; Kottler & Schofield, 2001; Patrick, 2007):

- *Cognitive functioning:* Individuals may experience confusion, memory problems, organizational difficulties, irrational thinking, negativity, rigidity, disillusionment, and decreased creativity.
- *Emotional functioning:* Common emotional expressions associated with burnout include irritability, sadness, anxiety, numbness, apathy, and a sense of being "out of control" or "emotionally drained" or "not oneself."
- *Behavioral functioning:* People may withdraw from colleagues, friends, and activities; be critical or detached; and engage in inappropriate risk taking. Struggles with interpersonal relationships may be evidenced, and productivity may decrease.
- *Physical functioning:* A host of physical problems are associated with burnout, including headaches, sleep problems, nervousness, addictions, fatigue, chest or back pains, loss of appetite, increased blood pressure levels, and weakened immune systems.

Kottler and Schofield (2001) categorize sources of counselor stress and burnout into four primary areas: the work environment, specific events, client-induced stress, and self-induced stress. **Work environment stressors** include excessive paperwork, demanding time pressures, managed care constraints, inflexible rules and regulations, unsupportive colleagues, and incompetent supervisors. **Event-related stressors** tend to stem from individuals' personal lives and may include developmental transitions (e.g., getting married, having children, entering midlife), health-related issues, and financial concerns. In contrast, **client-induced stressors** include difficult or resistant clients, clients experiencing trauma or crisis, and clients who terminate prematurely. Finally, examples of **self-induced stressors** include perfectionism, unrealistic expectations, an unhealthy lifestyle, exhaustion, and fear of failure on the part of the clinician. All counselors will experience stress of some type. The question is not whether stress will be experienced but, instead, how counselors will choose to cope with it.

To be effective helpers, it is essential for counselors to find ways to take care of themselves (Baird, 2014). Remember what flight attendants say: Secure your own oxygen mask first—then tend to others. The same principle applies to counseling. Just as prevention in counseling is preferable to remediation, a proactive approach to managing stress and avoiding burnout can help counselors balance professional and personal challenges more effectively. Four areas in which clinical mental health counselors can take steps to achieve balance are establishing limits, modeling self-care, cultivating self-awareness, and maintaining a sense of humor.

Establishing Limits

Some of the very characteristics that inspire people to become counselors—wanting to help others, idealism, and high motivation—can lead them to take on more responsibilities than can be managed realistically or effectively. Counselors often work extra hours, engage in volunteer activities, and make themselves accessible to clients and others long after the normal workday is finished. Swenson (1998) labels the tendency to take on too much and continually push personal limits as **overload syndrome**. Many counselors are not very adept at defining their personal limits, and consequently, it is easy for them to overextend. However, living in a state of constant overload, with no margins or buffers to protect one's time and energy, can lead to exhaustion and stagnation. Setting limits at work and elsewhere is essential to healthy, effective living. The following suggestions, made by various authors (e.g., Baird, 2014; MacCluskie & Ingersoll, 2001; Patrick, 2007; Swenson, 1998) can help counselors establish and maintain limits in their personal and professional lives.

- *Use appropriate assertiveness and say no.* People often set unrealistic expectations for themselves, believing that they can accomplish more in a 24-hour period than is feasible. Other people accept additional responsibilities because they fear the repercussions of declining them. Setting necessary limits involves prioritizing what is important, recognizing that we have more control over our schedules than we realize, and learning how to say no, even to good things, to avoid overcommitment.
- *Consider doing less, not more.* It is easy to saturate our schedules, leaving little room for empty space or margins. Overly packed schedules provide the fuel for stress responses. Counselors can intentionally create margins in their schedules by (a) ending sessions on time; (b) building in breaks during the day for note writing, physical activity, and rejuvenation; and (c) periodically pruning, or cutting out, activities that are unnecessary or unrewarding.
- *Create boundaries around the private spaces of life.* Often, the boundary between work and home becomes blurred or even nonexistent, making burnout more likely. With the continual advances in technology, which can make people accessible 24/7, the need to set boundaries becomes even more important. Belson (1992) facetiously advises counselors who want to "achieve" burnout to do the following:

  a. Work long hours, especially weekends and evenings, telling yourself that this doesn't interfere with family relationships.

  b. Think about your most difficult cases, even when you are not at work.

  c. Worry continually about what you are not doing that you should be doing.

In contrast, counselors who maintain healthy boundaries recognize that it is desirable to establish and defend perimeters around their homes, communities, and leisure activities. Protecting boundaries allows counselors to nurture relationships with family members and friends, which are essential to healthy living.

Modeling Self-Care

In addition to setting limits, counselors can model physical, mental, emotional, and spiritual self-care. The counselor who pursues a wellness-oriented lifestyle is in a better position to provide services to clients and help them engage in their own self-care plans. Developing a personal wellness plan and sticking with it can be one way to model self-care, thereby reducing stress and avoiding burnout.

* *Physical self-care.*   Often, counselors place their own physical self-care on the back burner as they attempt to meet the multiple demands of clients and organizations. However, the cost of physical neglect can be high, resulting in outcomes such as illness, hypertension, bodily aches and pains, fatigue, and other forms of physical or mental malaise. Engaging in physical self-care is essential to one's personal health and effectiveness as a counselor.

Sleep, nutrition, and exercise are three areas that need ongoing attention if counselors are to maintain optimal health. Ongoing sleep deprivation can lead to poor concentration, disorganization, and exhaustion. Prioritizing the need for sleep and guarding that time are essential to stress management. Similarly, carving out time to exercise regularly and eat nutritiously yields physical, emotional, and cognitive benefits. The sedentary nature of counseling, combined with busy schedules that may not include formal lunch breaks, increases the need for ongoing physical exercise and attention to nutrition. Counselors also will want to monitor the physical tension associated with stress and find healthy ways to alleviate that tension through such activities as relaxation exercises, mindfulness, and yoga that are stress reducing.

* *Cognitive self-care.*   The beliefs counselors hold about themselves, their clients, and the counseling process can enhance health and well-being or create stress and negativity. Evaluating and modifying irrational stress-inducing cognitions promotes positive mental health. Several authors have identified faulty beliefs that may negatively affect counselor effectiveness (e.g., Baird, 2014; James, 2008; Kottler & Schofield, 2001). Examples of irrational beliefs associated with stress and burnout include the following:

* My job is my life; what I do is who I am.
* I must be totally competent and knowledgeable.
* I must help everyone all the time.
* I must be a model of mental health.
* I need to be available at all times.
* No one can do the job like I can.
* I am responsible for client change.
* I should not be anxious or uncertain.
* Any negative feedback indicates that there is something wrong with me.
* The client is always in counseling to change or get better.
* The client should appreciate my efforts.
* The client should be different from what he or she is.

Taking the time to evaluate one's beliefs about self, the counseling process, and clients is the first step toward enhancing cognitive functioning. Working with a supervisor, colleague, or personal counselor can help you identify and modify faulty beliefs and expectations.

* *Emotional and spiritual self-care.*   Some of the qualities that help make counselors effective—being empathic, sensitive, humane, people oriented, and highly committed—also can lead to difficulties and stress. For example, empathic, sensitive counselors may also be anxious, obsessive, overly conscientious, overly enthusiastic, and susceptible to identifying

too closely with clients (James, 2008). As noted earlier, counselors who work with traumatized clients may be especially vulnerable to experiencing compassion fatigue. Consequently, it is crucial for counselors to monitor their emotional reactions on an ongoing basis. Baird (2014) suggests engaging in "cleansing rituals" after demanding sessions. These rituals may include stretching, walking, splashing water on one's face, or deep breathing exercises. Moreover, counselors can symbolize leaving clients at work by placing client files in the file cabinet (or securing them on their computers), closing the door to the office, and literally and figuratively leaving them there.

Seeking support from friends, family members, and colleagues is a key element of emotional self-care. Taking time to nurture personal relationships with loved ones provides an important source of support. However, one of the difficulties related to counseling is the need to keep clients' stories confidential, which means that much of what goes on during the day cannot be shared with those closest to us. Consequently, having a professional colleague or supervisor with whom one can discuss difficult or unsettling cases can be an invaluable resource. Another source of support, especially when counselors are dealing with difficult personal issues, comes through personal counseling or therapy. Ironically, many counselors are reluctant or unwilling to seek help for themselves, even though they recommend it for others. However, participating in counseling can help counselors deal with personal issues, the stresses of practice, and their understanding of the therapeutic practice (Baird, 2014; Kottler & Schofield, 2001).

In addition to emotional self-care, spiritual nurturing can help counselors manage stress more effectively. Myers and Williard (2003) define **spirituality** as "the capacity and tendency present in all human beings to find and construct meaning about life and existence and to move toward personal growth, responsibility, and relationship with others" (p. 149). Finding ways to nurture and enhance one's spiritual development—whether through prayer, meditation, mindfulness, worship, or some other practice—can promote personal growth and facilitate optimal functioning. Intentional practice of "alonetime"—a devoted period in silence and solitude or reflectively within oneself when in a group—can also be helpful (Wicks & Buck, 2014).

The Case of Dale

Recently Dale has been feeling stressed out and fatigued. She has not felt this way before but she recognizes that her feelings are interfering with her effectiveness as a counselor. She is not pleased about that, but to counter these feelings she has come up with a plan. She has a golden lab who is very gentle and able to accompany her to work. She thinks if she brings in the dog and pets him in between clients, she will feel better and actually do better. She has even thought of bringing the dog into sessions.

What do you think of Dale's ideas? What are their positive points? What are their negatives? What else might Dale consider so that her stress is lessened and she feels more energetic?

Cultivating Self-Awareness

One of the key characteristics of effective counselors is **self-awareness**—an in-depth knowledge of their attitudes, values, and feelings, as well as the ability to recognize ways situations and events affect them. Self-awareness enables counselors to identify early symptoms of stress and overload and then select coping responses more effectively. Kottler and Schofield (2001, p. 429) suggest that counselors use the following questions to guide reflection and increase self-awareness:

- What haunts you the most and continues to plague you during vulnerable moments?
- In what ways are you less than fully functioning in your personal and professional life?
- What are some aspects of your lifestyle that are unhealthy?
- What are your most difficult, conflicted, and dysfunctional relationships?
- How does all of this affect your work with clients?

Counselors can increase personal self-awareness by practicing reflection, which allows time and space for self-examination (Boyatzis, McKee, & Goleman, 2002). Reflection provides time away from work and responsibilities for the purpose of being alone with one's thoughts. It involves a conscious, disciplined effort at self-examination and provides an opportunity to contemplate past experiences, current relationships, and future hopes. Through reflection, counselors may encounter themselves and their deepest feelings in ways that are surprising, unexpected, and perhaps a little frightening. Such encounters put counselors in a better position to take stock and move in directions that are personally and professionally enhancing.

Maintaining a Sense of Humor

The physiological benefits of humor are extolled in Norman Cousins's (1979) *Anatomy of an Illness*. Having a **sense of humor**—being able to laugh at oneself and absurd life events—can be a primary source of energy for rejuvenation. As Oscar Wilde once stated, "Life is too important to be taken seriously." Or, to paraphrase the title and content of a book by Paul Watzlawick (1983), humor allows one to know that many human problems are "hopeless but not serious" or "serious but not hopeless" and, therefore, solvable.

Humor has the remarkable ability to promote insight, generate creativity, and defuse tense situations (Gladding, 1995). Laughter releases endorphins, which can help improve our mood and induce relaxation. It is easy to take ourselves too seriously, thus missing out on the ability to see things through a different lens (Gladding & Wallace, 2016). Being able to laugh at ourselves and our mistakes can help put things in perspective and create pathways for healing.

In the following narrative (Box 8–6), Gladding shares an example of how humor sometimes arises unexpectedly in counseling situations.

BOX 8–6   Maintaining Effectiveness as a Counselor

I learned about the value of humor in counseling during my first years of work as a counselor. I had completed intake information on a man and asked him what he would like to work on in the session. He looked at me a bit negatively and simply stated, "I am not talking until you get rid of the rabbits in this room."

We were in a rural area, so I surveyed our surroundings. Not seeing any rabbits, I asked where they were. He pointed to an imaginary hare (that I assumed was wild), and I went over, grabbed it by its invisible ears, then opened the door, and threw it outside. As I went to sit down, he pointed to a second imaginary furry creature, so I proceeded to do the same thing. Again, as I went back to my chair, he pointed to a third unseeable furry critter with long ears and a cotton tail (so he said). As I approached this third imaginary hare and started to grab it by its long ears and toss it out with a flair, I suddenly stopped and thought, "Who really needs help here?" I laughed to myself and proceeded to get my client the help he needed.

From that experience, I began to develop better confrontation skills. I probably would have eventually learned these necessary helping techniques in counseling, but the bizarre nature of my client's experience accelerated the process and let me laugh at myself in the process. Levity can sometimes be enlightening, and there often is a humorous side to even the most serious of situations.

Samuel Gladding, PhD, LPC, NCC, CCMHC

Counseling is serious business. However, it also provides multiple opportunities for joy, enthusiasm, and continued mastery of personal and professional skills. As you develop that mastery, it is helpful to keep in mind the words of Robert Brown, a leader in the counseling profession, who died of cancer several years ago:

What do I have to say to counselors in the field who are trying to find their way, to create meaning in their lives? Don't take yourself seriously, but take yourself measurably. Don't take yourself in a manner that is cavalier, but take yourself in a manner that has sincerity and thoughtfulness about it. (Kottler & Brown, 2000, p. 383)

Summary and Conclusion

Clinical mental health counseling is a challenging yet rewarding profession that requires mental health professionals to develop the skills and knowledge to help clients with a wide range of issues. Professional helpers are challenged to be skilled in many different areas so that they can provide high-caliber counseling services. In this chapter, two particularly challenging services have been discussed: crisis and disaster response and suicide assessment and intervention.

Crises can be developmental, situational, existential, and ecosystemic. Ways to assess, intervene, and manage crises, especially the six-step model of crisis intervention, were discussed, as well as the importance of becoming skilled in disaster mental health and being able to offer psychological first aid when needed. Preventing compassion fatigue, traumatic stress, and vicarious traumatization were also highlighted. Suicide assessment and intervention were also covered in this chapter. Ways of assessing suicide and identifying risk and protective factors were focused on, as well as ways of responding to suicidal clients.

The chapter closed with a focus on maintaining personal effectiveness as a counselor by managing stress and burnout. Stress and burnout are occupational hazards in the counseling field. However, consciously engaging in self-care and boundary setting can positively contribute to keeping one's passion, focus, and mental health as a counselor.

PART 3

Working with Specific Populations

CHAPTER 9

Working with Groups

SpeedKingz/Shutterstock

Who am I in this pilgrim group
*   whose members differ so in perception?*
Am I timid like a Miles Standish,
*   letting others speak for me*
*   because the experience of failure is softened*
*   if a risk is never personally taken?*
Or am I more like a John Alden
*   speaking boldly for others in the courting of beauty*
*   but not seeking such for myself?*
Perhaps I am more than either man
*   or maybe I'm both at different times!*
In the silence and before others, I ponder the question anew.

Reprinted from "A Restless Presence: Group Process as a Pilgrimage," by S. T. Gladding, 1979, *School Counselor, 27,* p. 126. Copyright © 1979 by Samuel T. Gladding. Used with permission.

CHAPTER OVERVIEW

From reading this chapter, you will learn about

- The place of groups in counseling
- The four major types of groups counselors use: psychoeducational, task/work, psychotherapy, and counseling
- The advantages and limitations of groups
- Stages of and issues in groups
- Qualities of effective group leaders

As you read, consider

- What groups have worked well for you in the past
- What the dynamics are that make groups successful
- Issues you have seen arise in groups and ways they were or were not settled successfully
- What skills you may need to develop if you are to become a group leader
- The differences you notice in group work compared with individual counseling

Working in groups is a counseling specialty that is relatively new, but one that is often effective in helping individuals resolve personal and interpersonal concerns. Organized groups make use of people's natural tendency to gather and share thoughts and feelings as well as work and play cooperatively.

This chapter examines multiple aspects of groups, including the place of groups in counseling, types of groups counselors use, advantages and limitations of groups, stages and issues in group work, and qualities of effective group leaders. Clinical mental health counselors, especially in community and agency settings, who restrict their competencies to individual counseling and do not learn how to run groups limit their options for helping.

THE PLACE OF GROUPS IN COUNSELING

A **group** is generally considered to be "a collection of two or more individuals who meet in face-to-face interaction, interdependently, with the awareness that each belongs to the group and for the purpose of achieving individual and/or mutually agreed upon goals" (Gladding, 2016b, p. 4). The exception to this definition is found in some groups who meet on the Internet, where there is no face-to-face interaction (Page et al., 2000).

Groups have a unique place in counseling. Everyone typically spends some time in group activities each day, for example, with colleagues, schoolmates, neighbors, or business associates. Gregariousness is a part of human nature, and many personal and professional skills are learned through group interactions. It is only natural, then, for counselors to make use of this primary way of human interaction. Groups are an economical and effective means of helping individuals who share similar problems and concerns.

Groups are not a new phenomenon in clinical mental health work. They have a long and distinguished place in the service of counseling. Joseph Hersey Pratt is generally credited with starting the first psychologically oriented group. He did so in 1905 with tuberculosis outpatients at Massachusetts General in Boston. He found their regular group experience to be informative, supportive, and therapeutic. The following professionals were also pioneers in the group movement in the 20th century (see Figure 9–1):

- Jacob L. Moreno, who introduced the term **group psychotherapy** into the counseling literature in the 1930s
- Kurt Lewin, whose field theory concepts in the 1930s and 1940s became the basis for the Tavistock small study groups in Britain and the T-group movement in the United States
- Fritz Perls, whose Gestalt approach to groups attracted new energy and interest in the field
- W. Edwards Deming, who conceptualized and implemented the idea of quality work groups to improve the processes and products people produced and to build morale among workers in businesses
- William Schutz and Jack Gibb, who emphasized a humanistic aspect to groups that focused on personal growth as a legitimate goal
- Carl Rogers, who devised the basic encounter group in the 1960s that became the model for growth-oriented group approaches

Thus, organized therapeutic and growth groups are over 100 years old. Those who have engineered and created ways of conducting them have established various types of groups as a main component within counseling.

Therapist	Time	Contribution to Group Work
Joseph Hersey Pratt	1905	Started first psychotherapy/counseling group
Jacob Moreno	1920s	Began psychodrama; introduced the term *group psychotherapy*
Kurt Lewin	1930s	His field concept theory became the basis for T-groups
Fritz Perls	1940s	Founder of Gestalt groups
W. Edward Demmings	1950s	Originated total quality groups
William Schutz/Jack Gibbs	1960s	Worked to humanize T-groups, personal growth
Carl Rogers	1960s/1970s	Started growth-oriented basic encounter groups

FIGURE 9–1   Early Pioneers in Group Work

TYPES OF GROUPS

Groups come in many forms: "There seems to be a group experience tailored to suit the interests and needs of virtually anyone who seeks psychotherapy, personal growth, or simply support and companionship from others" (Lynn & Frauman, 1985, p. 423). A number of group models are appropriate for a wide variety of situations. Although lively debate persists about how groups should be categorized, especially in regard to goals and process (Waldo & Bauman, 1998), the following four types of groups have training standards developed by the Association for Specialists in Group Work (ASGW; 2000): psychoeducational, counseling, psychotherapy, and task/work.

Psychoeducational Groups

Psychoeducational groups were originally developed for use in educational settings, specifically in schools. There they were known simply as educational or guidance groups. However, now psychoeducational groups are frequently implemented in agency and community settings as well (Champe & Rubel, 2012). The primary function of these groups is the prevention of personal or societal disorders through the conveying of information and/or the examining of values. Psychoeducational groups stress growth through knowledge. Content includes, but is not limited to, personal, social, vocational, and educational information. For instance, group participants may be taught how to deal with a potential threat (e.g., the Zika virus), a developmental life event (e.g., growing older), or an immediate life crisis (e.g., the death of a loved one). Preventive and growth activities can take many forms but usually are presented as nonthreatening exercises or group discussions (Carroll, Bates, & Johnson, 2004).

As indicated, psychoeducational group activities are offered throughout the life span in a variety of settings. How they are offered differs, though, depending on the group involved. Sometimes these groups take the form of life-skills development, especially for those who have a deficit of appropriate interpersonal behaviors (Gazda et al., 2005). This how-to approach may include the use of films, plays, demonstrations, role plays, and guest speakers. At other times, psychoeducational groups focus on learning new skills and information. Psychoeducational groups often are found in agency and community settings.

The size of the group varies with the setting (e.g., a self-contained classroom), but the typical group size ranges from 10 to 40 individuals. The group leader has expertise in the topic being discussed and is in charge of group management and disseminating information. One of the most important parts of the process that goes on in such groups revolves around group discussion of how members will personalize the information presented in the group context. These groups are designed to meet the needs of generally well-functioning people.

Counseling Groups

Counseling groups focus on prevention, growth, and remediation. They focus on interpersonal problems or concerns. They seek to help group participants resolve the usual, yet often difficult, situations connected with living in an ever-changing society. An additional goal is to help participants develop their existing interpersonal problem-solving competencies so they may be better able to handle future problems. Non-severe career, educational, personal, social, and developmental concerns are frequently addressed.

Because the focus of group counseling is on each person's behavior and growth or change within the group, the interaction among persons, especially in resolving concerns and difficulties, is highlighted. Group dynamics and interactive relationships are emphasized. Whereas psychoeducational groups are recommended for everyone on a continuous basis, group counseling is more selective. It focuses on individuals experiencing common complications of living that information alone will not solve, such as changing careers.

The size of these groups varies with the ages of the individuals involved, ranging from 3 or 4 in a children's group to 8 to 12 in an adult group. The number of group meetings also fluctuates but generally ranges from 6 to 16 sessions. The leader is in charge of facilitating the group interaction but becomes less directly involved as the group develops and members become more connected and interactive. Usually, the topics covered in group counseling are developmental or situational in nature, such as educational, social, career, and personal issues. Counseling groups tend not to be of long-standing duration. Compared with psychoeducational groups, this type of group offers a more direct approach to dealing with troublesome behaviors. The major advantages of group counseling are the collaboration, feedback, and contribution of group members with each other over a period of time.

Psychotherapy Groups

Psychotherapy groups are set up to help individual group members resolve their in-depth and sometimes serious psychological problems. These groups are described in the professional literature as remedial types of groups. "Because the depth and extent of the psychological disturbance is significant, the goal is to aid each individual to reconstruct major personality dimensions" (ASGW, 1992, p. 13).

At times, there is overlap in group counseling and group psychotherapy, but the emphasis on major reconstruction of personality dimensions generally distinguishes the two. The setting of group psychotherapy is often in inpatient facilities, such as hospitals or mental health facilities, because of greater control of the people involved. As an entity, psychotherapy groups may be either open ended (i.e., admitting new members at any time) or closed (i.e., not admitting new members after the first session). Certain types of individuals are poor candidates for outpatient, intensive group psychotherapy: for example, individuals with depression; those who are incessant talkers; people with paranoia or with schizophrenic, sociopathic, or suicidal personalities; and individuals with extreme narcissism

(Yalom & Leszcz, 2005). It may be easier to identify group psychotherapy candidates who should be excluded than to pick those who should be included. Regardless, group psychotherapy is an American form of treatment and has provided much of the rationale for group counseling.

One of the primary aims of the group psychotherapy process is to reconstruct, through in-depth analysis, the personalities of those involved (Gazda, Ginter, & Horne, 2001). The size of the group varies from two or three to a dozen. Members meet for a period of months, or even years. The group leader has expertise in one of the mental health disciplines (i.e., psychiatry, psychology, clinical mental health counseling, social work, or psychiatric nursing), as well as training and expertise in dealing with people who have severe emotional problems. The responsibilities of the leader are to confront as well as to facilitate.

Task/Work Groups

Task/work groups assist their members in applying group dynamics principles and processes to improve work practices and to accomplish identified work goals. "The task/work group specialist is able to assist groups such as task forces, committees, planning groups, community organizations, discussion groups, study circles, learning groups, and other similar groups to correct or develop their functions" (ASGW, 1992, p. 13). The prototype of a task/work group is a **quality circle** in which members of a work unit discuss the processes under which they operate and try to make continuous improvements.

There are as many types of task/work groups as there are kinds of tasks and work. Regardless of type or form, however, all such groups emphasize accomplishment and efficiency in completing identified work goals. They are united in their emphasis on achieving a successful performance or a finished product through collaborative efforts. Unlike other groups examined here, there is no emphasis in task/work groups on changing individuals. Whether the group is successful or not depends on group dynamics, which are the interactions fostered through the relationships of members and leaders in connection with the complexity of the task involved. Because task/work groups run the gamut from informal subcommittees to major film production, the number of members within a task/work group may be large, but such a group usually works best when kept below 12. The length of a task/work group varies, but most are similar to other groups in that they have a beginning, a working period, and an ending. One difference is that often little attention is paid by members or leaders to the termination stage, and some of these groups end abruptly.

Mixed Groups

Most groups belong in one of the four categories of specialty groups just discussed. However, some do not fit well into any category. The most notable of these, often called **mixed groups**, encompass multiple ways of working with members and may change emphasis frequently. For example, some groups that are instructive are simultaneously or consequentially therapeutic. The prototype for such a mixed group is a self-help group (Gladding, 2016b).

Self-help groups take two forms: those that are organized by an established professional helping organization or individual (i.e., **support groups**) and those that originate spontaneously and stress their autonomy and internal group resources—self-help groups in the truest sense (Riordan & Beggs, 1987). Although there are distinctions between support groups and self-help organizations, these groups share numerous common denominators, including the fact that they are composed of individuals who have a common focus and purpose. They are psychoeducational, therapeutic, and usually task driven as well. In addition, members of these groups frequently employ counseling techniques, such as reflection, active listening, and confrontation.

Many support and self-help groups seem to be successful in helping their members to take more control over their lives and to function well. Some that lack professional leadership make up for this deficiency in terms of experienced lay leaders. The narrow focus of these groups is both an asset in achieving a specific goal and a deficit in helping participants expand their horizons.

The Case of Cassie

Cassie has been a volunteer in a low-income neighborhood. She has mainly worked with children, organizing them into teams that compete as well as cooperate with each other on various levels, from playing stickball to cleaning up trash on the street. The children seem to have thrived under Cassie's leadership, even though she is a young, White female, and they are predominantly people of color. Now Cassie's supervisor wants her to stretch herself and do more for the neighborhood. The supervisor specifically wants Cassie to lead a parent/child group and focus on family relationships. The kids she has worked with will be in the group.

Cassie is not sure she should switch roles. She is only 23 and is not a parent. She also worries that she may accidentally divulge information about the children she has worked with to their parents. Thus, there are boundary issues. Furthermore, her role as an educational leader would be quite different from her role now as a recreational leader. So the questions playing in Cassie's mind are these: Can she switch roles and not alienate the children she has been working with? Does she know enough and have enough credibility as an outsider with no parental experience to help educate low-income parents on techniques that would be helpful in creating a healthy family environment? If you were Cassie, what would you do?

REALITIES AND MISPERCEPTIONS ABOUT GROUPS

Despite the long history of different types of groups in society, certain misperceptions about groups are still prevalent in the general public (Gladding, 2016b). Most misperceptions involve counseling and psychotherapy groups (as opposed to psychoeducational and task/work groups). The following are some prevalent myths about groups:

- They are artificial and unreal experiences.
- They are second-rate structures for dealing with problems.
- They force people to lose their identity by tearing down psychological defenses.
- They require that people become emotional and spill their guts.
- They are touchy-feely, confrontational, hostile, and brainwashing experiences (Childers & Couch, 1989).

The reality is that none of these myths are true, at least in well-run groups. Indeed, quite the contrary is actually the case. Therefore, it is important that individuals who are unsure about groups ask questions before they consider becoming members. In such a way, doubts and misperceptions can be addressed, anxiety may be lessened, and people may benefit significantly within a group environment.

USES, ADVANTAGES, AND LIMITATIONS OF GROUPS

Although there are specialty groups and best practices associated with such groups, whether a person is right for a group is always a question that should be asked. Furthermore, the advantages and limitations of groups should be considered before establishing or joining a group.

Uses of Groups

Most clinical mental health counselors must make major decisions about when, where, and with whom to use groups. There are some situations in which groups are not appropriate. For instance, a counselor employed by a company would be unwise to use groups to counsel employees with personal problems who are unequal in rank and seniority in the corporate network. Similarly, a clinical mental health counselor would be foolish to use a group setting as a way of working with children who are all behaviorally disruptive. But a group may be ideal for helping people who are not too disruptive or unequal in status and who have common concerns. In such cases the procedure is for counselors to schedule a regular time in a quiet, uninterrupted setting for such people to meet and interact together.

Groups differ in purpose, composition, and length, but basically they all involve work. Gazda et al. (2001) describe work as "the dynamic interaction between collections of individuals for prevention or remediation of difficulties or for the enhancement of personal growth/enrichment" (p. 297). Hence, the term **group work** is often used in connection with what goes on in groups. Group work is

> a broad professional practice involving the application of knowledge and skill in group facilitation to assist an interdependent collection of people to reach their mutual goals, which may be intrapersonal, interpersonal, or work related. The goals of the group may include the accomplishment of tasks related to work, education, personal development, personal and interpersonal problem solving, or remediation of mental and emotional disorders. (ASGW, 2000, p. 3)

Advantages of Groups

Groups have a number of general advantages. For example, group members can come to realize that they are not alone, unique, or abnormal in their problems and concerns. Through their interaction with one another, they learn more about themselves in social situations. In groups, clients can try out new behaviors and ways of interacting because the group atmosphere provides a safe environment to experiment with change and receive feedback. Members also observe how others attack and resolve problems, thereby picking up skills vicariously. Finally, the group may serve as a catalyst to help persons realize a want or a need for individual counseling or the accomplishment of a personal goal.

If set up properly, groups have specific advantages that can be beneficial in helping individuals with a variety of problems and concerns. For instance, research has shown that breast cancer patients live longer and have a better quality of life when they undergo group therapy as a part of their recovery (Sleek, 1995). Groups can also be powerful and effective experiences for clients dealing with social phobias, developmental disabilities, and insomnia. Literally hundreds of studies describe group approaches and statistically support the effectiveness of various forms of groups. Documentation of group experiences is occurring at such a fast rate that it is difficult to stay abreast of the latest developments.

Some researchers in the field regularly write comprehensive reviews on select group activities that help practitioners become better informed. The following are some relevant findings that are advantages of groups:

- Group counseling appears to be a positive resource for support and skill building for adolescents who have been arrested for first-time misdemeanor offenses (Choate & Manton, 2014).
- School-based counseling groups using mindfulness meditation have the potential to help alternative high school students enhance their social, emotional, and academic strengths (Wisner & Norton, 2013).
- Group counseling can be used to help improve the test scores and social skills of low-performing students (Webb, Brigman, & Campbell, 2005).
- Groups can promote career development in general (Santos, 2004) and can be used effectively in vocational planning with some underserved populations, such as battered and abused women (Peterson & Priour, 2000).
- Psychoeducational support groups for serious mental illness can help participants manage their illness better, combat social isolation, and increase self-esteem and hope (Lefley, 2009).
- Group therapy is an efficient and cost-effective way to provide treatment for socially anxious college students (Damer, Latimer, & Porter, 2010).
- Support groups can be of benefit in helping older women cope with divorce and its aftermath (Blatter & Jacobsen, 1993).
- Group intervention with female adolescent offenders can help them increase their self-confidence and self-esteem and achieve a sense of relationship with others (Calhoun, Bartolomucci, & McLean, 2005).
- Group counseling and psychoeducational programs can help persons who have sustained a heart attack improve their quality of life (Bagheri, Memarian, & Alhani, 2007).

Limitations of Groups

Yet despite their many uses and advantages, groups are not a panacea for all people and problems. They have definite limitations and disadvantages (Gladding, 2016b). For example, many client concerns and personalities are not well suited for groups. The problems of individuals may not be dealt with in enough depth in groups. In addition, group pressure may force a client to take action, such as self-disclosure, before being ready. Groups may also lapse into a **groupthink** mentality, in which stereotypical, defensive, and stale thought processes become the norm while creativity and problem solving are squelched.

Another drawback to groups is that individuals may try to use them for escape or for selfish purposes and thereby disrupt the group process. Furthermore, it may be difficult for leaders to find a suitable time to conduct groups so that all who wish to can participate.

An additional concern is whether groups reflect the social milieu in which individual members normally operate. If they do not, what is learned from the group experience may not be relevant. Finally, if groups do not work through their developmental stages successfully, they may become regressive and engage in nonproductive and even destructive behaviors such as scapegoating, group narcissism, and projection (McClure, 1994).

THEORETICAL APPROACHES IN CONDUCTING GROUPS

Theoretical approaches to counseling in groups vary as much as individual counseling approaches. In many cases, the theories are the same. For instance, within group work different approaches are based on psychoanalytic, Gestalt, person-centered, behavioral, rational-emotive behavior, transactional analysis, and cognitive theories. Yet the implementation of any theoretical approach differs when employed with a group because of group dynamics.

In an evaluation of seven major theoretical approaches to groups, Ward (1982) analyzed the degree to which each approach pays attention to the (a) individual, (b) interpersonal, and (c) group levels of the process (see Box 9–1). The psychoanalytic, Gestalt, and behavioral approaches to groups were strong in focusing on the individual but weak on the other two components of the group process, whereas the Rogerian approach was strong on the individual level and medium on the interpersonal and group levels. Ward points out the limiting aspects of each theoretical approach and the importance of considering other factors, such as the group task and membership maturity, in conducting comprehensive group assignments.

BOX 9–1   Three Levels of Groups

Individual—Interpersonal—Group

In a similar way, Frey (1972) outlines how eight approaches to group work can be conceptualized on continuums from insight to action and from rational to affective, and Hansen, Warner, and Smith (1980) conceptualize group approaches on continuums from process to outcome and from leader centered to member centered. Group leaders and potential group members must know how theories differ on dimensions such as these in order to make wise choices.

Overall, multiple theoretical models provide richness and diversity for conducting groups. Three additional factors are useful for group leaders to consider in arriving at a decision on what approach to take:

1. Does one need a theoretical base for conducting the group?
2. What uses will the theory best serve?
3. What criteria will be employed in the selection process?

A theory is a lot like a map. In a group, a theory provides direction and guidance in examining basic assumptions about human beings. Theory is also useful in determining goals for the group, in clarifying one's role and functions as a leader, and in explaining the group interactions. Finally, a theory can help in evaluating the outcomes of the group. Trying to lead a group without an explicit theoretical rationale is similar to attempting to fly an airplane without a map and knowledge of instruments. Either procedure is foolish, dangerous, and likely to lead to injury.

A good theory serves practical functions, too (Gladding, 2016b). For example, it gives meaning to and a framework for experiences and facts that occur within a setting. Good theory helps make logical sense out of what is happening and leads to productive research. With so many theories from which to choose, the potential group leader is wise to be careful in selecting an approach.

Ford and Urban (1963) contend that four main factors should be considered when selecting a theory: personal experience (does it work for you as a group leader?), consensus of experts (i.e., is it seen as useful?), prestige (i.e., is it held in high esteem?), and a verified body of knowledge (what does the research confirm about its effectiveness?) (see Box 9–2).

BOX 9–2   Four Main Factors for Selecting a Theory

Personal Experience—Consensus of Experts—Prestige—Verified Body of Knowledge

---

There are liabilities and advantages to all the criteria for selecting a theory. Therefore, it is crucial for counselors to listen to others and to read the professional literature critically to evaluate the theories that are most verifiable and that fit their personality styles.

STAGES IN GROUPS

Groups, like other living systems, go through stages. If an individual or group leader is not aware of these stages, the changes that occur within the group may appear confusing rather than meaningful, and the benefits may be few. Leaders can maximize learning by setting up conditions that facilitate the development of the group and by "using developmentally based interventions, at both individual and group levels" (Saidla, 1990, p. 15).

There is debate within the professional literature about which groups go through stages and when. Developmental stages have been identified in various types of groups, such as learning groups and training groups, yet much of the debate about stages focuses on group counseling. The most agreed-on number of group counseling stages is four or five, but there are models for as few as three and as many as six stages. Tuckman's stage model, which is presented here, is considered mainstream.

Tuckman (1965) was one of the first theorists to design a stage process for group counseling. He believed there were four **stages of group development**: forming, storming, norming, and performing. This concept was later expanded to include a fifth stage: adjourning (Tuckman & Jensen, 1977), or mourning/morning (Waldo, 1985). In each stage certain tasks are performed. For example, in the **forming stage**, the foundation is usually laid for what is to come and who will be considered in or out of group deliberations. In this stage (the group's infancy), members express anxiety and dependency. They talk about nonproblematic issues. One way to ease the transition into the group at this stage is to structure it so that members are engaged with one another by participating in group activities (Hagedorn & Hirshhorn, 2009). For example, G. A. Miller (2012) has compiled a volume of activities that leaders can use to help participants warm up and get to know each other and themselves better. Another way to start the forming stage is to help group members relax and know in advance what is expected of them. For instance, prior to the first meeting, members might be told they will be expected to spend three minutes telling others who they are.

In the **storming stage**, sometimes called the **transition stage** (Greason, 2011), there is "increased tension and testing of the group environment" (p. 104). Sometimes turmoil, conflict, and unevenness occur, as in adolescence. Group members seek to make sure they are safe and to understand the relationships in the group. They focus on establishing themselves in the hierarchy of the group and on dealing successfully with issues of anxiety, power, and future expectations. Sometimes the group leader is attacked at this stage. At other times the group becomes dependent on the group leader. Ideally neither of the two preceding paths is followed, and group members develop a sense of comfortableness with one another and the leader. When such occurs, it helps the group move on interpersonally and as an entity to the next stage.

The **norming (or working) stage** is similar to young adulthood, when "having survived the storm, the group often generates enthusiasm and cohesion. Goals and ways of working together are decided on" (Saidla, 1990, p. 16). This stage is sometimes combined with the storming, or transition, stage and leads to the **performing stage**, which parallels adulthood in a developmental sense. At this stage, the group members become involved with each other and with their individual and collective goals. This is the time when the group, if it works well, is productive. Finally, in the **adjourning (or mourning/morning) stage**, the group comes to an end, and members say good-bye to one another and to the group experience. In this closing stage, members feel either fulfilled or empty. There is often a celebration experience at this point or at least a closure ceremony.

One of the easiest ways to conceptualize groups, regardless of the type, is through the four-stage group model: forming, norming, working, and terminating. Table 9–1 gives a brief breakdown of the emphasis of each stage, its dynamics/characteristics, the role of the leader, the role of the members, possible problems, interventions, and ideal outcomes.

Overall, the developmental stages of a group are not readily or even clearly differentiated. "A group does not necessarily move step by step through life stages, but may move backward and forward as a part of its general development" (Hansen et al., 1980, p. 476). However, to be most effective, it is necessary for a group to have at least a beginning, a middle, and a closing (Jacobs, Schimmel, Masson, & Harvill, 2016). Beyond that, the question of what stage a group is in and where it is heading is primarily answerable through either retrospection or insightful perception.

ISSUES IN GROUPS

A number of issues are involved in conducting successful groups. Some deal with procedures for running groups; others deal with training and ethics.

Selection and Preparation of Group Members

Screening and preparation are essential procedures for conducting a successful group. Some individuals who wish to be members of groups are not appropriate for them. If such persons are allowed to join a group, they may end up being difficult group members (e.g., by monopolizing or manipulating) and cause the group leader considerable trouble (Kottler, 1994). They may also join with others at an equally low level of functioning and contribute to the regression of the group. When this happens, members become psychologically damaged, and the group is unable to accomplish its goals (McClure, 1990).

Screening and preparation are usually accomplished through pregroup interviews and training sessions that take place with the group leader and prospective members. During a pregroup interview, members should be identified whose needs and goals are compatible with the established goals of the group, whose functioning does not impede the group process, and whose well-being is not jeopardized by the group experience. Research indicates that pregroup training, in which members learn more about a group and what is expected of them, provides important information for participants and gives them a chance to lower their anxiety (Sklare, Petrosko, & Howell, 1993).

TABLE 9–1 Four Stages of Groups

	Forming	Norming	Working	Terminating
Emphasis	Help members feel they are part of the group. Develop trust and inclusiveness.	Leader and members work through overt and covert tension, frustration, and conflict as they find their place in the group and develop a sense of cohesiveness (i.e., "we-ness").	Productivity, purposefulness, constructiveness, achievement, and action are highlighted.	Completeness, closure, and accomplishment of tasks/goals are highlighted along with celebration and ultimately the dismissal of the group.
Dynamics/ Characteristics	Members initiate conversations/ actions that are safe; interactions are superficial.	Energy, anxiety, and anticipation increase temporarily. Focus on functioning of group as an entity heightens. Cooperation and security increase toward end of this stage.	Members are more trusting of self and others. Risk taking increases, along with hopefulness, problem solving, and inclusiveness of others in achieving goals/objectives. Leader is less involved in directing or structuring group. Members become increasingly responsible for running group.	About 15% of the group's time is spent concentrating and reflecting on events signifying the end of the group, such as completion of a task. Members deal with the issue of loss, as well as celebration, individually or collectively.
Role of Leader	Leader sets up a structured environment where members feel safe, clarifies purpose of group, establishes rules, makes introductions. Leader models appropriate behaviors, initiates ice-breaker activities, engages in limited self-disclosure, outlines vision of the group.	Leader manages conflict between members, emphasizes rules and regulations regularly, helps group become a more unified entity.	Leader concentrates on helping members and group as a whole achieve goals by encouraging interpersonal interactions; prevents problems through use of helping skills and renewed focus on reaching goal(s); models appropriate behavior(s).	Leader helps members assess what they have learned from the group and encourages them to be specific; provides a structure for dealing with loss and celebration of group, as well as its ending; arranges for follow-up and evaluation.

(continued)

TABLE 9–1 Four Stages of Groups (*Continued*)

	Forming	Norming	Working	Terminating
Role of Members	Members need to dedicate themselves to "owning" the group and becoming involved. They need to voice what they expect to get out of the group as well as what they plan to give to it.	Members seek and receive feedback from others, which changes from more negative to neutral/ positive as group works through power issues and becomes more unified. "I statements" become more necessary and prevalent.	Members concentrate on individual and group accomplishments; they give and receive input in the form of feedback about their ideas and behaviors.	Members focus on the work they have accomplished and what they still need to achieve; celebrate their accomplishments; resolve unfinished business with others; incorporate their group experiences in both unique and universal ways.
Problem Areas	Inactive, unfocused, or uninvolved group members will inhibit the group from progressing. Too much openness is also detrimental. Anxiety that is denied or unaddressed will surface again.	Group may deteriorate and become chaotic and conflictual with less involved members. Corrective feedback may be misunderstood and underused. A sense of cohesiveness may fail to develop, and group may regress and become more artificial.	Unresolved conflicts or issues may resurface. Inappropriate behaviors may be displayed and inhibit the growth of the group. Rules may be broken.	Members may deny the group is ending and be unprepared for its final session(s). Members may be reluctant to end the group and may ask for an extension. Leaders may not prepare members for the ending and may foster dependency.
Intervention Techniques	Set up the group room so that it is conducive to interpersonal interaction, such as arranging chairs in a circle. Help group members feel relaxed, welcomed, and valued. Invest energy in giving group members a say or air time so they are energized and invested in the group.	Introduce structured experiences, rely more on spontaneity, and use increased self-disclosure. Employ helping skills, such as active listening and linking, to build trust and sense of togetherness and purposefulness. Along with members, take limited risks. Acknowledge differences as strengths.	Allot more time for discussion and interaction of goals and processes. Acknowledge with group what is occurring, and use the ideas of the group in reaching a resolution. Remind group of agreed-on goal(s) and the finiteness of the group's time.	Actively remind each other of the conclusion of the process. Use goodbye events, such as celebrations; written or verbal feedback assignments on what has been learned from the group experience; joint planning of last sessions and date of follow-up.

(*continued*)

TABLE 9–1   Four Stages of Groups (*Continued*)

	Forming	Norming	Working	Terminating
Ideal Outcome	Leader and members are clear on purpose of group, dedicated to that purpose, and feel a sense of trust in the group and their ability to contribute to it. Anxiety within the group lessens as members get to know each other and the purposes of the group better. Enthusiasm and commitment are heightened.	Differences and similarities among group members are recognized and used. Group becomes cooperative, and leader/members invest in it with shared goals/ objectives. Conflicts between members are resolved. Group becomes poised to begin the working stage.	Group stays focused and productive; works as a team. Risk taking, creativity, and pride in the group and its accomplishments occur. Group makes a transition toward termination.	Group members have pride in having accomplished planned projects/ goals and are able to point to tangible results. Everyone in the group has dealt successfully with losing the group. Everyone leaves the group stronger and better connected with other group participants. Everyone makes a successful transition back to everyday life.

In the process of setting up a group, certain individuals may need to be screened out or may elect to screen themselves out. **Screening** is a two-way process. Potential group members may not be appropriate for a certain group at a particular time with a designated leader. Prospective group members should be advised of their options if they are not selected for a group—for example, joining another group or waiting for a group to form that is better able to address their needs or situation. A group leader should select individuals for the group who can identify with other group members, at least on some issues. In essence, the screening interview "lays the foundation upon which the group process will rest" (McCoy, 1994, p. 18).

Group members need to be informed as much as possible about group process before the group begins. Group process has to do with at least three basic questions:

- Who am I?
- Who am I with you?
- Who are we together? (Hulse-Killacky, Killacky, & Donigian, 2001)

In other words, group process is the interaction of group members based on intrapersonal and interpersonal dynamics. **Group process** can be thought of as the chemistry among members; that is, how they are attracted to or repelled by each other. It is the process of the group—not the content, focus, or purpose—that will eventually determine whether a group succeeds. However, group process must be balanced with group content (Donigian, 1994). "When either the content or the process of . . . groups becomes disproportionate, the group may experience difficulty accomplishing work" (Nelligan, 1994, p. 8). Veterans of group experiences usually need minimal information about how a group will be conducted; novice participants may require extensive preparation. The point is that members who are informed about the procedures and focus of a group before they begin will do better in the group once it starts. This is true for any of the major types of groups, that is, psychoeducational, counseling, therapy, or task/work.

Before joining a group, potential members should learn from the group organizer what possibilities and outcomes are expected in the group experience. Corey (2016) lists a number of items that potential participants have a right to expect before they enroll in a group. Among the most important are these:

- A clear statement of the group's purpose
- A description of the group format, ground rules, and basic procedures
- A statement about the educational and training qualifications of the group leader(s)
- A pregroup interview to determine whether the potential group leader and other group members are compatible with the individual's needs at the time
- A disclosure of the risks involved in being in a group and the rights and responsibilities of group members
- A discussion of the limitations of confidentiality and the roles group leaders and participants are expected to play within the group setting

Regardless of the perceived need for information, research supports the idea that "providing a set of expectations for participants prior to their initiation into a group improves the possibility of members having a successful group . . . experience" (Sklare, Keener, & Mas, 1990, p. 145). Specific ways group leaders can facilitate "here and now group counseling are by discouraging 'you' and 'we' language, questioning, speaking in the third person, seeking approval, rescuing, and analyzing." Group leaders must model the behaviors they wish members to emulate. They must also be able to make the covert overt and do away with hidden agendas.

The Case of Allison

Allison joined a counseling group to work on her shyness. She attended faithfully but by the end of six sessions she found she was no more assertive than when she began. She thought something must be wrong with her or the group. Therefore, without telling anyone of her dissatisfaction, she stopped attending the group.

What other actions might Allison have taken? What do you think would have been the result? What would you do about Allison's behavior if you were the leader of this counseling group?

Group Size and Duration

The size of a group is determined by its purpose and preference. Large groups are less likely to spotlight the needs of individual members, whereas small groups may limit the scope of interaction among the members. A generally agreed-on number of group members is 6 to 8, though Gazda (1989) notes that if groups run as long as six months, up to 10 people may productively be included. Group size and duration affect each other. Corey (2016) states that

> for ongoing groups with adults, about eight members with one leader seems to be a good size. Groups with children may be as small as three or four. In general, the group should have enough people to afford ample interaction so it doesn't drag and yet be small enough to give everyone a chance to participate frequently without . . . losing the sense of "group." (p. 75)

Open versus Closed Groups

Open-ended groups admit new members after they have started; closed-ended groups do not. **Open-ended groups** are able to replace lost members rather quickly and maintain an optimal size. Many long-term outpatient groups are open-ended (Gladding, 2016b). **Closed-ended groups**, though not as flexible in size, promote more cohesiveness among group members and may be very productive in helping members achieve stated goals.

Confidentiality

Groups function best when members feel a sense of confidentiality; that is, what has been said within the group setting will not be revealed outside. To promote this sense of confidentiality and build trust, a group leader must be active. The subject of confidentiality should be raised in the prescreening interview. In addition, the importance of confidentiality needs to be stressed during the first meeting of the group and on a regular basis thereafter (Corey et al., 2015). ACA and a number of other professional groups have published guidelines on confidentiality that emphasize the role group leaders have in protecting their members by clearly defining confidentiality and the importance and difficulty of enforcing it. Any question about the betrayal of confidentiality within a group should be dealt with immediately. Otherwise, the problem grows, and the cohesiveness of the group breaks down. Olsen (1971) points out that counselors must realize they can guarantee only their own adherence to the principles of confidentiality. Still, they must ensure the rights of all group members.

Physical Structure

Where a group is conducted is either an asset or a liability. Yalom and Leszcz (2005), among other prominent specialists in group work, emphasize the need for a physical structure (i.e., a room or other setting) that ensures the safety and growth of group members. Groups within community agencies need to be conducted in places that promote the well-being of the group. Attractive furnishings and the way the group is assembled (preferably in a circle) can facilitate the functioning of the group.

Coleaders

It is not necessary for groups to have **coleaders** (i.e., two leaders); however, such an arrangement can be beneficial to the group and to the leaders, especially if the group has over 10 members. With coleaders, one leader can work with the group while the other monitors the group process. A coleader arrangement may also be beneficial when an inexperienced leader and an experienced leader are working together. In such a setup, the inexperienced leader can learn from the experienced one. Many group specialists advocate that an inexperienced leader colead a group first before attempting the process alone.

Dinkmeyer and Muro (1979) suggest that successful, experienced coleaders (a) possess a similar philosophical and operational style, (b) have similar experience and competence, (c) establish a model relationship for effective human interaction, (d) be aware of splitting member loyalty ties to one leader or the other and help the group deal with this, and (e) agree on counseling goals and the processes to achieve them so that power struggles are avoided.

Pietrofesa, Hoffman, and Splete (1984) recommend that coleaders sit opposite each other in a group so that leader responsibility and observation are maximized. They point out that it is not necessary for group coleaders to be of the opposite sex; skills, not gender, matter most.

Case Study: Delilah's Dilemma

Delilah has been interested in self-growth all her life. She figured that with the wellness trend sweeping the nation, others would be, too. She was right. Her friends therefore urged her to start a wellness group because they knew she was an expert in self-growth and wellness. Delilah gave in and succumbed to their wishes. She was sure there was much she could add to the lives of others.

Delilah thought it might be best if she ran her group according to a group counseling model instead of conducting it as a psychoeducational group. She also thought it best to keep the group open. To her surprise, Delilah found herself frustrated in her effort to steer the group in a positive way. New people kept asking old questions, and members kept dropping in and out of the group as their schedules dictated.

What would you do in this situation now if you were Delilah? What do you think she should have done in the first place? Do you think this group is salvageable, and if so, would it be worth the effort?

Self-Disclosure

Self-disclosure is defined as "here and now feelings, attitudes, and beliefs" (Shertzer & Stone, 1981, p. 206). The process of self-disclosure is dependent on the trust that group members have for one another. If there is high trust, there will be greater self-disclosure. An interesting aspect of this phenomenon is that self-disclosure builds on itself and also builds cohesion among group members (Forsyth, 2014). During the first stages of a group, self-disclosure may have to be encouraged. Morran (1982) suggests that in the beginning sessions of a group, leaders make self-disclosures often to serve as a model for others and to promote the process. As Stockton, Barr, and Klein (1981) document, group members who make few verbal self-disclosures are more likely than others to drop out of a group or have a less positive experience in the group.

Feedback

Feedback is a multidimensional process that consists of group members' responding to the verbal messages and nonverbal behaviors of one another. It is one of the most important and abused parts of any group experience. When feedback is given honestly and with care, group members can gauge the impact of their actions on others and attempt new behaviors. Corey (2016) distinguishes between group feedback given at the end of a session and that given at the termination of a group. During the latter process, Corey encourages group members to be clear, concise, and concrete with one another. Group members should also give feedback about how they have changed during the group experience. After processing feedback information, group members should record some of the things said during final feedback sessions so they will not forget and can make use of the feedback experience in evaluating progress toward their goals.

To promote helpful feedback, the following criteria should be taken into consideration (Donigian & Hulse-Killacky, 1999; Gladding, 2016b; Yalom & Leszcz, 2005):

- Feedback should be beneficial to the receiver and not serve the needs of the giver.
- Feedback is more effective when it is based on describable behavior.
- In the early stages of group development, positive feedback is more beneficial and more readily accepted than negative feedback.
- Feedback is most effective when it immediately follows a stimulus behavior and is validated by others.
- Feedback is of greater benefit when the receiver is open and trusts the giver.

Follow-Up

Follow-up is used to keep in touch with members after a group has terminated, to determine how well individuals are progressing on personal or group goals. Often group leaders fail to conduct proper follow-up, especially with short-term counseling groups or with groups led by an outside leader. Follow-up helps group members and leaders assess what was gained in the group experience and allows the group leader to make a referral of a group member for help, if appropriate. Follow-up sessions maximize the effects of a group experience and encourage members to keep pursuing original goals (Jacobs et al., 2016).

Corey (2016) suggests that a follow-up session for a short-term group be conducted about three months after termination of the group experience. He points out that the process of mutual feedback and support from other group members at this time can be very valuable. If group members are aware during the termination stage of their group that they will meet again for a follow-up, they are more likely to continue pursuing their goals. In addition to a whole-group follow-up, individual follow-up between leaders and group members is important, even if these sessions are conducted by phone. See Figure 9–2 for a summary of issues in conducting a group.

- Screen potential group members for suitability in the group
- Inform members of group process before group begins
- Provide a set of expectations for group participants before group begins
- Address issue of confidentiality
- Limit group size (six to eight adults is ideal)
- Decide if group is open-ended (admit new members after group has started) or closed-ended
- Select a physical structure that ensures safety and growth of group members
- Decide on a single leader or coleaders
- Encourage appropriate self-disclosure
- Model appropriate behaviors
- Provide descriptive and timely feedback promoting growth
- Follow up with group members within three to six months to check on their status and encourage pursuit of goals

---

FIGURE 9–2 Issues in Conducting Groups

QUALITIES OF EFFECTIVE GROUP LEADERS

There are distinguishing qualities of effective and ineffective group leaders (Johnson & Johnson, 2013). For instance, group leaders who are authoritarian, aggressive, confrontational, or removed emotionally from the group are ineffective and produce group casualties (i.e., members who drop out or are worse after the group experience; Yalom & Lieberman, 1971). The following are **four leadership qualities** or skills that have a positive effect on the outcome of groups, if not used excessively:

1. *Caring:* the more the better
2. *Meaning attribution:* clarifying, explaining, and providing a cognitive framework for change
3. *Emotional stimulation:* being active, challenging content, taking risks, and self-disclosing
4. *Executive function:* developing norms, structuring, and suggesting procedures (Yalom & Leszcz, 2005)

It is vital that group leaders find a position between extreme degrees of emotional stimulation and executive function for the well-being of the group. Group leaders should not allow members to experience so much emotion that they are unable to process the material being discovered in the group; nor should leaders structure the situation so rigidly that no emotion is expressed.

Ohlsen (1977) states that effective leaders are those who understand the forces operating within a group, recognize whether these forces are therapeutic, and if they are not, take steps to better manage the group with the assistance of its members. His assessment of leadership complements that of Yalom and Leszcz (2005), who believe that good group leaders behave with intentionality because they are able to anticipate where the group process is moving and recognize group needs. An example of this phenomenon is the ability of group leaders to treat group members homogeneously when there is a need to manage group tensions and protect group members and to treat them heterogeneously when the group has become too comfortable and is not working.

In addition, Corey (2016) maintains that effective group leaders are committed "to the never-ending journey" to become more effective as human beings. He lists a number of personal qualities that are "vitally related to effective group leadership" (pp. 15–16), among which are presence, personal power, courage, willingness to confront oneself, sincerity, authenticity, enthusiasm, sense of identity, and inventiveness/creativity.

A final quality of effective group leaders is that they are well educated in group theory and practice. In 1984, CACREP adopted ASGW guidelines for the education of group leaders. These detailed guidelines, which were revised in both 1990 and 2000, are vital for potential group leaders to consult and follow. To be effective, group leaders must be courageous and not be afraid to conduct groups with underserved but needy populations (see Box 9–3).

BOX 9–3   Group Counseling in a Prison Setting

There are some barriers to providing an effective group experience to inmates in a prison setting. For instance, a disadvantage is the limited amount of privacy, with closed-circuit television and windowed doors. Institutional furniture in a room with tables and no carpeting ordinarily is not conducive to physical comfort and emotional closeness. Materials used in the group must be approved in advance and examined by prison guards. Out-of-group contact also can be a problem, even in a very large institution.

Some counselors might be reluctant to hold groups in this milieu due to concerns for personal safety. Though unfounded, these fears may be difficult to overcome until trust has been established. Also, there is ambivalence in society as to whether an inmate, who is in prison for punishment, is entitled to grief groups.

The advantages, however, greatly outweigh the disadvantages. The prison chaplains publicize the group, interview prospective members, and collect evaluations after the group ends. A mixture of self-referrals and men encouraged by the psychologist or social worker brings a variety of experiences and awareness to the group. Many of the participants have experience with groups and have learned to communicate directly and with great insight. They are enthusiastic about (and have time for) homework assignments, often taking great care with written activities such as letter writing and closing comments. They are open to experiential exercises, genuine with each other, and appreciative of facilitators who treat them as "real people." Our experience with these groups has been growth promoting for all involved.

Margaret (Peg) J. Olson, PhD, Counselor Educator; Margaret (Peg)
A. McEwen, MSN, Family Nurse Practitioner

GROUP ORGANIZATIONS

Because group work is so important and prevalent in counseling and therapeutic circles, national organizations have been established for professionals engaged primarily in leading groups. Prominent group organizations include the American Group Psychotherapy Association (AGPA), the American Society of Group Psychotherapy and Psychodrama (ASGPP), and the Society of Group Psychology and Group Psychotherapy (Division 49 of the American Psychological Association).

Probably the most comprehensive of any group organization, and the one to which most professional counselors belong, is the Association for Specialists in Group Work (ASGW), a division of ACA. This organization, which has a diverse membership, was chartered by ACA in 1974. It has been a leader in the establishment of educational and best practices guidelines for group leaders (ASGW, 1998, 2000). It publishes a quarterly periodical, the *Journal for Specialists in Group Work.*

Summary and Conclusion

Groups are an exciting, diversified, necessary, and effective way to help people. They can take an educational, preventive, or remedial form. Standards have been formulated by the Association for Specialists in Group Work for psychoeducational groups, counseling groups, psychotherapy groups, and task/work groups. Yet there are still many misconceptions and myths about groups that make some people wary of them. Overall, there is supportive research evidence that groups can be helpful in increasing learning, facilitating coping, improving career decision making, and promoting healing.

The theories used in groups are often the same as those used in working with individuals. There are differences in application, however, especially in regard to an emphasis on dynamics, process, and content. Groups go through stages, with most practitioners agreeing that groups form, storm, norm, perform, and adjourn over time. How well groups work depends on a number of factors, such as the screening of members, the size of the group, confidentiality, self-disclosure, feedback, and follow-up.

Group leadership is another important variable in how well groups work. Leaders must be competent in dealing with individual as well as group issues if they are to be maximally effective. They must know what types of groups they are leading and share this information with potential members. Effective group leaders are concerned with the general well-being of their groups and the people in them. They display caring, carry out their executive function of structuring the group, emotionally stimulate the group, and provide a cognitive framework for change so that group members find meaning in what they are doing.

Overall, groups are a stage-based, effective, and expanding way of working with people to achieve individual and collective goals. Professional counselors, especially those in clinical mental health community and agency settings, must acquire group skills if they are to be well rounded and versatile.

MyCounselingLab

Try the Topic 9 Assignments: *Group Counseling*.

CHAPTER 10

Couple and Family Counseling

Fotoluminate LLC/Shutterstock

CHAPTER OVERVIEW

From reading this chapter, you will learn about

- The family life cycle
- Different types of families and their issues
- Family life stressors
- Couple and family counseling theories
- Couple and family enrichment

As you read, consider

- Where you are in the family life cycle and how that affects your worldview
- How you might treat different family types and why
- What family life stressors you have seen and what impact they have had on families you have known
- Various theories of marital and family counseling and how they appeal to you
- The place of enrichment as a way of helping couples and families

At thirty-five, with wife and child
   a Ph.D.
      and hopes as bright as a full moon
         on a warm August night,
He took a role as a healing man
   blending it with imagination,
      necessary change and common sense
To make more than an image on an eye lens
   of a small figure running quickly up steps;
Quietly he traveled
   like one who holds a candle to darkness
   and questions its power
So that with heavy years, long walks,
   shared love, and additional births
He became as a seasoned actor,
   who, forgetting his lines in the silence,
   stepped upstage and without prompting
   lived them.

Reprinted from "Without Applause," by S. T. Gladding, 1974, *Personnel and Guidance Journal, 52,* p. 586. Copyright © 1974 by Samuel T. Gladding. Used with permission.

The profession of couple and family counseling is relatively new. Its formal beginnings are traced to the 1940s and early 1950s, but its real growth occurred in the 1970s and 1980s (Nichols, 1993). It differs from individual counseling and group counseling in both its emphasis and its clientele (Gladding, 2015). For instance, couple and family counseling usually concentrates on making changes in systems, whereas individual counseling and group counseling primarily focus on intrapersonal and interpersonal changes.

This chapter explores various aspects of couple and family counseling as they relate to clinical mental health counselors. It begins with an examination of what a family is, the family life cycle, various family life forms, and the issues prevalent in each. It then looks at family life stressors and some of the major theories used in both couple counseling and family counseling, including those that are systemic as well as nonsystemic. Couple and family enrichment is then briefly examined, followed by an overview of outcome research and the organizations and associations of those most involved in the profession.

Counselors who know how to work with couples and families are at a distinct advantage in offering services to a wide variety of clientele. It is essential for those who are employed as clinical mental health counselors in community and agency settings to master the skills of helping couples and families.

WHAT IS A FAMILY?

Families come in many forms (e.g., nuclear, single-parent, remarried, multigenerational, gay or lesbian) and may be defined in a number of ways (Goldenberg & Goldenberg, 2013). In this chapter, a **family** is considered to be those persons who are biologically and/or psychologically related through historical, emotional, or economic bonds and who perceive themselves to be a part of a household (Gladding, 2015). Such a definition allows for maximum flexibility in defining the boundaries of family life and fosters an understanding of the different forms of family life available, without describing each in great detail. Furthermore, this definition engenders an appreciation of persons within family units and the roles they play.

Overall, families are characterized in multiple ways, and those that are healthy function efficiently according to form and need. Within most families there is a dual emphasis on fostering the development of individuals while simultaneously offering family members stability, protection, and preservation of the family unit structure (Strong, DeVault, & Cohen, 2011).

FAMILY LIFE AND THE FAMILY LIFE CYCLE

Family life and the optimal growth and development that take place within it are at the heart of couple and family counseling. The **family life cycle** is the name given to the stages a family goes through as it evolves over the years (Walsh, 2012). These stages sometimes parallel and complement those in the individual life cycle (e.g., Erikson, 1959; Levinson, Darrow, Klein, Levinson, & McKee, 1978), but often they are unique because of the number of people involved and the diversity of tasks to be accomplished. Table 10–1 illustrates a nine-stage family life cycle model, derived from several sources. This particular cycle, which is primarily applicable to middle-class Americans, begins with the unattached adult and continues through the family years into later life. In each stage of the family life cycle, there are practical, emotional, and relational challenges as well as potential crises that need to be addressed in a timely and adequate way.

TABLE 10–1   Stages of the Family Life Cycle

Stage	Emotional Issues	Stage-Critical Tasks
1. Unattached adult	Accepting parent–offspring separation	a. Differentiation from family of origin b. Development of peer relations c. Initiation of career
2. Newly married adults	Committing to the couple	a. Formation of marital system b. Making room for spouse with family and friends c. Adjusting career demands
3. Childbearing adults	Accepting new members into the system	a. Adjusting couple to make room for child(ren) b. Taking on parenting roles c. Making room for grandparents
4. Adults with preschool-age child(ren)	Accepting the new personality/-ies	a. Adjusting family to the needs of specific child(ren) b. Coping with energy drain and lack of privacy c. Taking time out to be a couple
5. Adults with school-age child(ren)	Allowing child(ren) to establish relationships outside the family	a. Extending family/society interactions b. Encouraging the child(ren)'s educational progress c. Dealing with increased activities and time demands
6. Adults with teenage child(ren)	Increasing flexibility of family boundaries to allow independence	a. Shifting the balance in the parent–child relationship b. Refocusing on midlife career and marital issues c. Dealing with increasing concerns with older generation
7. Adults launching adult child(ren)	Accepting exits from and entries into the family	a. Releasing adult child(ren) to work, college, couple b. Maintaining supportive home base c. Accepting occasional returns of adult child(ren)
8. Middle-aged adults	Letting go of child(ren) and facing each other again	a. Rebuilding the couple b. Welcoming child(ren)'s spouse(s), grandchild(ren) into family c. Dealing with aging of one's own parents
9. Retired adults	Accepting retirement and old age	a. Maintaining individual and couple functioning b. Supporting child(ren)'s family unit c. Coping with death of parents, spouse d. Closing or adapting family home

Source: Family Therapy: A Systematic Integration (7th ed.), by Dorothy Stroh Becvar and Raphael J. Becvar, 2009, Boston, MA: Allyn & Bacon. Copyright © 2009 by Allyn & Bacon. Reprinted with permission.

Some families and family members are more "on time" in achieving stage-critical tasks that go with the family cycle of life shown here. In such cases, a better sense of well-being is achieved (McGoldrick, Preto, & Carter, 2016). Other families—such as those in poverty, those who are affluent, or new immigrants—have different ways of navigating through the life cycle, and indeed their life cycles are usually quite different from that of the middle class. Regardless of timing, all families have to deal with **family cohesion** (i.e., emotional bonding) and family **adaptability** (i.e., ability to be flexible and change). Each of these two dimensions has four levels; the cohesion dimension runs from a low of disengaged to a high of enmeshed, and the adaptability dimension runs from a low of rigid to a high of chaotic. This model has been named by Olson (1986; Olson & Gorall, 2003) as the circumplex model of marital and family systems. The two dimensions—cohesion and adaptability—are curvilinear. Families that are very low or very high on both dimensions seem dysfunctional (e.g., rigidly disengaged or chaotically enmeshed), whereas families that are balanced, such as those that are flexibly separated or structurally connected, seem to function more adequately (Maynard & Olson, 1987). Families that are most successful, functional, happy, and strong are not only balanced but also highly social (Watts, Trusty, & Lim, 2000). According to researchers (Stinnett & DeFrain, 1985), **healthy families** (a) are committed to one another, (b) appreciate each other, (c) spend time together, (d) have good communication patterns, (e) have a high degree of religious or spiritual orientation, and (f) are able to deal with crisis in a positive manner.

Wilcoxon (1985) notes that in working with families, counselors need to be aware of the different stages the families are in while being concurrently attuned to the developmental tasks of individual members. Counselors who are sensitive to individual family members and to the family as a whole are able to realize that some individual manifestations—such as depression (Lopez, 1986; Weitzman, 2006), career indecisiveness (Kinnier, Brigman, & Noble, 1990), and substance abuse (Clark, 2003; Stanton, 1999)—are related to family structure and functioning as well as to personal behaviors. Consequently, these counselors are able to be more inclusive in their treatment plans.

When evaluating family patterns and the mental health of everyone involved, it is crucial that an assessment be based on the form and developmental stage of the family constellation. To facilitate this process, McGoldrick et al. (2016) have proposed sets of developmental tasks for traditional and nontraditional families. Bowen (1978, 1994) suggests specific terms to describe family dysfunctionality: **Enmeshment** refers to family environments in which members are overly dependent on each other or are undifferentiated, such as a mother and daughter being inseparable. **Triangulation** refers to family fusion situations in which one person is pulled in two different directions by the other members of the triangle, such as an adolescent who is trying to please two parents who disagree with each other. Clinical mental health counselors who work effectively with couples and families have guidelines for determining how, where, when, or whether to intervene in the family process. These counselors do not fail to act, such as neglecting to engage everyone in the therapeutic process, nor do they overreact, such as placing too much emphasis on verbal expression (Gladding, 2015).

DIFFERENT TYPES OF FAMILIES AND THEIR ISSUES

Prior to the 1980s, couple and family counseling, with some notable exceptions, concentrated on working with traditional, middle-class nuclear couples and families. Since that time, however, it has become evident that the future of the profession of family therapy is dependent on the ability and flexibility of professionals to work with a wide variety of families. Some of the most prevalent of these family forms are minority ethnic, dual-career, single-parent, childless, remarried, gay/lesbian, aging, multigenerational, and military families.

Minority Ethnic Families

Past research has indicated that distinct and relatively small-sized ethnic family groups are often misunderstood by majority cultures (Wright, Mindel, Van Tran, & Habenstein, 2012). This misunderstanding is associated with cultural prejudices, flaws in collecting data about minorities, stereotyping, and unrecognized economic differences (McGoldrick, Giordano, & Garcia-Preto, 2005). Bias is unfortunate because it perpetuates myths that may cause harm. Ethnic families need to be seen in regard to their strengths and liabilities, both collectively and individually.

One trend now is to study ethnic families from the perspective of their competencies, social class, and observed family styles (McGoldrick et al., 2005). This approach makes it more likely that differences and similarities among families from various backgrounds will be reported accurately and fairly in research studies and that counselors will select culturally sensitive and appropriate interventions.

Dual-Career Families

Dual-career families are those in which both marital partners are engaged in developing careers to which they have a high commitment (Hertz & Marshall, 2001). Over 50% of married couples in the United States are pursuing dual careers, and the likelihood is that their numbers will continue to increase. The reasons for this trend are complex, but they are related to the large number of women in the workforce, economic pressures, and the tendency for professionals to marry other professionals.

"Balancing the dual-career and family life can lead to conflict and create a considerable source of stress" (Thomas, 1990, p. 174). Such a situation is likely if one or both members of the couple are inflexible in redefining traditional gender roles related to their careers and family obligations. In the past, men have reported that their career interests interfered with their fathering roles, and women have stated that parenting interfered with their career roles (Gilbert, 1985; Nicola, 1980). Research indicates that working women are more likely to experience conflict between their work and family roles than are working men (Blair-Loy, 2003; Hochschild & Machung, 2012; Werbel, 1998). Learning new skills, staying flexible, and continually assessing and revising work and family life are necessary if dual-career couples are to thrive. Because there are multiple variables in family life that affect the quality of these couples' relationships, their coping strategies over time must often be dealt with, as well as their career and personal patterns.

Single-Parent Families

Single-parent families are those headed by either a mother or a father as the sole parent responsible for taking care of her- or himself and a child(ren) (Gladding, 2015; Klein & Noel, 2006). These families are often some of the poorest, neediest, and most challenging that clinical mental health counselors work with (Sussman, Hanson, Helms, & Julian, 2017; Waggonseller, Ruegamer, & Harrington, 1998). Although mothers predominantly head single-parent families (85%), each year there are an increasing number of fathers who gain custody of their children (Davis & Borns, 1999).

The primary challenge for family counseling professionals is determining how to help these families find the support and services they need. The work of Boszormenyi-Nagy

(1987), which emphasizes community connectedness, is probably one of the most functional yet least utilized theories to date available for working with single-parent families.

Childless Families

For many couples, the decision of whether to have a child(ren) is one they consciously make by choice. For others, that decision is made by chance or the situation (such as marrying late) or biology (infertility). Regardless, a record number of couples are opting not to have children. A significant rate of childlessness is expected to continue for younger women because of a number of changes in society, including less pressure to have children, the cost of raising a child, and double duty demands put on women both professionally and domestically (Gray, 2015).

Childless couples, especially women, who elect not to have children are sometimes stigmatized and made to feel out of place in social gatherings. Extended family relationships are sometimes strained, especially when siblings of the childless couple have children. These childless couples may have difficulty coming to terms with the choices they made not to have children. They may actually mourn the children they never had (McGoldrick & Walsh, 1999).

In any of these situations, clinical mental health counselors may need to involve other family members related to the couple. They may also need to emphasize the opportunities available to childless couples and the advantages of being childless, such as having less stress, more discretionary income, and greater opportunities to serve in the community.

Remarried Families

Remarried families (along with first-married and single-parent families) are one of three predominant types of American families. They are composed of a couple and children where at least one spouse has been previously married. One reason for the growth of this type of family is the fact that approximately three of every four people who divorce eventually remarry (Goldenberg & Goldenberg, 2013).

Overall, remarried families are quite complex in regard to relationships. Individuals within these families often have to establish new roles and new rules (Papernow, 2013). Ways of functioning efficiently, effectively, and harmoniously have to be established. Clinical mental health counselors need to be prepared to deal with the multifaceted nature of these families and help individual members bridge physical and psychological gaps in connecting with each other.

Gay and Lesbian Families

Since the 1990s, there has been an increase in the number of openly **gay and lesbian families** in the United States. These families are made up of a parent who is gay or lesbian or two partners who are gay or lesbian. Gay and lesbian couples and families may come to therapy with concerns such as communication problems, parenting issues, or concerns related to intimacy; or they may come with concerns specifically related to being in a same-sex relationship. Counselors can be most effective by (a) not assuming that the reason for therapy has to do with sexual orientation; (b) building awareness of personal prejudice and biases so that they are never imposed on clients (see *ACA Code of Ethics*, 2014, Standard A.4); (c) being knowledgeable about the political, social, and legal implications of being in a lesbian or gay family; and (d) being able to refer clients to places of support in the community (Nichols, 2010; Spitalnick & McNair, 2005).

Although research is lacking regarding the particular therapeutic needs of gay and lesbian families, the following concerns have been shown to be relevant (Falkner & Starkey, 2009; Nichols, 2010; Spitalnick & McNair, 2005): internalized homophobia, which can affect either the counselor or the couple/family; lack of role models either in the media or in the couple's family of origin, resulting in insufficient feedback and validation; traditional gender roles, which are often less useful in same-sex relationships; and systemic prejudice and heterosexism.

When working with a sexual minority couple, a social empowerment model may be helpful (Falkner & Starkey, 2009). The goal of **empowerment counseling** is to increase self-advocacy and to overcome inequities that may undermine the development of healthy relationships (Savage, Harley, & Nowak, 2005).

Aging Families

An **aging family** is generally considered one where both partners are age 65 or older. It is estimated that by the year 2020, the typical American family will consist of at least four generations. Furthermore, by the year 2040, nearly a quarter of the population of the United States will be 65 years old and older. Yet the study of aging families is a new frontier that "still lacks identifiable landmarks and road maps" (Goldberg, 1992, p. 1).

What we do know is that with increased age, families become concerned with different personal, family, and societal issues. For instance, on an individual level there is more emphasis on physical health (Goldin & Mohr, 2000). This focus spills over into family and institutional relationships as well (Piercy, 2010). In addition to health, aging families are involved with the launching or relaunching of their young adult children. This task is especially challenging during hard financial times, such as recessions, when increasing numbers of young unmarried adults return to live with their parents.

Another factor associated with aging families is increased stress and rewards as older relatives move into their children's homes or into retirement homes (Montalvo & Thompson, 1988). In these situations, couples and families have to change their household and community routines and sometimes become involved in taking care of their parents (Goeller, 2004). This type of situation can increase tension, anger, joy, guilt, gratitude, and grief among all involved. It is an uneven experience that fluctuates in its rewards and restrictions. It is also a process that counselors who work with couples and families must become familiar with if they are to help aging family units and their members cope.

Multigenerational Families

The number of **multigenerational families** has grown over the years (Anderson & Sabatelli, 2011). These are households that include a child, a parent, and a grandparent, according to the U.S. Bureau of the Census definition. Common before World War II, the number of multigenerational families decreased from that time until the 1980s. Now there are two factors influencing the increase in the number of these families. The first is economic, that is, when the economy is in recession, fewer people maintain separate households. The second factor is medical. People are living longer, partly because of advances in medicine. However, many individuals, especially those past their mid-70s, cannot maintain a house by themselves and, therefore, move in with their children.

The advantages of multigenerational families are many. Different generations get to interact and enjoy each other more directly. There are often more people to help with household and child-care duties, which can lessen stress. However, the disadvantages of this type of arrangement can be considerable. For instance, there may be increased stress on the parent subunit to take care of children and grandparents. There can also be new financial and psychological difficulties as the parent subunit has to take care of more people with the same amount of money and is simultaneously squeezed to provide adequate living space.

Military Families

Military families are those that have at least one family member enlisted in the armed services. These families are part of a unique culture that differs from that of civilian families (Blaisure, Saathoff-Wells, Perelra, Wadsworth, & Dombro, 2016; Weiss, Coll, Gerbauer, Smiley, & Carillo, 2010). Many military families face special concerns related to the nature of the work military personnel perform. One such concern is frequent relocation. Approximately 33% of military families relocate each year, as compared to 5% of civilian families (Baker, 2008). Frequent moves require military families to face repeatedly the challenge of finding new support, making adjustments, and building or rebuilding relationships and a sense of community (Kay, 2003). Another major concern is the emotional stress associated with deployment and/or redeployment. Military families live with ongoing uncertainty about how world or national events may unfold. When a family member is deployed, the entire family must cope with the reality of potential danger (Pavlicin, 2003).

Current global events have increased the need for counseling services for military families (Hall, 2017). However, the stigma associated with seeking mental health services continues to be a barrier for service members and their families. Civilian counselors can be trained to work effectively with military families, but as Hall points out, "It is essential that [counselors] understand the worldview, mind-set, and culture of the military before attempting to intervene and work with those families" (p. 5). Her book, *Counseling Military Families*, is one tool clinical mental health counselors can use to gain a better understanding of how to work effectively with military personnel.

A summary of family types can be found in Figure 10–1.

Family—those persons who are biologically and/or psychologically related through historical, emotional, or economic bonds and who perceive themselves to be a part of a household

Nuclear family—two parents and a child or children

Dual-career family—a family in which both marital partners are engaged in developing careers to which they have a high commitment

Single-parent family—a family headed by either a mother or a father as the sole parent responsible for taking care of her- or himself and a child(ren)

Childless couple—a couple that does not have children voluntarily (by choice) or because of circumstances (e.g., infertility)

Remarried family—a family where at least one spouse has been previously married

Gay and lesbian family—a family in which the parent is or spouses are gay or lesbian

Aging family—one where both partners are age 65 or older

Multigenerational family—a household that includes a child, a parent, and a grandparent

Military family—a family that has at least one family member enlisted in the armed services

---

FIGURE 10–1 Types of Families

FAMILY LIFE STRESSORS

Stress is a reaction to a stimulus that disturbs an organism's physical or mental equilibrium. It is an inevitable part of life in all families. It is found in the daily routine of family members as they move in and out of the family home. As individuals do, families attempt to keep stressful events from becoming distressful (Selye, 1976). They do this through a variety of means, some of which are healthier than others. The ways that families cope with stressors is sometimes related to whether they are prepared to deal with these situations.

McGoldrick et al. (2016) have categorized family stressors into two types: vertical and horizontal (see Figure 10–2). Among the **vertical stressors** are those dealing with family patterns, myths, secrets, and legacies. These are stressors that are historical and that families inherit from previous generations, for example, an ancestor who was imprisoned or committed suicide. **Horizontal stressors** are those related to the present, for example, current work or marital relationships. Among horizontal stressors are those that are developmental, such as life cycle transitions, and those that are unpredictable, such as an accident. The Carter and McGoldrick model is systemic and in line with how most family therapists view families.

Although families have universally expected stressors that accompany life transitions, families are unique, too. For example, the rates at which families plan for their children to grow up, leave home, and start families of their own differ. Families with a British American background usually expect a much faster shift in these events than Italian American families do. Anticipating when events may happen helps family members prepare themselves mentally and physically for changes and even failure. In many cases, family life stages and individual life stages complement each other (Bowen, 1978).

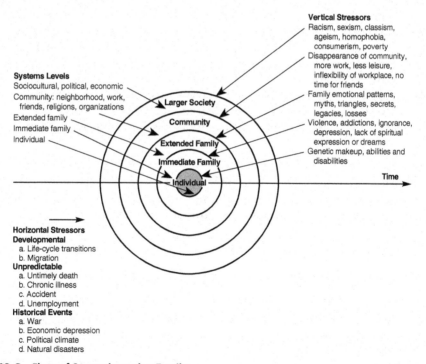

FIGURE 10–2 Flow of Stress through a Family
Source: CARTER, BETTY A.; MCGOLDRICK, MONICA, THE EXPANDED FAMILY LIFE CYCLE: INDIVIDUAL, FAMILY, AND SOCIAL PERSPECTIVES, 3rd Ed., © 1999. Reprinted and Electronically reproduced by permission of Pearson Education, Inc., New York, NY.

Expected Life Stressors

There are a number of stressors that families can expect, regardless of their level of functioning (McGoldrick et al., 2016). Some are **developmental stressors** (i.e., age and life stage related), and others are **situational stressors** (e.g., interpersonal interactions; Figley, 1989). Some stressors are related to present events, such as work, school, and social functions (Kaslow, 1991); others are more historical in nature (i.e., family life heritage).

When surveyed, family members frequently cite prevalent stressors in their families as those associated with (a) economics and finances, (b) children's behaviors, (c) insufficient couple time, (d) communication with children, (e) insufficient personal time, and (f) insufficient family play time (Curran, 1985). Some of these everyday stressors deal with deficiencies, such as not having enough time. In these types of stress situations, families can resolve problems through planning ahead, lowering their expectations, or both. They are then better able to cope. The flip side of this stress relief, however, is that families and their members may experience stress from not accomplishing enough of what they had planned and from overscheduling family calendars.

Unexpected Life Stressors

Unexpected life stressors are life events that take family members by surprise or are beyond the control of the family. If life events come too soon, are delayed, or fail to materialize, the health, happiness, and well-being of all involved may be affected (Goodman, Schlossberg, & Anderson, 2006). Intensified emotionality and/or behavioral disorganization in families and their members are likely to occur as a result.

Timing is crucial to the functioning of families and their members, especially in dealing with the unexpected. If timing is off, families struggle. For example, if a first wedding is either relatively early in one's life (e.g., before age 20) or relatively late (after age 40), the difficulty of accepting or dealing with the circumstances surrounding the event, such as interacting with the new spouse, is increased for both the couple and their families (Carter & McGoldrick, 2005). See Figure 10–3 for an overview of stress and stressors that affect families.

Family development and environmental fit (Eccles et al., 1993) is a crucial variable in unexpected stress as well. Some environments are conducive to helping families develop

---

Stress—a reaction to a stimulus that disturbs a person's physical or mental equilibrium

Vertical Stressors—stressors dealing with family patterns, myths, secrets, and legacies, for example, an ancestor who was imprisoned or committed suicide

Horizontal Stressors—stressors related to the present, for example, current work or marital relationships

Developmental Stressors—stressors that are age and life stage related

Situational Stressors—stressors that deal with interpersonal interactions

Unexpected Life Stressors—stressors that take family members by surprise or are beyond the control of the family, for example, life events come too soon, are delayed, or fail to materialize

---

FIGURE 10–3   Stress and Stressors That Affect Families

and resolve unexpected crises; others are not. For example, a family that lives in an impoverished environment and loses its major source of income may not recover to its previous level of functioning, despite that family's best effort. Such would probably not be the case with a family living in a more affluent and supportive environment.

The Sanchez Family

Maria and Juan Sanchez met in high school and immediately fell in love. After their graduations, they decided to marry. Both wanted a large family. However, after years of trying without success, they went to a fertility clinic to get help. Unfortunately, two years of work with clinic personnel produced no results.

The Sanchezes have been referred to you for counseling. You recognize that they are in some distress because they have not had the children they wanted and expected. How do you help them express their feelings of frustration, and perhaps sadness, and find appropriate ways of dealing with their situation?

COUPLE COUNSELING

Couples, whether married or not, seek **couple counseling** (working with two partners on their relationship) for a wide variety of reasons, including issues of finance, children, fidelity, communication, and compatibility. Almost any difficult situation can serve as the impetus to seek help.

Regardless of who initiates the request, it is crucial in almost all cases that clinical mental health counselors see both members of the couple from the beginning. Trying to treat one spouse alone for even one or two sessions increases both the other spouse's resistance to counseling and his or her anxiety. Also, if one member of a couple tries to change without the knowledge or support of the other, conflict in the form of negative feedback is bound to ensue. Thus, if clinical mental health counselors are not able to structure sessions so that both partners can attend, they will probably not help the couple and possibly will do harm.

To combat possible negative results when one member of a couple is reluctant or refusing to attend counseling, Wilcoxon and Fenell (1983) developed a therapist-initiated letter explaining the process of couple therapy to an absent partner. It outlines the perils of treating just one partner and is sent by counselors to the nonattending partner to help clarify the potential benefits that can accrue when both members of the couple participate.

When both partners decide to enter couple counseling, a variety of approaches can be taken. Among the most popular approaches are psychoanalytic, social learning, Bowen family systems, structural–strategic, rational emotive behavior therapy, and emotionally focused therapy.

Psychoanalytic Theory

Psychoanalytical couple counseling is based on the **theory of object relations**, a theory that addresses how relationships are developed across the generations (Scarf, 1995; Slipp, 1988). **Objects** are significant others in one's environment, such as a mother, with whom children form an interactive emotional bond. The basis of preferences for certain objects as opposed to others is developed in early childhood in parent–child interactions. Individuals bring these unconscious forces into a couple relationship.

To help the couple, the counselor focuses with each partner on obtaining emotional insight into early parent–child relationships. The treatment may be both individual and conjoint. The counselor uses the process of **transference**, through which each partner restructures internally based perceptions of, expectations of, and reactions to self and others and projects them onto the counselor. Other techniques used in this approach include taking individual histories of each partner and of the couple relationship. Interpretation, dream work, and an analysis of resistance are often incorporated into the treatment. **Catharsis**, the expression of pent-up emotion, is a must. The goal of this approach is for individuals and couples to gain new insights into their lives, leading to changed behaviors.

Social-Learning Theory

Social-learning theory is a form of behaviorism that stresses learning through modeling and imitation (Bandura, 1977b; Horne & Sayger, 2000). The premises underlying the theory are that behaviors are learned through observing others and that couple partners have either a deficit or an excess of needed behaviors. A deficit may be the result of one or both partners never having witnessed a particular skill, such as how to fight fairly. An excess may come as a result of one or both partners thinking that just a little more of a certain behavior will solve their problems. For example, one partner may tell the other everything he or she likes and does not like in the couple in the hope that honest communication will be beneficial. Although such honesty may be admired, research shows that couples grow more through positive reciprocity than through negative feedback (Gottman & Silver, 2015). Selective communication and interaction with one's spouse seem to work best.

The focus in social-learning couple counseling is on skill building in the present. Events that have disrupted the couple in the past may be recognized but receive little focus. Within the treatment process, clinical mental health counselors may use a wide variety of behavioral strategies to help couples change, such as self-reports, observations, communication-enhancement training exercises, contracting, and homework assignments (Stuart, 1980, 1998). Much of social-learning theory is based on linear thinking.

Bowen Family Systems Theory

The focus of Bowen family systems marital theory is on **differentiation**, or distinction, of one's thoughts from one's emotions and of oneself from others (Bowen, 1994; Kerr & Bowen, 1988; Titelman, 2014). Couples marry at varying levels of emotional maturity, with those who are less mature having a more difficult time in their couple relationships. When there is a great deal of friction within a couple, the partners who compose it are often characterized by a high degree of **fusion** (undifferentiated emotional togetherness) or **cutoff** (physical or psychological avoidance). These individuals have not separated themselves from their families of origin in a healthy way, nor have they formed stable self-concepts. When they experience stress within the couple, they tend to **triangulate**, or focus on a third party (Gilbert, 2006; Sprenkle & Piercy, 2005). The third party can be the couple itself, a child, an outside agency, or even a somatic complaint. Regardless, it leads to unproductive interactions for the couple.

Techniques used in this approach focus on ways to differentiate oneself from one's extended family-of-origin system. In the process, there is an attempt to create an individuated person with a healthy self-concept who can be part of a couple and not experience undue anxiety every time the relationship becomes stressful. Ways of achieving this goal include assessment of self and family through the use of a **genogram** (i.e., a visual representation of a person's family tree depicted in geometric figures, lines, and words) and a focus on **cognitive** (intellectual or mental) **processes**, such as asking content-based questions of one's family (Bowen, 1976). The sequencing and pacing of this process differ from spouse to spouse, and the therapeutic interaction takes place either with one spouse and the counselor or, ideally, with both spouses and the counselor together.

Structural–Strategic Theory

Structural–strategic theory is based on the belief that when dysfunctional symptoms occur in a couple, they are an attempt to help couples adapt. This approach combines the best techniques of the structural and strategic schools of couple and family therapy and sees problems as occurring within a developmental framework of the family life cycle. Marital difficulties are generated by the system the couple is in, and these symptoms consequently help maintain the marital system in which they operate (Todd, 1986). Therefore, the job of a structural–strategic couple counselor is to get couples to try new behaviors because their old behaviors are not working. Usually, a specific behavior is targeted for change. If this behavior can be modified, it will tend to have a spillover effect, helping the couple make other behavior changes as well.

To bring about change, clinical mental health counselors who work from this perspective are active, direct, and goal oriented as well as problem focused, pragmatic, and brief. **Relabeling**, or giving a new perspective to a behavior, is frequently used, as are **paradoxing**, or insisting on just the opposite of what one wants, and **prescribing the symptom**, or having the couple display voluntarily what they have previously manifested involuntarily, such as fighting. The counselor often asks clients to pretend to make changes or to carry out homework assignments (Madanes, 1984; Minuchin, 1974). The objective is to bring about new functional behaviors that will help couples achieve a specific goal.

Rational Emotive Behavior Theory

The premise behind rational emotive behavior theory (REBT) is that couples, like individuals, often become disturbed because of what they think rather than what has occurred in the relationship (DiGiuseppe, Doyle, Dryden, & Backx, 2014; Ellis, 2000; Ellis & Dryden, 2007). **Irrational thinking** that is "highly exaggerated, inappropriately rigid, illogical, and especially absolutist" is what leads to neurosis and relationship disturbance (Ellis, Sichel, Yeager, DiMattia, & DiGiuseppe, 1989, p. 17). To combat disturbances, couples need to challenge and change their belief systems about activating events. Otherwise they continue to "awfulize" and "catastrophize" themselves and their couple. The essence of this theory is essentially what Ellis (1988) calls **double systems therapy**, in which emphasis is placed on personal and family systems change.

As with individual counseling, the REBT counselor concentrates on thinking, but within the context of a couple. The focus is on helping individuals first and couples second. After assessing what is occurring with the couple, the REBT counselor works with the individuals separately and together in the ABC method of REBT. There is a special emphasis, however, on some particular marital problems, such as jealousy and issues of sexuality.

Emotionally Focused Therapy

Emotionally focused therapy (EFT) was originated by Susan Johnson and is a systemic approach to working with couples. It is based on an assimilative integration of experiential psychotherapy with structural family therapy. It focuses on **intrapsychic processes** (i.e., how

Psychoanalytic	Goal of counseling is making the unconscious more conscious and helping each partner in a couple obtain emotional insight into early parent–child relationships and how they affect present relationships
Social Learning	Goal of counseling is helping couples learn through modeling and imitation
Bowen	Goal of counseling is on differentiation, or distinction, of one's thoughts from one's emotions and of oneself from others
Structural–Strategic	Goal of counseling is get couples to try new behaviors because their old behaviors are not working. Usually, a specific behavior is targeted for change
Rational Emotive Behavior	Goal of counseling is helping individuals first and couples second; approach is placed on personal and family systems change
Emotionally Focused	Goal of counseling is helping couples feel better about themselves and their partners. Techniques in this approach concentrate on disclosure of feelings, self-awareness, catharsis, and increasing empathy

FIGURE 10–4   Six Couple Counseling Theories

partners process their emotional experiences) and **interpersonal processes** (i.e., how partners organize their interactions into patterns and cycles; Kowal, Johnson, & Lee, 2003). The roots of the approach are based on attachment theory, first posited by John Bowlby.

EFT strives to foster the development of more secure attachment styles in couples by seeing emotions "as a positive force for change in couple therapy" rather than "something to be overcome and replaced with rationality" (Johnson, 1998, p. 451). Treatment in EFT focuses on helping couples feel better about themselves and their partners. Thus, techniques in this approach concentrate on disclosure of feelings. There are several ways feelings are mined. One technique is for the therapist to probe and ask partners to acknowledge immediate feelings, such as anger, and to be accepting of that emotion. Therapists may also interrupt couples' arguments and disagreements. In doing so, they reflect with each member of the couple and defuse hostility. In addition, EFT therapists explore the perceptions that underlie partners' emotional responses, which, up to that point in time, they have kept hidden. Both catharsis and self-awareness are encouraged. During this process, the partner receiving the emotional response is provided with the opportunity to become aware of the other's viewpoint and to develop empathic closeness (Young & Long, 2007). If such understanding is achieved, empathy becomes instrumental in the couple's relationship, and the couple becomes closer. See Figure 10–4 for a summary of the six couple counseling theories just discussed.

FAMILY COUNSELING

Families enter counseling for a number of reasons. Usually, there is an **identified patient (an IP)**, or an individual who is seen as the cause of trouble within the family structure (the family scapegoat). Family members use that individual as their ticket of entry. Most family counseling practitioners do not view one member of a family as the problem but instead work with the whole family system, especially when there is a major family problem such as sex abuse.

BOX 10–1   Challenges of Working with A Family who has Sexually Offended

"I'm here because I inappropriately touched my sister." These words sound unnatural when uttered by a 12-year-old, and this sentence forced a family and their counselor to acknowledge the pervasiveness of sexual abuse. Sexual abuse does not differentiate across demographics, and children who have committed sexual offenses present unique challenges and rewards to counselors working with them and their families.

Sexual abuse affects all individuals within the family system, and an initial challenge may be gaining family support in treatment. Families vary in their perceptions of the child: Some unknowingly utilize the child as a family scapegoat, while others view the child's behaviors through a minimizing lens that renders the family unable to see the problems. These perceptions may be equally detrimental to a child's self-image as children often adapt and internalize the roles their families impose. Treatment encourages families to grow and better understand broader patterns and dynamics in the child's behavior and to serve as a healthy and reliable support system.

Bethany Montplaisir, LPCA, NCC (Systemic Treatment after Sexual Abuse for Families)

Because family counseling has a proven track record of helping individuals, couples, and families, it has expanded rapidly since the mid-1970s and now encompasses many aspects of couples counseling. Seven of its main theoretical orientations will be covered here. Although some family counselors are linearly based and work on cause-and-effect relationships, most are not. Rather, the majority of counselors who work with families operate from a general systems framework and conceptualize the family as an open system that evolves over the family life cycle in a sociocultural context. Functional families follow rules and are flexible in meeting the demands placed on them by family members and outside agencies. Family systems counselors stress the idea of **circular causality**; that is, family members affect each other for better or worse, as well as the family as a whole, through their multiple interactions. These counselors, often clinical mental health counselors, also emphasize the following concepts:

- *Nonsummativity:*   The family is greater than the sum of its parts. It is necessary to examine the patterns within a family rather than the actions of any specific member alone.
- *Equifinality:*   The same origin may lead to different outcomes, and the same outcome may result from different origins. Thus, the family that experiences a natural disaster may become stronger or weaker as a result. Likewise, healthy families may have quite dissimilar backgrounds. Therefore, the focus of treatment is on interactional family patterns rather than on particular conditions or events.
- *Communication:*   All behavior is seen as communicative. It is important to attend to the two functions of interpersonal messages: *content* (i.e., factual information) and *relationship* (i.e., how the message is to be understood). The *what* of a message is conveyed by how it is delivered, for example, the way the words are said.
- *Family rules:*   A family's functioning is based on both explicit and implicit rules. Family rules provide expectations about roles and actions that govern family life. Most

families operate on a small set of predictable rules, a pattern known as the **redundancy principle**. To help families change dysfunctional ways of working, counselors have to help them define and/or expand the rules under which they operate.

• *Morphogenesis:*   The ability of the family to modify its functioning to meet the changing demands of internal and external factors is known as **morphogenesis**. Morphogenesis usually requires a **second-order change** (i.e., an entirely new response) instead of a **first-order change** (i.e., repeating the same things that have been done previously; Watzlawick, Weakland, & Fisch, 1974). For example, instead of just talking, family members may need to try new behaviors to get their points across to one another, such as writing or illustrating what they are trying to convey.

• *Homeostasis:*   As with biological organisms, families have a tendency to remain in a steady, stable state of equilibrium unless otherwise forced to change. When a family member unbalances the family through his or her actions, other members quickly try to rectify the situation through **negative feedback loops (morphostasis)**. The model of functioning is similar to a furnace that comes on when a house falls below a set temperature and cuts off once the temperature is reached. Sometimes homeostasis can be advantageous in helping a family achieve life cycle goals, but often it prevents the family from moving on to another stage in its development.

Counselors who operate from a family systems approach work according to the concepts just covered. For instance, if family rules are covert and cause confusion, the counselor helps the family make these regulations overt and clear. For example, instead of saying, "Someone should clean up this mess," a father might say to an adolescent, "Jon, please help me clean up this mess." The point is that when all members of a family know what is expected of them, they are much more likely to be engaged with each other and have open communication channels. Often, a genogram is constructed to help family members and counselors detect intergenerational patterns of family functioning that have an impact on the present (McGoldrick, 2012).

Overall, the popularity of counseling with families may be attributed to the realization that persons become healthier when their families function better. The economy of using family counseling and its encompassing nature are intrinsically appealing and make it attractive for clinical mental health counselors who wish to work on complex, multifaceted levels within their communities.

Psychodynamic Family Counseling

As traditionally practiced, psychoanalysis concentrates on individuals instead of social systems such as the family. Ackerman (1966) broke with tradition by working with intact families. He believed that family difficulties resulted from **interlocking pathologies**, or unconscious and dysfunctional ways of acting, present in the couple and family system. An initial goal of psychodynamic family counseling is to change the personalities of family members so they can work with one another in a healthy and productive way. Psychodynamic-oriented counselors who follow Ackerman most often use an eclectic mix of psychoanalytic and systems concepts.

A unique contribution that psychodynamic practitioners have made to the field of family counseling is the use of **object relations** as a primary emphasis in treatment. Object relations, as mentioned previously, are internalized residues of early parent–child interactions. In dysfunctional families, object relations continue to exert a negative influence in present interpersonal relationships. Dysfunctional families are those with a greater degree of unconscious, unresolved conflict or loss. Three main ways of working with these families are (a) developing a stronger parent coalition, (b) defining and maintaining generation boundaries, and (c) modeling sex-linked roles.

Overall, psychodynamic family counselors concentrate on (a) helping family members obtain insight and resolve family-of-origin conflicts/losses, (b) eliminating distorted projections, (c) reconstructing relationships, and (d) promoting individual and family growth (Walsh, 2012). Prominent practitioners associated with this approach are Nathan Ackerman, James Framo, Theodore Lidz, and Norman Paul.

Experiential Family Counseling

Experientialist family counselors are concerned as much with individuals as with family systems and consider intrapsychic problems when explaining psychopathology. Unlike most other family counselors, experientialists describe patterns of family dysfunction using the individual or a dyad as the unit of analysis. They believe that dysfunctional families are made up of people who are unaware of their emotions; or if they are aware of their emotions, they suppress them, making real intimacy very difficult. This tendency not to feel or express feelings creates a climate of **emotional deadness**. Therefore, the goal of counseling is to emphasize sensitivity and feeling expression, thus opening family members to new experiences.

Two historically prominent practitioners in the experiential school were Virginia Satir and Carl Whitaker. Satir (1967, 1972) stressed the importance of clear communications in her approach. She believed that when family members are under stress, they may handle their communications in one of four nonproductive roles:

1. *Placater:* agrees and tries to please
2. *Blamer:* dominates and finds fault
3. *Responsible analyzer:* remains emotionally detached and intellectual
4. *Distractor:* interrupts and constantly chatters about irrelevant topics

The Satir method helps families by teaching members to own personal feelings and express them clearly, a process she called **leveling**. In leveling, individuals are instructed to listen to one another to promote intimacy. Satir further stressed the importance of obtaining and providing feedback and negotiating differences when they arise. Her primary focus was on communication skills. She used experiential exercises and props to help families and their members become more aware.

Whitaker (1976, 1977, 1989) was more of an existential maverick whose interactions with families were sometimes unconventional but always very creative. He took a less structured approach to working with families and represented the extreme side of the experiential school. Whitaker advocated nonrational, creative experiences in family counseling and let the form of his methods develop as he worked. He sometimes used **absurdity** (i.e., a statement that is half-truthful and even silly if followed out to its conclusion) in working with families. To be effective, he also used a cotherapist. Whitaker was known to go to sleep, have a dream, and share it with a family. Messages that come from such events are hard for family members to dismiss or resist. Thus, as Whitaker found, families began to change their patterns of behaving and became more honest, open, and spontaneous with each other. Overall, Whitaker (Keith, 2015) emphasized uncovering and utilizing the unconscious life of the family.

Behavioral Family Counseling

Behavioral family counselors use theory techniques originally devised for treating individuals. With the exception of functional family therapists (e.g., Alexander & Parsons, 1982; Sexton & Lebow, 2016), they are nonsystemic in conceptualizing and in clinically working with families. Most behavioral family counselors, whether clinical mental health counselors or not, stress the importance of learning. They emphasize the importance of family rules and skill training and believe that behaviors are determined by consequences rather than by antecedents.

The goals of behavioral family counseling are specific and limited. Behaviorists try to modify troublesome behavior patterns to alleviate undesirable interactions. Much of their work focuses on changing dyadic interaction through teaching, modeling, and reinforcing new behaviors. Behaviorists believe that change is best achieved through accelerating positive behavior rather than decelerating negative behavior. Most of their work is concentrated in three main areas of (a) behavioral parent training (Patterson, 1971), (b) behavioral couple counseling (Stuart, 1980), and (c) treatment of sexual dysfunctions (LoPiccolo, 1978; Masters & Johnson, 1970).

Structural Family Counseling

Structural family counseling, founded by Salvador Minuchin (1974), is based on general systems theory. Its practitioners advocate structural changes in the organization of the family unit, with particular attention on changing interactional patterns in subsystems of the family, such as the marital dyad, and establishing clear boundaries between family members (Minuchin, Montalvo, Guerney, Rosman, & Schumer, 1967; Minuchin, Reiter, & Borda, 2014).

In working with families, structural family counselors join with the family in a position of leadership. They try to formulate a structure in their minds of the family to determine how it is stuck in dysfunctional patterns. These counselors then use a number of techniques aimed at getting the family to change the way it operates (Minuchin & Fishman, 1981). One primary technique is to work with the family's interaction patterns. When family members repeat nonproductive sequences of behavior or demonstrate either a detached or enmeshed position in the family structure, the counselor will rearrange the physical environment so they have to act in a different way. The technique may be as simple as having people face each other when they talk. Structural family counselors also use **reframing**, or helping the family see its problem from a different and more positive perspective. For example, if a child is misbehaving, the behavior may be relabeled "naughty" instead of "crazy." As a consequence, the child and actions will be viewed as less pathological. By helping families change their structure, reframe their problems, establish a hierarchy with the parents in charge, and create clear boundaries and appropriate ways of interacting, structuralists help families use their own inner resources to function in a productive and healthy way.

Strategic Family Counseling

Jay Haley (1973), Cloe Madanes (1991), and the Mental Research Institute were prominent leaders in initiating the strategic school of family counseling. Strategic counselors take a systemic view of problem behaviors and focus on the process rather than on the content of dysfunctional interactions. They strive to resolve presenting problems and pay little attention to instilling insight. One powerful technique often used by strategic counselors is to **prescribe the symptom**. This approach places targeted behaviors, such as family fights, under the control of the counselor by making a behavior voluntary if family members comply and eliminating a behavior if the family group resists the counselor's instructions. Strategic family counselors accept the presenting problems of families and view symptoms as serving the positive purpose of communication.

The technique of **ordeals**—for example, doing something a person does not want to do, such as buying a gift for somebody who is disliked—is sometimes used during the treatment process. The idea is that if families have to make sacrifices to get better, then the long-term improvements of treatment are enhanced. A major aspect of strategic family counseling is the assignment of original homework tasks, often given in the form of prescriptions that are to be completed between sessions. Many strategic counselors work in teams and limit the number of treatment sessions as a motivational factor. Overall, this treatment is short term and pragmatic.

Brief Solution-Focused Family Counseling

Brief solution-focused family counseling is both an extension of strategic family counseling and a distinct entity. It traces its roots to the work of Milton Erickson (1954), particularly his **utilization principle**, which involves using whatever clients present in counseling "as a basis and means for client solutions and change" (Lawson, 1994, p. 244). Erickson believed that people have within themselves the resources and abilities to solve their own problems. "Additionally, Erickson . . . believed that a small change in one's behavior is often all that is necessary to lead to more profound changes in a problem context" (Lawson, 1994, p. 244). This viewpoint was adopted from Erickson by Jay Haley and has been formulated into brief solution-focused family counseling by Steve deShazer and Bill O'Hanlon.

The essence of brief solution-focused family counseling is that clients create problems because of their perceptions, such as "I am always depressed." Brief solution-focused family counselors try to help clients get a different perspective on their situations through having them notice exceptions. Client families are then directed toward solutions that already exist, as found in these exceptions. Thus, the focus of sessions and homework is on positives and possibilities either now or in the future (Ratner, George, & Iveson, 2013; Walter & Peller, 1992). One way to help individuals change perspective, from concentrating on the negative to emphasizing the positive, is by asking the **miracle question** (de Shazer, 1991). In this intervention clients are asked to imagine that their problem is suddenly solved. What will then happen in regard to their behaviors, and how will they know the problem is solved?

Narrative Family Therapy

Narrative family therapy emphasizes the reauthoring of their life stories by individuals and families. The most prominent professionals associated with narrative family therapy are Michael White and David Epston from Australia and New Zealand, respectively. The approach distinguishes between **logicoscientific reasoning**, which is characterized by empiricism and logic, and **narrative reasoning**, which is characterized by stories, substories, meaningfulness, and liveliness. According to the narrative viewpoint, "People live their lives by stories" (Kurtz & Tandy, 1995, p. 177). Thus, the emphasis within narrative family therapy is helping people change their life stories by reauthoring their lives (see Figure 10–5).

The process of changing life stories is undertaken by **externalizing the problem**, which means that all family members can objectively address unproductive behaviors (White, 1995). In addition, the influence of the problem on a person(s) is noted, as well as

Psychodynamic	Goal of counseling is to change the personalities of family members so they can work with one another in a healthy and productive way
Experiential	Goal of counseling is to emphasize sensitivity and feeling expression, thus opening family members to new experiences
Behavioral	Goal of counseling is to modify troublesome behavior patterns to alleviate undesirable interactions and focus on accelerating positive behavior
Structural	Goal of counseling is to make structural changes in the organization of the family unit, with particular attention on changing interactional patterns in subsystems of the family, such as the marital dyad, and establishing clear boundaries between family members
Strategic	Goal of counseling is to resolve presenting problems; pays little attention to instilling insight
Solution Focused	Goal of counseling is to help clients get a different perspective on their situations through having them notice exceptions and focus on the possible and the positive
Narrative	Goal of counseling is to help people change their life stories, reauthor their lives, and externalize problems

FIGURE 10–5   Seven Family Counseling Theories

the influence of a person(s) on the problem. Narrative family therapists also predict setbacks in treatment so families and individuals can plan ahead for how they will act when those times come. As with solution-focused family counseling, there is a major focus on exceptions to the problem and on how families act when there is not a problem. The goal is to challenge a family's view of the world and to offer them hope that their lives can be different because some changes have taken place and they are moving toward putting other changes in place. When the family or individuals have been successful in overcoming the externalized problem, narrative family therapists offer them certificates of achievement and celebrations to signify their victory or achievement (White & Epston, 1990).

Which Theory for the Thurbers?

John and Shelia Thurber are the parents of four children: John, Jr. (age 18), Kathy (age 16), Tom (age 12), and Mimi (age 10). Kathy is struggling. She thinks her parents are not protecting her from the verbal insults of her older and younger brothers. She considers her sister a pest. Furthermore, Kathy is alienated from her former friends at school and has actually skipped school for the past week. She is now beginning to experiment with drugs, and her new friends are certainly not the type of people her parents want her hanging out with.

The Thurbers have come to you as a family, although it is obvious that they want you to "fix" Kathy and to do so quickly. You know the full range of theoretical approaches to working with a family like the Thurbers. At first you think you might work from a structural– strategic perspective. However, you are not quite sure that it is a good fit.

How do you go about choosing a theoretical approach that will be helpful to a family such as the Thurbers? What if the approach you choose does not seem to work well? Is there any one approach that you think might be one you could drop back to if all else fails?

COUPLE AND FAMILY ENRICHMENT

Although the majority of this chapter focuses on different treatment modalities for working with couples and families, a primary prevention emphasis—enrichment—can also be a part of helping families. The idea of **couple enrichment** is based on the concept that couples, and consequently their families, stay healthy or get healthier by actively participating in certain activities with other couples (Mace & Mace, 1977). In such settings, couples learn about themselves; they also learn from other couples. There are over two dozen enrichment organizations in the United States on a national level, and the material in this field has mushroomed.

Couples retreats, engagement in interactive cooperative activities, and involvement in family-level councils are among the most recommended ways of achieving health in couples and families. The research on enrichment shows that it can be helpful to couples and families who are not in distress. However, enrichment experiences, especially those involving couple encounter weekends, can be quite disruptive and damaging to distressed couples and can lead to further deterioration of their relationships (Doherty, Lester, & Leigh, 1986). Care must be exercised in selecting couples and families to participate in these programs.

A part of couple and family enrichment involves self and couples help (Love & Stosny, 2007). This type of help is often in the form of information as well as structured exercises that theoretically and practically bring couples closer together through sharing experiences (Olson, DeFrain, & Skogrand, 2014). For instance, couples may learn to give and receive nonverbal and verbal messages and to reflect on positive times in their lives together. They may also be able to give and receive feedback on important relationship topics such as sexuality, finance, parenting, and household chores (Johnson, Fortman, & Brems, 1993).

RESEARCH AND ASSOCIATIONS

Interest in couple and family counseling has grown rapidly since the 1970s, and the number of individuals receiving training in this specialty has increased accordingly. One reason for these increases is the growing need for services. Approximately 50% of all problems brought to counselors are related to couple and family issues (Gurman & Kniskern, 1981; Gurman, Lebow, & Synder, 2016). These issues include unemployment, poor school performance, spouse abuse, depression, rebellion, and self-concept.

Further, research studies summarized by Pinsof and Wynne (1995, 2000) report a number of interesting findings. First, family counseling interventions are at least as effective as individual interventions for most client complaints and lead to significantly greater durability of change. Second, some forms of family counseling (such as using structural–strategic family therapy with substance abusers) are more effective in treating problems than are individual counseling approaches. Third, the presence of both parents, especially noncompliant fathers, in family counseling situations greatly improves the chances for success. Similarly, the effectiveness of couple counseling when both partners meet conjointly with the counselor is nearly twice that of counselors working with just one spouse. Finally, when couple and family counseling services are not offered to couples conjointly or to families systemically, the results of the intervention may be negative, and problems may worsen. Overall, the basic argument for using couple and family counseling is its proven efficiency. This form of treatment is logical, fast, satisfactory, and economical. Working with couples and families can be both challenging and rewarding (see Box 10–2).

Four major professional associations attract specialists in this area. The largest and oldest (established in 1942) is the American Association for Marriage and Family Therapy (AAMFT). The second association, the International Association of Marriage and Family Counselors (IAMFC), which is a division within the American Counseling Association, was chartered in 1986. The third association, Division 43 (Family Psychology), which is a division within the American Psychological Association, was formed in 1984 to provide a professional affiliation for family practitioners who wanted to maintain their identity as psychologists. Finally, the American Family Therapy Association (AFTA), which was formed in 1977, is identified as an academy of advanced professionals interested in the exchange of ideas.

BOX 10–2   Reflections on Working with Couples and Families

I have found, both personally and professionally, that life is a series of losses and opportunities often reshaping the very structure of families. To learn about each family's *story* and community is a privilege, responsibility, and challenge. To effect positive change on individual, family, group, and community levels is intrinsically rewarding. My role as a practitioner is to restore or instill choice; help clients pass through transitions; and when appropriate, engage in advocacy. In working with problems relating to partner abuse, child abuse, suicide, physical health, and poverty, I have found that all problems have a family and social context; however, the appropriate treatment is not always couple/family therapy. Practicing in a time when services are limited by managed care requires the engagement of clients in understanding/creating their *story* (individual, couple, and family) while also problem solving, and establishing links to community resources in a brief time frame. As a social worker and educator with an interdisciplinary background, I have found that *joining* and *letting go* ultimately shapes the pain and the promise of working with couples and families.

Nicholas Mazza, PhD, MSW, Professor of Social Work, Florida State University

---

Summary and Conclusion

Family life in the United States is very diverse with a variety of family forms. Regardless of form, all families go through life cycles that influence their development. Expected and unexpected events can lead to stress and even distress. One way to help couples and families is through couple and family counseling, and clinical mental health counselors can get special training in this area.

The profession of couple and family counseling has grown rapidly in recent years for a number of reasons, including theory development, needs within the population, and proven research effectiveness. There are six main approaches to couple counseling: psychoanalytic, social-learning, Bowen family systems, structural–strategic, rational emotive behavior, and emotionally focused therapy. Family counseling has a wider range of approaches (e.g., psychodynamic, behavioral, brief solution-focused, strategic, structural, and narrative), but the dominant ones are family systems oriented.

In working as either a couple counselor or a family counselor, the helping professional must be aware of the theoretical basis of the approach being implemented and must keep in mind where couple and/or family members are in their individual and family life cycles. Counseling couples and families is important and gratifying for counselors, including clinical mental health counselors. Likewise, primary prevention in the form of enrichment experiences can and should be a part of the work in community and agency settings. Through enrichment experiences and exercises, couples learn more about each other and ways to relate to one another and their families.

MyCounselingLab

Try the Topic 8 Assignments: *Family Counseling*.

CHAPTER 11

Counseling Children and Adolescents

Shutterstock

There you sit Alice Average
   midway back in the long-windowed classroom
     in the middle of Wednesday's noontime blahs,
Adjusting yourself to the sound of a lecture
   and the cold of the blue plastic desk that supports you.
In a world full of light words, hard rock, Madonnas,
   long hair, high tech, confusion, and change
     dreams fade like blue jeans
And "knowing" goes beyond the books and disks
   that are packaged for time-limited consumption
     and studied until the start of summer. . . .

Reprinted from "Thoughts on Alice Average Midway Through the Mid-day Class on Wednesday," by S. T. Gladding, 1980, *Humanist Educator, 18*, p. 203. Copyright © 1980, 1986 by S. T. Gladding.

CHAPTER OVERVIEW

From reading this chapter, you will learn about

- Mental health issues that affect children and adolescents
- Developmental, biological, and contextual issues that contribute to young people's mental health
- Effective ways of working with children and adolescents
- Specific concerns young people face, including depression, eating disorders, ADHD, family disruption, grief and loss, and maltreatment

As you read, consider

- What developmental issues clinical mental health counselors need to consider when they work with young people
- What specific biological and contextual factors affect children's mental health and well-being
- How common depression is among children and adolescents
- Why eating disorders are so prevalent among adolescents and how they are manifested

overty, violence, illness, school difficulties, and family disruption, as well as typical transitions associated with development, are factors that influence the mental health and well-being of a growing number of children and adolescents. Whether the increased prevalence of mental health issues in this population is due to a higher level of vulnerability or to increased efforts to identify problems, currently more young people are in need of mental health services than were in years past (Erford, 2015). According to the surgeon general's report (U.S. Department of Health and Human Services, 2000) and the National Institute of Mental Health (NIMH; 2016b), approximately 20% of children and adolescents are estimated to have mental disorders of some type, and 5% to 9% of youth have serious emotional disturbances. Although many youth are affected by mental health issues, an estimated 80% of young people who need treatment do not receive the mental health services they need (U.S. Department of Health and Human Services, 2016). Clearly, youth are not immune from mental health disorders, and a large majority of young people needing help are not getting it.

Mental health problems appear in youth of all social classes and backgrounds. Some children are at greater risk than others because of a wide range of factors, including genetic vulnerability, temperament, family dysfunction, poverty, caregiver separation, and abuse (Moore et al., 2011; Surgeon General Report, 2000). Clinical mental health counselors who work with children and adolescents need to be aware of these risk factors, as well as of the developmental factors that affect mental health. They also need to be skilled at implementing prevention and intervention strategies that target multiple levels, including the individual, the family, and the broader community.

This chapter describes developmental and bioecological influences on children's mental health and focuses on the counseling process as it applies to children and adolescents. Following that, an overview is given of some of the specific issues that affect children and adolescents living in today's society. Treatment suggestions for working with these issues are then described.

The Case of Brian

Four-year-old Brian is always on the go, according to his mother, Louise. He attends a local preschool for a half day, three days a week. Brian's preschool teacher says that he is "very active" and that he frequently interrupts other children when they are playing, often pushing them when they won't let him join them in their activities. Brian has one close friend, Bart, who tends to go along with whatever Brian wants to do. During circle time in preschool, Brian has trouble sitting still. He is easily distracted and will often try to leave the circle to go play with some of the toys in the room.

Brian has a new baby sister, Tamara, who is 3 months old. Louise, who is a single mother, enrolled Brian in preschool for the first time this fall, two months before Tamara was born. Tamara cries a lot and requires a lot of her mother's attention. Last week, Louise discovered Brian pinching Tamara until she cried. Distressed, Louise called Family Services, a community mental health agency in town, to request help for Brian.

If you were one of the clinical mental health counselors at this agency, what additional information would you like to have? What issues raise the biggest concerns for you? How would you conduct an intake interview with Brian and Louise? If counseling is warranted, what are some ways you might proceed?

DEVELOPMENTAL CONSIDERATIONS

Childhood and adolescence are characterized by dramatic developmental changes physically, cognitively, socially, and emotionally. To a large degree, mental health during these years is defined by achieving expected developmental milestones, establishing secure attachments, negotiating relationships with family members and peers, and learning effective coping skills. Mental health practitioners who work with young people need to be guided by developmental theory as they select strategies for prevention, support, and treatment.

Development is multidimensional and complex and is marked by qualitative changes that occur in multiple domains. A summary of developmental theories and counseling implications, which was adapted from several sources (e.g., Berk, 2014; Nystul, 2016), is presented in Table 11–1. Although it is not our intent to describe the full range of developmental characteristics associated with children and adolescents, in the section that follows, an overview of some general characteristics of early childhood, middle childhood, and adolescence is provided.

Early Childhood

Children between the ages of 2 and 6 are in the early childhood stage, sometimes called the **play years** (Berk, 2014). During this period, motor skills are refined, children begin to build ties with peers, and thought and language skills expand rapidly. To understand the way young children think and use language, it is helpful to refer to Jean Piaget's stage-constructed theory of cognitive development. Although current research indicates that the stages of cognitive development are more fluid than Piaget hypothesized, his descriptions of cognitive development provide a relatively accurate picture of how children think and reason at different ages (Bjorklund, 2000).

According to Piaget, children between 2 and 7 years of age are **preoperational**, which means they are developing the ability to represent objects and events through imitation, symbolic play, drawing, and spoken language. They are likely to be egocentric, implying that they cannot comprehend the viewpoint of another. Preoperational children may attribute lifelike qualities to inanimate objects and may have difficulty with abstract nouns and concepts, such as time and space (Vernon, 2009). For the first time, these children are entering into a stage where they are able to represent and recall their feelings. As they near the end of the preoperational stage, their emotional self-regulation improves.

Erik Erikson's psychosocial theory provides another way to understand children's development. Erikson describes development as a series of psychological crises that occur at various stages. The way in which a crisis is resolved, along a continuum from positive to negative, influences healthy or maladaptive outcomes at each stage. Young children are in the process of resolving the developmental crisis of **initiative versus guilt** (Erikson, 1968). Initiative refers to being enterprising, energetic, and purposeful. Children in this stage are discovering what kinds of people they are, particularly in regard to gender. Because of their increased language and motor skills, they are capable of imagining and trying out many new things. To navigate this period successfully, children need to be given a variety of opportunities to explore, experiment, and ask questions. The guidance of understanding adults can help young children develop self-confidence, self-direction, and emotional self-regulation.

Play is an extremely important activity for children in this age group. Through play, children find out about themselves and their world. Counselors who work with young children will want to use some form of play when counseling them. Play provides a way for

TABLE 11–1   Developmental Theories and Implications for Counseling

Developmental Theory	Founder	Key Concepts	Implications for Counseling
Cognitive theory	Piaget and Elkind	Conceptualizes cognitive development in four stages: sensorimotor (birth to 2), preoperational (2 to 7), concrete operations (7 to 11), formal operations (usually after 11).	Counselors can adjust their approaches and select interventions to match a child's level of cognitive functioning. For example, counselors working with young children will want to use some form of play media.
Moral development	Kohlberg and Gilligan	Kohlberg: Identifies three levels of moral development, beginning with a punishment and obedience orientation and progressing to higher stages of moral reasoning. Gilligan: Posits that feminine morality emphasizes an ethic of care, focusing on interpersonal relationships.	An understanding of moral reasoning can help children learn self-control and help parents with discipline issues. Girls and boys may make moral judgments in different ways.
Sociocultural theory	Vygotsky	Focuses on the *zone of proximal development*, which emphasizes a range of tasks too difficult for a child to complete alone but possible with the help of others.	Counselors can use groups to facilitate learning and accomplishment.
Psychosocial development	Erikson	Identifies eight psychosocial stages and their associated developmental tasks (e.g., from birth to 1 year of age, the central task is trust).	Counselors can help clients obtain the coping skills necessary to master developmental tasks so the clients can move forward in their development.
Developmental psychopathology	Kazdin, Kovacs, and others	Considers child and adolescent psychopathology in the context of maturational and developmental processes.	Counselors have a framework for understanding child psychopathology as unique from adult psychopathology, aiding in accurate assessment.
Classic theories of personality	Freud, Adler, and Jung	Emphasize the role of early life experiences on child and adolescent development.	Counselors can understand the dynamics of behavior *before* selecting counseling techniques to promote change.
Attachment theory	Ainsworth, Bowlby, and others	Focuses on the relationship between the emotional parent–child bond and the child's psychosocial development over the life span.	An understanding of attachment relationships can provide useful insights into how to move toward optimal psychosocial development.
Emotional intelligence	Salovey and Mayer	Focuses on the role that emotions play in social and psychological functioning.	Counselors can help promote emotional intelligence through such activities as group social skills training.

Source: Adapted from *Introduction to Counseling: An Art and Science Perspective* (3rd ed., p. 303; 4th ed., p. 284), by Michael S. Nystul, 2006/2011, Boston: Allyn & Bacon.

children to express feelings, describe experiences, and disclose wishes. Although young children may not be able to articulate feelings, toys and other play media serve as the words they use to express emotions (Landreth, 1993). Materials used to facilitate play include puppets, art supplies, dolls and dollhouses, construction tools, and toy figures or animals.

Middle Childhood

Children between 7 and 11 years of age are in middle childhood. During this time period, children develop literacy skills and logical thinking. Cognitively, they are in Piaget's **concrete operational** stage, meaning that they are capable of reasoning logically about concrete, tangible information. Concrete operational children are able to mentally reverse actions, although they can generalize only from concrete experiences. They grasp logical concepts more readily than before, but they typically have difficulty reasoning about abstract ideas. Children in this stage learn best through questioning, exploring, manipulating, and doing. As a rule, their increased reasoning skills enable them to understand the concept of intentionality and to be more cooperative.

From a psychosocial perspective, children in this age group are in the process of resolving the crisis of **industry versus inferiority** (Erikson, 1968). To maximize healthy development, they need opportunities to develop a sense of competence and capability. When adults provide manageable tasks, along with sufficient time and encouragement to complete the tasks, children are more likely to develop a strong sense of industry and efficacy. Alternatively, children who do not experience feelings of competence and mastery may develop a sense of inadequacy and pessimism about their capabilities. Experiences with family, teachers, and peers all contribute to children's perceptions of efficacy and industry.

Negotiating relationships with peers is an important part of middle childhood. Acceptance in a peer group and having a "best friend" help children develop competence, self-esteem, and an understanding of others (Vernon, 2009). Some of the interpersonal skills children acquire during middle childhood include learning to get along with age mates, learning the skills of tolerance and patience, and developing positive attitudes toward social groups and institutions (Havighurst, 1972). Clinical mental health counselors can help children develop their interpersonal skills by implementing preventive strategies targeting social skills development.

Adolescence

Adolescence is the period when young people transition from childhood to adulthood. During adolescence, youth mature physically, develop an increased understanding of roles and relationships, and acquire and refine skills needed for performing successfully as adults. In many modern societies, the time span associated with adolescence can last for nearly a decade. Puberty marks the beginning of adolescence, with girls typically reaching puberty earlier than boys. As adolescence ends, young people ideally have constructed an identity, attained independence, and developed more mature ways of relating to others. In years past, adolescence was referred to as a time of **storm and stress**, but current research indicates that, although the period can be emotionally turbulent for some young people, the term *storm and stress* exaggerates what most adolescents experience (Berk, 2014).

As young people enter adolescence, they begin to make the shift from concrete to formal operational thinking. The transition takes time and usually is not completed until at least age 15, if then. Adolescents moving into the **formal operational** stage are able to deal

with abstractions, form hypotheses, engage in mental manipulation, and predict consequences. As formal operational skills develop, they become capable of reflective abstraction,
the ability to reflect on knowledge, rearrange thoughts, and discover alternative routes to
solving problems. Consequently, counseling approaches that provide opportunities to generate alternative solutions are more likely to be effective with adolescents than with younger
children. However, some adolescents and even adults do not become fully formal operational, perhaps because of restricted experiences (Kuhn & Franklin, 2006).

A new form of **egocentrism** often emerges during adolescence, characterized by a
belief in one's uniqueness and invulnerability. This egocentrism may be reflected in reckless
behavior and grandiose ideas. Consequently, preventive strategies are warranted, addressing
such issues as substance abuse, teenage pregnancy, reckless driving, and unsafe Internet
use. Related to a heightened sense of uniqueness is the adolescent phenomenon of feeling
constantly "on stage" or playing to an imaginary audience. It is not uncommon for adolescents to feel that everyone is looking at them, leading to increased anxiety and self-
consciousness. These feelings tend to peak in early adolescence and then decline as formal
operational skills improve (Bjorklund, 2000).

The onset of puberty often triggers the psychosocial crisis of **identity versus role
confusion** (Erikson, 1968). A key challenge during adolescence is the formation of an identity, including self-definition and a commitment to goals, values, beliefs, and life purpose. To
master this challenge, adolescents need opportunities to explore options, try on various
roles and responsibilities, and speculate about possibilities. Sometimes adolescents enter a
period of role confusion, characterized in part by overidentification with heroes or cliques,
before they develop a true sense of individuality and recognize that they are valuable members of society.

Spending time with peers continues to be important throughout adolescence. As they
develop self-confidence and sensitivity, adolescents base their friendships on compatibility
and shared experiences. Intimate friendships increase, as do dating and sexual experimentation. Counseling may involve helping these young people deal with issues of complex relationships and decision making about the future.

It is important to keep in mind that developmental generalizations may not be applicable to all ethnic or cultural groups. For example, the search for self-identity may be delayed,
compounded by a search for ethnic identity, or even nonexistent among certain groups of
adolescents (Herring, 1997). Also, research on Piagetian tasks suggests that some forms of
logic do not emerge spontaneously according to stages but are socially generated, based on
cultural experiences (Berk, 2014). Developmental theories provide useful guides for understanding children and adolescents; however, no theory provides a complete explanation of
development, nor does any theory take into account all cultural perspectives.

BIOECOLOGICAL CONSIDERATIONS

> *The characteristics of the person at a given time in his or her life are a joint function of the
> characteristics of the person and of the environment over the course of that person's life up
> to that time.*

Bronfenbrenner, 1989, p. 190

Bronfenbrenner's (1979, 1989, 1995) bioecological model illustrates the way development
is influenced by multilayered interactions of specific characteristics of a child (e.g., genetic,

biological, and psychological factors), the immediate environment (e.g., family, school, peers, neighborhood, and community), and the more global culture, or **macrosystem**, within which the young person lives. The systems that compose Bronfenbrenner's bioecological model are depicted in Box 11–1. These systems are not static, but instead are constantly changing. To work effectively with children and adolescents, counselors need to assess individual, environmental, and cultural factors and their interactive effects on development and adjustment. Teasing the different influences apart can be difficult, if not impossible.

BOX 11–1   Bronfenbrenner's Bioecological Model: Five Interactive Systems

MICROSYSTEM: A specific environment in which an individual develops. Young people are members of many different microsystems, such as family, peer groups, school, and church.

MESOSYSTEM: A system defined by interrelations among two or more microsystems. For example, what is going on with a child at school may affect what is going on in the family, or vice versa.

EXOSYSTEM: A context that exerts an indirect influence on a child's development. For example, a parent's workplace may affect the parent in ways that then indirectly affect the child.

MACROSYSTEM: An overarching belief system or culture that exerts its effects indirectly through cultural tools and institutions.

CHRONOSYSTEM: The evolution of the four other systems over time. An awareness of the chronosystem allows counselors to take into account ways the particular systems and their interactions develop and change through a young person's life.

Psychological, Biological, and Genetic Influences

A wide array of individual characteristics—including physical appearance, personality traits, cognitive functioning, and genetic predisposition—influence the manner in which children and adolescents adjust and adapt to their environments. A key factor affecting children's development is **temperament**, which refers to specific traits with which each child is born and which influence the way the child reacts to the surrounding environment. Defined more simply, temperament refers to a person's **emotional style** (Berk, 2014). Temperament includes traits such as attention span, goal orientation, activity level, curiosity, and emotional self-regulation. Differences in temperament are evidenced when one child is easily excitable and impulsive, another is shy and withdrawn, and a third is calm and attentive. Although there is some continuity in temperamental traits across the life span, temperament may be modified during development, particularly through interaction with family members (Thomas & Chess, 1977).

Cognitive factors also influence child and adolescent adjustment and well-being. **Cognitive factors** include intelligence, information processing skills, and neurological conditions. Cognitive skills can serve as protective factors, increasing children's chances for success in school and their ability to solve problems effectively. In contrast, neurological deficits and lower levels of intellectual functioning increase the risk of school failure, thereby placing youth at a greater risk for delinquency (Calhoun, Glaser, & Bartolomucci, 2001). Genetic factors and biological abnormalities of the central nervous system caused by injury, exposure to toxins, infection, or poor nutrition can lead to deficits in cognitive development.

Faulty cognitive processing skills, such as **attributional bias**, can adversely affect an individual's reactions to people and situations. For example, juvenile offenders often attribute hostility to others in neutral situations, resulting in unwarranted acts of aggression (Calhoun et al., 2001). As another example, depressed youth often have negative attributional styles, believing that they are helpless to influence events in their lives and that they are responsible for any failures or problems being experienced. In contrast, young people with more realistic attributional styles tend to be more adaptable and less likely to form misperceptions, leading to healthier coping and adjustment skills.

Just as genetic inheritance influences individual characteristics such as temperament and cognitive functioning, it also influences mental health. Although the precise manner in which heredity influences mental health is not fully understood, certain mental health conditions—including depression, anxiety, and chemical abuse—appear to have a genetic component. For example, children of depressed parents are three times as likely as children of nondepressed parents to experience a depressive disorder (U.S. Department of Health and Human Services, 2016). It is theorized that multiple gene variants act in conjunction with environmental factors and developmental events to make a person more likely to experience mental health problems. Children and adolescents who are genetically vulnerable to specific conditions may benefit from prevention efforts targeting certain areas, such as building resiliency and improving coping responses.

Contextual Influences

Even as genetic inheritance and other biological factors help determine individual traits and set the stage for child development, contextual influences also play critical roles in child and adolescent development. The many contexts in which young people live and interact have powerful effects on their mental health and well-being. Family, school, and peers are examples of contextual factors that influence psychological adjustment.

FAMILY INFLUENCES.   One of the most significant influences on the development of young people is the family, within which interactions typically occur on a daily basis. Within the family, unique bonds are formed that serve as models for relationships in the greater community. Family relationships are complex and influence development both directly and indirectly. A number of family-related variables have been identified as risk factors for adverse mental health, including severe parental discord, parent psychopathology, poor living conditions, and economic hardship (U.S. Department of Health and Human Services, 2016). In contrast, healthy interactions among family members can lead to positive outcomes, as well as serve as buffers against negative influences, such as illness or poverty, over which the family has little control.

The quality of the relationships between children and their caregivers is of principal importance to well-being across the life span. Parent–child interactions have been associated with a wide range of developmental outcomes, including self-confidence, academic achievement, psychological health, and conduct. In particular, parent–child interactions that are marked by high levels of parental support and behavioral control help children develop mastery and competence (Maccoby & Martin, 1983). Supportive behaviors are those that facilitate socialization through warmth, nurturance, responsiveness, and open communication. Controlling behaviors—including rule setting, negotiation, and consistent discipline—help establish guidance and flexibility within the power hierarchy of the family. By combining the dimensions of support and control along high and low extremes, parenting styles can be classified into four types: authoritative, authoritarian, indulgent, and neglecting (Baumrind, 1991; Maccoby & Martin, 1983). These four parenting types are depicted in Figure 11–1.

Authoritative families are characterized by emotional support, high standards, appropriate granting of autonomy, and clear communication (Darling & Steinberg, 1993). Authoritative parents monitor their children and set clear standards for conduct. Disciplinary methods are inductive (i.e., they explore the consequences of the child's actions on others) rather than punitive, and parental responses are consistent. Children are listened to, and they participate in family decision making. Goals for children in an authoritative family include social responsibility, self-regulation, and cooperation.

Authoritative parenting has been linked with a wide range of positive child outcomes, including social competence, psychological well-being, fewer conduct problems, and higher scholastic performance (e.g., Baumrind, 1991; Supple & Small, 2006). Systematic efforts to educate parents about effective parenting processes and authoritative parenting practices can help improve the quality of family life and parent–child relationships. A variety of forums can be used to implement the teaching of parenting skills, including community-based parent education programs and school-sponsored clinics for parents.

Authoritative parenting style
- *High in support* (accepting, responsive, child-centered)
- *High in control* (clear standards, high level of monitoring)
- Goals for child: social responsibility, self-regulation, cooperation

Authoritarian parenting style
- *Low in support* (low in acceptance and responsiveness, parent-centered)
- *High in control* (directive and demanding, high level of monitoring)
- Goals for child: obedience, achievement, orderly environments

Indulgent parenting style
- *High in support* (warm, overly accepting of child's behaviors and attitudes)
- *Low in control* (few rules, permissive, low level of monitoring)
- Goals for child: warm relationships, minimal confrontation or conflict in family

Neglecting parenting style
- *Low in support* (not responsive to child's needs, ignoring or indifferent)
- *Low in control* (little structure or monitoring of child's activities, uninvolved)
- Goals for child: minimal goals, if any. (This style is associated with the most negative outcomes for children, as compared to the other typologies.)

FIGURE 11–1 Four Parenting Styles
Source: Adapted from Baumrind, 1991; and Maccoby and Martin, 1983.

In addition to parenting styles and practices, several other family-related factors influence child adjustment. Family structure (e.g., divorced, single-parent, married), family size, socioeconomic status, the amount of time family members spend together, and issues such as neglect and abuse all influence adjustment in various ways. Clinical mental health counselors who work with children and adolescents need to be aware of these influences, help families build on strengths, and target areas in which improvement is needed.

SCHOOL INFLUENCES.   The unique characteristics of the school context give it special prominence in child and adolescent development. Through interactions with peers, teachers, and other adults in the school, young people make judgments about themselves, their capabilities, and their goals for the future. Consequently, experiences in school play a major role in the development of individual differences in children and adolescents.

Schools in which support, trust, respect, optimism, and intentionality are demonstrated foster the development of positive student attitudes and behaviors. In particular, supportive teachers can positively influence students' self-confidence and performance (Newsome, 1999). Also, schools that are orderly and organized, with consistent and fair enforcement of rules, are conducive to positive student behaviors, although excessive teacher control and discipline can be detrimental to adolescent adjustment and achievement (Eccles & Roeser, 2011).

Clinical mental health counselors need to be aware of the powerful influence the school context has on young people. This awareness enables them to work collaboratively with school counselors, teachers, and other school personnel to optimize child and adolescent development.

PEER INFLUENCES.   Relationships with peers—at home, at school, and in the community—become increasingly important as children grow older. Peer interaction plays a key role in helping children learn to take different perspectives and understand other points of view. **Peer acceptance**, which refers to being liked by other children, shapes the views children have of themselves as well as their views of others.

Whereas some children are well liked and make friends easily, others are rejected or neglected. Unfortunately, some children are the victims of frequent verbal and/or physical attacks by other children (i.e., bullying). Such victimization leads to a variety of adjustment difficulties, including depression, loneliness, and school avoidance. Counselors can intervene at various levels to assist children who are having difficulties with peers. Depending on the situation, it may be necessary to help children develop social skills or assertiveness skills. Individual and group counseling interventions can include coaching, modeling, reinforcing positive social skills, and teaching perspective taking. Clinical mental health counselors can intervene systemically by working collaboratively with schools to develop codes against bullying and by conducting parent education groups to help eliminate all forms of bullying.

During adolescence, young people begin spending more time with peers and less time with family members. Typically, friendships are formed with peers who have similar interests, values, and behaviors. Most often, peer group association positively influences well-being, as teenagers learn adaptive skills that benefit adjustment. In some cases, however, the peer group provides a negative context in which antisocial behaviors are the norm. For example, young people who were aggressive and rejected as children and who feel distanced from their families are likely to become involved with deviant peers and engage in antisocial behaviors (Berk, 2014). Difficult temperament, low intelligence, poor school performance, peer rejection in childhood, and involvement with antisocial peer groups are associated with juvenile delinquency, a widespread problem that accounts for a substantial proportion of criminal offenses committed in the United States.

NORMATIVE AND NONNORMATIVE LIFE EVENTS. Many of the developmental challenges young people face are expected: physical changes, school transitions, emerging sexuality, changes in cognitive functioning, and changes in family and peer relationships. Developmental transitions of this nature are considered **normative life events**; that is, they are anticipated generic challenges that everyone encounters. In some contexts, developmental challenges are compounded by **chronic stressors**, which are enduring aspects of the environment that involve deprivation or hardship. Poverty, physical disability, and family dysfunction are examples of chronic stressors that can exert taxing demands on families.

Whereas normative life events are expected, **nonnormative life events** are those unexpected, acute demands that may alter the course of development, either directly or transactionally (Compas, 1987). Nonnormative life events include parental divorce, death of a family member, onset of illness or disability, and job loss. **Catastrophic phenomena—** sudden, powerful events (e.g., natural disasters, accidents, and terrorism) that require major adaptive responses from the groups sharing the experience—also are considered nonnormative events. Nonnormative events are not always negative, however. Examples of positive nonnormative events include inheriting a large amount of money or being selected for a coveted position.

Some students, the gifted, have nonnormative lives. By definition, gifted individuals are not normal on some metric. This nonnormative aspect of their lives can manifest itself in unexpected responses to others or from others. The exceptional abilities of gifted individuals contribute to different experiences from other students, which may be academic, interpersonal, or intrapersonal. These unique experiences and characteristics of gifted individuals tend to revolve around four issues: (a) unhealthy perfectionism, (b) anxiety, (c) depression, and (d) suicidality (Cross & Cross, 2015). It is as important for counselors to attend to these students and their issues as it is to focus on others who are having more normative experiences.

Normative and nonnormative events occur in multiple contexts and have a wide range of effects on the people experiencing them. The frequency, intensity, and timing of the events can affect a youth's mental health, with outcomes moderated by subjective perceptions, parental and peer support, and coping skills. To understand young clients' developmental trajectories, counselors need to assess the normative and nonnormative life events these clients have experienced. Counselors can help children handle negative life events more effectively by implementing stress management interventions that are tailored to helping children use active, problem-focused coping strategies.

CULTURAL INFLUENCES. A key ecological factor that exerts a powerful influence on the development and adjustment of young people is the broader culture in which they live. Cultural beliefs, values, and institutions compose what Bronfenbrenner (1979, 1995) referred to as the macrosystem. On one level, children are influenced by the dominant culture of a society: its values, laws, customs, and resources. When children are members of one or more minority groups, they are affected not only by the belief system of the dominant culture but also by the values that guide the minority culture(s). The various sociocultural influences interact, and sometimes conflict, to shape a developing child's subjective worldview.

McClure and Teyber (2003) illustrate the effects cultural influences can have on the counseling process:

> An adolescent African-American male who is "paranoid" around authority figures is often accurately discerning a persecutory or hostile environment given his life experiences. A counselor who diagnoses him as paranoid (which frequently occurs) and focuses on helping him see "reality" (i.e., the *counselor's* subjective worldview) would quickly lose credibility. Similarly, encouraging a young adult from a traditional Asian family to emancipate and become more autonomous from her family may only engender increased distress. (pp. 7–8)

Competent counselors are aware of the array of cultural issues that influence child and adolescent development. They recognize the importance of evaluating which cultural aspects are relevant to a particular individual and plan interventions that build on cultural strengths.

COUNSELING CONSIDERATIONS

Working effectively with young people requires a special knowledge of child development, contextual influences, and child-related counseling procedures. Children's needs, wishes, behaviors, and ways of viewing the world differ significantly from those of adults. Indeed, interventions that are appropriate for adults may be ineffective or even detrimental when applied to children and adolescents (Sherwood-Hawes, 1993). Through all stages of the counseling process, counselors need to take into account universal developmental principles as well as the unique, subjective way in which each child views the world.

Building a Counseling Relationship

The key to any successful counseling experience is developing an effective working relationship based on mutual trust and acceptance. The most important first step is being willing to enter completely into a child's world, with no preconceptions, expectations, or agenda. All judgment needs to be suspended so that the counselor can remain open to what the child is sharing, either verbally or nonverbally. As the therapeutic relationship is being established, listening and observational skills are more important than questioning skills (Erdman & Lampe, 1996). By listening carefully to what young clients have to say, giving them undivided attention, and responding sensitively to feelings, reactions, and cultural cues, counselors can create bridges of trust and understanding.

ESTABLISHING RAPPORT. To build relationships successfully, counselors need to tailor their responses and interactions to fit the specific needs of each child, taking into account developmental experiences, sociocultural background, and reasons for referral (McClure & Teyber, 2003). With these considerations in mind, counselors can select from a variety of approaches to help establish rapport. When working with young children who have difficulty verbalizing, play and art media can be especially effective. With older children, age-appropriate games or activities can provide a nonthreatening introduction to the counseling process.

One of the factors that make building a relationship with children different from building a relationship with adults is that children often do not understand what counseling is. They may be confused about the nature and process of counseling, fearful of being in an unknown situation, and/or resistant to talking about issues with a stranger. Typically, children are brought to counseling by parents or by other significant adults in their lives, and it is these adults, not the children, who want change to occur. This is particularly true when children or adolescents are referred because of behavioral patterns that bother adults (Sommers-Flanagan & Sommers-Flanagan, 2007). The counselor's task is to find ways to involve the child in the counseling process, first by clarifying the counseling role.

CLARIFYING THE COUNSELING ROLE. During the initial session, counselors need to find ways to explain to the children what counseling is all about. Any delay in getting to the reason for counseling can cause undue anxiety for children. Many times, parents or caregivers are included in the initial sessions with children. When this is the case, it is helpful to clarify the counseling role with everyone involved. It is especially important to dissipate any misconceptions about the purpose of counseling, such as beliefs that counseling will "fix" the children. It also is wise to let parents know that things may get worse before they get better. Depending on a child's age, it may be helpful to meet with everyone together at the outset and then meet separately with the child and the caregiver.

EXPLAINING CONFIDENTIALITY. Issues related to confidentiality can create challenging legal and ethical dilemmas for counselors who work with minors (Lawrence & Kurpius, 2000). Counselors have a responsibility to protect information received through confidential counseling relationships with all clients, including children. However, this responsibility often conflicts with legal rights of parents or guardians, which include the right to determine the need for counseling, the right to access pertinent information about their children's treatment, and the right to control the release of information that results from counseling (Glosoff, 2001). It is important to clarify with parents and their children the conditions and limits of confidentiality before counseling begins. Ethical and legal guidelines related to confidentiality and other topics pertinent to counseling with minors are presented in Figure 11–2.

In many cases, it is in the child's best interest to involve the parents in the counseling process. Taylor and Adelman (2001) maintain that keeping information from parents can impede the counselor's efforts to help the child. They recommend orienting the parents to the counseling process, educating them about confidentiality with minors, and letting them know that any vital information that affects their child's well-being will be shared. If parents are oriented in this way, they are more likely to support the process and respect their child's right to privacy (Welfel, 2016).

The way counselors approach the issue of confidentiality with children depends on their ages. Young children typically do not have an understanding of confidentiality or the need for it (Remley & Herlihy, 2016). It is important to explain the concept in words a child can understand. Therefore, the counselor might say, "Most of the things you and I talk about in here are between you and me, unless you tell me that you are planning to hurt yourself or someone else. If you tell me something that I think your mom [dad, other caregiver] needs to know, you and I will talk about it first."

Adolescents often have a heightened concern about privacy and confidentiality in the counseling relationship (Remley & Herlihy, 2016). Clinicians who work with adolescents can help them understand confidentiality and its limits from the outset. It also is important for them to feel free to disclose their concerns in an atmosphere of trust. Balancing issues related to trust and minor consent laws can often be challenging.

It is not unusual for clinical mental health counselors to encounter dilemmas related to the requirements of confidentiality and counselors' responsibilities to parents or other caregivers. By keeping the lines of communication open and taking responsibility for

Professional Competence: ACA's (2014) *Code of Ethics* mandates that counselors practice only within the bounds of their competence, based on education, training, supervised practice, and appropriate experience (C.2.a). Knowledge and skills needed to work effectively with minor clients differ from those needed to work with adult clients. Counselors who work with children need to be trained in child development and child counseling theory, as well as have an understanding of child psychopathology.

Informed Consent: Informed consent is "the formal permission given by a client that signals the beginning of the legal contractual agreement that allows treatment to be initiated" (Lawrence & Kurpius, 2000, p. 133). Legally, minor clients cannot enter into contracts. The ACA Code (2014) states that when minors or other individuals cannot give voluntary informed consent, parents or guardians should be included in the counseling process (B.5). Ideally, if clients are minors, counselors should obtain signed informed *consent* from the parent(s) and *assent* from the minor client (Glosoff, 2001).

There are some instances in which minor clients can enter into treatment without parental consent, although the exceptions differ from state to state, depending on legal statutes. Typical exceptions include these:

- Mature or emancipated minors: A mature minor is usually over the age of 16 (in some states, 14) and is capable of understanding the nature and consequences of agreeing to a proposed treatment. An emancipated minor is a child under the age of 18 who lives separately from parents or guardians and manages his or her own financial affairs (American Bar Association, 1980). Being head of a household, employed, in the armed forces, or married may constitute an exception in which the adolescent can give informed consent (Welfel, 2016).
- In some states, parental informed consent may not be required when the minor is in treatment for drugs or narcotics, for sexually transmitted diseases, for pregnancy and birth control counseling, or when waiting for parental consent would endanger the minor client's life or health.

Confidentiality: Counselors have the *ethical* obligation to protect minor clients' privacy, but parents and guardians have the *legal* right to determine the need for treatment and to access pertinent information about their children's treatment. At times, ethical dilemmas arise in trying to balance legal requirements and ethical responsibilities. Because state laws differ, counselors need to be familiar with the legal requirements of the states in which they practice. Counselors can motivate minor clients to disclose on their own when such disclosures would be beneficial and can involve the parents in creating mutually agreed on guidelines for disclosure (Lawrence & Kurpius, 2000).

Counselors need to discuss confidentiality and its limits with parents and children before counseling begins. Minor clients need to know that if they make a threat to hurt themselves or others, counselors will be required to breach confidentiality. In some instances, duty to warn also applies to threats to destroy property (e.g., *Peck v. Counseling Service of Addison County*, 1985).

Reporting Abuse: All states have statutes requiring counselors and other professionals to report suspected child abuse and neglect (Kemp, 1998). Counselors are advised to become familiar with the wording of the statutes for their particular states. In general, statutes require counselors to report if they have reason to believe that (a) a child is currently being abused or neglected or (b) the child has been abused or neglected in the past. Requirements for reporting past abuse differ when the child is no longer in danger. Reporters are protected from liability as long as reports are made in good faith. When making the decision to report, it may be helpful to consult with professional colleagues or to gain legal advice. As with other counseling decisions, it is important to document the report and the reasons for making it.

FIGURE 11–2   Legal and Ethical Issues Related to Counseling Minors
Source: From Glosoff, 2001; Lawrence and Kurpius, 2000; and Remley and Herlihy, 2016.

knowing state and federal law, it may be possible to circumvent potential problems before they arise (Welfel, 2016). Some helpful references regarding minors' rights include the following (cited in Henderson & Thompson, 2016):

- *State Minor Consent Laws: A Summary* (English, Bass, Boyle, & Eshragh, 2010)—Provides a state-by-state description of the legal status of minors.
- Guttmacher Institute (www.guttmacher.org)—Publishes policy briefs and summaries of laws that pertain to young people.
- American Bar Association (www.abanet.org/public.html)—Provides information about state laws and minors.
- Books on ethical and legal issues in counseling and psychotherapy (e.g., Barnett & Johnson, 2015; Remley & Herlihy, 2016; Welfel, 2016; Wheeler & Bertram, 2015).

Assessment and Evaluation

Assessment is an integral part of the counseling process. Assessment is an ongoing process in which counselors gather information about clients from several different sources and then use that information to make decisions about treatment planning. Assessment also provides a way to evaluate counseling progress and outcomes. Assessment methods, which can be formal or informal, help counselors understand children's current problems or concerns within the context of their unique developmental histories.

INTERVIEWS.   Initial assessment typically begins with an intake that involves the child and the child's parents or guardians. The amount of time spent with everyone together versus time spent with each individual depends on the age of the child, the nature of the problem, family dynamics, agency policy, and the particular work setting (e.g., an inpatient setting will differ from a private practice setting). During the intake session, the types of rapport-building activities described earlier can be used to gather important information about the child. In many agencies, intake forms are available for use with children and families.

Early and ongoing assessment is necessary for accurate case conceptualization and effective intervention planning. Orton (1997) suggests conducting a complete developmental assessment that provides the counselor with the following information:

- *The specific concerns that brought the child to counseling.*   The manifestation, intensity, frequency, and duration of the concerns should be explored. In what settings or around which individuals are the concerns evidenced? Expression, manifestation, and course of a disorder in children may be quite different from that in adults (U.S. Department of Health and Human Services, 2016). Certain behaviors may be normal at one age but represent a problem at another age (e.g., temper tantrums exhibited by a 3-year-old child versus tantrums exhibited by a 6-year-old). Assessment, diagnosis, and treatment planning need to occur within the context of the child's overall development.
- *Physical, cognitive, emotional, and social development.*   Evaluating each of these areas of development is essential to conducting a thorough assessment. When possible, the counselor will want to obtain information about the child's medical history, perinatal history, motor development, cognitive functioning, and ability to express and regulate emotions. The counselor also will want to gather information about socioeconomic and sociocultural factors that have affected development. To facilitate information gathering,

the counselor can ask parents or guardians to complete an information form prior to or immediately following the initial counseling session (Orton, 1997). The counselor can then use the form—which includes questions about the child's physical, cognitive, emotional, and social development—to guide exploration of any areas that may be contributing to the problem.

- *Relationships with parents, siblings, and peers.* Understanding the nature and quality of relationships the child has with family members and peers is a key component of child assessment. Topics to be addressed include the child's living arrangements, home responsibilities, methods of discipline used, the child's response to discipline, typical family activities, and a "typical day." Interview questions or qualitative assessment methods, such as a genogram or a **kinetic family drawing** (i.e., a picture of everyone in the family doing something), can provide rich information about relationships, as can ongoing observation of interactions as the counselor works with the child and the family.

- *School experiences, including academics, attendance, and attitude.* Academic and social successes or failures play an important part in children's overall development. Children who experience repeated failures often have poor self-esteem and may engage in disruptive behaviors as a way of compensating. Also, school failure may signify a learning disorder that typically requires formal testing for diagnosis. Because of the pervasive effect school has on children's lives, it is advisable to ask parents to sign a consent form for release of information so that the school can be contacted early in the counseling process.

- *Strengths, talents, and support system.* Implementing a strengths-based approach to assessment can help take the focus off the problem so that it is possible to begin moving toward solutions. Creative activities, checklists, and various qualitative assessment methods provide useful tools for evaluating strengths and supports. After learning about children's special skills and interests, counselors can incorporate them into treatment planning. For example, if a child enjoys art, the counselor can select expressive art interventions to facilitate the change process.

INFORMAL AND FORMAL ASSESSMENT. Informal assessment includes direct observation and qualitative assessment methods. **Qualitative assessment** emphasizes holistic procedures that typically are not standardized and do not produce quantitative raw scores. A variety of qualitative assessment methods can be used with children and adolescents, including informal checklists, unfinished sentences, decision-making dilemmas, writing activities, games, expressive arts, storytelling, role-play activities, and play therapy strategies (Gladding, 2016a; Vernon, 2009). Informal assessment procedures of this nature can reveal patterns of thought and behavior relevant to concerns and issues. Such methods are especially helpful with young children, who may not know exactly what is bothering them or may lack the words to express their concerns verbally.

Formal assessment instruments that have been standardized and have sound psychometric properties provide a way for counselors to gain a somewhat more objective view of children's behaviors or attributes than informal methods provide. Whereas some instruments are designed to assess specific disorders—for example, the Children's Depression Inventory (Kovacs, 1992)—others assess a full range of behavioral and emotional symptoms and disorders—for example, Achenbach System of Empirically Based Assessment. A number of questionnaires, scales, and checklists designed to assess attributes, behaviors, interests, and emotional states of children and adolescents have been published in recent years. The *Mental Measurements Yearbook*, published by the Buros Institute, provides descriptions and reviews of a wide range of published instruments. Carefully selected formal assessment tools can supplement and enhance the information counselors gather through less formal methods of assessment.

By appraising children's therapeutic needs through interviews, informal assessment, and formal assessment, counselors gain a better understanding of the children's development and concerns. This understanding can then be used to set goals, design and implement interventions, and evaluate the counseling process. As with adults, the information gained through assessment sometimes leads to a diagnosis, using an established diagnostic classification system such as the most current edition of the *DSM*. However, the criteria for diagnosing many mental disorders in children are derived from adult criteria, and less research has been conducted on children to verify their validity. Consequently, diagnosing childhood mental disorders is a challenging task and requires training and supervision.

Designing and Implementing a Treatment Plan

Several factors affect treatment planning for child and adolescent clients. The age and characteristics of the child; the nature of the presenting issue; and the counselor's theoretical approach, past training, and current skills all influence the selection of interventions. Competent counselors take each of these factors into consideration. If they realize that the presenting issues are beyond their competence, they take steps to match the children with counselors who are prepared to work with those issues.

INTENTIONALITY AND FLEXIBILITY.   Counselors who work with children and adolescents need to be intentional and flexible as they conceptualize cases and design interventions. Being intentional refers to taking steps to set counseling goals collaboratively with the children and, in many cases, the children's parents or caregivers. Being flexible refers to the counselors' ability to adapt strategies to meet the specific needs of the children in their contexts. No single counseling approach is best for all children or all problems. Counselors who are familiar with a wide array of interventions and child-based counseling strategies can personalize a treatment plan so that the possibility of a positive outcome is enhanced. Also, to work effectively with children (as well as with adults), counselors need to be cognizant of ethnicity, gender, socioeconomic status, and other areas of diversity and respond accordingly.

One way counselors can intentionally plan interventions is by asking specific questions related to the following areas (Vernon & Clemente, 2004):

- *Vision:*   What could be different? How could things be better? What would be ideal?
- *Goal setting:*   What is going well? What needs to be worked on?
- *Analysis:*   What is enabling or interfering with achieving these goals? What is getting in the way of solving the problem?
- *Objective:*   What specifically does the child want to change?
- *Exploration of interventions:*   What has already been tried, and how did it work? Who else will be involved in the counseling process? What types of activities does the child respond to best? What has research shown to be the most effective interventions for this type of concern?

SELECTING INTERVENTIONS.   Using information gathered through assessment and goal setting, counselors can begin making decisions about which interventions to implement. No one theoretical approach to counseling children and adolescents has been found to be generally more effective than another (Sexton, Whiston, Bleuer, & Walz, 1997). Instead, a systematic, eclectic approach enables counselors to work constructively with the many different needs and concerns that bring young people to counseling.

Although more outcome-based research has been conducted with adults than with children, a body of information is beginning to accumulate matching efficacious interventions with specific concerns and needs. Consequently, clinical mental health counselors need to be familiar with current outcome research on effective treatment when selecting interventions. For example, an empirically supported approach to providing treatment for children with ADHD is a multimodal, multisystemic approach that involves parent training, counseling, and school interventions (Edwards, 2002). For adolescents with conduct disorder, a promising treatment is multisystemic therapy (MST), an intensive home- and family-focused treatment (U.S. Department of Health and Human Services, 2016). MST integrates empirically based treatment approaches such as cognitive skills training into an ecological framework that addresses the family, peer, school, and neighborhood contexts (Schoenwald, Brown, & Henggeler, 2000). Other examples of efficacious treatments include play or art therapy for sexually abused children and cognitive–behavioral approaches for children who are depressed or anxious. It is the counselors' responsibility to keep up with current research to provide the best possible care for their young clients.

Creative Interventions

Counseling young people effectively often requires a departure from traditional talk therapy. In many cases, an integrative approach that uses a variety of techniques—including art, music, clay, puppetry, storytelling, drama, bibliotherapy, sand play, and other forms of directive and nondirective play therapy—can guide the counseling process and promote healing and growth. Counselors who work with children are encouraged to refer to the many excellent resources that are available to enhance their expertise in using play and expressive arts in counseling (Gladding, 2016a) (see Box 11–2).

BOX 11–2 Using Expressive Arts in Counseling Young People

Expressive arts have been a part of my counseling since I began working as a counselor. I have worked with different ages and in different settings, and I have found that expressive arts easily transfer everywhere. My clients quickly come to understand that I may ask them to draw, paint, string beads, tell stories, act things out, or play, in addition to traditional talking. I may initially encounter surprise, disbelief, reluctance, or fear, but I have yet to be turned down.

What I have found by using creative arts is that my clients relax, have a sense of playfulness, and open up more quickly. I have used creative arts to draw out depressed clients who are locked up in their despair; gain trust with a mistrustful child; help a family learn to positively interact with one another; give an adolescent a chance to express herself in new ways; calm an anxious parent; and join a group together. The possibilities are only as limited as my mind. When I encounter my own limitations, I ask my clients for options. They often come up with the most creative ideas.

There are also personal advantages for me in using expressive arts as a counselor. I find my sessions to be exciting and packed with energy. I look forward to helping people find new ways to express themselves. As a counselor, I feel it is important to be myself. Being creative is a natural part of who I am. Using expressive arts in counseling is a perfect match for me.

Elizabeth Vaughan, MA Ed, LPC

CONCERNS AFFECTING CHILDREN AND ADOLESCENTS

Clinical mental health counselors who work with children and adolescents are likely to see a wide range of presenting problems, including mood disorders, anxiety disorders, ADHD, aggressive or antisocial behaviors, learning disorders, and eating disorders. They also are likely to work with young people coping with family disruption, poverty, abuse, violence, unemployment, and grief. In this section, an overview of three common disorders that may be experienced by young people—depression, eating disorders, and ADHD—is provided. To work effectively with young clients, counselors need to consult resources that deal specifically with children's mental health issues and participate in additional educational experiences, training, and supervision.

Depression

Depression is a mood disorder that can affect thoughts, feelings, behaviors, and overall health. It can affect relationships, academic performance, sleep, appetite, self-esteem, and thought processes. A depressed child may pretend to be sick, refuse to go to school, become isolated, cling to caretakers, or worry that a caretaker may die. Depressed adolescents may exhibit excessive anger, frustration, moodiness, and/or destructive behaviors. The onset of major depressive disorders typically is between the ages of 13 and 19, with depression being one of the most common psychological problems of adolescence (Costello, Erkanli, & Angold, 2006). Unless treated, early onset of depression can predict more severe and negative symptoms later in life. Untreated mood disorders also increase the risk of suicide (Sburlati, Lyneham, Mufson, & Schniering, 2012). The Child Welfare League of America (2008) reports that suicide is the third leading cause of death for 15- to 24-year-olds and the sixth leading cause of death for 5- to 14-year-olds. Suicide attempts are even more common.

MANIFESTATION OF DEPRESSION.   Levels of depression in young people can vary, ranging from depressed mood, which is not a clinical disorder, to more severe diagnosable mood disorders. Approximately one-third of adolescents experience depressed mood for short or extended periods of time. Depressed mood is characterized by negative emotions, which may include sadness, anxiety, guilt, disgust, anger, and fear.

For a clinical diagnosis of depression, a young person must exhibit a specific collection of symptoms that are of a specified intensity and duration and that meet the diagnostic criteria of a standardized classification system, such as the *DSM-5* (APA, 2013). Symptoms must be serious enough to interfere with a young person's level of functioning. Depressive disorders can include major depressive disorder, bipolar disorder, dysthymic disorder, cyclothymic disorder, and adjustment disorder with depressed mood (or mixed anxiety and depressed mood). Mood disorders due to medical conditions or substance abuse can also be diagnosed as depressive disorders.

Diagnosing depression in young people may be more challenging than in adults because young people have more difficulty articulating their feelings and often mask the symptoms. Instead, their behavior may be more indicative of depression. Depressed children and adolescents may withdraw or display anxiety symptoms, acting out or appearing irritable, or they may have more somatic complaints than adults do. A list of common signs and symptoms of depression in young people is presented in Figure 11–3.

Some two-thirds of children and adolescents with clinical depression also have another clinical disorder (U.S. Department of Health and Human Services, 2016). The most commonly

- Feeling sad, empty, or hopeless
- Increased emotional sensitivity
- Lack of interest or ability to engage in pleasurable activities
- Decreased energy level
- Physical complaints (e.g., headaches, stomachaches, tiredness)
- Frequent absences from school (or poor performance)
- Outbursts (e.g., shouting, complaining, crying)
- Being bored
- Substance abuse
- Fear of death
- Suicidal ideation
- Sleep/appetite disturbances
- Reduced ability to think clearly and make decisions
- Increased irritability, anger, or restlessness
- Failure to make expected weight gains
- Reckless behavior
- Difficulty with relationships

FIGURE 11–3   Signs and Symptoms of Depression in Children and Adolescents
Source: "Depression in Children and Adolescents," National Institute of Mental Health, 2011. Retrieved from www.nimh.nih.gov/health/publications/depression-in-children-and-adolescents/index.shtml.

associated disorders include anxiety disorders, disruptive disorders, eating disorders, substance abuse, and personality disorders. When a young person has more than one disorder, depression is more likely to begin after the onset of the other disorder, with the exception of substance abuse. Counselors will want to be alert to the possibility of dual or multiple diagnoses and be prepared to plan interventions accordingly.

ETIOLOGY AND RISK FACTORS. Several factors are associated with the **etiology** (i.e., causes) of depression, including biological, cognitive, and environmental variables. Biological explanations focus on the role of genetics and biochemical factors associated with depression. It is theorized that multiple gene variants, rather than a single gene, act in conjunction with environmental factors and developmental events to make a person more likely to experience depressive symptoms (NIMH, 2011a). Various neurotransmitters—including serotonin, norepinephrine, and dopamine—are associated with depression. These neurotransmitters function within structures of the brain that regulate emotions, reactions to stress, and various physical drives (e.g., sleep, appetite, and sexuality).

Cognitive theory can help clinicians conceptualize depression because of the way it links thoughts, emotions, and behaviors. In other words, emotions and moods are affected by people's interpretations of events, rather than the events themselves. Because these interpretations can influence how young people view themselves and the world around them, they can be affected by maladaptive information processing, such as **negative attributions** (e.g., when children believe they are helpless to influence events in their lives) and **cognitive distortions** (e.g., minimizing positive accomplishments and maximizing negative events). These inaccurate interpretations of events can lead to symptoms of depression.

Other explanations of depression emphasize the role played by stressful life events. Youth who experience numerous stressors may be more likely to experience depression than those who do not. Stressors can be categorized as normative life events (i.e., expected changes, such as school entry and puberty), nonnormative events (e.g., divorce, abuse, moving away), and daily hassles (e.g., conflict with friends, excessive schoolwork). Exposure to stress triggers several physical, emotional, and cognitive changes in the body, and long-term exposure can lead to physical and psychosocial difficulties, including depression (Sharrer & Ryan-Wenger, 2002). The manner in which stress is experienced varies from child to child. Preventive strategies, such as teaching constructive coping skills, can help children manage stress more effectively.

A number of other factors have been linked with depression, including family conflict, the emotional unavailability of parents, poor peer relationships, being considered "different," loss of a loved one, breakup of a relationship, chronic illness, and abuse. A thorough developmental assessment can alert counselors to the presence of conditions that might make children more vulnerable to depression and thus can inform treatment planning.

TREATMENT STRATEGIES. Because of the increased attention given to child and adolescent depression during the past three decades, treatments for this serious condition are getting more effective. Counselors who work with depressed young people typically involve both the individual and the family (McWhirter & Burrow, 2001). In some settings, counselors conduct group interventions, which can be especially effective with older children and adolescents.

Research has demonstrated the efficacy of certain approaches, especially cognitive–behavioral therapy (CBT), in alleviating depressive symptoms in young people (Gledhill & Hodes, 2011). The goal of CBT is to help clients develop cognitive structures that will positively influence their future experiences (Kendall, 2012). The cognitive component of CBT helps individuals identify and change negative, pessimistic thinking, biases, and attributions. Examples of cognitive-based strategies include the following:

1. Recognizing the connections among thoughts, feelings, and behaviors
2. Monitoring automatic negative thoughts
3. Examining evidence that refutes distorted automatic cognitions
4. Substituting more realistic interpretations for distorted cognitions
5. Regulating emotions and controlling impulses (McWhirter & Burrow, 2001, pp. 201–202)

The behavioral component, important to the process, focuses on increasing positive behavior patterns and improving social skills. Other behavioral strategies include relaxation training, social skills training, and behavioral rehearsal.

CASE STUDY: Nick's Group for Depressed Kids

Nick was a counselor in a large public school. His course work in clinical mental health had taught him a lot about depression and he wanted to help the kids in his school who were depressed get better. Thus, he decided to run a group for depressives. He reserved a quiet room away from foot traffic, talked with teachers about a good time to hold the group, and prepared materials announcing the beginning of the group. When the day came for the group to begin, Nick was surprised no one showed up. What do you think Nick could have done that would have attracted kids to his group? What do you think of conducting such a group with children?

Another type of counseling, **interpersonal therapy for adolescents (IPT-A)**, was adapted from IPT for adults (Mufson, Moreau, Weissman, & Klerman, 1993; Sburlati et al., 2012).

Depression is viewed as a conflict taking place in the context of interpersonal relationships. The two primary goals of IPT are to reduce depressive symptoms and to improve disturbed relationships that may contribute to depression. In treatment, five potential areas of concern are addressed: grief, interpersonal role disputes, role transitions, deficits in interpersonal skills, and single-parent families.

FAMILY INTERVENTIONS.   Concurrent family consultation or family counseling is nearly always indicated when working with depressed children and adolescents (McWhirter & Burrow, 2001). Frequently, counselors need to consult with parents to educate them about depression and help them learn ways to encourage their children's use of new skills (Stark et al., 2006). Moreover, family factors such as inconsistent parenting, family conflict, and divorce may contribute to the onset of depression (Gledhill & Hodes, 2011). Family interventions are designed to modify negative interactions and increase cohesion. Significant goals may include developing communication skills, enhancing family interactions, and sharing information about specific issues.

ANTIDEPRESSANT MEDICATIONS.   Certain antidepressant medications—usually selective serotonin reuptake inhibitors (SSRIs)—may benefit children and adolescents with depression (Gledhill & Hodes, 2011). However, our knowledge of the ways antidepressants affect young people, as compared to adults, is limited. The NIMH published research, the Treatment of Adolescents with Depression Study (TADS), in *The Archives of General Psychiatry*. In this study (March et al., 2007), a combination of psychotherapy and antidepressant medication appeared to be the most effective treatment for adolescents with major depressive disorder. However, because some studies have suggested that SSRIs and other antidepressants may have adverse effects on young people, in particular an increased risk of suicidal thinking, in 2004 the Food and Drug Administration (FDA) adopted a **black box warning label** on antidepressant medications. This label emphasizes that children, adolescents, and young adults (up through age 24) taking antidepressants should be closely monitored for adverse side effects of the medication, including suicidal ideation.

Early identification and treatment of depression can help alleviate symptoms and put young people on a healthy developmental trajectory. Through individual, group, and family counseling, clinical mental health counselors can help depressed youth address depressive symptoms and meet the challenges of development in ways that provide positive mental health.

Eating Disorders

Eating disorders often appear for the first time in pre- or early adolescence or during the transition to young adulthood, although they may develop during childhood or later life (NIMH, 2011b). Eating disorders involve serious disturbances in eating behaviors (e.g., unhealthy reduction of body weight or extreme overeating), as well as feelings of distress or excessive concern about body shape or weight. Girls and young women tend to exhibit eating problems at a much higher frequency than do boys or young men, although the prevalence rate in males is increasing. Although eating disorders have been more frequently associated with young, affluent, White females, it appears that disorders also exist among various ethnic and cultural minority groups (Kalodner & Van Lone, 2001). Counselors need to be aware of early warning signs in all populations so that preventive interventions can be implemented when necessary.

TYPES OF EATING DISORDERS. There are several types of feeding and eating disorders in the *DSM-5*, but the three most prevalent are anorexia nervosa, bulimia nervosa, and binge-eating disorder.

Individuals with **anorexia nervosa** weigh less than 85% of what is considered normal for their age and height (APA, 2013). They have a resistance to maintaining minimally normal weight, an intense fear of gaining weight or becoming fat, and a distorted view of their own bodies and weight. Youth with anorexia often stop (or fail to start) menstruating. Unusual eating habits develop, such as avoiding food, picking out only a few foods and eating them in small quantities, or weighing food servings. Whereas some young people with anorexia severely restrict eating (i.e., **restricting type**), others engage in compulsive exercise or purge by means of vomiting or use of laxatives (i.e., **binge-eating/purging type**). Youth with anorexia tend to deny that they have a problem, making treatment difficult.

Bulimia nervosa is characterized by recurrent episodes of binge eating, typically twice a week or more, followed by attempts at compensating by purging or exercising (APA, 2013). **Binge eating** is defined by excessive, rapid overeating, often to the point of becoming uncomfortably full. An episode of binge eating is usually accompanied by a sense of lack of control, as well as by feelings of disgust, depression, and guilt. Subsequently, the individual engages in activities to compensate for overeating: vomiting or laxative use for the **purging type** of bulimia and excessive exercise or fasting for the **nonpurging type**. Youth with bulimia do not meet the severe underweight criterion associated with anorexia; indeed, they may appear to be within the normal weight range for their age and height. However, they are dissatisfied with their bodies and desire to lose weight or fear gaining weight.

Binge-eating disorder is characterized by recurrent binge-eating episodes with no purging, excessive exercise, or fasting. Consequently, young people with this disorder may be overweight or obese. They also are likely to experience guilt, shame, and distress about their binge eating (NIMH, 2011b).

Youth with eating disorders tend to be high achieving and sensitive to rejection. Eating disorders often coexist with other disorders, including depression, substance abuse, and anxiety disorders. Eating disorders are considered medical illnesses with complex psychological and biological causes. To make sure that these issues are addressed in treatment, clinicians need to conduct a thorough biopsychosocial assessment.

A number of physical complications are associated with eating disorders. In anorexia, the physical problems are related to malnutrition and starvation. In the most severe cases, major organ systems in the body are affected. The mortality rate associated with anorexia is around 5% per decade with death resulting "from medical complications rather than suicide" (Fishman, 2016, p. 25). In bulimia, the medical complications are due to vomiting or the use of laxatives or diuretics and can include dental problems, esophageal inflammation, gastrointestinal problems, and metabolic imbalances (NIMH, 2011b). With binge eating, individuals lose control over their eating. However, because young people diagnosed with binge-eating disorder do not purge, exercise excessively, or fast, they tend to be overweight or obese. They often have low self-esteem and may be at higher risk for developing cardiovascular disease and high blood pressure.

ETIOLOGY AND RISK FACTORS. An interplay of biological, psychological, and sociocultural factors are thought to contribute to the development of disordered eating. Anorexia often arises during the transition to adolescence, when the chief developmental task is identity formation. Peer pressure, puberty, self-esteem issues, and societal messages that glorify thinness may all coalesce to trigger problematic eating patterns. Some of the factors that appear to be linked to eating disorders include media promotion of thinness as healthy and a sign of success, perfectionism, highly competitive environments (e.g., dance, gymnastics) that stress body thinness, a loss in personal relationships (e.g., family breakups or death), low sense of self-esteem, and a heightened concern for appearance and body shape (Manley, Rickson, & Standeven, 2000). Overall, eating disorders often reflect struggles with unmet needs, including the need to be loved, cared for, and respected, and disordered eating becomes a means of coping with feelings that are painful (McClure & Teyber, 2003).

TREATMENT STRATEGIES.   When eating disorders are treated early, positive outcomes are more likely. A comprehensive treatment plan is required that involves medical care and monitoring, counseling, nutritional consultation, and, at times, medication management. In some cases, when body weight is dangerously low, hospitalization is required. Treatment involves a team process, with the counselor working closely with the young person's physician and nutritionist. The most effective treatment for anorexia nervosa is structural family therapy (SFT) where parents (or parental figures of a child) are charged with feeding their anorexic teenager together. This parsimonious intervention quickly addresses "the ubiquitous parental split (central to maintaining AN)" while successfully getting a teen to eat again (Reichenberg & Seligman, 2016, p. 25).

To successfully treat anorexia, NIMH recommends three phases:

1. Restoring the person to a healthy weight
2. Treating psychological issues related to the eating disorder
3. Reducing or eliminating thoughts and behaviors that lead to disordered eating, and then preventing relapse

For bulimia, the primary treatment goal is to reduce or eliminate binge eating and purging behaviors. Nutritional counseling and psychotherapy can be used to help the young person develop healthier patterns of thinking, feeling, and behaving. The counselor works collaboratively with the client to establish a pattern of regular meals that are not followed by binging, improve attitudes related to the eating disorder, encourage healthy but not excessive exercise, and alleviate co-occurring conditions such as mood or anxiety disorders. Cognitive–behavioral approaches, including group counseling, and interpersonal psychotherapy are usually effective in helping young people with bulimia. At times, medication may be prescribed.

Interventions for binge-eating disorder are similar to those used to treat bulimia. Cognitive–behavioral therapy that is tailored to the individual can be effective, and antidepressants are sometimes prescribed to reduce binge-eating episodes and lessen depression (NIMH, 2011b).

Attention-Deficit/Hyperactivity Disorder

Attention-deficit/hyperactivity disorder (ADHD), the most common neurobehavioral disorder of childhood, can influence children's emotional, behavioral, and social adjustment. To be diagnosed with ADHD, symptoms of inattention, impulsivity, and hyperactivity must appear prior to age 12 (APA, 2013). Boys are twice as likely as girls to be diagnosed with ADHD.

The *DSM-5* (APA, 2013) identifies three types of ADHD: **predominantly inattentive type**, **predominantly hyperactive–impulsive type**, or a **combined type**. The two symptom clusters used to diagnose ADHD are the *inattention cluster* and the *hyperactivity–impulsivity cluster*. A child must exhibit at least six of the nine behaviors in the cluster to be considered significantly inattentive or hyperactive. Children with the combined subtype of ADHD, which is the most common presentation, exhibit six or more symptoms in both categories.

Children with ADHD are thought to have an underdeveloped inhibition of behavior, thus making it a disorder of impulse control (Barkley, 1997, 2015). They typically have difficulty staying on task for more than a few minutes, are disorganized, and often ignore social rules. Children who have the inattentive type of ADHD have difficulty focusing (e.g., listening, following directions) and sustaining attention (e.g., staying on task, completing assignments). They frequently lose things and are forgetful. Children who have the hyperactive–impulsive type may act as though they are always on the go. They have difficulty sitting still and taking turns. Their social skills tend to be impaired, as evidenced by excessive talking, interrupting, and blurting out answers in class (McClure & Teyber, 2003).

ADHD can create numerous difficulties for children, their families, and their teachers. Because of impaired social skills and lack of behavioral control, children with ADHD may experience peer rejection, academic difficulties, and negative family interactions. Careful assessment is needed to ensure that counselors "look beyond the hallmark symptoms of the disorder and consider interventions that address comorbid problems as well" (Nigg & Rappley, 2001, pp. 183–184).

ETIOLOGY AND RISK FACTORS.   There is no conclusive proof of what causes ADHD. Some of the causal factors attributed to the development of ADHD include neurological factors, genetic factors, pre- and postnatal factors, and toxic influences (Brown, 2000; NIMH, 2016a). In particular, physical differences in brain structure and brain chemistry appear to play roles in the myriad symptoms associated with ADHD (Lyoo et al., 1996). Family factors also have been attributed to the development of ADHD; however, stressful home life does not cause ADHD. Instead, the disruptions brought about in a family as a result of the expression of ADHD symptoms can cause family stress and disorganization, which can then exacerbate preexisting symptoms.

TREATMENT STRATEGIES.   A multimodal, multicomponent approach to treatment is recommended for children with ADHD (e.g., Brown, 2000; NIMH, 2016a). Prior to treatment, a comprehensive assessment is conducted that includes a developmental history, interviews with the child and significant adults, child observation, and a medical examination by the child's physician. Typically, behavior rating scales such as the Conners–3 (Conners, 2008) or the Behavior Assessment System for Children–2 (BASC–2; Reynolds & Kamphaus, 2004) are used with parents and teachers to supplement information gathered during clinical interviews. If the assessment indicates that the child has ADHD, multimodal interventions that address the child, the family, and the environment are suggested. To develop a comprehensive treatment program, the following areas should be considered:

- Behavioral interventions in the family that include parent and child education about ADHD, parent training for behavior management, and ancillary family counseling when necessary are essential to treatment (Nigg & Rappley, 2001). Helping families develop predictable daily routines, organized households, and firm but affectionate discipline can improve family functioning. Barkley (2015) developed a comprehensive training program for parents that can be especially helpful.

- Individual and group counseling can provide a setting in which children feel understood and where issues of self-esteem and social relationships can be addressed. In particular, *cognitive–behavioral self-regulation approaches* to help children control their behavior and *social-skills training* to help children learn to take turns, follow rules, and develop hobbies or sports activities can be helpful (McClure & Teyber, 2003).
- Medication can be particularly effective in addressing the core symptoms of ADHD, although it is a controversial intervention for some educational and mental health professionals. The medications that appear to be most effective are stimulant medications. Not all children with ADHD need medication, and the decision to use it depends on several factors. Physicians who prescribe medication follow up with the child to determine whether the medication is working and to monitor potential side effects (NIMH, 2016a).
- School interventions are often instigated by clinical counselors as they work with teachers and school counselors to coordinate a child's treatment plan (Edwards, 2002). Counselors can consult with teachers about behavior management and academic interventions. Pfiffner and Barkley (1998) have suggested a number of classroom interventions that can help children with ADHD experience school success.
- Intensive summer camp programs may benefit children with ADHD (Edwards, 2002). Such programs include sports-skill training, behavior management interventions, and opportunities for positive peer interactions.

As with any disorder, training is needed for counselors to work effectively with children who have ADHD and with their families. With training, clinical mental health counselors can coordinate multimodal, multicomponent treatment approaches that include parent management training, counseling, school interventions, and medication.

CASE STUDY: Ellen and the Active First Graders

Ellen had taught first grade for three years and had a good experience with her children. This year was different though. She had three boys in her class who were out of their seats constantly and disturbing other children. She was not sure what to do so she asked the counselor in the school to come observe. He did and the disruptive behavior never materialized while he was in the room. When he left, the boys ran wild once more. Ellen was frustrated and talked to the counselor about the situation. He came again and the disruptive behavior failed to materialize until he left. Instead of having the counselor come a third time, Ellen thought there might be something she could do. If you were Ellen what would you do? Would you consult with the counselor about your plans?

Specific Issues of Concern

Young people in today's society are faced with myriad issues that can affect development and adjustment. Child maltreatment, drug and alcohol abuse, cyberbullying, changing family situations, life-threatening illnesses, trauma, and the death of loved ones are just some of the many concerns that may affect children and precipitate a need for counseling. Divorce, grief and loss, maltreatment, and cyberbullying will be examined here.

CHILDREN OF DIVORCE. Postdivorce family relationships are among the most common issues seen by counselors who work with young people (McClure & Teyber, 2003). Nearly half of all first marriages end in divorce, a statistic that has remained stable for several years (Henderson & Thompson, 2016). Research indicates that the children involved are often confronted with a wide range of adjustment challenges. Many studies document negative consequences for children whose parents divorce, particularly in regard to psychological adjustment, academic achievement, and behavior problems (e.g., Hetherington, 2006; Wallerstein, 2008). However, there is a marked variability in children's responses to divorce, with some children adjusting well and even showing improved behavior after the breakup, particularly if there has been a lot of conflict in the home.

Some of the factors that influence young people's responses to divorce include their developmental level at the time of the separation, social support systems, individual resilience and coping styles, the level of parental conflict prior to and during the divorce, parenting quality after the divorce, and the degree of economic hardship experienced. There also may be gender differences in responses, with some studies indicating that boys appear to experience greater adjustment difficulties (e.g., Morrison & Cherlin, 1995; Wallerstein, 2008).

Although responses vary, the initial experience of family disruption is painful for most children. Their responses to the experience tend to differ based on their developmental level. Preschoolers may feel frightened and insecure, experience nightmares, and regress to more infantile behaviors. Children between the ages of 6 and 8 may experience pervasive sadness, view the divorce as their fault, feel rejected, fear abandonment, and hold unrealistic hopes for reconciliation. Older children are more likely to feel anger and anxiety, develop psychosomatic symptoms, blame one parent or the other, and engage in troublesome behavior. Responses vary even more in adolescents than in younger children. Some adolescents feel betrayed, disengage from the family, and become depressed. Others show a positive developmental spurt and demonstrate maturity, compassion, and helpfulness toward their parents and younger siblings (McClure & Teyber, 2003).

It is important for counselors and parents to remember that adjusting to divorce takes time and requires continued patience and reassurance. During the adjustment period, children may benefit from individual or group counseling. Counselors can help children with the adjustment process by giving them opportunities to express their feelings and concerns. They also can assist children as they work through the following psychological tasks (Henderson & Thompson, 2016; Wallerstein & Blakeslee, 2003):

- Acknowledging the reality of the marital breakup
- Disengaging from parental conflict and distress and resuming typical activities
- Resolving the loss of what used to be
- Resolving anger and self-blame
- Accepting the permanence of the divorce
- Achieving realistic hope regarding relationships

Counselors may also work with the parents of children involved in divorce. Parent support groups and counselor–parent consultation can help parents cope more effectively with the changes brought about by the divorce. Counselors can encourage parents to do the following:

- Talk with children about the divorce in a way that is developmentally appropriate, making sure that they do not consider the divorce their fault
- Plan for ways to make the child's life as stable and consistent as possible
- Arrange for regular visits from the absent parent to assure the child of both parents' love

- Talk with children about the future, and involve them in the planning without overwhelming them
- Avoid asking children to take on responsibilities beyond their capabilities (Henderson & Thompson, 2016)

GRIEF AND LOSS.   At one time or another, all children are affected by death, either of a pet, a grandparent, a parent or sibling, or a friend. Accepting the reality of death as part of life is a developmental task that often needs to be facilitated in counseling.

Children may experience a range of physical and emotional responses to grief experiences. Some of the physical reactions to loss include headaches, chest pains, and stomachaches. Children may experience a distortion in time or find it difficult to start new projects or begin new relationships. Some children regress to an earlier period in development, when they felt safer. Emotional responses may vary widely, ranging from feelings of anger or guilt to those of sadness, fear, or denial of pain.

As with divorce, several factors influence children's responses to death, including their developmental level, support systems, and the manner in which the adults in their lives deal with grieving. The grief process is unique for each individual, and it is important not to assume that children in the same age group will respond in the same manner. Counselors can let children take the lead in sharing their grief experiences by requesting, "Help me find ways to help you tell me about what you feel." One of the most beneficial things counselors can do is listen carefully to the children, trusting the children's wisdom and giving them unhurried time to express their thoughts, feelings, and concerns.

In addition, the following counseling strategies can help children deal with loss from a death:

- Focus on what the child shares about specific thoughts, feelings, and concerns. Respond clearly and thoughtfully, keeping in mind the child's cognitive level.
- Allow children to express their grief, talk freely, and ask questions. Play therapy, creative expression, puppetry, bibliotherapy, imagery, and letter writing are just a few of the methods that facilitate children's expression of death.
- Help the children commemorate their loss and say good-bye, perhaps through compiling a scrapbook of their loved one or memorializing the loss in some significant way.
- Work collaboratively with parents to help the children learn more about the process of death and dying. Child-appropriate books about death, which are available in most libraries, can help answer questions, stimulate conversation, and provide new understanding (Redcay, 2001).
- Help families reduce stress in their children's lives by maintaining structure and being aware of the possibility of regression. Family counseling may be needed.
- Be aware of triggers of grief, including birthdays, holidays, and the anniversary of the death.
- Help children give themselves permission to go on with life without feeling guilty. (Henderson & Thompson, 2016)

CHILD MALTREATMENT.   Child maltreatment, which refers to abuse and neglect, is a serious concern. Approximately 905,000 cases of substantiated maltreatment were documented in the United States in 2014, with an estimated 1,580 fatalities (U.S. Department of Health and Human Services, Administration for Children and Families, Administration on Children,

Youth and Families, Children's Bureau, 2016). That same year, over 3,600,000 cases of maltreatment were reported that received an investigation and/or assessment. Child abuse and neglect occur at all socioeconomic and educational levels (Henderson & Thompson, 2016). Maltreatment categories and associated conservative statistics include neglect (64%), physical abuse (16%), sexual abuse (8.8%), and psychological or emotional maltreatment (6.6%). Rates of maltreatment have fluctuated only slightly during the decade. Descriptions of each maltreatment category are presented in Figure 11–4.

A particular concern is the fact that childhood maltreatment has escalated with advances in technology. Specifically, minors may be enticed or persuaded to meet online

Child Neglect	**Physical Abuse**
• Deliberate failure by a caretaker to provide a child with shelter, food, clothing, education, supervision, medical care, and other basic necessities	• Any act that results in a nonaccidental physical injury; includes punching, beating, kicking, burning, cutting, twisting limbs, or otherwise harming a child
• Represents an ongoing pattern of inadequate care	• Often represents unreasonable and unjustified punishment of a child by a caregiver
• Physical signs and symptoms: poor hygiene, poor weight gain, inadequate medical care, dressing inadequately for weather, being chronically late for or absent from school, constant complaints of hunger, severe developmental lags	• Physical signs and symptoms: bruises, burns, and fractures
	• Affective-behavioral signs and symptoms: aggression, hopelessness, depression, low self-esteem, defiance, running away, property offenses, delinquency, substance abuse
• Affective-behavioral signs and symptoms: low self-esteem, aggression, anger, frustration, conduct problems	
Sexual Abuse	**Psychological Maltreatment**
• Any act that forces, coerces, or threatens a child to have any form of sexual contact or engage in any type of sexual activity	• A pattern of behavior that can seriously interfere with a child's positive emotional development
• Includes both touching and nontouching offenses (e.g., indecent exposure)	• Acts that communicate to a child that he or she is worthless, unloved, or unwanted
• Physical signs and symptoms: genital bleeding, odors, eating or sleep disturbances, somatic complaints, enuresis or encopresis	• Includes emotionally neglectful behaviors and emotionally abusive behaviors
• Affective-behavioral signs and symptoms: anxiety, nightmares, guilt, anger/hostility, depression, low self-esteem, sexualized behavior, aggression, regression, hyperactivity, self-injurious behavior, delinquency, running away, substance abuse	• Affective-behavioral signs and symptoms: self-abusive behavior, aggression, anxiety, shame, guilt, anger/hostility, pessimism, dependency
	• Social deficits: insecure attachments, poor social adjustment

FIGURE 11–4 Definitions, Signs, and Symptoms of Child Maltreatment
Sources: American Humane Association, 1996; and Miller-Perrin, 2001.

predators for sexual acts. The National Center for Missing and Exploited Children (NCMEC) provides information for parents and caretakers about ways to protect their children. Federal and state laws related to child pornography and other types of child sexual exploitation are summarized on the website at www.ncmec.org (Henderson & Thompson, 2016; NCMEC, 2016).

Every state has laws requiring professionals who work with children to report suspected child abuse or neglect to local child protective services. Also, each state and most counties have social services agencies that provide protective services to children. Counselors who work with children need to be aware of the agencies in their region to contact in cases of suspected abuse.

Victims of child maltreatment differ in regard to their preabuse histories, the nature of the abuse experiences, family and system responses to the abuse, available social supports, and individual coping resources. They also differ in regard to the types of symptoms displayed, with some children displaying many symptoms and others displaying few or none. Consequently, there is no single treatment approach that is appropriate or effective for all clients. Depending on the individual client's presentation, clinicians should consider treatment approaches that include the following (Miller-Perrin, 2001):

- *Managing negative thoughts and feelings associated with the maltreatment, including guilt, anxiety, shame, fear, and stigmatization.*   Counseling can give children opportunities to diffuse negative feelings by confronting the abuse experience within the safety of the therapeutic relationship. Older children and adolescents may be able to talk about their experiences. For younger children, reenacting the experiences through play or art may be helpful.
- *Providing clarification of cognitions and beliefs that might lead to negative attributions.*   Confronting issues of secrecy and stigmatization are important. Cognitive–behavioral approaches that help children restructure their beliefs about themselves (e.g., being "different," being at fault) can be effective. Group counseling may facilitate cognitive restructuring.
- *Reducing problem behavior.*   Behavioral problems such as impulsivity, aggression, and sexualized behavior often need to be addressed in counseling. Parent training typically accompanies the counseling process when the parent is not the perpetrator.
- *Empowering the child survivor.*   Prevention training that includes self-protection skills is often necessary. Self-protection skills involve teaching children to identify potential abuse situations, providing them with protective responses, and encouraging them to disclose any abuse experiences.
- *Enhancing developmental skills.*   Children may have deficits in problem-solving skills and social skills. Depending on the age of the children when the abuse occurred, there also may be lags in regard to psychosocial development (e.g., learning to trust). Individual and group counseling can facilitate growth in these areas.
- *Improving parenting skills.*   In many cases of child maltreatment, parent-focused interventions are warranted. Such interventions include educating parents about developmental processes to correct misperceptions and unrealistic expectations, teaching parents about appropriate disciplinary techniques, and teaching anger management and stress reduction skills.

Because of the complex nature of child maltreatment, counselors should consider accessing community resources and services to help families manage difficult situations more effectively. Examples of such services include substance abuse treatment, money management training, crisis hotlines, respite care services, preschool services, and parent education classes.

CYBERBULLYING.   Over 93% of youth are active users of the Internet, and at least 75% own their own cell phones. Although the extent of cyberbullying and its prevalence are unclear, studies have found that anywhere from 9% to 40% of students are victims of cyberbullying (Schneider, O'Donnell, Stueve, & Coulter, 2012). The National Crime Prevention Council defines *cyberbullying* as using the Internet, cell phones, or other electronic devices to send or post text or images intended to hurt or embarrass another person (see www.NCPC.org).

In many ways, online attacks differ from and can cause more harm than traditional bullying (Paterson, 2011). Online attacks can take place anonymously and can quickly involve hundreds of participants and onlookers. Cyberbullying "isolates its intended targets and haunts its victims relentlessly because the attacks reside and proliferate throughout a primary social network for today's youth—the Internet" (Paterson, 2011, p. 44).

Cyberbullying occurs over a number of media. Among the most prominent are social networking websites, such as Facebook; video-sharing websites, such as YouTube; instant messaging on the Internet; text messaging on cell phones; and "trash-polling" sites, where visitors are invited to post unflattering comments about someone, often based on photos (Hinduja & Patchin, 2016).

The harmful effects of cyberbullying are numerous. They include but are not limited to psychological distress (such as feeling scared, angry, and unable to trust others), decreased self-esteem, increased depression, social isolation, embarrassment, decreased confidence, feelings of worthlessness, and harassment. The most serious one is increased suicidal ideation and instances of suicide. Two widely reported tragic examples in the early part of the 21st century of young teenagers taking their lives as a result of cyberbullying concerned Ryan Halligan, from Vermont, and Megan Meier, from Missouri. Halligan committed suicide at the age of 13 after being bullied by his classmates in real life and cyberbullied online. Meier died of suicide attributed to cyberbullying through social networking by hanging three weeks before her 14th birthday.

Clinical mental health counselors can help in instances of adolescent cyberbullying by taking the issue seriously and learning more about it, for example, consulting the Cyberbullying Research Center website at www.cyberbullying.us. They can also provide psychoeducation to parents about being proactive and setting limits on social media for their teenagers, offer support groups for people who have been targets of cyberbullying, and provide supportive individual therapy that includes skill training. Clinical mental health counselors can also work with perpetrators of cyberbullying to help them gain a greater understanding of their actions, as well as advocate for laws and regulations that prohibit cyberbullying. A useful resource is the book *Cyberbullying: What Counselors Need to Know* (Bauman, 2011).

OTHER ISSUES.   Divorce, grief, maltreatment, and cyberbullying are just a few of the many issues with which children and adolescents may struggle. Other issues include living in chemically dependent families, being homeless, having poor nutrition, living with chronic or terminal illness, adjusting to blended families, managing teenage pregnancy, and engaging in delinquent activities. It is beyond the scope of any text to cover all the concerns faced by young people; therefore, counselors who work with this population can acquire more expertise through continuing education workshops and online webinars.

Summary and Conclusion

Working with children and adolescents provides unique and exciting challenges for clinical mental health counselors. Clinicians who work with this population need to have a comprehensive understanding of the developmental issues that influence young people's well-being. They also need to be aware of the various contextual influences on development, including the family, school, peers, life events, and culture.

Knowledge of development and bioecological influences provides a strong foundation for counseling children and adolescents. When counseling young people, special attention needs to be given to building a therapeutic relationship, assessing and evaluating, and selecting and implementing developmentally appropriate interventions.

Young people in today's society are confronted with a wide array of issues, ranging from diagnosable mental health disorders to specific concerns related to life events. Some of the disorders discussed in this chapter include depression, eating disorders, and ADHD. Other concerns that may precipitate the need for counseling include parental divorce, death of a loved one, cyberbullying, and child maltreatment. These are just a few of the multiple concerns that may bring young people to counseling.

MyCounselingLab

Try the Topic 15 Exercise 15.4(a): *Legal Issues Working with Minors.*

CHAPTER 12

Rawpixel.com/Shutterstock

My father tells me
  my mother is slowing down.
He talks deliberately and with deep feelings
  as stooped shouldered he walks to his garden
    behind the garage.
My mother informs me
  about my father's failing health.
"Not as robust as before," she explains,
  "Lower energy than in his 50s."
Her concerns arise as she kneads dough for biscuits.
Both express their fears to me
  as we view the present from the past.
In love, and with measured anxiety,
  I move with them into new patterns.

Reprinted from "A Day in the Life of Aging," in *Family Therapy: History, Theory and Practice* (4th ed., p. 155), by S. T. Gladding, 2008, Upper Saddle River, NJ: Prentice Hall. © Samuel T. Gladding.

Counseling Adults

CHAPTER OVERVIEW

From reading this chapter, you will learn about

- The transition model and ways it can be used in counseling adults
- Descriptions of four developmental stages of adulthood: emerging adulthood, early adulthood, middle adulthood, and later adulthood as well as transitions and counseling implications associated with each stage
- Ways to combat ageism
- Gender-aware counseling and its application to women and men

As you read, consider

- Your current life stage and the transitions you've faced
- Which age group you understand best and which age group you'd like to learn more about
- What examples of ageism you have noticed
- The degree to which gender roles are socially constructed
- Whether you would find it easier to counsel women or men and why

People are defined by their age, by the time in which they grew up, and by a wide range of intersecting cultural factors. Clinical mental health counselors work with people across the life span. In our current social milieu of global connectedness, a central theme is change, which reflects the "dynamic impact of forces across demographic, social, cultural, technological, political, and historical domains" (Anderson, Goodman, & Schlossberg, 2012, p. 3). Consequently, counseling goals often include coping, adapting, and developing self-advocacy skills.

In working with adults of all ages and backgrounds, it is crucial that counselors keep in mind that individuals, as well as groups, change over time. What once may have been accurate in assessing adults in a particular decade may have lost validity over the years. Likewise, gender roles for men and women have changed and will continue to do so. Accordingly, clinical mental health counselors need to be knowledgeable about development and able to help clients cope with the multiple transitions that have an impact on their lives. Counselors also need to be sensitive to ways gender and aging affect the overall well-being of clients.

Human development is traditionally defined as any kind of systematic change that is lifelong and cumulative (Papalia & Martorell, 2015). Development occurs on a number of levels throughout the life span. Adults continue to develop physically, cognitively, emotionally, socially, and spiritually. A strong knowledge of traditional and emerging developmental theories helps provide a framework that informs clinical mental health work with clients of all ages. The Association for Adult Development and Aging (AADA), a division of the ACA, focuses on adult development and aging issues.

Throughout the life span, people face transitions both during and between developmental stages and phases. Nancy Schlossberg (e.g., 1981, 1991) proposes a **transition model** that emphasizes the importance of life transitions affecting adults of all ages. Transitions occur over a period of time and may be anticipated or unanticipated. When life events are accelerated or delayed or fail to materialize (i.e., become **nonevents**), the well-being of adults may be negatively affected (Anderson et al., 2012). In this chapter, the transition model is described and its relevance is illustrated in counseling adults within a developmental framework. Attention is also focused on gender issues in counseling.

BOX 12–1

Adults are individuals—some are healthy, some are unhealthy; some are sexually alive, others are uninterested; some are happy, some are sad; some are productive, others are disintegrating; some are coping, some are collapsing.

(Anderson et al., 2012, p. 37)

THE TRANSITION FRAMEWORK

The transition framework provides a way of understanding pivotal events and nonevents that people encounter throughout the course of a lifetime. Levinson (1986) describes **transitions** as turning points: periods between times of relative stability. Transitions often trigger changes in relationships, routines, and roles (Anderson et al., 2012). They can be identified as anticipated, unanticipated, or nonevents.

Anticipated transitions are considered "normative"; that is, they are expected to occur in a somewhat predictable sequence across the life span. Leaving home, starting a job, getting married, having children, becoming "empty nesters," and retiring are examples of anticipated life events. In contrast, **unanticipated transitions**, also called **unscheduled events**, are not predictable or expected and may be positive or negative. Developing an acute or chronic illness, being fired, getting a divorce, and experiencing the unexpected death of a family member are examples of unanticipated events. Other examples include being unexpectedly promoted or suddenly becoming wealthy. Whereas people can usually plan for anticipated transitions, unanticipated transitions most often catch people unprepared and may result in feelings of turmoil and chaos.

Nonevent transitions are events that people expect to happen but that do not occur. For example, a couple may try for years to have a child, only to find that the event is not likely to happen. The expected transition then becomes a nonevent transition, which can alter the way the couple views themselves and their future. Nonevents can be positive as well, such as anticipating a job layoff that never occurs.

Two other important terms associated with transitions are **perspective** and **context** (Anderson et al., 2012). Perspective refers to an individual's appraisal of the transition. To illustrate, one person may view retirement negatively, whereas another person may see it as a time of new opportunities and challenges. Context refers to factors such as environment, gender, culture, socioeconomic status, and other variables that influence the effects transitions have on people. Context can also be viewed chronologically. Each generation is affected by the unfolding history of influences that have an impact on their particular life course. In today's world, for example, people are affected by rapidly advancing technology and terrorism, whereas people living in the 1930s and 1940s were affected by the Great Depression and World War II.

The transition model is composed of three major parts (Anderson et al., 2012):

1. *Approaching transitions:* identifying types of transition and the transition process itself
2. *Taking stock of coping resources:* identifying potential assets and liabilities as they apply to the *situation, support systems, self,* and *strategies* for coping—also known as the **4 S's** (see Figure 12–1)
3. *Taking charge:* strengthening resources to facilitate coping and moving through the transition toward a positive outcome

---

1. The **situation** variable—What is happening? Does the transition come at a time that the individual is experiencing multiple stressors?
2. The **self** variable—To whom is the transition happening? Each person is different in terms of life issues and personality. These differences affect the way people respond to transitions.
3. The **support** variable—What help is available? What support systems are already in place? Is the individual getting whatever is needed for moving through this particular transition?
4. The **strategies** variable—How does the person typically cope? Coping represents the ways people respond to life strains and stressors. What ways of coping would be most helpful for the current situation?

FIGURE 12–1   Taking Stock of Coping Resources: The 4-S System
Source: Adapted from Anderson et al., 2012.

Many theorists (e.g., Bloch, Bridges, Lorenz) have discussed the transition process from various perspectives. Although their perspectives differ, each theorist views transitions as integral components of development, transformation, and growth. Clinical mental health counselors who understand the significance of transitions are better equipped to help clients work through multiple layers of feelings and adjustments associated with transitions across the life span.

Different stages of development and the various developmental components of it (e.g., psychosocial, cognitive, spiritual, physical) affect adults during their life span. They are described here.

EMERGING ADULTHOOD

Emerging adulthood is a new, distinct stage of development that was introduced as a theory by Jeffrey Arnett (2000, 2004, 2006). Emerging adulthood represents a time of transition between adolescence and young adulthood. According to Arnett, the sweeping demographic shifts of the past several decades have contributed to the emergence of a new stage of development that focuses on young people between the ages of 18 and the late 20s. In the past, developmental trajectories for young people typically moved from adolescence to young adulthood. Markers of young adulthood included choosing a stable occupation, getting married, and having a first child. However, rapid changes in society have altered that stage and paved the way for the emerging adulthood stage.

Emerging adulthood is "historically embedded and culturally constructed" (cf. Tanner & Arnett, 2009, p. 39.) Three significant societal changes gave rise to this new stage: (a) the change from an industrial-based economy to an information-based economy, leading to an increased need for postsecondary education; (b) significant increases in educational and occupational opportunities available to women, which meant that many women were delaying marriage or partnerships to pursue those opportunities; and (c) greater tolerance of premarital sex, which allowed young people in many societies to engage in sexual activity long before considering marriage.

BOX 12–2   The Emerging Adult Brain

Emerging adult thinking, feeling, and acting reveal underlying physiological and neurological development unique to this developmental stage. The brain's center for reasoning and problem-solving fully develops during the emerging adult age period. Cognitive capacities, strategies, and organization shift during emerging adulthood, as does the attainment of wisdom-related knowledge and judgment.

(Tanner & Arnett, 2009, p. 41)

Emerging adults do not view themselves as adolescents; however, many of them do not characterize themselves as "fully adult" either. When questioned about whether they viewed themselves as adults, the majority of emerging adults said yes in some respects, no in other respects. In normative development, emerging adulthood is characterized by five features, which have received empirical support. Arnett (2007) identifies these features:

- *The age of identity explorations.*   Much has changed since Erikson first proposed his theory of psychosocial adjustment. For many decades, explorations of identity were primarily associated with adolescence. However, now explorations that relate to work, love relationships, and ideology characterize emerging adulthood. Postsecondary educational opportunities, aspirations and goals related to work, and finding someone to be a life partner often take place not during adolescence but during emerging adulthood (Arnett, 2007).

- *The age of instability.* Instability is "a normal characteristic of emerging adulthood" (Arnett, 2007, p. 154). Young people in this developmental stage typically change jobs nearly every year for a decade and may also change residences every year. They may leave home, return home again, cohabitate, and move to new locations to pursue educational or occupational opportunities. Emerging adulthood represents a stage of life when transitions, both anticipated and unanticipated, are the norm.
- *The self-focused age.* Arnett (2004, 2010) describes this feature as the time of life in which there is freedom from binding relationships and an opportunity for making independent decisions. *Self-focused* does not imply selfishness. Instead, emerging adults are less egocentric than adolescents and better equipped to consider other people's perspectives. They are self-focused because they are developing the skills needed for adult life. However, they also realize that the time of being self-focused is limited—emerging adults have the freedom of self-direction that they did not have as children or adolescents and will probably not experience in adulthood.
- *The age of feeling in between.* As stated earlier, emerging adulthood represents a developmental time period between adolescence and adulthood. In the United States and in other industrialized countries, much ambiguity is associated with emerging adults' perceptions of themselves as adults. Interestingly, the markers traditionally associated with adulthood—entering full-time work, marriage or partnership, and parenthood—are not considered markers of adulthood by this age group. Instead, they identify the most important markers of adulthood as (a) taking responsibility for one's actions, (b) making independent decisions, and (c) becoming financially independent.
- *The age of possibilities.* Many emerging adults have high hopes for their future. This attitude cuts across social class and educational opportunities. They anticipate finding work that is meaningful, the right love partner, and ways to be financially stable. Although they tend to be optimistic, they are usually able to adapt their dreams and goals to match reality.

Counseling Implications for Emerging Adults

Emerging adulthood is characterized by change and exploration. As such, it is a developmental stage replete with transitions. As is the case with all developmental stages, there is much variation among emerging adults and the way in which they navigate the process of becoming young adults. Because emerging adulthood is a new developmental stage that evolved as a function of rapid social, historical, and cultural changes in the global world, many counselors may not be aware of the challenges and opportunities faced by these young people. Thus, one implication for counselors is to become knowledgeable about this life stage.

Three developmental tasks have been associated with emerging adulthood: leaving home, advancing in the capacity for mature intimacy, and developing individuation (Scharf, Mayseless, & Kivenson-Baron, 2004). Clinical mental health counselors can provide psychoeducation, individual counseling, and group counseling to help emerging adults accomplish those tasks. Group counseling can be especially helpful for clients who may feel isolated and alone, believing that everyone else has it together except them. Group and individual counseling can provide ways for emerging adults to explore their personality types, values, interests, beliefs, work options, and sense of self. Accepting clients wherever they are in regard to their developmental trajectories is crucial, as is the need to provide support and encouragement.

The issues described up to this point are developmental in nature. Clinicians working with emerging adults during this major time of transition can help normalize their clients' experiences and help them develop coping skills for dealing with ambiguity. Clinicians may also work with emerging adults who find the transition from adolescence to adulthood especially challenging because of specific clinical issues. Some of the more common issues that arise during adolescence and emerging adulthood include depression, anxiety, bipolar disorder, eating disorders, substance abuse, and an inability to regulate or control emotions (Galambos, Barker, & Krahn, 2006). Schizophrenia, which afflicts over 2 million people in the United States, typically begins between the ages of 15 and 25. The average onset is age 18 for men and age 25 for women. Although schizophrenia is not curable, it is treatable. People who are diagnosed and treated early have a better prognosis for positive outcomes (Schizophrenia.com, 2016). Thus, counselors need to be aware of the signs and symptoms associated with schizophrenia to ensure that clients with this disorder receive the kind of intensive help they need.

EARLY ADULTHOOD

Early adulthood (approximately 25 to 40 years of age) and middle adulthood (approximately 40 to 65 years of age) are age brackets that are somewhat arbitrary. They have changed over the years because of societal norms and biological factors. People today are living considerably longer than they did half a century ago. The average life expectancy (ALE) for an American born in 2015 is estimated to be 79 years, although ALE varies by race/ethnicity, gender, and region (U.S. Census Bureau, 2015). Women currently have a higher life expectancy than men do, although the gap is narrowing. Greater longevity also affects the way life stages are demarcated by age. For example, age 35 used to be considered the onset of middle adulthood. That is no longer the case. Moreover, the age at which people are considered young, or early, adults has changed.

Early adulthood has traditionally been identified by several indicators: finishing education, entering full-time work, beginning marriage or partnership, and parenting. However, the most important criteria emerging adults identified as markers of adulthood were making independent decisions, accepting personal responsibility, and becoming financially independent (Arnett, 2004). Reaching certain markers may be meaningful for some young adults and less so for others. According to Arnett (2007), "Becoming an adult today means learning to stand alone as a self-sufficient person" (p. 157).

Developmental Issues

One of the most important issues faced by young adults, according to Erikson (1963), is successfully resolving the psychosocial crisis of intimacy vs. isolation. Traditionally, **intimacy** refers to making a long-term commitment to another person. Another way of conceptualizing intimacy is the ability to form meaningful relationships with others, even if those relationships do not result in marriage or partnership. To achieve true intimacy with another requires having already developed a sense of personal identity. Young adults who achieve intimacy tend to be cooperative, tolerant, and able to respond to the needs of a significant other. An individual who is not able to develop one or more close relationships risks feeling **isolated**. An inability to develop a meaningful relationship with another can have deleterious effects, including loneliness, depression, and diminished self-esteem (Santrock, 2016).

One of the challenges of early adulthood is balancing intimacy and commitment with independence and freedom. Developing **autonomy** includes increasing one's independence from parents, becoming financially stable, and being able to make decisions. Ideally, young adults are able to experience healthy independence in conjunction with an intimate relationship. For example, two young adults, deeply committed to each other and planning to get married, might both, at the same time, have a strong sense of self-identity, be comfortable pursuing their own career paths, and have individual friendships as well as "couple" friendships.

Early Adult Lifestyles

Young adults have many lifestyle options. Some are self-selected, and others are affected by a range of factors, including the economy, personal convictions, divorce, remarriage, and a host of other variables. Adults may choose to live alone, cohabitate, marry, form committed partnerships, and/or have children. Additionally, lifestyles often do not remain constant. For example, a young married couple may experience problems that lead to divorce. Some divorced adults remarry; others choose to return to a single lifestyle. So although early adulthood is typically associated with higher levels of stability than emerging adulthood, early adulthood is also a period of much transition.

SINGLE ADULTS. When people leave their parents' homes, they usually do so as single adults. They may go to college, enter the workforce, join the military, or spend time working with organizations such as Americorps or the Peace Corps. Often when people move out of their family homes, they are in the emerging adulthood stage. As time passes, they may form an intimate relationship that leads to marriage or partnership, or they may choose to remain single.

The number of single adults has increased dramatically since 1970. According to the 2015 U.S. Census Bureau, over 50% of all Americans over the age of 18 are single. Some single people are living with children, others are widowed or divorced, and others have not married or entered into partnerships. One reason that many young adults are single is that people today often enter into marriage at later ages than in years past. In 2015, the median age for a man's first marriage was 29 years, and the median age for a woman's first marriage was 27 (U.S. Census Bureau, 2015).

Some of the advantages of being single include having time to make decisions about one's life course, time to develop personal resources, and freedom to make autonomous decisions and pursue personal interests and opportunities (Santrock, 2016). Being single and mentally healthy requires that individuals establish social networks, find meaning in their work or avocations, and live a balanced life physically and psychologically. Singles must also develop coping strategies to avoid becoming overwhelmed by stress, loneliness, or isolation (Kleinke, 2002). For some singles, overcoming internal and external expectations to marry or form partnerships, even when they do not wish to do so, can be a major challenge.

COHABITATION.   **Cohabitation** refers to the lifestyle of unmarried couples living together in an intimate, sexual relationship. For some young adults, cohabitation is a precursor to marriage. For others, it is an alternative to marriage—an ongoing lifestyle. Although Americans are more open to cohabitation than in years past, their attitudes are less positive than those of Western Europeans (Berk, 2014). Cohabitating combines some of the rewards of marriage (e.g., intimacy, shared expenses) without the obligations (e.g., it is easier to leave the relationship because there is no legal bond). Research on the benefits of cohabitation, particularly as a precursor to marriage, yields mixed reports. In general, researchers have found that cohabitation either leads to no difference or has a negative effect on marital satisfaction (cf. Santrock, 2016).

NEWLY MARRIED.   The newly married lifestyle pertains to the first few years of marriage. Marriage as an institution can have many benefits. Adults often thrive when another person is committed to their well-being, and children benefit when they have two parents who are legally and emotionally dedicated to them. Studies indicate that married people as a whole tend to be "a little happier, healthier, and richer than never-married [people], but not by much" (Berger, 2014, p. 472).

During the **honeymoon stage** of marriage (i.e., approximately the first 6 months), couples tend to be happiest. The excitement of starting a new life together and a propensity to idealize each other contribute to this high level of happiness. This idealization is likely to dissipate naturally with the passage of time. Overall, this stage of the family life cycle is one filled with challenge and compromise. For example, new couples must learn how to share space, meals, chores, and leisure time. **Egalitarian marriages**—in which spouses relate as equals, share household tasks, and engage in conflict resolution—are associated with greater marital satisfaction than marriages in which there is an imbalance of power or division of labor. When each partner is committed to the marriage and willing to make compromises and manage conflicts, the marriage is more likely to be successful. Couples that are most satisfied are those whose partners believe they are receiving as much as they are giving.

It is not surprising that the new-couple stage of marriage (approximately the first two years) is one of the most likely times for couples to divorce, because of an inability to resolve differences or make adaptations (Gladding, 2015). On the other hand, it is a time when couples may experience the greatest amount of satisfaction in their marriage, especially if they negotiate satisfactory arrangements early and have children later. The new couple is free to experiment with life and engage in a variety of activities. Financial and time constraints are two common challenges for couples during this period.

GAY AND LESBIAN COUPLES.   Gay and lesbian couples are similar to heterosexual couples in several ways. Many same-sex couples are committed, faithful, and supportive. However, problems associated with communication, finances, and abuse may arise, just as they do with heterosexual couples. Heterosexual couples and same-sex couples are similar in overall satisfaction (Herek, 2006; Kurdek, 2006). Same-sex couples with children may be more likely than their married heterosexual counterparts to exhibit an equal division in household labor (Kurdek, 2006).

PARENTS WITH YOUNG CHILDREN.   Becoming a parent marks the beginning of a new phase of young adulthood. Parenting, especially when children are under 3 years of age, is physically, psychologically, and interpersonally demanding (Bauman, 2002). The arrival of a child can have an impact on a couple's living arrangements (e.g., place of residence), marital relationship (e.g., intimacy), and stress level (e.g., new demands and roles). When a newborn enters a family, the family becomes unbalanced, at least temporarily. A rebalancing occurs in a couple's investment of time, energy, and focus. Changing roles, exhaustion, and increased responsibilities can be especially challenging. Couples who have strong support systems, open communication systems, realistic expectations, and friendships with other new parents are likely to navigate the transition more easily.

One of the most important tasks for young adult families is meeting the physical demands that accompany having preschool children. This challenge becomes especially great when both partners are working outside the home, as do a large percentage of couples in the United States with children under the age of 6 (Bauman, 2002). Dual-earner couples need to develop strategies that help them combine work and family roles. Juggling multiple roles can lead to frustration and dissatisfaction unless necessary adjustments are made. To increase marital and family satisfaction, it is important for partners to develop egalitarian gender-role expectations and negotiate effective methods of role sharing.

Counseling Implications for Young Adults

Many of the tasks engaged in during early adulthood, such as developing an identity and establishing intimacy, continue over the life span and influence future outcomes. As is the case with emerging adults, young adults experience a wide array of transitions. One of these transitions relates to work and career. Other transitions include adapting to a new lifestyle—whether that be singlehood, cohabitation, marriage, partnership, having children, or remaining childless. Also during this time period, separation, divorce, and sometimes remarriage are major changes that can affect young adults.

Premarital education and counseling can be especially helpful for young adults considering marriage or committed partnerships. Making the decision to marry or commit to a partner represents a major life transition. Research has shown that premarital education is linked to a higher level of commitment and satisfaction, a lower level of destructive conflict, and a decreased likelihood of divorce (Stanley, Amato, Johnson, & Markman, 2006).

Counselors can provide psychoeducation about the normal, expected changes that occur during early adulthood. For example, if young couples with preschool children expect their lives to be more hectic and less intimate, they may be better prepared to deal with their circumstances, delay gratification, and not get discouraged with or withdraw from each other. Cautioning young adults about the consequences of too much change can help them realize that they cannot do everything at once, thus preparing them to make intentional choices in pursuing or declining opportunities.

Young adults benefit when clinicians lead counseling groups designed to help people cope with unanticipated transitions, such as divorce, and with nonevents, such as not being able to have children. Adults facing negative transitions may find individual counseling helpful. For example, a man who believes that his wife is having an affair may be unsure about how to confront her, and if he does confront her, he may question what will happen to their marriage. Individual counseling can give him a safe place to express his anger and fears. It can also give him an opportunity to examine and explore various possibilities and their potential outcomes.

Yet another way to help young adults is to provide ways to explore patterns and recognize transitions within their families of origin. This process can help them conceptualize the positive and negative influences their families have had on them. It can help them avoid repeating negative patterns as they develop their own lifestyles. One way to do this is to construct a genogram, such as the one shown in Figure 12–2.

A genogram is a visual representation of a person's family tree, depicted in geometric figures, lines, and words (Gladding, 2015). Genograms include generational information about employment, health, and family relationships over at least three generations. Genograms help people see and understand patterns in the context of historic and contemporary events (McGoldrick, 2012). The tangibility and nonthreatening nature of this process helps counselors and clients gather a large amount of information in a relatively brief period of time.

Genograms allow young adults "to go 'back, back, back; and up, up, up' their family tree to look for patterns . . . getting not just information but a feel for the context and milieu that existed during each person's formative years" (White, 1978, pp. 25–26). This process promotes a shift from emotional reactivity to clear cognition. Data in a genogram are scanned for (a) repetitive patterns, such as triangles, cutoffs, and coalitions; (b) coincidences of dates, such as the death of members or the age of symptom onset; and (c) the impact of change and untimely life cycle transitions, such as off-schedule events like marriage, death, and the birth of children.

The Case of Whitney

Whitney is a 28-year-old who has graduated with her MBA. She hopes to move out of state, where she has been offered a lucrative position with a large company. However, she feels obligated to take a job that will allow her to live with her mother, who lost her job two months ago. Whitney's younger sister Camille, who also is unemployed, lives in the home with her 3-year-old son, Nathaniel.

Whitney tells you that she thinks that she should put her dream job on hold. She worries about what will happen if she doesn't go home and help support her family. Her mother has been unsuccessful in her job search and is now using her savings to keep up with the bills. Meanwhile, Camille spends most of her nights out clubbing, leaving Nathaniel at home with his grandmother. Whitney is frustrated that her mother is allowing Camille to live a carefree, party-filled lifestyle when there are so many bills to be paid. She also worries about her nephew and wants to provide a positive role model for him.

What transitions is Whitney going through? What developmental issues need to be considered? How might moving back home affect her personal growth as a young adult? If you were Whitney's counselor, where would you begin? What approaches might be helpful?

MIDDLE ADULTHOOD

Middle adulthood can be conceptualized as the developmental period that spans ages 40 to 60–65. For many healthy adults, midlife is a stage that lasts longer than in years past. Some researchers divide this period into **early middle life** (ages 40–54) and **late middle life**

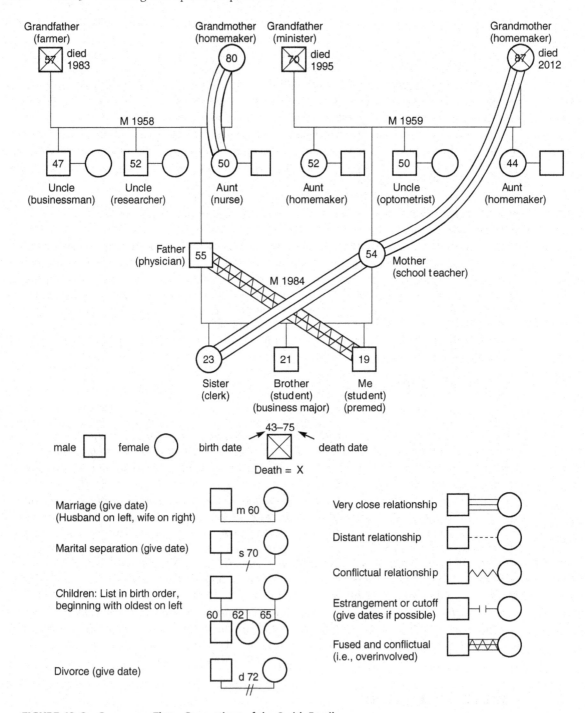

FIGURE 12–2 Genogram: Three Generations of the Smith Family

(ages 55–65; Deeg, 2005). During midlife, people experience a multitude of transitions, including physical changes, psychosocial challenges, relationship adjustments, and caring for aging parents. For many, midlife represents a period of questioning one's sense of purpose, mattering, and meaning (Anderson et al., 2012). It is a time for evaluating, deciding, and making adjustments. Because of the many changes associated with midlife, the entire period can be labeled **midlife transition**. There is no one set path for any given individual. Midlifers' paths are affected by life circumstances, sociocultural norms, and historical context.

Physical Changes

Overall, there is some physical decline in men and women during middle adulthood, including losses in hearing, sight, hormonal levels, height, and strength. As a society, Americans value youth and fitness, but during midlife, many of the visible signs of youth change. For example, wrinkles (due to changes in skin structure and sun exposure), graying hair, balding, bone density loss, and weight changes are some of the more visible signs of aging (Lee, Jordan, Stevens, & Jones, 2017). To combat those changes, some midlifers take many steps to "slow down" the aging process such as undergoing cosmetic procedures and Botox injections.

On a more positive note, people in middle adulthood are less susceptible to accidents, colds, and injuries than they are in other stages of the life span (Santrock, 2016). Many people in this age group develop or maintain healthy wellness plans that can reduce some of the visible signs of aging and increase longevity. Moreover, a healthy lifestyle helps them cope with stress, depression, anxiety, and a host of other challenges, as illustrated in Box 12–3.

BOX 12–3

I have engaged in regular physical exercise and healthy eating habits since my mid-20s. I realize that running, swimming, and other forms of regular exercise make a tremendous difference in the ways I manage stress, anxiety, and frustrations. Also, I enjoy it. My head is clearer, making it easier to concentrate. Furthermore, the network of friends I have formed as a result of working out with other people my age has been socially rewarding. I realize that the medical and mental health benefits of a healthy lifestyle are numerous. However, my primary motivator is to gain the sense of well-being that accompanies regular exercise. On the days that I don't exercise, I find myself irritable and less able to focus. In some ways, my stress outlet is a form of addiction, but I consider it a positive one.

Debbie Newsome, PhD, LPC, NCC

An important transition that accompanies middle age is a change in hormonal levels. For most women, menopause occurs sometime in the late 40s or early 50s when they cease to have menstrual cycles and become infertile. Perimenopause is a transitional phase leading up to menopause. During perimenopause and menopause, levels of estrogen decline dramatically. Some women experience uncomfortable side effects, including moodiness, "hot flashes," fatigue, and rapid heartbeats. Other women experience very few symptoms. The loss of fertility, particularly when menopause starts early, can cause distress for women who delay having children.

Men also experience hormonal declines, although they tend to be slower and less extreme. Unlike women, men do not lose their fertility during middle age. Although some men experience a decline in energy as they take on more roles at work and at home, these symptoms usually are not hormone related. However, the gradual decline in testosterone levels can reduce men's sexual drive. During middle age, men often experience erectile dysfunction for the first time.

Physical changes during middle age may have significant effects on adults' mental health and well-being. Clinical mental health counselors who are aware of the many physical transitions midlifers experience are better equipped to help them with concurrent clinical issues.

Psychosocial Issues

During middle adulthood, Erikson proposes that adults are resolving the psychosocial crisis of generativity vs. stagnation. **Generativity** refers to finding ways to give to and guide the next generation. Generativity can take many forms, including taking care of others, producing something that benefits society, and engaging in meaningful work (Belsky, 2016). In contrast, **stagnation** refers to becoming detached from important relationships and becoming self-centered and even narcissistic. People experiencing stagnation become less interested in being productive at work or in developing their talents and creativity.

Generative adults are usually better adjusted, more self-accepting, and more caring. Their overall life satisfaction is higher than that of their counterparts. In many ways, generativity leads to an increased sense of meaning and purpose.

Another theory of psychosocial development in midlife is Levinson's (1978, 1996) seasons-of-life theory based on interviews with middle-aged men. Although females were not included in his original study, he later reported that the stages and transitions associated with midlife were applicable to women as well as men. Levinson suggests that midlife begins with a *transition* (ages 40–45) followed by a *life structure* (ages 45–50). The structure is reevaluated between the ages of 50 and 55 and ends in a culminating life structure (ages 55–60). During midlife transition, people evaluate their lives in regard to goals, successes, and failures. They realize that there is more time behind them than in front of them, contributing to a sense that the years go by more and more quickly as they age. At this time, adults may make big changes in their lives—in family, relationships, and work (Belsky, 2016).

Midlife Relationships

Most midlife adults live in families, either with a spouse or a partner (Belsky, 2016). They may raise and "launch" children, remain childless, have grandchildren, and/or be caregivers for aging parents. They also may divorce, remarry, or choose to remain single. Since many deal with the transitions associated with raising children and having them leave home, matters pertaining to divorce, and caring for aging parents, these aspects of middle age will be covered here.

PARENTING CHANGES.   As children in families begin to grow up, parent–child relationships change. For example, relationships with young children and relationships with adolescents differ in multiple ways. One of the challenges of parenthood is learning to adapt to children's different ages and stages. The types of relationships parents have with their children vary greatly, depending on cultural and societal factors. For example, a dual-career family may experience the stress of **role strain** (Goode, 1960), as parents and children attempt to juggle work, school, extracurricular activities, and social relationships, while a family living in poverty may experience stress just trying to put food on the table.

When stressors are less, however, the quality of parent–child relationships increases. A significant stage in midlife occurs when children leave home. Although people still use the term "empty nest" to describe this stage, it can also be defined as "launching children and moving on" (Belsky, 2016). Parents begin to relate to their children as adults and find time to explore new interests and friendships. As time progresses, the family may expand to include in-laws and grandchildren. Unfortunately, during difficult economic times, adult children may return home for an indefinite period of time—a phenomenon that gave rise to the term **boomerang generation**. When adult children return home, it is important for everyone in the household to make adjustments. Discussing expectations and roles for adult children living at home can facilitate the transition process.

DIVORCING.   Another relationship transition that may occur during midlife is divorce. Although most divorces occur during the first 5 to 10 years of marriage, about 10% of divorces occur during midlife (U.S. Department of Health and Human Services, 2016). Approximately 50% of marriages in the United States end in divorce (Gladding, 2015). Although divorce is common, it can be one of life's most painful experiences and is a primary reason people seek counseling (Anderson et al., 2012). Multiple factors influence midlife adults' decision to divorce. Sometimes the desire to dissolve the marriage is mutual— the partners have grown apart through the years, and once the children are grown, they decide that they would be better off living apart. Extramarital affairs, escalating conflict, poor communication, and the desire to try out a new life on one's own terms are just a few of the many reasons a couple may separate and/or divorce.

People respond to divorce in a variety of ways. For many women, the financial implications can be extreme. Divorce leads to a 39% drop in income for women between the ages of 30 and 44 (Belsky, 2016). A spouse or partner who leaves because of substance abuse, physical abuse, or emotional/verbal abuse is likely to adjust to divorce more positively, although the same is not true for the other partner. Ramifications of divorce can run the gamut from increased satisfaction with life to emotional and psychic devastation. Moreover, the decision to divorce has an impact on other family members—including children, in-laws, and the extended family. Consider the scenario presented in Box 12–4.

BOX 12–4   Making Decisions about Divorce

One woman in her late 40s recently told a counselor, "My marriage doesn't do it for me anymore, but I don't know if I have the guts to leave. What will happen to me? to him? to our families? Both of us have aging parents, and I don't know how they will handle this." This woman is grappling with a major decision about whether to initiate a divorce, thus embarking on a major transition. She could benefit from help in examining her resources for coping, regardless of the decision she makes.

Source: Adapted from Anderson et al., 2012.

CARING FOR AGING PARENTS.   Approximately 50% of middle-age adults have parents who are living. Depending on health, finances, and other issues, many older adults choose to live independently, although there is much variation among cultures. For example, many Asian families reside with aging parents (Belsky, 2016). When aging parents become less healthy and need help to engage in the daily activities of living, middle-age adults may need to quit their jobs or make other adjustments in order to provide needed care.

The **sandwich generation** is a term used to describe midlifers who are caring for children under age 18 as well as for aging parents. Often, it is the woman who provides care for the elderly parent who needs assistance. Caring for a parent whose once-robust life is now characterized by dependence is emotionally difficult for all parties involved. It can lead to role overload, depression, exhaustion, and illness (Belsky, 2016). Financial strain is a consideration when aging adults need more help than the caregiver can provide. Counselors can help caregivers explore their coping strategies, social support systems, and community resources.

Caregiving is not restricted to helping elderly parents. Middle adults may also find themselves in unexpected caregiving roles when a child, spouse, or partner is diagnosed with a condition that can devastate the family and require major adaptations. Consider the case of Roger.

The Case of Roger

Roger, a 50-year-old Gulf War veteran, is one of your clients at the Veterans Health Administration Center. Roger has a diagnosis of PTSD. He demonstrates high levels of anxiety and talks about feeling meaningless. You have been working with Roger for several months. Prior to his next scheduled appointment, his wife, Monica, contacts you and asks to be included in Roger's next session. (Roger agreed to this before Monica called.) During the session, Monica tells you that Roger has stopped listening to her and has become very forgetful. Roger is frustrated because he doesn't think anything has changed, stating that Monica is just "nagging a lot."

Roger's PTSD has been relatively well managed by group and individual therapy and medications. According to Monica, however, his nightmares and flashbacks have been getting progressively worse during the past few months. After further discussion, Roger admits the PTSD symptoms are increasing. He knows he is having more nightmares but doesn't always remember them by the time he awakens the next day.

After the session, you consult with colleagues about Roger. They recommend additional medical analysis to determine whether an underlying medical condition is related to the changes Monica has reported. Roger agrees to the recommendation and is found to have early-onset Alzheimer's disease. Although Monica seems to understand the diagnosis, she is in denial about what that means for the future. Roger is confused by the diagnosis and is angry about the turn his life has taken.

If you were Roger's counselor, how would you help him? What would be the best way to help Monica? What developmental, transitional, and clinical considerations are significant? Do you think that individual counseling, couples counseling, or a combination of both would be best at this point?

Counseling Implications

Clinical mental health counselors need to be aware of the many transitions associated with middle adulthood. Many life events that the current cohort of middle adults experience have been associated with younger adults, such as the birth of a first child, going to college, and beginning a new career. Moreover, individuals vary greatly in the experiences they have during midlife and their reactions to those experiences. As a result, it helps for clinicians "to consider the entire midlife period as a time of growth, development, movement, and challenge" (Degges-White & Myers, 2006, p. 147).

One way mental health counselors can work effectively with midlife clients experiencing transitions is by using the 4-S transition model (Schlossberg, 1984). To understand a client's experiences, it is important to first assess the **situation** (e.g., triggers, timing, control, role changes, duration, concurrent stressors). Next, counselors can assess clients' **sense of self**. One of the most effective ways to do that is to listen to clients tell their stories (Anderson et al., 2012). Counselors can use a **narrative approach** (e.g., Savickas, 2005, 2010) to get a rich sense of clients' experiences and perceptions. Creative art techniques—including time lines, collages, and other art forms that depict a client's past, present, and anticipated future—can help the counselor gain a better understanding of the client's perspective and sense of self (Gladding, 2016a).

Assessing a client's sense of self also includes evaluating the client's **hardiness**, a term that describes an individual's stress resistance (Maddi, 1999). Dimensions associated with hardiness include openness to change, commitment (i.e., sense of purpose), control (i.e., ability to determine personal responses to circumstances), and confidence (i.e., feeling personally valuable and capable; Anderson et al., 2012). Learning about a client's spiritual beliefs is important, as is recognizing a client's sense of self-efficacy.

Assessing **supports** means finding out what external resources clients can depend on. Support systems can include family, friends, and communities. In assessing support systems, counselors will want to find out how readily clients can access support or make the needed connections. Coupled with assessing support is the need to recognize which perceived "supports" may actually be toxic, leading to increased stress and less positive outcomes (Anderson et al., 2012).

Finally, counselors will want to assess the **strategies** their clients use to navigate transitions. In some cases, the strategies used in the past may have been counterproductive. Finding new ways to cope includes building on strengths, remembering strategies that have proved helpful in the past, and recognizing that some strategies that were helpful in the past may not work effectively in the present. The client and counselor work toward developing plans to manage transitions in ways that contribute to growth and well-being.

The 4-S system provides a framework counselors can use to help clients manage anticipated transitions, unanticipated transitions, and nonevents. Within that framework, cognitive–behavioral approaches, affective approaches, existential approaches, and specific interventions (e.g., grief work, support groups) can be used to help clients cope more effectively with changes and challenges associated with middle adulthood.

LATER ADULTHOOD

The average life span expectancy has increased dramatically since 1900, particularly in countries with adequate and accessible medical care. In the United States, the **graying of America** is a term that addresses this fact (see Figure 12–3). In 2014, 46.2 million Americans, or 14.5% of the population, were aged 65 or older. By the year 2030, that older population will be 70 million people or approximately 20% of the U.S. population (Fullen, 2016). Because people are living longer, the time period associated with later adulthood encompasses almost four decades!

Although aging and accompanying physical declines are inevitable, many people who are living longer are living better. Because of the increased emphasis on prevention and wellness, older adults are much more likely to experience healthy, active lifestyles than ever before (Newsome, Yancu, Wilkerson, & Matthews, 2017). They also report the highest levels of life satisfaction when compared to young and middle-aged adults (Fullen, 2016, p. 45). In

- More than one in every seven people in the U.S. population was an older adult.
- Persons reaching age 65 have an average life expectancy of an additional 19.3 years (20.5 years for females and 17.9 years for males).
- Older women outnumbered older men (25.1 million older women to 19.6 million older men, or a ratio of 128.1 women for every 100 men).
- Older men were much more likely to be married than older women were (70% of men vs. 45% of women).
- Racial and ethnic minority populations increased from 6.3 million in 2003 (17.5% of the older adult population) to 9.5 million in 2013 (21.2% of older adults) and are projected to increase to 21.1 million in 2030 (28.5% of older adults).

FIGURE 12–3   A Profile of Older Americans: 2015
Source: Data from Administration on Aging, 2015.

this section, developmental issues, activities in later adulthood, relationships, and responses to adversity are focused on, as well as related counseling implications.

Developmental Issues

Not everyone experiences developmental changes in the same way or at the same time. The Administration on Aging (2015) describes three categories of older adulthood: **65–74 (young old), 75–84 (old),** and **85 and beyond (old old)**. These are merely groupings and have little to do with the actual physical and mental health of persons in them since aging is a nonuniform process.

ERIKSON: EGO INTEGRITY VS. DESPAIR.   Erikson (1963) describes the psychosocial task of older adulthood as one of resolving the conflict between ego integrity and despair. Older adults have an opportunity to look back over their lives and reflect on the sense of meaning and purpose. Individuals who believe that they have accomplished what they set out to do often are able to achieve a sense of ego integrity. However, some older adults regret the way they have lived their lives. They may fear death and feel that their lives have been meaningless and experience what Erikson describes as despair (Belsky, 2016). Older adults experiencing despair may benefit from individual or group counseling in which they are encouraged to rewrite their self-narratives, coming to realize that they are worthwhile individuals. Even though they still may experience regret over things they have done (or not done) throughout the life span, older adults who have an opportunity to reframe their experiences and gain a sense of hope may be able to overcome the sense of despair.

The Case of Bill: Despair

Bill's wife of 40 years died after a long battle with cancer. Bill spent the last 8 years of his wife's life as her sole caregiver, rarely accepting help from well-meaning friends. After her death, Bill (age 78) believed that there was no reason to continue living. He found little joy in the activities he had enjoyed earlier in life, such as gardening and playing cards with friends. He rejected reaching out for help from his support network and refused to see a counselor. In his own world of despair, he insulated himself from his community and spent the last 2 years of his life watching TV, eating microwaved meals, and becoming increasingly isolated and resentful.

The Case of Pearl: Experiencing Ego Integrity

Pearl, age 83, views life optimistically. Several years ago, she retired from her job as a profes-
sor and moved to a retirement community. She remains active and engaged in life and in
learning. Pearl socializes regularly with family and friends. When asked to reflect on her life,
she stated that she had few regrets and is looking forward to her "golden years."

REMINISCENCE AND LIFE REVIEW. The process of **reminiscence** (recalling memories and
reflecting on their significance) facilitates the development of ego integrity (Haber, 2006).
For older adults, reminiscence helps strengthen one's sense of identity and prepare for the
inevitability of death. Reminiscing includes talking with peers and younger generations
about personal life experiences. In most cases, reminiscing is a healthy activity that helps
adults achieve a sense of inner continuity as they age (Atchley, 1989). Narrative therapists
contend that reminiscence allows us to construct our identities over time by telling and
retelling our life stories.

Life review is an intervention that counselors can use with older adults to build on
the therapeutic potential of reminiscence. A structured life review process can help older
adults reflect on the past and prepare for the future. During the life review process, older
adults often focus on experiences related to childhood, family, career, values, and aging
(Haber, 2006).

A structured life review can take place during individual counseling, group counseling,
or counseling that includes family members. There are many ways counselors can facilitate
life review. For example, counselors can encourage older adults to share photographs from
the past that depict important events and people in their lives. Another option is to ask older
adults to share music or stories that are meaningful to them. A life review intervention is
potentially less threatening and more familiar to older adults than other therapeutic
approaches are (Haight & Haight, 2007; Weiss, 1995).

A life review with older adults has many benefits. It typically increases ego integrity,
life satisfaction, and positive feelings, while decreasing feelings of depression and despair
(Bohlmeijer, Roemer, Cuijpers, & Smit, 2007). MacKinlay and Trevitt (2010) demonstrated
that a carefully facilitated reminiscence group can improve the quality of life and spiritual
well-being of individuals with dementia. Life review can also help older adults gain a sense
of control over their personal narratives, which is especially important as they lose other
forms of control and independence. Assisted reminiscence can help older adults discover
existential meaning as they reflect on the purpose of their lives within in a larger context.
Finally, life review completed with family members can enrich both the storyteller and the
listeners, thus strengthening the bonds between them (Luepker, 2010).

GEROTRANSCENDENCE. The concept of **gerotranscendence** is attributed to Erik Erikson's
wife, Joan Erikson (1997). Some theorists view the process of gerotranscendence as a ninth
stage of psychosocial development, whereas others view it as an extension of ego integrity
vs. despair. Researchers (e.g., Degges-White, 2005; Tornstam, 2000) describe gerotranscendence as a period when an older adult begins to withdraw from the material world and focus
on a world that is more spiritual. Adults in this stage may turn inward and spend more time
in self-reflection. Often, older adults experiencing gerotranscendence possess an inner calm
and sense of contentment. Although the process of turning inward may be misidentified as

depression, Degges-White (2005) suggests that counselors and caregivers need to respect the older adults' right to spend more time in solitude and reflection and less time with other people.

Activities in Late Adulthood

It is ageist to assume that older people are no longer active (Berger, 2014). On the contrary, older adults engage in a variety of activities (see Box 12–5), although the nature of those activities typically changes with physical decline.

BOX 12–5   The Iron Nun

Madonna Buder is a Roman Catholic religious sister who also is known as the Iron Nun (Buder & Evans, 2010). After training for several years, she ran her first marathon at the age of 55 and has continued competing into her 80s. In 2005, at the age of 75, she was the oldest woman to compete in the prestigious Ironman triathlon in Hawaii. She completed it again the following year, just 1 minute before the cutoff time of 17 hours.

Clearly, Sister Madonna represents an exception among older adults, but even those adults unwilling or unable to participate in the grueling training regimen required to complete an Ironman triathlon can still be active. Walking and swimming are less strenuous than running, as are water aerobics, chair exercises, and stretching.

The theory of **selective optimization with compensation (SOC)** is particularly applicable to older adults (Baltes, 1997; Heidemeier & Staudinger, 2012). According to SOC, successful aging involves three primary factors: **selection** (choosing goals and activities that are meaningful and important), **optimization** (enhancing positive changes to achieve a set of desirable outcomes), and **compensation** (counteracting certain losses in ways that make it possible to reach those outcomes). SOC is rooted in finding ways to adapt to life changes. It may include searching for new goals, reconstructing goal hierarchies, and focusing on goals that are most meaningful (Baltes, 1997, p. 372). Clinical mental health counselors can help older clients explore ways to adapt work- or leisure-related pursuits so that they can continue to engage in activities that are meaningful.

WORK AND RETIREMENT.   Whether it involves paid employment, volunteer activities, or continuing education, work provides psychological and practical benefits for people, including older adults (Moen & Spencer, 2006). Whether or not an older adult chooses to continue working for pay or to retire is dependent on many factors—for example, affordability, physical health, occupational identity, the meaning attached to work, and living situations. Sometimes retirement is voluntary: A person decides that it is time to transition from paid work into another phase of life. At other times, the decision is involuntary: An individual may be laid off, develop a health condition, or need to retire to take care of a loved one.

Older adults approach retirement in many ways. For example, some people choose to continue working full time until it is no longer possible to do so. Others may select **phased retirement**, cutting back on work hours with the intent of retiring completely sometime in the future. Some older adults retire and then pursue other opportunities, either paid or unpaid. In general, adults who are financially stable and who were satisfied in their lives before retirement tend to adjust best to retirement (Santrock, 2016). Older adults burdened by financial concerns, health issues, and other stressors may find adjustment to retirement more difficult. Still other older adults—those whose identity is strongly connected with work—may struggle with retirement because of a perceived loss of self-worth.

Retirement represents a major life transition and is a process rather than a single event. As with other major transitions, it takes time to adjust to a new way of living. During the process, people often grieve the lives left behind, flounder as they try out new paths, and then begin to integrate new ways of living with their integral sense of self (Schlossberg, 2011). Often, personal or group counseling can be especially helpful at this juncture. Counselors can help older adults explore their thoughts and feelings about work and retirement and the impact it has on their lives and sense of worth. Schlossberg highlights the need for retirees to check in with themselves by asking, "Can I change what is going on?" If the answer is no, then ask, "Can I change the way I look at the situation?" "Can my stress be reduced through meditation, exercise, counseling, or some combination of the three?" Group counseling for older adults working through retirement transitions can be especially helpful (Maples, 2009). It can help older adults identify common issues, concerns, and problems, as well as positive anticipations for "what comes next."

Relationships

The people who accompany us through life's journey make up our **social convoy** (Antonucci, Akiyama, & Merline, 2001). Bonds are formed over a lifetime, including bonds with spouses, partners, siblings, neighbors, and friends. The importance of having a social convoy continues throughout the life span and is particularly important in late adulthood (Berger, 2014). Older adults who have high-quality, diversified networks and social support have an advantage in late adulthood. The quality of social relationships held in later life may be a key indicator of the needs and risks older adults encounter as they age (Newsome et al., 2017).

MARRIAGE AND PARTNERSHIPS. Many older adults live with a spouse or partner. In 2014, 58.6% of adults age 65 and older were married (U.S. Census Bureau, 2015). Being married provides protection across the life course. Studies show that marriage or partnership increases the likelihood of good mental and physical health and economic well-being (Grundy & Tomassini, 2010). When compared with their unmarried counterparts, married older adults tend to have better cognitive function, life satisfaction, and well-being, particularly in the case of long-term first marriages.

LGBT PARTNERSHIPS. Just as with younger individuals, the population of older adults is diverse in sexual orientations, attitudes, and behaviors. Many older adults live in same-sex partnerships, and projections suggest that the number of self-identified LGBT seniors will double from approximately 3 million in 2009 to over 6 million by 2030 (Goldsmith & Kurpius, 2015).

The social stigma associated with being LGBT can be stronger for older adults than it is for younger generations. LGBT seniors are more likely than heterosexual seniors to be single and childless, and because they are often estranged from their biological families, they instead rely on families of choice (e.g., friends, other loved ones). These seniors may be more isolated, because of prejudice and societal biases. This combination of factors can negatively influence their self-concepts and put them at a greater risk for depression and anxiety (Knauer, 2009). Clinical mental health counselors need to be aware of the unique concerns experienced by the older LGBT population, particularly in regard to marginalization. With that said, however, nonheterosexual partnerships can provide many of the same benefits associated with marriage, and same-sex marriages are now legal nationally.

FRIENDSHIPS.   Older adults benefit greatly from friendships maintained throughout later life (Newsome et al., 2017). Although shrinking social networks due to changes in work-related roles, family structure, and the deaths of loved ones are inevitable with the passage of time, older adults benefit from the intimacy, companionship, and connectedness of relationships with friends. Friendships can strongly influence older adults' mental and physical health throughout the aging process. Clinicians can help older adults explore opportunities to socialize with peers through community-based programs, religious affiliations, and social clubs. Friendships are especially important for older people who do not have a living spouse or children (Berger, 2014).

Response to Adversity

To a large extent, the way older adults managed adverse circumstances when they were younger parallels the way they handle hardships in later adulthood. Many factors contribute to the way older adults respond to adversity, including individual personality traits, coping skills, stress management skills, and the nature and number of negative life events they experience. Physical health, social networks, and community resources also play large roles in regard to adversity responses. Managing adversity well is associated with *resiliency*, or the ability to "bounce back."

The Case of Bernice

Bernice, an 85-year-old widow, has dealt with many challenging life events. Her husband of 40 years died of Alzheimer's disease 15 years ago. Bernice spent many of those years as sole caregiver. Now, Bernice is experiencing several age-related health concerns, including tremors, failing eyesight, and arthritis. Last year, she made the decision to give up driving, so she depends on her adult children and certain friends to help her with tasks that she used to perform independently, like grocery shopping.

Many aging adults have similar experiences, especially age-related health concerns and loss of partners or loved ones. Older adults experience more negative life events than younger adults do, and the older adults' resilience is the key to how well they adapt to adversity.

Resilience has enabled Bernice to continue aging successfully. She is able to rely on her social support system for help and make informed decisions about how to manage change. She continues to be actively involved with her family, friends, and church community, all of which contribute to her resilience and ability to handle life's challenges.

WHAT IS ADVERSITY?   **Adversity** refers to negative life events that affect people throughout the life span. Examples of adversity include declining health, death of a spouse or life partner, death of a loved one, financial burdens, and chronic life stressors. Other adverse circumstances that may affect older adults include losing driving privileges, being forced to retire or relocate, and experiencing cognitive decline (Hildon, Montgomery, Blane, Wiggins, & Netuvili, 2009). As adults age, the number of cumulative adverse events tends to increase.

The way in which older adults cope with adversity affects their personal health, subjective well-being, and life satisfaction (Hildon et al., 2009; Ong & Bergeman, 2004).

WHAT IS RESILIENCE? "**Resilience** is the ability to adapt in a positive way to difficult and trying situations" (Skolvolt & Trotter-Mathison, 2016, p. 3). Individuals may demonstrate resilience in one aspect of their lives but not in another (Hildon et al., 2009). Some of the dimensions associated with resilience include these:

- Personality factors, including openness to change, agreeableness, and extraversion
- Sense of humor and optimism
- Adaptive and solution-focused coping skills that center on solving problems
- Religiosity/spirituality
- A sense of personal control and optimism
- Support from family, friends, and community
- Cultural influences

In contrast, adults who are less resilient, or whose resilience has eroded, are more vulnerable to a cascade of negative events, such as complicated grief and loneliness, perceived loss of control, and financial difficulty. Counselors who work with older adults need to be aware of the factors that can contribute to resilience or to vulnerability leading to a sense of isolation and despair (Hildon, Smith, Netuveli, & Blane, 2008). These counselors can provide a safe space for exploring emotions and reactions to negative life events and can design interventions that contribute to feelings of mastery and control (Ong & Bergeman, 2004).

AGEISM

For counselors to assume that the ageism so pervasive in U.S. society either does not affect them or does not apply to them represents a very serious form of denial and makes them all contributors to the problems faced by older persons.

Myers & Shannonhouse, 2013, p. 153

What Is Ageism?

Ageism is a form of prejudice exhibited when people are categorized and judged on the basis of their chronological age (Belsky, 2016). As with any form of prejudice, ageism has short- and long-term negative consequences for the older adults who experience it. For example, ageism can reduce social and economic opportunities, damage self-esteem, exacerbate health problems, and dampen the optimal potential of aging adults (Myers & Shannonhouse, 2013; North & Fiske, 2012). Some of the stereotypes people have about older adults include the following (Myers & Shannonhouse, 2013):

- Old age represents a time of unwelcome physical, emotional, social, and financial losses. *Reality:* Although physical decline is inevitable, many older adults report being happier than their younger counterparts.
- People who are older are more likely to live in poverty, experience disabilities, and be depressed. *Reality:* According to the Administration on Aging (2015), four out of five older people live above the poverty level, and more than 95% of older people live in communities as opposed to institutional settings. Rates of depression peak in middle adulthood rather than later life.

- Older adults do not engage in sexual activities. *Reality:* Not true.
- Older adults are dependent on the younger generation. *Reality:* Although 86% of adults experience some form of impairment, most are able to live actively and independently. Moreover, many older adults are resilient and experience a lower incidence of mental health issues than young people do (Whitbourne, 2010, as cited in Myers & Shannonhouse, 2013).

The point is this: Older adults are valuable members of society. Most have learned to adapt to life's changes and stressors, give back to the community through paid and unpaid work, and have a collective wisdom that benefits younger generations.

How Is Ageism Expressed?

Ageism is expressed in multiple ways—sometimes subtly and at other times blatantly (see Box 12–6). Many younger people are unaware that they are expressing ageism. For example, one manifestation of ageism is **elderspeak**, which is a condescending way of speaking to older adults. It often resembles baby talk, as evidenced by simple, short sentences, exaggerated emphasis, a slower rate, and a higher pitch (Belsky, 2016). Overuse of terms like *dear* or *honey* or *sweetie* can come across as patronizing. Older people may react with resentment, anger, or self-doubt.

Another form of ageism is expressed in the workplace. Although federal legislation prohibits employers from discriminating against employees on the basis of age, companies often offer older workers "packages," which provide financial incentives to retire. This practice occurs in spite of research findings that suggest that abilities and performance can continue to develop throughout our working lives, that the brain is much more "plastic" than previously assumed, and that new learning can occur at any age (e.g., Langer, 2009). Although some older workers do experience cognitive decline, dementia, and disabilities that keep them from performing effectively, many other older adults perform as effectively or more effectively than their younger counterparts do (Moore, 2012).

Elder abuse refers to maltreatment, neglect, and exploitation of older adults. It has become a serious problem in the United States and other countries (Nelson, 2005). Mandatory reporting laws regarding elder abuse exist in every state; however, not all mental health workers are aware of them (Myers & Shannonhouse, 2013). Negative attitudes toward older adults make it easier for a perpetrator to view their welfare and humanity as less important than that of younger adults (Nelson, 2005). The increasing problem of elder abuse, which often goes unreported, needs to be addressed by clinical mental health counselors and other healthcare providers.

BOX 12–6   Recognizing Ageism

Ageism is reflected in words, deeds, and actions. It is reflected in the things people do for older persons (e.g., speaking more loudly or slowly than normal to be sure one is heard and/or understood), people's responses to older persons (e.g., becoming visibly frustrated when standing behind them in the grocery line or demonstrating anger when driving behind them), and the things people fail to do (e.g., consider them for paid tasks, not just volunteer opportunities). Whenever people make choices and perform actions based on age, they may have succumbed to ageism.

Source: Adapted from Myers & Shannonhouse, 2013, p. 156.

Clinical mental health counselors are in a position to combat ageism on multiple levels. First and foremost, they need to examine their own attitudes and biases, recognizing that prejudice on any level is detrimental to individuals and society. They also can educate themselves about later adulthood and take part in training to work effectively with older adults. Also, they can engage in advocacy by working with policymakers and legislators and be more intentional about their language (e.g., omitting the term "the elderly" from their vocabulary). They can increase their outreach efforts to offer services to older adults. Most people will enter the later adulthood stage, barring premature death, and are likely to experience ageism on a personal level. By advocating for older adults and by combating ageism on all levels, clinical mental health counselors contribute not only to the well-being of society but also to the welfare of their future selves.

GENDER-AWARE COUNSELING

In addition to being aware of the issues and transitions that accompany varying ages and stages across the adult life span, counselors need to be aware of ways gender differences can affect the counseling process. **Gender-aware counseling** involves (a) recognizing the ways gender roles are socially and culturally constructed (e.g., Belsky, 2016; Langer, 2010); (b) recognizing that gender development is influenced by a multitude of factors, including biology, cognition, culture, and socialization by caregivers (Root & Denham, 2010); and (c) recognizing that gender refers to socially constructed roles, whereas biological sex refers to the possession of an XY chromosome pair for genetically healthy males and an XX chromosome pair for genetically healthy females (Robinson-Wood, 2017).

Societal beliefs about women and men have undergone many changes during the past century. Consider, for example, the fact that until 1920 women were not allowed to vote. Their socially prescribed role was in the home, where they cooked, took care of children, and managed the household while men worked and provided financial security for the family. These traditional roles were maintained to a large degree until the women's movement of the late 1960s, when feminism and the political fight for equality radically altered the traditional views society had of women. So it has only been since the 1970s that significant attention has been directed toward gender bias, gender equity, and differences between counseling women and men.

Counseling Women

Consider the following demographics that compare women with men.

- Approximately 57% of women are now in the workforce (U.S. Department of Labor, 2015).
- More men take an active role in child care than in years past, although women continue to provide most of the child care.
- Men own the majority of corporations in America.
- On average, women earn approximately 77% of what men earn in similar occupations, and the wage gap persists at all levels of education (National Committee on Pay Equity, 2012).
- Women outlive men by approximately five years.
- Elderly women are less likely to commit suicide than elderly men.
- Many diagnosed mental health disorders differ in prevalence by gender (Schwartz, Lent, & Geihsler, 2011).

The majority of clients who seek counseling services are women (e.g., Choate, 2009; Evans, 2013). The issues they bring to counseling are as unique as the individuals themselves. Women "are more likely than men to be diagnosed with depression, anxiety, phobias, eating disorders, borderline personality disorders, dissociative disorders, somatization disorders, agoraphobia, and posttraumatic stress disorder (PTSD)" (Evans, 2013, p. 139). The prevalence of diagnoses in women may be based, in part, on the stereotyping of female gender roles and behavior (American Psychological Association, 2007). Apart from diagnoses, women in counseling present with many common concerns, including grief and loss, the balancing of multiple roles, career concerns, negative body image, intimate partner violence, sexual and emotional abuse, parenting concerns, a lack of relationship boundaries, and the overvaluing of others' approval (Shallcross, 2012d). Three of those issues are examined here: the balancing of multiple roles, negative body image, and the overvaluing of others' approval.

THE BALANCING OF MULTIPLE ROLES.   Both women and men may find it difficult to manage multiple roles in today's society. For women, taking care of children and/or aging parents, meeting the demands of work, maintaining a healthy marriage or partnership, attending to friendships, engaging in spiritual and/or religious activities, and sustaining personal wellness goals are just a few of the roles they may be juggling at any given point in time. In addition to balancing these more tangible roles, Manley (cited in Shallcross, 2012d) states that both women and men frequently explore ways to balance their internal masculine and feminine traits.

Clinical mental health counselors can help women struggling to manage multiple roles and identities by emphasizing the importance of self-care. It is difficult, if not impossible, to take care of others and perform well at work without first taking care of oneself. Holistic approaches that emphasize physical, spiritual, relational, and emotional wellness can be helpful. Moreover, helping women with assertiveness skills, including learning when and how to say no, can enhance well-being and self-respect.

NEGATIVE BODY IMAGE.   Girls are socialized at an early age to believe that being accepted, loved, and respected requires meeting a certain standard of beauty (Brown & May, 2009). Moreover, beauty is often associated with prevalent media images of unrealistically thin, attractive women. When girls and women internalize these images as ideals to be achieved, they may develop disordered eating, low self-esteem, and body dissatisfaction (Evans, 2013).

Other negative body images can also cause distress for women. Some concerns are relatively common (e.g., "My breasts are too small," "I don't have a waist," "My hair is too thin," "I'm getting wrinkles"). Others are more overwhelming. For example, women who are diagnosed with cancer and receive treatment—whether it be surgery, chemotherapy, and/or radiation—deal with myriad challenges, the most important being survival. The challenge of adjusting to an altered body can be very real as well. Counselors who specialize in working with women diagnosed with breast cancer, ovarian cancer, and other types of cancer can help their clients with a range of concerns, including finding ways to adapt to a new body image.

THE OVERVALUING OF OTHERS' APPROVAL.   Women are socialized to be nurturing, emotionally expressive, agreeable, and nonassertive (Evans, Kincade, & Seem, 2011). These traits can contribute to the need for women to seek approval from others. Women who overvalue the approval of others may not have a well-developed internal locus of control. They equate their personal self-worth with others' approval. For example, a highly qualified professional woman may feel undervalued when her boss does not validate her work, even though she knows that both her efforts and the final product were superior. Without validation, she may question the value of her contribution and her worth to the company, thus undermining her self-esteem.

Counselors can help women move from a position of depending on others for approval to a place of respecting their own self-evaluations. In part, the tendency of women to look to others for approval is related to gender socialization. In American society, males are rewarded for exhibiting behaviors and attitudes that are assertive, independent, and competitive. A primary goal is to help women learn to rely on personal evaluation, rather than the evaluations of others (Shallcross, 2012d). Working toward this goal helps create emotional autonomy—freedom from the persistent need for external approval and reassurance (Robinson-Wood, 2017).

COUNSELING IMPLICATIONS.   Gender-sensitive counselors are aware of the unique concerns faced by women. Many counseling theories can be applied when working with women; however, counselors need to be cognizant of the *way* they are applied (Enns, 2003). Feminist therapy, relational–cultural therapy, narrative approaches, cognitive–behavioral therapy, person-centered therapy, and interpersonal therapy are just a few of the theory-based approaches that can be used successfully with women.

FEMINIST THERAPY.   Feminist therapy is a form of gender-aware counseling that views gender as central to the counseling process. It is rooted in feminist theory, which developed during the feminist political movement of the 1960s and 1970s. Initially, the women's movement was a challenge to patriarchal power, but as the movement grew, the focus included the development of females as unique individuals. Beginning with the publication of Carol Gilligan's *In a Different Voice* (1982), there has been an increased integration of feminist theory into counseling.

Feminist theory focuses on the influence of gender, the oppression of women, and the influence of politics (Neukrug, 2016). Feminist therapy is informed by feminist theory and has evolved considerably over the past several decades. The primary goal of feminist therapy is to empower clients, both female and male. Empowered individuals "know what they feel as they are feeling it and can use their feelings as a useful source of information" (Brown & Bryan, 2007, p. 1124).

Three basic tenets of feminist therapy, which are all connected with empowerment, can be summarized as follows (Evans, 2013):

1. *The personal is political.*   Personal problems have a social cause and a political solution. Feminist therapists encourage clients to change the status quo rather than simply adjust to it. They focus on the context of a client's life that contributed to the presenting concern.
2. *The relationship between counselor and client is egalitarian.*   Counselors focus on developing a therapeutic relationship that is nonhierarchical and collaborative. They intentionally demystify the counseling process and treat the client as an equal partner in the therapeutic process. The counselor acknowledges the client's expertise in knowing what is best for her life (Brown & Bryan, 2007).

3. *Women's experiences have priority.*   Feminist therapists give priority to a client's lived experiences. They consider women's and oppressed persons' concerns as primary, not an afterthought. Brown and Bryan (2007) describe this tenet somewhat differently. They emphasize a focus on wellness. Feminist therapists do not view problems as arising from psychopathology; instead, they view problems as coping responses to societal and political stress and subjugation.

Evans (2013) describes three strategies that make multicultural feminist therapy unique: gender-role analysis, power analysis, and cultural analysis. **Gender-role analysis** entails examining the gender socialization that has shaped clients' lives. Its purpose is to help clients learn how to differentiate between gender socialization beliefs that enhance their lives and those that hinder them. **Power analysis** helps clients learn about how they use power and how power is used against them. Clients are encouraged to use their power in ways that boost self-esteem and self-efficacy to fit their beliefs about themselves. **Culture analysis** enables clients to examine the multiple identities that have shaped their lives and explore ways cultural beliefs have affected their lives, both positively and negatively.

Counseling Men

Men face distinctive challenges related to masculine socialization experiences and changing cultural expectations (Good, Thomson, & Brathwaite, 2005; Reed, 2014). In general, men's traditional gender roles are more narrowly defined than women's. Beginning in childhood, stricter sanctions exist against boys adopting "feminine" behaviors than against girls adopting behaviors deemed "masculine" (Robinson-Wood, 2017). Furthermore, girls are rewarded for being emotionally expressive, whereas boys learn to restrict and repress their emotions (Good et al., 2005). Instead, they are socialized to be rational, independent, competitive, and aggressive. These internalized gender roles are frequently carried into adulthood. Men are less likely to seek counseling than women; however, they are more likely to be treated for severe psychiatric diagnoses (Vogel, Wester, & Larson, 2007). The male gender role, which emphasizes independence and control, could be one reason that fewer men seek counseling than women. Men may associate seeking help for emotional issues with weakness because it implies that they are unable to handle problems on their own (Addis & Mahalik, 2003). Seeking out and engaging in counseling may especially undermine a young man's sense of identity that has been developed and reinforced socially (Reed, 2014).

Neukrug (2016) cites a number of sources that illustrate differences based on gender. Some of the general characteristics of men that need to be considered in counseling are listed here. These are broad statements that cannot be generalized to all men since there are more within-group differences than between-group differences in men and women (Spurgeon, 2013). Nevertheless, many of these statements have considerable merit.

- Men are more restrictive emotionally, less communicative, and less comfortable with sad feelings, self-disclosure, and intimacy.
- Men tend to be more comfortable with angry feelings, aggression, and competitiveness.
- Men internalize negative messages about expressing traditionally feminine feelings, yet they are criticized for not being more sensitive.
- Men are criticized for being too controlling, yet they may be made to feel inadequate if they do not take control.

- Men are placed in positions of being in charge of others, which sometimes results in oppression of women. Such oppression not only harms women, but also harms men's psyches.
- Men commit the vast majority of crimes and have higher rates of substance abuse than women do.

CLINICAL CONCERNS. Men and women share many clinical concerns, although the concerns may be manifested differently by the two sexes. Depression, anxiety, substance abuse, violence, emotional restriction, career issues, gender-role identity, trauma, and stress management are just a few of the clinical issues that affect men (Reed, 2014). Depression and emotional restriction are dealt with here, as well as ways clinical mental health counselors can counsel men effectively.

Depression.   More than 6 million men in the United States experience depression each year (NIMH, 2016c). This number probably underestimates the number of men who experience depression but do not seek treatment. No one is immune to depression. Factors such as family history, excessive stress, the loss of a loved one, or serious illness can make men more vulnerable to depression. If untreated, depression can lead to personal, family, and financial difficulties.

Men experience depression differently than women do. Some indicators of depression in men include feeling tired and irritable, feeling angry and aggressive, experiencing difficulties sleeping, and losing interest in work, family, or hobbies (NIMH, 2016c). As noted earlier, men may be reluctant to seek help for this treatable condition because they believe that they can handle it themselves and consider seeking outside help a sign of weakness. However, depression is a serious condition. Although women with depression are more likely to attempt suicide, men with depression are more likely to die by suicide.

Several types of therapy can help treat depression. Cognitive–behavioral approaches, interpersonal therapy, and psychopharmacological interventions are especially efficacious (Good et al., 2005). Restrictive emotionality and conflicts between work and family relations are associated with men's depression. Clinical mental health counselors who are aware of the signs and symptoms of depression in men and who understand the contributing factors are in a better position to help men in treatment.

Emotional Restriction.   Men are socialized from an early age to demonstrate the essential features of masculinity: toughness, fearlessness, assertiveness, and denial of vulnerability (Mejia, 2005). Although many of these age-old characteristics of masculinity are now being challenged, many adult men today are likely to have already internalized them. Thus, they have been socialized to restrict or suppress emotions, exhibit independence and achievement, and avoid characteristics associated with femininity. Several researchers have identified links between aspects of masculinity and men's health concerns. For example, men reporting greater masculinity-related conflicts "are more psychologically distressed, experience greater depression, have more difficulty with interpersonal intimacy, and have greater biomedical concerns and poorer health behaviors" (Good et al., 2005, p. 700). Although clinical mental health counselors do not want to scare men away from treatment by immediately delving into the world of feelings, counselors need to be aware of the gender-associated characteristic of emotional restriction.

APPROACHES FOR COUNSELING MEN.   Many theoretical approaches, even feminist therapy, can be used to counsel men (Mejia, 2005). The strength of the therapeutic alliance is the best predictor of therapeutic outcomes (Wampold, 2000). However, masculine socialization toward stoicism and self-reliance may make it more challenging to establish a strong therapeutic alliance (Good et al., 2005). To facilitate the process, men need to feel supported, understood, and not judged. Counselors need to understand the ways gender socialization has affected male clients and develop the knowledge and skills needed to work effectively with men's issues. Neukrug (2016) has established a set of guidelines, based on the work of various researchers, that can help counselors working with male clients. An adapted version of those guidelines includes the following:

- *Accept men where they are.* This practice strengthens the therapeutic alliance and builds trust.
- *Don't push men to express what they may consider to be "softer feelings."* Pushing men to express feelings may push them out of counseling.
- *Validate feelings as they are expressed.* Early in the relationship, men may blame others and society for their problems. Validate their feelings without falling into the "blame game." Also, validate clients' perceptions of male sex-role stereotypes.
- *Have a plan for the counseling process.* Collaborate with men in developing a plan. Men generally like structure and tend to be goal-oriented.
- *Introduce developmental issues.* Discussing developmental issues can help normalize particular issues, such as questioning one's career choice.
- *Slowly encourage the expression of new feelings.* When new feelings are validated, men may begin to feel more comfortable sharing more vulnerable feelings.
- *Explore underlying issues, and reinforce new ways of understanding the world.* As counseling progresses, deeper concerns may emerge, such as feelings of inadequacy or family-of-origin issues.
- *Encourage behavioral change.* As new insights emerge, encourage men to try out new behaviors.
- *Encourage the integration of new feelings, new cognitions, and new behaviors.*

In addition to individual interventions, group counseling with men has been empirically supported (Gladding, 2016b). Group counseling can be powerful in cutting through defenses and building a sense of community. It can help men normalize experiences by interacting with men dealing with similar issues. Group work also allows men to reprocess many of the negative aspects of traditional masculinity—such as emotional restrictiveness, homophobia, and autonomy—and learn to value emotional connection and vulnerability (Good et al., 2005).

Summary and Conclusion

In this chapter, developmental issues and related counseling concerns encountered by adults throughout the life span were examined. Adults experience many transitions as they age—transitions that differ with each stage of life. The transition framework, which provides a way of understanding pivotal events and nonevents that people encounter throughout the course of a lifetime, was described.

Although the age divisions are somewhat fluid, there are four major stages of adulthood: emerging adulthood (ages 18 to 25–29), early adulthood (ages 25–29 to 40), middle adulthood (ages 40 to 60–65), and later adulthood (ages 65 and beyond). There is a need to pay particular attention to later adulthood for several reasons: (a) It is a stage of life that encompasses approximately four decades; (b) it represents a stage of life that has not been given much attention, even though the population of older adults is increasing more rapidly than any other age group; and (c) older adults are negatively affected by ageism, or prejudice based on age.

Gender-aware counseling enables clinical mental health counselors to work effectively with women and men. Gender roles are socially constructed and significantly influence the way women and men experience life and view the world. As a result, although women and men experience many of the same clinical concerns, the manner in which they experience them differs. Moreover, some counseling issues are germane to men, whereas others are experienced more frequently by women. Counselors need to develop awareness, knowledge, and skills related to gender and gender-aware counseling so as to provide efficacious treatment to the clients they serve.

PART 4

Clinical Mental Health Counseling: Settings and Services

CHAPTER 13

College and Career Counseling

Shutterstock

Far in the back of his mind, he harbors thoughts
  like small boats in a quiet cove
    ready to set sail at a moment's notice.
I, seated on his starboard side,
  listen for the winds of change
    ready to lift anchor with him
      and explore the choppy waves of life ahead.
Counseling requires a special patience
  best known to seamen and navigators—
    courses are only charted for times
      when the tide is high and the breezes steady.

Reprinted from "Harbor Thoughts," by S. T. Gladding, 1985,
Journal of Humanistic Education and Development, 23, p. 68.
Copyright © 1985 by Samuel T. Gladding. Used with permission.

CHAPTER OVERVIEW

From reading this chapter, you will learn about

- The history of college counseling and the ways that college counseling has changed over time, including the way it is structured
- Prevalent issues and mental health concerns faced by today's college students
- Crisis management in college settings
- Career counseling, career services, and current influences on the world of work
- Prominent theories of career counseling and specific skills associated with career counseling

As you read, consider

- What are some of the prominent concerns and more serious mental health issues that college students face
- Why it is important to have a crisis management team on college campuses
- How workers have been affected by economic conditions
- What specific skills career counselors possess
- What specific services career counselors provide

Clinical mental health counselors provide services in many different settings, and those services vary in purpose, nature, and duration. In this chapter, the ways clinical mental health counselors practice in college and career counseling are covered. Counseling in college and university settings requires a knowledge of life span development, mental health issues, and career-related concerns. Career counselors, whether in a college setting or not, need to be well versed in developmental issues as well as knowledgeable about the world of work.

COUNSELING IN COLLEGE AND UNIVERSITY SETTINGS

History of College Counseling

College health services first came into existence in 1861 at Amherst College with a focus on students' physical health. Mental health at the time was the responsibility of teachers and clergy who emphasized guidance and character development.

The importance of mental health on college campuses began in 1908 when Clifford Beers published a seminal book, *A Mind That Found Itself,* which promoted the concept of mental hygiene. In his book, Beers, who had had mental difficulties while a student at Yale, discussed the significance of providing psychosocial therapy and a community-based support system for psychiatric patients so they would receive the best possible treatment and increase their chances for a recovery from mental illness. American psychiatry and subsequent mental health fields were heavily influenced by the mental hygiene movement. Beers's initial goals within this movement became the foundation for future mental health practices and guided initial college mental hygiene clinics, which were a part of student health services (Barreira & Snider, 2010).

In 1910, Dr. Stewart Paton of Princeton University opened the first official mental hygiene clinic on a college campus after noticing that students were leaving the university without finishing their degrees because of emotional and personal difficulties (Kraft, 2011). Paton realized that colleges were not providing students with adequate skills to cope with the challenges and stressors of adult life. Therefore, he advocated for institutions of higher education to promote the concept of emotional stability and to teach students skills that would help in coping with stress (Barreira & Snider, 2010). Subsequently, several more colleges and universities introduced similar mental hygiene clinics, all of which were operated by psychiatrists.

In 1920, Dr. Frankwood Williams addressed the members of the American Student Health Association and discussed the importance of mental hygiene. He stated that it was imperative to start focusing on mental health for several reasons, such as retaining students, preventing mental illness, and helping students reach their full intellectual potential. In 1931, a set of standards for college health and mental hygiene was adopted at the first National Conference on Health in Colleges (Kraft, 2011). The University of Wisconsin opened the University Testing Bureau in 1932, which was the first counseling center independent of health services on a college campus. During that time period, counseling centers were still primarily used for academic and vocational counseling and for support of student development (Barreira & Snider, 2010).

After World War II, college counseling centers became more prevalent as institutions of higher education realized veterans returning from combat often had serious mental and emotional issues. During this period, a study committee of the Group for the Advancement of Psychiatry (GAP) concluded that colleges and universities should focus not only on educational and intellectual development, but also on emotional maturity. In the late 1940s and early 1950s, college counseling centers, influenced by the mental hygiene movement, focused on prevention and development rather than clinical issues. With the publication of the *Diagnostic and Statistical Manual* in 1952, the focus of college counselors began to change as they used a combination of developmental and clinical approaches in their work with students (Barreira & Snider, 2010). Many college counseling centers began utilizing a multidisciplinary approach to focus on wellness and development as well as on more serious mental illness (Kraft, 2011).

Counseling psychologists were the main mental health professionals, outside of psychiatrists, who provided therapy to students when counseling centers began focusing on emotional concerns in addition to academic and vocational concerns. College counseling centers became even more distinct from student health services with the introduction of a separate accrediting body called the International Association of Counseling Services (IACS), which remains the primary accreditation body for college counseling centers. Additionally, the Association for University and College Counseling Center Directors (AUCCCD), established in the 1950s, gave college counseling center directors and college counselors opportunities to discuss trends, concerns, and best practices (Barreira & Snider, 2010).

During the early 1960s, the community mental health model was introduced, and mental health practitioners, including those in college counseling centers, embraced prevention and community-based support as ways to address mental health issues (Barreira & Snider, 2010). Thus developing campus prevention programs and advancing health education became prevalent (Kraft, 2011). Currently, the community mental health model is a framework that many colleges and universities utilize to structure the responsibilities of their counseling centers. The main components include serving a certain population, attending to the whole person, and promoting overall wellness through psychoeducation and prevention techniques. Centers utilize a multidisciplinary team method and identify concerning issues in students as quickly and efficiently as possible.

In 1992, the American College Counseling Association (ACCA) was formed as a division within ACA. Counselors, including clinical mental health counselors, are members of ACCA and are now quite involved in college counseling centers.

Campus Counseling Centers and Areas of Clinical Focus

The number of students and severity of issues that college counseling centers currently face are significant matters of concern. The demand for counseling on college campuses often exceeds the time and resources available from counseling staffs. The community mental health model stresses the importance of a multidisciplinary approach and identification of individual needs so that appropriate mental health care is implemented. The counseling response to student mental health concerns may depend on the size of the institution and the availability of staff and resources. Larger colleges and universities are usually better equipped to provide care for a wide array of developmental, emotional, and clinical issues, whereas smaller colleges and universities often work with students facing developmental and minor clinical issues, referring more severe cases to clinical mental health agencies (Barreira & Snider, 2010).

The common factor among all college counseling centers is that they offer some type of individual counseling or psychotherapy. Beyond that aspect, the structural nature of centers and the services offered vary widely. Centers may provide group counseling, support groups, couples counseling, substance abuse counseling, career counseling, eating disorders treatment, psychiatric services, and psychological assessment and testing. Some counseling centers are independent organizations, whereas other centers are combined with student health services. A joint organization of counseling services and health services can lead to increased collaboration, more holistic care, and streamlining of resources. However, a merged office can also present issues with confidentiality, budget and resource allocation, administration, and marketing of services (American College Health Association, 2015).

Even though contemporary college counseling centers have to be cognizant of the wide array of psychiatric illnesses that may affect students, counseling centers generally approach therapy through a developmental lens. Counselors often spend the first and perhaps the second session completing an intake with the student to gain a better understanding of the presenting concerns and to discuss treatment goals. The intake appointments focus on information gathering regarding such topics as family history, academic progress, social and developmental history, current or past trauma, suicidal or homicidal ideation, medical problems, current and past levels of functioning and coping, and psychiatric history. The first few sessions also focus on rapport building in order to foster the therapeutic alliance, which is integral in the counseling process.

Therapy in a college counseling center is time sensitive because of session limits and the overwhelming demand on counselors to work with large numbers of students. Therefore, many counselors use a brief therapy or solution-focused approach with clients so that a certain area of concern is emphasized and worked on throughout the counseling process. In addition, counselors in a college setting may approach treatment with developmental issues in mind and may use psychoeducation in sessions to normalize experiences and increase awareness. College counseling must take into account the concerns of this exclusive population and the realistic capabilities of the setting. Effective college counselors practice collaborative treatment planning that meets the developmental level and presenting concerns of clients (Eichler & Schwartz, 2010).

Prevalent Mental Health Issues among College Students

The American College Health Association administers the National College Health Assessment II to college students each year in order to gather information about students' physical and mental health. As evidenced by the reported statistics, college students face a number of issues that pertain to their mental health, relationships, and behaviors throughout their time on campus. The following sections address key issues found in college student populations, such as stress, homesickness, interpersonal difficulties, and substance use and abuse.

STRESS.   During emerging adulthood (18 to 25 years), college students face a number of new obstacles, such as academic challenges and independent daily living. Almost 86% of college students (American College Health Association, 2015) reported feeling overwhelmed sometime in the last 12 months. Transitioning from high school to college can be a significant change for many students who face the challenge of learning how to thrive independently of their parents. This transition usually causes students to redefine roles in their lives and to take on new roles. Additional stress in college is elicited by such factors as academics, social relationships, finances, daily living, cognitive deficits, illness, depression and anxiety, poor nutrition, decreased life satisfaction, and decreased amounts of sleep (Brougham,

Zail, Mendoza, & Miller, 2009; Degges-White & Borzumato-Gainey, 2014; Kadison & Digeronimo, 2004).

A study by Brougham et al. (2009) demonstrates that college women experience higher overall stress levels than men over such factors as family relationships, social relationships, daily living, and finances. The American College Health Association (2015) reports that college women experience feeling hopeless, very sad, very lonely, exhausted, overwhelmed, depressed, and anxious to a higher degree than their male counterparts. In addition, women are more likely to screen positively for an anxiety disorder (Eisenberg, Gollust, Golberstein, & Hefner, 2007).

College-age women tend to use **emotion-focused strategies**, such as self-help and self-punishment, as coping mechanisms to a greater degree than men do to deal with life stressors. College men are more likely to use **adaptive emotion-focused coping strategies** for certain stressors, whereas women are found to use **maladaptive emotion-focused strategies**. However, in both groups, emotion-focused coping strategies are used to a greater extent than **problem-focused coping strategies**. In general, coping strategies that utilize problem-focused techniques—such as action, planning, and acceptance—are healthier and more adaptive for college students than are emotion-focused strategies that rely on avoidance, self-punishment, and excessive emotional reactivity (Brougham et al., 2009). Moreover, students who demonstrate negative coping skills and perfectionism are more likely to have health issues and/or use alcohol than are students who exhibit optimism and greater self-esteem (Pritchard, Wilson, & Yamnitz, 2007).

HOMESICKNESS AND ADJUSTMENT.   The transition to college is likely to evoke a range of feelings for college students. It is normal for most students to experience mild forms of homesickness and then develop coping skills to address these issues. However, some students exhibit extreme difficulty and undergo severe distress when leaving home and adjusting to the college environment. Students who suffer from homesickness may report symptoms of anxiety and depression, may become socially withdrawn, and may not be able to concentrate on academic work. Homesickness can also intensify preexisting mood disorders or other mental health concerns.

Adjustment concerns can be exacerbated by cultural differences between the home environment and the college environment. If the student is from a different culture or different part of the country than the institution, transitional issues may be more significant. International students can be at greater risk of experiencing adjustment issues because they often have to cope with a new cultural environment, a new language, different foods and clothing styles, and diverse beliefs, values, and religions. Additionally, many students face the fear of finding a place to belong at their new college or university. If students do not initially find a social network or feel accepted, they may experience homesickness more intensely or for a longer period of time. For international students and students from minority cultures, discrimination and stereotyping can pose challenges in finding supportive and accepting peer networks.

Some risk factors for experiencing intense homesickness include being young in age, having spent little time away from home, perceiving the distance between school and home as great, relying heavily on family members, feeling low levels of control, possessing an insecure attachment to parents, and perceiving discrimination on campus. Conversely, students who are older in age, have spent time away from home, possess higher self-efficacy, make friends easily, and feel connected to their institution are likely to experience less homesickness (Thurber & Walton, 2012).

College counselors and other student affairs staff and faculty can be proactive in helping students adjust to the campus environment. Staff can present a positive image of the school to prospective students through personal interaction and website information. Social networking websites and established social connections prior to campus entry can assist students in feeling welcome and can decrease stress about finding a group of friends. When students arrive on campus, staff can provide helpful information about campus resources, university history, student groups, and student culture. Events can be set up to help international students feel welcome on campus; for example, campus leaders can help international students meet students from their home country (if possible), as well as students from the host country.

When students seek out counselors or other staff to talk about feeling homesick, counselors and staff members can help normalize students' feelings and encourage them to discuss their thoughts and emotions. Students can work with counselors to regain a sense of control, resolve family-of-origin issues, make plans for how and when to communicate with family members and friends at home, learn about pertinent campus resources, establish healthy coping mechanisms and lifestyle choices, and understand how to develop self-compassion (Thurber & Walton, 2012).

COMPLEX TRAUMA AND DATING VIOLENCE.   Many students arrive at college after living in unstable home environments and/or enduring years of physical, emotional, or sexual abuse by family members. Experiencing traumatic events repeatedly over time can result in **complex trauma**, which usually develops in the context of a particular relationship or setting (Courtois, 2008). Although complex trauma can occur in adulthood, it is more often associated with childhood abuse, which results in insecure attachment to the abusive caregiver and leads to symptoms of PTSD (Pearlman & Courtois, 2005). Partly because of insecure attachment, individuals who have experienced complex trauma may exhibit an array of symptoms that are associated with the unresolved and destructive child–caregiver relationship. Some of these symptoms include emotional lability, dissociation, feelings of guilt and shame, lack of trust in others, medical issues, and hopelessness about being understood (Courtois, 2008; Ford & Courtois, 2013).

Successful and effective treatment for complex trauma often occurs in three stages. The first stage consists of stabilization, psychoeducation regarding trauma, skill development, and safety planning. The second stage involves discussion and exploration of the complex trauma events. The third stage represents a culmination of all the stages and involves working on daily relationships within the context of a normal life (Courtois, 2008). In addition to individual therapy, support groups or group therapy in the college setting may be helpful. Groups can assist students in recognizing that other students have gone through similar types of trauma. Groups also help students who have a history of trauma learn how to cope more effectively within the college environment.

Relationship violence, or intimate partner violence, is another prevalent abuse issue on college campuses. Studies have shown that about 90% of college relationships involve some form of emotional or psychological abuse, and about 20% of relationships include sexual violence (Amar & Gennaro, 2005). Additionally, physical abuse affects as many as one-fifth to one-third of college-age couples (Amar & Gennaro, 2005; Kaukinen, Gover, & Hartman, 2011). Contrary to popular belief regarding women's roles in abusive relationships, women have been found to be victims, perpetrators, and both victims and perpetrators within dating relationships. Some of the symptoms that counselors may witness in clients involved in abusive relationships include depression, anxiety, psychosomatic complaints, anger, suicidal ideation, fear, and hopelessness.

Campus leaders can help educate students about relationship violence and provide resources describing safe places on campus for reporting and discussing relationship violence. Peer-initiated prevention and education strategies are often effective in capturing the attention of fellow students. Additionally, educational awareness events can be targeted toward certain populations and settings, including sororities and fraternities, residence life, and student groups. Directors of such events can provide facts regarding relationship violence, lead discussion-based forums that give students an opportunity to share personal experiences, and teach skills for healthy conflict management. Although students can lead these programs, counselors should be present to address any issues that arise with individual students during the event (Schwartz, Griffin, Russell, & Frontaura-Duck, 2006). Finally, counselors can provide resources and a solid support system to students who have been (or are still) in abusive relationships.

SUBSTANCE USE.   In their newly independent states, college students often find a sense of thrill and excitement in experimentation. They also may feel pulled to fit in with peer groups. Therefore, substance use is a prevalent occurrence on college campuses and has been linked with risky behaviors and various health problems. Approximately 80% of American college students drink (National Council on Alcoholism and Drug Dependence, 2017). In addition, the number of students who use marijuana is approximately 38% (Donaldson James, 2016). Males tended to use drugs slightly more than females did, but there was not a reported difference in alcohol consumption. Overall, alcohol use on college campuses has not changed significantly in the last 25 years (Anderson, 2011).

Because college students are in a developmental phase in which long-term consequences are not contemplated as often as short-term rewards, substance use behavior can be impulsive and perilous. A number of consequences—including automobile accidents, sexual assaults, and unprotected sexual intercourse—frequently occur after students binge drink with peers (Halligan, Pohl, & Smith, 2006). Injuries—such as falls, automobile accidents, and drowning—are the most common adverse physical consequences of alcohol use on college campuses. In addition, medical complications, such as gastrointestinal bleeding and coma, can occur when students drink an excessive amount of alcohol (Rimsza & Moses, 2005). Tragically, about 1,800 students each year die because of alcohol-related incidents (National Institute on Alcohol Abuse and Alcoholism, 2014).

Alcohol consumption and substance use are often dependent on the student's environment. For example, fraternities and sororities have a high rate of alcohol use, followed by residence halls and dormitories. About 80% of fraternity and sorority members and 45% of students in residence halls report binge drinking (Rimsza & Moses, 2005). According to the National Institute on Alcohol Abuse and Alcoholism, binge drinking is defined as consuming four or more drinks for women and five or more drinks for men in less than two hours. Frequent episodes of binge drinking can damage the liver and various other organs. About half of underage college students find alcohol very accessible, and the same number of students engage in binge drinking.

Many students report consuming alcohol because of peer pressure and a desire to fit in. Social anxiety can motivate students to drink as a way to cope with worries, conform, experience intoxication, and appear more social (Ham, Zamboanga, Bacon, & Garcia, 2009). Students often drink because they believe that their peers are also consuming a similar amount of alcohol at a comparable frequency (American College Health Association, 2015). However, the American College Health Association survey results indicate that the perception of substance use is much greater than the actual reported amount of use. For example, 65.9% of students reported having used alcohol in the past 30 days, but students perceived that about 93% of students had consumed alcohol in the past 30 days. Similarly, about 15% of students reported having used marijuana in the last 30 days, but students perceived that over 80% of students had smoked marijuana in the last 30 days. The difference between the statistics surrounding students' perceptions and students' actual use is staggering.

Because of students' perceptions regarding peer substance use and the consequences associated with student substance use, it is vital that college administrators, faculty, and staff take a vested interest in educating students about the topic. In response, colleges and universities have made concerted efforts over the years to reduce binge drinking. However, despite such efforts, the rate of binge drinking has remained relatively constant, with a little less than half of students reporting binge drinking behavior.

Some of the factors related to this trend are as follows. First, alcohol use is not simply a campus issue, but also a societal issue. Many students learn drinking behaviors in high school but do not receive sufficient alcohol awareness education to motivate them to change. Second, campuses often deal with alcohol issues in a judicial or disciplinary capacity instead of exploring the causes behind the drinking behavior. Additionally, college staff who plan alcohol awareness programs often do not carry out appropriate research or have adequate resources to execute successful initiatives (Anderson, 2011).

To increase the effects of campus interventions, campus officials need to implement strategies on various levels in order to make an impact on students. Although policies and disciplinary procedures are integral to addressing inappropriate behavior, educational programs and interventions need to be implemented to increase student awareness. Programs dealing with alcohol and drug use should not simply address the benefits of abstaining but should also address how to engage in such behaviors safely and carefully. Counselors and other staff who deal with alcohol and drug issues on campus should participate in programs that train them to work effectively with at-risk students. A campus alcohol and drug education coordinator can plan and oversee various initiatives, but the entire campus community needs to be involved in addressing substance use and abuse. Giving students opportunities to get involved with awareness initiatives can help gain peer support from other students. Students are more likely to be influenced by their own peers' thoughts and behaviors than by the thoughts and behaviors of staff and faculty. Finally, faculty members have a unique opportunity to incorporate alcohol awareness into courses through projects, class discussions, and service-learning opportunities (Anderson, 2011).

Severe Mental Illness and Suicide

In recent years, the prevalence of severe mental illness and suicidal ideation has increased on college campuses. Suicide is the third leading cause of death for traditionally aged college students (Suicide.org, 2016). Therefore, college counselors, who used to view their work as primarily developmental in nature, now have to contemplate how to address presenting concerns of severe psychopathology (Beamish, 2005). A significant issue lies in getting those students who have more severe concerns to seek counseling services. Even though the suicide rate for students who are clients at counseling centers is three times higher than that of students who are not clients, the *risk* of suicide for student clients is

18 times higher than that of the general student population. Therefore, college counseling centers play a critical role in reducing harm to students who present with serious mental and emotional issues (Schwartz, 2006a, 2011).

There is a strong association between students who screen positively for generalized anxiety disorder and major depression and students who screen positively for major depression and suicidal thoughts (Eisenberg et al., 2007). There also are strong associations between feeling hopeless and having suicidal ideation and between loneliness and suicidal ideation. Additionally, students who express suicidal thoughts are more likely to use tobacco, alcohol, and other drugs than are students who do not express suicidal thoughts. Consequently, it is imperative that college counselors understand the risk factors associated with suicide when assessing a student for suicidal ideation. Because many students may not come directly to campus counseling centers to discuss their mental health, counseling services should collaborate with primary care providers and other mental health professionals in the community (Schwartz & Friedman, 2009).

A significant protective factor for students on college campuses is the restricted access to firearms, which account for half of completed suicides. Restricted access to firearms helps keep students from having the means to attempt suicide using lethal weapons. Another factor that campuses must consider is the accessibility of buildings from which students might jump (Schwartz, 2006b). Counselors can be leaders in suicide prevention by making crisis resources available to students, having crisis protocol in place for staff, and educating staff and students about issues related to suicide.

Crisis Management on College Campuses

One approach to addressing severe mental illness, suicidality, and other serious concerns facing college students is a comprehensive model entitled the **new diversity initiative** (Nolan, Ford, Kress, Anderson, & Novak, 2005). This model addresses mental illness in an inclusive manner by involving faculty, staff, and students throughout the college campus. It is composed of seven elements and can be implemented on any college campus.

- The first element of the model involves helping faculty and student affairs staff to become comfortable discussing mental illness and suicide. Staff and faculty participate in a workshop to help them understand their own biases and sensitivities about mental illness, to educate them about the wide range of mental health issues on college campuses, and to increase awareness of the services available at the college counseling center. A second purpose of the workshop is to educate faculty and staff about the myths and realities associated with mental illness.
- The second element of the model involves forming a counseling center research team, which compares student mental illness on campus with regional and national trends. Campus research focuses on clinical issues of individual clients as well as spirituality, self-injurious behavior, family history of medical and mental illness, stress management, and conflict resolution skills. The information from the study is then shared with administrators, faculty, and staff and can be utilized to inform best practices in college counseling.
- The third element of the initiative is the development of a video about the most common issues seen in college counseling centers, which is used as a training tool for faculty, staff, and students for conveying the gravity of severe mental illness and suicide. The video can also be useful in educating various campus constituents about how to address and assist students who appear to be struggling with mental health issues.

- The fourth element consists of a program called "Because We Care." The program is designed to identify students in psychological distress who might not otherwise be identified. Anyone who is concerned about a student can complete a form describing the student's behavior and appearance and then return the form to a designated student affairs official, who addresses the concerns and makes referrals to the counseling center as needed. The program provides an avenue for students to share their concerns about fellow students.
- The fifth element consists of an academic misconduct research group composed of university staff and faculty members. The group is directed to investigate any type of disorderly conduct or disruption caused by a student on campus. It is in charge of handling such cases, providing resources, making referrals, or dismissing students from the university.
- The sixth element provides for the program's long-term continuation through ongoing training. A team of faculty and staff designs a training module for presentations on campus. The module is adapted to target specific audiences, such as students who are concerned about fellow students and faculty who are concerned about in-class disruptive behavior.
- The final element of the initiative involves using pretests and posttests to assess knowledge gained by faculty and staff who have participated in the trainings. Further assessment occurs on an ongoing basis to evaluate their utilization of materials presented in the trainings.

Addressing severe mental illness, suicidal ideation, and incidence of suicide on a college campus must be a collaborative effort designed to assist as many students as possible and to identify issues as early as possible. Because campus counselors are not in every student environment (e.g., classrooms, residence halls, student groups), it is imperative that campus administrators, faculty, staff, and students learn what to do if a student is struggling with severe mental health issues. Additionally, college administrators need to clearly articulate policies regarding suicide to campus faculty and staff. Ethical and legal concerns have become prevalent as a result of the tragic deaths that have occurred across the country on college campuses (Kay, 2010).

Another issue that has become significant is threat assessment and consultation. Violent and tragic occurrences on campuses such as Virginia Tech and Northern Illinois University have prompted campus officials to reexamine their own protocol regarding students of concern who exhibit disturbing behavior. Counseling centers are often directly involved in assessing students and in providing consultation services to campus departments. Many campuses have instigated crisis team meetings or students-of-concern meetings that involve various campus constituents who provide input on students who have exhibited troubling behaviors. A crisis team is vital for detecting issues early, cross-examining information across departments, developing protocol for reporting and resolving concerns, and training and supporting various departments in addressing students of concern. Counselors usually serve on such committees to provide consultation but still must adhere to ethical codes of confidentiality unless imminent suicidal or homicidal danger is present. It is helpful for faculty and staff members on crisis committees to understand that students who intend to commit targeted violence typically exhibit disturbing behavior over a period of time and are often suicidal. Institutions must develop effective and efficient protocol to address and investigate students who could pose a risk to the campus community (Eels & Rando, 2010).

Other Issues of Concern

Eating disorders and body image issues are commonly encountered in the college community and can be associated with a number of other symptoms. Symptoms of depression are often associated with eating disorders and the desire to be thin (Booth & Phiipps, 2014; Grossbard, Atkins, Geisner, & Larimer, 2012). Eating disorders can lead to severe medical complications such as heart and kidney failure, osteoporosis, reproductive issues, and even death (Nelson, Castonguay, & Locke, 2011). The typical client who presents with an eating disorder in college settings is a Caucasian, heterosexual female; however, many men are starting to report issues with their body image and eating. Men who experience body image issues are often striving for bulked-up, muscular bodies. They do not exhibit depressive symptoms and disordered eating behaviors as frequently as men and women with eating disorders who strive to be thin (Grossbard et al., 2012; Smith, Hawkeswood, Bodell, & Joiner, 2011). A multidisciplinary approach to treatment is the best way to provide comprehensive care for clients experiencing eating disorders.

Multicultural and diversity factors also need to be considered when working on a college campus. Colleges and universities are composed of students who vary in race, ethnicity, nationality, religious or spiritual practices, gender identity, sexual orientation, ability, socioeconomic status, and age (Zavadil & Kooyman, 2014). Therefore, college counselors cannot afford to be culturally encapsulated. Because culture can play a prominent role in a student's life, college counselors need to acknowledge and respect cultural issues during counseling sessions. Counselors also can be advocates for clients who experience discrimination, bias, and prejudice based on personal characteristics. Moreover, college counselors can help instigate policies that denounce all forms of discrimination, prejudice, and marginalization.

To summarize, college students face unique opportunities and challenges within the college environment. Although college is a time of great excitement, new opportunities, and growth, it can present a time of uncertainty, social insecurity, and internal turmoil. College counselors and other college staff are valuable resources for students as they learn to navigate the multifaceted college experience.

CAREER COUNSELING

Choosing a career is more than simply deciding what one will do to earn a living. Occupations influence a person's whole way of life, including physical, mental, and emotional health. Work roles and other life roles are intricately interconnected. Thus, income, stress, social identity, meaning, education, clothes, hobbies, interests, friends, lifestyle, place of residence, and even personality characteristics are all linked to one's work life (Niles & Harris-Bowlsbey, 2013). In some cases, work groups serve as cultures in which social needs are met and values are developed. The nature and purpose of work relate to a person's sense of identity, well-being, and life satisfaction. Qualitative research indicates that individuals who appear most happy in their work are committed to following their interests; exhibit a breadth of personal competencies and strengths; and function in work environments characterized by freedom, challenge, meaning, and a positive social atmosphere (Henderson, 2000).

The Need for Career Development Services

The need for career development services is high on college campuses and elsewhere (Brown, 2016). People seek career services for many reasons. Young people in college often need help understanding their values, interests, motivations, personality, and skills. They typically are exploring options as they relate to their majors, minors, advanced fields of study, and the world of work. People who are unemployed and underemployed may seek career or vocational counseling to get help with their job search. Some individuals seek career services because they are dissatisfied with their jobs and want to find work that is more fulfilling. Yet other individuals may struggle with workaholism, work–life balance, work stress, and mental health issues related to work (see Box 13–1). In this section, a general overview of career counseling and career services, particularly as they relate to clinical mental health counseling, is presented.

BOX 13–1 Work and Stress

The nature of work means that stress can crop up at any given time, but new research published in the *Journal of Occupational and Environmental Medicine* indicates that work-related stress drastically increases during a recession and that stress leads to an accompanying rise in employee absenteeism. When people feel overloaded and stressed at work, they are more likely to bring that stress home with them (cf. Shallcross, 2012a).

Career Development Process

Many factors influence the process of career development. For instance, personality styles, developmental stages, values, skills, and cultural factors all affect career development and career choice. Serendipity and happenstance (Mitchell, Levin, & Krumboltz, 1999), family background (Chope, 2012), gender (Whitmarsh & Wentworth, 2012), giftedness (Maxwell, 2007), and age (Newsome et al., 2017) may also influence career options and choices. Other important factors include local and global economic conditions, trends in the workplace, and the accessibility of career information.

The world of work and the role work plays in clients' lives have changed tremendously throughout history, as has the process of career counseling. Career counselors in contemporary society need to have skills in personal counseling, an understanding of career development theories, knowledge about projections for occupational opportunities, and an ability to use technology to assist clients with career-related decisions. Career counselors also need to possess multicultural competencies and follow the ethical codes that guide the practice of career counseling, such as the *ACA Code of Ethics* (2014), the National Career Development Association *Code of Ethics* (2015), and the NCDA *Guidelines for Use of the Internet for Career Information and Planning Services* (available online at www.ncda.org).

The National Career Development Association (NCDA) and the National Employment Counseling Association (NECA) are the two divisions within the ACA primarily devoted to career development and career counseling. NCDA, the oldest division within the ACA, traces its roots back to 1913. The association is composed of professionals in business and industry, rehabilitation agencies, government, private practice, and educational settings. Its mission is to inspire and empower the achievement of career and life goals (NCDA, 2013). Services include professional development activities, publications, research, public information, professional standards, advocacy, and professional recognition for achievement. Among the organization's publications is a description of career counseling competencies, adopted by the NCDA in 1997 and revised in 2009 (www.ncda.org).

NECA offers professional leadership to people who counsel in employment services or career development settings and to people employed in related areas of counselor education, research, administration, or supervision. The organization's goal is to provide the best possible resources for people seeking employment and for the counselors who work with them (NECA, 2016). NECA's website (www.employmentcounseling.org/) provides links to a range of career-related online resources, including blogs, social networking sites, and Twitter feeds from career and employment counselors.

Career Counseling and Related Terminology

Changes that have taken place in society and the world of work have resulted in changes in the practice and definition of **career counseling**. Several current definitions of career counseling are worth examining. D. Brown (2016) defines career counseling as "a service provided to a single client or group of clients who come seeking assistance with career choice or career adjustment problems" (p. 16). Niles and Harris-Bowlsbey (2013) define career counseling as "a formal relationship in which a professional counselor assists a client or group of clients to cope more effectively with career concerns (e.g., making a career choice, coping with career transitions, coping with job-related stress, or job searching)" (p. 16).

Each of these definitions illustrates the broad scope of career counseling—a complex process that is both a counseling specialty and a core element of general counseling practice. By necessity, career counselors possess a wide range of competencies that include general counseling skills as well as skills, knowledge, and awareness specific to the career domain. According to the NCDA (2013), career counseling can include any combination of the following activities:

- Administering and interpreting assessments to help clients clarify and specify relevant self-characteristics, including values, skills, interests, and personality traits
- Encouraging career exploration activities, such as job shadowing, internships (or externships), and occupational information interviews
- Using career planning systems and occupational information systems to help individuals understand the world of work
- Providing opportunities for improving decision-making skills
- Assisting in the development of individualized career plans
- Teaching job-search strategies, interview skills, and resumé development skills
- Helping resolve potential personal conflicts on the job through practice in developing relevant interpersonal skills, such as assertiveness training or anger management
- Providing support for clients experiencing job stress, job loss, and/or career transition

Throughout its history, several different names have been associated with career counseling and development, including *vocational guidance, occupational counseling,* and *vocational counseling*. Differences in terminology reflect changes in viewpoints about the meaning of work and its significance in our society. To understand the process of career counseling in our current society, it is important to first clarify terms associated with career and career counseling.

Three terms associated with the term *career* are job, occupation, and vocation. A **job** is an activity undertaken for economic returns, whereas an **occupation** is a group of similar jobs found in different industries or organizations (Herr, Cramer, & Niles, 2004). The term **vocation** implies a psychological commitment or calling to a particular field. Each of these terms is somewhat limited in scope. In contrast, the term *career* is broader and more inclusive.

Career development specialists have defined **career** in a number of ways. According to Sears (1982), a career is the totality of work one does in a lifetime. Super (1976) views career as the course of events that constitute a life. Similarly, Herr et al. (2004) define career as the total constellation of roles played over the life span. The overarching themes of life span and roles are key to conceptualizing the term *career*.

The balance of leisure and work is also an important consideration in career counseling. Liptak (2001) describes the interaction between work and leisure activities, maintaining that effective career counseling involves helping clients combine work and leisure experiences to gain greater life satisfaction.

Five additional terms related to the process of career counseling include career education, career information, career intervention, career development facilitator, and career coaching. To help build a foundation for what follows, we briefly define those terms here and elaborate on them later in the chapter:

- *Career education:* A systematic attempt to influence the career development of students and adults through various educational strategies, including providing occupational information, infusing career-related concepts into the academic curriculum, and offering career-planning activities (Brown, 2016).
- *Career information:* Information about the labor market, including job trends, industries, and comprehensive information systems. Career counselors need to be aware of where to acquire occupational information and how to assess the quality of that information. The Internet provides a wealth of career-related information. In addition, the U.S. Department of Labor (www.dol.gov), as well as other government departments, is a premier source of occupational information and one that publishes numerous career-related resources.
- *Career intervention:* A deliberate act designed to empower people to cope effectively with career development tasks (Spokane, 1991). Career interventions include individual and group career counseling, career development programs, computer information delivery systems, and career education (Niles & Harris-Bowlsbey, 2013).
- *Career development facilitator (CDF):* An occupational title that designates individuals working in a variety of career development settings. These individuals, who may or may not be professional counselors, have participated in at least 120 hours of career development training by a nationally trained instructor. A CDF may serve as a career group facilitator, job search trainer, career resource center coordinator, career coach, career development case manager, intake interviewer, occupational and labor market information resource person, human resource career development coordinator, employment/placement specialist, or workforce development staff person (NCDA, 2017).
- *Career coaching:* An interactive process that helps individuals and organizations improve their performances. Through the process of career coaching, clients learn skills such as goal setting, taking positive action, making decisions, and building on their natural strengths (International Coach Federation, 2016).

Career Development Theories

Just as it is important for counselors to be familiar with current terminology related to career development and career counseling, it also is essential for them to be informed about the different theories of career development that guide career counseling practice. Career development theories try to explain why individuals choose careers. They also deal with the career adjustments people make over time, because people living in the 21st century are likely to change jobs several times over their life span. Some of the more prominent career development theories first appeared in the counseling literature in the 1950s (Gysbers, Heppner, & Johnston, 2014). The theories of Donald Super and John Holland are perhaps the most utilized and/or recognized theories of career development (Weinrach, 1996), although a number of other career theories have been generated, and some are currently evolving. Four prominent theories of career development that have been extensively researched and that often guide career counseling practice are examined here.

TRAIT-AND-FACTOR THEORY.   Trait-and-factor theory, which currently is referred to as **trait-and-type theory**, originated with Frank Parsons (1909). This theory stresses that the traits of clients should first be assessed and then systematically matched with factors inherent in various occupations. Its most widespread influence occurred during the Great Depression, when E. G. Williamson (1939) championed its use. Trait-and-factor theory fell out of favor during the 1950s and 1960s but has resurfaced in a more modern form: John Holland's (1997) theory of vocational choice.

Holland's theory of vocational choice stresses the interpersonal nature of careers and associated lifestyles, as well as the performance requirements of a work position. Holland (1997) identifies six categories that classify personality types and job environments: realistic, investigative, artistic, social, enterprising, and conventional (RIASEC; see Figure 13–1). Individuals of a particular type are attracted to environments of similar types. People typically achieve the most work satisfaction when their work environment matches their personality type (Platt & Drew, 2013).

Counselors grounded in Holland's approach use instruments to assess a client's personality type and then explore corresponding work orientations (Platt & Drew, 2013). The Strong Interest Inventory, the Self-Directed Search, and the Kuder Career Planning System are examples of instruments frequently used to assess personality type. These assessment

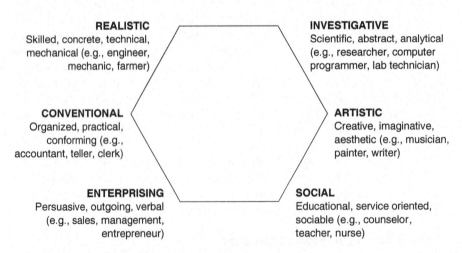

FIGURE 13–1   Holland's Six Categories of Personality and Occupation
Source: Reproduced by special permission of the publisher, Psychological Assessment Resources, Inc., from *Making Vocational Choices: A Theory of Careers* (3rd ed.), by J. L. Holland. Copyright © 1973, 1985, 1992, 1997 by Psychological Assessment Resources, Inc. All rights reserved.

tools provide clients with a three-letter personality code that represents their modal personality orientation. For example, a person's code might be SAE (social, artistic, enterprising). A person with this code would have interests in helping others (S), using creative talents (A), and leading or influencing others (E). Holland codes for multiple occupations can be found in the O*NET occupational database, which is the official online publication of the U.S. Department of Labor (www.online.onetcenter.org). Holland's *Occupations Finder* (Holland, 1994) and the *Dictionary of Holland Occupational Titles* (Gottfredson & Holland, 1996) also help clients find occupations that are similar to their codes.

Three constructs that are central to the theory of vocational choice are congruence, consistency, and differentiation (Holland, 1997). **Congruence** refers to a match between personality type and work environment type. For example, a counselor, whose code is SAE, would be in a profession considered congruent with his or her type. **Consistency** refers to the relative proximity of the letters of a person's personality code on the Holland hexagon (see Figure 13–1). People with letters that are adjacent, such as SA or SE, are more likely to find working environments that are consistent with their interests than are individuals whose code letters are inconsistent (i.e., the first two letters are opposite each other on the hexagon, such as SR). **Differentiation** indicates the degree to which an individual's interests are defined. For example, a person who has a clearly differentiated profile will have at least one code letter that is markedly higher than the lowest code letter. Someone with clearly differentiated interests is likely to have less difficulty making career decisions than an undifferentiated person. Work environments also differ in levels of differentiation, with some environments providing more flexibility than others. Career counselors who utilize Holland's theory consider these constructs as they explore career options with their clients.

SUPER'S DEVELOPMENTAL THEORY.   Developmental theories, such as the one developed by Donald Super, are generally more inclusive, more concerned with longitudinal expression of career behavior, and more inclined to highlight the importance of self-concept than other career theories. Super's life span–life space approach (1957, 1980, 1990) posits that career development is the lifelong process of implementing a self-concept. Self-concept evolves throughout the life span and is influenced by biological, psychological, and support factors (Platt & Drew, 2013). People's self-images are reflected in what they do. Super suggests that vocational development unfolds in five stages, each of which contains a developmental task to be completed. These five stages, each consisting of several substages, constitute the *life span* concept of Super's theory.

The first stage, according to Super, is the **growth** stage (from birth to age 14). During this stage, children form a mental picture of themselves in relation to others. They develop interests and skills, and their self-concept begins to develop. Throughout the growth stage, children become oriented to the world of work.

The second stage, **exploration**, takes place during later adolescence and early adulthood. The major tasks of this stage include a general exploration of the world of work and the initial specification of a career preference. With the millennial generation specification appears to be less common than it was during the time Super developed his theory. Only a few millennials have prior job experience as they enter emerging adulthood, and many lack the basic knowledge of the world of work that young people from previous generations typically possessed (Kennedy, 2008). Moreover, the world of work today is fluid, as some jobs become obsolete and new jobs are created. In addition, the global financial crisis, which began in late 2007, affected the millennial generation negatively because of the high levels of unemployment among young people, making it difficult for them to establish any type of financial security.

Super's third stage is known as **establishment** (ages 25–44). During this stage, adults choose and implement a career and become established in that career. According to Super, once a career is selected, persons can concentrate on advancement until they reach the top of their professions, tire of their jobs, or are forced to change jobs. Again, in contemporary society, people typically change jobs several times over the course of a lifetime. Therefore, the establishment stage may look quite different now than it did a few decades ago.

The fourth stage, **maintenance** (ages 45–64), includes the major task of preserving what one has already achieved. Continued efforts to improve skills and knowledge and to keep up with technological advancements are especially critical during this stage. The final stage, **disengagement** (formerly called *decline*—a term with negative connotations), was theorized to occur from the age of 65 and older. Major tasks of disengagement include detaching from work and aligning with other sources of life satisfaction. Activities associated with this stage include deceleration, retirement planning, and retirement living (Niles & Harris-Bowlsbey, 2013).

The age demarcations associated with the different developmental stages are not static. For example, many people choose to work well beyond the age of 65. Moreover, Super (1990) suggests that people often **recycle** through stages at various points in life, particularly when they are considering career changes and/or are destabilized by downsizing, illness, injury, or other socioeconomic or personal events. For example, if a 40-year-old woman loses the job she has had with a particular company for the past 20 years, she is likely to reenter the exploration stage as she reexamines options and opportunities.

Whereas Super's concept of life span is characterized by five stages and recycling, the concept of **life space** refers to the combination of life roles in which people participate (Super, 1980). These roles include those of son or daughter, student, "leisurite," citizen, worker, spouse or partner, homemaker, parent, and retiree. People participate in various roles in specific arenas, such as the home, school, the workplace, and the community. Super's **Life-Career Rainbow** illustrates how six life roles can be depicted within a person's life space (see Figure 13–2). The degree of importance people attach to different roles, the amount of time allotted to each, and the extent to which life roles overlap and/or interact all influence life satisfaction. When life seems out of balance or stressful, it may be due to attempts at balancing multiple roles in a manner that is not satisfying. Issues related to balancing roles and expectations can be a source of angst that leads people to seek career counseling.

The major contributions of developmental career counseling theories such as Super's are their emphases on the importance of life span development in career decision making and on ways career decisions are influenced by other processes and events in a person's life. This "life pattern paradigm for career counseling encourages counselors to consider a client's aptitudes and interests in a matrix of life experiences, not just in comparison to some normative group" (Savickas, 1989, p. 12).

Career counselors using Super's developmental theory may include any of the following in their work with clients:

- Identifying a client's level of **career maturity** (i.e., the readiness of a client to make sound career choices)
- Attempting to reduce potential deficits related to needed attitudes, skills, knowledge, and accomplishment of career development tasks

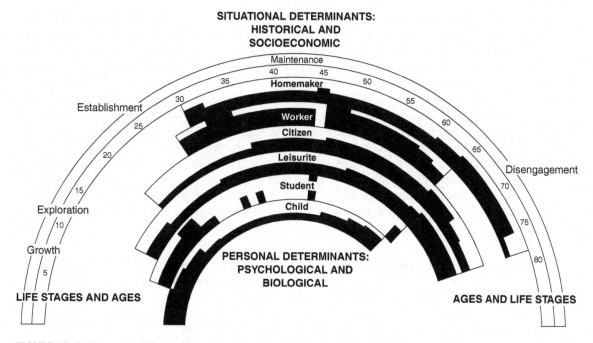

FIGURE 13–2 **Super's Rainbow Theory: Six Life Roles in Schematic Life Space**
Source: From "Career and Life Development," by D. F. Super, in *Career Choice and Development: Applying Contemporary Theories to Practice* (2nd ed.), 1990, San Francisco: Jossey-Bass. Copyright © 1990 by Donald Super. Used with permission of John Wiley and Sons, Inc.

- Analyzing a client's self-concept and strengthening it through assessment and counseling, if needed
- Identifying interests, abilities, and values and helping clients examine how they are distributed across life roles
- Understanding that a career is a combination of interacting life roles and helping clients define those roles and their importance as they attempt to achieve balance in life (Amundson, Harris-Bowlsbey, & Niles, 2009, p. 22)

LEARNING THEORY OF CAREER COUNSELING. A third influential career development theory was originally proposed by John Krumboltz in 1979, at which time it was called the **social learning theory** of career decision making and was based on Bandura's (1977a, 1986) social cognitive theory. In recent years, Krumboltz and his colleagues have expanded the theory to include specific applications of social learning theory to the practice of career counseling. The expanded theory is called the **learning theory of career counseling (LTCC)**.

According to LTCC (Mitchell & Krumboltz, 1996), four factors influence a person's career decision making: **genetic endowment** (innate traits and abilities), **environmental conditions and events** (which may be planned or unplanned), **learning experiences** (instrumental and associative learning), and **task-approach skills** (work habits, expectations of performance, cognitive processes, and emotional response patterns). Through the interaction of these four factors, people form beliefs about their own abilities (i.e., self-observation generalizations) and beliefs about the world (i.e., worldview generalizations). These generalizations affect actions and decisions relevant to the career-planning process.

The goal of career counseling from an LTCC perspective is to help clients develop skills, interests, beliefs, values, work habits, and personal qualities that will enable them to have satisfying lives within a dynamic work environment (Swanson & Fouad, 2010). Often, career counselors serve as coaches or mentors as they help clients develop new beliefs, attitudes, and skills. Interventions may be developmental and preventive (e.g., career education, job clubs) or targeted and remedial (e.g., directed toward unhelpful cognitions and behaviors).

Krumboltz amended the learning theory of career counseling to include the construct of **planned happenstance** (Krumboltz & Levin, 2010). The term, which at first glance appears oxymoronic, refers to the "creating and transforming of unplanned events into opportunities for learning" (Mitchell et al., 1999, p. 117). Career counselors can help clients develop attitudes that enable them to recognize, create, and use events that happen by chance as career opportunities. Moreover, counselors can help their clients learn to be comfortable with ambiguity and indecision, thereby making it possible for them to capitalize on unforeseen future events.

SOCIAL COGNITIVE CAREER THEORY. A theory of career development that has been the subject of much current research is **social cognitive career theory (SCCT)**. Proposed by Lent, Brown, and Hackett (1994), SCCT provides a framework for explaining career development that focuses on the "(a) formation and elaboration of career-relevant interests, (b) the selection of academic and career choice options, and (c) performance and persistence in educational and occupational pursuits" (p. 79). Like Krumboltz's LTCC theory, SCCT derived from Bandura's (1977a, 1977b, 1986) social cognitive theory. As with LTCC, a primary assumption of SCCT is that a complex array of factors—including culture, gender, genetic endowment, and health—affect people's beliefs, interests, and subsequent career decision-making behaviors. However, Lent et al. emphasize two additional constructs—self-efficacy beliefs and outcome expectations—in a manner that differs from Krumboltz's approach.

Self-efficacy refers to an individual's beliefs about his or her ability to perform successfully a particular task. **Outcome expectations** are the consequences a person expects to occur following a particular course of action. According to SCCT, self-efficacy beliefs and outcome expectations influence the development of career-related interests. These interests, in turn, influence the development of career-related aspirations and goals.

Two other key constructs believed to influence career interests and goals are people's perceptions of *barriers* and their perceptions of *supports* (Lent, Brown, & Hackett, 2000). To illustrate, even if a person possesses high levels of self-efficacy, high expectations, and interests that coincide with a particular career, that person may avoid pursuing the career if barriers toward that pursuit appear insurmountable. For example, people may lower their aspirations because of financial concerns or perceived discrimination. In contrast, their perception of certain supports (e.g., family, community) may enhance the likelihood that they will embark on a particular career path.

SCCT has particular relevance for the career development of women, ethnic minorities, gay and lesbian individuals, and others who are members of cultural minorities (e.g., Fouad, 2007; Leong & Gupta, 2007; McWhirter & Flojo, 2001). Career counselors who follow an SCCT approach acknowledge the influence of contextual factors on cognitions, interests, and goals. Counselors working from this perspective may implement interventions that help clients:

- Identify options that may have been foreclosed because of unrealistic or faulty self-efficacy beliefs or outcome expectations.

- Identify perceived barriers that may have led clients to eliminate career possibilities prematurely and then examine how realistic those perceptions of barriers are.
- Modify and counteract faulty beliefs and expectations as well as faulty occupational information (Swanson & Fouad, 2010).

Theories of career development serve as road maps to help counselors understand their clients' career-related beliefs, behaviors, and aspirations (Krumboltz, 1993). Theoretical approaches help career counselors make sense of the information clients bring them about work-related issues. Many career counselors adopt a holistic approach to career counseling that integrates key constructs from various theories with particular relevance for particular clients dealing with particular issues. A strong understanding of career development theories and their applications guides counselors as they become skilled in implementing effective career interventions.

Career Counseling Process and Skills

As mentioned previously, career counseling is a complex process that has evolved through the years. A number of factors have contributed to rapid changes in the world of work and the delivery of career counseling services, including the following:

- Global recessions
- An interdependent global economy and other economic factors
- Evolving occupational projections and trends
- Continued advancements in technology
- An increasingly diverse workforce
- Corporate downsizing
- An increased number of dual-career families and of people working from locations away from the workplace
- Large-scale unemployment and underemployment
- Blurred boundaries between work lives and lives outside of work
- Increased work-related stress and associated mental health issues (e.g., depression, anxiety)

To help career counselors practice effectively, NCDA developed a set of career counseling competency statements, which focus on a range of general counseling skills and specific career-related skills. Three of these essential skill areas are conducting career-related assessment, providing career information, and counseling diverse clientele.

CAREER ASSESSMENT. It is not uncommon for clients to enter career counseling with the misconception that counselors will give them tests that will reveal the perfect career match. Perhaps this misconception stems from the early days of trait-and-factor theory, when Frank Parsons's model of career counseling predominated. In today's society, the complex process of career counseling goes well beyond the test-and-tell method, and counselors recognize the limitations associated with standardized testing. Therefore, it is important for career counselors to clarify their role from the outset.

Although career assessment does not act as a crystal ball, it does serve a key role in career counseling. Assessment is an ongoing activity that takes place throughout the entire counseling process, from referral to follow-up (Hohenshil, 1996). Formal and informal methods of assessment help counselors gather information to determine the nature of clients' issues, the prevalence of their problems, and the clients' strengths and skills (Whiston, 2017). Similarly, career-related assessment may be formal or informal, is used to gather client information, and helps evaluate individual strengths and areas of concern. The purposes of career assessment are to help clients examine career possibilities, assess personal strengths, acquire a structure for evaluating career alternatives, clarify expectations, and implement plans of action.

Conceptually, it is helpful to divide career assessment into two major categories: assessment of individual differences and assessment of the career choice process (see Betz, 1992, Whiston, 2017). Career counselors assess individual differences to increase client self-awareness in multiple areas, including interests, values, needs, personality attributes, and abilities. In contrast, assessing the career choice process involves measuring where clients are in the decision-making process. Assessment in this area may include measuring the degree of career maturity or level of decidedness. Many different career assessment instruments have been developed during the past several decades, some of which have stronger psychometric properties than others. Publications such as *A Counselor's Guide to Career Assessment Instruments* (Wood, 2013) and *Using Assessment Results for Career Development* (Osborn & Zunker, 2016) can be especially helpful in describing the characteristics of various instruments, including purpose, reading level, validity, reliability, and cultural fairness.

Technology-assisted assessment is frequently a component of career counseling. Career assessment can be conducted online, or instruments can be purchased for computerized administration and interpretation. When computers are used in career assessment, scoring errors are avoided, and results are obtained quickly, thus saving time for the professionals and eliminating the wait period for clients. However, several concerns have been raised concerning technology-assisted assessment. Whiston (2017) summarizes some of those concerns:

> With the ease of technology-generated reports, clinicians may be lulled into a false sense of security and may use the technology-generated results without becoming educated about the instrument. Instruments used in counseling are validated for specific purposes; therefore, a counselor cannot use a general technology-generated report in isolation. . . . Simply using a technology-generated report without knowledge of the instrument's strengths and limitations would be considered by the courts to be negligent and unprofessional. Technology-generated reports are designed to supplement or complement the clinician's interpretation of the results, not replace them. (p. 354)

Qualitative methods of assessment, which encourage active client participation, are especially applicable to career counseling. Career counselors can use qualitative assessment alone or in conjunction with quantitative instruments. Through qualitative assessment procedures, clients have opportunities to tell their stories and explore the meaning they take from those stories (McMahon, Patton, & Watson, 2003). Examples of qualitative assessment processes include card sorts, lifelines, and career genograms. The career genogram is similar to the family genogram in that it creates a graphic representation of a client's family spanning three generations. It provides a framework for examining many topics, including personal worldviews, possible environmental barriers, potential role conflicts, and cultural variables (Gysbers et al., 2014). The career genogram provides a venue through which the client can describe family relationships and prevailing attitudes about the various occupations that have been charted.

Qualitative and quantitative forms of career assessment can help clients clarify values, interests, skills, and personality traits that affect career development and choice. In summarizing important points related to the use of assessment in career counseling, Niles and Harris-Bowlsbey (2013) offer valuable reminders:

- The results of assessment tools are only one piece of data that the client and counselor use to consider career options. Counselors interpret assessments in conjunction with other data, including the client's self-knowledge, past experiences, and knowledge about the world of work.
- Career assessment is most effective when used to identify new concepts of self, areas of potential growth, and possibilities for exploration, rather than to make predictions about an unpredictable future.
- It is best to work collaboratively with the client in making decisions about whether to engage in assessment, determining what procedures to use, and interpreting results. (pp. 167–168)

CAREER INFORMATION AND PLANNING. Career information refers to the many types of resources available in print and electronic form that career counselors can use to help clients make informed career choices. The NCDA has developed a comprehensive set of guidelines describing counselors' responsibilities for selecting high-quality information resources of all types (see NCDA website at www.ncda.org/ under the Guidelines section). The NCDA's website assists career counselors in evaluating career software, career and occupational literature, and video media.

The **Occupational Information Network (O*NET)** is a technology-based career information system that provides the most up-to-date occupational information available (www.onetcenter.org/). The O*NET database contains information about occupations and is continually updated by surveying workers from various occupations. O*NET also provides a set of career exploration tools, which can help workers and students looking to find or change careers. The site is sponsored by the U.S. Department of Labor/Employment and Training Administration, which is a branch of the U.S. Department of Labor. The Department of Labor places all its major publications, such as the *Occupational Outlook Handbook* and the *Bureau of Labor Statistics Employment and Unemployment Data*, online.

Skilled career counselors know how to access, evaluate, and utilize various types of printed and electronic career-related resources. Knowledge alone, however, is not sufficient. Effective career counselors also are able to work collaboratively with their clients so that the information retrieved can be translated into something that is meaningful and useful.

Career counselors are likely to work in any number of settings, including college and university settings, job placement services, rehabilitation facilities, employment offices, businesses and industries, or in private practice (Hodges, 2012). Typically, career counselors in clinical mental health settings work with adults rather than children, whereas counselors in educational settings focus on career development interventions and activities for young people. Career counselors who work in college settings, such as a career and professional development center, assist students in many areas, including exploration of majors, career exploration, and internship placement. These counselors may also teach career exploration courses, review resumés and cover letters, and plan career fairs.

CAREER COUNSELING WITH DIVERSE POPULATIONS. Regardless of the setting, being able to counsel effectively with diverse populations is an essential skill needed by career counselors. Many of the assumptions inherent in traditional theories of career development were based on working with heterosexual, able-bodied, middle- to upper-class White men and consequently fall short in their application to diverse populations (Luzzo & McWhirter, 2001; Platt & Drew, 2013). Social activism, combined with a growing body of research, helps challenge constraining negative forces and create models of career counseling for diverse groups (Peterson & Gonzalez, 2000). A career counselor's ability to work effectively with diverse populations is dependent on a willingness to reflect carefully on the appropriateness of any assumption, theory, or intervention when working with specific individuals.

Several career development textbooks and journals provide excellent suggestions for conducting career counseling with diverse populations. For example, Duggan and Jurgens (2007) focus on career development and counseling with the following groups:

- Single parents
- Homemakers reentering the workforce
- Welfare-to-work clients
- The working poor
- Victims of intimate partner violence
- Dislocated or displaced workers
- Homeless individuals
- Older adults
- Offenders and ex-offenders
- People with physical and/or mental disabilities
- People with chemical dependencies
- Veterans
- Newly immigrated individuals

In addition to these groups, issues related to gender, sexual orientation, and ethnicity need to be considered, as those issues also relate to career development, choice, and advancement. To that end, McWhirter, Joyce, and Aranda (2009) assert the following:

> Is it possible to be knowledgeable about all cultures and all types of disability or to fully understand the complexities of gender and sexual orientation as they interact with career development? Of course, the answer to this question is no. It certainly is possible, and in fact is a professional obligation, to develop an approach to all clients that explores and honors their multiple identities and orientations. Such an approach requires continuous education through reading, contact with diverse clientele, consultation with colleagues, seminars and workshops, and ongoing critical self-reflection. (p. 273)

Before concluding this section on career counseling, it is important to note how career counseling may be integrated with personal counseling. Although distinctions are sometimes drawn between career counseling and personal counseling, the two processes are not dichotomous but instead are intricately related. Often, a client will present with a career-related issue that is rooted in personal problems (e.g., job loss stemming from anger management problems). Or the reverse can occur, with a toxic work environment resulting in stress and decreased coping skills that negatively affect family interactions. Competent career counselors are able to work holistically with clients, helping them deal effectively with personal issues and career-related issues that arise during the counseling process.

The Case of Jeremy

Jeremy has worked as a computer analyst for a major company for 23 years. Recently, the company decided to outsource its information technology department, and Jeremy was told that he would lose his job in 6 months. During the past several years, Jeremy has considered pursuing another career, but he wondered how to go about making a change. He likes inter- acting with people, and he does not have many opportunities to do that in his current posi- tion. He views the layoff as an opportunity to train for a new career, possibly in education or the healthcare field. His severance package will be significant; however, he is concerned that changing careers at this stage of life is too risky. His current company is providing career counseling for employees who will be laid off.

If you were his career counselor, what approach would you take to assist Jeremy? How would you help him with the transition? What factors might you and he discuss during the process? What additional information would you like to have to work effectively with Jeremy? Think about these questions.

Summary and Conclusion

In this chapter, two fields in which clinical mental health counselors practice were described: college counseling and career counseling. The history of college counseling illustrates the many ways college counseling has changed since its inception and some of the reasons dif- ferent college counseling centers are structured the way they are. The primary focus of col- lege counseling centers is on the prevalent issues and mental health concerns faced by today's college students. College counselors work with students facing common issues, such as managing stress, adjusting to college life, and coping with homesickness. In addition to these relatively typical developmental concerns, many college students face a range of more serious issues, including trauma, dating violence, and substance use and abuse.

In recent years, the prevalence of severe mental illness, suicidal ideation, and self- harming behavior has increased. Moreover, incidences of suicide, homicide, and other forms of crisis have increased. College counseling centers can lead the way in developing crisis management teams to combat these behaviors. Clinical mental health counselors who work on college campuses are working within a system, and the system functions best when col- laborative methods are used campuswide to improve the quality of campus life in general and the quality of life for those individuals who need additional support.

Career counseling and some of the prominent theories of career counseling were dis- cussed next, including specific skills associated with career counseling, for example, con- ducting career assessment, providing career information, and working with diverse groups of clients. Some of the specific services career counselors provide include the following:

- Administering and interpreting tests and inventories
- Conducting personal counseling sessions
- Developing individualized career plans
- Helping clients integrate vocational and avocational life roles
- Facilitating decision-making skills
- Providing support for persons experiencing job stress, job loss, or career transitions

MyCounselingLab

Try the Topic 2 Assignments: *Career/Individual/Development Counseling*.

CHAPTER 14

Olimpik/Shutterstock

As our sessions go on you speak of your scars
    and show me the places where you have been burned.
Sadly, I hear your fiery stories
    reliving with you, through your memories and words,
    all of the tension-filled blows and events
    that have beaten and shaped your life.
"I wish I were molten steel," you say,
"And you were a blacksmith's hammer.
Maybe then, on time's anvil, we could structure together
    a whole new person, with soft smooth sounds,
    inner strength and glowing warmth."

Reprinted from "Scars," by S. T. Gladding, 1977, *Personnel and Guidance Journal, 56,* p. 246. Copyright © S. T. Gladding. Used with permission.

Community Agencies, Medical Settings, and Other Specialized Clinical Settings

CHAPTER OVERVIEW

From reading this chapter, you will learn about

- Community mental health centers, the ways they have evolved, and services that often are provided in these settings

- Hospitals and behavioral healthcare settings and services, including various levels of care offered by psychiatric services in hospitals

- Additional services provided by clinical mental health counselors in some medical settings, including cancer support services and services for patients and caregivers affected by Alzheimer's disease and other dementias

- Other specialized clinical settings in which clinical mental health counselors work, including hospice centers, substance abuse treatment centers, and child and family service agencies

As you read, consider

- The rewards and challenges that might accompany working in each setting

- Which settings appeal most to you, and why

- Whether there are settings in which you do not see yourself working and what would make these settings more appealing to you

- What ethical concerns might arise for clinical mental health counselors working in the settings described

During the past four decades, professional counselors' opportunities for employment have increased significantly. Prior to the passage of the Community Mental Health Act of 1963 (Title II, Public Law 88-164), counselors worked primarily in educational settings. With the passage of the Community Mental Health Act, funding was provided for the nationwide establishment of community mental health centers, thereby opening the door for large numbers of counselors to work in agency settings. Today, clinical mental health counselors are employed in many different clinical sites, including government-funded agencies, hospitals, rehabilitation agencies, family service agencies, shelters for victims of domestic violence, probation settings, and faith-based settings. Within these settings, counselors provide a wide range of direct and indirect services to people of all ages who struggle with problems ranging from developmental transitions to serious mental disorders.

In this chapter, we describe some of the publicly and privately funded settings where clinical mental health counselors are often employed. These include community agencies, healthcare facilities, child and family agencies, and specialized clinical sites.

COMMUNITY MENTAL HEALTH CENTERS AND AGENCIES

Evolution of Community Mental Health Centers

Prior to 1963, people with mental illness were primarily hospitalized in state institutions. Unsafe and inhumane conditions in many of these institutions precipitated a reform movement that led to the enactment of the Community Mental Health Centers Act (CMHC Act), resulting in the **deinstitutionalization** of people with chronic and severe mental illness. The purpose of deinstitutionalization was to remove people with severe mental health issues from state institutions and public hospitals and to provide them with quality care in their communities. The CMHC Act provided federal matching funds for the state construction of community mental health centers in **catchment areas**—geographic areas of 75,000 to 200,000 people.

These community-based agencies were expected to provide a comprehensive continuum of care to all Americans in need of mental health services. Five core elements of service were identified: (a) outpatient care, (b) inpatient care, (c) consultation and education, (d) partial hospitalization, and (e) emergency/crisis intervention. In addition to providing a comprehensive system of care, community agencies were expected to engage in outreach to the community and form linkages with other service providers. A primary purpose of community mental health centers was to serve as many clients as possible in the least-restrictive setting.

In subsequent years, funding of CMHCs shifted primarily from federal monies to state and local funding. By 1981, with the passage of the Omnibus Budget Reconciliation Act, federal funding of mental health services was allocated through block grants "to be used by states as they saw fit" (MacCluskie & Ingersoll, 2001, p. 230). Block grants were grouped into nine areas of preventive health, with one of the largest being the alcohol, drug abuse, and mental health block grant (ADAMHA). In 1992, Congress passed the ADAMHA Reorganization Act, which abolished ADAMHA and replaced it with a new federal organization called Substance Abuse and Mental Health Services Administration (SAMHSA; www.samhsa.gov/), which is a division of the Department of Health and Human Services (DHHS). Currently, although states still bear the primary funding burden for mental health services, federal government funds help finance mental health care through Medicaid, Medicare, and federally funded special programs for adults with serious mental illness and children with serious emotional disability. Medicaid is unique in that it is funded by federal, state, and local funds; is run by state guidelines; and is designed to assist low-income persons by paying for most medical expenses.

Although community mental health centers were designed to provide a broad range of community care, community members often needed more support than the CMHCs could provide, resulting in many people not receiving treatment and increased rates of homelessness and rehospitalization. The National Institute of Mental Health (NIMH) reports that approximately one quarter of American adults experience one or more mental disorders within a given year, and that the lifetime prevalence of experiencing a disorder is 46.4% (NIMH, 2014). According to the Surgeon General's report (U.S. Department of Health and Human Services, 1999), our community mental health system is "multifaceted and complex, comprised of public and private sectors, general health and specialty mental health providers, and social services, housing, criminal justice, and education agencies" (p. 11). The complex systems do not always provide the coordinated service delivery they were designed to provide. Making adequate support available to all people in need of mental health assistance continues to be a challenge for community mental health service providers.

Many state and community mental health programs currently are in a state of organizational transition, as attempts are made to manage human and financial resources while providing quality mental health services. However, good intentions do not always lead to positive results. For example, in 2001 the General Assembly of North Carolina voted for mental health reform in the state, which was designed "to tear down, then rebuild the way the state treats mentally ill people, about 210,000 of whom seek state help each year" (Stith & Raynor, 2008, p. 2). Instead of providing services through traditional community mental health centers, the state was divided into geographic areas served by 25 local management entities (LMEs). The LMEs served as administrative behavioral health authorities that outsourced treatment to a network of providers in the area, some of which are more successful than others in providing an effective system of care for individuals with mental health needs. For example, many of the LME providers hired high school graduates, rather than licensed professionals, to provide services (Stith & Raynor, 2008). In addition, more than 500 hospital beds were eliminated. The outcome was that the state's cost of mental health care increased and many people needing mental health services did not receive the treatment they needed. The importance of mental health advocacy becomes even more vital when plans to improve mental health treatment are not executed successfully.

Service Delivery

The way in which community mental health services are delivered varies from state to state, especially because of national, state, and local budgeting concerns. In some states, CMHCs still exist and are required to provide certain core services. In other states, community-based mental health services are delivered through state-endorsed providers. Still other states use different methods of mental health service delivery. The National Association of State Mental Health Program Directors (NASMHPD; www.nasmhpd.org) provides summaries of the various ways states use mental health block grants to deliver mental health services. Each state is required to develop a comprehensive mental health plan and to demonstrate how funds are being used.

The goal of **community-based mental health** (also called community behavioral health) is to provide a comprehensive system of care designed in partnership with the community, service providers, and payers. The following principles guide community mental health practices:

1. Services should be accessible and culturally sensitive to those who seek treatment.
2. Services should be accountable to the entire community, including the at-risk and underserved.
3. Services should be comprehensive, flexible, and coordinated.
4. Continuity of care should be assured.
5. Behavioral health care needs to be holistic: personalized to meet individual needs.
6. Prevention and early intervention are the most essential services provided.
7. Treatment providers should utilize a multidisciplinary team approach to care. (National Council for Behavioral Healthcare, 2012)

Multidisciplinary teams that provide services typically include counselors, psychiatrists, psychologists, social workers, psychiatric nurses, and paraprofessionals. The following areas of service are frequently offered by community mental health providers:

• *Outpatient counseling services.* The goal of outpatient services is to help clients improve personal and social functioning through the use of individual, group, and/or family counseling, and possibly medication management. Most often, social workers, counselors, and psychologists provide these services, which address both acute and chronic mental health needs.

• *Day programs.* Day programs provide intensive treatment to clients who do not need 24-hour care but who have significant impairment due to psychiatric, emotional, behavioral, and/or addictive disorders. These programs provide a combination of individual and group therapy, psychoeducation, recreational therapy, life-skills training, vocational rehabilitation, medication management, and other activities designed to help participants acquire skills needed for adjustment to everyday-life tasks and roles (Viger, 2001). In many community agencies, day programs include two types of service: **partial hospitalization programs (PHPs)** and **intensive outpatient programs (IOPs)**. PHPs provide brief, intensive, structured treatment for clients who need a high level of care, whereas IOPs usually serve more stable individuals who still need structured treatment programs but on a more flexible basis.

• *Emergency services/crisis intervention.* These services provide for the delivery of center- and community-based crisis intervention in psychiatric emergencies. Community members experiencing acute distress can contact emergency and crisis intervention agencies and receive immediate crisis intervention assistance (Staton, Revenson, & Tennen, 2007). Services are available on a 24-hour basis through telephone crisis lines, mobile crisis units, walk-in treatment, or agencies specifically designated to provide emergency care.

• *Substance abuse services.*   Substance abuse services address the recovery of individuals who are dealing with addiction to, dependence on, or abuse of substances (Smith, 2015). Addictive substances can include alcohol, prescription medications, or illegal drugs. Because recovery is an ongoing process, treatment may include outpatient services, residential care, inpatient treatment, emergency care, and the coordination of community drug abuse resources. In addition, counseling and educational programs for family members are usually available to help the family understand and cope with the effects of a substance abuse environment.

• *Case management and outreach.*   Case management links clients to essential services and supports in the community. Essential services include securing financial benefits, health care, and psychiatric treatment. Goals of case management include preventing hospitalization, improving quality of life and levels of functioning, and empowering clients to maximize their independence (MacCluskie & Ingersoll, 2001). Outreach involves engaging people in need of services who are unable or unwilling to seek services on their own (Viger, 2001).

Because clients with severe mental health conditions may require a variety of services but may not have a central location in which those services are delivered (such as long-term-care mental institutions), finding ways to meet the needs of chronically mentally ill clients is challenging. One case management model that is designed to assist clients in accessing, coordinating, and integrating mental health services is called **assertive community treatment (ACT)**. ACT programs typically include a "team of professionals representing counseling, social work, nursing, rehabilitation, and psychiatry" who have small caseloads and who share responsibilities among team members. Other shared common elements include the philosophy that the community is the proper place to care for people with severe and persistent mental disorders because "it is in the community where they face daily, ongoing stressors." In addition, community-based treatment must be "comprehensive and capable of addressing all areas of the client's life." Furthermore, treatment must be "flexible and individualized" as well as "well-organized and available 7 days a week, 24 hours a day" (Gerig, 2014, p. 268).

• *Education and consultation.*   These services include support for family members of clients who are mentally ill, community-wide education programs describing the nature of mental health, preventive programs that teach participants about skills such as stress management, and informational programs describing ways to link with various community resources (Lewis et al., 2003). Education and consultation play key roles in primary and secondary prevention, which are geared toward promoting and maintaining mental health. Funding challenges can impede the delivery of these services, which may not translate into billable hours. However, grants, contracts with other organizations, and pro bono work can help ensure that these crucial services are delivered.

• *Residential programs.*   Residential programs include transitional facilities where individuals recently discharged from hospitals learn to function in the community, youth homes for troubled or delinquent adolescents, homes for individuals with developmental delays, and other residential homes that vary in the degree to which clients are supervised. Residential supervision can range from 24-hour staffed supervision to independent living options that allow participants to receive care based on their level of functioning. In some cases, intensive outpatient programs for substance abuse and other disorders provide a temporary residential option for clients during the course of treatment.

• *Inpatient services.* Most community mental health agencies are affiliated with either community or state hospitals that provide intensive, inpatient mental health services to stabilize symptoms of acute mental illness and prepare clients to return to community-based care. During the past several decades, the number of state psychiatric institutions providing inpatient services has shrunk dramatically, resulting in the discharge of many individuals who are severely mentally ill into nursing homes or board-and-care homes that are inadequately prepared to provide necessary services. The average length of stay in state mental hospitals varies but usually is less than eight days (Lee, Rothbard, & Noll, 2012; Levine, Perkins, & Perkins, 1997). Although reducing the length of time in psychiatric facilities is one way to support the contemporary mental health philosophy of least-restrictive treatment to maximize a client's personal freedom, there have been serious consequences for shortened stays. "Some clients are admitted, stabilized, released to out-patient care, and then readmitted," resulting in the "revolving door" phenomenon (Gerig, 2014, p. 260). Lack of sufficient treatment can lead to increased hospital emergency room visits or incarceration.

BOX 14–1 Negative Consequences of Early Release from Inpatient Treatment

Lack of proper treatment is causing more people who are mentally ill or who have a substance-abuse problem to be taken to hospital emergency rooms—or jail. And they're rotating in and out of the state's psychiatric hospitals. On some days, state hospitals are so full, they are refusing to accept new patients.

Since 2001 [in North Carolina], at least 13 people committed suicide or overdosed on drugs less than a week after being discharged from state hospitals. Some died within hours.

(Stith & Raynor, 2008, p. 2)

Direct and Indirect Services

Clinical mental health counselors who work in community agencies provide services that focus on promotion of mental health and prevention, as well as on treatment of mental disorders and dysfunctions. Some of the services are direct while some are indirect. They target individual clients as well as the community at large. Examples of direct and indirect services that might be provided by clinical mental health counselors are illustrated in Figure 14–1.

To provide direct and indirect services effectively, counselors who work in community mental health centers must have basic counseling skills as well as specialty skills related to particular populations and problems. These counselors need to be skilled in assessment and diagnosis, which requires a comprehensive knowledge of the most current edition of the *DSM* and its classifications. They also need to be familiar with medications used to treat mood, anxiety, substance abuse, and psychotic disorders, as well as the medications' common side effects. Knowledge and skills related to evidence-based treatment services are indispensable. Other essential skills include being able to plan, implement, and evaluate prevention programs designed for individuals, groups, and the community at large. Community mental health agencies treat a diverse set of clients, many of whom come from lower socioeconomic backgrounds and present with a broad spectrum of issues. Consequently, multicultural awareness, knowledge, and skills are necessary for effective service delivery.

	Community Services	Client Services
Direct	• Educational programs on the nature of mental health • Preventive education programs that teach about mental health and life skills	• Counseling and crisis intervention services • Outreach programs for persons dealing with life transitions and difficult situations
Indirect	• Helping the local community organize to work for positive environmental change • Taking action on policies affecting community mental health	• Advocacy for groups such as underserved populations dealing with chronic mental health problems • Consultation within clients' helping networks • Promoting self-help programs; linking clients with other helping systems in the community

FIGURE 14–1   Direct and Indirect Community and Client Services in Community Mental Health Agencies
Source: Community Counseling: Empowerment Strategies for a Diverse Society (3rd ed.), by J. A. Lewis, M. D. Lewis, J. A. Daniels, and M. J. D'Andrea, 2003, Pacific Grove, CA: Brooks/Cole. Adapted with permission of Wadsworth, a division of Thomson Learning.

In most community mental health sites, counselors are expected to meet the organization's productivity objectives, which vary from agency to agency (MacCluskie & Ingersoll, 2001). **Productivity** refers to the number of billable hours a clinician generates. Many agencies have a specified number of client hours that must be averaged over a period of time and that often affect salary and promotion. Being able to meet productivity expectations, complete paperwork requirements, provide crisis intervention when needed, and attend staff meetings and supervision can prove to be challenging, making it all the more necessary for counselors to practice self-care to maintain wellness and avoid burnout (see Box 14–2).

BOX 14–2   Urban Community Mental Health: Adult Outpatient Services

The greatest challenge of working in a community mental health center (CMHC) is to effectively meet administrative (agency) and clinical (consumer) needs without burning out over time. All settings have paperwork and difficult clients, yet a CMHC, as a public agency, is subject to a high volume of documentation requirements and a high volume of clients. There is also the burden of meeting productivity expectations (quotas) each month. This is not an easy task when 50% of new clients are no-show for first appointments. The challenge is to work with as many clients as you can, as skillfully as you can, and not get behind in paperwork, productivity, or passion.

Many days the benefits of working in a CMHC setting outweigh the struggles. The benefits include the ease of consulting with, and referring clients to, colleagues under the same roof; stable work hours; and no personal responsibility for emergency crisis coverage. Additionally, the pay is good, the organization values high practice standards, and clients do improve. A CMHC is a great place to grow professionally and to make a difference in the lives of those who seek therapy.

Ellen Nicola, PhD, Senior Psychologist/Team Leader at a CMHC

Professional Affiliation and Certification

Professional counselors who work in mental health settings may choose to affiliate with the American Mental Health Counselors Association (AMHCA), a division of ACA. Members of AMHCA have been active in supporting federal and state legislation that recognizes mental health counselors as core practitioners, or reimbursable providers of services. The organization also has helped to define the areas in which mental health counselors work and to establish guidelines for involvement in those areas. AMHCA has initiated several different task forces that focus on prevention and treatment in relation to specific populations and concerns. Such concentrations are important because they enable counselors who work in mental health settings to obtain in-depth knowledge and skills in particular areas. AMHCA also publishes a quarterly periodical, the *Journal of Mental Health Counseling*, which provides readers with up-to-date information on prevention, treatment, and emerging issues in the mental health field.

AMHCA was instrumental in establishing the **certified clinical mental health counseling credential (CCMHC)**, a specialty credential within the field of professional counseling, which is now administered by NBCC (www.nbcc.org/Certification/Certified-ClinicalMentalHealthCounselor). Professionals seeking this credential first need to be national certified counselors (NCCs). Requirements for earning the CCMHC credential include the following:

- 60 semester or 90 quarter hours of graduate-level academic coursework from a regionally accredited university with a major study in counseling covering 10 content areas
- 100 hours of counseling supervision
- 3,000 hours of clinical client contact
- A passing score on the National Clinical Mental Health Counseling Examination (NCMHCE)
- A taped video or audio clinical session

HOSPITALS AND OTHER HEALTHCARE SETTINGS

Many clinical mental health counselors work in hospitals and other healthcare facilities, which are essential components of community healthcare systems. Most hospitals offer behavioral healthcare or psychiatric services to assist people struggling with mental health concerns, and many provide preventive and maintenance programs for patients with cardiac disease, diabetes, stroke, and other illnesses (Browers, 2005). Hospitals and other healthcare settings also provide counseling through programs such as cancer patient support, rehabilitation services, HIV/AIDS clinics, geriatric services, and hospice care. People receiving care in healthcare facilities are usually referred to as *patients* rather than *clients*. Many behavioral healthcare systems demonstrate their commitment to quality standards by seeking accreditation from organizations such as the Joint Commission on Accreditation of Healthcare Organizations (JCAHO) or the Commission on Accreditation of Rehabilitation Facilities (CARF).

Inpatient Medical Settings

Inpatient services are designed to treat patients with mental health disorders such as major depression, bipolar disorder, schizophrenia, substance abuse, and dementia. Inpatient services provide crisis stabilization, evaluation, and intensive monitoring based on medical assessment conducted by a multidisciplinary team. Team members include psychiatrists, psychiatric nurses, social workers, counselors, occupational therapists, and other health professionals. Usually within 24 hours of admission, patients are given a complete medical, nursing, and biopsychosocial assessment. Each team member participates in the assessment process and then works collaboratively to formulate a diagnosis and treatment plan.

When possible, the patient and the patient's family members work with the interdisciplinary team in developing a treatment plan. That plan, which is reviewed periodically, includes a description of patient problems and assets, goals and objectives, target dates, interventions and desired outcomes, and discharge information. Interventions may include medication; individual, group, and/or family counseling; psychoeducation; recreation therapy; and support groups. To provide a continuum of care, after patients have been stabilized in an inpatient setting, they may be discharged and then moved to another level of treatment.

Other Behavioral Health/Psychiatric Services

Many hospitals offer a broad spectrum of treatment options that represent a continuum of care, ranging from outpatient services to more intensive services. Treatment options include several of the services just described; for example, partial hospital programs (PHPs) and intensive outpatient programs (IOPs) provide services to patients who continue to need intensive treatment but do not need 24-hour supervised care. An additional service, the 23-hour observation bed, is an option for intensive monitoring and evaluation without formal admission to an inpatient unit and the associated expensive inpatient costs. Residential treatment programs provide supervised housing and treatment for specific problems, particularly for substance abuse. Outpatient clinics or services provide individual, group, and/or family counseling, based on the patient's need. Examples of outpatient, partial hospitalization, and residential treatment services that may be found in hospitals include the following:

- Marital and family therapy clinics, providing services to families and couples
- Memory disorders clinics, which assist in the evaluation of individuals with declines in memory, concentration, and thinking, followed by appropriate referral
- Sleep centers, which evaluate sleep disorders and recommend treatment
- Substance abuse intensive outpatient programs, which help patients recovering from chemical abuse or dependency and may include detoxification, medication management, dual diagnosis treatment, 12-step orientation, family education, and relapse prevention
- Child and adolescent outpatient services, which use multimodal approaches to treat the needs of youth and their families
- Child and adolescent partial hospitalization services, which help reduce psychological symptoms and improve the psychosocial functioning of troubled youth
- Residential treatment for sexually aggressive children and adolescents, where treatment focuses on relapse prevention in a safe, structured, supportive environment
- Sexual abuse clinics, which provide evaluation and treatment for children who may have been abused sexually, prevention services for preschool youth, and community education
- Geriatric outreach services, in which healthcare professionals specializing in geriatric mental health offer services to seniors in their homes and work with family members to access community resources
- Student wellness services for medical and graduate students (Wake Forest Baptist Health, 2016)

The Case of Anna

Anna is an 18-year-old female who has a history of bipolar disorder with severe manic epi-sodes. When she was 15, she was hospitalized for attempting to commit suicide by taking over 50 Tylenol capsules. Six days ago, she was taken to the emergency room by her mother, who found her unconscious on the bathroom floor with deep vertical cuts in both wrists.

After Anna was stabilized, she was assessed by one of the hospital psychiatrists. He rec-ommended inpatient hospitalization. Anna was then evaluated by an interdisciplinary team consisting of a psychiatric nurse, the psychiatrist, and a clinical social worker. During the assessment, Anna revealed that she had not been taking her medication for the past two months and that her suicide attempt came after breaking up with her boyfriend. After Anna was released from the inpatient program, she began attending daily outpatient treatment where you work as a clinical mental health counselor. The outpatient treatment program includes group counseling, recreation therapy, and some individual counseling.

What goals might be part of Anna's treatment plan? What would be some ways to help her achieve those goals? What resources can she access as she learns to develop new coping mechanisms? What do you consider to be the top priority regarding her treatment?

Cancer Patient Support Services

Statistics indicate that men have a one in two risk and women a one in three risk of develop-ing cancer during the course of a lifetime, with three out of four families in the United States being affected by some form of cancer (American Cancer Society, 2016). Cancer accounts for approximately one quarter of all deaths in the United States, exceeded only by cardiac dis-ease. When cancer is diagnosed, feelings of fear, anxiety, and confusion often emerge, plac-ing the patient and frequently the entire family in a state of crisis (Johnson, 1997). In many medical settings, oncology clinics provide counseling and other forms of psychosocial sup-port to help families through the diagnosis, treatment, and posttreatment process of a loved one developing cancer. Examples of the services provided by cancer patient support pro-grams include the following:

- New patient orientation services that provide information about the oncology center, treatment procedures, and support services
- Individual counseling to help the patient cope with the cancer diagnosis, treatment ramifications, and related life issues
- Family counseling that focuses on helping family members learn ways to help the patient and themselves as they cope with new stresses on the family system
- Support and educational groups for caregivers, cancer patients, and cancer survivors
- Therapeutic music, guided imagery, yoga classes, and pastoral care
- Appearance consultation to assist patients receiving chemotherapy who may need help with various appearance-related issues, including the provision of wigs, turbans, and hats
- Resource rooms that provide information for patients and family members on all aspects of cancer care, including diagnosis, treatment, and coping strategies; may offer books, brochures, videotapes, and computer access to Internet information

Many cancer patient support programs use mental health professionals and trained volunteers as service providers. Mental health professionals can recognize the psychosocial, spiritual, and other concerns that come with a cancer diagnosis and respond accordingly. For example, we interviewed the associate director of a local cancer patient support program who has worked with cancer patients and their families for over 25 years. When we asked her to describe her work, she stressed the importance of just being there to *listen*—to let people tell their stories. She explained, "You just see them visibly relax. Telling their stories gives them a sense of control: It is something that they need to do time and time again." She went on to say, "Even though many people in today's society are cancer survivors, there is still a feeling in the general public that a diagnosis of cancer is a death sentence. A lot of what I do is to normalize what they are experiencing" (DeChatelet, personal communication, July 15, 2001; July 30, 2012).

BOX 14–3 Receiving a Cancer Diagnosis

Receiving a diagnosis of cancer is a little like being pushed out of a helicopter into a jungle war without any training, any familiarity with the terrain, or any sense of how to survive.

(Lerner, 1994, p. 28)

Clinical mental health counselors who work with cancer patients and their families need to be aware that the impact cancer has on the family system varies, depending on the nature of the cancer diagnosis, the clinical course of the cancer, and the developmental stage of the family. Counselors also need to have worked through their own issues related to cancer, illness, and loss so that they are capable of helping others facing difficult circumstances.

Memory Assessment Counseling Services

Another example of a hospital-based setting in which clinical mental health counselors work is a center designed to help patients with memory loss, cognitive dysfunction, and dementia. Although many hospitals do not yet offer this service, those that do work with individuals, couples, and families affected by Alzheimer's disease and other dementias. One such center located at Wake Forest Baptist Hospital is administered by Dr. Ed Shaw. He describes the Memory Assessment Clinical Counseling Center (MACCC) in Box 14–4.

BOX 14–4 An Interdisciplinary Counseling Center for Individuals, Couples, and Families Affected by Alzheimer's Disease and Other Dementias

Currently, there are 5 million people diagnosed with Alzheimer's disease in the United States. In 20 years, as the baby boomers age, this number is expected to triple to 15 million. Most clients diagnosed with dementia typically have a primary caregiver (PCG) and several other family members involved in their care.

Significant mental health issues exist for patients and their caregivers when Alzheimer's disease or other forms of dementia are diagnosed. The Memory Assessment Clinic Counseling Center (MACCC) is staffed by a full-time clinic coordinator, a physician with a master's degree in counseling, and one or two second-year counseling graduate students. Patients are referred to the center by a geriatrician following a diagnosis of mild cognitive impairment (MCI, predementia), Alzheimer's disease, fronto-temporal dementia, Lewy body dementia, or one of several other dementia diagnoses. In general, referrals to the MACCC revolve around major events in the dementia patient's life span, including initial diagnosis, transitions from independence to partial dependence, transitions from partial dependence to complete dependence, and the time when a patient is nearing the end of life's journey.

Both patient-centered and caregiver-centered issues are of concern. Caregivers, in particular, frequently are in need of support. The most common mental health issues seen in both patients and caregivers include depression, anxiety, and grief. Suicidal ideation, substance abuse, conflict management, and family discord are often evidenced as well. Depending on the stage of the patient's dementia, other problems that arise include agitation, aggression, delusions/hallucinations, disinhibition, and safety issues (e.g., wandering, possession of weapons in the home). In addition, challenges with performing the instrumental activities of daily living are commonly seen. The staff meet on a biweekly basis to discuss patients being seen during which geriatricians provide medical updates on their patients, and members of the staff provide mental health updates, followed by an interdisciplinary discussion of ongoing care.

Services offered by the MACCC include individual counseling (patient, PCG, or other family members as needed), couple counseling (patient and spouse/partner), family counseling, and support groups. After assessment of a patient, the staff develops a treatment plan that may include individual, couple, and/or family counseling. Mental health services focus on the dementia-related issues. For a given life span issue (e.g., new diagnosis of dementia), the patient/PCG/family are provided up to 12 counseling sessions. When chronic mental health issues exist, a referral is made to a licensed professional counselor (LPC), psychologist, or psychiatrist; however, the MACCC counselor remains involved for dementia-associated problems. The MACCC also offers two support groups: a Caregiver's Support Group (CSG) and an Early Journey Support Group (EJSG).

Edward G. Shaw, MD

Other Hospital-Based Counseling Services

Additional counseling-related services offered in hospital settings include pastoral counseling, wellness programs, patient support groups, rehabilitation counseling, and trauma center work (see Box 14–5). The opportunity for clinical mental health counselors to work in medical settings continues to increase as medical personnel recognize the significant contributions made by mental health professionals.

BOX 14–5   Level I Trauma Centers, Alcohol Screening, and Brief Counseling Interventions

In 2007 the American College of Surgeons Committee on Trauma (ACS COT) changed its standards and now requires alcohol screening and brief counseling interventions for accrediting Level II Trauma Centers (ACS COT, 2006). The National Highway Traffic Safety Administration (2007) notes that someone suffers an alcohol-related injury in an automobile crash every two minutes. Up to half of hospitalized trauma patients test positive for alcohol-related concerns (Saitz, 2005). Patients experiencing alcohol-related trauma injuries may be at a point where they are ready to consider the impact alcohol is having on their lives. Offering screening and brief counseling interventions in trauma centers can lead to the prevention of future alcohol problems.

Mary Claire O'Brien, MD, and Laura J. Veach, PhD, recipients of the Robert Wood Johnson Foundation Grant for Substance Abuse Policy Research Programs

In addition to hospital settings, counselors work in a variety of public and private non-profit agencies and clinics that are medically connected. Whereas centralized community mental health centers and medical facilities provide a wide array of treatment options, other agencies intentionally provide a narrower range of specialized services. Specialized agencies usually focus on a specific problem (e.g., domestic violence, substance abuse) or a specific group (e.g., older adults, children, at-risk youth), or both. Examples of specialized settings and services include AIDS care centers, child abuse prevention services, drop-in crisis counseling centers, child and family services, homeless shelters, and services for at-risk youth. Some of the specialized services described are occasionally delivered in medical settings; thus, the distinctions between settings may be blurred. It is like a Venn diagram with some settings overlapping.

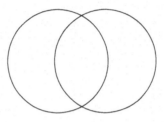

OTHER SPECIALIZED CLINICAL SETTINGS

Hospice and Palliative Care

Although hospice and palliative care programs function outside hospitals, they are connected with the medical world and hence are included in this section. Hospice and palliative care programs assist individuals and their families as they cope with grief, loss, and change. **Hospice care** specifically refers to the care needed by an individual during the last months or weeks of life. Medicare guidelines for hospice care specify that a physician believes, upon assessment, that a person has six months or less to live. **Palliative care** includes hospice care and refers to a compassionate, comprehensive team approach to care that focuses on quality of life for anyone coping with a serious illness, including the patient and the family members (National Hospice and Palliative Care Organization [NHPCO], 2016). Hospice and palliative care centers provide help to families dealing with many life-limiting illnesses, including Alzheimer's disease, amyotrophic lateral sclerosis (ALS), cancer, chronic lung disease, AIDS, pediatric conditions, congestive heart failure, and more. Hospice interdisciplinary team (IDT) members traditionally include physicians, nurses, nurse aids, social workers, chaplains, and bereavement counselors. Some hospices also include art and music therapists, physical and occupational therapists, nutritionists, pharmacists, and trained volunteers (NHPCO, 2012).

BOX 14–6   Death as a Process

The great events of life, as we observe them, are still clearly recognizable as journeys. . . . Out of centuries of experience has come the repeated observation that death appears to be a process rather than an event, a form of passage for human life.

Source: Adapted from Stoddard, 1992

The Worst Things to Say	The Best Things to Say
At least she lived a long life; many people die young.	I am so sorry that you are going through this painful process.
He is in a better place.	I wish I had the right words—just know I care.
I understand how you are feeling.	I don't know how you feel, but I am here to help in any way I can.
Aren't you over him yet? He has been dead for a while now.	Grieving takes time. The experience is different for everyone.
You can have another child still.	Please know that I am here for you.
She was such a good person. God wanted her to be with Him.	She meant a lot to you. Will you tell me about her?
He lived a long and full life.	I did not know _____ that well. What was he like?
She did what she came here to do, and it was her time to go.	I am usually up early or late, if you need anything.
Be strong.	[Say nothing; just be with the person.]

FIGURE 14–2   **Unhelpful and Helpful Things to Say to Someone Who Is Grieving**
Source: Adapted from Kessler, 2012; and Klein, 1998.

An important role of hospice and palliative care centers is to provide bereavement support services, including counseling, to individuals and families who are facing or have experienced the death of a loved one. The types of bereavement support services offered through the centers vary widely, depending on the resources available at the particular site. Support can include home visits, grief workshops, grief support groups, individual grief counseling, telephone calls, and the provision of brochures and other materials that describe how individuals deal with the sorrow and uncertainty surrounding death (Foliart, Clausen, & Siljestrom, 2001). Figure 14–2 provides a list of helpful and unhelpful things to say to people who have experienced the death of a loved one.

Counselors working in hospice settings need to be skilled in grief and bereavement counseling, knowledgeable about death education, aware of their own feelings and beliefs about death, capable of maintaining personal and professional boundaries, and practicing effective and meaningful self-care. Issues related to countertransference, dealing with the loss of a client, and fostering overdependence can be especially challenging to manage in this particularly emotional field. Counselors working in hospice programs can begin to navigate boundary issues more effectively by asking themselves the following questions (Hampton, 2002, 2012):

- Have I experienced less patience and increased irritability?
- Am I giving out any telephone number other than my work number?
- Is the family becoming overly dependent on me (or vice versa)?
- Do I feel as if no one can support the family like I can?

By maintaining healthy boundaries, working as part of a team, and engaging in consultation or supervision on a regular basis, clinical mental health counselors can play vital roles in meeting the needs of hospice patients and their families, as well as the needs of bereaved members of their communities.

Substance Abuse Treatment Programs

Substance-related disorders represent the most commonly occurring mental health problem in the United States. About half of the people treated in mental health settings have had at least one substance use problem in their lifetime (Behavioral Health Evolution, 2016). It is estimated that 25% of the patients seen by primary care physicians have an alcohol or drug problem (Doweiko, 2015). Although the statistics change from year to year, substance use disorders (SUDs) represent a major public health problem, affecting individuals, families, and society at large. Substances that frequently are abused include alcohol, marijuana, cocaine, heroin and other opiates, methamphetamine, and a wide range of prescription drugs. Problems related to substance use transcend gender, ethnicity, socioeconomic levels, geography, and almost all other domains (Stevens & Smith, 2013).

Substance abuse is the number one cause of preventable death in the United States, and between 20% and 50% of all hospital admissions are related to the effects of substance abuse and addiction (Doweiko, 2015; Kelly, 2016). Unfortunately, many people with substance use problems are in denial, and their conditions often go undiagnosed and untreated. When people with SUDs do present for treatment, either voluntarily or involuntarily, they typically are diagnosed with either a substance abuse or a substance dependency disorder.

Substance abuse is characterized by continued use of a substance in the presence of significant adverse consequences. An individual who exhibits one or more of the following symptoms within a 12-month period is considered to have a substance abuse problem:

- Substance use is responsible for failure to fulfill role obligations at work, school, or home.
- Recurrent substance use occurs in situations in which it is physically hazardous.
- Legal problems related to substance use recur.
- Continued substance use occurs despite the difficulties it is causing in significant relationships. (APA, 2013)

Substance dependence refers to the repeated, nonmedical use of a substance that harms the user or precipitates behavior in the user that harms others; it is characterized by physical or psychological dependence, which is diagnosed when three or more of the following symptoms are evidenced:

- Tolerance—that is, increased amounts of the substance are needed to experience the desired effect).
- Withdrawal—withdrawal symptoms occur, or individuals continue to use the substance to avoid withdrawal symptoms.
- The substance is taken in larger amounts or over a longer period of time than was intended.
- There is a persistent desire to cut down or control substance use.
- A lot of time is spent trying to acquire the substance.
- Important work, social, or leisure activities are given up or reduced because of the substance use.
- Substance use continues despite knowledge of recurrent physical or psychological consequences. (APA, 2013)

Frequently, individuals with substance-related disorders have co-occurring mental health issues, including mood disorders, anxiety, personality disorders, sleep disorders, posttraumatic stress disorder, psychotic disorders, and other psychological disorders. The coexistence of substance abuse and mental disorders is referred to as **dual diagnosis**, a condition that can be particularly intractable to treatment. Clients with a dual diagnosis are at greater risk for relapse, and those who do relapse are more likely to develop depression (Pidcock & Polansky, 2001). Another condition that makes the already-complex issue of SUDs more difficult to assess, diagnose, and treat is **polysubstance abuse**, which refers to the abuse of two or more substances simultaneously. Approximately 40% of people admitted for substance abuse treatment in recent years also have problems with at least one other drug (SAMHSA, 2016).

People with a substance dependency are considered to have an **addiction**: a complex, progressive behavior pattern with biological, psychological, sociological, and behavioral components (Kelly, 2016). Addiction has been defined as "a persistent and intense involvement with and stress upon a single behavior pattern, with a minimization or even exclusion of other behaviors, both personal and interpersonal" (L'Abate, Farrar, & Serritella, 1992, p. 2). Addictive disorders—which can include gambling, workaholism, sexual addictions, nonsuicidal self-injury, Internet addictions, and compulsive behaviors—continue to be major problems in the United States (Doweiko, 2015). Addictions like these, which are not the same as chemical addictions, are called **process addictions** (see Box 14–7). Counselors may work in sites that specialize in treating any of these addictions.

BOX 14–7   Technology Addiction

Technology addiction (TA), a growing concern in our society, is a relatively new phenomenon. To date, little is known about the impact of the addictive properties of technology on mental health. The instant gratification and accessibility offered by technological sources may exacerbate addictive behaviors among vulnerable individuals.

Although technology has advanced many facets of our society, its negative impact is prevalent. With casual use, technology may be used as a coping mechanism to escape from the stressors of daily living. For example, individuals may use television as a way to wind down from a stressful day, may play Farmville (a Facebook game) to pass the time, or may go into Second Life (a virtual reality world) to engage in fantasy play. For some individuals, however, casual use becomes addictive use of technology. As with other addictions, the risk of TA is further increased by the combination of stressors in the environment, greater accessibility, and genetic predisposition.

Current literature on TA offers multiple diagnostic concepts that focus on limited subtypes, such as Internet addiction or video game addiction. Within a biopsychosocial framework, TA can be viewed within the scope of process addictions. Therefore, the biological, psychological, and social aspects of individuals are all affected when TA is present. In order to continue learning about and understanding the effects of TA on the human psyche and society in general, clinicians can benefit from developing awareness of the following warning signs, which mirror chemical dependency risk factors:

- Neglect of responsibilities due to increasing use of technology
- Relationship changes with continued use of technology
- Preoccupation with technology and increasing forgetfulness
- Escalating reliance on technology
- Multiple unsuccessful attempts to stop or cut back on technology use
- Escape from stress by using technology
- Alienation from loved ones due to extensive use of technology

- Lying and defensiveness about technology use
- Development of physical health risks specifically related to overuse of technology (e.g., carpal tunnel syndrome)
- Loss of possessions

Counselors might use the proposed warning signs to explore technology behaviors, screen for harmful patterns of technology use, and consider referring clients identifying with the warning signs to an addiction specialist for intensive assessment.

Kristina M. Acosta, PhD, LCAS, LPC; Anya Lainas, MA, NCC, LPC;
and Laura Veach, PhD, LPC, LCAS, CCS

In this section, our focus is on the treatment of addictions to or abuse of chemical substances, including alcohol, illegal drugs, and prescription drugs. In the 1980s, the primary mode of treatment for chemical addiction was residential care. Now, however, the more frequently used level of care, after a client has been through detoxification and is stabilized, is intensive outpatient treatment (Veach & Madwid, 2005). Treatment for individuals who abuse substances occurs primarily in two general settings: substance abuse treatment facilities and community mental health centers or agencies (Von Steen, Vacc, & Strickland, 2002). Professionals and paraprofessionals, including rehabilitation counselors and other professional counselors, often are employed in substance abuse treatment centers. Many agencies provide education, prevention, and consultation services about substance use, as well as about treatment and rehabilitation services for substance abuse.

Although it is important for all clinical mental health counselors to have some training in addictions and substance abuse, counselors who work in substance abuse treatment facilities benefit from specialized training and certification (e.g., licensed clinical addiction specialist, certified clinical addiction specialist, certified substance abuse counselor, and certified substance abuse prevention consultant). The number of academic counselor-education programs with an emphasis on substance abuse is growing, and since 1994, the NBCC has provided a certification process for becoming a certified master addictions counselor (MAC).

CACREP (2016) created a new specialty area for counselors who want to work in the addictions field. Counselor education programs can now offer the specialty area of **addiction counseling**. Students preparing to work as addiction counselors develop knowledge and skills "necessary to work in a wide range of addiction counseling, treatment, and prevention programs, as well as in a mental health context" (CACREP, 2016, p. 17).

The dominant model for treating SUDs is the Minnesota Model of addiction treatment (Doweiko, 2015). The Minnesota Model, also known as the Hazelden Model, was designed in the 1950s and has evolved over time, particularly because of changes in reimbursement policies in the 1990s. The model is based on the disease concept of dependency, which asserts that chemical addiction is a treatable disease with specific origins, symptoms, progression, and outcomes. The multidisciplinary model asserts that recovery is possible only through abstinence accompanied by major emotional and spiritual changes. The model uses a treatment team composed of health professionals from different specialty areas, including physicians, counselors, certified substance abuse specialists, social workers, nurses, and clergy. In addition to advocating abstinence, the model places a strong emphasis on life change by orienting clients to 12-step programs—for example, Alcoholics Anonymous (AA) and Narcotics Anonymous (NA). The model provides a combination of didactic, educational, and psychotherapeutic interventions and values personal confrontation. Initially designed for the treatment of alcoholism, the model is now used to treat all forms of chemical dependency. It is characterized by a continuum of care that includes detoxification, inpatient and outpatient services, and aftercare services (Smith & Garcia, 2013).

- **Detoxification** (the process of removing toxic substances or qualities) is the first phase of dependency treatment. Three forms include **medical detoxification** (when withdrawal can be life threatening, thus requiring the help of medical professionals), **social detoxification** (when withdrawal symptoms are less severe, enabling detoxification to occur in a residential, nonmedical setting), and **self-detoxification** (unmanaged, unsupervised detoxification that often is unsuccessful). Detoxification serves as a gateway to treatment, with formal detoxification typically lasting from a few days to two weeks (Smith & Garcia, 2013).

- **Residential treatment** can occur in medical or nonmedical residential facilities, halfway houses, and therapeutic communities. Two widely recognized residential settings are the Betty Ford Center and Hazelden, both of which utilize the Minnesota Model of treatment.

> The programs [at Hazelden] are not defined by a number of days, but rather by individual needs. Lengths of stay in both outpatient and residential programs are dependent on the needs of the individual and are determined through an assessment and evaluation process. For most people, an average length of stay in primary care is four to six weeks but longer-term programs—often two or three months—are beneficial to some. Successful treatment is the ultimate goal, and time is necessary to win the battle.
>
> (Hazelden, 2016)

Other settings, which are less costly, are referred to as *freestanding programs*. They offer residential care in community-based settings with lower levels of direct medical monitoring. During the course of treatment, abstinence is required, and group therapy and psychoeducation are emphasized, although some programs also provide individual counseling. Residential programs focus on the attainment of short-term goals in treatment and the development of longer-term goals for posttreatment. In these confrontational but supportive environments, clients have an opportunity to live and act productively in a drug-free manner.

- **Outpatient treatment** is designed to follow more intensive inpatient or residential treatment as part of the continuum of care plan. In the past, outpatient treatment for substance abuse was either unlimited or had very liberal limits, allowing clients to continue in treatment for an indefinite period of time. However, insurance companies and funding agencies now impose stricter limits on the number of outpatient visits covered per year or per policy. An additional problem associated with outpatient treatment, particularly if it is not preceded by more intensive forms of treatment, is a high rate of missed appointments and relapse because individuals have not been removed from the pressures of the drinking or drug-using environments in which they live. To address this problem, many sites offer **intensive outpatient programs (IOPs)**, which may provide temporary housing for people in treatment. IOPs are the predominant level of care for clients in treatment for chemical dependency and consist of sessions three to five days or evenings per week, continuing for three to ten weeks overall. Counseling and psychoeducation in IOPs tend to be group focused, intensive, and multidimensional, in accordance with the Minnesota Model. Family members often are encouraged to participate, and clients are asked to attend AA or NA meetings during and after treatment.

   • **Aftercare** follows successful completion of a chemical dependency treatment program. These clients are not considered *cured*, that is restored to health; instead, their recovery has just begun and is considered to be a lifelong process. Clients who successfully complete treatment still have much work to accomplish. To help with recovery and to prevent relapse, the majority of inpatient addiction treatment programs in the United States incorporate AA and NA into plans for treatment and follow-up care (Smith, 2015; Stevens & Smith, 2013). These peer support groups provide guidance, support, sustenance, and solace to individuals seeking help with substance-related disorders (Benshoff, 1996).

   Typically, AA, NA, and other support groups, which are adjunctive to a comprehensive continuum of care, have at their foundation the 12 steps. The 12 steps utilize important counseling concepts, including *problem recognition* (Step 1), *hope* (Step 2), *help seeking* (Steps 3, 5, and 7), *insight development* (Steps 4, 6, and 10), *restitution* (Steps 8 and 9), and *adoption of new consciousness and forms of behavior* (Step 12; Benshoff & Janikowski, 2000).

   Working with clients who have substance-related disorders can be challenging for many reasons. **Denial**, which involves minimizing the effects of substance abuse on oneself or others, is a common defense mechanism and can sabotage successful treatment. Related to denial is the client's degree of motivation, or readiness for change. When clients are court ordered to receive treatment for substance use, they may not be at a point where they are willing to acknowledge that they have a problem or to consider changing their behaviors. Such individuals are in the precontemplation stage of change. Counselors working with clients in this stage are advised to use strategies such as motivational interviewing to help clients become more aware of their emotional responses to the negative consequences associated with their substance use habits (Prochaska & Norcross, 2014). Various forms of client resistance, unhealthy family dynamics, negative environmental influences, and stressful living conditions are other factors that can make working with this population problematic.

   Although there are challenges in working with people who are dealing with addictions, recovery is both a goal and a reality for many clients. The term **recovery** is frequently used in the addictions world, as well as in the broader world of mental health, to refer to "a process, a new way to live one's life beyond mere abstinence from alcohol and other drugs. Recovery defines how one lives life today, implying hope, healing, and restoration" (Adams & Grieder, 2005, p. 17).

Child and Family Service Agencies

Many communities have nonprofit agencies that specialize in treating the needs of children, couples, and families. Funding sources for child and family service agencies vary, with many of the private agencies getting support from the United Way, religiously affiliated organizations, charities, private endowments, and/or grants. Clinical mental health counselors with a background in family counseling may find excellent opportunities in agencies that specialize in child and family services. Depending on the agency, family services may include combinations of any of the following services:

   • Child and family assessment
   • Individual counseling
   • Couples counseling

- Family counseling
- Parent education
- Pregnancy testing and support/education services
- Adoption support services
- Domestic violence and rape crisis hotlines
- Shelters for women and children who are victims of domestic violence or sexual assault
- Victim assistance counseling
- Counseling and support groups for abusers
- Counseling and support groups for adult survivors of sexual abuse or incest
- Supervised, structured visitation for parents who are not allowed to be alone with their children
- Family preservation programs
- Counseling and support for abusive or potentially abusive families
- Community education programs to help prevent abuse and neglect

Clinical mental health counselors who work in child and family settings need to have a comprehensive understanding of systems-based counseling. Systems-based counseling embraces a circular causality approach and assumes that interactions within families are dynamic rather than static or linear. For counseling to be effective, both the family system and the larger systems within which the family is embedded need to be taken into account. Popular family counseling approaches include structural, strategic, experiential, solution focused, and narrative.

DOMESTIC VIOLENCE. Domestic violence is a pervasive problem that affects spouses, partners, children, and seniors. **Intimate partner violence (IPV)** is a form of domestic violence that occurs between two people in a close relationship and can include physical abuse, emotional abuse, sexual abuse, and/or threats of physical or sexual violence (Centers for Disease Control [CDC], 2015). Women are more likely than men to be victims of IPV, although there are many instances in which men are abused. Nearly 3 in 10 women and 1 in 10 men in the United States have experienced rape, physical violence, or stalking by a partner (CDC, 2015). These figures should be viewed as conservative estimates because many incidents of IPV go unreported. In addition to IPV, domestic violence includes abusive treatment of elders or children and the witnessing of violence by children.

Victims of violence are at increased risk for mental health problems as well as for physical injury and death (CDC, 2015). Anxiety, PTSD, depression, suicide, eating disorders, and substance abuse are among the many mental health issues associated with being abused. Children who witness abuse are at a greater risk for short- or long-term emotional disturbances, including nightmares, PTSD, depression, learning difficulties, and aggressive behavior.

Because of the prevalence and severity of domestic violence, many family service agencies include services designed to prevent domestic violence from occurring or recurring and to protect victims of domestic violence. To accomplish these goals, comprehensive programs may provide anger management programs, counseling groups for abusers, support groups for people who have been abused, and protective shelters for women and children.

What Is Abuse? According to the National Coalition Against Domestic Violence (NCADV, 2016), **abuse** is a pattern of behavior used to establish power and control over another person through the use of fear and intimidation. Abuse occurs when one person believes that he or she is entitled to control another person. Three major categories of abuse are these:

- **Physical abuse**, which can range from bruising to murder. Many times, physical abuse begins with trivial injuries that then escalate over time
- **Sexual abuse**, which refers to any forced sexual activity
- **Psychological or emotional abuse**, which includes constant verbal abuse, harassment, extreme possessiveness, deprivation of resources, isolation, and the destruction of physical property

A number of social, psychological, and cultural theories have been posited to explain battering and abuse. Among the more prominent of those theories are attachment theory, feminist theory, social learning theory, and systems theory (James, 2008; James & Gilliland, 2017). Counselors providing domestic violence services need to be familiar with theoretical frameworks about the causes of battering so that they can work more effectively with perpetrators and victims.

Who Are Batterers? Domestic violence cuts across socioeconomic, geographic, cultural, and religious boundaries. Several psychological and behavioral characteristics are associated with batterers, although no single typology characterizes all people who abuse. Men who abuse women may exhibit some of the following characteristics, attitudes, and behaviors:

- Objectifying women, who are not respected but instead are viewed as property
- Exhibiting low self-esteem, often feeling inadequate or powerless
- Blaming their behavior on external causes, perhaps a "bad day," alcohol, or drugs
- Denying the severity of the problem and its effects on their families
- Being characterized as jealous, possessive, demanding, and aggressive
- Abusing alcohol or other drugs
- Being unemployed or experiencing significant life stressors
- Having been abused as children or having seen their mothers abused
- Having strong, traditional, patriarchal beliefs
- Tending to overreact, having a short fuse
- Being likely to use force or violence to solve problems
- Cycling from being hostile, aggressive, and cruel to being charming, manipulative, and seductive, depending on the situation
- Having unrealistic expectations of marriage, their partners, and relationships in general (James, 2008; NCADV, 2016)

Why Do Women Stay? Reasons to remain in or terminate a relationship are seldom simple. In cases of domestic violence, reasons typically are quite complex. Often, the act of leaving is dangerous, as many batterers will attempt to retaliate. It has been noted that most women leave an abusive relationship an average of three to six times, with varying degrees of permanence (James, 2008). Some of the reasons a woman might choose to stay in an abusive relationship include these:

- She would suffer shame, embarrassment, and humiliation if her secret were revealed.
- She fears repercussion from her partner. Women who leave their batterers are at a 75% greater risk of being killed by the batterer than those who stay (Domestic Abuse Shelter, 2016).

- Financial circumstances make leaving difficult.
- Early role models of an abusive parent may have warped her view of the nature of relationships.
- She may not have access to safety or support.
- She may hold strong beliefs against separation or divorce.
- She may believe that her partner will reform.
- She fears the repercussions leaving may have on her children.
- She may focus on the good times rather than the battering. (James, 2008; Domestic Abuse Shelter, 2016)

What Services Are Available? During the last 30 years, as consciousness about domestic violence has been raised, programs have been established that target both the victim and the abuser. Crisis lines, shelters, and support groups are common forms of assistance for victims. Counselors who work with domestic violence issues need to be well trained in crisis intervention as well as in other forms of intervention appropriate for victims of violence. Examples of knowledge and skills that should be acquired by counselors who work with this population are listed in Figure 14–3. Ensuring the victim's safety is of primary concern, regardless of the setting. Counselors also often serve as victim advocates by providing assistance with legal, economic, housing, and parenting issues (NCADV, 2016). To advocate effectively, counselors need to understand the legal system and have a strong networking alliance so that help can be obtained quickly (James, 2008).

Many communities have created programs to treat people who have abused their partners, recognizing that treatment is necessary for change to occur. Although not all counselors who work in family services will choose to work with those who victimize, it is important to be aware of the types of services available to domestic abusers. Most **batterers** (i.e., those who inflict physical abuse), especially those who are adjudicated, do not enter intervention programs willingly and often exhibit denial, minimization, justification, or projection of blame (James, 2008). The prevalent mode of intervention for batterers is court-ordered group counseling, which provides opportunities for social learning, anger management, confrontation, and support. Groups typically are designed to help abusers learn to accept responsibility for their behavior, recognize the spectrum of abuse, resolve conflict without violence or abuse, and address personal concerns. A counselor who worked with batterers describes his experiences in Box 14–8.

- Knowledge about the phenomenon of partner abuse (definitions, prevalence rates, types of abuse, dynamics and consequences of abuse)
- Knowledge of the explanatory theories of abuse and violence
- Knowledge of feminist-informed and culturally sensitive theories and practices pertaining to partner abuse
- Effective assessment protocols for partner abuse
- Knowledge of the experiences, needs, and risks faced by battered individuals (including symptoms of PTSD)
- Key principles and practices for individual treatment
- Services and resources available for victims and abusers

FIGURE 14–3   Knowledge and Skills Needed to Work with Victims of Domestic Violence
Source: Adapted from Haddock, 2002.

BOX 14-8   Group Counseling with Male Batterers

"They" were not the people I expected to meet. I expected "them" to be the stereotype—uncaring, manipulative, harsh, and antisocial. I took the assignment because I needed the hours. I was already working with sexually and physically abused boys. I told myself I would only do the groups for a short time, just until the end of my internship. My first group was almost seven years ago, and I am still with the program.

Some male batterers personify the stereotype—a noxious soup of bullying, selfishness, narcissism, and sociopathology. They always try to tell me what they think I want to hear. They always think they can hide their true selves. They can't see themselves accurately, and they assume that I am similarly impaired. Their problems are always caused by others, and the deck is always stacked against them.

The majority of male batterers I encounter, however, value family, love their partners, and acknowledge that some of their behaviors are inappropriate. Many of these men enter the group believing that control will prevent abandonment, and the opposite is true. Many batterers enter the group believing that "taking care of her" is respectful and appropriate, and the opposite is true. Intimate relationships produce a frustrating paradox for most of these men. The harder they try, the more conflict, frustration, and failure they experience.

The purpose of the program is to produce a safer world for women and children. The goal is to educate and change beliefs. The process is one of engagement, confrontation, and encouragement. Success is measured with attendance, homework returned, and in-session behavior. Throughout the process, I always hope for healing and changes of heart.

Robin Daniel, PhD, LPC, NCC

CHILD ABUSE SERVICES. In many communities, specialized agencies focus on the prevention and treatment of child abuse. These agencies provide support services for abusive or potentially abusive families, parent training programs, and community education programs regarding the recognition of abuse and neglect. Lewis et al.'s (2003) community counseling model provides a helpful framework for conceptualizing the types of services that might be offered at a child abuse prevention and treatment agency (see Figure 14–4).

HOME-BASED SERVICES. Home-based services provide intensive interventions within the homes of children and youth with emotional disturbances. In most cases, home-based services are provided through child welfare, juvenile justice, or community mental health systems. Three major goals of home-based services are to (a) prevent out-of-home placements; (b) connect youth and their families with community resources, thereby creating an outside support system; and (c) strengthen the family's coping skills and capacity after crisis treatment is completed (Stroul, 1988). Services provided through these programs include evaluation, assessment, counseling, skills training, and coordination of services.

Two primary types of home-based services are family preservation programs and multisystemic therapy programs (MST; Promising Practices Network on Children, Families, and Communities, 2016; U.S. Department of Health and Human Services, 1999). **Family preservation programs** provide family-based services designed to keep dysfunctional families together. For example, the Surgeon General's mental health report (U.S. Department of Health and Human Services, 1999) describes the Homebuilders Program in Tacoma,

	Community Services	Client Services
Direct	• Community education programs regarding the recognition of abuse and neglect • Parent training classes offered to the community-at-large	• Individual and family counseling for children and parents • Assessment of and treatment for sexual offenders
Indirect	• Sponsoring community awareness events to make families aware of abuse and neglect issues • Working with local and state legislators to advance children's rights	• Sponsoring parent support groups that focus on effective parenting skills • Working with the department of social services to provide supervision and structured intervention for visits between children and parents who are not allowed to be alone with their children

FIGURE 14–4 **Direct and Indirect Community and Client Services in a Child Abuse Prevention and Treatment Agency**
Source: Community Counseling: Empowerment Strategies for a Diverse Society (3rd ed.), by J. A. Lewis, M. D. Lewis, J. A. Daniels, and M. J. D'Andrea, 2003, Pacific Grove, CA: Brooks/Cole. Adapted with permission of Wadsworth, a division of Thomson Learning.

Washington, and family reunification programs in both Washington State and Utah. The success of these programs was attributed to the following:

- Delivering services in a home and community setting
- Viewing family members as colleagues in defining a service plan
- Making backup services available 24 hours a day
- Building life skills based on individual needs of family members
- Offering marital and family interventions
- Efficiently coordinating community services
- Assisting with basic needs, such as clothing, food, and housing

MST programs (Henggeler, Schoenwald, Borduin, Rowland, & Cunningham, 1998) are intensive, short-term, home- and family-focused treatment services for youth with behavioral and emotional disturbances. MST is based on Bronfenbrenner's (1979, 1995) bioecological theory. Originally implemented with juvenile delinquents, MST intervenes directly in a young person's family, school, neighborhood, and peer group by identifying factors that contribute to the problem behaviors. Major goals of MST are to (a) empower caregivers with the skills needed to address the difficulties that accompany parenting youth with behavior problems and (b) empower youth to cope more effectively with family, peer, school, and neighborhood difficulties. By working intensively with the young person, the family, and the larger community, skills are developed across all groups that lead to improved behaviors and mental health. The efficacy of MST has been attributed to the fact that it is clearly specified, is based on solid empirical research, and uses quality assurance mechanisms to ensure that treatment protocol is followed (Schoenwald et al., 2000).

Other Clinical Services

Opportunities for community-based mental health counselors exist in many different settings, depending on the counselor's training, skills, interests, and professional certification. In addition to the sites already mentioned, opportunities for employment include wellness centers, for-profit agencies, faith-based counseling centers, career centers, private practice, correctional facilities, school-based mental health settings, colleges and universities, and government agencies. In particular, there is a growing need for civilian counselors to work with military personnel (Hall, 2017). National legislation has now recognized licensed professional counselors as legitimate providers of mental health services within the Veteran's Healthcare Administration.

The settings in which clinical mental health counselors work are numerous, and the varying needs for services are great. We conclude this section with narratives from a counselor working in an ecumenical, nonprofit counseling center (see Box 14–9). She describes some of the challenges and rewards that are inherent in this work.

BOX 14–9   Directing and Counseling in a Private, Nonprofit Community Counseling Center

Trinity Center, Inc.'s mission of wholeness—mind, body, and spirit—is inspired by the spirit of our shared Christian faith. We are ecumenical in our approach, serving with respect clients of varying faith backgrounds. We have been in operation since 1982 and are organized as a small, ecumenical community counseling center, operating on a budget of approximately $425,000 annually. Our staff consists of a 2/3 time executive director; a full-time director of client services; 3 half-time administrative and support staff; 4 clinical employees; 14 part-time contract clinicians; 1 part-time (6 hours per week) medical director; and a 16-member board of directors.

One of the rewards of directing Trinity Center is working alongside talented, committed professionals who bring creativity and energy into the work they do with their clients, each other's lives, and the life of the center. An ongoing challenge is continually adapting to changes that come from our professionals' evolving interests and the profession's evolving standards of acceptable practice. It is a challenge to hold both of these goals in balance—sacrificing neither procedural predictability and accountability nor professional creativity and growth.

Another challenge is maintaining financial stability as we combine the model of a standard private practice (i.e., with clients able to pay the full fee for services either through insurance or self-pay) with that of a nonprofit agency (i.e., serving appropriate clients, regardless of ability to pay, soliciting subsidy revenue from individual, church, and business donors and foundations). For over 30 years, we have shared the financial challenges as well as the professional enrichment—learning and adapting as we have grown.

Ann Dixon Coppage, MA Ed, LPCS, Director of Client Services

Summary and Conclusion

In this chapter, we have described a variety of settings in which clinical mental health counselors may be employed. Some of the venues, such as community mental health centers and hospitals, provide many different treatment options for diverse clientele who present with a spectrum of issues. Other settings—including hospice programs, substance abuse agencies, and family service agencies—allow counselors to focus on a specific population or mental health issue. Services in CMHCs, hospitals, clinics, and agencies can include inpatient treatment and day programs, residential treatment, outpatient services, home visits, prevention efforts, and multisystemic interventions.

Regardless of the setting in which they practice, counselors need to engage in ongoing training and supervision to update knowledge, skills, and professional certifications. The counseling profession and community mental health service programs continue to evolve, both as a result of changes in the profession itself and as a consequence of government and public policy. It is incumbent on counseling professionals to be cognizant of those changes, remaining open to new approaches, interventions, and service options.

MyCounselingLab

Try the Topic 16 Assignments: *Substance Abuse.*

CHAPTER 15

A and N photography/Shutterstock

Employee Assistance Programs, Private Practice, Coaching, and Managed Care

I feel at times that I'm wasting my mind
   as we wade through your thoughts and emotions.
With my skills I could be in a world-renowned clinic
   with a plush, private office, soft padded chairs,
     and a sharp secretary at my command.
Instead of here in a pink cinderblock room
   where it leaks when it rains
     and the noise seeps under the door like water.
But in leaving, you pause for a moment
   as your voice spills out in a whisper:
"Thanks for being here when I hurt."
With those words my fantasies end, as reality,
   like a wellspring begins filling me
     with life-giving knowledge, as it cascades through
      my mind,
That in meeting you, when you're flooded with pain,
I discover myself.

Reprinted from "Here and Now," by S. T. Gladding, 1975, *Personnel and Guidance Journal, 53*, p. 746. Copyright © Samuel T. Gladding. Used with permission.

CHAPTER OVERVIEW

From reading this chapter, you will learn about

- The purpose of employee assistance programs (EAPs)
- Different types of private practice and services offered by private practitioners
- Tips for building a successful private practice and pragmatic needs of private practitioners
- The field of coaching, different types of coaching, and coaching as it relates to clinical mental health counseling
- The history of managed care, the effects of managed care on the counseling profession, and ethical considerations associated with working in a managed care environment

As you read, consider

- What types of services are offered by EAPs and the difference between in-house and contracted EAP services
- Benefits and challenges associated with private practice as well as reasons clinical mental health counselors may elect to go into private practice

- How private practitioners market their services and remain accountable to their clients and the public
- What the purpose of coaching is and how coaching differs from counseling
- Advantages and disadvantages associated with working in a managed care environment and ways you can be placed on a managed care panel

Clinical mental health counselors are employed in a variety of professional settings, including community agencies, schools, colleges and universities, hospitals, clinics, treatment centers, government, the military, employee assistance programs, managed care companies, and private practice (Harrington, 2013). Two settings that are appealing to many clinical mental health counselors are employee assistance programs (EAPs) and private practice. EAP counselors work with companies and institutions, sometimes operating within a particular organization and sometimes operating on a referral basis. Their activities may include personal counseling, family counseling, providing seminars for organizations, and conducting wellness-focused initiatives with workers in employment settings. Private practitioners work independently or in a group with other clinicians. Many private practitioners specialize in helping people with specific issues, such as bereavement, mood disorders, anxiety, career or life coaching, and family transitions.

Coaching is closely related to counseling but differs in its scope and purpose. Indeed, the Center for Credentialing in Education (CCE), which is an affiliate of NBCC, now offers a coaching certification for counselors. Coaching is a growing field that provides another avenue for using the skills and knowledge gained in an accredited clinical mental health counseling program.

Managed care, which has had a pervasive effect on the delivery of many clinical mental health services, is also covered in this chapter. Clinical mental health counselors need to be aware of what it means to work in managed care environments. The development of managed care organizations, their influence on clinical mental health counseling, potential ethical issues, and recommendations for counselors who work in settings associated with managed behavioral health care are examined.

EMPLOYEE ASSISTANCE PROGRAMS

For many years, business, industry, government, educational, and private/public institutions in the United States have exhibited a strong interest in the overall health of their employees (Herlihy, 2000). Many corporate organizations now include mental health services as part of their employee benefits programs. Employee assistance programs (EAPs) provide mental health services to employees, recognizing that personal and professional issues can affect work performance, health, and general well-being. EAPs are designed to assist individual employees, their families, and work organizations.

The service has evolved to address a multitude of mental health issues, including the following (Employee Assistance Professionals Association, 2016):

- Emotional and mental distress (e.g., anxiety, grief, depression)
- Stress at home or work
- Family/personal relationship issues
- Work relationship issues

- Substance abuse and addictions
- Career issues
- Financial and legal concerns
- Child and elder care concerns
- Health and wellness
- Critical incidents (e.g., exposure to crises and trauma)
- Violence
- Company reorganization and change
- Retirement planning

EAP services are provided by approximately 10,000 mental health professionals, including counselors. Many of these professionals are represented by membership organizations such as the Employee Assistance Professionals Association (EAPA; www.eapassn.org) and EASNA, the Employee Assistance Trade Association (www.easna.org). About 5,000 professionals are certified employee assistance professionals (CEAP), a certification that is provided by EAPA (EAPA, 2016). Virtually all Fortune 500 companies in the United States have EAP programs, with most offering fourth-party payments (from the companies themselves) to EAP counselors. According to the 2008 National Study of Employers, 65% of employers provided EAPs in 2008, up from 56% in 1998 (Families and Work Institute, 2008).

The establishment of EAPs has positively affected the productivity of employees, resulting in savings to employers and healthier lifestyles for employees (EAPA, 2016). Employees and their household members have the opportunity to use EAPs to manage professional and personal issues that may affect their work performance. Typically, there is no charge for these services because they have been prepaid by the employer. Confidentiality is maintained in accordance with privacy laws and ethical guidelines. In self-referred cases, employers do not know who is using EAP services, unless there are extenuating circumstances and written release forms have been signed. In cases of formal referrals (i.e., supervisory referrals made for employees who are experiencing job performance problems), the client who was referred may be asked to sign a release form indicating that counseling appointments were kept; however, information about the content of the counseling sessions remains confidential unless otherwise specified.

In addition to providing direct services to individual clients, EAPs also provide services to their **corporate clients**—the organizations that either contract with the EAPs externally or have an in-house EAP provision. Examples of services an EAP might provide to an organization include these:

- *Workplace consultation:* Providing consultation to supervisors, work groups, union officials, and other individuals in the organization regarding performance issues and recommended approaches to specific situations.
- *Policy consultation:* Providing consultation to the organization regarding organizational policies that address human factors in the workplace (e.g., responding to violence, drug testing, organizing work teams, managing an aging workforce).
- *Training:* Skill building for supervisors, managers, and executives on topics such as conflict management, communication skills, performance management, violence prevention, and diversity.
- *Information and education activities:* Sharing information with workplace personnel through such activities as seminars, employee orientation, mailings, and emails.

- *Critical incident management:*   Responding to traumatic events that affect the work-place. Services may include situation assessment, debriefing, defusing, and family information management.
- *Special situations:*   Providing services that address specific company events, including downsizing, mergers, and celebratory events.
- *Program implementation and management:*   Managing the programs provided by the EAP or other vendors. This service promotes the efficient implementation and ongoing operation of the EAP and related workplace activities. (EAPA, 2016)

The Case of Peter

Peter is a 42-year-old Caucasian car sales manager who lives in a suburban West Coast town. His ex-wife, Lisa, divorced him 10 months ago. Since then, Peter has been living alone in an apartment and spending time with his teenage son off and on. Peter and Lisa avoid each other as much as possible, despite living in the same town. Meanwhile, Peter's parents, older sister, and extended family all live on the East Coast.

Peter moved across the country in his early 20s to pursue a job in acting. After years of playing bit parts, he began working at a car dealership to have a regular income. He met Lisa when he was 26, and they were married a year later. Peter stayed in car sales, getting promoted to manager of one shop and then to district manager.

Lately, Peter has been having difficulty in his role at work. Two direct reports have quit in response to Peter's angry outbursts and increasingly unrealistic sales goals. His drinking, one of the reasons for the divorce, is escalating in quantity and frequency. Peter has been spending his weekends bar-hopping with younger, unmarried coworkers and occasionally driving home intoxicated.

Peter's boss mandated that Peter seek counseling after he walked into a meeting still hung over from the night before. For Peter to keep his job, he must pass a sobriety test and complete a specified number of counseling sessions through his company's EAP.

If you were Peter's EAP counselor, what would your responsibilities be to Peter? to his supervisor? to the company? Which issue do you think needs to be addressed first? Can you work with Peter in a short period of time (i.e., six sessions)? Do you need to refer him to a substance abuse agency? What other factors will you want to consider?

Becoming an EAP Counselor

In a national survey of EAP programs, over 60% of the externally administered programs reported hiring counseling graduates with master's and doctoral degrees (Hosie & Spruill, 1990). This percentage was topped only slightly by EAP programs hiring master's-level social workers. From these statistics, it is evident that the need exists for counselors to provide preventive and remedial services to employees and to train supervisors to recognize troubled workers and refer them for help. Counselors can also actively contribute to the conceptual development of EAP prevention and intervention programs. For many clinical mental health counselors, EAPs represent an alternative to traditional community mental health agencies and provide a way for counselors to interact with the mental health world and the corporate world.

Employee assistance utilizes knowledge about human behavior and behavioral health to improve personal and professional productivity. Such a service integrates organizational development, behavioral health, human resources, and business management (EAPA, 2016). EAP professionals come from diverse professional backgrounds, including the fields of counseling and social work, substance abuse and addictions counseling, and human resources and organizational development. Many EAP organizations expect their mental health professionals to understand organizational practice and to be skilled in consultation, program management, evaluation, and marketing (Hosie, West, & Mackey, 1993).

Although some universities offer formal EAP training, most professional development for EAP workers comes through continuing education offered through EAPA and its local chapters. Joining EAPA provides a sense of professional identity as well as access to information and resources available to members. Among those resources is the *Journal of Employee Assistance* (JEA), which is published quarterly. The journal addresses a plethora of organizational- and employee-related topics, such as issues related to technology, including social media; emotional healing from workplace disasters; developments in HIPAA and Health Information Technology for Economic and Clinical Health (HITECH); veterans in the workplace; identifying and treating employees with personality disorders; and workplace bullying.

Serving as an EAP Counselor

Employee assistance counselors recognize that there are multiple ways of bringing about change in employees and institutions. One way is for EAP counselors to take a preventive approach by collaborating with others in the organization. One goal of this approach is to have the workplace culture reflect the company's mission so there is congruence between what employees expect from their work and what actually occurs (Kennedy, 2001). If this type of harmony is reached, workers are more likely to be pleased with their work environment.

A second approach is to work with employees directly. In this type of arrangement, EAP counselors attempt to move employees beyond their present range of behavior and help them find new solutions. Specific ways in which employees are served are dependent on the counselors' skills, employees' needs, and institutional resources (Sandhu, 2002). One general way for EAP counselors to be effective is to set up programs that deal with a variety of topics in which employees have an interest, for example, retirement planning, conflict resolution, and stress management. EAP counselors can conduct seminars themselves or may invite outside experts to make presentations. In either case, arrangements for evaluation and follow-up should be a part of the plan, because one-shot efforts at helping may not be entirely satisfactory.

Additionally, EAP counselors typically offer short-term counseling services to employees who may be experiencing difficulties. These services are usually time limited (e.g., three to eight sessions) and include assessment, a plan of action that may include short-term counseling or psychoeducation, and a follow-up plan (EAPA, 2016). As experts in community resources, EAP counselors may also make referrals to mental health professionals or outside agencies that can offer employees more extensive services than can be provided through the EAP program.

Many large corporations have in-house EAPs, in which EAP counselors are employees of the organizations. Other businesses and industries contract with private practitioners who serve employees as part of their client base but are paid on a contractual basis by the participating organization. In these cases, the employee typically contacts the company's insurance provider, who then preauthorizes a certain number of services. Typically, clinical mental health counselors who engage in contract work with organizations also work as private counselors with a separate caseload of non-EAP clients (Hodges, 2012).

BALANCE AND WELLNESS.   Among the present emphases in EAP settings are programs that focus on prevention and wellness. Two key concerns of many employees are balancing work and family life and maintaining a wellness-oriented lifestyle.

Achieving a good balance between one's work and family life is not always easy. The reasons are many, including increased responsibilities at work and/or home, self-imposed demands for perfection in either or both areas, and lack of adequate time for self and others. Often it is challenging to keep work-related problems from affecting family life and vice versa. One way EAP counselors can intervene is by initiating comprehensive work/life balance programs. These initiatives can include a personalized focus on employees' strengths, establishment of a cultural climate that is supportive and understanding of employee needs, and a solution-focused, empowerment-oriented approach to working with employees with diverse needs (e.g., Herlihy, 2000; Hobson, Delunas, & Kesic, 2001; Kennedy, 2001).

Positive wellness approaches (i.e., health-related activities that are preventive, holistic, and beneficial for individuals who practice them consistently) represent another current emphasis in EAP programs. Wellness approaches underscore ways to establish and maintain physical, psychological, intellectual, social, spiritual, and emotional health. EAP counselors frequently emphasize wellness as they deliver preventive and remediation services (Bennett & Lehman, 2003).

BOX 15–1   Rewards and Challenges of EAP Counseling

Employee assistance programs (EAPs) are work-based programs that address the personal problems of employees and their family members in order to improve the productivity of the workforce. EAPs grew from the alcohol programs of individual companies in the 1940s. They originally addressed alcohol issues but broadened in scope in the 1970s to include other drug issues, psychiatric issues, and a range of personal problems that do not conform to a *DSM* diagnosis. Today, most EAP work is done by an agency that provides the service to contracted companies.

Working as an EAP counselor is something I find rewarding for several reasons:

1. EAP counseling is short-term. A key emphasis in EAP work is on conducting a comprehensive assessment to determine the client's needs and the appropriateness of EAP counseling. I generally conduct three to six sessions, using brief counseling interventions, many of which are solution focused. When short-term counseling is not appropriate, I am responsible for referring the client to other services.
2. Efforts are made to impact the employer, not just the employee. EAP counselors design and implement various training programs and workshops, which can include stress management, substance abuse, and sexual harassment, to name just a few. We also consult with managers, supervisors, and human resource professionals about issues that influence work performance. These consultations may be about individual employees or about the impact of policies, procedures, or external events on the workplace.
3. EAP counseling is free to employees and their family members. As an EAP counselor, you do not get direct payment from the client. Instead, you generally contract with the client's employer to provide counseling services. This means the client's ability to pay does not interfere with the counseling relationship or process.

(continued)

As with any career, this one also comes with challenges. The biggest challenges for EAP counselors are protecting confidentiality and setting appropriate boundaries. This is largely because EAP counselors work with more than one set of clients. For example, I may be working with a client in my office, but I also have an obligation to the company for which that client works. This means that I must be very aware of confidentiality issues and articulate those issues to clients and the company. At times, the need to maintain confidentiality may mean losing a contract with a particular company.

Boundary and competency issues can also occur when EAP counselors are expected to take on ever-expanding roles that may go well beyond their levels of expertise. Counselors must be aware of personal and professional limits when making promises about providing services. Sometimes, it is necessary to direct a client or a company to other resources. This can be difficult, given the pressure that some companies may place on having certain services performed by EAPs. It is important, however, to maintain integrity of self, the program, and the relationships with various clients and customers. Ultimately, this will determine a counselor's long-term success in the EAP field.

Jay Hale, LPC, CEAP

PRIVATE PRACTICE COUNSELING

As the field of clinical mental health counseling continues to grow, there are more opportunities for counseling professionals to work in private practice. ACA is aware of the growing number of private practitioners and has done several things to help clinicians who already work in private practice settings or are considering starting or expanding a private practice. For example, ACA has a website called Private Practice Pointers for ACA members, which provides information and suggestions on a variety of topics, including working with managed care, buying or selling a private practice, and meeting HIPAA requirements. In addition, ACA's monthly publication, *Counseling Today*, regularly includes a column that focuses on private practice. The column addresses topics such as extending client coverage, communicating electronically, renting office space, and handling other practical issues relevant to private practice counseling.

BOX 15–2   Private Practice Work Settings: Three Scenarios

Elaine works as a solo private practitioner and owns her own office space. She specializes in couples and family counseling. Prior to opening a private practice, Elaine worked with a family services agency for 18 years. Her decision to work in private practice was based on several factors, including the desire to be her own boss and choose her own hours. She has been in private practice for 5 years and meets with approximately 15 couples or families each week. She and four other private practitioners meet weekly for peer consultation and support.

In contrast, Patricia rents office space in a building occupied by two other clinical mental health counselors, one social worker, and one psychologist. They each see clients independently and share monthly expenses. Patricia is trained in EMDR (eye movement desensitization and reprocessing) and works with people who have been traumatized or diagnosed with PTSD. Once a week, the five mental health practitioners meet for peer supervision. They have an office manager who has a business background and helps with billing, accounting, and marketing. They also have a receptionist who schedules clients and manages the front desk/reception area. The group is not incorporated;

that is, no legal document binds the group together as a corporation. However, each practitioner has signed a contract defining financial and business responsibilities (Palmo & Palmo, 2011).

Jamar is part of an incorporated group. He specializes in working with children and adolescents. Seven other people are part of the group, including a psychiatrist, a nutritionist, two social workers, two licensed professional counselors, and a neuropsychologist. A legal document binds the group members together, although the practitioners have their own client base and set their own hours. The legal document defines the group as an incorporated business, in which each group member is a legal partner who earns a salary based on contribution of time, status, or initial investment (Palmo & Palmo, 2011). Group members meet regularly for supervision and consultation. Although the group is legally defined as an incorporated business, each practitioner is considered to be in private practice.

As you read about Elaine, Patricia, and Jamar, what commonalities and differences did you notice in their work settings? Which setting is most appealing to you? Which one do you think would be most challenging? What hurdles do you think are associated with each type of private practice?

The three scenarios in Box 15–2 demonstrate three different private practice work settings: sole proprietors (or solo practitioners), expense-sharing groups, and incorporated groups. Each setting offers advantages and disadvantages. For clinicians who like to be around other clinicians on a regular basis, the idea of working as a solo practitioner may not be as appealing as working in either an expense-sharing group or an incorporated group. For others, having colleagues outside the actual office space, while having the autonomy of being a sole proprietor, represents an attractive option. On the other hand, the legal binding offered by an incorporated business composed of private practitioners may offer a sense of security to some clinicians. The choice of a private practice work setting is based on personal goals, professional goals, and available opportunities (Sheperis & Sheperis, 2015).

Services Offered by Private Practitioners

The services offered by private practitioners depend on a multitude of factors, including areas of specialization, community needs, and the settings in which they work. Although counseling services are basic to any private practice setting, other services that are often offered include consultation, supervision, and community involvement. Additional services that private practitioners may offer include career counseling, career coaching, life coaching, holistic practices, and rehabilitation counseling.

Typically, private practitioners have developed expertise in one or more areas. Training and practice are key to developing areas of specialization. More often than not, clinical mental health counselors work in settings such as community agencies, medical settings, addictions settings, career settings, and university settings before going into private practice (Shallcross, 2011). After gaining supervised experience and developing their skills, some clinical mental health counselors then decide that they want the freedom to be more creative as they grow professionally. In her March 2011 article in *Counseling Today*, Shallcross interviewed several clinicians who elected to go into private practice, and in December 2014, Meyers conducted similar interviews. The clinicians emphasized the importance of developing a niche, pursuing multiple training opportunities, and letting other people and agencies know about their services. Some of the areas of expertise developed by these practitioners include online counseling; life coaching; working with children, adolescents, and families; working with victims of trauma; spirituality-based counseling; and bereavement counseling.

An important first step in building a private practice is surveying community needs. One way clinicians can do this is by talking with social agencies, schools, medical establishments, and other recognized organizations to determine unmet needs in the broader community. For example, there may be a demand for more couples and family counseling—an area in which you have experience and expertise. Or there may be a need for counselors who specialize in process addictions, and you and several other clinicians decide to open a private practice that specializes in helping people who are addicted to such things as gambling, Internet pornography, and overeating. Yet another field that continues to expand is that of geriatric counseling. As baby boomers age, there is an even greater demand for counselors skilled in working with older populations.

CONSULTATION AND COLLABORATION.   Many private practitioners share their expertise with other clinicians, often on an unpaid basis, through the processes of consultation and collaboration. They do this to help the clinicians provide high-quality care for their clients. For example, a school counselor may refer to you a student who is having difficulty focusing and completing assignments. After consulting with the school counselor, you meet with the student and determine that it would be helpful to involve the parents and the student's pediatrician. (In such cases, appropriate releases are completed by the parents or guardians so that information can be exchanged among professionals.) Through consultation and collaboration, you make a provisional diagnosis of ADHD. In addition to working with the student and his parents, you stay in close communication with the school counselor and the pediatrician, making changes to treatment plans as needed.

At other times, private practitioners are paid for consultation and other services requested by organizations that have a need for their expertise. For example, you may be invited to consult with a family services agency about best practices for working with teens with eating disorders. In this case, you might present a seminar or work specifically with mental health professionals in the agency who want additional training on how to work with adolescents with eating disorders.

Sometimes private practitioners are asked to run counseling groups at schools, offer parenting classes at various agencies, or provide counseling services to assisted living sites. Private practitioners may also offer EAP services to various businesses and agencies. Contracting for EAP services can give professionals in the private sector new opportunities to market other counseling, consultation, and psychoeducational programs to the companies and their employees.

SUPERVISION.   Yet another service that is a component of private practice is supervision—both giving and receiving supervision. Clinicians in private practice need to get regular supervision, regardless of their level of training. Frequently, supervision takes place in peer supervision groups composed of other private practitioners. Participating in supervision groups or working individually with a supervisor is a necessity on an ethical, professional, and personal level (Palmo & Palmo, 2011). Furthermore, supervision groups offer collegial support and provide a sense of professional community.

Supervision within a private practice also provides an avenue for revenue. Licensed professional counselor supervisors (LPCSs) can provide newly degreed counselors with a needed service, and supervisors are expected to charge for their services. Private practice clinicians who supervise new counselors in need of direct clinical hours for licensure often make it possible for the new counselors to be accepted on managed care organization panels as providers.

COMMUNITY INVOLVEMENT.   Community involvement is another key component of private practice. It is important for private practitioners to be visible within their communities. Sometimes that means providing pro bono services for local groups and organizations. For example, a private practitioner may volunteer to lead a group for divorced parents at a neighborhood church. Giving back to the community not only helps people who may be underserved but also helps people in the community know more about the services offered by the clinician. The opportunities for providing pro bono work are numerous, so private practitioners need to be good time managers and know how to say no. Because counseling in a private practice means that the counselor is "essentially a small business owner" (Hodges, 2012, p. 136), profit versus overhead must be carefully considered.

Pragmatic Considerations

There are multiple pragmatic considerations that go into building a private practice. The advantages are clear: freedom to be the primary decision maker; choice in work location/ hours/fees/projects; ability to work from a preferred theoretical approach; and an elective decision by both client and clinician to work together. Disadvantages include complete responsibility for all financial matters (overhead; insurance policies; furnishings; equipment; continuing education; fees for extra services such as billing, accounting, administrative work, etc.); inconsistent revenue streams; and financial barriers for uninsured or underresourced clients to access service (Harrington, 2013). Most clinical mental health counselors do not have degrees in marketing or business. However, operating a private practice is, in reality, operating a small business. Thus, many clinicians considering opening a private practice take courses in business to help increase their knowledge about developing a small business.

Additional considerations include, but are not limited to, the following:

- *Office space:*   Do you want to buy or lease property? What type of office furniture do you need?
- *Billing:*   Will you accept insurance or require clients to pay directly for services? Will you hire a billing company to help with the financial aspects of the practice?
- *Paperwork:*   If you elect to accept insurance and get on managed care panels, the approval processes and requirements related to insurance and managed care can be overwhelming. Hiring a billing company is one way to help with this process.
- *Professional protection:*   Securing professional liability insurance is essential. Furthermore, insurance to cover emergencies that may involve loss of furniture, equipment, and other office materials is necessary.
- *Attorneys and accountants:*   Securing the services of an attorney and an accountant can help ensure that you have a legal advisor available to help with difficult questions, such as how to handle HIPAA compliance regulations. Having an accountant can help you with business arrangements, realistic financial goals, payroll, and taxes.
- *Emergency and contact procedures:*   Private practitioners are responsible for making sure that clients can reach them in cases of emergency. Pagers, answering machines that provide information on whom to contact if the counselor cannot be reached, and other ways to manage client crises help ensure that clients have a way to get the support they need.

Tips for Building a Successful Private Practice

In interviews with Shallcross (2011), several private practitioners offered tips for building a successful private practice. Colburn (2013) has also made pertinent suggestions especially in regard to diversifications. Here are some of their recommendations:

- Set up a well-designed website.
- Network with other professionals.
- Market yourself by providing workshops, business cards, and brochures.
- Participate in ongoing training.
- Meet regularly with a cohort of professional peers.
- Specialize in one or more clinical mental health areas.
- Return phone calls within 24 hours.
- Pay your bills on time.
- Establish good relationships with your accountant, your bank, and the licensure board in your state.
- Take a marketing or business class.
- Manage your time effectively, and learn how to say no. Block out time for emergencies, paperwork, and phone calls.
- Be practical, but also be willing to take risks.
- Believe in your ability to be successful.

Although private practice can be challenging, it can also be quite rewarding. Private practice gives clinicians an ability to set their own schedules and be their own bosses. It also provides opportunities to be creative, develop specialized skills, and communicate with professionals in different fields, such as medicine. Moreover, clinical mental health counselors who specialize in particular areas have the opportunity to fill a niche in the community that otherwise might not be filled. For clinicians who are entrepreneurial, who are willing to take risks, and who value autonomy, working in or owning a private practice can be an exciting endeavor.

BOX 15–3   Working in a Private Practice Setting

Being in private practice means living in two worlds. The first is the world of the clinician. It has the delight of working with clients, being challenged by them, and sometimes being inspired by them. Part of my focus is figuring out what sort of client I work best with—who is a good match for my skills, training, and interests. Knowing this helps refine my message when I'm getting the word out about my work. Being in solo practice, I also have to be intentional about finding support by connecting with formal or peer supervision groups.

As a counselor in private practice, I have the freedom to set my own hours, deciding what time in the morning to start and how late in the evening to work. I can block out time to tend to the demands of my own life, whether that means finding time for exercise or taking care of family commitments.

The other world I work in is the world of business. As a small business owner (my practice is a small business), I have to deal with the administrative side of the work. I choose to make my own appointments and file insurance claims. I keep records not only of my income but also of my business expenses.

As a business owner, I also have to market my practice, letting people know who I am and what kind of service I offer. One day I may work on a brochure about my practice. Another day I may meet with my networking group or speak to a community group. Another day I may work on my website or send thank-you cards to professionals (such as doctors) who refer clients to me. For me, the variety of tasks is part of what I enjoy.

Being in private practice requires having an entrepreneurial personality and being comfortable with a certain level of risk. Income may vary from week to week and can be impacted by snow-storms or flu epidemics. Being self-employed means being responsible for health insurance and retirement benefits. Being in private practice requires becoming comfortable with self-promotion and dealing with money issues. Fortunately, there are more and more resources out there for people who are looking for help in building a practice.

For those of us who love private practice, the freedom that we have in working with our clients and creating the shape of our practices outweighs the risks and demands.

Peggy Haymes, MDiv, MA, LPC

COACHING

What Is Coaching?

Coaching is a relatively new professional discipline designed to help clients who are not in psychological distress and are able to use their strengths and resources to pursue goals, actions, and outcomes that enhance their lives, either personally or professionally (Labardee, Williams, & Hodges, 2012). Coaching has roots in several disciplines, but the primary origins are in sports psychology and humanistic and existential psychology (Stelter, 2009). The International Coach Federation (ICF) defines **coaching** as "partnering with clients in a thought-provoking and creative process that inspires them to maximize their personal and professional potential" (ICF, 2016). The ICF describes the coaching process as collaborative, strengths-based, and goal-oriented (see Box 15–4).

BOX 15–4   The Coaching Process

Coaching honors the client as the expert in his or her life and work and believes that every client is creative, resourceful, and whole. Standing on this foundation, the coach's responsibility is to do the following:

- Discover, clarify, and align with what the client wants to achieve
- Encourage client self-discovery
- Elicit client-generated solutions and strategies
- Hold the client responsible and accountable

Coaches are trained to listen, to observe, and to customize their approaches to individual client needs. They seek to elicit solutions and strategies from the clients, believing that the clients are naturally creative and resourceful. The coach's job is to provide support to enhance the skills, resources, and creativity that the client already has.

(ICF, 2016)

Silsbee (2010), in his book *The Mindful Coach: Seven Roles for Helping People Grow*, compares coaching to providing a "fast track" to personal or professional development. It enables clients to reduce the learning curve in developing new skills. Coaching is not traditional therapy; instead, its purpose is to help motivated clients achieve more and at a faster rate than they previously achieved. Clients (or coachees) are encouraged to identify what they want, clarify the beliefs that will help them fulfill desired outcomes, specify action steps they need to take to achieve their goals, develop external support to help them meet their goals, and consistently take action to reach those goals (Davison & Gasiorowski, 2006).

The industry of coaching has grown considerably over the decades, and there are now tens of thousands of life coaches in the United States alone (Grant, 2003). A large number of organizations provide coach training, with some being more reputable than others. Coaches come from various professional fields. They typically are "trained mental health professionals, business people, and virtually anyone with a skill set that is necessary for individuals to have to achieve outcomes they set out to accomplish" (Davison & Gasiorowski, 2006, p. 190). Here the focus is on clinical mental health counselors who coach.

Clinical Mental Health Counseling and Coaching

The NBCC and its affiliate, the Center for Credentialing and Education (CCE), examined similarities and differences between coaching and counseling and determined that the professional education of counselors aligns closely with that of coaching (Labardee et al., 2012). They also determined that licensed professional counselors who are trained and qualified in coaching are better prepared to help meet the growing need for coaching services. Consequently, the CCE now offers the credential of board certified coach (BCC) for applicants holding a master's degree (or higher) from an accredited educational institution or program. The requirements for obtaining the BCC are listed on the CCE website at www.cce-global.org/. To be certified, counselors need to complete at least 30 hours of professional coach training from a CCE-approved coach training provider. They also must participate in 30 hours of postdegree coaching experience that is verified by a professional coach, supervisor, or colleague. To complete the process, applicants must pass the BCC examination and submit one letter of professional endorsement. BCC applicants also have the opportunity to apply for specialty designations in the following areas:

- Executive/corporate/business/leadership coach
- Health and wellness coach
- Career coach
- Personal/life coach

Counselors who become BCCs are expected to adhere to the BCC code of ethics and participate in continuing education.

In their article *Counselors Who Coach*, Labardee et al. (2012) describe how coaching fits into the counseling profession, what counselors need in terms of training, and what ethical and practice considerations there are for counselors who coach. The authors also share examples of clients who would benefit from coaching services (e.g., a 48-year-old married female who is contemplating going back to school for her nursing degree) and clients who would not benefit from coaching services but would benefit from counseling (e.g., a widowed 48-year-old female who is grieving the unexpected loss of her husband and is contemplating returning to school to complete her nursing degree). Clinical mental health counselors who also coach need to determine whether the focus of their work with clients is on mental health concerns (i.e., therapy) or on creating strategies for achieving specific goals in the clients' personal or professional lives (i.e., coaching; ICF, 2016).

Different Types of Coaching

As previously noted, coaches may choose to specialize in one of several areas. For example, a clinical mental health counselor can specialize in career coaching, executive coaching (see Box 15–5), health and wellness coaching, and life coaching. Life coaches help people with a range of life issues that may be challenging, such as balancing multiple roles, dealing with stress or lack of motivation, or questioning life's meaning or purpose. Health and wellness coaches work with clients who are interested in developing healthier lifestyles and/or examining their levels of wellness in various areas of life, including physical, social, emotional, spiritual, and intellectual domains. The coach can help pinpoint what may be out of balance, and the client then sets personal goals for change. Other specialty areas of coaching include small-business coaching and sports coaching. (Sports coaching helps athletes who are not fulfilling their potential; it is not "athletic coaching" in the traditional sense.) In most cases, a clinical mental health counselor has skill sets that align with specific types of coaching.

BOX 15–5   Comments from the Field of Executive Coaching

Executive coaching, as I see it, includes self-reflection, business acumen, and exploration of management styles. It is designed for people who are in executive management. More generally, "executive coaching" involves a one-to-one helping relationship between the coach and the client. The major aim of the relationship is to help the executive perform his or her duties more effectively. In each case, the client has encountered problems that require a change in the client's behaviors. My own practice of executive coaching provides opportunities to facilitate leadership development and personal growth that help the performance of executives. I collaborate with clients to help them determine and fulfill specific professional goals. The process often involves a discussion of personal problems that impede clients' accomplishment of their executive duties.

John P. Anderson, LPC, Executive Coach

Regulation of Coaching

Although organizations like NBCC, the ICF, and the International Institute of Coaching have brought some structure and standardization into the coaching profession, coaching remains an unregulated industry. Many people who call themselves coaches have not received formal training. During the past decade, some strides have been made to regulate coaching; however, regulation still is not mandatory. If mental health counselors choose to work as coaches as well as clinicians, they should participate in formal training that leads to certification and be aware of the distinction between providing therapeutic services and providing coaching.

MANAGED CARE

All clinical mental health counselors, including private practitioners, need to be familiar with the background and purpose of managed care organizations. Although some counselors do choose to work in environments that are not associated with managed care, they are in the minority. The explosive growth of managed care organizations (MCOs), especially during the past few decades, has had a tremendous impact on the counseling profession, creating significant changes in the manner in which mental health treatment is provided and financed.

Indeed, according to some mental health professionals, managed care has emerged as the "single most important influence on the practice of counseling and psychotherapy" (Davis & Meier, 2001, p. vii).

The Development of Managed Care Systems

In many ways, health care today is equated with managed care. Prior to the 1980s, however, managed care organizations were uncommon. Mental health care was generally funded by major medical insurance, which utilized a fee-for-service system. Within such a system, insurance companies paid for services rendered by practitioners after consumers met specified deductible amounts. These third-party healthcare systems were founded on the premise that a large group of persons would pay a premium to offset the cost of care for those who were ill (Cooper & Gottlieb, 2000).

When third-party insurance systems such as Blue Cross were first established, mental health benefits were not included in their plans. Indeed, it was not until the 1950s that such insurance plans began to include mental health benefits, with services provided more frequently on an outpatient, rather than inpatient, basis (Austad & Berman, 1991).

With more employers offering insurance coverage, and with the establishment of federally funded programs such as Medicare and Medicaid in 1965, the cost and the utilization of medical and mental health services increased dramatically. These escalating costs and growing demands for coverage and service led to increasingly greater portions of the federal budget and of corporate profits being earmarked for health insurance costs (Mitchell, 1998).

In response to the rising cost of health coverage, insurance companies, employers, and the federal government began to grapple with ways to curb expenses. Managed care provided an alternative to the traditional fee-for-service system. The Health Maintenance Organization Act of 1973 designated federal funding for the development of managed care programs and required employers to offer managed care options to employees (Cooper & Gottlieb, 2000). Health maintenance organizations (HMOs) are one of several forms of managed care systems designed to reduce total healthcare costs by shifting care to less expensive forms of treatment. By the late 1990s, 75% of Americans with health insurance were enrolled in some type of managed care plan (Kiesler, 2000). In the 21st century, managed health care strongly influences health care in general and mental health services in particular (Cooper & Gottlieb, 2000).

What Is Managed Care?

Managed care can be described as "a way of providing care, a philosophy of care, a way to finance care, and a way to control costs" (Talbott, 2001, p. 279). It refers to the administration of healthcare services by a party other than the client or practitioner. Managed care systems assume the financial risks as well as oversee the services provided by practitioners to clients. Generally speaking, the two primary goals of managed care systems are to (a) contain costs and (b) ensure quality of care. Costs are controlled by limiting the amount and type of services, monitoring services, and changing the nature of services offered. Managed care systems typically use treatment guidelines, peer review, and financial incentives and penalties to influence providers, payors, and financial intermediaries to manage the cost, financing, utilization, and quality of healthcare services.

Most of today's mental health professionals have at least some degree of involvement with managed care systems. Consequently, counselors need to be familiar with the terms and procedures associated with managed care environments. The three most common models of managed care are HMOs, preferred provider organizations (PPOs), and government-funded health programs (i.e., Medicaid, Medicare, and Civilian Health and Medical Programs of the Uniformed Services). Descriptions of various managed care systems and the terms associated with those systems are presented in Figures 15–1 and 15–2.

Today, hundreds of managed care companies operate in both the public and the private sectors. These companies contract with approved mental health providers and facilities to provide mental health services for consumers at reduced fees. Providers and facilities that contract with MCOs agree to comply with company procedures, including preadmission screening and utilization reviews. Some companies are more restrictive than others, so prospective providers are encouraged to explore the potential effects the policies may have on their work with clients (Glosoff, 1998).

Term	Definition
Managed care organization (MCO)	A third party that oversees healthcare delivery in order to limit costs and monitor and influence services. The term refers to any HMO or managed behavioral care entity.
Health maintenance organization (HMO)	An organization that provides comprehensive health care to its members in return for a fixed monthly membership fee. Health services are coordinated by a primary care physician, who serves as the gatekeeper and makes all decisions regarding referral for specialty examinations and services.
Individual or independent practice association (IPA)	An organization that typically is created by physicians and marketed to employers. An IPA may contract for services with several different HMOs. Practitioners in the IPA serve clients from the HMOs as well as their individual clients.
Preferred provider organization (PPO)	Groups of hospitals, physicians, or other practitioners who contract with employers, insurance companies, or third-party groups to provide comprehensive medical care for a fee that is typically discounted. This plan allows patients to visit specialists outside the plan's network, but at a higher cost.
Health Care Finance Administration (HCFA)	The federal agency that oversees health financing policies for Medicare and the Office of Prepaid Health Care.
Joint Commission on Accreditation of Healthcare Organizations (JCAHO)	A nonprofit organization whose goal is to improve the quality of healthcare services.
National Committee for Quality Assurance (NCQA)	A private, nonprofit group composed primarily of representatives from managed care companies and employers, whose purpose is to evaluate the quality of managed care plans and accredit MCOs based on standardized reviews.

FIGURE 15–1 **Types of Managed Care Organizations and Managed Care Regulators**
Source: Definitions compiled from various sources, including Davis and Meier, 2001; Lawless, Ginter, and Kelly, 1999; and Winegar and Hayter, 1998.

Term	Definition
Capitation	A form of payment in which the provider is paid on a per-member basis.
Carve-out	The separation, or carving out, of specific types of health care from the overall benefit package. For example, the mental health and substance abuse portion of healthcare benefits may be "carved out" of the overall package and separately contracted with managed behavioral care organizations.
Case/care management	A coordinated set of professional activities focused on treatment planning and assurance of treatment delivery that addresses clients' needs while maintaining good quality, cost-effective outcomes.
Case rate	A preestablished fee paid for the entire course of treatment for one case.
Clinical review criteria	The written protocols or decision "trees" used by a utilization review organization to determine medical necessity and level-of-care decisions.
Closed panel health plan	An agreement whereby an MCO requires participants to utilize practitioners, facilities, and pharmacies with which it has a contractual relationship.
Covered services	Professional services of healthcare providers that have been authorized by the healthcare plan or HMO.
Gatekeeper	An individual (usually a clinician) who controls the access to healthcare services for members of a specific group. Often, the gatekeeper is the primary care physician (PCP). In some healthcare delivery systems, the gatekeeper is a case manager.
Gag clause	A stipulation made by an MCO that prevents counselors from discussing alternative treatments outside the boundaries of approved services. Gag clauses are less common now than in the past, after having been successfully challenged in court.
Intensive outpatient program (IOP)	In behavioral health care, IOP refers to an outpatient treatment program that provides two to four hours of care two or more times per week (includes both individual and group counseling).
Level of care	Refers to treatment alternatives on a continuum of care (e.g., inpatient, partial hospitalization, outpatient, long-term residential treatment).
Medically necessary	The designation that a particular treatment or evaluation is required, appropriate, and in agreement with acceptable standards of medical practice and cannot be provided in a less intensive setting.
Network	The combining of two or more independent group practices under contract with an HMO to provide services to HMO members.
Open panel (HMO)	An agreement whereby an HMO allows members to receive services outside the provider network without referral authorization. Members usually pay an additional deductible and/or copay for these services.
Primary care physician (PCP)	Physician who oversees the provision of health care for defined subsets of HMO members. Some managed care plans require PCP screening and referral for mental health or substance abuse treatment as well as for other types of health care.
Practice guidelines	Recommended interventions and procedures for treatment of specific conditions so as to achieve optimum results as efficiently as possible.
Provider contract	A written agreement between a licensed healthcare provider (e.g., physician, counselor, facility) and a health plan.
Utilization review	Process by which an MCO reviews the diagnosis, treatment plan, and response to treatment before authorizing the use or extension of the client's benefit plan.

FIGURE 15–2 Terms Associated with Managed Care Systems
Source: Definitions compiled from various sources, including Davis and Meier, 2001; Lawless, Ginter, and Kelly, 1999; and Winegar and Hayter, 1998.

Implications for Counselors

How has managed care affected the work of professional counselors? According to C. E. Anderson (2000), working within managed care systems has changed the way mental health professionals perform clinical duties. Short-term, highly focused interventions that follow treatment guidelines and protocols are the norm. The emphasis is on demonstrating the efficacy of services while containing costs. Counselors working in managed care environments are expected to write specific treatment plans, participate in utilization reviews, and comply with the limits placed on the amount of therapy authorized by managed care organizations. Cooper and Gottlieb (2000), citing several sources, highlight the defining characteristics of counseling and psychotherapy in a managed care system:

- Brief therapy is mandated and characterized by immediate assessment of the client's presenting problem, clearly delineated treatment goals, and active counseling.
- The counselor forms a pragmatic therapeutic relationship with the client for the purpose of providing the most efficient and effective treatment.
- Communication with the client's PCP is usually required, as well as increased interaction with other healthcare professionals.
- The counseling process is monitored by the MCO and typically includes documentation of treatment necessity and regular submission of treatment plans. The process of monitoring the therapeutic process is called **utilization review (UR)** and may occur before, during, and after treatment.

Advantages and Disadvantages of Managed Care

Proponents of managed care assert that managed care services contain costs while simultaneously maintaining quality service. Supporters claim that time-limited treatment is a research-supported practice that is as effective as traditional treatment for most clients (see Austad & Berman, 1991; Hoyt, 1995; Paulson, 1996). Other potential advantages associated with managed care include greater access to mental health services, increased numbers of referrals for some practitioners, and the implementation of quality control and standards of practice (Lawless, Ginter, & Kelly, 1999). Accredited managed behavioral care organizations typically require providers to document the quality of their work in several areas, including client satisfaction, clinical outcomes, and adherence to best-practice guidelines, thus increasing practitioner accountability.

Even though working in managed care settings may benefit practitioners and clients in some ways, many studies indicate that most mental health professionals believe that managed care has negatively affected their work with clients and presents significant ethical challenges (e.g., Cohen, Marecek, & Gillham, 2006; Cooper & Gottlieb, 2000; Danzinger & Welfel, 2001). Practitioners have expressed several concerns related to counseling in managed care environments. One is that standardized treatment guidelines fail to take into account the unique nature of clients' needs and compromise counselors' autonomy in determining specific interventions (Cantor & Fuentes, 2008). The systems that set up treatment protocols usurp much of the clinical judgment and professionalism of the practitioner. Other concerns include arbitrary time limits, caps on the number of sessions approved, increased paperwork, difficulties in being placed on provider lists, increased job stress, and insufficient qualified personnel acting as gatekeepers (Cantor & Fuentes, 2008; Glosoff, Garcia, Herlihy, & Remley, 1999). Managed mental health care systems are based on a medical model, which requires the labeling of pathology before services are authorized, rather than on a growth-based developmental model, which characterizes the counseling profession. Services that do not constitute a medical necessity will not be reimbursed, and many policies exclude coverage for certain types of counseling and mental health conditions, including marriage counseling, career counseling, educational services, experimental interventions, and personality disorders (Braun & Cox, 2005; Luck, 1999). Particularly distressing to many clinicians are the ethical dilemmas encountered when attempting to balance managed care dictums with professional codes of ethics. Negative appraisals of managed care organizations often stem from the difficult ethical issues with which practitioners are faced.

Ethical Considerations

A growing body of literature addresses ethical dilemmas that face clinical mental health counselors working in managed care environments (e.g., Braun & Cox, 2005; Cooper & Gottlieb, 2000; Daniels, 2001; Danzinger & Welfel, 2001; Davis & Meier, 2001; Glosoff et al., 1999). Ethical concerns related to client welfare, confidentiality, informed consent, counselor competence, and integrity are among the issues frequently encountered in managed care environments, requiring counselors to engage in thoughtful decision-making practices.

CLIENT WELFARE. A professional counselor's first and foremost responsibility is to respect the dignity and promote the welfare of clients (ACA, 2014). At times, counselors working in managed care environments are faced with the difficulty of supporting a client's right to quality care as a priority over the counselor's relationship with the reimburser. According to the ACA (2014) *Code of Ethics*, treatment plans should be clinically viable, offer a reasonable likelihood of effectiveness, be consistent with the client's abilities and situations, and respect the client's freedom of choice (Standard A.1.c). However, because treatment plans must conform to MCO protocols and be approved by MCO representatives, counselors may not be free to plan and implement treatments independently. When professional judgments differ from MCO mandates, practitioners must decide whether to implement the approved but less suitable treatment plans or risk denial of reimbursement (Danzinger & Welfel, 2001).

Time-limited treatment imposed by MCOs also can affect client welfare in that it may compromise quality, providing the client with partial treatment, which may result in early termination. I. J. Miller (1996) refers to this practice as **rationing** and cautions that it is imperative for counselors to inform clients in advance about the possibility of rationed services. In some cases, clinicians may determine that clients will benefit from brief therapy. Even so, the number of sessions recommended by the clinician for a satisfactory outcome may be greater than the number allocated by the MCO (Davis & Meier, 2001). When this is the case, counselors need to make appropriate arrangements for those who cannot be served effectively following MCO guidelines. Such arrangements may include negotiating for longer treatment services with MCOs, having clients pay out of pocket, referring clients to alternative treatment sources, and working pro bono (Glosoff et al., 1999). Standard A.12 of the ACA (2014) *Code of Ethics* addresses the issue of early termination by stating that counselors are not to abandon their clients and are responsible for making arrangements for continuation of care.

There are legal as well as ethical ramifications of time-limited treatment and early termination. In court cases dealing with the issue of responsible treatment of clients, most decisions have found the *practitioners* primarily responsible for their clients' care, regardless of

MCO guidelines (Glosoff et al., 1999). For example, in *Wickline v. State of California* (1987), the service provider was held liable for the HMO's decision to limit hospitalization, even though the provider had recommended additional treatment. In this case, which dealt with the delivery of medical services rather than mental health services, the court maintained that the provider did not protest the HMO's denial of services aggressively enough (Davis & Meier, 2001). In another case, *Muse v. Charter Hospital of Winston-Salem, Inc.* (1995), the court ruled that it was the duty of the mental health facility to provide care to patients based on patients' medical conditions, not on the needs of insurance companies (see Box 15–6).

BOX 15–6 *Muse v. Charter Hospital of Winston-Salem, Inc.*

In *Muse*, plaintiffs brought an action for the wrongful death of their son, Joe, who was an inpatient in a psychiatric hospital being treated for depression with suicidal thoughts. When Joe's insurance was about to expire, the hospital sought a promissory note of payment from the parents. The parents agreed to pay for two extra days, after which Joe was released as an outpatient. Shortly thereafter, Joe took an overdose of drugs and killed himself. In this case, the court held that the hospital "had a duty not to institute a policy or practice which required that patients be discharged when their insurance expired and which interfered with the medical judgment of [the doctor]" (1995).

(Madonna, 2000, p. 26)

CONFIDENTIALITY. Assurance of confidentiality is at the heart of the counseling relationship. Without this assurance, many clients would not feel safe discussing private, intimate aspects of their lives (Remley & Herlihy, 2016). Section B of ACA's (2014) *Code of Ethics* extensively addresses the issue of confidentiality. Traditionally, counselors have been able to assure clients of confidentiality with certain exceptions (i.e., threat of harm to self or others). In the era of managed care, however, the issue of confidentiality has become much more complex. Danzinger and Welfel (2001) report that one of the most frequently listed ethical challenges associated with managed care was that of confidentiality. Eighty percent of the counselors and counselor educators surveyed in their study stated that interactions with MCOs either often or occasionally compromised client confidentiality.

MCOs often request extensive, personal information about clients and detailed reports of their treatment (Cooper & Gottlieb, 2000). Once information is shared with MCOs, counselors have little control over what happens to that information. Cooper and Gottlieb (2000) offer several recommendations to practitioners to help them address ethically the issue of confidentiality:

- Provide a comprehensive informed consent form to help clients understand the ramifications of MCO reimbursement policies.
- Release only the minimal amount of information needed so client privacy is protected.
- Make sure clients understand the nature of any release forms signed.
- Avoid sending case notes to MCOs; instead, send treatment summaries.
- Exercise caution when transmitting information electronically, being mindful of HIPAA regulations.

INFORMED CONSENT. Standard A.2.b of the ACA (2014) *Code of Ethics* states that counselors are to inform clients of the purposes, goals, procedures, limitations, risks, and benefits of counseling, both at the onset of the counseling relationship and throughout the process as necessary. The *Code of Ethics* also states that counselors should take steps to make sure clients understand the implications of diagnosis; the use of tests, reports, fees, and billing arrangements; and the limits of confidentiality. Counselors working within a managed care context may need to expand their informed consent procedures to ensure that clients are aware of their benefit plans, MCO-related limits to confidentiality, and potential limits to treatment (Daniels, 2001). It is helpful for practitioners to view informed consent as an *ongoing process* rather than as a single event (Cooper & Gottlieb, 2000). When clients begin counseling, they may not be fully able to understand what they are told, especially if they are experiencing stress, anxiety, or depression. Revisiting issues related to informed consent ensures that the client truly comprehends the information that was presented initially.

COMPETENCE.   Most MCOs endorse brief-therapy models of treatment. Although most counselor education programs now include brief-therapy models as part of their curricula, some counselors have not been adequately trained or prepared to practice brief therapy. Standard C.2.a of the *Code of Ethics* states that counselors are to practice only within the boundaries of their competence, based on their training, experience, and credentialing. If counselors are not adequately trained to provide treatments authorized by an MCO, then they must either receive proper training or refrain from joining particular managed care panels.

INTEGRITY.   **Integrity** refers to honesty and fairness and includes being accurate and unbiased when reporting to other parties, including MCOs (Cooper & Gottlieb, 2000). Honesty in diagnosing and reporting is addressed in Standard E.5.a of ACA's ethical code. However, when client diagnoses do not fall within reimbursement guidelines, counselors may be tempted to diagnose inappropriately to gain reimbursement (Danzinger & Welfel, 2001). For example, a practitioner might assign a more serious diagnosis than is warranted to obtain more authorized sessions, a process known as **upcoding** (Cooper & Gottlieb, 2000). In other situations, the counselor may be tempted to **downcode**, or apply a less serious diagnosis, so that the client is able to receive treatment. For example, if a client presents with borderline personality disorder—a condition that typically is not reimbursable—a counselor who downcodes would record only a condition such as anxiety. In a national survey of clinical counselors, over 70% of the respondents stated that they were aware of at least occasional occurrences of downcoding, and over 60% indicated awareness of upcoding (Mead, Hohenshil, & Singh, 1997). Both practices, sometimes called "diagnosing for dollars" (Wylie, 1995, p. 22), are unethical and constitute insurance fraud.

Recommendations for Counselors

Providing quality care without compromising ethical and legal concerns is a challenging but necessary goal for all counselors who work in managed care environments (Braun & Cox, 2005). If an ethical dilemma does arise, it is important to have a decision-making plan in place. In solving ethical dilemmas related to managed care, Cooper and Gottlieb (2000) suggest using Haas and Malouf's model of ethical decision making, which includes the following steps:

1. Gather information about the problem.
2. Consult with colleagues, and look at relevant literature to consider pertinent legal and ethical principles.
3. Create a list of appropriate responses.

- **A clear statement of the client's problem**
- **A statement of goals with specific, measurable criteria to measure goal attainment**
  Goals can be listed as short term, intermediate, and long term, depending on the issues that are addressed.
- **A clear statement of objectives or activities that will be implemented to help the client meet the established goals**
  Ask yourself, "How will I know if the client accomplished the objective?"
- **A time frame within which goals and objectives will be accomplished**

Example:
The client currently exhibits flat affect and depressed mood and reports disturbed sleep (no more than 4 hours a night for the past month) and decreased appetite (has been eating one meal a day for the past 2 weeks). The goals are (1) to make a list of three pleasurable activities from which client will choose one and perform 3 days out of the week, (2) to eat two well-balanced meals a day for 1 week, and (3) to identify triggers to depression by writing in a journal three times a week. I plan to see the client in weekly individual sessions. I will be using cognitive behavioral techniques to help identify triggers to depression as well as client-centered therapy to enhance the therapeutic relationship. I am requesting 12 sessions. At the end of these sessions, the client's progress will be reevaluated.

FIGURE 15–3   What to Include in a Treatment Plan Written for an MCO
Source: From "Dealing Constructively with Managed Care: Suggestions from an Insider," by C. E. Anderson, 2000, *Journal of Mental Health Counseling, 22,* p. 345. Reprinted with permission of AMHCA.

4. Conduct a cost–benefit analysis of each potential response.
5. Choose the option that best resolves the dilemma.
6. Act on that option, and evaluate its effectiveness.

In addition to knowing how to solve ethical dilemmas effectively, clinical mental health counselors can do several things to facilitate their work with clients affiliated with MCOs. As a clinical mental health counselor, you must gain a complete understanding of the terms and functions of MCOs, including preauthorization, cost containment, clinical criteria requirements, and review procedures. You also need to be aware of client benefits, referral procedures, criteria for medical necessity, procedures for completing claim forms, and emergency procedures (Anderson, 2000). Still other ways to prepare for work in a managed care environment include developing knowledge and skills related to *DSM* categories, treatment-plan writing (see Figure 15–3), brief and solution-focused counseling, and procedures for getting on provider panels. Combining clinical expertise with knowledge of MCO procedures and skill in working collaboratively with MCO personnel can help clinical mental health counselors provide quality mental health services in the age of managed care.

Summary and Conclusion

In this chapter, three settings in which clinical mental health counselors work were discussed: employee assistance programs, private practice settings, and coaching. These venues require counselors to be knowledgeable about both the business world and the counseling world. Services offered in each setting were described. Individuals who are interested in working with employees and their organizations and like the possibility of conducting short-term counseling, leading seminars, and helping improve organizational functioning may want to explore working as an EAP counselor. Those who like the concept of developing a particular area of expertise, have an entrepreneurial spirit, and recognize the need to gain skills in a variety of counseling-related areas prior to working independently may find private practice a fulfilling venue in which to work. Finally, professionals who like working to help people change outside of direct counseling settings but still using counseling skills may find coaching appealing.

Managed care now influences the field of clinical mental health counseling in multiple ways. Clinicians who work in managed care environments are likely to use brief, highly focused interventions that follow treatment guidelines. Advantages and disadvantages are associated with the proliferation of managed care organizations. Among the advantages that have been cited are increased access to mental health services, higher rates of referrals, controlled costs, and the implementation of quality control and standards of practice. However, many clinicians indicate that managed care has negatively affected their work with clients and has created significant ethical challenges. Clinical mental health counselors who work in managed care environments need to be aware of potential ethical concerns and engage in thoughtful, informed decision-making practices as they confront those concerns.

MyCounselingLab

Try the Topic 4 Assignments: *Counseling in Mental Health and Private Practice.*

Epilogue

Clinical mental health counseling, like other helping professions, has evolved over time. It is not the same as it was in 1977–1978, when the concepts surrounding this specialty were formulated. Counseling in the late 1970s had only recently been legally recognized as a profession separate and distinct from psychology. While Virginia licensed counselors starting in 1976, no other state did until 1979. Furthermore, there was no national certification of counselors, let alone counseling specialties, and no national standards or accreditation of counselor education programs. Most people who earned a master's degree in counseling completed a 30- to 36-semester-hour program, with or without an internship, and graduated mostly as generalists. Almost anyone could call him- or herself a counselor or a mental health counselor and many did. The profession that was to evolve was at the time unregulated and unfocused.

In addition to the weaknesses within the profession, American society, and indeed the world, was quite different from today. The United States was just calming down from the chaos surrounding the Vietnam War. Jimmy Carter was president and there was a malaise in the nation among many people. The Cold War between the Soviet Union and the United States was in full swing. Women and minorities in America were still fighting for their rights and recognition. Mental health as a federal concept was still being formulated and often took a backseat to physical health initiatives. The Internet, cell phones, and other social media had yet to be invented, mass produced, and extensively used. People still read newspapers and magazines regularly, and the processing of information was slower because the speed at which it reached the masses was more measured. The concepts of deinstitutionalization of individuals with mental health problems was still occurring, and fears associated with mental disorders were still prevalent in many places. The *DSM* was in its third version. In other words, the world where counseling and clinical mental health counseling were conceived was far different from the environments in which they exist today.

Yet as different as the times were, they still have much in common with the 21st century. People then, like today, got anxious, stressed, and depressed, and suffered mentally. Parents worried about their children, and adolescents were apprehensive about their future. Bullying occurred—just not online. Sexism, racism, and a host of other "isms" that discriminated against others were present and often unrecognized or tolerated. Academic, artistic, athletic, and business competitions were daily topics of conversation among most Americans. Big and bulky colored televisions with remotes kept families informed of the latest news just as computers and other streaming media do today. Politics and politicians fluctuated from being heated and unproductive to being constructive. Music by ABBA, the Bee Gees, Queen, and the Commodores played on car radios and in discos just as music by Adele, Justin Bieber, Drake, and Taylor Swift fills iPods, MP3 player, and clubs today. There was a search for meaning then as now, and self-help books as well as seminars were popular in the 1970s as they continue to be.

While the world has dramatically changed since the late 1970s, it has remained the same in many ways. Concerns over environment, migrants, trade, and how people live are prevalent topics of conversation now as then. Mental health services also continue to be of interest to most, although they are talked about in quieter and more subtle ways. Services for those with mental difficulties and everyday concerns have been transformed radically from that time in ways that few other professions have. Today managed care and insurance companies have replaced fee-for-service providers. New therapeutic approaches have been created, and evidence-based ways of working are emphasized more than ever before. In addition, there are many more options for receiving mental health and, as this book has pointed out, many more recognized places where mental health professionals work and more diverse populations whom they treat.

While the stigma with seeking counseling has not disappeared, it has faded some, and clients who seek out counselors and counseling have many more choices from which to choose. Psychiatrists, psychologists, psychiatric nurses, and social workers, among others, are still major players in working with individuals, groups, and families experiencing difficulties. However, so are counselors. They are at the forefront of those who assist the distressed and mentally anguished. The change in status for counseling as a profession and counselors regardless of specialty is thanks to national accreditation standards by the Council for Accreditation of Counseling and Related Educational Programs (CACREP), national certification by the National Board for Certified Counselors (NBCC), advocacy and ethics by the American Counseling Association (ACA), and regulations and oversight of counselors by state counselor licensing boards plus the American Association of State Counseling Boards (AASCB). The profession of counseling (and clinical mental health counseling in particular) has achieved equal status with sister helping professionals. It is something we occasionally take for granted.

We hope that you have recognized and appreciated the transition of counseling over the decades as you have read this book. Counselors and clinical mental health counselors have numerous opportunities today to address mental health issues from multiple perspectives. Settings such as colleges, schools, career centers, EAP programs, the military, mental health clinics, substance abuse agencies, and government institutions need the skills and services of clinical mental health counselors. The education of counselors is thorough, pragmatic, and focused on meeting the needs of people from all walks of life. Clinicians with a counseling background address preventative and developmental concerns as well as treatment situations. People from across the life span and in diverse walks of life are those whom clinical mental health counselors can and do help.

We hope that you will retain the emphasis of this book if not many of the facts. Clinical mental health counseling has a place in modern society. On its journey, clinical mental health counseling has progressed and faced changes and challenges, as have the professionals within its core. More alterations and transformation will occur in the profession and society going forward. Counselors and clinical mental health counselors are relevant and vital to the well-being of humanity. Their skills and approaches make them an integral part of the mental health field.

Samuel T. Gladding, PhD
Deborah W. Newsome, PhD

REFERENCES

Ackerman, N. W. (1966). *Treating the troubled family*. New York, NY: Basic Books.

Adams, N., & Grieder, D. M. (2005). *Treatment planning for person-centered care: The road to mental health and addiction recovery*. Burlington, MA: Elsevier.

Addis, M. E., & Mahalik, J. R. (2003). Men, masculinity, and the contexts of help-seeking. *American Counselor, 58*, 5–14.

Administration on Aging (AoA). (2015). *A profile of older Americans: 2015*. Retrieved from www.aoa.acl.gov/Aging_Statistics/Profile/index.aspx

Albee, G. W. (2000). Commentary on prevention in counseling psychology. *The Counseling Psychologist, 28*, 845–853.

Albee, G. W., & Gullotta, T. P. (1997). *Primary prevention works*. Thousand Oaks, CA: Sage.

Albee, G. W., & Ryan-Finn, K. D. (1993). An overview of primary prevention. *Journal of Counseling and Development, 72*, 115–123.

Alexander, J., & Parsons, B. V. (1982). *Functional family therapy*. Pacific Grove, CA: Brooks/Cole.

Allport, G. W. (1954). *The nature of prejudice*. Reading, MA: Addison-Wesley.

Amar, A. F., & Gennaro, S. (2005). Dating violence in college women: Associated physical injury, healthcare usage, and mental health symptoms. *Nursing Research, 54*(4), 235–242.

American Bar Association. (1980). *Standards relating to the rights of minors*. Cambridge, MA: Ballinger.

American Cancer Society. (2016). Cancer facts and figures. Retrieved from www.cancer.org/

American College Health Association. (2015). American College Health Association-National College Health Assessment II: Reference Group executive summary spring 2015. Hanover, MD: American College Health Association.

American College of Surgeons Committee on Trauma. (2006). *Resources for optimal care of the injured patient*. Chicago, IL: ACS.

American Counseling Association (ACA). (2014). *ACA code of ethics*. Alexandria, VA: Author.

American Counseling Association (ACA). (2016). What is counseling? Retrieved from www.counseling.org/about-us/about-aca

American Educational Research Association, American Psychological Association, & National Council on Measurement in Education. (2014). *Standards for educational and psychological testing*. Washington, DC: American Educational Research Association.

American Humane Association, Children's Division. (1996). *Fact sheets*. Englewood, CO: Author.

American Mental Health Counselors Association (AMHCA). (2009). About AMHCA. Retrieved from www.amhca.org/about

American Mental Health Counselors Association (AMHCA). (2015). *Code of ethics of the American Mental Health Counselors Association—2015 revision*. Alexandria, VA: Author.

American Mental Health Counselors Association (AMHCA). (2016). About AMHCA. Retrieved from www.amhca.org/about

American Psychiatric Association (APA). (1968). *Diagnostic and statistical manual of mental disorders* (2nd ed.). Washington, DC: Author.

American Psychiatric Association (APA). (2000). *Diagnostic and statistical manual of mental disorders* (4th ed., text rev.). Washington, DC: Author.

American Psychiatric Association (APA). (2013). *Diagnostic and statistical manual of mental disorders* (5th ed.). Washington, DC: Author.

American Psychiatric Nurses Association. (2016). Psychiatric-mental health nurses. Retrieved from www.apna.org/i4a/pages/index.cfm?pageid=3292

American Psychological Association. (2007). *Guidelines for psychological practice with girls and women: A joint task force of APA Divisions 17 and 35*. Retrieved from www.apa.org/practice/guidelines/girls-and-women.pdf

American Psychological Association. (2010, February 20). Ethical principles of psychologists and code of conduct. *American Psychologist, 57*, 1060–1073.

Ametrano, I. M. (2014). Teaching ethical decision making: Helping students reconcile personal and professional values. *Journal of Counseling and Development, 92*, 154–162.

Amos, W. E., & Williams, D. E. (1972). *Community counseling: A comprehensive model for developmental services*. St. Louis, MO: Warren H. Green.

Amundson, N. E., Harris-Bowlsbey, J., & Niles, S. G. (2009). *Essential elements of career counseling: Processes and techniques* (2nd ed.). Upper Saddle River, NJ: Merrill Pearson.

Anatasi, A., & Urbina, S. (1997). *Psychological testing* (7th ed.). Upper Saddle River, NJ: Prentice Hall.

Anderson, C. E. (2000). Dealing constructively with managed care: Suggestions from an insider. *Journal of Mental Health Counseling, 22*, 343–353.

Anderson, D. S. (2011). New directions for substance-abuse prevention-change. *Magazine of Higher Learning, 43*(6), 46–55.

Anderson, M. L., Goodman, J., & Schlossberg, N. K. (2012). *Counseling adults in transition: Linking Schlossberg's theory with counseling in a diverse world* (4th ed.). New York, NY: Springer.

Anderson, S. A., & Sabatelli, R. M. (2011). *Family interaction: A multigenerational developmental perspective* (5th ed.). Hoboken, NJ: Pearson.

Antonucci, T. C., Akiyama, H., & Merline, A. C. (2001). Dynamics of social relationships in midlife. In M. Lachman (Ed.), *Handbook of midlife development* (pp. 571–598). New York, NY: John Wiley & Sons.

Arnett, J. J. (2000). Emerging adulthood: A theory of development from the late teens through the twenties. *American Psychologist, 55,* 469–480.

Arnett, J. J. (2004). *Emerging adulthood: The winding road from the late teens through the twenties.* New York, NY: Oxford University Press.

Arnett, J. J. (2006). High hopes in a grim word: Emerging adults' views of their futures and of "Generation X." *Youth and Society, 31,* 267–286.

Arnett, J. J. (2007). Afterword: Aging out of care—Toward realizing the possibilities of emerging adulthood. *New Directions for Youth Development, 113,* 151–161.

Arnett, J. J. (2010). Oh, grow up! Generational grumbling and the new life stage of emerging adulthood—-Commentary on Trzesniewski & Donnellan (2010). *Perspective on Psychological Science, 5,* 89–92.

Arredondo, P., Toporek, R., Brown, S., Jones, J., Locke, D. C., Sanchez, J., & Stadler, H. (1996). *Operationalization of the multicultural counseling competencies.* Alexandria, VA: Association for Multicultural Counseling and Development.

Association for Assessment in Counseling and Education. (2012, May). *Standards for multicultural assessment* (4th ed.). Retrieved from http://aarc-counseling.org/assets/cms/uploads/files/AACE-AMCD.pdf

Association for Lesbian, Gay, Bisexual, and Transgender Issues in Counseling (ALGBTIC). (2012). *Competencies for counseling with lesbian, gay, bisexual, queer, questioning, intersex, and ally individuals.* Alexandria, VA: Author.

Association for Specialists in Group Work (ASGW). (1992). Professional standards for the training of group workers. *Journal for Specialists in Group Work, 17,* 12–19.

Association for Specialists in Group Work (ASGW). (1998). *Best practice guidelines.* Alexandria, VA: Author.

Association for Specialists in Group Work (ASGW). (2000). *Professional standards for the training of group workers.* Alexandria, VA: Author.

Association for Spiritual, Ethical, and Religious Values in Counseling (ASERVIC). (2009). *Competencies for addressing spiritual and religious issues in counseling.* Alexandria, VA: Author.

Atchley, R. C. (1989). A continuity theory of normal aging. *The Gerontologist, 29*(2), 183–190.

Attkisson, C. C., & Greenfield, T. K. (1994). Client Satisfaction Questionnaire-8 and Service Satisfaction Scale-30. In M. Maruish (Ed.), *The use of psychological testing for treatment planning and outcome assessment* (pp. 402–422). Hillsdale, NJ: Erlbaum.

Attneave, C. (1982). American Indian and Alaskan native families: Emigrants in their own homeland. In M. McGoldrick, J. Pearce, & J. Giordano (Eds.), *Ethnicity and family therapy* (pp. 55–83). New York, NY: Guilford Press.

Aubrey, R. F. (1977). Historical development of guidance and counseling and implications for the future. *Personnel and Guidance Journal, 55,* 288–295.

Aubrey, R. F. (1982). A house divided: Guidance and counseling in twentieth-century America. *Personnel and Guidance Journal, 61,* 198–204.

Aubrey, R. F. (1983). The odyssey of counseling and images of the future. *Personnel and Guidance Journal, 61,* 78–82.

Austad, C. S., & Berman, W. H. (1991). Managed care and the evolution of psychotherapy. In C. S. Austad & W. H. Berman (Eds.), *Psychotherapy in managed health care: The optimal use of time and resources* (pp. 3–18). Washington, DC: American Psychological Association.

Axelson, J. A. (1999). *Counseling and development in a multicultural society* (3rd ed.). Pacific Grove, CA: Brooks/Cole.

Bagheri, H., Memarian, R., & Alhani, F. (2007). Evaluation of the effect of group counselling on post myocardial infarction patients: Determined by an analysis of quality of life. *Journal of Clinical Nursing, 16*(2), 402–406.

Baird, B. N. (2014). *The internship, practicum, and field placement handbook: A guide for the helping professions* (7th ed.). Boston, MA: Pearson.

Baird, K., & Kracen, A. C. (2006). Vicarious traumatization and secondary traumatic stress: A research synthesis. *Counseling Psychology Quarterly, 19*(2), 181–188.

Baker, A. (2008). *Life in the U.S. armed forces: (Not) just another job.* Westport, CT: Praeger Security International.

Ballesteros, D., & Whitlock, J. (2012). Coping: Stress management strategies. Retrieved from www.crpsib.com/

Baltes, P. B. (1997). On the incomplete architecture of human ontogeny: Selection, optimization, and compensation—A foundation of developmental theory. *American Psychologist, 52*(4), 366–380.

Bandura, A. (1977a). Self-efficacy: Toward a unifying theory of behavioral change. *Psychological Review, 84,* 191–215.

Bandura, A. (1977b). *Social learning theory.* Upper Saddle River, NJ: Prentice Hall.

Bandura, A. (1986). *Social foundations of thought and action.* Upper Saddle River, NJ: Prentice Hall.

Barden, S. M., Conley, A. H., & Young, M. E. (2015). Integrated health and wellness in mental health counseling: Clinical, educational, and policy implications. *Journal of Mental Health Counseling, 37,* 152–163.

Barkham, M., Mellor-Clark, J., Connell, J., Evans, C., Evans, R., & Margison, F. (2010). Clinical outcomes in routine evaluation (CORE)—The CORE measures and system:

Measuring, monitoring, and managing quality evaluation in the psychological therapies. Retrieved from www.coreims.co.uk/

Barkley, R. A. (1997). Behavioral inhibition, sustained attention, and executive functions: Constructing a unifying theory of ADHD. *Psychological Bulletin, 121,* 65–94.

Barkley, R. A. (2015). *Attention deficit hyperactivity disorder: A handbook for diagnosis and treatment* (4th ed.). New York, NY: Guilford Press.

Barnett, J. E., & Johnson, W. B. (2015). *Ethics desk reference for counsellors* (2nd ed.). Alexandria, VA: American Counseling Association.

Barreira, P., & Snider, M. (2010). History of college counseling and mental health services and the role of the community mental health model. In J. Kay & V. Schwartz (Eds.), *Mental health care in the college community* (pp. 21–31). West Sussex, UK: Wiley-Blackwell.

Barros-Bailey, M., & Saunders, J. L. (2010). Ethics and the use of technology in rehabilitation counseling. *Rehabilitation Counseling Bulletin, 53*(4), 255–259.

Bauer, A. (2001). Responding to a community crisis: Frontline counseling. In E. R. Welfel & R. E. Ingersoll (Eds.), *The mental health desk reference* (pp. 239–245). New York, NY: Wiley.

Bauman, S. (2011). *Cyberbullying: What counselors need to know.* Alexandria, VA: American Counseling Association.

Bauman, S. S. M. (2002). Promoting parenting and child-rearing skills. In C. L. Juntenen & D. R. Atkinson (Eds.), *Counseling across the lifespan* (pp. 227–242). Thousand Oaks, CA: Sage.

Baumrind, D. (1991). The influence of parenting style on adolescent competence and substance use. *Journal of Early Adolescence, 11,* 56–95.

Bazelon Center for Mental Health Law. (2009). Where we stand. Retrieved from www.bazelon.org/Where-We-Stand/Community-Integration/Employment.aspx

Beamish, P. M. (2005). Introduction to the special section—Severe and persistent mental illness on college campuses: Considerations for service provision. *Journal of College Counseling, 8,* 138–139.

Beamish, P. M., Granello, D. H., & Belcastro, A. L. (2002). Treatment of panic disorder: Practical guidelines. *Journal of Mental Health Counseling, 24,* 224–246.

Beck, A. T., & Steer, R. A. (1991). *Manual for the Beck Scale for Suicide Ideation.* San Antonio, TX: Psychological Corporation.

Beck, A. T., Steer, R. A., & Brown, G. K. (1996). *Beck Depression Inventory II.* San Antonio, TX: Psychological Corporation.

Beck, J. S. (1995). *Cognitive therapy: Basics and beyond.* New York, NY: Guilford Press.

Becvar, D. S., & Becvar, R. J. (2009). *Family therapy: A systematic integration* (7th ed.). Boston, MA: Allyn & Bacon.

Beers, C. (1908). *A mind that found itself.* New York, NY: Longman Green.

Behavioral Health Evolution. (2016). Innovative resources for treating substance use, mental health, and co-occurring disorders. Retrieved from www.bhevolution.org/publicoverview_faqs.page

Belsky, J. B. (2016). *Experiencing the lifespan* (4th ed.). New York, NY: Worth.

Belson, R. (1992, September/October). Ten tried-and-true methods to achieve therapist burnout. *Family Therapy Networker,* 22.

Bennett, J. B., & Lehman, W. E.-K. (Eds.). (2003). *Preventing workplace substance abuse: Beyond drug testing to wellness.* Washington, DC: American Psychological Association.

Benshoff, J. J. (1996). Peer self-help groups. In W. Crimando & T. F. Riggar (Eds.), *Utilizing community resources: An overview of human services* (pp. 57–66). Delray Beach, FL: St. Lucie Press.

Benshoff, J. J., & Janikowski, T. P. (2000). *The rehabilitation model of substance abuse counseling.* Belmont, CA: Wadsworth.

Berecz, J. M., & Helm, H. W., Jr. (1998). Shame: The underside of Christianity. *Journal of Psychology and Christianity, 17*(1), 5–14.

Berger, K. S. (2014). *Invitation to the life span* (2nd ed.). New York, NY: Worth.

Berk, L. E. (2014). *Development through the life-span* (6th ed.). Upper Saddle River, NJ: Pearson.

Betz, N. E. (1992). Career assessment: A review of critical issues. In S. D. Brown & R. W. Lent (Eds.), *Handbook of counseling psychology* (2nd ed., pp. 453–484). New York, NY: Wiley. The Bisexual Index. (2016). What is bisexuality? Retrieved from www.bisexualindex.org.uk/index.php/Bisexuality

Bjorklund, D. F. (2000). *Children's thinking: Developmental function and individual differences* (3rd ed.). Belmont, CA: Wadsworth.

Black, J., & Underwood, J. (1998). Young, female, and gay: Lesbian students and the school environment. *Professional School Counseling, 1,* 15–21.

Blair-Loy, M. (2003). *Competing devotions: Career and family among women executives.* Cambridge, MA: Harvard University Press.

Blaisure, K., Saathoff-Wells, T., Perelra, A., Wadsworth, S. M., & Dombro, A. (2016). Serving military families: Theories, research, and application (2nd ed.). New York, NY: Routledge.

Blatter, C. W., & Jacobsen, J. J. (1993). Older women coping with divorce: Peer support groups. *Women and Therapy, 14,* 141–154.

Bloom, M. (1996). *Primary prevention practices.* Thousand Oaks, CA: Sage.

Boeree, C. G. (2002). General psychology: Limbic system. Retrieved from webspace.ship.edu/cgboer/limbicsystem.html

Boeree, C. G. (2003). General psychology: Neurotransmitters. Retrieved from webspace.ship.edu/cgboer/genpsyneurotransmitters.html

Bohlmeijer, E., Roemer, M., Cuijpers, P., & Smit, F. (2007). The effects of reminiscence on psychological well-being in older adults: A meta-analysis. *Aging and Mental Health, 11*(3), 291–300.

Booth, C. S., & Phipps, G. S. (2014). Understanding and treating eating disorders in college students. In S. Degges-White & C. Borzumato-Gainey (Eds.), *College student mental health counseling* (pp. 155–184). New York, NY: Springer.

Borrell-Carrió, F., Suchman, A. L., & Epstein, R. M. (2004). The biopsychosocial model 25 years later: Principles, practice, and scientific inquiry. *Annals of Family Medicine, 2,* 576–582.

Boszormenyi-Nagy, I. (1987). *Foundations of contextual therapy*. New York, NY: Brunner/Mazel.

Bowen, M. (1976). Theory in the practice of psychotherapy. In P. J. Guerin, Jr. (Ed.), *Family therapy: Theory and practice* (pp. 42–90). New York, NY: Gardner Press.

Bowen, M. (1978). *Family therapy in clinical practice*. New York, NY: Jason Aronson.

Bowen, M. (1994). *Family therapy in clinical practice*. New York, NY: Jason Aronson.

Boyatzis, R., McKee, A., & Goleman, D. (2002). Reawakening your passion for work. *Harvard Business Review, 80,* 86–93.

Boyce, B. (Ed.). (2011). *The mindfulness revolution*. Boston, MA: Shambhala.

Bradley, L. J., Hendricks, B., Lock, R., Whiting, P. P., & Parr, G. (2011). E-mail communication: Issues for mental health counselors. *Journal of Mental Health Counseling, 33*(1), 67–79.

Brammer, L. M. (1985). *The helping relationship: Process and skills* (3rd ed.). Upper Saddle River, NJ: Prentice Hall.

Brandt, R. (1959). *Ethical theory*. Upper Saddle River, NJ: Prentice Hall.

Braun, S. A., & Cox, J. A. (2005). Managed mental health care: Intentional misdiagnosis of mental disorders. *Journal of Counseling and Development, 83,* 425–433.

Brent, D. A., Baugher, M., Bridge, J., Chen, T., & Chiappetta, L. (1999). Age and sex-related risk factors for adolescent suicide. *Journal of the American Academy of Child and Adolescent Psychiatry, 38,* 1497–1505.

Brewer, J. M. (1932). *Education as guidance*. New York, NY: Macmillan.

Bringaze, T. B., & White, L. J. (2001). Living out proud: Factors contributing to healthy identity development in lesbian leaders. *Journal of Mental Health Counseling, 23,* 162–173.

Britzman, M. J., & Nagelhout, S. E. (2011, November). Professional counselors: Are we too overwhelmed to focus on prevention? *Counseling Today, 54,* 46–47.

Bronfenbrenner, U. (1979). *The ecology of human development*. Cambridge, MA: Harvard University Press.

Bronfenbrenner, U. (1989). Ecological systems theory. In R. Vasta (Ed.), *Six theories of child development: Revised formulations and current issues* (pp. 187–249). London, UK: Jessica Kingsley.

Bronfenbrenner, U. (1995). The bioecological model from a life course perspective: Reflections of a participant observer. In P. Moen, G. H. Elder, & K. Luscher (Eds.), *Examining lives in context: Perspectives on the ecology of human development* (pp. 599–647). Washington, DC: American Psychological Association.

Brougham, R. R., Zail, C. M., Mendoza, C. M., & Miller, J. R. (2009). Stress, sex differences, and coping strategies among college students. *Current Psychology, 28,* 85–97.

Browers, R. T. (2005). Counseling in mental health and private practice settings. In D. Capuzzi & D. R. Gross (Eds.), *Introduction to the counseling profession* (4th ed., pp. 357–380). Needham Heights, MA: Pearson/Allyn & Bacon.

Brown, D. (2016). *Career information, career counseling, and career development* (11th ed.). Hoboken, NJ: Pearson.

Brown, D., Pryzwansky, W. B., & Schulte, A. C. (2011). *Psychological consultation and collaboration* (7th ed.). Upper Saddle River, NJ: Pearson.

Brown, J. (1983). Consultation. In J. A. Brown & R. H. Pate, Jr. (Eds.), *Being a counsellor: Directions and challenges* (pp. 124–146). Pacific Grove, CA: Brooks/Cole.

Brown, L. S., & Bryan, T. C. (2007). Feminist therapy with people who self-inflict violence. *Journal of Clinical Psychology: In Session, 63*(11), 1121–1133.

Brown, M. B. (2000). Diagnosis and treatment of children and adolescents with attention-deficit hyperactivity disorder. *Journal of Counseling and Development, 78,* 195–203.

Brown, S. L., & May, K. M. (2009). Counseling with women. In C. M. Ellis & J. Carlson (Eds.), *Cross cultural awareness and social justice in counseling* (pp. 61–88). New York, NY: Routledge. *Bruff v. North Mississippi Health Services, Inc., 244F.3d 495 (5th Cir. 2001).

Bubenzer, D. L., Zimpfer, D. G., & Mahrle, C. L. (1990). Standardized individual appraisal in agency and private practice: A survey. *Journal of Mental Health Counseling, 12,* 51–66.

Buder, M., & Evans, K. (2010). *The grace to race: The wisdom of the 80-year-old world champion triathlete known as the Iron Nun*. New York, NY: Simon and Shuster.

Burck, H. D., & Peterson, G. W. (1975). Needed: More evaluation, not research. *Personnel and Guidance Journal, 53,* 563–569.

Burke, M. T., Chauvin, J. C., & Miranti, J. G. (2005). *Religious and spiritual issues in counseling: Applications across diverse populations*. New York, NY: Brunner-Routledge.

Buser, J. K. (2009). Treatment-seeking disparity between African Americans and Whites: Attitudes toward treatment, coping resources, and racism. *Multicultural Counseling and Development, 37,* 94–104.

Buser, J. K. (2013). Stress, spiritual coping, and bulimia: Feeling punishment from God/Higher Power. *Journal of Mental Health Counseling, 35,* 154–171.

Butcher, J. N., Dahlstrom, W. G., Graham, J. R., Tellegen, A., & Kaemmer, B. (1989). *Minnesota Multiphasic Personality Inventory-2 (MMPI-2): Manual for administration and scoring.* Minneapolis: University of Minnesota Press.

Butler, K. (1994, July/August). Duty of care. *Family Therapy Networker, 18,* 10–11.

Cadwallader, E. H. (1991). Depression and religion: Realities, perspectives, and directions. *Counseling and Values, 35,* 83–92.

Calhoun, G. B., Bartolomucci, C. L., & McLean, B. A. (2005). Building connections: Relational group work with female adolescent offenders. *Women & Therapy, 28*(2), 17–29.

Calhoun, G. B., Glaser, B. A., & Bartolomucci, C. L. (2001). The juvenile counseling and assessment model and program: A conceptualization and intervention for juvenile delinquency. *Journal of Counseling and Development, 79,* 131–141.

Calhoun, L. G., & Tedeschi, R. G. (Eds.). (2013). *Handbook of post traumatic growth.* New York, NY: Routledge.

Cameron, S., & turtle-song, i. (2002). Learning to write case notes using the SOAP format. *Journal of Counseling and Development, 80,* 286–292.

Cantor, D. W., & Fuentes, M. A. (2008). Psychology's response to managed care. *Professional Psychology Research and Practice, 39,* 638–645.

Carkhuff, R. R. (1969). *Helping and human relations.* New York, NY: Holt, Rinehart & Winston.

Carkhuff, R. R. (1972). *The art of helping.* Amherst, MA: Human Resource Development Press.

Carney, J. M., & Jefferson, J. F. (2014). Consultation for mental health counselors: Opportunities and guidelines for private practice. *Journal for Mental Health Counseling, 36,* 302–314.

Carroll, L., Gilroy, P. J., & Ryan, J. (2002). Counseling transgendered, transsexual, and gender-variant clients. *Journal of Counseling and Development, 80,* 131–139.

Carroll, M., Bates, M. M., & Johnson, C. D. (2004). *Group leadership: Strategies for group counseling leaders* (4th ed.). Denver, CO: Love.

Carter, B., & McGoldrick, M. (1989). *The changing family life cycle: A framework for family therapy* (2nd ed.). Boston, MA: Allyn & Bacon.

Carter, B., & McGoldrick, M. (Eds.). (2005). *Expanded family life cycle: Individual, family, and social perspectives* (3rd ed.). Boston, MA: Allyn & Bacon.

Carter, R. T. (1990). The relationship between racism and racial identity among white Americans: An exploratory investigation. *Journal of Counseling and Development, 69,* 46–50.

Casas, J. M. (2005). Race and racism: The efforts of counseling psychology to understand and address the issues associated with these terms. *The Counseling Psychologist, 33,* 501–512.

Cashwell, C. S., Bentley, D. P., & Bigbee, A. (2007). Spirituality and counselor wellness. *Journal of Humanistic Counseling, Education, and Development, 46,* 66–81.

Cashwell, C. S., Bentley, D. P., & Yarborough, J. P. (2007). The only way out is through: The peril of spiritual bypass. *Counseling and Values, 51,* 139–148.

Cashwell, C. S., & Young, J. S. (Eds.). (2011). *Integrating spirituality and religion into counseling: A guide to competent practice* (2nd ed.). Alexandria, VA: American Counseling Association.

Cass, V. C. (1979). Homosexual identity formation: A theoretical model. *Journal of Homosexuality, 4,* 219–235.

Cass, V. C. (1984). Homosexual identity formation: A concept in need of definition. *Journal of Homosexuality, 10,* 105–126.

Centers for Disease Control and Prevention. (2015). Injury prevention and control: Division of Violence Prevention. Retrieved from www.cdc.gov/violenceprevention/suicide/

Chamberlain, P., Goldney, R., Delfabbro, P., Gill, T., & Dal Grande, L. (2009). Suicidal ideation: The clinical utility of the K10. *Crisis, 30*(1), 39–42.

Champe, J., & Rubel, D. J. (2012). Application of focal conflict theory to psychoeducational groups: Implications for process, content, and leadership. *Journal for Specialists in Group Work, 37,* 71–90.

Cherry, K. (2016). What's the difference between a psychologist and a psychiatrist? Retrieved from www.psychology.about.com/od/psychotherapy/f/psychvspsych.htm

Cheung, F. K. (1991). The use of mental health services by ethnic minorities. In H. F. Myers, P. Wholford, L. P. Guzman, & R. J. Echemendia (Eds.), *Ethnic minority perspectives on clinical training and services in psychology* (pp. 23–31). Washington, DC: American Psychological Association.

Childers, J. H., Jr., & Couch, R. D. (1989). Myths about group counseling: Identifying and challenging misconceptions. *Journal for Specialists in Group Work, 14,* 105–111.

Child Welfare Information Gateway. (2012). *The risk and prevention of maltreatment of children with disabilities.* Retrieved from www.childwelfare.gov

Child Welfare League of America. (2008). *Child, youth, and family development: Childhood depression.* Retrieved from www.cwla.org/programs/health/healthtipschilddepression.htm

Chi Sigma Iota (CSI). (2016). About CSI. Retrieved from https://www.csi-net.org/?page=About_CSI

Choate, L. H. (2009). Girls' and women's issues in counseling: A theory-based course design. *Counselor Education and Supervision, 48,* 179–193.

Choate, L.H., & Manton, J. (2014). Teen court counseling groups: Facilitating positive change for adolescents who are first-time juvenile offenders. *Journal for Specialists in Group Work, 39,* 345–365.

Chope, R. C. (2012). *Family matters: The influence of the family in career decision making* (2nd ed.). Alexandria, VA: American Counseling Association.

Chung, R. C.-Y., & Bemak, F. (2002). The relationship of culture and empathy in cross-cultural counseling. *Journal of Counseling and Development, 80,* 154–159.

Clark, W. (2003, November/December). Substance abuse and evidence-based family interventions. *Family Therapy Magazine, 2*(6), 15–19.

Clarke, P. B., Adams, J. K., Wilkerson, J. R., & Shaw, E. G. (2016). Wellness-based counseling for caregivers of persons with dementia. *Journal of Mental Health Counseling, 38,* 263–277.

Cohen, J., Marecek, J., & Gillham, J. (2006). Is three a crowd? Clients, clinicians, and managed care. *American Journal of Orthopsychiatry, 76,* 251–259.

Colangelo, N. (1985). Overview. *Elementary School Guidance and Counseling, 19,* 244–245.

Colburn, A. A. N. (2013). Endless possibilities: Diversifying service options in private practice. *Journal of Mental Health Counseling, 35,* 198–210.

Cole, D. A. (1988). Hopelessness, social desirability, depression, and parasuicide in two college student samples. *Journal of Consulting and Clinical Psychology, 56,* 131–136.

Compas, B. E. (1987). Stress and life events during childhood and adolescence. *Clinical Psychology Review, 7,* 275–302.

Conners, C. K. (2008). *Conners Third Edition.* Los Angeles, CA: Western Psychological Services.

Conyne, R. K. (1991). Gains in primary prevention: Implications for the counseling profession. *Journal of Counseling and Development, 69,* 277–279.

Conyne, R. K. (2000). Prevention in counseling psychology: At long last, has the time now come? *The Counseling Psychologist, 28,* 838–844.

Conyne, R. K., Newmeyer, M. D., Kenny, M., Romano, J. L., & Matthews, C. R. (2008). Two key strategies for teaching prevention: Specialized course and infusion. *Journal of Primary Prevention, 29,* 375–401.

Cooper, C. C., & Gottlieb, M. C. (2000). Ethical issues with managed care: Challenges facing counseling psychology. *The Counseling Psychologist, 28,* 179–236.

Cooper, J. (2014). Essential crisis intervention skills. In L. R. Jackson-Cherry & B. T. Erford (Eds.), *Crisis assessment, intervention, and prevention* (2nd ed., pp. 67–84). Upper Saddle River, NJ: Pearson.

Corey, G. (2013). *The art of integrative counseling* (3rd ed.). Belmont, CA: Brooks/Cole.

Corey, G. (2016). *Theory and practice of group counseling* (9th ed.). Boston, MA: Cengage.

Corey, G., Corey, M. S., Corey, C., & Callanan, P. (2015). *Issues and ethics in the helping professions* (9th ed.). Stamford, CT: Cengage.

Cormier, L. S. (2016). *Counseling strategies and interventions for professional helpers* (9th ed.). Upper Saddle River, NJ: Pearson.

Cormier, L. S., Nurius, P. S., & Osborn, C. J. (2017). *Interviewing and change strategies for helpers* (8th ed.). Boston, MA: Cengage.

Corsini, R. J. (2008). Introduction. In R. J. Corsini & D. Wedding (Eds.), *Current psychotherapies* (8th ed., pp. 1–13). Belmont, CA: Thomson Brooks/Cole.

Costello, E. J., Erkanli, A., & Angold, A. (2006). Is there an epidemic of child or adolescent depression? *Journal of Child Psychology and Psychiatry, 47,* 1263–1271.

Cottone, R. R., & Tarvydas, V. M. (2016). *Ethics and decision making in counseling and psychotherapy* (4th ed.). New York, NY: Springer.

Council for Accreditation of Counseling and Related Educational Programs (CACREP). (2016). *CACREP standards.* Retrieved from www.cacrep.org/for-programs/2016-cacrep-standards/

Counselors for Social Justice (CSJ). (2011). CSJ mission statement. Retrieved from www.counselorsforsocialjustice.com/

Courtois, C. A. (2008). Complex trauma, complex reactions: Assessment and treatment. *Psychological Trauma: Theory, Research, Practice, and Policy, S*(1), 86–100.

Cousins, N. (1979). *Anatomy of an illness.* New York, NY: Norton.

Cross, J. R., & Cross, T. L. (2015). Clinical and mental health issues in counseling the gifted individual. *Journal of Counseling and Development, 93,* 163–172.

Curran, D. (1985). *Stress and the healthy family.* San Francisco, CA: Harper & Row.

Damer, D. E., Latimer, K. M., & Porter, K. H. (2010). "Build your social confidence": A social anxiety confidence group for college students. *Journal for Specialists in Group Work, 35,* 7–22.

D'Andrea, M., & Heckman, E. F. (2008). Contributing to the ongoing evolution of the multicultural counseling movement: An introduction to the special issue. *Journal of Counseling and Development, 86,* 259–260.

Daniels, J. A. (2001). Managed care, ethics, and counseling. *Journal of Counseling and Development, 79,* 119–122.

Daniels, J. A. (2002). Assessing threats of school violence: Implications for counselors. *Journal of Counseling and Development, 80,* 215–218.

Daniels, M., Mines, R., & Gressard, C. (1981). A meta-model for evaluating counseling programs. *Personnel and Guidance Journal, 59*(9), 578.

Daniels, M. J., Thompson, E. S., & Wolf, C. P. (2017). Program evaluation. In C. J. Sheperis, J. S. Young, & M. H. Daniels (Eds.), *Counseling research: Quantitative, qualitative, and mixed methods* (pp. 301–316). Hoboken, NJ: Pearson.

Danzinger, P. R., & Welfel, E. R. (2001). The impact of managed care on mental health counselors: A survey of perceptions, practices, and compliance with ethical standards. *Journal of Mental Health Counseling, 23,* 137–150.

Darden, C. A., Gazda, G. M., & Ginter, E. J. (1996). Life-skills and mental health counseling. *Journal of Mental Health Counseling, 18,* 134–141.

Darling, N., & Steinberg, L. (1993). Parenting style as context: An integrative model. *Psychological Bulletin, 188,* 487–496.

Davis, H. V. (1988). *Frank Parsons: Prophet, innovator, counselor.* Carbondale: University of Southern Illinois Press.

Davis, R. F., & Borns, N. E. (1999). *Solo dad survival guide: Raising your kids on your own.* New York, NY: NTC/Contemporary Publishing.

Davis, S. R., & Meier, S. T. (2001). *The elements of managed care.* Belmont, CA: Wadsworth.

Davison, M., & Gasiorowski, F. (2006). The trend of coaching: Adler, the literature, and the marketplace would agree. *Journal of Individual Psychology, 62,* 188–201.

Day-Vines, N. L., Wood, S. M., Grothaus, T., Craigen, L., Holman, A., Dotson-Blake, K., & Douglass, M. J. (2007). Broaching the subjects of race, ethnicity, and culture during the counseling process. *Journal of Counseling and Development, 85,* 401–409.

Deeg, D. J. M. (2005). The development of physical and mental health from late midlife to early old age. In S. L. Willis & M. Martin (Eds.), *Middle adulthood* (pp. 209–242). Thousand Oaks, CA: Sage.

Degges-White, S. (2005). Understanding gerotranscendence in older adults: A new perspective for counselors. *Adultspan, 4*(1), 36–48.

Degges-White, S., & Borzumato-Gainey, C. (Eds.). (2014). *College student mental health: A developmental approach.* New York, NY: Springer.

Degges-White, S., & Myers, J. E. (2006). Transitions, wellness, and life satisfaction: Implications for counseling midlife women. *Journal of Mental Health Counseling, 28*(2), 133–150.

De Los Reyes, A., & Kazdin, A. E. (2008). When the evidence says, "Yes, no, and maybe so": Attending to and interpreting inconsistent findings among evidence-based interventions. *Current Directions in Psychological Science, 17,* 47–51.

Derogatis, L. R. (1993). *The Brief Symptom Inventory (BSI): Administration, scoring, and procedures.* Minneapolis, MN: Pearson Assessments.

Derogatis, L. R. (1994). *The SCL-90-R: Administration, scoring and procedures manual* (3rd ed.). Minneapolis, MN: Pearson Assessments.

Derogatis, L. R., & Lazarus, L. (1994). SCL-90-R, Brief Symptom Inventory, and matching clinical rating scales. In M. Maruish (Ed.), *The use of psychological testing for treatment planning and outcome assessment* (pp. 217–248). Hillsdale, NJ: Erlbaum.

de Shazer, S. (1991). *Putting difference to work.* New York, NY: Norton.

Dharmalingam, K., Berg, L., & Hall, D. (2012, May 31). *Program and client outcome evaluation.* Presentation at Wake Forest University, Winston-Salem, NC.

DiGiuseppe, R. A., Doyle, K. A., Dryden, W., & Backx, W. (2014). A practitioner's guide to rational emotive behavior therapy (3rd ed.). New York, NY: Oxford University Press.

Dinkmeyer, D. C., & Muro, J. J. (1979). *Group counseling: Theory and practice* (2nd ed.). Itasca, IL: F. E. Peacock.

Doherty, W. J., Lester, M. E., & Leigh, G. (1986). Marriage encounter weekends: Couples who win and couples who lose. *Journal of Marital and Family Therapy, 12,* 49–61.

Domestic Abuse Shelter. (2016). *Why women stay.* Retrieved from www.domesticabuseshelter.org/InfoDomesticViolence.htm#why

Donaldson James, S. (2016, September 8). Pot use rises on college campuses, while other drug use declines: Study. *NBC News.* Retrieved from www.nbcnews.com/feature/college-game-plan/pot-use-rises-college-campuses-while-other-drug-use-declines-n645026

Donigian, J. (1994, Fall). Group reflections. *Together, 23,* 6.

Donigian, J., & Hulse-Killacky, D. (1999). *Critical incidents in group therapy* (2nd ed.). Pacific Grove, CA: Brooks/Cole.

Dougherty, A. M. (2014). *Psychological consultation and collaboration in school and community settings* (6th ed.). Belmont, CA: Brooks/Cole, Cengage Learning.

Doweiko, H. E. (2015). *Concepts of chemical dependency* (9th ed.). Stamford, CT: Cengage Learning.

Drapeau, C. W., & McIntosh, J. L. (for the American Association of Suicidology). (2015, January 22). *U.S.A. suicide 2013: Official final data.* Washington, DC: American Association of Suicidology. Retrieved from www.suicidology.org

Drummond, R. J., Sheperis, C. J., & Jones, K. D. (2016). *Assessment procedures for counselors and helping professionals* (8th ed.). Hoboken, NJ: Pearson.

Duggan, M. H., & Jurgens, J. C. (2007). *Career interventions and techniques: A complete guide for human service professionals.* Boston, MA: Pearson/Allyn & Bacon.

Eccles, J. S., Midgley, C., Wigfield, A., Buchanan, C. M., Reuman, D., Flanagan, C., & MacIver, D. (1993). Development during adolescence: The impact of stage–environment fit on young adolescents' experiences in schools and families. *American Psychologist, 48,* 90–101.

Eccles, J. S., & Roeser, R. W. (2011). Schools as developmental contexts during adolescence. *Journal of Research on Adolescence, 21,* 225–241.

Edwards, D., Burnard, P., Coyle, D., Fothergill, A., & Hannigan, B. (2000). Stress and burnout in community mental health nursing: A review of the literature. *Journal of Psychiatric and Mental Health Nursing, 7,* 7–14.

Edwards, J. H. (2002). Evidence-based treatment for child ADHD: "Real-world" practice implications. *Journal of Mental Health Counseling, 24,* 126–139.

Eels, G. T., & Rando, R. A. (2010). Components of an effective college mental health service. In J. Kay & V. Schwartz (Eds.), *Mental health care in the college community* (pp. 43–55). West Sussex, UK: Wiley-Blackwell.

Egan, G. (2014). *The skilled helper* (10th ed.). Belmont, CA: Brooks/Cole.

Eichler, R. J., & Schwartz, V. (2010). Essential services in college counseling. In J. Kay & V. Schwartz (Eds.), *Mental health care in the college community* (pp. 57–89). West Sussex, UK: Wiley-Blackwell.

Eisenberg, D., Gollust, S. E., Golberstein, E., & Hefner, J. L. (2007). Prevalence and correlates of depression, anxiety, and suicidality among university students. *American Journal of Orthopsychiatry, 77*(4), 534–542.

Ellis, A. (1988). *How to stubbornly refuse to make yourself miserable about anything—yes, anything!* Secaucus, NJ: Lyle Stuart.

Ellis, A. (2000). Rational–emotive behavior in marriage and family therapy. In A. M. Horne (Ed.), *Family counseling and therapy* (3rd ed., pp. 489–514). Itasca, IL: F. E. Peacock.

Ellis, A., & Dryden, W. (Eds.). (2007). *The practice of rational emotive behavior therapy* (2nd ed.). New York, NY: Springer.

Ellis, A., Sichel, J. L., Yeager, R. J., DiMattia, D. J., & DiGiuseppe, R. (1989). *Rational–emotive couples therapy.* New York, NY: Pergamon Press.

Emam, P. (2016, May/June). Disability as a cultural experience. *Family Therapy Magazine,* 9–11.

Employee Assistance Professionals Association (EAPA). (2016). About EAPA. Retrieved from www.eapassn.org

Engel, G. (1977). The need for a new medical model. *Science, 196,* 129–136.

English, A., Bass, L., Boyle, A. D., & Eshragh, F. (2010). *State minor consent laws: A summary* (3rd ed.). Chapel Hill, NC: Center for Adolescent Health and the Law.

Enns, C. Z. (2003). Contemporary adaptations of traditional approaches to the counseling of women. In M. Kopala & M. A. Keitel (Eds.), *Handbook of counseling women* (pp. 3–21). Thousand Oaks, CA: Sage.

Epp, L. R. (1998). The courage to be an existential counselor: An interview with Clemmont E. Vontress. *Journal of Mental Health Counseling, 20,* 1–12.

Erchul, W. P. (2003). Interpersonal process in consultation: Guest editor's comments. *Journal of Educational and Psychological Consultation, 14,* 105–107.

Erchul, W. P. (2009). Gerald Caplan: A tribute to the originator of mental health consultation. *Journal of Educational and Psychological Consultation, 19,* 95–105.

Erdman, P., & Lampe, R. (1996). Adapting basic skills to counsel children. *Journal of Counseling and Development, 74,* 374–377.

Erford, B. T. (2015). Helping students with mental and emotional disorders. In B. T. Erford (Ed.), *Transforming the school counseling profession* (4th ed.). Upper Saddle River, NJ: Prentice Hall.

Erickson, M. (1954). Special techniques of brief hypnotherapy. *Journal of Clinical and Experimental Hypnosis, 2,* 109–129.

Erikson, E. H. (1959). *Identity and the life cycle: Psychological issues.* New York, NY: International Universities Press.

Erikson, E. H. (1963). *Childhood and society* (2nd ed.). New York, NY: Norton.

Erikson, E. H. (1968). *Identity: Youth and crisis.* New York, NY: Norton.

Erikson, E. H., with Erikson, J. M. (1997). *The life cycle completed: Extended version.* New York, NY: Norton.

Evans, K. M. (2013). Issues in counseling women. In C. C. Lee (Ed.), *Multicultural issues in counseling: New approaches to diversity* (4th ed., pp. 139–150). Alexandria, VA: American Counseling Association.

Evans, K. M., Kincade, E. A., & Seem, S. (2011). *Introduction to feminist therapy: Strategies for social and individual change.* Thousand Oaks, CA: Sage.

Ezell, M. (2001). *Advocacy in the human services.* Belmont, CA: Wadsworth.

Fair Access Coalition on Testing (FACT). (2015). The National Fair Access Coalition on Testing mission. Retrieved from www.fairaccess.org/home.html

Falkner, J., & Starkey, D. (2009). Counseling lesbian, gay, bisexual, transgender, and questioning clients. In D. Capuzzi & D. R. Gross (Eds.), *Introduction to the counseling profession* (5th ed., pp. 501–529). Boston, MA: Pearson/Allyn & Bacon.

Falvey, J. E. (2001). Clinical judgment in case conceptualization and treatment planning across mental health disciplines. *Journal of Counseling and Development, 79,* 292–303.

Families and Work Institute. (2008). About FWI. Retrieved from www.familiesandwork.org

Faustman, W. O. (1994). Brief psychiatric rating scale. In M. Maruish (Ed.), *The use of psychological testing for treatment planning and outcome assessment* (pp. 371–401). Hillsdale, NJ: Erlbaum.

Field, T. A., Beeson, E. T., & Jones, L. K. (2015). The new ABCs: A practitioner's guide to neuroscience-informed cognitive-behavior therapy. *Journal of Mental Health Counseling, 37,* 206–220.

Figley, C. R. (1989). *Helping traumatized families.* San Francisco, CA: Jossey-Bass.

Figley, C. R. (1995). Compassion fatigue: Toward a new understanding of the costs of caring. In B. H. Stamm (Ed.), *Secondary traumatic stress: Self-care issues for clinicians, researchers and educators* (2nd ed., pp. 3–29). Baltimore, MD: Sidran Press.

First, M. B., & Wakefield, J. C. (2013). Diagnostic criteria as dysfunction indicators: Bridging the chasm between the definition of mental disorder and diagnostic criteria for specific disorders. *The Canadian Journal of Psychiatry, 58*(12), 663–668.

Fishman, C. (2016, May/June). Anorexia nervosa treatment and the family therapist. *Family Therapy Magazine,* 22–26.

Foliart, D. E., Clausen, M., & Siljestrom, C. (2001). Bereavement practices among California hospices: Results of a statewide survey. *Death Studies, 25,* 461–467.

Ford, D., & Urban, H. (1963). *Systems of psychotherapy: A comparative study.* New York, NY: Wiley.

Ford, D. A., & Courtois, C. A. (Eds.). (2013). *Treating complex traumatic stress disorders.* New York, NY: Guilford.

Forester-Miller, H., & Davis, T. D. (1998). *A practitioner's guide to ethical decision making.* Alexandria, VA: American Counseling Association. Retrieved from www.counseling.org/docs/ethics/practitioners_guide. pdf?sfvrsn=2

Forsyth, D. R. (2014). *Group dynamics* (6th ed.). Belmont, CA: Cengage.

Foster, S. (1996). October is National Disability Employment Awareness Month. *Counseling Today, 39*(4), 18.

Fouad, N. A. (2007). Work and vocational psychology: Theory, research, and applications. *Annual Review of Psychology, 58*(5), 1–22.

Fowler, J. W. (1981). *Stages of faith.* New York, NY: Harper and Row.

Frank, J. D., & Frank, J. B. (2004). Therapeutic components shared by all psychotherapies. In A. Freeman, M. J. Mahoney, P. Devito, & D. Martin (Eds.), *Cognition and psychotherapy* (2nd ed., pp. 45–78). New York, NY: Springer.

Fretz, B. R., & Mills, D. H. (1980). *Licensing and certification of psychologists and counselors.* San Francisco, CA: Jossey-Bass.

Frey, D. H. (1972). Conceptualizing counseling theories. *Counselor Education and Supervision, 11,* 243–250.

Frey, L. L., Beesley, D., & Liang, Y. (2009). The Client Evaluation of Counseling Inventory: Initial validation of an instrument measuring counseling effectiveness. *Training and Education in Professional Psychology, 3,* 28–36.

Fujiura, G. T. (2001). Emerging trends in disability. *Population Today, 29,* 9–10.

Fullen, M. (2016, July). Have you gone gray? *Counseling Today, 59*(1), 44–49.

Galambos, N. L., Barker, E. T., & Krahn, H. J. (2006). Depression, self-esteem, and anger in emerging adulthood: Seven-year trajectories. *Developmental Psychology, 42,* 350–365.

Gallagher, A. M. (2011, October 30). *Biopsychosocial assessment.* Presentation at Wake Forest University, Winston-Salem, NC.

Gazda, G. M. (1989). *Group counseling: A developmental approach* (4th ed.). Boston, MA: Allyn & Bacon.

Gazda, G. M., Balzer, F. J., Childers, W. C., Nealy, A., Phelps, R. E., & Walters, R. P. (2005). *Human relations development: A manual for educators* (7th ed.). Boston, MA: Allyn & Bacon.

Gazda, G. M., Ginter, E. J., & Horne, A. M. (2001). *Theory and practice of group psychotherapy.* Boston, MA: Allyn & Bacon.

Gerig, M. S. (2014). *Foundations for mental health and community counseling: An introduction to the profession* (2nd ed.). Upper Saddle River, NJ: Pearson.

Gibson, D. M., & Myers, J. E. (2006). Perceived stress, wellness, and mattering: A profile of first-year Citadel cadets. *Journal of College Student Development, 47,* 647–660.

Gilbert, L. A. (1985). *Men in dual-career families: Current realities and future prospects.* Hillsdale, NJ: Erlbaum.

Gilbert, R. M. (2006). *The eight concepts of Bowen theory.* Falls Church, VA: Leading Systems Press.

Gilligan, C. (1982). *In a different voice: Psychological theory and women's development.* Cambridge, MA: Harvard University Press.

Ginter, E. J. (1999). David K. Brooks' contribution to the developmentally based life-skills approach. *Journal of Mental Health Counseling, 21,* 191–202.

Giordano, A. L., Prosek, E. A., Daly, C. M., Holm, J. M., Ramsey, Z. B., Abernathy, M. R., & Sender, K. M. (2015). Exploring the relationship between religious coping and spirituality among three types of collegiate substance abuse. *Journal of Counseling and Development, 93,* 70–79.

Gladding, S. T. (1973). Reality sits in a green-cushioned chair. *Personnel and Guidance Journal, 54,* 222.

Gladding, S. T. (1974a). Patchwork. *Personnel and Guidance Journal, 53,* 39.

Gladding, S. T. (1974b). Without applause. *Personnel and Guidance Journal, 52,* 586.

Gladding, S. T. (1975). Autumn storm. *Personnel and Guidance Journal, 54,* 149.

Gladding, S. T. (1978). In the midst of the puzzles and counseling journey. *Personnel and Guidance Journal, 57,* 148.

Gladding, S. T. (1979). A restless presence: Group process as a pilgrimage. *The School Counselor, 27,* 126–127.

Gladding, S. T. (1984). Bittersweet. *Counseling and Values, 28,* 146.

Gladding, S. T. (1986/1995). Thoughts of a Wall Street counselor. *Journal of Humanistic Education and Development, 24,* 176.

Gladding, S. T. (1990). Coming full cycle: Reentry after the group. *Journal for Specialists in Group Work, 15,* 130–131.

Gladding, S. T. (1995). Humor in counseling: Using a natural resource. *Journal of Humanistic Education and Development, 34,* 3–12.

Gladding, S. T. (2015). *Family therapy: History, theory, and practice* (6th ed.). Hoboken, NJ: Pearson.

Gladding, S. T. (2016a). *The creative arts in counseling* (5th ed.). Alexandria, VA: American Counseling Association.

Gladding, S. T. (2016b). *Group work: A counseling specialty* (7th ed.). Hoboken, NJ: Pearson.

Gladding, S. T. (in press). *Counseling: A comprehensive profession* (8th ed.). Hoboken, NJ: Pearson.

Gladding, S. T., & Wallace, M. J. D. (2016). Promoting beneficial humor in counseling: A way of helping counselors help clients. *Journal of Creativity in Mental Health, 11*, 2–11.

Gladstein, G. A., & Apfel, F. S. (1987). A theoretically based adult career counseling center. *Career Development Quarterly, 36*, 178–185.

Gledhill, J., & Hodes, M. (2011). The treatment of adolescents with depression. *Current Medical Literature—Psychiatry, 22*, 1–7.

Glosoff, H. L. (1998). Managed care: A critical ethical issue for counselors. *Counseling and Human Development, 31*, 1–16.

Glosoff, H. L. (2001, November). *Ethical practice in a complex era: Clients' rights, counselors' responsibilities.* Workshop presentation at Wake Forest University, Winston-Salem, NC.

Glosoff, H. L., Garcia, J., Herlihy, B., & Remley, T. P. (1999). Managed care: Ethical considerations for counselors. *Counseling and Values, 44*, 8–16.

Glosoff, H. L., Herlihy, B., & Spence, E. B. (2000). Privileged communication in the counselor–client relationship. *Journal of Counseling and Development, 78*, 454–462.

Goeller, G. (2004). *Coming of age with aging parents.* Spokane, WA: Patina.

Gold, J. M. (2010). *Counseling and spirituality: Integrating spiritual and clinical orientations.* Upper Saddle River, NJ: Merrill Pearson.

Goldberg, J. R. (1992, August). The new frontier: Marriage and family therapy with aging families. *Family Therapy News, 23*, 1, 14, 21.

Goldenberg, H., & Goldenberg, I. (2013). *Family therapy: An overview* (8th ed.). Belmont, CA: Brooks/Cole.

Goldin, E., & Mohr, R. (2000). Issues and techniques for counseling long-term, later-life couples. *The Family Journal, 8*, 229–235.

Goldman, L. (1990). Qualitative assessment. *The Counseling Psychologist, 18*, 205–213.

Goldsmith, J. S., & Kurpius, S. E. R. (2015). Older adults and integrated health settings: Opportunities and challenges for mental health counselors. *Journal of Mental Health Counseling, 37*, 124–137.

Good, G. E., Thomson, D. A., & Brathwaite, A. D. (2005). Men and therapy: Critical concepts, theoretical frameworks, and research recommendations. *Journal of Clinical Psychology, 61*, 699–711.

Goode, W. J. (1960). A theory of role strain. *American Sociological Review, 25*, 483–496.

Goodman, J. E. (2009). Starfish, salmon, and whales: An introduction to the special section. *Journal of Counseling and Development, 87*, 259.

Goodman, R. D. (2015). Trauma counseling and interventions: Introduction to the special issue. *Journal of Mental Health Counseling, 37*, 283–294.

Goodman, J., Schlossberg, N., & Anderson, M. (2006). *Counseling adults in transition: Linking practice with theory* (3rd ed.). New York, NY: Springer.

Goodyear, R. K. (1981). Termination as a loss experience for the counselor. *Personnel and Guidance Journal, 59*, 349–350.

Goodyear, R. K. (1984). On our journal's evolution: Historical developments, transitions, and future directions. *Journal of Counseling and Development, 63*, 3–9.

Gottfredson, G. D., & Holland, J. L. (1996). *Dictionary of Holland occupational codes* (3rd ed.). Odessa, FL: Psychological Assessment Resources.

Gottman, J., & Silver, N. (2015). *The seven principles of making marriage work* (Rev. ed.). Easton, PA: Harmony Books.

Gould, M. S., Marrocco, F. A., Kleinman, M., Thomas, J. G., Mostkoff, K., Cote, J., & Davies, M. (2005). Evaluating iatrogenic risk of youth suicide screening programs. *Journal of the American Medical Association, 293*(13), 1635–1643.

Granello, D. H., & Gibbs, T. A. (2016). The power of language and labels: "The mentally ill" versus "people with mental illnesses." *Journal of Counseling and Development, 94*, 31–40.

Granello, D. H., & Young, M. E. (2012). *Counseling today: Foundations of professional identity.* Upper Saddle River, NJ: Pearson.

Granello, P. (2013). *Wellness counseling.* Upper Saddle River, NJ: Pearson.

Granello, P. F., & Witmer, J. M. (2013). Theoretical models for wellness counseling. In P. F. Granello (Ed.), *Wellness counseling* (pp. 29–36). Upper Saddle River, NJ: Pearson.

Grant, A. M. (2003). The impact of life coaching on goal attainment, metacognition and mental health. *Social Behavior and Personality, 31*, 253–265.

Grant, B. (1992). The moral nature of psychotherapy. In M. T. Burke & J. G. Miranti (Eds.), *Ethical and spiritual values in counseling* (pp. 27–35). Alexandria, VA: American Counseling Association.

Gray, E. (2015, April 9). A record percentage of women don't have kids. Here's why that makes sense. *The Huffington Post.* Retrieved from www.huffingtonpost.com/2015/04/09/childless-more-women-are-not-having-kids-says-census_n_7032258.html

Greason, D. P., Newsome, D. W., Henderson, D. A., McCarthy, C. C., & Wyche, B. E. (2012, March). *Mindfulness and ADHD.* Presentation for the American Counseling Association National Conference, San Francisco, CA.

Greason, D. P. B. (2011). The transition stage in group work. In B. T. Erford (Ed.), *Group work process and application* (pp. 103–120). Upper Saddle River, NJ: Pearson.

Grossbard, J. R., Atkins, D. C., Geisner, I. M., & Larimer, M. E. (2012). Does depressed mood moderate in the influence of drive for thinness and muscularity on eating disorder symptoms among college men? *Psychology of Men and Masculinity.* doi:10.1037/a0028913

Grundy, E., & Tomassini, C. (2010). Marital history, health and mortality among older men and women in England and Wales. *BMC Public Health, 10,* 554.

Gurman, A., & Kniskern, D. (Eds.). (1981). Family therapy outcome research: Knowns and unknowns. In A. Gurman & D. Kniskern (Eds.), *Handbook of family therapy* (pp. 742–775). New York, NY: Brunner/Mazel.

Gurman, A. S., Lebow, J. L. & Synder, D. K. (2016). Clinical handbook of couple therapy (5th ed.). New York, NY: Guilford Press.

Gysbers, N. C., Heppner, J. A., & Johnston, J. A. (2014). *Career counseling: Process, issues, and techniques* (4th ed.). Alexandria, VA: American Counseling Association.

Haber, D. (2006). Life review: Implementation, theory, research, and therapy. *The International Journal of Aging and Human Development, 63*(2), 153–171.

Haddock, S. A. (2002). Training family therapists to assess for and intervene in partner abuse: A curriculum for graduate courses, professional workshops, and self-study. *Journal of marital and family therapy, 28,* 193–202.

Hadley, R. G., & Mitchell, L. K. (1995). *Counseling research and program evaluation.* Pacific Grove, CA: Brooks/Cole.

Hagedorn, W. B. (2011). Using therapeutic letters to navigate resistance and ambivalence: Experiential implications for group counseling. *Journal of Addictions and Offender Counseling, 31,* 108–126.

Hagedorn, W. B., & Hirshhorn, M. A. (2009). When talking won't work: Implementing experiential group activities with addicted clients. *Journal for Specialists in Group Work, 34,* 43–67.

Hagermoser L. M., Sanetti, L. M. H., & Kratochwill, T. R. (2009). Treatment integrity assessment in the schools: An evaluation of the Treatment Integrity Planning Protocol (TIPP). *School Psychology Quarterly, 24,* 24–35.

Haight, B. K., & Haight, B. S. (2007). *The handbook of structured life review.* Baltimore, MD: Health Professions Press.

Haley, J. (1973). *Uncommon therapy.* New York, NY: Norton.

Haley, M., & Vasquez, J. (2009). Technology and counseling. In D. Capuzzi & D. R. Gross (Eds.), *Introduction to the counseling profession* (5th ed., pp. 156–186). Boston, MA: Pearson/ Allyn & Bacon.

Hall, L. K. (2017). *Counseling military families: What mental health professionals need to know* (2nd ed.). New York, NY: Routledge.

Halligan, F. R., Pohl, J. A., & Smith, M. K. (2006). Weeding and seeding: Programming for alcohol abuse prevention and wellness enhancement in an undergraduate population. *Journal of College Student Psychotherapy, 20*(3), 33–51.

Ham, L. S., Zamboanga, B. L., Bacon, A. K., & Garcia, T. A. (2009). Drinking motives as mediators of social anxiety and hazardous drinking among college students. *Cognitive Behaviour Therapy, 38*(3), 133–145.

Hamachek, D. E. (1988). Evaluating self-concept and ego development within Erikson's psychosocial framework: A formulation. *Journal of Counseling and Development, 66,* 354–360.

Hamilton, M. (1960). A rating scale for depression. *Journal of Neurology, Neurosurgery, and Psychiatry, 23,* 56–62.

Hampton, D. (2002, 2012). *Grief counseling: It's all about loss.* Unpublished manuscript.

Hanna, F. J., & Cardona, B. (2013). Multicultural counseling beyond the relationship: Expanding the repertoire with techniques. *Journal of Counseling and Development, 91,* 349–357.

Hansen, J. C., Rossberg, R. H., & Cramer, S. H. (1994). *Counseling: Theory and process* (5th ed.). Boston, MA: Allyn & Bacon.

Hansen, J. C., Warner, R. W., & Smith, E. J. (1980). *Group counseling* (2nd ed.). Chicago, IL: Rand McNally.

Harold, M. (1985). Council's history examined after 50 years. *Guidepost, 27*(10), 4.

Harrington, J. A. (2013). Contemporary issues in private practice: Spotlight on the self-employed mental health counselor. *Journal of Mental Health Counseling, 35,* 189–197.

Harris, A. H. S., Thoresen, C. E., & Lopez, S. J. (2007). Integrating positive psychology into counseling: Why and (when appropriate) how. *Journal of Counseling and Development, 85,* 3–13.

Harris, E. C., & Barraclough, B. (1997). Suicide as an outcome for mental disorders. A meta-analysis. *British Journal of Psychiatry, 170,* 205–228.

Harris, R. (2013). *Getting unstuck in ACT: A clinician's guide to overcoming common obstacles in Acceptance and Commitment Therapy.* Oakland, CA: New Harbinger.

Hartung, P. J., & Blustein, D. L. (2002). Reason, intuition, and social justice: Elaborating on Parsons' career decision-making model. *Journal of Counseling and Development, 80,* 41–47.

Hattie, J. A., Myers, J. E., & Sweeney, T. J. (2004). A factor structure of wellness: Theory, assessment, analysis, and practice. *Journal of Counseling and Development, 82,* 354–364.

Havighurst, R. J. (1972). *Developmental tasks and education* (3rd ed.). New York, NY: David McKay.

Hay, C. E., & Kinnier, R. T. (1998). Homework in counseling. *Journal of Mental Health Counseling, 20,* 122–132.

Hayes, R. L. (1984, March). Report on community counseling. *ACES Newsletter,* 15.

Hays, D. G. (2013). *Assessment in counseling: A guide to the use of psychological assessment procedures.* Alexandria, VA: American Counseling Association.

Hays, D. G., & Erford, B. T. (Eds.). (2014). *Developing multicultural counseling competence* (2nd ed.). Upper Saddle River, NJ: Pearson.

Hays, P. A. (2016). *Addressing cultural complexities in practice: Assessment, diagnosis, and therapy* (3rd ed.). Washington, DC: American Psychological Association.

Hazelden. (2016). *What is treatment like at Hazelden and how is it done?* Retrieved from www.hazelden.org/web/public/faqtreatment.page

Health Information Technology for Economic and Clinical Health (HITECH) Act, Title XIII of Division A and Title IV of Division B of the American Recovery and Reinvestment Act of 2009 (ARRA), Pub. L. No. 111-5 (2009).

Health Insurance Portability and Accountability Act of 1996 (HIPAA), Pub. L. No. 104-191. (See also HIPAA Privacy Rule, 45 C.F.R. § §160.101-160.312, 2010.)

Heidemeir, H., & Staudinger, U. M. (2012). Self-evaluation processes in life satisfaction: Uncovering measurement non-equivalence and age-related differences. *Social Indicators Research, 105*(1), 39–61.

Hemingway, M. (2015). *Out came the sun.* New York, NY: Regan Arts.

Henderson, D. A., & Thompson, C. L. (2016). *Counseling children* (9th ed.). Boston, MA: Cengage.

Henderson, S. J. (2000). "Follow your bliss": A process for career happiness. *Journal of Counseling and Development, 78,* 305–315.

Henggeler, S. W., Schoenwald, S. K., Borduin, C. M., Rowland, M. D., & Cunningham, P. B. (1998). *Multisystemic treatment of antisocial behavior in youth.* New York, NY: Guilford.

Henriksen, R. C., Jr., & Maxwell, M. J. (2016). Counseling the fastest growing population in America: Those with multiple heritage backgrounds. *Journal of Mental Health Counseling, 38,* 1–11.

Heppner, P. P. (1990). Life lines: Institutional perspectives [Feature editor's introduction]. *Journal of Counseling and Development, 68,* 246.

Herek, G. M. (2006). Legal recognition of same-sex relationships in the United States: A social science perspective. *American Psychologist, 61,* 607–621.

Herlihy, B., & Corey, G. (2015). *ACA ethical standards casebook* (7th ed.). Alexandria, VA: American Counseling Association.

Herlihy, P. A. (2000). Employee assistance and work/family programs: Friends or foes? *Employee Assistance Quarterly, 16,* 33–52.

Hermann, M. A. (2011, April 29). *Legal and ethical issues in counseling.* Presentation at Wake Forest University, Winston-Salem, NC.

Hermann, M. A., & Herlihy, B. R. (2006). Legal and ethical implications of refusing to counsel homosexual clients. *Journal of Counseling and Development, 84,* 414–418.

Heron, M. (2016, February 16). Deaths: Leading causes 2013. *National Vital Statistics Reports, 65*(2). Retrieved from www.cdc.gov/nchs/data/nvsr/nvsr65/nvsr65_02.pdf

Herr, E. L. (1985). AACD: An association committed to unity through diversity. *Journal of Counseling and Development, 63,* 395–404.

Herr, E. L., Cramer, S. H., & Niles, S. G. (2004). *Career guidance and counseling through the lifespan: Systematic approaches* (6th ed.). Boston, MA: Allyn & Bacon.

Herr, E. L., & Fabian, E. S. (1993). The *Journal of Counseling and Development*: Its legacy and its aspirations. *Journal of Counseling and Development, 72,* 3–4.

Herring, R. D. (1997). *Multicultural counseling in schools.* Alexandria, VA: American Counseling Association.

Hershenson, D. B. (1998). Systemic, ecological model for rehabilitation counseling. *Rehabilitation Counseling Bulletin, 42,* 40–50.

Hershenson, D. B., Power, P. W., & Waldo, M. (1996). *Community counseling: Contemporary theory and practice.* Needham Heights, MA: Allyn & Bacon.

Hertz, R., & Marshall, N. L. (2001). *Working families: The transformation of the American home.* Berkeley: University of California Press.

Hetherington, E. M. (2006). The influence of conflict, marital problem solving, and parenting on children's adjustment in nondivorced, divorced, and remarried families. In A. Clarke-Stewart & J. Dunn (Eds.), *Families count* (pp. 203–236). New York, NY: Oxford University Press.

Hettler, W. (1984). Wellness: Encouraging a lifetime pursuit of excellence. *Health Values: Achieving High Level Wellness, 8,* 13–17.

Hildon, Z., Montgomery, S. M., Blane, D., Wiggins, R. D., & Netuveli, G. (2009). Examining resilience of quality of life in the face of health-related and psychosocial adversity at older ages: What is "right" about the way we age? *The Gerontologist, 5*(1), 36–47.

Hildon, Z., Smith, G., Netuveli, G., & Blane, D. (2008). Understanding adversity and resilience at older ages. *Sociology of Health and Illness, 30,* 726–740.

Hill, N. R., & Beamish, P. M. (2007). Treatment outcomes for obsessive-compulsive disorder: A critical review. *Journal of Counseling and Development, 85,* 504–510.

Hill, R. (1949). *Families under stress.* Westport, CT: Greenwood Press.

Hinduja, S., & Patchin, J. W. (2016). Cyberbullying research center. Retrieved from www.cyberbullying.us

Hinkle, J. S. (1999). A voice from the trenches: A reaction to Ivey and Ivey (1998). *Journal of Counseling and Development, 77,* 474–483.

Hobson, C. J., Delunas, L., & Kesic, D. (2001). Compelling evidence of the need for corporate work/life balance initiatives: Results from a national survey of stressful life-events. *Journal of Employment Counseling, 38,* 38–44.

Hochschild, A., & Machung, A. (2012). *The second shift: Working families and the revolution at home*. New York, NY: Penguin.

Hodges, S. (2012). *101 careers in counseling*. New York, NY: Springer.

Hohenshil, T. H. (1996). Role of assessment and diagnosis in counseling. *Journal of Counseling and Development, 75*, 64–67.

Hohenshil, T. H., Amundson, N. E., & Niles, S. G. (2013). *Counseling around the world: An international handbook*. Alexandria, VA: American Counseling Association.

Holland, J. L. (1994). *The occupations finder*. Odessa, FL: Psychological Assessment Resources.

Holland, J. L. (1997). *Making vocational choices: A theory of vocational preferences and work environments* (3rd ed.). Odessa, FL: Psychological Assessment Resources.

Hollis, J. W. (2000). *Counselor preparation 1999–2001: Programs, faculty, trends* (10th ed.). Philadelphia, PA: Taylor & Francis.

Hollis, J. W., & Wantz, R. A. (1980). *Counselor preparation*. Muncie, IN: Accelerated Development.

Hood, A. B., & Johnson, R. W. (2007). *Assessment in counseling: A guide to the use of psychological assessment procedures* (4th ed.). Alexandria, VA: American Counseling Association.

Hoogestraat, T., & Trammel, J. (2003). Spiritual and religious discussions in family therapy: Activities to promote dialogue. *The American Journal of Family Therapy, 31*, 413–426.

Horne, A. M., & Sayger, T. V. (2000). Behavioral approaches to couple and family therapy. In A. M. Horne (Ed.), *Family counseling and therapy* (3rd ed., pp. 454–488). Itasca, IL: F. E. Peacock.

Horowitz, J. L., & Newcomb, M. D. (1999). Bisexuality, not homosexuality: Counseling issues and treatment approaches. *Journal of College Counseling, 2*, 148–164.

Hosie, T. W., & Spruill, D. (1990, November). *Counselor employment and roles in three major types of EAP organizations*. Paper presented at the Southern Association for Counselor Education and Supervision Convention, Norfolk, VA.

Hosie, T. W., West, J. D., & Mackey, J. A. (1993). Employment and roles of counselors in employee assistance programs. *Journal of Counseling and Development, 71*, 355–359.

Howard, K. I., Orlinsky, D. E., & Bankoff, E. A. (1994). The research project on long-term psychotherapy: A qualitative analysis. *Journal of Counseling Psychology, 43*, 207–217.

Hoyt, M. F. (1995). *Brief therapy and managed care: Readings for contemporary practice*. San Francisco, CA: Jossey-Bass.

Hulse-Killacky, D., Killacky, J., & Donigian, J. (2001). *Making task groups work in your world*. Upper Saddle River, NJ: Prentice Hall.

Hutchins, D. E., & Vaught, C. G. (1997). *Helping relationships and strategies* (3rd ed.). Pacific Grove, CA: Brooks/Cole.

Ingersoll, R. E. (1994). Spirituality, religion, and counseling: Dimensions and relationships. *Counseling and Values, 38*, 98–111.

Ingram, B. L. (2012). *Clinical case formulations: Matching the integrative treatment plan to the client* (2nd ed.). Hoboken, NJ: John Wiley & Sons.

International Coach Foundation. (2016). What is professional coaching? Retrieved from www.coachfederation.org/

Ivanoff, A., Jang, S. J., Smyth, N. F., & Linehan, M. M. (1994). Fewer reasons for staying alive when you are thinking of killing yourself: The Brief Reasons for Living Inventory. *Journal of Psychopathology and Behavioral Assessment, 16*(1), 1–13.

Ivers, N. N., Johnson, D. A., Clarke, P. B., Newsome, D. W., & Berry, R. A. (2016). The relationship between mindfulness and multicultural counseling competence. *Journal of Counseling and Development, 94*, 72–82.

Ivey, A. E. (1971). *Microcounseling: Innovations in interviewing training*. Springfield, IL: Charles C Thomas.

Ivey, A. E., & Ivey, M. B. (2007). *Intentional interviewing and counseling* (7th ed.). Belmont, CA: Thomson Brooks/Cole.

Jackson, B. R., & Bergeman, C. S. (2011). How does religiosity enhance well-being? The role of perceived control. *Psychology of Religion and Spirituality, 3*(2), 149–161.

Jackson-Cherry, L. R., & Erford, B. T. (Eds.). (2014). *Crisis assessment, intervention, and prevention* (2nd ed.). Upper Saddle River, NJ: Pearson.

Jacobs, E. E., Schimmel, C. J., Masson, R. L. L., & Harvill, R. L. (2016). *Group counseling: Strategies and skills* (8th ed.). Boston, MA: Cengage.

Jaffee v. Redmond, WL 314841 (U.S. June 13, 1996).

James, M. D., & Hazler, R. J. (1998). Using metaphors to soften resistance in chemically dependent clients. *Journal of Humanistic Education and Development, 36*, 122–133.

James, R. K. (2008). *Crisis intervention strategies* (6th ed.). Belmont, CA: Thompson Brooks/Cole.

James, R. K., & Gilliland, B. E. (2017). *Crisis intervention strategies* (8th ed.). Boston, MA: Cengage Learning.

Jobes, D. A., Jacoby, A. M., Cimbolic, P., & Hustead, L. A. T. (1997). Assessment and treatment of suicidal clients in a university counseling center. *Journal of Counseling Psychology, 44*(4), 368–377.

Johnson, D. W., & Johnson, F. P. (2013). *Joining together: Group theory and group skills* (11th ed.). Upper Saddle River, NJ: Pearson.

Johnson, J. D. (1997). *Cancer-related information seeking*. New York, NY: Hampton Press.

Johnson, M. E., Fortman, J. B., & Brems, C. (1993). *Between two people: Exercises toward intimacy*. Alexandria, VA: American Counseling Association.

Johnson, S. M. (1998). Emotionally focused couple therapy. In F. M. Dattilio (Ed.), *Case studies in couple and family therapy* (pp. 450–472). New York, NY: Guilford.

Kabat-Zinn, J. (1990). *Full catastrophe living.* New York, NY: Delta.

Kabat-Zinn, J. (2005). *Wherever you go there you are: Mindfulness meditation in everyday life.* New York, NY: Hachette.

Kabat-Zinn, J. (2012). *Mindfulness for beginners: Reclaiming the present moment and your life.* Boulder, CO: Sounds True Inc.

Kadison, R., & Digeronimo, T. F. (2004). *College of the overwhelmed.* San Francisco, CA: Jossey-Bass.

Kalodner, C. R., & Van Lone, J. S. (2001). Eating disorders: Guidelines for assessment, treatment, and referral. In E. R. Welfel & R. E. Ingersoll (Eds.), *The mental health desk reference: A sourcebook for counselors and therapists* (pp. 119–128). New York, NY: Wiley.

Kaplan, D. M. (2002, July). Celebrating 50 years of excellence. *Counseling Today, 1,* 45.

Kaplan, D. M., & Coogan, S. L. (2005). The next advancement in counseling: The bio-psycho-social model. In G. R. Walz & R. K. Yep (Eds.), *VISTAS: Compelling perspectives on counseling 2005* (pp. 17–25). Alexandria, VA: American Counseling Association.

Kaplan, D. M., & Gladding, S. T. (2011). A vision for the future of counseling: The 20/20 principles for unifying and strengthening the profession. *Journal of Counseling and Development, 89,* 367–372.

Kaplan, D. M., Tarvydas, V. M., & Gladding, S. T. (2014). A vision for the future of counseling: The new consensus definition of counseling. *Journal of Counseling and Development, 92,* 366–372.

Kaplan, M., Kocet, M. M., Cottone, R. R., Glosoff, H. L., Miranti, J. G., Moll, E. C., & Tarvydas, V. M. (2009). New mandates and imperatives in the revised *ACA Code of Ethics. Journal of Counseling and Development, 87,* 241–256.

Kaplan, M. S., Huguet, N., McFarland, B. H., & Newsom, J. T. (2007). Suicide among male veterans: A prospective population-based study. *Journal of Epidemiology and Community Health, 61,* 619–624.

Kaplan, R. (2000). Two pathways to prevention. *American Psychologist, 55,* 382–396.

Kaslow, F. W. (1991). The art and science of family psychology. *American Psychologist, 46,* 621–626.

Kaukinen, C., Gover, A. R., & Hartman, J. L. (2011). College women's experiences of dating violence in casual and exclusive relationships. *American Journal of Criminal Justice, 37*(2), 146–162.

Kay, E. (2003). *Heroes at home.* Minneapolis, MN: Bethany House.

Kay, J. (2010). The rising prominence of college and university mental health issues. In J. Kay & V. Schwartz (Eds.), *Mental health care in the college community* (pp. 1–20). West Sussex, UK: Wiley-Blackwell.

Kazdin, A. E. (2008). Evidence-based treatment and practice: New opportunities to bridge clinical research and practice, enhance the knowledge base, and improve patient care. *American Psychologist, 63,* 146–159.

Keeton v. Anderson-Wiley, 664 F.3d 865 (11th Cir. 2011).

Keith, D. (2015). Continuing the experiential approach of Carl Whitaker: Process, practice and magic. Phoenix, AZ: Zeig, Tucker & Theisen.

Kelly, E. W., Jr. (1995). *Spirituality and religion in counseling and psychotherapy.* Alexandria, VA: American Counseling Association.

Kelly, V. A. (2016). *Addiction in the family: What every counselor needs to know.* Hoboken, NJ: Wiley.

Kemp, A. (1998). *Abuse in the family: An introduction.* Pacific Grove, CA: Brooks/Cole.

Kendall, P. C. (2012). Guiding theory for therapy with children and adolescents. In P. C. Kendall (Ed.), *Child and adolescent therapy: Cognitive-behavioral procedures* (4th ed., pp. 3–26). New York, NY: Guilford Press.

Kennedy, A. (2008, July). Next stop, adulthood. *Counseling Today, 51*(1), 42–45.

Kennedy, S. (2001). Organizational change affects work stress and work-family balance. *Australian and New Zealand Journal of Family Therapy, 22,* 105–106.

Kerr, M. E., & Bowen, M. (1988). *Family evaluation: An approach based on Bowen theory.* New York, NY: Norton.

Kessler, D. (2012). *10 best and worst things to say to someone in grief.* Retrieved from grief.com/helpful-tips/the-10-best-and-worst-things-to-say-to-someone-in-grief/

Kiesler, C. A. (2000). The next wave of change for psychology and mental health services in the health care revolution. *American Psychologist, 55,* 481–487.

Kinnier, R. T., Brigman, S. L., & Noble, F. C. (1990). Career indecision and family enmeshment. *Journal of Counseling and Development, 68,* 309–312.

Kinsey, A. C., Pomeroy, W. B., & Martin, C. E. (1948). *Sexual behavior in the human male.* Philadelphia, PA: Saunders.

Kiselica, M. S., & Look, C. T. (1993). Mental health counseling and prevention: Disparity between philosophy and practice? *Journal of Mental Health Counseling, 15,* 3–14.

Kiselica, M. S., & Robinson, M. (2001). Bringing advocacy counseling to life: The history, issues, and human dramas of social justice work in counseling. *Journal of Counseling and Development, 79,* 387–397.

Kitchener, K. S. (1984). Intuition, critical evaluation, and ethical principles: The foundation for ethical decisions in counseling psychology. *The Counseling Psychologist, 12,* 43–55.

Klein, A., & Noel, B. (2006). *The single parent resource* (rev., exp. ed.). Naperville, IL: Sourcebooks.

Klein, S. (1998). *Heavenly hurts: Surviving AIDS-related deaths and losses.* New York, NY: Baywood.

Kleinke, C. L. (2002). *Coping with life challenges* (2nd ed.). Prospect Height, IL: Waveland.

Kleist, D. M. (1999). The state of prevention in mental health counseling and counselor education. In J. S. Hinkle (Ed.), *Promoting optimum mental health through counseling: An overview* (pp. 35–40). Greensboro, NC: ERIC/CASS.

Knauer, N. J. (2009). LGBT elder law: Towards equity in aging. *Harvard Journal of Law and Gender, 32,* 308–358.

Kocet, M. M., & Herlihy, B. J. (2014). Addressing value-based conflicts within the counseling relationship: A decision-making model. *Journal of Counseling and Development, 92,* 180–186.

Koenig, H. G., George, L. K., & Titus, P. (2004). Religion, spirituality, and health in medically ill hospitalized older patients. *Journal of the American Geriatrics Society, 52,* 554–562.

Kottler, J. A. (1993). *On being a therapist.* San Francisco, CA: Jossey-Bass.

Kottler, J. A. (1994). Working with difficult group members. *Journal for Specialists in Group Work, 19,* 3–10.

Kottler, J. A., & Brown, R. W. (2000). *Introduction to therapeutic counseling: Voices from the field* (4th ed.). Belmont, CA: Wadsworth.

Kottler, J. A., & Schofield, M. (2001). When therapists face stress and crisis: Self-initiated coping strategies. In E. R. Welfel & R. E. Ingersoll (Eds.), *The mental health desk reference* (pp. 426–431). New York, NY: Wiley.

Kovacs, M. (1992). *Children's Depression Inventory.* North Tonawanda, NY: Multi-Health Systems.

Kowal, J., Johnson, S. M., & Lee, A. (2003). Chronic illness in couples: A case of emotionally focused therapy. *Journal of Marital and Family Therapy, 29,* 299–310.

Kraft, D. P. (2011). One hundred years of college mental health. *Journal of American College Health, 59*(6), 477–481.

Krumboltz, J. D. (Ed.). (1966). *Revolution in counseling.* Boston, MA: Houghton Mifflin.

Krumboltz, J. D. (1979). *Social learning and career decision making.* New York, NY: Carroll.

Krumboltz, J. D. (1993). Integrating career and personal counseling. *Career Development Quarterly, 42,* 143–148.

Krumboltz, J. D., & Levin, A. S. (2010). *Luck is no accident* (2nd ed.). Atascadero, CA: Impact.

Kuhn, D., & Franklin, S. (2006). The second decade: What develops (and how)? In W. Damon & R. Lerner (Eds.), *Handbook of child psychology* (6th ed., pp. 953–993). New York, NY: Wiley.

Kurdek, L. A. (2006). Differences between partners from heterosexual, gay, and lesbian cohabitating couples. *Journal of Marriage and the Family, 68,* 509–528.

Kurtz, P. D., & Tandy, C. C. (1995). Narrative family interventions. In A. C. Kilpatrick & T. P. Holland (Eds.), *Working with families* (pp. 177–197). Boston, MA: Allyn & Bacon.

Labardee, L., Williams, P., & Hodges, S. (2012, November). Counselors who coach. *Counseling Today, 11,* 62–64.

L'Abate, L., Farrar, J. E., & Serritella, D. A. (1992). *Handbook of differential treatments for addictions.* Boston, MA: Allyn & Bacon.

Lambert, M. J., & Bergin, A. E. (1994). The effectiveness of psychotherapy. In A. E. Bergin & S. L. Garfield (Eds.), *Handbook of psychotherapy and behavior change* (pp. 143–189). New York, NY: Wiley.

Lambert, M. J., Hansen, N. B., Umpress, V., Lunnen, K., Okishi, J., & Bulingame, G. M. (1996). *Administration and scoring manual for the OQ-45.2.* Stevenson, MD: American Professional Credentialing.

Landreth, G. (1993). Child-centered play therapy. *Elementary School Guidance and Counseling, 28,* 17–29.

Langer, E. J. (2009). *Counter clockwise: Mindful health and the power of possibility.* New York, NY: Ballantine Books.

Langer, S. (2010). Gender differences in experimental disclosure: Evidence, theoretical explanations, and avenues for future research. *Sex Roles, 63,* 178–183.

Lapsley, D. K., & Quintana, S. M. (1985). Recent approaches to the moral and social education of children. *Elementary School Guidance and Counseling, 19,* 246–259.

Lawless, L. L., Ginter, E. J., & Kelly, K. R. (1999). Managed care: What mental health counselors should know. *Journal of Mental Health Counseling, 21,* 50–65.

Lawrence, G., & Robinson Kurpius, S. E. (2000). Legal and ethical issues involved when counseling minors in nonschool settings. *Journal of Counseling and Development, 78,* 130–136.

Lawson, D. (1994). Identifying pretreatment change. *Journal of Counseling and Development, 72,* 244–248.

Lazarus, R. S., & Folkman, S. (1984). *Stress, appraisal and coping.* New York, NY: Springer.

Lease, S. H., Horne, S. G., & Noffsinger-Frazier, N. (2005). Affirming faith experiences and psychological health for Caucasian lesbian, gay, and bisexual individuals. *Journal of Counseling Psychology, 52,* 378–388.

Lee, C. C. (2001). Defining and responding to racial and ethnic diversity. In D. C. Locke, J. E. Myers, & E. L. Herr (Eds.), *The handbook of counseling* (pp. 581–588). Thousand Oaks, CA: Sage.

Lee, C. C. (Ed.). (2007). *Counseling for social justice* (2nd ed.). Alexandria, VA: American Counseling Association.

Lee, C. C. (Ed.). (2013). *Multicultural issues in counseling: New approaches to diversity* (4th ed.). Alexandria, VA: American Counseling Association.

Lee, C. C., & Park, D. (2013). A conceptual framework for counseling across cultures. In C. C. Lee (Ed.), *Multicultural issues in counseling: New approaches to diversity* (4th ed., pp. 3–12). Alexandria, VA: American Counseling Association.

Lee, C. C., & Rodgers, R. A. (2009). Counselor advocacy: Affecting systemic change in the public arena. *Journal of Counseling and Development, 87,* 284–287.

Lee, C. C., & Walz, G. R. (Eds.). (1998). *Social action: A mandate for counselors*. Alexandria, VA: American Counseling Association.

Lee, J. M. (1966). Issues and emphases in guidance: A historical perspective. In J. M. Lee & N. J. Pallone (Eds.), *Readings in guidance and counseling*. New York, NY: Sheed & Ward.

Lee, R., Jordan, J., Stevens, M., & Jones, A. (2017). Middle adulthood: Physical and cognitive development. In B. T. Erford (Ed.), *An advanced life span odyssey for counseling professionals* (pp. 345–366). Boston, MA: Cengage.

Lee, S. L., Rothbard, A. B., & Noll, E. L. (2012). Length of inpatient stay of persons with serious mental illness: Effects of hospital and regional characteristics. *Psychiatric Services, 63,* 889–895.

Lee, S. M., Cho, S. H., Kissinger, D., & Ogle, N. T. (2010). A typology of burnout in professional counselors. *Journal of Counseling and Development, 88,* 131–138.

Lefley, H. P. (2009). A psychoeducational support group for serious mental illness. *Journal for Specialists in Group Work, 34,* 369–381.

Leibert, T. W. (2006). Making change visible: The possibilities of assessing mental health counseling outcomes. *Journal of Counseling and Development, 84,* 108–113.

Lemoire, S. J., & Chen, C. P. (2005). Applying person-centered counseling to sexual minority adolescents. *Journal of Counseling and Development, 83,* 146–154.

Lent, R. W., Brown, S. D., & Hackett, G. (1994). Toward a unifying social cognitive theory of career and academic interest, choice, and performance. *Journal of Vocational Behavior, 45,* 79–122.

Lent, R. W., Brown, S. D., & Hackett, G. (2000). Contextual supports and barriers to career choice: A social cognitive analysis. *Journal of Counseling Psychology, 47,* 36–49.

Leong, F. T., & Gupta, A. (2007). Career development and vocational behaviors of Asian Americans. In F. T. Leong, A. Ebreo, L. Kinoshita, A. G. Inman, & L. H. Yang (Eds.), *Handbook of Asian American psychology* (2nd ed., pp. 159–178). Thousand Oaks, CA: Sage.

Leppma, M., & Young, M. E. (2016). Loving-kindness meditation and empathy: A wellness group intervention for counseling students. *Journal of Counseling and Development, 94,* 297–305.

Lerner, M. (1994). Training for cancer: An interview with Michael Lerner. *Journal of Mind-Body Health, 10,* 27–37.

Levers, L. L. (2012). An introduction to counseling survivors of trauma: Beginning to understand the context of trauma. In L. L. Levers (Ed.), *Trauma counseling: Theories and interventions* (pp. 1–22). New York, NY: Springer.

Levers, L. L., & Buck, R. P. (2012). Contextual issues of community-based violence, violence-specific crisis and disaster, and institutional response. In L. L. Levers (Ed.), *Trauma counseling: Theories and interventions* (pp. 317–334). New York, NY: Springer.

Levine, M., Perkins, D. V., & Levine, M. (1997). *Principles of community psychology*. New York, NY: Oxford University Press.

Levinson, D. J. (1978). *The seasons of a man's life*. New York, NY: Ballantine.

Levinson, D. J. (1986). A conception of adult development. *American Psychologist, 41,* 3–13.

Levinson, D. J. (1996). *The seasons of a woman's life*. New York, NY: Knopf.

Levinson, D. J., Darrow, C. N., Klein, E. B., Levinson, M. H., & McKee, B. (1978). *The seasons of a man's life*. New York, NY: Random House.

Lewis, J. A., & Bradley, L. (2000). Introduction. In J. Lewis & L. J. Bradley (Eds.), *Advocacy in counseling: Counselors, clients, and community* (pp. 3–4). Greensboro, NC: Caps Publications.

Lewis, J. A., & Lewis, M. D. (1977). *Community counseling: A human services approach*. New York, NY: Wiley.

Lewis, J. A., Lewis, M. D., Daniels, J. A., & D'Andrea, M. J. (2003). *Community counseling: Empowerment strategies for a diverse society* (3rd ed.). Pacific Grove, CA: Brooks/Cole.

Lewis, J. A., Lewis, M. D., Packard, T., & Soufleé, F., Jr. (2001). *Management of human service programs* (3rd ed.). Belmont, CA: Wadsworth.

Lieberman, J. A., III, & Stuart, M. R. (1999). The BATHE method: Incorporating counseling and psychotherapy into the everyday management of patients. *Primary Care Companion to The Journal of Clinical Psychiatry, 1,* 35–38.

Liptak, J. J. (2001). *Treatment planning in career counseling*. Pacific Grove, CA: Brooks/Cole.

Liu, W. M. (2011). *Social class and classism in the helping professions: Research, theory, and practice*. Thousand Oaks, CA: Sage.

Liu, W. M., Pickett, T., Jr., & Ivey, A. E. (2007). White middle class privilege: Social class bias and implications for training and practice. *Journal of Multicultural Counseling and Development, 35,* 194–207.

Liu, W. M., & Watt, S. K. (2013). Counseling and the culture of economic disadvantage. In C. Lee (Ed.), *Multicultural issues in counseling: New approaches to diversity* (4th ed., pp. 259–274). Alexandria, VA: American Counseling Association.

Livneh, H., & Evans, J. (1984). Adjusting to disability: Behavioral correlates and intervention strategies. *Personnel and Guidance Journal, 62,* 363–368.

Livneh, H., & Wosley-George, E. T. (2001). Counseling clients with disabilities. In D. Capuzzi & D. R. Gross (Eds.), *Introduction to the counseling profession* (3rd ed., pp. 435–462). Needham Heights, MA: Allyn & Bacon.

Locke, D. C. (2001). ACES at its best: Celebrating the human spirit. *Counselor Education and Supervision, 40,* 242–251.

Loesch, L. C. (2001). Counseling program evaluation: Inside and outside the box. In D. C. Locke, J. E. Myers, & E. L. Herr (Eds.), *The handbook of counseling* (pp. 513–525). Thousand Oaks, CA: Sage.

Lopez, F. G. (1986). Family structure and depression: Implications for the counseling of depressed college students. *Journal of Counseling and Development, 64*, 508–511.

LoPiccolo, J. (1978). Direct treatment of sexual dysfunction. In J. LoPiccolo & L. LoPiccolo (Eds.), *Handbook of sex therapy* (pp. 1–17). New York, NY: Plenum.

Love, P., & Stosny, S. (2007). *How to improve your marriage without talking about it.* New York, NY: Broadway.

Luck, R. S. (1999). Rehabilitation counseling credentialing as a professional specialty. In G. L. Gandy, E. D. Martin, & R. E. Hardy (Eds.), *Counseling in the rehabilitation process: Community services for mental and physical disabilities* (2nd ed., pp. 271–288). Springfield, IL: Charles C Thomas.

Luepker, E. T. (2010). Videotaped life review: Its personal and intergenerational impact. *Clinical Social Work Journal, 38*(2), 183–192.

Lusky, M. B., & Hayes, R. L. (2001). Collaborative consultation and program evaluation. *Journal of Counseling and Development, 79*, 26–38.

Lustig, D. C., Rosenthal, D. A., Strauser, D. R., & Haynes, K. (2000, Spring). The relationship between sense of coherence and adjustment in persons with disabilities. *Rehabilitation Counseling Bulletin, 43*, 134–141.

Luzzo, D. A., & McWhirter, E. H. (2001). Sex and ethnic differences in the perception of educational and career-related barriers and levels of coping efficacy. *Journal of Counseling and Development, 79*, 61–67.

Lynch, R. K., & Maki, D. (1981). Searching for structure: A trait-factor approach to vocational rehabilitation. *Vocational Guidance Quarterly, 30*, 61–68.

Lynn, S. J., & Frauman, D. (1985). Group psychotherapy. In S. J. Lynn & J. P. Garske (Eds.), *Contemporary psychotherapies: Models and methods* (pp. 419–458). Columbus, OH: Merrill.

Lyoo, K., Noam, G. G., Lee, C. K., Lee, H. K., Kennedy, B. P., & Renshaw, P. F. (1996). The corpus callosum and lateral ventricles in children with attention-deficit hyperactivity disorder: A brain magnetic resonance imaging study. *Biological Psychiatry, 40*, 1060–1063.

MacCluskie, K. C., & Ingersoll, R. E. (2001). *Becoming a 21st century agency counselor: Personal and professional explorations.* Belmont, CA: Wadsworth.

Maccoby, E. E., & Martin, J. A. (1983). Socialization in the context of the family: Parent–child interaction. In R. H. Mussen (Series Ed.) & E. M. Hetherington (Vol. Ed.), *Handbook of child psychology: Vol. 4. Socialization, personality, and social development* (pp. 1–101). New York, NY: Wiley.

Mace, D., & Mace, V. (1977). *How to have a happy marriage: A step-by-step guide to an enriched relationship.* Nashville, TN: Abington.

MacKinlay, E., & Trevitt, C. (2010). Living in aged care: Using spiritual reminiscence to enhance meaning in life for those with dementia. *International Journal of Mental Health Nursing, 19*(6), 394–401.

Madanes, C. (1984). *Behind the one-way mirror: Advances in the practice of strategic therapy.* San Francisco, CA: Jossey-Bass.

Madanes, C. (1991). Strategic family therapy. In A. S. Gurman & D. P. Kniskern (Eds.), *Handbook of family therapy* (Vol. 2, pp. 396–416). New York, NY: Brunner/Mazel.

Maddi, S. (1999). The personality construct of hardiness: Effects on experiencing, coping, and strain. *Consulting Psychology Journal, 51*, 83–94.

Madonna, T. I. (2000). Providing mental health services under managed care arrangements: The challenges. *Hospital Topics, 78*, 23–27.

Mahaffy, K. A. (1996). Cognitive dissonance and its resolution: A study of lesbian Christians. *Journal for the Scientific Study of Religion, 35*, 392–402.

Manderscheid, R. W., & Sonnenschein, M. A. (1992). *Mental health in the United States, 1992* (DHHS Publication No. [SMA] 92–1942). Washington, DC: U.S. Government Printing Office.

Manley, R. S., Rickson, H., & Standeven, B. (2000). Children and adolescents with eating disorders: Strategies for teachers and school counselors. *Intervention in School and Clinic, 35*, 228–231.

Maples, M. F. (2009). The "transition experience": Group counseling for baby boomers. In L. B. Golden (Ed.), *Case studies in counseling older adults* (pp. 29–37). Upper Saddle River, NJ: Pearson.

March, J. S., Silva, S., Petrycki, S., Curry, J., Wells, K., Fairbank, J., … Severe, J. (2007). The treatment of adolescents with depression study (TADS): Long-term effectiveness and safety outcomes. *Archives of General Psychiatry, 64*(10), 1132–1143.

Martin, E. D., Jr. (1999). Foundations of rehabilitation. In G. L. Gandy, E. D. Martin, Jr., & R. E. Hardy (Eds.), *Counseling in the rehabilitation process: Community services for mental and physical disabilities* (2nd ed., pp. 5–31). Springfield, IL: Charles C Thomas.

Maslach, C. (2003). *Burnout: The cost of caring.* Cambridge, MA: Malor Books.

Masters, W. H., & Johnson, V. E. (1970). *Human sexual inadequacy.* Boston, MA: Little, Brown.

Matthews, D. A., McCullough, M. E., Larson, D. B., Koenig, H. G., Swyers, J. P., & Milano, M. G. (1998). Religious commitment and health status: A review of the research and implications for family medicine. *Archives in Family Medicine, 7*, 118–124.

Matthews, G. G. (2001). *Neurobiology: Molecules, cells and systems.* Malden, MA: Blackwell Science.

Maxmen, J. S., & Ward, N. G. (1995). *Essential psychopathology and its treatment* (2nd ed.). New York, NY: Norton.

Maxwell, M. (2007). Career counseling is personal counseling: A constructivist approach to nurturing the development of gifted female adolescents. *Career Development Quarterly, 55,* 206–224.

Maynard, P. E., & Olson, D. H. (1987). Circumplex model of family systems: A treatment tool in family counseling. *Journal of Counseling and Development, 65,* 502–504.

McCarn, S. R., & Fassinger, R. E. (1996). Revisioning sexual minority identity formation: A new model of lesbian identity and its implications for counseling and research. *The Counseling Psychologist, 24,* 508–534.

McClure, B. A. (1990). The group mind: Generative and regressive groups. *Journal for Specialists in Group Work, 15,* 159–170.

McClure, B. A. (1994). The shadow side of regressive groups. *Counseling and Values, 38,* 77–89.

McClure, F. H., & Teyber, E. (2003). *Casebook in child and adolescent treatment: Cultural and familial contexts.* Pacific Grove, CA: Brooks/Cole.

McCoy, G. A. (1994, April). A plan for the first group session. *The ASCA Counselor, 31,* 18.

McCrae, R. R., & Costa, P. T. (2010). *NEO inventories: Professional manual.* Lutz, FL: PAR.

McCubbin, H. I., & Patterson, J. M. (1982). Family adaptation in crisis. In H. I. McCubbin, A. E. Cauble, & J. M. Patterson (Eds.), *Family stress, coping, and social support* (pp. 26–47). Springfield, IL: Charles C. Thomas.

McCulloch, J., Ramesar, S., & Peterson, H. (1998). Psychotherapy in primary care: The BATHE technique. *American Family Physician.* Retrieved from www.aafp.org/afp/980501ap/mcculloc.html

McGoldrick, M. (2012). *The genogram journey* (Rev. ed.). New York, NY: W. W. Norton.

McGoldrick, M., Giordano, J., & Garcia-Preto, N. (Eds.). (2005). *Ethnicity and family therapy.* New York, NY: Guilford Press.

McGoldrick, M., Preto, M. A. G., & Carter, B. A. (2016). *The expanding family life cycle: Individual, family, and social perspectives* (5th ed.). Hoboken, NJ: Pearson.

McGoldrick, M., & Walsh, F. (1999). Death and the family life cycle. In B. Carter & M. McGoldrick (Eds.), *The expanded family life cycle* (3rd ed., pp. 185–201). Boston, MA: Allyn & Bacon.

McMahon, M., Patton, W., & Watson, M. (2003). Developing qualitative career assessment processes. *Career Development Quarterly, 51,* 194–202.

McNamara, S. (2000). *Stress in young people: What's new and what can we do?* New York, NY: Continuum.

McWhirter, B. T., & Burrow, J. J. (2001). Assessment and treatment recommendations for children and adolescents with depression. In E. R. Welfel & R. E. Ingersoll (Eds.), *The mental health desk reference* (pp. 199–205). New York, NY: Wiley.

McWhirter, E. H. (1994). *Counseling for empowerment.* Alexandria, VA: American Counseling Association.

McWhirter, E. H. (1997). Empowerment, social activism, and counseling. *Counseling and Human Development, 29,* 1–14.

McWhirter, E. H., & Flojo, J. R. (2001). Career counseling: Counseling for life. In D. Capuzzi & D. R. Gross (Eds.), *Introduction to the counseling profession* (3rd ed., pp. 188–207). Needham Heights, MA: Allyn & Bacon.

McWhirter, E. H., Joyce, J., & Aranda, C. L. (2009). *An introduction to career counseling.* In D. Capuzzi & D. R. Gross (Eds.), *Introduction to the counseling profession* (5th ed., pp. 263–291). Upper Saddle River, NJ: Pearson.

Mead, M. A., Hohenshil, T. H., & Singh, K. (1997). How the *DSM* system is used by clinical counselors: A national study. *Journal of Mental Health Counseling, 19,* 383–401.

Meisenhelder, J. B., & Chandler, E. N. (2002). Spirituality and health outcomes in the elderly. *Journal of Religion and Health, 42,* 243–252.

Mejia, X. E. (2005). Gender matters: Working with adult male survivors of trauma. *Journal of Counseling and Development, 83,* 29–40.

Merriman, J. (2015). Enhancing counsellor supervision through compassion fatigue education. *Journal of Counseling and Development, 93,* 370–378.

Meyers, H. H. (2007). Counseling and spirituality: Integrating wellness into practice. In P. K. S. Patrick (Ed.), *Contemporary issues in counseling* (pp. 320–338). New York, NY: Pearson/Allyn & Bacon.

Meyers, L. (2014, December). Look before you leap. *Counseling Today,* 37–45.

Miller, G. A. (2012). *Group exercises for addiction counseling.* Hoboken, NJ: Wiley.

Miller, I. J. (1996). Managed care is harmful to outpatient mental health services: A call for accountability. *Professional Psychology: Research and Practice, 27,* 349–363.

Miller, J. L., & House, R. M. (2005). Counseling gay, lesbian, and bisexual clients. In D. Capuzzi & D. R. Gross (Eds.), *Introduction to the counseling profession* (4th ed., pp. 430–464). Boston, MA: Pearson/Allyn & Bacon.

Miller, M. J. (2007). A bilinear multidimensional measurement model of Asian American acculturation and enculturation: Implications for counseling interventions. *Journal of Counseling Psychology, 54,* 118–131.

Miller, R. M., & Barrio Minton, C. A. B. (2016). Experiences learning interpersonal neurobiology: An interpretative phenomenological analysis. *Journal of Mental Health Counseling, 38,* 47–61.

Miller, W. R., & Rollnick, S. (2013). *Motivational interviewing: Preparing people for change* (3rd ed.). New York, NY: Guilford Press.

Miller-Perrin, C. L. (2001). Child maltreatment: Treatment of child and adolescent victims. In E. R. Welfel & R. E. Ingersoll (Eds.), *The mental health desk reference* (pp. 169–177). New York, NY: Wiley.

Millon, T., Davis, R., & Millon, C. (1997). *MCMI-III manual* (2nd ed.). Minneapolis, MN: National Computer Systems.

Minuchin, S. (1974). *Families and family therapy.* Cambridge, MA: Harvard University Press.

Minuchin, S., & Fishman, C. H. (1981). *Family therapy techniques.* Cambridge, MA: Harvard University Press.

Minuchin, S., Montalvo, B., Guerney, B., Rosman, B., & Schumer, F. (1967). *Families of the slums.* New York, NY: Basic Books.

Minuchin, S., Reiter, M. D., & Borda, C. (2014). The craft of family therapy: Challenging certainties. New York, NY: Routledge.

Mitchell, C. G. (1998). Perceptions of empathy and client satisfaction with managed behavioral health care. *Social Work, 43,* 404–411.

Mitchell, J. T. (2012). Crisis incident stress management. Retrieved from www.info-trauma.org/

Mitchell, K. E., Levin, A. S., & Krumboltz, J. D. (1999). Planned happenstance: Constructing unexpected career opportunities. *Journal of Counseling and Development, 77,* 115–124.

Mitchell, L. K., & Krumboltz, J. D. (1996). Krumboltz's learning theory of career choice and counseling. In D. Brown, L. Brooks, & Associates (Eds.), *Career choice and development* (3rd ed., pp. 233–280). San Francisco, CA: Jossey-Bass.

Mitchell, R. M. (2007). *Documentation in counseling records: An overview of ethical, legal, and clinical issues* (3rd ed.). Alexandria, VA: American Counseling Association.

Moen, P., & Spencer, D. (2006). Converging divergencies in age, gender, health, and well-being: Strategic selection in the third age. In R. H. Binstock & L. K. George (Eds.), *Handbook of aging and the social sciences* (6th ed., pp. 129–145). Burlington, MA: Academic Press.

Montalvo, B., & Thompson, R. F. (1988, July/August). Conflicts in the caregiving family. *Family Therapy Networker, 12,* 30–35.

Moore, K. (2012). Building a robustness against ageism: The potential role of coaching and coaching psychology. *Coaching Psychologist, 8*(1), 12–19.

Moore, K. A., Mbwana, K., Theokas, C., Lippman, L., Bloch, M., Vandivere, S., & O'Hare, W. (2011). Children's developmental contexts: An index based on data of individual children. *Child Trends Research Brief* (Publication #2011-11). Retrieved from www.childtrends.org

Morran, D. K. (1982). Leader and member self-disclosing behavior in counseling groups. *Journal for Specialists in Group Work, 7,* 218–223.

Morrison, D. R., & Cherlin, A. J. (1995). The divorce process and young children's well-being: A prospective analysis. *Journal of Marriage and the Family, 57,* 800–812.

Mostade, J. (2009). Affirmative counseling with transgendered persons. In C. Lee (Ed.), *Multicultural issues in counseling: New approaches to diversity* (3rd ed., pp. 303–318). Alexandria, VA: American Counseling Association.

Moursund, J., & Kenny, M. C. (2002). *The process of counseling and therapy* (4th ed.). Upper Saddle River, NJ: Prentice Hall.

Mufson, L., Moreau, D., Weissman, M. M., & Klerman, G. L. (1993). *Interpersonal psychotherapy for depressed adolescents.* New York, NY: Guilford Press.

Muse v. Charter Hospital of Winston-Salem, Inc., 117 N.C. App. 468 (1995).

Myer, R. A. (2001). *Assessment for crisis intervention: A triage assessment model.* Belmont, CA: Wadsworth.

Myer, R. A., Williams, R. C., Ottens, A. J., & Schmidt, A. E. (1992). Crisis assessment: A three-dimensional model for triage. *Journal of Mental Health Counseling, 14,* 137–148.

Myers, I. B., McCaulley, M. H., Quenk, N. L., & Hammer, A. L. (1998). *MBTI manual: A guide to the development and use of the Myers-Briggs Type Indicator* (3rd ed.). Palo Alto, CA: Consulting Psychologists Press.

Myers, J. E., & Shannonhouse, L. R. (2013). Combating ageism: Advocacy for older persons. In C. C. Lee (Ed.), *Multicultural issues in counseling: New approaches to diversity* (4th ed., pp. 151–170). Alexandria, VA: American Counseling Association.

Myers, J. E., & Sweeney, T. J. (2005a). *Counseling for wellness: Theory, research, and practice.* Alexandria, VA: American Counseling Association.

Myers, J. E., & Sweeney, T. J. (2005b). *Five Factor Wellness Inventory: Adult, teenage, and elementary school versions.* Menlo Park, CA: Mind Garden.

Myers, J. E., & Sweeney, T. J. (2008). Wellness counseling: The evidence base for practice. *Journal of Counseling and Development, 87*(4), 482–493.

Myers, J. E., Sweeney, T. J., & White, V. E. (2002). Advocacy for counseling and counselors: A professional imperative. *Journal of Counseling and Development, 80,* 394–402.

Myers, J. E., Sweeney, T. J., & Witmer, J. M. (2000). The wheel of wellness counseling for wellness: A holistic model for treatment planning. *Journal of Counseling and Development, 78,* 251–266.

Myers, J. E., & Williard, K. (2003). Integrating spirituality into counselor preparation: A developmental, wellness approach. *Counseling and Values, 47,* 142–155.

Nasar, J. L., & Devlin, A. S. (2011). Impressions of psychotherapists' offices. *Journal of Counseling Psychology, 58*(3), 310–320.

National Association of Social Workers (NASW). (2008). *Code of ethics.* Retrieved from www.socialworkers.org/pubs/code/code.asp

National Board for Certified Counselors (NBCC). (2012). *NBCC Code of Ethics.* Retrieved from www.nbcc.org/

National Board for Certified Counselors (NBCC). (2016a). *National certification and state licensure.* Retrieved from www.nbcc.org/Certification-Licensure

National Board for Certified Counselors (NBCC). (2016b). *Standards for distance professional services*. Retrieved from www.nbcc.org/Assets/Ethics/NBCCPolicyRegardingPracticeofDistanceCounselingBoard.pdf

National Career Development Association (NCDA). (2013). About NCDA. Retrieved from ncda.org/aws/NCDA/pt/sp/about

National Career Development Association (NCDA). (2015). *Code of ethics*. Broken Arrow, OK: Author.

National Career Development Association (NCDA). (2017). NCDA career development facilitator training. Retrieved from http://ncda.org/aws/NCDA/pt/sp/facilitator_overview

National Center for Missing and Exploited Children (NCMEC). (2016). *Child safety and prevention*. Retrieved from www.ncmec.org

National Child Traumatic Stress Network & National Center for PTSD. (2006, July). *Psychological first aid: Field operations guide* (2nd ed.). Retrieved from www.ncptsd.va.gov

National Coalition Against Domestic Violence (NCADV). (2016). *National Coalition Against Domestic Violence*. Retrieved from www.ncadv.org/

National Committee on Pay Equity (NCPE). (2012). The wage gap over time: In real dollars, women see a continuing gap. Retrieved from www.pay-equity.org/

National Council for Community Behavioral Healthcare. (2012). About us: Mission and vision. Retrieved from www.thenationalcouncil.org/cs/mission_and_vision

National Council on Alcoholism and Drug Dependence. (2017). Underage and college drinking. Retrieved from www.ncadd.org/about-addiction/underage-issues/underage-and-college-drinking

National Employment Counseling Association (NECA). (2016). About NECA. Retrieved from www.employment-counseling.org/About-NECA.aspx

National Fair Access Coalition on Testing. (2015). Mission. Retrieved from www.fairaccess.org/

National Highway Traffic Safety Administration. (2007). *Traffic safety facts*. Retrieved from nhtsa.gov/

National Hospice and Palliative Care Organization (NHPCO). (2016). *Advancing care at the end of life*. Retrieved from www.nhpco.org/

National Institute of Mental Health (NIMH). (2011a). *Depression in children and adolescents (fact sheet)*. Retrieved from www.nimh.nih.gov/health/publications/depression-in-children-and-adolescents/index.shtml

National Institute of Mental Health (NIMH). (2011b). *Eating disorders*. Retrieved from www.nimh.nih.gov/health/publications/eating-disorders/index.shtml

National Institute of Mental Health (NIMH). (2014). *Any disorder among adults*. Retrieved from www.nimh.nih.gov/health/statistics/prevalence/any-mental-illness-ami-among-us-adults.shtml

National Institute of Mental Health (NIMH). (2016a). *Attention deficit hyperactivity disorder (ADHD)*. Retrieved from www.nimh.nih.gov/health/publications/attention-deficit-hyperactivity-disorder/index.shtml

National Institute of Mental Health (NIMH). (2016b). *Child and adolescent mental health*. Retrieved from www.nimh.nih.gov/health/topics/child-and-adolescent-mental-health/ndex.shtml

National Institute of Mental Health (NIMH). (2016c). *Depression in men*. Retrieved from www.nimh.nih.gov/health/publications/men-and-depression/index.shtml

National Institute on Alcohol Abuse and Alcoholism. (2014). Alcohol facts and statistics. Retrieved from http://pubs.niaaa.nih.gov/publications/AlcoholFacts&Stats/AlcoholFacts&Stats.htm

National Organization for Victim Assistance (NOVA). (2016). Victims relation training. Retrieved from www.trynova.org/help-crisis-victim/relations-training

National Organization on Disability. (2010). 2010 gap survey of Americans with disabilities. Retrieved from www.2010disabilitysurveys.org/

National Victim Assistance Academy (NVAA). (2002). Victimization of individuals with disabilities. Retrieved from www.ovcttac.gov/views/TrainingMaterials/-dspSupportingCrimeVictims.cfm

National Wellness Institute. (n.d.). Dimensions of wellness. Retrieved from www.nationalwellness.org/index.php?id_tier=2&id_c=25

Nations, R. (2006, November). *Spirituality issues in counseling: Applying attachment theory in understanding spirituality and counseling*. Paper presented at Wake Forest University, Winston-Salem, NC.

Nauert, R. (2008). Stress hormone affects immune system. *PsychCentral*. Retrieved from http://psychcentral.com/news/2008/07/15/stress-hormone-affects-immune--system/2608.html

Nelligan, A. (1994, Fall). Balancing process and content: A collaborative experience. *Together, 23*, 8–9.

Nelson, D. L., Castonguay, L. G., & Locke, B. D. (2011). Challenging stereotypes of eating and body image concerns among college students: Implications for diagnosis and treatment of diverse populations. *Journal of College Counseling, 14*, 158–172.

Nelson, T. (2005). Ageism: Prejudice against our feared future self. *Journal of Social Issues, 61*, 207–221.

Neukrug, E. S. (2016). *The world of the counselor: An introduction to the counseling profession* (5th ed.). Boston, MA: Cengage.

Neukrug, E. S., & Fawcett, R. C. (2015). *Essentials of testing and assessment: A practical guide for counselors, social workers, and psychologists* (3rd ed.). Stamford, CT: Cengage.

Newsome, D., Yancu, C., Wilkerson, J., & Matthews, S. (2017). Relationships and psychosocial aspects of later adulthood. In B. T. Erford (Ed.), *An advanced life span odyssey for counseling professionals* (pp. 423–450). Boston, MA: Cengage.

Newsome, D. W. (1999). *Parental and school influences on adolescent academic achievement.* Unpublished doctoral dissertation, University of North Carolina, Greensboro.

Nichols, M. P. (2010). *Family therapy: Concepts and methods* (9th ed.). Upper Saddle River, NJ: Prentice Hall.

Nichols, W. C. (1993). *The AAMFT: 50 years of marital and family therapy.* Washington, DC: AAMFT.

Nicola, J. S. (1980). *Career and family roles of dual-career couples: Women in academia and their husbands.* Ann Arbor, MI: University Microfilms International.

Nigg, J. T., & Rappley, M. D. (2001). Interventions for attention-deficit/hyperactivity disorder. In E. R. Welfel & R. E. Ingersoll (Eds.), *The mental health desk reference* (pp. 183–190). New York, NY: Wiley.

Niles, S. G., & Harris-Bowlsbey, J. H. (2013). *Career development interventions in the 21st century* (4th ed.). Upper Saddle River, NJ: Merrill/Prentice Hall.

Nolan, J. M., Ford, S. J. W., Kress, V. E., Anderson, R. I., & Novak, T. C. (2005). A comprehensive model for addressing severe and persistent mental illness on campuses: The new diversity initiative. *Journal of College Counseling, 8,* 172–179.

North, M. S., & Fiske, S. T. (2012). An inconvenienced youth? Ageism and its potential intergenerational roots. *Psychological Bulletin, 138*(5), 982–997.

Nugent, F. A. (1981). *Professional counseling.* Monterey, CA: Brooks/Cole.

Nugent, F. A., & Jones, K. D. (2009). *An introduction to the profession of counseling* (5th ed.). Upper Saddle River, NJ: Pearson.

Nye, E. C., & Bell, J. B. (2007). Specific symptoms predict suicidal ideation in Vietnam combat veterans with chronic post-traumatic stress disorder. *Military Medicine, 172,* 144–147.

Nystul, M. S. (2016). *Introduction to counseling: An art and science perspective* (5th ed.). Thousand Oaks, CA: Sage.

Oestmann, J. (2007). The bio-psycho-social model: Integrating science and practice. In P. K. S. Patrick (Ed.), *Contemporary issues in counseling* (pp. 122–155). New York, NY: Pearson/Allyn & Bacon.

Ohlsen, M. M. (1977). *Group counseling* (2nd ed.). New York, NY: Holt, Rinehart & Winston.

Okun, B. F., & Kantrowitz, R. E. (2015). *Effective helping: Interviewing and counseling techniques* (8th ed.). Samford, CT: Cengage.

Olsen, L. D. (1971). Ethical standards for group leaders. *Personnel and Guidance Journal, 50,* 288.

Olson, D. H. (1986). Circumplex model VII: Validation studies and FACES III. *Family Process, 25,* 337–351.

Olson, D. H., DeFrain, J., & Skogrand, L. (2014). *Marriages and families: Intimacy, diversity, and strengths* (8th ed.). New York, NY: McGraw Hill.

Olson, D. H., & Gorall, D. M. (2003). Circumplex model of marital and family systems. In F. Walsh (Ed.). *Normal family processes* (3rd ed., pp. 514–548). New York, NY: Guilford Press.

O'Neil, J. M., & Carroll, M. R. (1988). A gender role workshop focused on sexism, gender role conflict, and the gender role journey. *Journal of Counseling and Development, 67,* 193–197.

Ong, A. D., & Bergeman, C. S. (2004). Resilience and adaptation to stress in later life: Empirical perspectives and conceptual implications. *Ageing International, 29*(3), 219–246.

Oravec, J. A. (2000). Online counselling and the Internet: Perspectives for mental health care supervision and education. *Journal of Mental Health, 9,* 121–135.

Orozco, G. L., Lee, W. M. L., Blando, J. A., & Shooshani, B. (2014). *Introduction to multicultural counseling for helping professionals* (3rd ed.). New York, NY: Taylor & Francis/Routledge.

Orton, G. L. (1997). *Strategies for counseling with children and their parents.* Pacific Grove, CA: Brooks/Cole.

Osborn, D. S., & Zunker, V. G. (2016). *Using assessment results for career development* (9th ed.). Boston, MA: Cengage Learning.

Ottens, A. J., & Klein, J. F. (2005). Common factors: Where the soul of counseling and psychotherapy resides. *Journal of Humanistic Counseling, Education, and Development, 44,* 32–45.

Page, B. J., Delmonico, D. L., Walsh, J., L'Amoreaux, N. A., Danninhirsh, C., & Thompson, R. S. (2000). Setting up on-line support groups using The Palace software. *Journal for Specialists in Group Work, 25,* 133–145.

Palma, T. V., & Stanley, J. L. (2002). Effective counseling with lesbian, gay, and bisexual clients. *Journal of College Counseling, 5,* 74–89.

Palmo, A. J. (2006). Highlight section: The professional counselor's role in prevention. In A. J. Palmo, W. J. Weikel, & D. P. Borsos (Eds.), *The foundations of mental health counseling* (3rd ed., pp. 415–421). Springfield, IL: Charles C Thomas.

Palmo, A. J., & Palmo, L. A. (2011). Counselors in private practice. In A. J. Palmo, W. J. Weikel, & D. P. Borsos (Eds.), *The foundations of mental health counseling* (4th ed., pp. 181–202). Springfield, IL: Charles C Thomas.

Papalia, D. E., & Martorell, G. (2015). *Experience human development* (13th ed.). Boston, MA: McGraw-Hill.

Papernow, P. L. (2013). *Surviving and thriving in stepfamily relationships: What works and what doesn't.* New York, NY: Routledge.

Parsons, F. (1909). *Choosing a vocation.* Boston, MA: Houghton Mifflin.

Parsons, R. D. (2009). *Translating theory to practice: Thinking and acting like an expert counselor.* Upper Saddle River, NJ: Pearson.

Paterson, J. (2011, June). Bullies with byte. *Counseling Today, 53,* 44–48.

Patrick, P. K. S. (2007). Stress-induced challenges to the counselor role: Burnout, compassion fatigue, and vicarious traumatization. In P. K. S. Patrick (Ed.),

Contemporary issues in counseling (pp. 210–250). Boston, MA: Pearson/Allyn & Bacon.

Patterson, G. R. (1971). *Families: Applications of social learning to family life.* Champaign, IL: Research Press.

Patton, M. (2008). *Utilization-focused evaluation* (4th ed.). Thousand Oaks, CA: Sage.

Paul, G. L. (1967). Strategy of outcome research in psychotherapy. *Journal of Consulting Psychology, 31,* 109–118.

Paulson, R. I. (1996). Swimming with the sharks or walking in the Garden of Eden: Two visions of managed care and mental health practice. In P. R. Raffoul & C. A. McNeece (Eds.), *Future issues of social work practice* (pp. 85–96). Needham Heights, MA: Allyn & Bacon.

Pavlicin, K. M. (2003). *Surviving deployment: A guide for military families.* St. Paul, MN: Elva Resa.

Pearlman, L. A., & Courtois, C. (2005). Clinical applications of the attachment framework: Relational treatment of complex trauma. *Journal of Traumatic Stress, 18*(5), 449–459.

Pearlman, L. A., & MacIan, P. (1995). Vicarious traumatization: An empirical study of the effects of trauma work on trauma therapists. *Professional Psychology: Research and Practice, 26*(6), 558–565.

Pearson, J. E. (1988). A support group for women with relationship dependency. *Journal of Counseling and Development, 66,* 394–396.

Peck v. Counseling Service of Addison County, 499 A.2d (Vt. 1985).

Pedersen, P. B. (1990). The constructs of complexity and balance in multicultural counseling theory and practice. *Journal of Counseling and Development, 68,* 550–554.

Pedersen, P. B. (2002). Ethics, competence, and other professional issues in culture-centered counseling. In P. B. Pedersen, J. G. Draguns, W. J. Lonner, & J. E. Trimble (Eds.), *Counseling across cultures* (5th ed., pp. 3–27). Thousand Oaks, CA: Sage.

Perls, F. S. (1969). *Gestalt therapy verbation.* Lafayette, CA: Real People Press.

Peterson, N., & Gonzalez, R. C. (Eds.). (2000). *Career counseling models for diverse populations.* Pacific Grove, CA: Brooks/Cole.

Peterson, N., & Priour, G. (2000). Battered women: A group vocational counseling model. In N. Peterson & R. C. González (Eds.), *Career counseling models for diverse populations* (pp. 205–218). Pacific Grove, CA: Brooks/Cole.

Petrocelli, J. V. (2002). Processes and stages of change: Counseling with the transtheoretical model of change. *Journal of Counseling and Development, 80,* 22–30.

Pfiffner, L. J., & Barkley, R. A. (1998). Treatment of ADHD in school settings. In R. A. Barkley (Ed.), *Attention deficit hyperactivity disorder: A handbook for diagnosis and treatment* (pp. 458–490). New York, NY: Guilford Press.

Piazza, N. J., & Baruth, N. D. (1990). Client record guidelines. *Journal of Counseling and Development, 68,* 313–316.

Pidcock, B. W., & Polansky, J. (2001). Clinical practice issues in assessing for adult substance use disorders. In E. R. Welfel & R. E. Ingersoll (Eds.), *The mental health desk reference: A sourcebook for counselors and therapists* (pp. 128–135). New York, NY: Wiley.

Piercy, K. W. (2010). *Working with aging families: Therapeutic solutions for caregivers, spouses, & adult children.* New York, NY: W. W. Norton.

Pietrofesa, J. J., Hoffman, A., & Splete, H. H. (1984). *Counseling: An introduction* (2nd ed.). Boston, MA: Houghton Mifflin.

Pinsof, W. M., & Wynne, L. C. (Eds.). (1995). Special issue: The effectiveness of marital and family therapy. *Journal of Marital and Family Therapy, 21,* 339–613.

Pinsof, W. M., & Wynne, L. C. (2000). Toward progress research: Closing the gap between family therapy practice and research. *Journal of Marital and Family Therapy, 26,* 1–8.

Platt, A., & Drew, M. (2013). Career counseling. In D. Capuzzi & D. Gross (Eds.), *Introduction to the counseling profession* (pp. 369–395). New York, NY: Routledge.

Polanski, P. J., & Hinkle, J. S. (2000). The mental status examination: Its use by professional counselors. *Journal of Counseling and Development, 78,* 357–364.

Ponterotto, J. G., & Casas, J. M. (1987). In search of multicultural competence within counselor education programs. *Journal of Counseling and Development, 65,* 430–434.

Pope, J. F., & Arthur, N. (2009). Socioeconomic status and class: A challenge for the practice of psychology in Canada. *Canadian Psychology, 50,* 55–65.

Pope, K., Sonne, J. L., & Greene, B. A. (2006). *What therapists don't talk about and why.* Washington, DC: American Psychological Association.

Pope, K. S., & Wedding, D. (2008). Current issues in psychotherapy. In R. J. Corsini & D. Wedding (Eds.), *Current psychotherapies* (8th ed., pp. 512–540). Belmont, CA: Thomson Brooks Cole.

Pope, M., Barret, B., Szymanski, D. M., Chung, Y. B., Singaravelu, H., McLean, R., & Sanabria, S. (2004). Culturally appropriate career counseling with gay and lesbian clients. *Career Development Quarterly, 53,* 158–177.

Pope, M., & Sweinsdottir, M. (2005). Frank, we hardly knew ye: The very personal side of Frank Parsons. *Journal of Counseling and Development, 83,* 105–115.

Pressly, P. K., & Heesacker, M. (2001). The physical environment and counseling: A review of theory and research. *Journal of Counseling and Development, 79,* 148–160.

Preston, J. D., O'Neal, J. H., & Talaga, M. C. (2010). *Handbook of clinical psychopharmacology for therapists* (6th ed.). Oakland, CA: New Harbinger.

Prieto, L. R., & Scheel, K. R. (2002). Using case documentation to strengthen trainees' case conceptualization skills. *Journal of Counseling and Development, 80,* 11–21.

Pritchard, M. E., Wilson, G. S., & Yamnitz, B. (2007). What predicts adjustment among college students? A longitudinal panel study. *Journal of American College Health, 56*(1), 15–21.

Prochaska, J. O., DiClemente, C. C., & Norcross, J. C. (1992). In search of how people change: Applications to addictive behaviors. *American Psychologist, 47,* 1102–1114.

Prochaska, J. O., & Norcross, J. C. (2014). *Systems of psychotherapy: A transtheoretical analysis* (8th ed.). Stamford, CT: Cengage Learning.

Promising Practices Network on Children, Families, and Communities. (2016). *Multisystemic therapy.* Retrieved from www.promisingpractices.net/program.asp?programid=81

Prosser, J. (1997). Transgender. In A. Medhurst & S. R. Munt (Eds.), *Lesbian and gay studies: A critical introduction* (pp. 309–326). Herndon, VA: Cassell.

Pueleo, S., & McGlothlin, J. (2014). Overview of crisis intervention. In L. R. Jackson-Cherry & B. T. Erford (Eds.). *Crisis assessment, intervention, and prevention* (pp. 1–25). Upper Saddle River, NJ: Pearson.

Quenk, N. (2000). *Essentials of Myers-Briggs Type Indicator assessment.* New York, NY: Wiley.

Quinnett, P. G. (2012). *Counseling suicidal people* (3rd ed.). Spokane, WA: QPR Institute.

Rajeski, W. J. (2008). Mindfulness: Reconnecting the body and mind in geriatric medicine and gerontology. *The Gerontologist, 48,* 135–141.

Ratner, H., George, E., & Iveson, C. (2013). *Solution focused brief therapy: 100 key points and techniques.* New York, NY: Routledge.

Ratts, M. J., Singh, A. A., Nassar-McMillan, S. N., Butler, S. K., & McCullough, J. R. (2015). Multicultural and social justice counseling competencies. Retrieved from www.counseling.org/docs/default-source/competencies/multicultural-and-social-justice-counseling-competencies.pdf?sfvrsn=20

Ratts, M. J., Toporek, R. L., & Lewis, J. A. (2010). *ACA advocacy competencies: A social justice framework for counselors.* Alexandria, VA: American Counseling Association.

Redcay, S. (2001). Helping children deal with loss. *The Counseling Corner from the American Counseling Association.* Retrieved from www.counseling.org/site/PageServer?pagename=publications_ccorner_corner801

Reed, E. E. (2014). Man up: Young men's lived experiences and reflections on counseling. *Journal of Counseling and Development, 92,* 428–437.

Reichenberg, L. W. (2014). *DSM-5 essentials: The savvy clinician's guide to the changes in criteria.* Hoboken, NJ: Wiley.

Reichenberg, L. W., & Seligman, L. (2016). *Selecting effective treatments: A comprehensive, systematic guide to treating mental disorders* (5th ed.). Hoboken, NJ: Wiley.

Reiner, S. M., Dobmeier, R. A., & Hernández, T. J. (2013). Perceived impact of professional counselor identity: An exploratory study. *Journal of Counseling and Development, 91,* 174–183.

Remley, T. P., Jr. (1992, Spring). You and the law. *American Counselor, 1,* 33.

Remley, T. P., Jr., & Herlihy, B. (2016). *Ethical, legal, and professional issues in counseling* (5th ed.). Hobokon, NJ: Pearson.

Remley, T. P., Jr., Herlihy, B., & Herlihy, S. B. (1997). The U.S. Supreme Court decision in *Jaffee v. Redmond:* Implications for counselors. *Journal of Counseling and Development, 75,* 213–218.

Reynolds, C. R., & Kamphaus, R. W. (2004). *Behavior assessment system for children* (2nd ed.). Circle Pines, MN: Pearson Assessment Group.

Rimsza, M. E., & Moses, K. S. (2005). Substance abuse on the college campus. *Pediatric Clinics of North America, 52,* 307–319.

Riordan, R. J., & Beggs, M. S. (1987). Counselors and self-help groups. *Journal of Counseling and Development, 65,* 427–429.

Ritter, K. Y., & Terndrup, A. I. (2002). *Handbook of affirmative psychotherapy with lesbians and gay men.* New York, NY: Guilford Press.

Robinson-Wood, T. L. (2017). *The convergence of race, ethnicity, and gender: Multiple identities in counseling* (5th ed.). Thousand Oaks, CA: Sage.

Rodriguez, C. P. (2004, September). *The biopsychosocial model.* Paper presented at Wake Forest University, Winston-Salem, NC.

Rogers, C. R. (1942). *Counseling and psychotherapy.* Boston, MA: Houghton Mifflin.

Rogers, C. R. (1987). The underlying theory: Drawn from experience with individuals and groups. *Counseling and Values, 32,* 38–46.

Roland, J. (1994). *Families, illness and disability.* New York, NY: Basic Books.

Rollins, J. (2008, July). Emerging client issues. *Counseling Today, 51*(1), 30–41.

Romano, J. L. (2001). Stress, coping, and well-being: Applications of theory to practice. In E. R. Welfel & R. E. Ingersoll (Eds.), *The mental health desk reference* (pp. 44–50). New York, NY: Wiley.

Romano, J. L., & Hage, S. M. (2000). Prevention and counseling psychology: Revitalizing commitments for the 21st century. *The Counseling Psychologist, 28,* 733–763.

Root, A. K., & Denham, S. A. (2010). The role of gender in the socialization of emotion: Key concepts and critical issues. *New Directions for Child and Adolescent Development, 128,* 1–9.

Rothrock, J. A. (1999). A personal experience of acceptance and adjustment to disability. In G. L. Gandy, E. D. Martin, Jr., & R. E. Hardy (Eds.), *Counseling in the rehabilitation process: Community services for mental and physical disabilities* (2nd ed., pp. 204–217). Springfield, IL: Charles C Thomas.

Rudd, M. D. (1989). The prevalence of suicidal ideation among college students. *Suicide and Life-Threatening Behavior, 19*, 173–183.

Rudow, H. (2012, May 22). Researcher of reparative therapy study retracts claims, says he owes gay community apology. *Counseling Today (CT) Daily*. Retrieved from ct.counseling.org/2012/05/researcher-of-reparative--therapy-study-retracts-claims-says-he-owes-gay--community-apology/

Russell-Chapin, L. (2016). Integrating neurocounseling into the counseling profession: An introduction. *Journal of Mental Health Counseling, 38*, 93–102.

Sager, J. B. (2001). Latin American lesbian, gay, and bisexual clients: Implications for counseling. *Journal of Humanistic Counseling, Education, and Development, 40*, 13–33.

Saidla, D. D. (1990). Cognitive development and group stages. *Journal for Specialists in Group Work, 15*, 15–20.

Saitz, R. (2005). Clinical practice: Unhealthy alcohol use. *New England Journal of Medicine, 10*, 596–607.

Sandhu, D. S. (Ed.). (2002). *Counseling employees: A multi-faceted approach*. Alexandria, VA: American Counseling Association.

Santos, P. J. (2004). Career dilemmas in career counseling groups: Theoretical and practical issues. *Journal of Career Development, 31*(1), 31–44.

Santrock, J. W. (2016). *Life-span development* (15th ed.). Boston: McGraw-Hill Higher Education.

Satir, V. M. (1967). *Conjoint family therapy*. Palo Alto, CA: Science and Behavior Books.

Satir, V. M. (1972). *Peoplemaking*. Palo Alto, CA: Science and Behavior Books.

Savage, T. A., Harley, D. A., & Nowak, T. M. (2005). Applying social empowerment strategies as tools for self-advocacy in counseling lesbian and gay male clients. *Journal of Counseling and Development, 83*, 131–137.

Savickas, M. L. (1989). Annual review: Practice and research in career counseling and development, 1988. *Career Development Quarterly, 38*, 100–134.

Savickas, M. L. (2005). The theory and practice of career construction. In S. D. Brown & R. W. Lent (Eds.), *Career development and counseling: Putting theory and research to work* (pp. 42–70). Hoboken, NJ: Wiley.

Savickas, M. L. (2010). *Life design: A general model for career intervention in the 21st century*. Paper presented at the Colloque International INETOP-CNAM.

Sburlati, E. S., Lyneham, H. J., Mufson, L. H., & Schniering, C. A. (2012). A model of therapist competencies for the empirically supported interpersonal psychotherapy for adolescent depression. *Clinical Child Family Psychological Review, 15*, 93–112.

Scarf, M. (1995). *Intimate worlds: Life inside the family*. New York, NY: Random House.

Schaffer, N. (2010). Do you still have social media privacy concerns? Retrieved from socialmediatoday.com/neals-chaffer/166038/do-you-still-have-social-media-privacy-concerns

Scharf, M., Mayseless, O., & Kivenson-Baron, I. (2004). Adolescents' attachment representations and developmental tasks in emerging adulthood. *Developmental Psychology, 40*, 430–444.

Schizophrenia.com. (2016). Schizophrenia facts and statistics. Retrieved from www.schizophrenia.com/szfacts.htm

Schlossberg, N. A. (1981). A model for analyzing human adaptation to transition. *The Counseling Psychologist, 9*, 2–18.

Schlossberg, N. A. (1984). *Counseling adults in transition*. New York, NY: Springer.

Schlossberg, N. A. (1991). *Overwhelmed: Coping with life's ups and downs*. Lexington, MA: Lexington Books.

Schlossberg, N. K. (2011, August 17). Transitions through life: Surviving every stage of life [Web blog post]. Retrieved from www.psychologytoday.com/blog/transitions-through-life/

Schneider, S. K., O'Donnell, L., Stueve, A., & Coulter, R. W. S. (2012, February). Cyberbullying, school bullying, and psychological distress: A regional census of high school students. *American Journal of Public Health, 102*, 171–177.

Schoenwald, S. K., Brown, T. L., & Henggeler, S. W. (2000). Inside multisystemic therapy: Therapist, supervisory, and program practices. *Journal of Emotional and Behavioral Disorders, 8*, 113–127.

Schure, M. B., Christopher, J., & Christopher, S. (2008). Mind-body medicine and the art of self-care: Teaching mindfulness to counseling students through yoga, meditation, and qigong. *Journal of Counseling and Development, 86*, 47–56.

Schwartz, A. J. (2006a). College student suicide in the United States: 1990–1991 through 2003–2004. *Journal of American College Health, 54*(6), 341–352.

Schwartz, A. J. (2006b). Four eras of study of college student suicide in the United States: 1920–2004. *Journal of American College Health, 54*(6), 353–366.

Schwartz, A. J. (2011). Suicidal behavior among college students. In D. A. Lamis & D. Lester (Eds.), *Understanding and preventing college student suicide* (pp. 5–32). Springfield, IL: Charles C. Thomas.

Schwartz, J. P., Griffin, L. D., Russell, M. M., & Frontaura-Duck, S. (2006). Prevention of dating violence on college campuses: An innovative program. *Journal of College Counseling, 9*, 90–96.

Schwartz, L. J., & Friedman, H. A. (2009). College student suicide. *Journal of College Student Psychotherapy, 23*, 78–102.

Schwartz, R. C., Lent, J., & Geihsler, J. (2011). Gender and diagnosis of mental disorders: Implications for mental health counseling. *Journal of Mental Health Counseling, 33*, 347–358.

Scilerppi, J. A., Teed, E. L., & Torres, R. D. (2000). *Community psychology: A common sense approach to mental health*. Upper Saddle River, NJ: Prentice Hall.

Sears, R., Rudisill, J., & Mason-Sears, C. (2006). *Consultation skills for mental health professionals.* Hoboken, NJ: John Wiley & Sons.

Sears, S. (1982). A definition of career guidance terms: A National Vocational Guidance Association perspective. *Vocational Guidance Quarterly, 31,* 137–143.

Seiler, G., Brooks, D. K., Jr., & Beck, E. S. (1987). Training standards of the American Mental Health Counselors Association: History, rationale, and implications. *Journal of Mental Health Counseling, 9,* 199–209.

Seligman, L. (2009). Diagnosis in counseling. In D. Capuzzi & D. R. Gross (Eds.), *Introduction to the counseling profession* (5th ed., pp. 373–394). Needham Heights, MA: Allyn & Bacon.

Seligman, L., & Reichenberg, L. W. (2014). *Theories of counseling and psychotherapy: Systems, strategies, and skills* (4th ed.). Upper Saddle River, NJ: Merrill/Prentice Hall.

Selye, H. (1976). *The stress of life* (2nd ed.). New York, NY: Guilford Press.

Sexton, T. L., & Lebow, J. (Eds.). (2016). *Handbook of family therapy* (2nd ed. rev.). New York, NY: Routledge.

Sexton, T. L., & Whiston, S. C. (1996). Integrating counseling research and practice. *Journal of Counseling and Development, 74,* 588–589.

Sexton, T. L., Whiston, S. C., Bleuer, J. C., & Walz, G. R. (1997). *Integrating outcome research into counseling practice and training.* Alexandria, VA: American Counseling Association.

Shallcross, L. (2011, March). Breaking away from the pack. *Counseling Today,* 28–36.

Shallcross, L. (2012a, April). Bringing work home. *Counseling Today, 54*(10), 32–38.

Shallcross, L. (2012b, February). A calming presence. *Counseling Today, 54*(8), 28–32, 38–39.

Shallcross, L. (2012c, March). What the future holds for the counseling profession. *Counseling Today, 54*(11), 32–44.

Shallcross, L. (2012d, August). Working with women from all walks of life. *Counseling Today, 55,* 30–38.

Shanker, T. (2008, April 6). Army is worried by rising stress of return tours to Iraq. *The New York Times.* Retrieved from www.nytimes.com/2008/04/06/washington/06military.html

Shannonhouse, L., Barden, S., Jones, E., Gonzalez, L., & Murphy, A. (2016). Secondary traumatic stress for trauma researchers: A mixed methods research design. *Journal of Mental Health Counseling, 38,* 201–216.

Shapiro, S. L., Carlson, L. E., Astin, J. A., & Freedman, B. (2006). Mechanisms of mindfulness. *Journal of Clinical Psychology, 62,* 373–386.

Sharrer, V. W., & Ryan-Wenger, N. A. (2002). School-age children's self-reported stress symptoms. *Pediatric Nursing, 28,* 21–27.

Sheperis, C. J., Young, J. S., & Daniels, M. H. (Eds.). (2017). *Counseling research: Quantitative, qualitative, and mixed methods* (2nd ed.). Hoboken, NJ: Pearson.

Sheperis, D. S., & Sheperis, C. J. (2015). *Clinical mental health counseling: Fundamentals of applied practice.* Upper Saddle River, NJ: Pearson.

Shertzer, B., & Stone, S. C. (1981). *Fundamentals of guidance* (4th ed.). Boston, MA: Houghton Mifflin.

Sherwood-Hawes, A. (1993). Individual counseling: Process. In A. Vernon (Ed.), *Counseling children and adolescents* (pp. 19–50). Denver, CO: Love.

Shipler, D. (2004). *The working poor: Invisible in America.* New York, NY: Knopf.

Shneidman, E. S. (1996). *The suicidal mind.* New York, NY: Oxford University Press.

Shulman, L. (2016). *The skills of helping individuals, groups, families, and communities* (8th ed.). Boston, MA: Cengage.

Silsbee, D. (2010). *The mindful coach: Seven roles for helping people grow* (Rev. ed.). San Francisco, CA: Jossey-Bass.

Simpson, L. R. (2009). Counseling and spirituality. In D. Capuzzi & D. R. Gross (Eds.), *Introduction to the counseling profession* (5th ed., pp. 292–313). Boston, MA: Pearson/Allyn & Bacon.

Singh, A. A., Boyd, C. J., & Whitman, J. S. (2010). Counseling competency with transgender and intersex individuals. In J. Cornish, L. Nadkarni, B. Schreier, & E. Rodolfa (Eds.), *Handbook of multicultural competencies* (pp. 415–442). New York, NY: Wiley & Sons.

Singh, A. A., & Chun, K. Y. S. (2013). Counseling lesbian, bisexual, queer, questioning, and transgender women. In C. Lee (Ed.), *Multicultural issues in counseling: New approaches to diversity* (4th ed., pp. 195–220). Alexandria, VA: American Counseling Association.

Singh, A. A., Hays, D. G., & Watson, L. S. (2011). Strength in the face of adversity: Resilience strategies of transgender individuals. *Journal of Counseling and Development, 89,* 20–27.

Sklare, G., Keener, R., & Mas, C. (1990). Preparing members for "here-and-now" group counseling. *Journal for Specialists in Group Work, 15,* 141–148.

Sklare, G., Petrosko, J., & Howell, S. (1993). The effect of pregroup training on members' level of anxiety. *Journal for Specialists in Group Work, 18,* 109–114.

Skovholt, T. M., & Trotter-Mathison, M. (2016). *The resilient practitioner* (3rd ed.). New York, NY: Routledge.

Sleek, S. (1995, July). Group therapy: Tapping the power of teamwork. *APA Monitor, 26*(1), 38–39.

Sleezer, C. M., Russ-Eft, D., & Gupta, K. (2014). *A practical guide to need assessment* (3rd ed.). San Francisco, CA: John Wiley & Sons.

Slipp, S. (1988). *The technique and practice of object relations family therapy.* New York, NY: Aronson.

Smart, J. F. (2013). Counseling individuals with physical, cognitive, and psychiatric disabilities. In C. Lee (Ed.), *Multicultural issues in counseling: New approaches to diversity* (4th ed., pp. 221–234). Alexandria, VA: American Counseling Association.

Smart, J. F., & Smart, D. W. (2006). Models of disability: Implications for the counseling profession. *Journal of Counseling and Development, 84,* 29–40.

Smith, A. R., Hawkeswood, S. E., Bodell, L. P., & Joiner, T. E. (2011). Muscularity versus leanness: An examination of body ideals and predictors of disordered eating in heterosexual and gay college students. *Body Image, 8,* 232–236.

Smith, R. L. (2015). *Treatment strategies for substance and process addictions.* Alexandria, VA: American Counseling Association.

Smith, R. L.., & Garcia, E. E. (2013). Treatment setting and treatment planning. In P. Stevens & R. L. Smith, *Substance abuse counseling: Theory and practice* (pp. 155–187). Upper Saddle River, NJ: Pearson.

Society of Counseling Psychology. (2007). About the Society of Counseling Psychology. Retrieved from www.div17.org

Sommers-Flanagan, J., & Sommers-Flanagan, R. (1995). Intake interviewing with suicidal patients: A systematic approach. *Professional Psychology: Research and Practice, 26*(1), 41–47.

Sommers-Flanagan, J., & Sommers-Flanagan, R. (2007). *Tough kids, cool counseling* (2nd ed.). Alexandria, VA: American Counseling Association.

Sperry, L. (2005a). Case conceptualizations: The missing link between theory and practice. *The Family Journal, 13,* 71–76.

Sperry, L. (2005b). Case conceptualizations: A strategy for incorporating individual, couple and family dynamics in the treatment process. *American Journal of Family Therapy, 33,* 353–364.

Sperry, L. (2012). *Spirituality in clinical practice: Theory and practice of spiritually oriented psychotherapy* (2nd ed.). New York, NY: Routledge/Taylor & Francis Group.

Spitalnick, J. S., & McNair, L. D. (2005). Couples therapy with gay men and lesbian clients: An analysis of important clinical issues. *Journal of Sex and Marital Therapy, 31,* 43–56.

Spokane, A. R. (1991). *Career intervention.* Upper Saddle River, NJ: Prentice Hall.

Sprenkle, D. H., & Piercy, F. P. (Eds.). (2005). *Research methods in family therapy* (2nd ed.). New York, NY: Guilford.

Spurgeon, S. L. (2013). Issues in counseling men. In C. C. Lee (Ed.), *Multicultural issues in counseling: New approaches to diversity* (4th ed., pp. 127–138). Alexandria, VA: American Counseling Association.

Stanley, S. M., Amato, P. R., Johnson, C. A., & Markman, H. J. (2006). Premarital education, marital quality, and marital stability: Findings from a large, household survey. *Journal of Family Psychology, 20,* 117–126.

Stanton, M. D. (1999, May). Alcohol use disorders. *AAMFT Clinical Update, 1*(3), 1–8.

Stanton, A. L., Revenson, T. A., & Tennen, H. (2007). Health psychology: psychological adjustment to chronic disease. *Annual Review of Psychology, 58,* 565–592.

Stark, D. D., Hargrave, J., Sander, J. B., Custer, G., Schnoebelen, S., Simpson, J., & Molnar, J. (2006). Treatment of childhood depression: The ACTION treatment program. In P. C. Kendall (Ed.), *Child and adolescent therapy: Cognitive–behavioral procedures* (3rd ed., pp. 160–216). New York, NY: Guilford Press.

Statista. (2016). Number of monthly active Facebook users worldwide as of 3rd quarter 2016 (in millions). Retrieved from www.statista.com/statistics/264810/number-of-monthly-active-facebook-users-worldwide/

Steenbarger, B. N., & Smith, H. B. (1996). Assessing the quality of counseling services: Developing accountable helping systems. *Journal of Counseling and Development, 75,* 145–150.

Steinhauser, L., & Bradley, R. (1983). Accreditation of counselor education programs. *Counselor Education and Supervision, 25,* 98–108.

Stelter, R. (2009). Coaching as a reflective space in a society of growing diversity—Towards a narrative, postmodern paradigm. *International Coaching Psychology Review, 4,* 209–219.

Stevens, P., & Smith, R. L. (2013). *Substance abuse counseling: Theory and practice* (5th ed.). Upper Saddle River, NJ: Pearson.

Stinnett, N., & DeFrain, J. (1985). *Secrets of strong families.* Boston, MA: Little, Brown.

Stith, P., & Raynor, D. (2008, February 26). Reform wastes millions, fails mentally ill. *The News and Observer.* Retrieved from www.newsobserver.com/2771/v-print/story/962049.html

Stockton, R., Barr, J. E., & Klein, R. (1981). Identifying the group dropout: A review of the literature. *Journal for Specialists in Group Work, 6,* 75–82.

Stoddard, S. (1992). *The hospice movement: A better way of caring for the dying* (Rev. ed.). New York: Random House.

Streatfield, N. (2012, February). Measuring outcomes. *Therapy Today, 24*(2), 28–31. Retrieved from www.therapy-today.net/article/show/2899

Stripling, R. O. (1978). ACES guidelines for doctoral preparation in counselor education. *Counselor Education and Supervision, 17,* 163–166.

Strong, B., DeVault, C., & Cohen, T. F. (2011). *The marriage and family experience: Intimate relationships in a changing society* (11th ed.). Belmont, CA: Wadsworth.

Strong, E. K., Jr. (1943). *Vocational interests of men and women.* Stanford, CA: Stanford University Press.

Stroul, B. A. (1988). *Home-based services.* Washington, DC: CASSP Technical Assistance Center.

Stuart, R. B. (1980). *Helping couples change: A social learning approach to marital therapy.* New York, NY: Guilford Press.

Stuart, R. B. (1998). Updating behavior therapy with couples. *The Family Journal: Counseling and Therapy for Couples and Families, 6,* 6–12.

Substance Abuse and Mental Health Services Administration (SAMHSA). (2016). Data, outcomes, and quality. Retrieved from www.samhsa.gov/

Sue, D. W. (1981). *Counseling and the culturally different: Theory and practice.* New York, NY: Wiley.

Sue, D. W., Arredondo, P., & McDavis, R. J. (1992). Multicultural counseling competencies and standards: A call to the profession. *Journal of Counseling and Development, 70,* 477–486.

Sue, D. W., Ivey, A. E., & Pedersen, P. (1996). *A theory of multicultural counseling and therapy.* Pacific Grove, CA: Brooks/Cole.

Sue, D. W., & Sue, D. (2016). *Counseling the culturally diverse: Theory and practice* (7th ed.). Hoboken, NJ: Wiley.

Suicide.org. (2016). College student suicide. Retrieved from www.suicide.org/college-student-suicide.html

Summit results in formation of spiritual competencies. (1995, December). *Counseling Today,* 30.

Super, D. E. (1955). Transition: From vocational guidance to counseling psychology. *Journal of Counseling Psychology, 2,* 3–9.

Super, D. E. (1957). *The psychology of careers.* New York, NY: Harper.

Super, D. E. (1976). *Career education and the meaning of work* [Monograph]. Washington, DC: Office of Career Education, U.S. Office of Education.

Super, D. E. (1980). A life-span, life space approach to career development. *Journal of Vocational Behavior, 16,* 282–298.

Super, D. E. (1990). A life-span, life-space approach to career development. In D. Brown, L. Brooks, & Associates (Eds.), *Career choice and development: Applying contemporary theories to practice* (2nd ed., pp. 197–261). San Francisco, CA: Jossey-Bass.

Supple, A. J., & Small, S. A. (2006). The influence of parental support, knowledge, and authoritative parenting on Hmong and European American adolescent development. *Journal of Family Issues, 27,* 1214–1232.

Surgeon General Report. (2000). *Mental health: A report of the Surgeon General.* Retrieved from www.surgeongeneral.gov/Library/MentalHealth

Sussman, M. B., Hanson, S., Helms, M. L., & Julian, D. J. (2017). *Single parent families: Diversity, myths, and realities.* New York, NY: Routledge.

Suzuki, L. A., & Kugler, J. F. (2001). Multicultural assessment. In E. R. Welfel & R. E. Ingersoll (Eds.), *The mental health desk reference: A sourcebook for counselors and therapists* (pp. 279–286). New York, NY: Wiley.

Suzuki, L. A., Ponterotto, J. G., & Meller, P. J. (Eds.). (2008). *Handbook of multicultural assessment: Clinical, psychological, and educational applications* (3rd ed.). San Francisco, CA: Jossey-Bass.

Swanson, C. D. (1983). Ethics and the counselor. In J. A. Brown & R. H. Pate, Jr. (Eds.), *Being a counselor* (pp. 47–65). Monterey, CA: Brooks/Cole.

Swanson, J. L., & Fouad, N. A. (2010). *Career theory and practice: Learning through case studies* (2nd ed.). Thousand Oaks, CA: Sage.

Sweeney, T. J. (1989). Excellence vs. elitism. *Newsletter of Chi Sigma Iota, 5*(1), 11.

Sweeney, T. J. (1995). Accreditation, credentialing, professionalization: The role of specialties. *Journal of Counseling and Development, 74,* 117–125.

Sweeney, T. J. (2001). Counseling: Historical origins and philosophical roots. In D. C. Locke, J. E. Myers, & E. L. Herr (Eds.), *The handbook of counseling* (pp. 3–26). Thousand Oaks, CA: Sage.

Sweeney, T. J., & Witmer, J. M. (1991). Beyond social interest: Striving toward optimal health and wellness. *Individual Psychology, 47,* 527–540.

Swenson, R. A. (1998). *The overload syndrome: Learning to live within your limits.* Colorado Springs, CO: NavPress.

Talbott, J. A. (2001). The economics of mental health care in the USA and the potential for managed care to expand to Europe. *Current Opinion in Psychiatry, 14*(4), 279–285.

Tanigoshi, H., Kontos, A. P., & Remley, T. P., Jr. (2008). The effectiveness of individual wellness counseling on the wellness of law enforcement officers. *Journal of Counseling and Development, 86,* 64–74.

Tanner, J. L., & Arnett, J. J. (2009). The emergence of "emerging adulthood": The new life stage between adolescence and young adulthood. In A. Furlong (Ed.), *Handbook of youth and young adulthood: New perspectives and agendas* (pp. 39–45). New York, NY: Routledge.

Tarasoff v. Board of Regents of the University of California. (1976). 551 p2d 334, 131, Cal Rptr 14 (Cal. Sup. Ct. 1976).

Tarvydas, V. M., & Ng, H. K. Y. (2012). Ethical perspectives on trauma work. In L. L. Levers (Ed.), *Trauma counseling: Theories and interventions* (pp. 521–539). New York, NY: Springer.

Taylor, L., & Adelman, H. (2001). Enlisting appropriate parental cooperation and involvement in children's mental health treatment. In E. R. Welfel & R. E. Ingersoll (Eds.), *The mental health desk reference: A sourcebook for counselors and therapists* (pp. 219–224). New York, NY: Wiley.

Thomas, R. (2002). Supreme Court limits ADA disability definition. Retrieved from www.ppspublishers.com/biz/ada.htm

Thomas, R. M., & Chess, S. (1977). *Temperament and development.* New York, NY: Brunner/Mazel.

Thomas, S. C. (1996). A sociological perspective on contextualism. *Journal of Counseling and Development, 74,* 529–536.

Thomas, V. G. (1990). Determinants of global life happiness and marital happiness in dual-career black couples. *Family Relations, 39,* 174–178.

Thompson, A. (1990). *Guide to ethical practice in psychotherapy.* New York, NY: Wiley.

Thompson, I. A., Amatea, E. S., & Thompson, E. S. (2014). Personal and contextual predictors of mental health counselors' compassion fatigue and burnout. *Journal of Mental Health Counseling, 36*, 58–77.

Thompson, M. N., Cole, O. D., & Nitzarim, R. S. (2012). Recognizing social class in the psychotherapy relationship: A grounded theory exploration of low-income clients. *Journal of Counseling Psychology, 59*, 208–221.

Thurber, C. A., & Walton, E. A. (2012). Homesickness and adjustment in university students. *Journal of American College Health, 60*(5), 415–419.

Titelman, P. (Ed.). (2014). *Differentiation of self*. New York, NY: Routledge.

Todd, T. C. (1986). Structural-strategic marital therapy. In N. S. Jacobson & A. S. Gurman (Eds.), *Clinical handbook of marital therapy* (pp. 71–105). New York, NY: Guilford Press.

Toporek, R. L. (2000). Developing a common language and framework for understanding advocacy in counseling. In J. Lewis & L. J. Bradley (Eds.), *Advocacy in counseling: Counselors, clients, and community* (pp. 5–14). Greensboro, NC: Caps Publications.

Toporek, R. L., Lewis, J. A., & Crethar, H. C. (2009). Promoting systemic change through the ACA advocacy competencies. *Journal of Counseling and Development, 87*, 260–268.

Tornstam, L. (2000). Gerotranscendence: The contemplative dimension of aging. *Journal of Aging Studies, 11*, 143–154.

Truax, C. B., & Carkhuff, R. R. (1967). *Toward effective counseling and psychotherapy: Training and practice*. Chicago, IL: Aldine.

Trzepacz, P. T., & Baker, R. W. (1993). *The psychiatric mental status examination*. New York, NY: Oxford University Press.

Tuckman, B. W. (1965). Developmental sequence in small groups. *Psychological Bulletin, 63*, 384–399.

Tuckman, B. W., & Jensen, M. A. (1977). Stages of small group development revisited. *Group and Organizational Studies, 2*, 419–427.

Tyiska, C. (1998). Working with victims with disabilities. *Office for Victims of Crime Bulletin*. Washington, DC: U.S. Department of Justice, Office for Victims of Crimes.

U'Ren, R. (2012). *Social perspective: The missing element in mental health practice*. Toronto, Canada: University of Toronto Press.

U.S. Census Bureau. (2012, July 25). Nearly 1 in 5 people have a disability in the U.S., Census Bureau reports. Retrieved from www.census.gov/newsroom/releases/archives/miscellaneous/cb12-134.html

U.S. Census Bureau. (2015). Census briefs. Retrieved from www.census.gov

U.S. Department of Health and Human Services. (1999). Mental health: A report of the Surgeon General. Rockville, MD: U.S. Department of Health and Human Services, Substance Abuse and Mental Health Services Administration, Center for Mental Health Services, National Institutes of Health, National Institute of Mental Health.

U.S. Department of Health and Human Services. (2000). Mental health: A report of the Surgeon General—Executive summary. Retrieved from www.surgeongeneral.gov/library/mentalhealth/summary.html

U.S. Department of Health and Human Services. (2016). Mental health. Retrieved from www.hhs.gov/ash/oah/resources-and-publications/publications/mental-health.html

U.S. Department of Health and Human Services, Administration for Children and Families, Administration on Children, Youth and Families, Children's Bureau. (2016). *Child maltreatment 2014*. Retrieved from http://www.acf.hhs.gov/sites/default/files/cb/cm2014.pdf#page=10

U.S. Department of Labor. (2015). Statistics. Retrieved from www.dol.gov/wb/stats/stats_data.htm

Utsey, S. O., Ponterotto, J. G., & Porter, J. S. (2008). Prejudice and racism, year 2008—still going strong: Research on reducing prejudice with recommended methodological advances. *Journal of Counseling and Development, 86*, 339–347.

Vacc, N. A., & Juhnke, G. A. (1997). The use of structured clinical interviews for assessment in counseling. *Journal of Counseling and Development, 75*, 470–480.

Vacc, N. A., & Loesch, L. (2000). *Professional orientation to counseling* (3rd ed.). Philadelphia, PA: Brunner-Routledge.

Van Hoose, W. H., & Kottler, J. (1985). *Ethical and legal issues in counseling and psychotherapy* (2nd ed.). San Francisco, CA: Jossey-Bass.

Veach, L. J., & Madwid, R. (2005). Older adults and the issue of addiction. In V. A. Kelly & G. A. Juhnke (Eds.), *Critical incidents in addictions counseling*. Alexandria, VA: American Counseling Association.

Vernon, A. (2009). Working with children, adolescents, and their parents: Practical application of developmental theory. In A. Vernon (Ed.), *Counseling children and adolescents* (4th ed., pp. 1–34). Denver, CO: Love.

Vernon, A., & Clemente, R. (2004). *Assessment and intervention with children and adolescents: Developmental and cultural approaches* (2nd ed.). Alexandria, VA: American Counseling Association.

Vickio, C. J. (1990). The goodbye brochure: Helping students to cope with transition and loss. *Journal of Counseling and Development, 68*, 575–577.

Viger, J. (2001). Community mental health centers. Retrieved from www.echoman.com/knowledgesource/Community_Mental_Health_Centers.htm

Vogel, D. L., Wester, S. R., & Larson, L. M. (2007). Avoidance of counseling: Psychological factors that inhibit seeking help. *Journal of Counseling and Development, 85*, 410–422.

Von Steen, P. G., Vacc, N. A., & Strickland, I. M. (2002). The treatment of substance-abusing clients in multi-service mental health agencies: A practice analysis. *Journal of Addictions and Offender Counseling, 22,* 61–71.

Waggonseller, B. R., Ruegamer, L. C., & Harrington, M. C. (1998). *Coping in a single-parent home.* New York, NY: Rosen.

Wake Forest Baptist Health. (2016). Our services. Retrieved from www.wakehealth.edu/Patient-Care/

Waldo, M. (1985). Curative factor framework for conceptualizing group counseling. *Journal for Counseling and Development, 64,* 52–58.

Waldo, M., & Bauman, S. (1998). Regrouping the categorization of group work: A goal and process (GAP) matrix for groups. *Journal for Specialists in Group Work, 23,* 164–176.

Wallace, B. A., & Shapiro, S. L. (2006). Mental balance and well-being: Building bridges between Buddhism and Western psychology. *American Psychologist, 61,* 690–701.

Wallerstein, J. S. (2008). Divorce. In M. M. Haith & J. B. Benson (Eds.), *Encyclopedia of infancy and early childhood.* Oxford, UK: Elsevier.

Wallerstein, J. S., & Blakeslee, S. (2003). *What about the kids?* New York, NY: Hyperion.

Walsh, F. (2012). *Normal family processes: Growing diversity and complexity* (4th ed.). New York, NY: Guilford.

Walsh, R. (2000). Asian psychotherapies. In R. J. Corsini & D. Wedding (Eds.), *Current psychotherapies* (6th ed., pp. 407–444). Itasca, IL: F. E. Peacock.

Walter, J., & Peller, J. (1992). *Becoming solution-focused in brief therapy.* New York, NY: Brunner/Mazel.

Walz, G. R. (2000). Preface. In J. W. Bloom & G. R. Walz (Eds.), *Cybercounseling and cyberlearning: Strategies and resources for the new millennium* (pp. xi–xvii). Alexandria, VA: American Counseling Association.

Wampold, B. E. (2000). Outcomes of individual counseling and psychotherapy: Empirical evidence in addressing two fundamental questions. In S. Brown & R. Lent (Eds.), *Handbook of counseling psychology* (4th ed., pp. 711–739). New York, NY: Wiley.

Ward v. Polite, 667 F.3d 727 (6th Cir. 2012).

Ward, D. E. (1982). A model for the more effective use of theory in group work. *Journal for Specialists in Group Work, 7,* 224–230.

Ward, D. E. (1984). Termination of individual counseling: Concepts and strategies. *Journal of Counseling and Development, 63,* 21–25.

Warden, S. P., & Nations, J. R., (2016, February). *Faith based counseling: Challenges and opportunities.* Paper presented at the North Carolina Counseling Association Annual Conference, Greensboro, NC.

Watts, R. E., Trusty, J., & Lim, M. G. (2000). Characteristics of healthy families as a model of social interest. *Canadian Journal of Adlerian Psychology, 26,* 1–12.

Watzlawick, P. (1983). *The situation is hopeless, but not serious.* New York, NY: Norton.

Watzlawick, P., Weakland, J., & Fisch, R. (1974). *Change: Principles of problem formation and problem resolution.* New York, NY: Norton.

Webb, L. D., Brigman, G. A., & Campbell, C. (2005). Linking school counselors and student success: A replication of the student success skills approach targeting the academic and social competence of students. *Professional School Counseling, 8*(5), 407–413.

Webber, J., & Mascari, B. (Eds.). (2016). *Disaster mental health counseling: A guide to preparing and responding* (4th ed.). Alexandria, VA: American Counseling Association.

Weikel, W. J. (1996). The mental health counselors association. In W. J. Weikel & A. J. Palmo (Eds.), *Foundations of mental health counseling* (2nd ed., pp. 30–37). Springfield, IL: Charles C Thomas.

Weinrach, S. G. (1987). Microcounseling and beyond: A dialogue with Allen Ivey. *Journal of Counseling and Development, 65,* 532–537.

Weinrach, S. G. (1996). The psychological and vocational interest patterns of Donald Super and John Holland. *Journal of Counseling and Development, 75,* 5–16.

Weinrach, S. G., & Thomas, K. R. (1998). Diversity sensitive counseling today: A postmodern clash of values. *Journal of Counseling and Development, 76,* 115–122.

Weiss, E. L., Coll, J. E., Gerbauer, J., Smiley, K., & Carillo, E. (2010). The military genogram: A solution-focused approach to resiliency building in service members and their families. *The Family Journal, 18,* 395–406.

Weiss, J. C. (1995). Cognitive therapy and life review therapy: Theoretical and therapeutic implications for mental health counselors. *Journal of Mental Health Counseling, 17*(2), 157–172.

Weitzman, J. (2006). The family's role in adolescent depression and treatment: Recent findings. *Journal of Psychotherapy and the Family, 17,* 37–48.

Welfel, E. R. (2016). *Ethics in counseling and psychotherapy: Standards, research, and emerging issues* (6th ed.). Boston, MA: Cengage.

Welfel, E. R., & Patterson, L. E. (2005). *The counseling process: A multitheoretical integrative approach* (6th ed.). Belmont, CA: Thomson Brooks/Cole.

Werbel, J. (1998). Intent and choice regarding maternal employment following childbirth. *Journal of Vocational Behavior, 53,* 372–385.

West-Olatunji, C. A. (2001). Counseling ethnic minority clients. In D. Capuzzi & D. R. Gross (Eds.), *Introduction to the counseling profession* (3rd ed., pp. 415–434). Needham Heights, MA: Allyn & Bacon.

Wheeler, A. M., & Bertram, B. (2015). *The counselor and the law: A guide to legal and ethical practice* (7th ed.). Alexandria, VA: American Counseling Association.

Whiston, S. C. (2017). *Principles and applications of assessment in counseling* (5th ed.). Boston, MA: Cengage.

Whitaker, C. (1976). The hindrance of theory in clinical work. In P. J. Guerin (Ed.), *Family therapy: Theory and practice* (pp. 154–164). New York, NY: Gardner Press.

Whitaker, C. (1977). Process techniques of family therapy. *Interaction, 1,* 4–19.

Whitaker, C. (1989). *Midnight musings of a family therapist.* New York, NY: Norton.

Whitbourne, S. B. (2010). The intersection of physical and mental health in aging: Minding the gap. In J. C. Cavanaugh, C. K. Cavanaugh, S. Qualls, & L. McGuire (Eds.), *Aging in America: Vol. 2. Physical and mental health* (pp. 141–170). Santa Barbara, CA: Praeger.

White, H. (1978). Exercises in understanding your family. In *Your family is good for you.* New York, NY: Random House.

White, M. (1995). *Re-authoring lives.* Adelaide, South Australia: Dulwich Centre Publications.

White, M., & Epston, D. (1990). *Narrative means to therapeutic ends.* New York, NY: Norton.

Whitely, J. M. (1984). Counseling psychology: A historical perspective. *The Counseling Psychologist, 12,* 2–109.

Whitmarsh, L., & Wentworth, D. K. (2012). Gender similarity or gender difference? Contemporary women's and men's career patterns. *Career Development Quarterly, 60,* 47–64.

Wickline v. State of California, 239 Cal. Rptr. 805, 741 P.2d 613 (1987).

Wicks, R. J., & Buck, T. C. (2014). "Alonetime": Recovering a rich classical resource for counselor self-renewal. *Journal of Mental Health Counseling, 36,* 288–301.

Wilcoxon, S. A. (1985). Healthy family functioning: The other side of family pathology. *Journal of Counseling and Development, 63,* 495–499.

Wilcoxon, S. A., & Fenell, D. (1983). Engaging the non-attending spouse in marital therapy through the use of therapist-initiated written communication. *Journal of Marital and Family Therapy, 9,* 199–203.

Williamson, E. G. (1939). *How to counsel students: A manual of techniques for clinical counselors.* New York, NY: McGraw-Hill.

Williamson, E. G., & Biggs, D. A. (1979). Trait-factor theory and individual differences. In H. M. Burks, Jr., & B. Stefflre (Eds.), *Theories of counseling* (3rd ed., pp. 91–131). New York, NY: McGraw-Hill.

Wilmarth, R. R. (1985, Summer). Historical perspective, part two. *AMHCA News, 8,* 21.

Winegar, N. (1993). Managed mental health care: Implications for administrators and managers of community-based agencies. *Families in Society: The Journal of Contemporary Human Services, 74,* 171–178.

Winegar, N., & Hayter, L. M. (1998). *Guidebook to managed care and practice management terminology.* New York, NY: Haworth Press.

Winter, J. M. (2002, February). *Counseling lesbian, gay, and bisexual clients.* Paper presented at the North Carolina Counseling Association Annual Conference, Greensboro, NC.

Wisner, B. L., & Norton, C. L. (2013). Capitalizing on behavioral and emotional strengths of alternative high school students through group counseling to promote mindfulness skills. *Journal for Specialists in Group Work, 38,* 207–224.

Witmer, J. M. (2013). Evolution of wellness. In P. F. Granello (Ed.), *Wellness counseling* (pp. 11–28). Upper Saddle River, NJ: Pearson.

Witmer, J. M., & Sweeney, T. J. (1992). A holistic model for wellness and prevention over the life span. *Journal of Counseling and Development, 71,* 140–148.

Witmer, J. M., Sweeney, T. J., & Myers, J. E. (1998). *The wheel of wellness.* Greensboro, NC: Author.

Wolf, C. P., Thompson, I. A., & Smith-Adcock, S. (2012). Wellness in counselor preparation: Promoting individual well-being. *Journal of Individual Psychology, 68,* 164–181.

Wood, C. (Eds.). (2013). *A counselor's guide to career assessment instruments* (6th ed.). Broken Arrow, OK: NCDA.

Woods, T. E., Antoni, M. H., Ironson, G. H., & Kling, D. W. (1999). Religiosity is associated with affective status in symptomatic HIV-infected African-American women. *Journal of Health Psychology, 4,* 317–326.

Worthington, R. L., Dillon, F. R., & Becker-Schutte, A. M. (2005). Development, reliability, and validity of the lesbian, gay, and bisexual knowledge and attitudes scale for heterosexuals. *Journal of Counseling Psychology, 52,* 104–118.

Wrenn, C. G. (1962a). *The counselor in a changing world.* Washington, DC: American Personnel and Guidance Association.

Wrenn, C. G. (1962b). The culturally encapsulated counselor. *Harvard Educational Review, 32,* 444–449.

Wright, K. C., & Martin, E. D., Jr. (1999). The rehabilitation process: A perspective for the rehabilitation counselor. In G. L. Gandy, E. D. Martin, Jr., & R. E. Hardy (Eds.), *Counseling in the rehabilitation process: Community services for mental and physical disabilities* (2nd ed., pp. 117–129). Springfield, IL: Charles C Thomas.

Wright, R. H., Jr., Mindel, C. H., Van Tran, T., & Habenstein, R. H. (2012). *Ethnic families in America: Patterns and variation.* Upper Saddle River, NJ: Pearson.

Wylie, M. S. (1995, May/June). The power of the *DSM-IV:* Diagnosing for dollars. *Networker,* 22–32.

Yakushko, O. (2005). Influence of social support, existential well-being, and stress over sexual orientation on self-esteem of gay, lesbian, and bisexual individuals. *International Journal for the Advancement of Counseling, 27*(1), 131–143.

Yalom, I. D., & Leszcz, M. (2005). *The theory and practice of group psychotherapy* (5th ed.). New York, NY: Basic Books.

Yalom, I. D., & Lieberman, M. (1971). A study of encounter group casualties. *Archives of General Psychiatry, 25,* 16–30.

Yoon, E., Langrehr, K., & Ong, L. Z. (2011). Content analysis of acculturation research in counseling and counseling psychology: A 22-year review. *Journal of Counseling Psychology, 58,* 83–96.

Young, J. S., Wiggins-Frame, M., & Cashwell, C. S. (2007). Spirituality and counselor competence: A national survey of American Counseling Association members. *Journal of Counseling and Development, 85,* 47–52.

Young, M. E. (2013). *Learning the art of helping: Building blocks and techniques* (5th ed.). Upper Saddle River, NJ: Merrill/Pearson Education.

Young, M. E., & Long, L. L. (2007). *Counseling and therapy for couples* (2nd ed.). Belmont, CA: Brooks/Cole.

Zavadil, A., & Kooyman, L. (2014). Understanding diverse populations on college campuses. In S. Degges-White & C. Borzumato-Gainey (Eds.), *College student mental health counseling* (pp. 51–68). New York, NY: Springer.

Zylowska, L. (2012). *The mindfulness prescription for adult ADHD.* Boston, MA: Trumpeter Books.

Zytowski, D. (1985). Frank! Frank! Where are you now that we need you? *The Counseling Psychologist, 13,* 129–135.

NAME INDEX

SUBJECT INDEX

f denotes figure; *t* denotes table.

A

ABCS model of crisis, 194, 195*f*
Ableism, 81
Absurdity, defined, 255
Abuse. *See also* Elder abuse; Emotional abuse; Physical abuse;
    Polysubstance abuse; Psychological abuse; Reporting abuse;
    Sexual abuse; Substance abuse
  according to NCADV, 369
  described, 370
  therapy with abused child, 121
ACA advocacy competencies, 182
ACA Code of Ethics, 39–42, 43–44, 46, 55, 56, 57, 58, 59, 60, 68, 73,
    111, 112, 118, 123, 136, 337, 394, 395–396
ACA Ethics Committee, 47, 54
ACA Office of Public Policy Information, 184
Acculturation, 68, 135
Acetylcholine, 153
Achenbach System of Empirically Based Assessment, 277
Acquired disabilities, 86–87
Action factors, effective counseling, 115
Action limits, 97–98
Active listening, 109
Activities of daily living (ADLs), 82, 84, 361
ADAMHA Reorganization Act (1992), 352
Adaptability, 242
Adaptive emotion-focused coping strategies, 330
Addiction counseling, 366
Addictions, 365
Addictive disorders, 143
ADDRESSING model, 64
Adjourning stage, groups, 227, 228
Administration on Aging, 310, 315
Administrative law, 48, 49
Adolescence/Adolescents
  concerns affecting, 280–292
  counseling of. *See* Counseling children/adolescents
  described, 266–267
Adults
  counseling of. *See* Counseling adults
  early adulthood, 299–303
  emerging adulthood, 297–299
  later adulthood. *See* Later adulthood
  middle adulthood. *See* Middle adulthood
  older adults. *See* Older adults
  single adults, 300–301
Advanced practice registered nurses (APRNs), 30
Adversity, 314–315
Advocacy
  ACA advocacy competencies, 182
  Buffkin's first role in, 181
  challenges of, 183–184
  continuum of, 180*f*
  defined, 179–180
  overview, 178–179
  for the profession, 184
  skills and attributes, 183

Affectional orientation, 73
Affective experiencing, as learning and action factor, 115, 116–118
Afghanistan, war in, 20, 197
African Americans, 64, 66, 273
Aftercare, for substance abuse treatment, 368
Ageism, 247*f*, 315–317, 323
Aging families, 245, 246*t*
Aging population, working with, 22
Agreeableness, as personality factor, 130
Alcohol, drug abuse, and mental health block grant (ADAMHA), 352
Alcohol consumption, college students, 332–333
Alcoholics Anonymous (AA), 366, 368
Alcohol screening, 361
ALGBTIC Competencies for Counseling LGBQQIA Individuals, 73
Alzheimer's disease, 360
American Association for Counseling and Development
    (AACD), 16, 17, 18
American Association for Marriage and Family Therapy (AAMFT), 260
American Association of State Counseling Boards (AASCB), 22
American Bar Association, 276
American College Counseling Association (ACCA), 18, 25, 328
American College Health Association, 329, 330, 333
American College of Surgeons Committee on Trauma (ACS COT), 361
American College Personnel Association, 11
American Counseling Association (ACA)
  ACA Code of Ethics. See ACA Code of Ethics
  advocacy competencies, 182
  as affiliation for clinical mental health counselors, 32
  Ethical Standards Casebook, 39, 45
  Ethics Committee, 47, 54
  and license portability, 22
  name change in 1992, 18
  NVGA as forerunner of, 7
  Office of Public Policy Information, 184
  previously APGA, 3, 15
  Private Practice Pointers website, 382
  as Red Cross partner, 203
  Risk Management Helpline, 54
  specialty divisions of, 24–25
  summary of outcome research by, 114
  theme (1999), 178
American Family Therapy Association (AFTA), 260
American Group Psychotherapy Association (AGPA), 237
American Mental Health Counselors Association (AMHCA), 3, 4, 14,
    16, 22, 25, 32, 39, 357
American Nurses Credentialing Center, 30
American Personnel and Guidance Association (APGA), 3, 11, 13,
    14, 15, 16
American Psychiatric Association (APA), 79, 114, 145
American Psychological Association (APA), 11, 12, 16, 30, 39, 79,
    114, 237, 260
American Red Cross, 20, 203
American Rehabilitation Counseling Association (ARCA), 24, 85
American School Counselor Association, 24
American Society of Group Psychotherapy and Psychodrama
    (ASGPP), 237
American Student Health Association, 327
Americans with Disabilities Act of 1990 (ADA), 81, 83

C

California State Counselor Association, 16
Campus counseling centers, areas of clinical focus, 328–329
Cancer patient support services, 359–360
Capacity, defined, 55
Capitation, 392*f*
Card sort, 133
Career
    defined, 339
    use of term, 338
Career assessment, 345–347
Career coaching, 339
Career concerns, sexual identity and, 80
Career counseling
    career development process, 337–338
    career development theories, 339–345
    defined, 338
    with diverse populations, 347–348
    need for career development services, 336–337
    overview, 336
    process and skills of, 345–348
    and related terminology, 338–339
Career development
    Super's work in, 12
    theories of, 337
Career development facilitator (CDF), 339
Career education, 339
Career genogram, 346
Career information, 339, 347
Career intervention, 339, 345, 347
Career maturity, 342
Career planning, 347
Carve-out, 392*f*
Case/care management, 392*f*
Case conceptualization/formulation, 110
Case law, 48
Case management and outreach, at CMHCs, 354
Case management plan, 113
Case notes, 118–119, 120*f*
Case rate, 392*f*
Cass's model of sexual identity development, 75
Catastrophic phenomena, defined, 272
Catchment areas, 351
Catharsis, 117, 250
Center for Credentialing in Education (CCE), 377, 388
Center for Mental Health Services, 18
Centers for Medicare and Medicaid Services, 49
Certification
    for counselors in mental health settings, 357
    standardization of, 16
    as type of professional credential, 29, 30*t*
Certified Clinical Mental Health Counselor (CCMHC), 32, 357
Certified employee assistance professionals (CEAP), 378
Change
    first-order change, 254
    helping clients initiate, 104
    second-order change, 254
    stages of, 103*f*
Charity myth, persons with disabilities, 82
Chat room counseling, 60
Checklists, as method of assessment, 129–130
Child abuse services, 372, 373*f*

Child and family service agencies, 368–373
Childless families/couples, 244, 246*f*
Child maltreatment
    definitions, signs, and symptoms of, 290*f*
    issues for children with, 289–292
Child neglect, described, 290*f*
Children. *See also* Counseling children/adolescents
    bioecological considerations of, 267–273
    concerns affecting, 280–292
    developmental considerations of, 264–267
    psychological, biological, and genetic influences on, 268–269
Children's Depression Inventory, 277
Child Welfare League of America, 280
Chi Sigma Iota, 16, 19, 25
Choice Program (VA), 24
Choosing a Vocation (Parsons), 6
Chronic phase, for families of persons with disabilities, 87
Chronosystem, 268
Circular causality, 253
Circumplex model of marital and family systems, 242
Civilian Health and Medical Programs of the Uniformed Services, 391
Civil law, 48–49
Civil rights movement, impact of, 13, 14
Classic theories of personality, 265*f*
Classism, 89, 91, 92, 180, 247
Cleansing rituals, 214
Client-centered case consultation, 175–176
Client-centered theories, 12
Client–environment interaction, 33
Client Evaluation of Counseling Inventory (CEC), 186
Client-induced stressors, 211
Client-observation skills, 108
Client outcome evaluation
    challenges and benefits of, 187
    definition and purpose of, 185
    examples of methods, 186*t*
    multifaceted approaches to, 185–187
    overview, 184–185
Client records
    confidentiality and access to, 111–112
    reasons for careful record keeping, 111
    suggestions for, 112–113
    use of term, 110
Client(s)
    documenting work with high-risk clients, 119, 121
    professional boundaries and roles with, 56–57
    reluctant clients, 101
    resistant clients, 101, 102
    welfare of as ethical consideration in managed care, 394–395
Clinical entries, 118
Clinical interviews
    as method of assessment, 130–131
    role of counselor in, 207
Clinical mental health counseling
    certified clinical mental health counseling credential (CCMHC), 357
    and coaching, 388
    development of, 5
    as merger of community counseling and mental health counseling, 3, 4
    not recognized as specialty area prior to 2009, 3
Clinical Mental Health Counseling Standards. *See* Standards for Clinical Mental Health Counseling (CACREP)

ethics and, 39–47
evidence-based counseling, 19–20, 114
evolution of, 5
globalization of, 21
history of, 3–4
influence of culture on, 13, 14
initial interviews, 104–108, 106–107*f*
internalization of, 22–23
the law and, 47–51
legal recognition of as profession, 28
of LGB/LGBT individuals, 58, 73–80. *See also* Bisexual couples/
  individuals; Gay couples/families/individuals; Lesbian couples/
  families/individuals; Transgender couples/individuals
marriage and family counseling, 8, 13. *See also* Family counseling
of military families/personnel. *See* Military families/personnel
of minors, legal and ethical issues related to, 275*f*
multicultural counseling. *See* Multiculturalism/Multicultural
  counseling
neurocounseling, 153
nondirective approach to, 10
occupational counseling, 338
online counseling, 21, 60, 383
physical setting of, 95–96
rehabilitation counseling, 84, 85, 361, 383
role, clarification of, 274
special populations. *See* Special populations
specialty defined, 27–28
standards for master's degree in, 15, 16
synchronous counseling, 60
theories of, 9, 10, 12. *See also* Theories
trait-factor counseling, 9, 12
ways to use Indivisible Self Model in, 163–164
working phase of, 113–121
Counseling adults. *See also* Counseling men; Counseling women;
  Couple counseling
early adulthood, 299–303
emerging adulthood, 297–299
implications for emerging adults, 298–299
later adulthood, 309–315
middle adulthood, 303–309
transition framework, 295–297
Counseling and Psychotherapy (Rogers), 10
Counseling around the World, 22
Counseling Association for Humanistic Education and
  Development, 24
Counseling children/adolescents
  assessment and evaluation, 276–278
  building counseling relationship, 273–276
  creative interventions, 279
  designing and implementing treatment plan, 278–279
Counseling groups, 221
Counseling in college/university settings
  campus counseling centers and areas of clinical focus, 328–329
  crisis management, 334–336
  history of college counseling, 327–328
  other issues of concern, 336
  prevalent mental health issues among college
    students, 329–333
  severe mental illness and suicide among college
    students, 333–334
Counseling men, 320–322
Counseling Military Families (Hall), 246
Counseling program evaluation (CPE), 188

Counseling psychology, as distinguished from clinical psychology,
  11–12
The Counseling Psychologist, 13, 14
Counseling relationship
  building of during initial sessions, 108
  closing of, 121–126
  counselor-client interactions/relationship, 56–57
  helping clients initiate change, 104
  initial sessions of, 96–113
  initiative in, 101
  Motivational Interviewing Behavior Matrix, 102*f*
  seriousness of presenting problem, 97
  structure of, 97–98
Counseling Today, 162, 382, 383
Counseling women, 317–320
The Counselor and the Law: A Guide to Legal and Ethical Practice
  (Wheeler and Bertram), 50
Counselor-client interactions/relationship, 56–57
The Counselor in a Changing World (Wrenn), 13
Counselors
  becoming/serving as EAP counselor, 379–382
  burnout, 210
  certification, 8
  distance certified, 21
  education programs for, 14, 15, 22, 165
  maintenance of effectiveness by, 215–216
  management of stress by, 210–216
  numbers of (US), 18
  self-awareness as multicultural competency, 69
A Counselor's Guide to Career Assessment Instruments
  (Wood), 346
Counselors for Social Justice (CSJ), 18, 25, 182
Counselors Who Coach (Labardee), 388
Couple counseling, 249–252, 259–260
Couple enrichment, 259
Court appearances, reasons for, 50–51
Court order, 50
Covered services, 392*f*
Covert rehearsal, 118
Credentialing, professional identification through, 28–29
Criminal law, 48
Crisis
  assessment, 197, 199–200
  categories of, 196
  in Chinese characters, 195
  defined, 194
  models of, 194
  reflections on counseling after crisis, 202
Crisis incident stress management (CISM), 203
Crisis intervention
  at CMHCs, 353
  counselor functions in, 197, 198*f*
  defined, 197
  goals of, 197
  six-step model of, 198*f*, 200–202, 201*f*
Crisis management
  on college campuses, 334–335
  as other term for crisis intervention, 197
Crisis phase, for families of persons with disabilities, 87
Crisis Response Planning Task Force, 20
Cross-cultural assessment, 136–137
Cultural empathy/Culturally sensitive empathy, 71–72, 108
Culturally encapsulated, 66

Technology
  addiction to, 365–366
  understanding and responding to, 21
  use of, 59–62
Technology addiction (TA), 365–366
Technology-assisted distance counseling, 60–62
Temperament, defined, 268
Ten Commonalities of Suicide, 208
Terminal phase, for families of persons with disabilities, 87
Terminating stage, groups, 229–231*t*
Termination, 121
Tertiary prevention, 166
Testing. *See also* Assessment; Inventories
  intelligence tests, 8
  National Fair Access Coalition on Testing (FACT), 30
  Psychological testing, 8, 129
  Standards for Educational and Psychological Testing, 136
  University Testing Bureau (University of Wisconsin), 327
Text messaging, 60, 292
T-group movement, 219
Theories
  attachment theory, 252, 265*f*, 370
  bioecological theory, 373
  Bowen family systems theory, 250–251
  career development theories, 337, 339–345
  classic theories of personality, 265*f*
  cognitive theory, 265*f*, 281. *See also* Social cognitive theory
  developmental psychopathology, 265*f*
  directive theories, 12
  emotional intelligence, 265*f*
  feminist theory, 17, 319, 370
  four main factors for selecting, 227
  human development theory, 177
  insight theory, 12
  learning theory, 12
  learning theory of career counseling (LTCC), 343–344
  moral development, 265*f*
  psychoanalytic theory/psychoanalysis, 6, 10, 12, 13, 249–250, 252*f*, 254
  psychosocial development, 265*f*
  psychosocial theory, 264
  rational emotive behavior theory (REBT), 251, 252*f*
  relational-cultural theory, 21
  seasons-of-life theory, 306
  selective optimization with compensation (SOC), 312
  seven family counseling theories, 258*f*
  six couple counseling theories, 252*f*
  social cognitive theory, 343, 344
  social learning theory, 250, 252*f*, 343, 370
  sociocultural theory, 265*f*
  structural-strategic theory, 251, 252*f*
  systemic theories, 21
  systems theory, 256, 370. *See also* Bowen family systems theory
  theory of object relations, 249
  trait-and-factory theory/trait-and-type theory, 340, 345
  vocational choice theory, 340–341, 340*f*
Theory of object relations, 249
Therapeutic professionals, identification and definition of, 29–32
Therapies
  cognitive-behavioral therapy (CBT), 57, 282, 285, 319
  cognitive therapy, 13, 87, 162
  conversion therapy, 79
  dialectical behavior therapy, 162

double systems therapy, 251
emotionally focused therapy (EFT), 249, 251–252, 252*f*, 260
feminist therapy, 319–320, 322
group psychotherapy, 203, 219, 220*f*, 221–222
Internet therapy, 60
interpersonal therapy, 319, 321
interpersonal therapy for adolescents (IPT-A), 282–283
multisystemic therapy (MST), 279, 372, 373
narrative family therapy, 257–258, 258*f*
psychotherapy, 10, 203, 219, 220*f*, 221–222
Rational-emotive therapy, 12
Reparative therapy, 79
Time limits, 97
Time management, 169, 170*f*
Tort, 49
Training
  disaster mental health training, 202–203
  of rehabilitation counselors, 85
  social-skills training, treatment of ADHD, 287
  standardization of, 4, 15, 16
Trait-and-factor theory/Trait-and-type theory, 340, 345
Trait-factor counseling, 9, 12
Transactional analysis, 12
Transamerica (movie), 80
Transference, 250
Transgender couples/individuals, 73, 80–81, 313–314
Transgender/Trans, use of terms, 80
Transition
  defined, 295
  in middle adulthood, 306
Transition framework, 295–297
Transition model, 295, 296
Transition stage, of groups, 227
Transphobia, 80
Transprejudice, 80
Transsexual individuals, 80
Transtheoretical model of change, 102
Trash-polling Internet sites, 292
Trauma, dealing with, 20
Trauma-based interventions, 22
Trauma-related disorders, 142
Treatment integrity, 185
Treatment of Adolescents with Depression Study (TADS), 283
Treatment plans
  design and implementation of with child and adolescent clients, 278–279
  in managed care, 397*f*
  in working phase of counseling, 113–114
Triad role-play model, 70
Triage assessment model, 199
Triangulation, defined, 242, 250
TRICARE, 24
Trinity Center, Inc., 374
12 step programs, 368
20/20: A Vision for the Future of Counseling, 21, 27

U

Unanticipated transitions, 296
Unethical behavior, 46–47
Unexpected life stressors, 248, 248*t*
Unintentional torts, 49
United Way, 368